Planet Wedding

Planet Wedding

A Nuptial-pedia

Sandra and
Harry Choron

Houghton Mifflin Harcourt
Boston New York 2010

For Livnat and Casey

It is written: When children find true love, parents

find true joy. Here's to our shared happiness.

Copyright © 2010 by March Tenth, Inc.

For information about permission to reproduce selections from this book, write to
Permissions, Houghton Mifflin Harcourt Publishing Company,
215 Park Avenue South, New York, New York 10003.

www.hmhbooks.com

Library of Congress Cataloging-in-Publication Data
Choron, Sandra.
Planet wedding : a nuptial-pedia / Sandra and Harry Choron.
p. cm.
ISBN 978-0-618-74658-3
1. Weddings. 2. Weddings—Planning. I. Choron, Harry. II. Title.
HQ745.C45 2009   395.2'2—dc22   2008052953

Book design by Lisa Diercks

Printed in the United States of America
DOC 10 9 8 7 6 5 4 3 2 1

This book is not intended as a substitute for professional advice. The author and publisher
disclaim any responsibility for any adverse effects resulting directly or indirectly from
information contained in this book.

Acknowledgments

This book was assembled with the help of hundreds of bridal professionals, consultants, magazine editors, and writers whose credits appear throughout the text. In addition, we thank Ron Schaumburg, Elliot Pravda, Heidi Greenberg, Meg Heister of Schaefer Gardens in Haworth, New Jersey, and Ofer Bendor for helping us in ways too subtle to explain.

Nancy Jaeger and USABride.com were especially helpful in giving us direction and supplying us with the last word on so many wedding subjects; we are happy to promote them shamelessly. In addition, the following individuals gave us their time and attention and have only our gratitude to show for it: Margaret Adamic, Jeff Behrendt, Lorna Beich, Kyle Elizabeth Bryner, Ricky Byrd, Joanna Cali, Kristin Ciccolella, Linda Daniels, Elizabeth Davies, Magda van Deventer, Lydia Dorsey, Jennifer Hattam, Ron Jacobs, Chris Jaeger, Brinna Jannenga, Patty and Greg Kuhlman, Reverend Amy Long, Lori McDonald, Christine McFarland, Claire Pettibone, Hank Reinhart, Evan Reitmeyer, Joann Rockwell, Cori Russell and Elegala.com, Diane Sollee, Kim Waldman, and Debbie Weckesser.

For their help in obtaining the artwork in this book, we're grateful to Myles Aronowitz, Bill and Donna Barr, Steven R. Berkshire, Carrie Biggers, Rebecca Burns, Ricky Byrd, Dalisa and John Michael Cooper, Linda Daniels, Ron Ducar, David Duncan, Marlow Gates, Dan Harris, Karen J. Harris, Eric Harshbarger, Henna Artisans, Eric Larson of CardCow.com, Caryn Nash, Daniel Ostrov, Brandon Reed, Mary Seid, Dawn Stubitsch, and Kimberely Waldman. Special thanks to Vlad and Marina Fridlyand, of Garden State Photo, for so many of the wedding photos here.

Most of all, we're grateful to our talented editor Susan Canavan for championing this book and our others, for keeping us on track, and for not making us cut our favorite lists. She is our honorary Maid of Honor. We're also indebted to her assistant, Elizabeth Lee, for stepping in with wisdom and enthusiasm.

A tip of the hat to Judy Linden, who inspired the advice on page 339 and who will no doubt be surprised to find her name here.

Finally, we thank those who show us constant support for no reason we can fathom: Casey Choron, Livnat Hai-Choron, Shirley Glickman, Shannon Garrahan, Dave Marsh, Wendy Leeds, Alison Oscar, Rochelle Diogenes, and Elvis.

Contributors

We are grateful to the following contributors for their material, time, expertise, and enthusiasm:

Stephanie Coontz and the Council of Contemporary Families for "Polygamy Fact Sheet"

Dr. Rictor Norton for "A History of Gay Marriage"

Barbara Rosewicz and the Pew Forum on Religion for "Same-Sex Marriage: A Timeline"

Mike Milton and WeddingFlorist.co.uk for "The Origin of 'Something Old, Something New . . .'"

Elizabeth Davies for "7 Centuries of British Bridal Gowns"

Diane Ferraro of Robbins Brothers for "Pre-Wedding and Engagement Traditions Around the World"

MyExpression.com for "A History of the Wedding Invitation"

Rose Smith of Wedding Themes and More (WedThemes.com) for "Flowers and Their Meanings"

Cornelia Powell of WeddingsOfGrace.com for "To Gather Orange Blossoms: Brides and the Orange Blossom Legend"

Judy Lewis of HudsonValleyWeddings.com for "A History of Wedding Cakes" and "What to Expect at a Military Wedding"

Joseph Kohn of IQPhoto.com for "A Brief History of Wedding Photography"

Sarah Stefanson and WeddingFashion.Suite101.com for "Bridal Attire Across the Globe"

David Boyer and Patrick Price for "7 Infamous Bachelor Parties"

Ron Schaumburg for "The Ballad of John and Yoko" and "In a Church Where a Wedding Has Been: Four Beatles Marriages"

Jade Nirvana Ingmire and Bridezilla.com for "The Bridezilla Hall of Fame"

Pagewise.com for "A History of Weddings in Las Vegas," copyright © 2001 by PageWise, Inc. Used with permission.

Erica Johnson of Vegas.com for "37 Celebrity Vegas Weddings"

Cele Otnes and Elizabeth Pleck of the College of Business, University of Illinois at Urbana-Champaign, for the excerpt from *Cinderella Dreams: The Allure of the Lavish Wedding*

The National Association of Wedding Ministers and the Bridal Association of America for "Weddings by the Numbers"

Jean Sanders Torrey for "17 Reasons Why Men Get Married"

Sabina Freedman and Eventective.com for "Top Wedding Venues in 5 Major American Cities"

Elizabeth Joyce for "Wedding Day Numerology"

Diana Mercer of Peace Talks Mediation Services for "5 Myths About Premarital Agreements"

Christine Friedrichsen of Intimate-Wedding.com for "9 Reasons to Have a Small Wedding"

Ron Decar of VivaLasVegasWeddings.com for "13 Themed Las Vegas Weddings"

Rev. Dr. Aurore Leigh Barrett of WeddingsLasVegas.com for "7 Great Las Vegas Wedding Chapels" and "The Rev. Barrett's Most Memorable Wedding Moments"

Roger Masterson of CelticCastles.com for "10 British Castle Weddings"

Gino and Mike Meriano of PinkWeddings.biz for "9 Outrageous Gay Weddings in the United Kingdom"

Nancy Jaeger and USABride.com for "When Money Is No Object" (by Lisa Akers); "20 Ways to Panic-Proof Your Wedding Day"; "9 Ways to Stay Relaxed During the Hours Before Your Wedding" (by Sandy Erzine); "Tired of Tossing Rice?" (by Elizabeth Watts); "How to Preserve Your Wedding Gown"; and "10 Unusual Honeymoons"

Massachusetts Wedding Guide for "Wedding Consultants 101"

Laurie Pawlik-Kienlien of Wedding-Planning.Suite101.com for "I Now Pronounce You—Online! Top 13 Wedding Planning Websites"

Gina Romanello for "10 Ways to Avoid the BS: Preventing the Bridezilla Syndrome"

Rose Giffin of Rosann's Bridal, Greentown, Ohio, for "How to Tell if You're a Bridezilla" and "How to Tell if You Are a Momzilla"

Angela Ann Holloway and Joy Guegler of Marriage.Suite101.com for "Premarital Counseling: Considerations in Preparing for Marriage"

Elise MacAdam of IndieEtiquette.com for "7 Antiquated Rules of Wedding Etiquette"

Patricia Lee of WeddingExpress.com for "A Deadly Combination: Your Wedding and Your Job" (copyright © Patricia Lee)

Deborah Spence and GlassLady.com for "Favorite Bible Verses for Wedding Ceremonies"

Joyce L. Gioia of MultiFaithWeddings.com for "6 Tips for Planning the Multi-Faith Wedding Ceremony"

Erica Tevis and LittleThingsFavors.com for "What Your Color Choice Really Means" and "A History of the Honeymoon"

Justin Alexander of JustinAlexanderBridal.com for "Which White?"

Blake Kritzberg and FavorIdeas.com for "9 Ways to Involve the Groom" and "Beyond the Unity Candle"

Michael Tomes of VegasVIP.com for "Top 10 Rules for the Ideal Bachelor Party"

Darsi Pizzolato and FrugalBride.com for "A Groom's Planning Tips"

Ramin Ramhormozi for "117 Things for the Groom to Do Before the Wedding"

Ron Rabon of Genesis Diamonds for "9 Most Common Mistakes People Make When Buying Diamonds"

Syerah Vivani and Payal Mirchandani of MyBindi.com for "In-Laws and Outlaws: 8 Ways to Cope"

Gerald Foley and Longevity.com for "14 Rules for Fighting Fair"

Shane McMurray and The Wedding Report for "Trends in Wedding Invitations"

Steven Brower of Steven Brower Design for "Wedding Fonts"

Terrica R. Skaggs of Fabu-Luxe.com for "How to Choose a Wedding Gown"

Crystal Unrau of Chrys Cross Bridal for "The 5 Wedding Gown Train Lengths"

Linda Daniels and Northampton Wools for "How to Knit Your Own Wedding Dress"

Jennifer Gay and Suite101.com for "Wedding Headpieces and Veils"

Sapphire Solutions of Stoughton, Massachusetts, and Massachusetts Wedding Guide for "How to Choose a Tuxedo to Match Your Body Type"

Minskytux.com for "A Groom's Guide to Formalwear"

Liztiany Zakaria and FavorIdeas.com for "How to Choose the Right Wedding Bouquet"

Patrick Rice of PRFisheye.com for "Photography Tips"

Lisa Robinson of CrystalClearVideoProductions.com for "How to Choose a Videographer"

DiscJockeys.com for "The Most Popular Wedding Songs"

Dale V. Atkins for "Why People Cry at Weddings"

Philip K. Dunn and EZWeddingPlanner.com for "Standing on Ceremony: Who Sits Where?"

Rick Pieczonka of InstantWeddingToasts.com for "How to Deliver a Toast"

Larry James of CelebrateIntimateWeddings.com for "The Blended Family Ceremony"

Janus of Spawnfar.net for "The 10 Essentials of a Wiccan Wedding"

Ronald A. Haller and Michelle McKenzie of HoneymoonersReviewGuide.com for "18 Great Honeymoon Tips"; "The 10 Most Romantic Cities in the World"; and "Honeymoon Weather Guide"

Chris Payne and Dollar Thrifty Automotive Group for "7 Winners of Thrifty Car Rental's 'Honeymoon Disasters Contest'"

Darlene Berkel and Every1Loves2Travel.com for "3 Honeymoon Capitals of the World Right Here in the U.S.A."

Hugh Durkin of WeddingsIreland.com for "12 Ways to Beat Post-Nuptial Syndrome (PNS)"

Janet Bodnar and Kiplinger's *Personal Finance* for "Savings Advice for Newlyweds." Copyright © 2008 by Kiplinger's *Personal Finance*. All rights reserved. Used by permission.

Contents

Introduction

If you've just landed on Planet Wedding, congratulations are in order, not only for the impending nuptials but also because in preparing for a wedding you embark on a journey that covers a variety of terrains and a range of experience. Rocky roads lie up ahead, as do glittering skies and rolling green hills. But that lovely landscape conceals some troublesome spots that may be difficult to negotiate, and you know what they say about all that glitters.

This is a guide to Planet Wedding.

Two things will surprise you upon your arrival. First, it's not just about white tulle and familiar songs, and second, it's a much bigger planet than you imagined. It encompasses thousands of years of tradition and practice, and each of its continents, separated by oceans of experience, offers a different global view.

Planet Wedding was actually a quiet place up until about seventy-five years ago. That is, wedding practice has changed more in the past six or seven decades than it has in the past 750 years. What's notable is that the change was brought about by commercial and industrial developments, and this, more than anything, tells us a great deal about the connections between weddings and our history. For just as wedding gifts became common only when technology made the manufacturing of "fake" treasures possible, so the glasses that are smashed at Jewish weddings, the food that is shared at Chinese nuptials, and the henna designs worn by Muslim and Hindu brides all have their origins in historical events. In reading about the history and culture of weddings, then, we read about ourselves.

Why do we do the things we do? How long have we actually been doing them? And what alternatives do we have? And most important of all, how does one save money on a wedding in this day and age of celebrated consumerism? These are some of the questions that our tour of the planet will answer. We'll guide you along the major highways, but we'll take plenty of side trips as well. You'll need comfortable shoes and an open mind to enjoy it all, and the souvenirs you take away are liable to last you a lifetime. More than anything, we're hoping that no matter what your ultimate destination may be, you'll take time to explore the entire planet.

— Sandy and Harry Choron

Chapter 1
A History of Weddings

These days, weddings may be all about white tulle and good wishes for a happy future, but take a look at the history of weddings and you'll find that they have a checkered past. Love and marriage didn't always go together like a horse and carriage, and in examining the history of weddings, it's difficult to believe that the ancient marriages of the polygamists of Africa have anything at all in common with the Guatemalan ritual during which a bride's and groom's hands are lovingly bound together with silver. Nevertheless, in taking a look back, we find the "placage" marriage in which simple promises are made, sans religious or government sanction, as practiced in Haiti, right alongside the customs of Thailand, which once required years of labor on the part of the groom before he could earn his bride.

Yet while wedding customs may vary so much that we barely recognize the connections between them, all weddings, from the beginning of time, seem to have had a few things in common.

For one thing, marriage has always served as a steadying hand on society. Marriage has also played a great role in the evolution of our culture, and it has always been noted as an important passage from one phase of life to another. In addition, it has always marked the joining of families rather than individuals, making weddings a central issue where fortunes and bloodlines are concerned.

Finally, no matter how disparate the methods of celebrating their union, everyone seems to agree that the bride and groom are especially vulnerable to a variety of threats on their wedding day. "There is a very general feeling or idea that the bride and bridegroom are in a state of danger, being particularly exposed to other persons' magical tricks

An American wedding procession, ca. 1907
LIBRARY OF CONGRESS

or evil looks, or to the attacks of evil spirits," wrote historian Edward Westermarck in his 1930 book *A Short History of Marriage.* With the bridal pair in constant need of protection, then, a body of rituals and customs, all designed to keep bad luck at bay, has grown up around marriages, and this, more than anything, gives all weddings, whether attended by four or four hundred, a certain commonality.

Understanding the history of weddings will help the modern bride understand the rituals in which she is about to participate, and it will serve as a guide for anyone who might want to "reinvent" an old tradition. Focusing on the history of marriages, this chapter, covering all corners of Planet Wedding, tells us much about who we are and how we got here.

Depiction of an ancient Egyptian wedding AUTHORS' COLLECTION

Once Upon A Wedding . . .

Paleolithic Period

No one has been able to discover when the first real wedding took place or what the bride wore, if anything. But we do know that the people of this period lived in nomadic tribes that were formed for protection against predators both human and animal. Conflicts between tribes sometimes led to serious battles during which women and children were abducted, and these were probably the first marital unions, although evidence shows that Stone Age man was not necessarily as barbaric as we once suspected—clobbering a woman over the head and dragging her off by her hair was something that happened mostly on *The Flintstones.* Nevertheless, when these first brides entered their new homes for the first time, they left behind everything they had—their belongings, their family, their name, and often their childhood.

Even if they had their origins in warfare, as tribes settled and formed agricultural communities, the first marriages, absent of any sort of emotion, were formed peaceably. Experts suggest that these were group weddings, held solely for the purpose of strengthening tribal relations. The institution gained popularity for its perks: sexual release, procreation, and cheap domestic help. A barter system soon developed: wives were traded for livestock, cash, crops, or goodwill. Families took shape, and the unions became a way of passing on property to future generations.

Weddings on the Nile

The first legal marriages in the region were created in order to stem incest, which was rampant in early Egypt. Pharaohs included sisters and even daughters among their wives in order to keep dynastic bloodlines strong, although this practice was rare among the middle and lower classes. The first legally enforceable marriage contract gave women a variety of rights, including the right to divorce.

Egyptians felt that it was in everyone's interest for a bride and groom to get to know each other before the wedding, and so an engagement period was created. Dowries existed in Egypt (see "The History of the Dowry," page 7), but in reverse: the groom and his family presented the bride's family with a sum of money to demonstrate his ability to care for his wife. He also presented his bride with a gift, commonly a gemstone.

The wedding reception was a colorful affair that featured feasting, dancing, and singing, and it ended with the couple leaving for private time as they were showered with wheat, which symbolized fertility.

As other civilizations soon became aware of the benefits of marriage—family resources could be strengthened, there was less feuding between clans, and men and women both seemed more contented in a familial atmosphere—the idea caught on.

1903 photograph of a bridegroom in Samaria being escorted to his wedding AUTHORS' COLLECTION

Ancient Rome

The early Romans hardly stood on ceremony when it came to weddings. Couples could be married by declaring their intentions in front of a witness, by signing a legal document, or simply by having the bride go to her spouse's home. But by about 30 B.C. the marriage union began to take on formality; this is the period when weddings as we know them today originated. (The Romans, in fact, gave us the word *matrimony,* which derives from mater, meaning "mother.") Emperor Augustus, aka Octavius (63 B.C.–14 A.D.), believed that marriage offered stability and harmony to society and that these qualities would bolster the empire. He went so far as to pass the first law on the subject, making it illegal for a man to put off his wedding day.

It was shortly after this time that wedlock first became holy with the emergence of another form of marriage known as a *conferreatio.* This form of marriage was administered by a member of the church and, unlike its civil counterpart, could not be annulled. It was largely reserved for the upper classes.

Typically in ancient Rome, a girl's father would arrange a marriage for her, largely to form political

The Bride Price

Also known as bride wealth, the bride price is the amount of money paid by a groom or his family to the bride's family in return for the right to marry their daughter. The payment is intended to reimburse the family for the loss of the daughter's labor and possible contributions to her clan.

The practice is mentioned at least as far back in history as the sixth-century Babylonian Code of Hammurabi and in the Hebrew Bible and Talmud, and it continues to this day in a wide variety of cultures:

• In Islamic marriages, the payment is made to the bride. After long being considered a social evil in India, however, the practice was eventually eradicated.

• In China, a special day was traditionally chosen to establish the bride price, and on the day of the wedding the bride's family would return a portion of the bride price to show good faith.

• A groom of the Roma people (or gypsies) pays the bride's family for the loss of their daughter. Negotiations between the families can become quite extensive, with the bride's father calculating how much his daughter has cost him since her birth, and how much she could be expected to earn during her lifetime. When agreement is reached, a ceremony called a *pliashka* is held. The groom's father brings a bottle of wine or brandy wrapped in a colorful silk handkerchief and attached to a necklace of coins. He puts the necklace around the bride's neck and embraces her. This indicates that she is now engaged and unavailable to any other man. The wine is drunk, but the bottle is refilled for use at the wedding ceremony.

• According to Hindu tradition, a young man repaid his debt to his ancestors by marrying. Brides lived with their husband's family, and poor families often saw the bride as another pair of hands. Therefore, the groom's family compensated the bride's family for their economic loss. On the other hand, in Brahman, or upper-caste, households, the bride was seen as a burden, requiring the support of her husband's family. The bride's family had to pay the groom's family with a dowry for taking her off their hands. Such traditional wedding rituals are often followed today in India, especially in rural areas.

A Hindu bridal party, ca. 1922 LIBRARY OF CONGRESS

or financial links. The match was made with the consent of the couple, between whom there had to be a conudium: the couple could not be related by blood; neither could be already married or engaged; and neither could be a slave. If the man was a soldier, he needed to complete his service before marrying, and there were restrictions on marrying foreigners as well. The final restriction involved the ages of the couple to be married: the bride had to be at least 12, and the husband at least 13.

A series of events leading to the marriage then took place: a betrothal celebration, known as a *sponsalia* (the woman was known as the *sponsa*, the man as the *sponsus*), was held at which the impending marriage was announced and the groom, with 10 witnesses present, solemnly pronounced his pledge to marry the girl. He presented her with a gift—usually one of fine jewelry, such as a ring—to seal the deal, and she gave him a gift of cloth, such as a toga.

On the morning of the wedding day, the bride would make a special offering to the gods of all of her childhood toys (some brides were still children themselves), demonstrating her willingness to leave her girlhood behind and take on the responsibilities of a wife. Then the bride, surrounded by female attendants offering advice and led by the bride's mother, called the *pronuba*, would be bathed and dressed for her wedding. Her dress would typically be a simple one that she might have made herself of white wool, but to good-naturedly confound the groom on his wedding night, it would have a very complicated knot. Her hair would be styled in six locks in the style of the Vestal Virgins, with fresh flowers and a veil, which symbolized her intent to remain married until her death.

> "Let her beauty be her dower."
> —William Shakespeare, *Two Gentlemen of Verona*

The groom, on the other hand, had no attendants and no special costume. His job was simply to show up. Some things never change.

The wedding was attended by friends and family in addition to 10 male citizens who acted as witnesses, ensuring the legality of the marriage. The actual ceremony consisted of the couple joining their right hands and stating their intent to marry. Details varied according to family tradition and income, but it is said that once a dowry (see page 4) was agreed upon, the couple was considered to be married.

After the ceremony, which was typically held in the home of the bride, the groom and his family would slip away to prepare their home for the new bride. Soon the bride, escorted by three boys, two holding her hands and one leading the way with a torch, and followed by a processional of all the guests, would make her way to her new home. There she performed traditional rituals such as tying wool and spilling oil on the doorposts for good luck, after which the groom would make a show of carrying his wife over the threshold. Inside, a welcoming celebration that included refreshments and musicians

A Medieval Wedding Feast

Here is an actual banquet menu for a medieval wedding feast, taken from a book called *Two Fifteenth-Century Cookery Books,* edited by Thomas Austin. The introduction explains: "Medieval feasts were traditionally served in three courses. Each course included a soup, followed by a wide range of baked, roasted, and boiled dishes, and finally an elaborate 'sotelty,' a lifelike (often edible) scene sculpted in colored marzipan or dough. The bounty of medieval feasts is legendary.

Oystres en Grauey (oysters steamed in almond milk)

Brede (bread flavored with ale)

Chawettys (tarts filled with spicy pork or veal)

Pigge Ffarced (stuffed roast suckling pig)

Goose in Sawse Madame (goose in a sauce of grapes and garlic)

Caboches in Potage (stewed cabbage flavored with cinnamon and cloves)

Crustade Lombarde (fruited custard in a pie)

Hippocras (spicy mulled wine)

would take place around the wedding bed, and the couple would be presented with gifts. Of course, they all lived happily ever after.

The Middle Ages

The myth: during the Middle Ages, June was the most popular month for weddings because most people took their yearly bath around that time; flowers were introduced to hide the bride's lingering body odor.

The reality: people of the Middle Ages bathed regularly, thank you. There were even laws against slovenliness, and soap, which had been invented before Christ's time, was in good supply throughout Europe.

Actually, the most popular months for weddings were January, November, and October—times between harvest and planting when animals could easily be slaughtered for a wedding feast. June was popular for the good weather it promised and for the arrival of new crops as well as flowers.

The Middle Ages saw the first major insinuation into the marriage pact by the Church. In 1076, the Council of Westminster decreed that all unions had to be blessed by a priest. By 1563, the Council of Trent required that a priest not only attend the ceremony but actually perform it. (Jewish marriages came to require the participation of a religious official during the fourteenth century.)

At least among the upper classes, marriages were arranged for children who were often no older than 10 or 11, and they did not meet until their wedding day, some five or six years later. The union was intended for the sharing of a lord's property; love was optional. The wedding ceremony took place in a castle (only later did church weddings become popular), and the event was cause for colorful celebrations that included dancers, jugglers, and feasting. The father of the bride or groom might even be moved to mark the occasion by releasing political prisoners, and beggars would be allowed to gather at the castle gate for leftovers.

It was during this time that betrothal became a legal, binding agreement, and to make sure that no betrothal was based on a misunderstanding or any type of fraud, a couple who wished to marry had their names read in church at three successive services to allow for any objections. These announcements, known as banns, still exist today in the form of the minister's "forever hold your peace" pronouncement.

Betrothals died out in England by the eighteenth century, allowing couples to pursue one another much more freely without the threat of legal action and bringing ever more romance to the wedding experience.

The History of the Dowry

A dowry refers to a gift or payment by a bride's family to the groom or his family made at the time of marriage. It began as a means by which families could build power and wealth by creating political alliances through marriage. Even when his daughter was just a baby, a father would begin to set aside the contents of a dowry, which would be used in bargaining for the best possible marriage.

• Sometimes the dowry took the form of household items that were helpful to the newlyweds as they set up their own home. If the dowry consisted of property or jewelry, it served as an insurance policy that would help support the bride in the event of her husband's death. It also served to protect her against ill treatment by her husband, since dowries were often a conditional gift.

• The tradition has a long history in Europe, South Asia, Africa, and other parts of the world:

• The Code of Hammurabi, created in ancient Babylon around 1760 B.C., set specific regulations for dowries and bride prices. If a woman, for instance, died without bearing sons, her husband had to refund the dowry, but he could deduct the value of the price he had paid for his bride. The wife became entitled to her dowry at her husband's death. Her dowry was also protected in that only her own children could inherit it.

• In ancient Rome, dowries were generally agreed upon at the time of betrothal and paid after the wedding. The bride's family would pay a dowry to the groom, who would then give his bride a monetary gift and an iron engagement ring in exchange. If the marriage was in manum (a marriage that conferred upon her all the rights of a daughter in her new family), all her property came under the control of her husband. If the marriage was not in manum, the bride's father controlled her and her property.

• In Victorian England, a number of laws stressed the importance of a dowry. It was seen as an early payment of a bride's inheritance, and if the couple died without children, the dowry was returned to the bride's family. A common penalty for the kidnapping and rape of an unmarried woman was requiring the abductor or rapist to provide the victim's dowry, and providing dowries for poor women was regarded as a form of charity. These dowry practices disappeared by the late nineteenth century.

• In some parts of Europe, land dowries were common. In Germany, for example, a new son-in-law was given land by his in-laws if they did not have a son of their own, the only condition being that he had to take his bride's last name.

• According to Hindu tradition, a lower-caste bride would live with her husband's family, who often saw her merely as another worker. The groom's family in this case paid the bride's family for their economic loss. However, in upper-caste households, the bride, not being a worker, was seen as a burden who needed the support of her husband's family. The bride's family had to pay the groom's family with a dowry for taking her off their hands. These traditions continue to be observed today.

Victoria and Albert Tie the Knot

The first reigning British queen to be married became famous in wedding history for setting a new standard. The white dress and the orange blossoms she wore became instant traditions that are alive and well today.

On the day of the wedding, February 10, 1840, thousands braved damp weather to witness a wedding procession that traveled from Buckingham Palace to the chapel at St. James's. The event captured the imagination of the public and the press alike, leaving us with many eyewitness accounts of the spectacle, including this one from *Victoria, Queen of England* (1868) by James Parton:

> The queen, as brides generally do, looked pale and anxious. Her dress was a rich white satin, trimmed with orange blossoms, and upon her head she wore a wreath of the same beautiful flowers. Over her head, but not so as to conceal her face, a veil of honiton lace was thrown. She was sparingly decorated with diamonds. She wore, however, a pair of very large diamond ear-rings, and a diamond necklace. Her twelve bridesmaids were attired in similar taste, and they were all young ladies of remarkable beauty.

By the second half of the nineteenth century, girls everywhere strove to follow in Victoria's footsteps, publicity and all. Weddings became public affairs, church weddings became the norm, and for the first time ever weddings were defined not by ritual but by romance.

Meanwhile, advances in technology and transportation facilitated the movement of ideas across the globe, and the weddings that were taking place throughout the world began to resemble one another—with variations, of course. Some celebrations lasted for days, and others were short, businesslike transactions. Matrimonial laws developed differently across countries and regions, and attitudes toward women and property varied greatly, even within a continent. In France, after the French Revolution, religion was banned from French culture and marriage became a secular event. Across the pond, those wacky colonialists came up with yet another nutty idea. Formal weddings were spurned for the more practical common-law marriage: a couple was considered legally married if they had cohabited for an extended period or if they signed in as husband and wife at public hotels.

The Nineteenth Century

By the beginning of the nineteenth century, wealthy urban families throughout the world were well on their way to defining weddings as we know them today. Girls were encouraged to marry and rarely dreamed of other options. A couple became engaged, and a betrothal period followed during which the business and logistical aspects of the marriage were determined. The bride's family issued invitations, the couple married in their best clothes in the parlor of the bride's or groom's home, and an elaborate meal and cake followed.

This basic procedure was the distillation of hundreds of years of wedding practices. Yet it took only one wedding to capture the imagination of a culture and change the history of weddings forever.

The influence of the 1840 wedding of Queen Victoria and Prince Albert on fashion and culture soon trickled down to the middle class, which had grown to huge proportions and now required a method for separating into various subclasses. An individual's adherence to a strict code of manners, etiquette, and style became the basis on which he or she was judged by society at large. Weddings proved to be the perfect arena for societal competition, giving rise to a complicated system of wedding etiquette.

Weddings had long been seen as dignified private events intended for family and close friends, but now it seemed that everyone wanted to get in on the action—suppliers and customers alike. For the first time in wedding history, families could hire outside vendors to take care of the chores that had once been family responsibilities: caterers, one of the first industries to enter the bridal marketplace, replaced the potluck offerings, and florists were now commonly hired to add professional artistry to the occasion. Printing advances allowed the distribution of many more invitations, and the white wedding dress finally became the staple it is today. More invitations meant more gifts, and these too changed as middle-class consumers became enamored of the many "fakes" that technology was making possible: jacquard looms produced an inexpensive version of brocade; pressed glass was passed off for the hand-blown and hand-cut varieties; and nickel and copper could be covered with a thin veneer of silver to look almost like the real thing. The plethora of treasures added to the frenzy as brides proudly displayed their gifts, to the envy of future brides.

> "By the 1870s, exhibiting presents for the public gaze was a common—if not universally approved—feature of middle class weddings. Conspicuous consumption and domesticity were served equally well by the array of bridal gifts."
>
> — Ellen K. Rothman, *A History of Courtship in America* (1987)

But not everyone could afford a "white wedding." Girls from wealthy families were able to afford the luxury, but the working class remained traditional. Louisa May Alcott points to the folly of conspicuous weddings when Meg, in *Little Women*, muses, "People who hire all these things done for them never know what they lose, for the homeliest tasks get beautified if loving hands do them." Meg shuns the finery that is offered to her, stating, "I don't want to look strange or fixed up today. I don't want a fashionable wedding but only those about me whom I love, and to them I wish to look and be my familiar self."

While Meg's sentiment is still voiced today in the decisions of brides who spurn the pomp in favor of privacy, this important period in wedding history is best known for popularizing the pageantry that defines today's traditional wedding.

> "So popular were brides [in the 1930s] that Hollywood studios, when promoting a new starlet, would often dress her up in a white satin gown with a veil and release the photo to the press.… The iconic white outfit caught the eye and could net these girls the coverage the studio was after."
>
> — Carol McD. Wallace, *All Dressed in White: The Irresistible Rise of the American Wedding* (2004)

The Twentieth Century

In 1912 *Suburban Life* magazine took a stand by publishing an article by Margaret Woodward called "The Evil of Elaborate and Showy Weddings." Its subtitle proclaimed: "Money lavished on ostentatious display—sacredness of marriage forgotten in preparation of a gorgeous, extravagant pageant." The article chronicled the hardships that such events created as the author told of a neighbor who mortgaged his house in order to afford the terraces and gardens that his engaged daughter demanded. Woodward's criticism wasn't limited to the ostentatious; she wagged her finger at the poor for aping those useless displays. "At their pitifully cheap festivities, they squander their hard-won earnings," she complained.

Heiress-brides have percale sheets, of course… Now Cannon brings them to budget-brides too!

Woodward criticized an unheeding public who went on to turn the wedding industry into the $70 billion behemoth it is today. Not only was the industry successful in parting young brides, grooms, and their unsuspecting families from dollars the couple hadn't yet earned, but it also created the illusion that the "modern wedding" had some grounding in history. It didn't. The jewelry industry invented the "tradition" of diamond-embellished rings and double-ring ceremonies, neither of which existed before this time. The engagement ring became a symbol of success, while the DeBeers Company convinced the world that "diamonds are forever."

Bridal magazines became part of wedding culture; especially during the 1930s and 1940s, the craze to conform generated a need for a central clearinghouse for all things wedding. *Brides* magazine, the maid of honor of them all, supplied that and more; to the delight of advertisers everywhere, it went on to dictate an even more lavish approach to weddings. The bridal shows that made their first appearance around this time toured the country to herald new fashions to brides everywhere, and department stores stepped up their efforts by creating gift registries and booking upscale hotels for fashion shows. By 1950, these marketing tools had become immensely popular among retailers and their dreamy-eyed clientele.

Caterers came of age during this time. Now

hotels and "wedding palaces" offered package-deal ceremonies and receptions, and as weddings became news, their sites became more and more important.

During the 1960s and 1970s, when society at large assumed the mantle of individuality, brides were encouraged to become more creative, and the new antiestablishment wedding was born. Now nothing was etched in stone. The miniskirted bride celebrated her mod wedding, while hippies popularized outdoor ceremonies. Marriages between members of different religions and cultures and second and even third marriages for some became more common during this period, and ceremonies began to be shaped by the needs of new family combinations.

By the 1990s, weddings had become a pastiche of customs and traditions, both new and invented, owing in great part to the choices that were now becoming available to the Internet bride. By 2000, 30 percent of couples were using the Internet to plan their weddings, and The Knot, a website that offered advice on all things wedding, went on to become the largest Internet supplier of favors, gifts, and other wedding accoutrements; a book series, a magazine, and various TV shows further helped to make The Knot a wedding staple. In 2002, the company acquired the backing of the May Department Stores Company, the second-largest department store chain in the United States, with some $14.2 billion in annual revenue from stores such as Lord and Taylor, Strawbridge, Foley's, and Filene's. The merger was typical of the time, when retailers were pushed toward consolidation. (May eventually merged with Federated, making The Knot a sister company of both David's Bridal at one end of the wedding gown spectrum and Priscilla of Boston at the other.)

The Vikings viewed weddings as little more than an excuse to party. Their wedding feasts sometimes lasted for as long as a month and were accompanied by wild revelry and a few of the Seven Deadly Sins thrown in for good measure.

And Onward

Today's marrying couple defies description, as they are a product of myriad choices that have been made available to them through wedding expos and e-commerce. Today's bride is sexy where she once exuded virginity, she is original where she once craved conformity, and she draws from various cultures and practices to create an event that expresses her personality and values. Sadly, she often falls victim to the "bridezilla" mind-set that a rabid industry thrusts upon her. Most important, she not only makes her own choices with respect to her wedding and its trappings, but more significantly, she also chooses her husband.

As for the institution itself, marriage continues to evolve as societies grow and change. The subject of gay marriage is central to political campaigns and raises questions about just what marriage really means. Multi-faith and independent church ministers create ceremonies for all occasions, and those who spurn the experience altogether turn to marriage alternatives. As weddings evolve, they raise interesting questions about their role in society. Ultimately, the answers reveal much about who we are.

Polygamy Fact Sheet

Stephanie Coontz, the author of this fact sheet, is a professor of history and family studies at Evergreen State College, in Olympia, Washington, and director of research and public education at the Council of Contemporary Families. She is the author of *Marriage, a History: How Love Conquered Marriage*. Here are some interesting facts about polygamy:

• Polygamy means multiple spouses. The most common form is polygyny, where a man can have many wives. Less common, but found in some societies such as Tibet, is polyandry, where a woman can have many husbands.

• Polygyny was accepted or even preferred in three-fourths of pre-industrial traditional societies, though it was seldom practiced by the commoners or lower classes. It tended to occur most frequently in societies where the route to winning wealth and political power was through attracting followers or having lots of sons to hunt for the family or defend the family's land. So a man might marry several wives and have them produce textiles he could trade, or grow food for elaborate feasts he could use to put poorer members of the community in his debt.

• In other cases, wealthy men accumulated many wives to produce more sons. It was very common for kings and other royalty to have many wives, both as a way to make alliances with other states or noble families and to ensure that they would have plenty of heirs. The king of the Merina in the highlands of Madagascar had 12 wives, each with a palace in a different part of his country. He stayed with whichever one was nearest when he traveled through the kingdom.

• Polygyny is not usually associated with a high status for women, and in many cultures it involved very young women being forced to marry older men. Still, in a society where gender roles are very rigid and women do most of the work around the farm and household, some women like having a cowife. In Botswana, women claim that having other wives to help meet some of their husband's demands and to share the child-rearing gives them more freedom than women in monogamous unions.

• Polygamy of either sort is far less common than it used to be, and is now concentrated in Africa, the Middle East, India, Thailand, and Indonesia. The trend over the past century has been toward limiting polygamy. Some societies have introduced a gradual reduction in the number of wives permitted, while others have relegated the status of secondary wives to that of concubines, and some have outlawed it outright.

Biblical Polygamists

1. Abijah, the second son of Samuel, had 14 wives.

2. Izban, an ancient Hebrew judge, had 60 wives.

3. Abijah, King of Judah, had 14 wives.

4. King Solomon had 700 wives and 300 concubines.

5. King David had at least 18 wives and 10 concubines.

6. Rehoboam, Solomon's son, took 78 wives.

7. Abraham had 3 wives.

8. Caleb, son of Jephunneh, had 5 wives.

9. Jacob, father of the 12 patriarchs of the tribes of Israel, had 4 wives.

10. Esau, Abraham's grandson, had 3 wives.

11. Muhammad, prophet and the founder of Islam, is thought to have had between 10 and 22 wives.

• The Mormons are an exceptional case of polygyny being adopted in an industrializing society. Early Mormons condemned much of nineteenth-century Christianity as a corruption of the true church, and sought to return to a purer faith, one which harkened back to God's ancient law. Polygyny was instituted and patriarchal marriage, as it was often called, was believed to elevate the family in this world and the next. Once the Mormons began migrating to Utah in 1847, polygyny was more openly practiced. Brigham Young had more than 50 wives. Nineteen of them were connubial wives, and they bore him 56 children.

The U.S. government moved to penalize Mormons through a series of federal statutes that outlawed polygamy. In 1890, the Church issued a manifesto forgoing plural marriage, and since 1904 the Church has had a policy of excommunicating followers who practice it.

Groups of disaffected former Mormons who have generally refused to accept the ruling have formed polygamous communities. These groups have stimulated much public discussion and debate and have led to the rise of advocacy groups such as Tapestry Against Polygamy, composed of former plural wives.

> "I think I have monogamy. I must have caught it from you people."
> — Samantha, *Sex and the City*

Wedding Customs Around the World

The familial marriages embraced by some societies may offend or even horrify others. In Judaism, a bride price expresses a certain attitude of respect for the rite of passage that is taking place; in India, it has been outlawed. In examining wedding styles around the world, we glimpse the essence of cultures. These customs tell us a great deal about how different societies approach the major events in their lives.

In world customs, it is often difficult to distinguish between ancient and modern practices. In many cases, the modern practice has evolved from its traditional predecessor. Sometimes customs have been abandoned by a society only to be rediscovered and reshaped centuries later. In addition, as people have moved from region to region, voluntarily or otherwise, they have brought their ethnicities with them, often adapting traditions to new social climates.

Thus, although the following provides only a small taste of each region, we offer it in the hopes that readers will use this information as a springboard from which to learn more. Incorporating ethnic rituals into a ceremony, whether or not the bride or groom is a member of the culture, can enhance a wedding and remind all present of the basic premise of marriage: two families, and the worlds from which they hail, are being brought together.

Love and Marriage

They didn't always go together like a horse and carriage. In fact, in ancient cultures they weren't connected in any way at all. When marriage was primarily intended to unite and strengthen families and clans, love and marriage were considered incompatible. Plato depicted love as an emotion that led men to behave honorably, but most societies felt that there was no place for it in marriage. In fact, the newly wedded couple was expected to join society and work for the community; love could prove to be a harmful distraction. Here are some other views on the subject:

1. In ancient India, falling in love was viewed as an antisocial act that disrupted society.

2. The Greeks believed that lovesickness was a true infirmity.

3. The French viewed love as "a derangement of the mind"; the only cure was sexual intercourse.

4. The Chinese believed that love was a direct threat to the extended family and that it would keep both husband and wife from performing their societal duties. If it happened, the parents of the husband could send the girl back to her parents. (Historically, the only Chinese word for love was usually used to describe illicit relationships; in the 1920s another word was invented for the love between man and wife.)

> **"It is most unwise for people in love to marry."**
> — George Bernard Shaw

Afghanistan

In Afghanistan, where the population is primarily Muslim, Hindu, and Sikh, marriages are normally arranged by parents, who are seeking to strengthen families; marriage among cousins is common. Although a Muslim man may have up to four wives, most Afghani men can afford the bride price for only one. Men here often marry girls who are 10 to 15 years younger than themselves.

The Durrani wedding ceremony in Afghanistan begins on the night before the ceremony, when the mother of the groom hosts a party at which young females prepare gifts for the bride. The gifts are then carried to the bride's home, accompanied by a cook and the groom's relatives as well as camels carrying food wrapped in colorful handkerchiefs. The bride is bathed and decorated with henna, as are the hands of the groom. When the sun rises on the following day, musicians play as the groom and his family make their way to the bride's home. A meal is served, after which the bride and groom proceed back to the groom's home, where the actual ceremony takes place.

Amish

Located primarily in Pennsylvania, Ohio, and Indiana, the Amish belong to a Mennonite sectarian Christian society of German descent. Mostly farmers, they disdain the use of machinery, and the values of the simple lives they lead are reflected in their marriage laws.

The wedding ceremony of the Amish is plain and wonderfully simple. The bride and groom personally deliver to each guest an invitation to their bonding. The wedding is planned to be celebrated after the harvesting season, so that all can attend, usually in the middle of the week. The ceremony is simple, as is the bride's dress, which is new but ordinary enough so that it can be worn to church on Sunday.

Armenia

Marriages in Armenia—until the 1990s part of the Soviet Socialist Republic—take place in the Armenian Christian Church or the Armenian Orthodox Church and typically celebrate the union of families.

Harsaniks, or weddings, traditionally take place on Fridays in the fall. The bride and groom wear gold or silver crowns and carry lit candles as they proceed to the church on horseback. The bride wears an outer and inner veil (the latter is removed by her husband in private). Godparents are prominent participants; they hold a cross over the couple's heads and tie their wrists with a special thread. Two doves may be released from a cage to symbolize the couple's love. At the reception, the bridal party holds up their arms to create an arch of flowers beneath which the newlyweds make their entrance. A godmother collects money for the couple and distributes gifts of dried fruit and nuts to guests, who toast the couple with a traditional Armenian wedding toast, "May you grow old on one pillow."

Belgium

The handkerchief tradition is perhaps the most unique custom of Belgium, where the mostly Catholic population marries in civil ceremonies. The family of the bride takes a handkerchief embroidered with the bride's name to the wedding. After the event, the handkerchief is displayed proudly in the family's home. As subsequent daughters in the family marry, their names are added to the handkerchief.

Bermuda

In Bermuda, part of the United Kingdom, a marriage can take the form of a civil or Christian ceremony. At many weddings, islanders top their wedding cakes with a tiny sapling. The newlyweds then

In 2004, Christelle Demichel, 35, became both bride and widow after marrying her dead boyfriend at Nice City Hall on the French Riviera. He had died two years before, but she remained so madly in love with the man that she wanted to take his name and be referred to as his wife even though he was dead.

Marriage by Any Other Name

In 1949, anthropologist George Peter Murdock defined marriage as a universal institution that involves a man and a woman living together, engaging in sexual activity, and co-operating economically. Here are some forms of marriage that he overlooked:

The Ashanti men of Ghana live with their mothers and sisters after marriage.

Among the Gururumba people in New Guinea, husbands and wives live and work separately. They are together only at mealtime.

In eighteenth-century Europe, married men and women among the lower classes often lived apart, as servants in separate homes, and visited one another only on their days off.

In certain West African societies, a woman may marry a woman as long as one of them agrees to act as the "female husband," and many sects recognize male-male marriages.

In China and Sudan, when families wanted to unite but there was only one son or daughter between them, that youth could be given in marriage to the spirit of a dead child. These "ghost marriages" existed right up until the early twentieth century, when they were popular among female silk workers in the Canton delta who sought the societal approval of marriage but also preferred economic independence.

Among the Toda of southern India, a girl could be married at the age of two or three, at which time she became the wife of all the brothers of the boy she married. When she came of age, she engaged in sex with all of them.

plant the tree in their garden at home, where they can watch it grow along with their marriage. Others top the cake with a miniature of the moon gate (a good-luck arch made of coral) through which the bride and groom pass on their way to the reception.

Buddhist
During the ceremony, the bride and groom are given a string of 21 ojuju beads: 1 represents Buddha, 2 are for each of the families, and 18 represent the bride and groom. All of these beads on one string represent the union of the families with Buddha.

Bulgaria
In Bulgaria, where the various influences of Romania, Greece, Turkey, and Serbia have roots, weddings vary from region to region. The population is primarily Eastern Orthodox, but under Communist rule (prior to 1991) religious ceremonies were outlawed. Today church weddings are the norm.

Once a girl becomes engaged in Bulgaria, she stays with her betrothed's parents until the wedding day, helping her prospective mother-in-law in keeping house. After marriage, things pretty much remain the same, since the couple usually resides with the groom's parents.

It is the duty of the maid of honor to place the veil over the bride's face before they set out for the church where the wedding will take place. It is a custom for the bride to show her modesty by rejecting the veil on the first two attempts but to finally agree to wear it on the third.

The bride and groom are instructed to enter the church right foot first, to ensure happiness.

Before the newlyweds enter the wedding feast, the groom's mother lays down a special cloth for their path and strews it with flowers, to wish them happiness in the future. She then feeds them from a special loaf of bread called a *pitka*, and they each grab an end. Whoever gets the biggest piece will rule the home.

After the marriage documents are signed, the bride and groom each try to be the first to step on the other one's toes. It is said that whoever is first will be the one to rule the roost.

Cajun
Before the reception begins at a traditional Louisianan Cajun wedding, the dance floor is cleared and the bride and groom, holding hands, march around the room as a song is played just for them.

When they have completed the rounds, guests choose partners and join the wedding march.

During the reception, guests pin money on the bride's veil in exchange for a dance with her or a kiss. Dollar bills are also pinned to the groom's jacket.

It's a Cajun tradition for older unmarried brothers and sisters of the bride or groom to dance with a broom at the wedding reception—thus mocking their single status.

Cambodia

Traditionally, the Buddhist marriages that took place here were arranged; today most Cambodians marry for love. The bride is elegantly adorned with bracelets on her wrists and ankles, and she wears a traditional sampot (lower body wrap). The wedding begins with a procession to the home of the bride, where she and the groom sit before a table elaborately laden with fruit, candles, and a sword to ward off evil. A monk cuts hair from each of their heads and mixes the hairs in a container. The process ends with the tying of knots on a string bracelet that the bride will wear; each knot represents a wish for future happiness. In some ceremonies, the priest ties the wrists of the couple together with red thread that has been dipped in holy water.

Central America

Central America has a wonderful mixture of Catholic, Protestant, and Mayan cultures and wedding customs, and any one custom is rarely free from the influence of the others. Catholic weddings in Central America routinely have aspects of Mayan traditions tossed in for good measure and contain many of the Hispanic elements found elsewhere (see Hispanic wedding traditions, page 22). Family is at the center of all wedding traditions in Central America, where celebrations are large, boisterous, happy affairs filled with friends and family, and children are always welcomed. The abundant varieties of flowers that grow throughout the region are ever-present at these celebrations.

In a traditional Guatemalan wedding, unlike in a more sedate North American wedding, the bride may waltz or strut or dance to the altar accompanied by her father or another male member of the family. It is

A Turkish bride in her wedding dress, ca. 1914 LIBRARY OF CONGRESS

also common for the bride and her bridesmaids and flower girls to all wear matching white wedding gowns. During the ceremony, the bride and groom are bound together with a silver rope symbolizing their eternal union.

In this country where family means everything, it is common for girls to marry quite young and to have many children. It is important that everyone, from the youngest baby to the oldest grandparent or great-grandparent, attend the wedding.

In Belize, weddings are especially joyous. Friends and family fill the church while the rest of the villagers peer in through the doors and windows, anxious not to miss a moment. While the groom and his best man stand at the altar, the bride waits outside the church until the moment of her grand entrance.

Simple and brief was the wedding, as that of Ruth and of Boaz.
Softly the youth and the maiden repeated the words of betrothal,
Taking each other for husband and wife in the Magistrate's presence,
After the Puritan way, and the laudable custom of Holland.
—From Henry Wordsworth Longfellow, "The Courtship of Miles Standish"

China

Ancient practices, including arranged marriages, marriages between relatives, and polygamy, were still practiced up until present times throughout many areas of China, whose people are primarily Buddhist. When the Communist Party enacted the Marriage Law of 1950, these practices, along with child betrothal, the keeping of concubines, and the sale of sons and daughters for marriage purposes, were banned. To curb the country's overpopulation problem, couples were encouraged to delay marriage until their midtwenties. The Marriage Law of the People's Republic of China, passed in 1981, further modernized marriage; now it became illegal for a bride price to be paid, monogamy was emphasized, and both bride and groom had to be completely willing to enter into the marriage. In China today women keep their maiden names after marriage (see also "The Buddhist Wedding," page 286).

Red (not white), representing joy, is the predominant color at a Chinese wedding. The bride's dress, the candles, and the decorations are all likely to be red. The invitations sent to the guests are wrapped in red gift wrap, and gifts of money to the newlyweds are presented in red envelopes.

Gold jewelry–filled purses are presented to the bride by women relatives and close friends in honor of her new status.

The 15-day period from the middle to the end of the seventh lunar month is considered inauspicious for marriages because that is the time of the Hungry Ghost Festival, when the gates of Hell are opened and the lost spirits are allowed to wander the

Above: Vintage illustration of a Chinese wedding processional **AUTHORS' COLLECTION**

Upper left: The Chinese calligraphy symbol "double happiness" is commonly seen on wedding invitations and programs. **AUTHORS' COLLECTION**

Right: Two bridal couples in China, ca. 1905 **LIBRARY OF CONGRESS**

earth. It is imperative that these spirits do not attend a wedding.

During the ceremony, both bride and groom pay homage and respect to their parents and elders for the guidance and wisdom they have bestowed upon the young pair.

During a special "capping" ceremony, the groom, dressed in a long gown, red shoes, and a red silk sash with a silk ball on his shoulder, kneels at the family altar while his father places a cap decorated with cypress leaves on his head. The groom bows to all, including his ancestors, and his father then removes the silk ball from the sash and places it on top of the bridal sedan chair that will carry the married couple.

After the ceremony, firecrackers are lit to chase any evil spirits and demons away from the couple. During the reception, the bride is presented typically in at least three different wedding outfits.

Cuba

When Fidel Castro came to power in 1956, he discouraged religious weddings. Today only the most devout Catholics in Cuba have church ceremonies. Weddings are largely performed by state employees and held in elegant state buildings called "Palaces of Matrimony." Because food is rationed in Cuba, only finger food and a cake are served. The state provides the wedding couple with a flower bouquet, which is placed on the shrine of a Cuban hero after the nuptials. During the reception, guests pin money to the bride's gown to help the couple set up their new household.

Cyprus

In the legendary birthplace of Aphrodite, brides and grooms are crowned as kings and queens as they are wed, largely in Greek Orthodox ceremonies.

A festivity called the "Spreading of the Mattress" takes place during the engagement celebration: the female friends of the bride take the couple's bedding, which has been blessed by a priest, to the party and dance with it. At the bachelor party, the groom is shoved by his friends, and he is instructed to be extremely kind to them lest the blade slip.

During the wedding ceremony, when the priest directs the bride to "love and obey" her husband, the groom steps on the bride's toes to underscore the message.

Czech Republic

On the steps of the church, the couple is formally presented and gets a "stern" lecture on their duties as husband and wife from the *starosta*, their male sponsor.

The bridesmaids' duties include pinning pieces of rosemary, a symbol of fertility, on each guest.

After the ceremony, the bride's veil is removed and replaced by the traditional matron's bonnet while the guests sing "Pisen Svatebni," a traditional Czech wedding song.

Czechs throw peas instead of rice.

Denmark

On the day of the wedding, an arch of pine, beech, or oak branches is erected in front of the home of the bride's parents as a show of respect. This "gate of honor" tradition is repeated on the couple's silver (25th) anniversary.

At the reception, guests dance around the groom and cut his tie (and possibly his socks) with a pair of scissors. Pieces are "auctioned off" to raise money for the honeymoon.

At some point during the celebration, someone persuades the groom to leave the room; after he's gone, all the men in the room kiss the bride. Later, the bride is lured away and the women kiss the groom.

Eastern Orthodoxy

Closely related to the Roman Catholic ceremony, the Eastern Orthodox wedding ceremony, as practiced in Albania, Bulgaria, Romania, Serbia, and Russia, requires certain rituals to be performed three times to symbolize the Holy Trinity: the best man moves the bride's and groom's rings from their left hands to their right hands three times; the crowns that are placed on their heads are switched from the bride to the groom three times; the couple takes three sips of wine from a cup; and the couple walks around a ceremonial table three times.

England

Most British weddings take place in a religious setting—either the Church of England or the Roman Catholic Church. In addition, a sizable portion of the English population are members of the Church of Scotland.

The traditional English wedding celebration began on the way to the ceremony: guests processed to the church as young girls scattered flower petals in the bride's path in hopes of providing her with a happy path in life. The bride carried a horseshoe decorated with ribbons for good luck.

Because seeing a chimney sweep on the way to a wedding was supposed to be good luck for the bride, one was often hired to attend the wedding.

In the north of England, it was customary for one of the oldest inhabitants of the neighborhood to be standing on the threshold of the bride's new home before she entered. There she would toss some shortbread over her head, making sure all the pieces landed outside. Guests would scramble for pieces, which were said to bring good luck.

Fishermen in Norfolk and Suffolk always got married at high tide for good luck.

The Jewish *ketubah* is, in essence, a prenuptial agreement in which the husband commits to providing food, clothing, and marital relations to his wife, and it is an integral part of the wedding ceremony. COURTESY OF GARDENSTATEPHOTO.COM

Ethiopian Jews

Among the small Jewish population of Ethiopia (most of the population is either Muslim or Ethiopian Orthodox), many of whom have now emigrated to Israel, preparations for a wedding began a week before the actual ceremony with the building of a wedding hut by the groom and his family that would be blessed by a *cahanet*. The ceremony began with a purification rite during which a *keherah*—one or more cords painted white for the groom's purity and red for the bride's virginity—was placed at the groom's feet, leading upward and tied to his forehead.

On the eve of the wedding, the bride painted her fingernails, palms, and feet with red dye.

If it was discovered that the bride was not a virgin, the marriage contract was torn into shreds, after which the woman would be shunned by the community.

Finland

Although most Finnish weddings are Lutheran, with ceremonies varying a great deal from region to region, a common theme is the royalty bestowed on the bride and groom on their special day. They are given gold crowns to wear and are seated in special places of honor. The seated bride holds a sieve, covered with a silk shawl,

and guests come by to slip money into the sieve. Their names and the amounts of their gifts are announced publicly by a groomsman.

During the reception, the single guests form a circle and dance around the blindfolded bride. Whomever she crowns will be the next to wed.

Finnish brides were once required to go door to door with a pillowcase to collect their wedding gifts.

France

Since 1791, the French Constitution has recognized marriage solely as a civil contract; religious weddings are rare in France, although 90 percent of the population is Roman Catholic. Historically, however, French weddings were routinely church affairs.

Traditionally, marriages were arranged by families more concerned with the household experience than with romance. During the 1800s, in rural areas, a husband who was not happy with his bridal choice could sell his wife in the marketplace. The practice was illegal but popularly accepted.

Guests at a traditional French wedding brought the flowers and floral decorations with them to the ceremony.

Today, as the French couple departs from their wedding ceremony, laurel leaves are scattered outside the exit, just as happened centuries ago. And at the reception, many French newlyweds still toast using a special two-handled cup called the *Coupe de marriage.* This is often an object that has been passed down through generations of a family.

The French wedding ring often comes in two parts: the bride's name and half of the wedding date are engraved on one part, and the groom's name and the other half of the date are engraved on the other; at the wedding ceremony, the two halves become whole.

The French throw wheat instead of rice.

Germany

The population of Germany is almost entirely Protestant and Catholic, and even though the church weddings here resemble the Western variety, many traditional customs survive.

Only about half of German couples wear engagement rings; among those who do, the rings are worn by both the bride and the groom.

In an eighteenth-century tradition known as "the Bride's Bush," a bush was positioned on a stake outside the tavern (where weddings usually took place), letting all passersby know that they were invited to attend the party within.

Even today three-day celebrations are the norm in Germany and break down as follows.

Day 1: Usually on a Thursday, the obligatory civil ceremony takes place and is followed by a dinner with family and friends.

Day 2: On Friday evening, the real fun begins. A party called a *Polterabend* includes joyful celebrating and the smashing of plates and other breakables for good luck ("May nothing else ever be broken in your home"). Before the couple is allowed to leave the party, friends block the exits with garlands of greenery and ribbon, and the groom must pay a "ransom" with promises of money and future festivities.

Day 3: The religious ceremony and the traditional reception are held. At the ceremony, when the couple kneels, the groom may put his knee on the bride's hem as a sign that he plans to "keep her in line." The bride, in turn, may step on his foot as she rises, to show that she is reasserting herself.

During the reception, the bride is abducted by the best man and then taken to a nearby bar. It is then the groom's job to find them and pay a "ransom"—usually the price of their drinks.

Greece

Because the Greek population is 97 percent Greek Orthodox, weddings take place in church, and no union is recognized until the couple has completed premarital counseling to discuss the religious and personal ramifications of this important step.

Traditionally, Greek couples become engaged in the presence of their families, and the engagement is considered to be as binding as the wedding itself.

An outdoor wedding might easily be attended by over a thousand people, usually representing the entire population of the village. Relatives of the bride and groom all chip in for expenses.

The *koumbaros*, traditionally the groom's godfather, was an honored guest who participated in the wedding ceremony. Today the *koumbaros* is usually the best man. It is his responsibility to help crown the couple. The crowns generally are white or gold, or they are made of either long-lasting flowers such as orange blossoms or "twigs of love and vine" wrapped in silver and gold paper. Other attendants may read Scripture, hold candles, and help by packing the crowns in a special box after the ceremony.

To seal their own good luck in making a match, single women once signed their names under the hem of the bride's dress.

Greek brides wear yellow or red veils, which symbolize fire and were thought to protect the bride from evil spirits in ancient times. A Greek bride also carries a lump of sugar with her to ensure that her life will be sweet. Traditionally, and still today, a pair of scissors is inserted into her bouquet to "cut" the evil eye of Vaskania, who embodied the devil.

At Greek weddings, dishes are smashed on the floor during the reception, for good luck, and the party can easily last all night.

A Greek bride may throw a pomegranate, whose seeds symbolize fertility, instead of the traditional bouquet.

Haiti

While the elite upper classes in Haiti routinely hold Christian weddings, the lower classes rely on the "placage" marriage, in which the groom, in the home of the bride, makes promises to provide for his new wife and the bride agrees to keep house. Although the government does not sanction these marriages, they are common practice.

Although virginity is not demanded of the Mirebalais bride of the Haitian Valley, she must divulge, at the time she weds, whether she has had sexual relations. While very few brides prove to be virgins, an unmarried girl who gives birth may be beaten, and the male culprit must face angry parents.

Hawaii

(SEE ALSO POLYNESIAN WEDDING CUSTOMS, PAGE 32)

In the nineteenth century, before the influx of Christianity, polygamy and polyandry were both acceptable in Hawaii. The purity of noble blood was of primary interest, and a chief would often take his sister for his bride. Distinguished families were likely to arrange marriages before birth.

Today Hawaiian marriages are monogamous just as they are throughout the rest of the United States, and weddings are largely held Western-style. But some ancient traditions are still practiced, sometimes as theater and sometimes as a nod to history.

The twining of two lives is symbolized by coconut fibers that have been braided into a rope known as an *aha*.

The *honi* is a tender gesture shared by the bride and groom after the nuptial kiss: they gently touch noses.

The Hawaiian lei is a symbol of love, and it is worn by the marrying couple to show their commitment to one another. A lei is also used to bind the couple together as a symbol of their new union.

In a custom known as *kuilama*, the couple holds hands during the entire ceremony.

The wedding cake is not cut at the reception party but later at the couple's home.

According to custom, the wedding guests bring gifts to the wedding, but these may not be gifts of money.

Hindu

Among Indian Hindus, compatibility of caste and cultural background are still often more important than the similarity of a couple's educational and financial backgrounds.

In a traditional Hindu wedding, the ceremony begins when the groom comes to the bride's home to ask her father for his blessing. When the father approves, Brahman priests read the families' genealogies.

There are three traditional requirements for an Indian Hindu bridegroom:

1. He can't be insane.

2. He can't be impotent.

3. He can't have a terrible disease.

There are seven traditional requirements for the bride:

1. She cannot have been married before.

2. If she isn't the oldest, then her older sisters must already be married.

3. She must want to bear children for her husband.

4. She must be physically attractive.

5. She must be practical and know how to manage a household.

6. She must be docile.

7. She must be eager to satisfy her husband sexually.

Hispanic

In examining Hispanic wedding traditions, it is often impossible to distinguish between Spanish, Mexican, and Latin American customs. While many of the rituals closely resemble one another, each is usually performed with its own slight twist or different sentiment (see also Central American wedding customs, page 17).

Hispanic wedding ceremonies in Spain, Mexico, and throughout Latin America take place in Catholic churches and commonly include a "Blessing of Rings and Coins." The presiding priest blesses the rings the couple will wear as well as the 13 coins that the groom will soon present to his bride: "May these coins be a symbol of mutual help throughout your lives." After the exchange of rings, the groom gives the bride the coins, symbolic of the care he promises to provide.

In Mexico and elsewhere, weddings traditionally were held much as they were throughout the rest of the world, except that the ceremony took place outside the church; only when it was over would the wedding party enter the church to attend Mass. During the ceremony, in a tradition that is still popular today, the bride and groom would be tied together, by either a very long rosary, ribbons, or a garland of flowers, at the shoulders, waists, and wrists in a figure-eight looping. Just before the wedding feast began, guns would be shot (could this have been the first shotgun wedding?), and when the dancing began, all the guests, arm in arm, would surround the couple, creating the shape of a heart.

Mehendi Wedding Customs

The art of Mehendi has existed for centuries. The exact place of its origin is difficult to track, given that people have traveled the globe for centuries, leaving their customs behind. Some historical evidence suggests that Mehendi started in India, or at least in the region.

• The occasion of Mehendi, or Mehandi, is a fun-filled ritual celebrated mainly by the bride's family. Just as modern Hindu weddings are far more elaborate than their earlier counterparts, so pre-wedding functions, and the Mehendi celebration in particular, are celebrated with enthusiasm.

• Mehendi has great significance in all Eastern wedding traditions. Mehendi night is something like a hen night in the West, with all the bride's female friends and relatives getting together to celebrate. They spend the evening singing traditional Mehendi songs, which tell of the good luck and blessings that Mehendi will bring.

• The Mehendi night is common in the Gulf regions of Saudi, Bahrain, Kuwait, and the United Arab Emirates. Here the celebration is generally held a few days prior to the wedding and is strikingly similar to the Indian version. The bride has her hands and feet painted, and traditional songs are sung by the mothers and grandmothers, who tease her about her future. Mehendi also features in other Middle Eastern celebrations such as births and christenings. In Gujarat, Mehendi tattooing is part of the Adivasi women's wedding traditions. Leaves and flowers are used as templates around which complex designs are painted on the bride's face and arms.

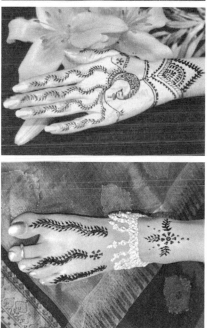

While the Mehendi ritual is practiced in many cultures, indications are that it originated in India. COURTESY OF HENNA ARTISANS

• The Mehendi ceremony is considered so sacred in some religions that unless the mother-in-law has applied the first dot of Mehendi to the bride's hand, the painting cannot go ahead. The Mehendi dot is considered a symbolic blessing, the bestowal of which permits the new daughter-in-law to beautify herself for the groom.

• Many brides believe that the deeper the color of the Mehendi, the deeper the love they will receive from their in-laws, in particular the mother-in-law, whose blessing is particularly important to an Asian bride. Hence, the bride does whatever she can to ensure that the Mehendi stain is deep. A deeply colored design is a sign of good luck for the marital couple. It is common for the names of the bride and groom to be hidden in the Mehendi design, and the wedding night cannot commence until the groom has found the names. A bride is not expected to perform any housework until her wedding Mehendi has faded.

In some areas, the bridegroom's hands are also decorated; communities in Kashmir and Bangladesh have evolved particular men's designs. A current trend in the United Kingdom has both brides and grooms decorating themselves with patterns in the form of rings or bracelets.

In Spain, the bride's parents represent the roles of the best man and maid of honor. The bride and groom are blessed at home by their parents before the ceremony.

Throughout the Hispanic countries, *padrinos* and *madrinos* (god-fathers and godmothers) are especially honored participants in the wedding. They assist with—and pay for—all aspects of the wedding arrangements, including the wedding site, the wedding songs, the flowers, and even the invitations.

The pillows on which the couple kneel at the altar have become an art form unto themselves. They are elaborately designed and hand-stitched with pearls and lace and usually contain a romantic sentiment.

At the reception, all of the male guests who dance with the bride have to pin money to her gown.

Special pins, called *capias*, are displayed on a doll, which is dressed like the bride. The capias have the bride's and groom's names and the wedding date inscribed on them and are given as favors to the guests.

After the reception, some observe the tradition of staging a mock recapture of the bride by her family, and only after the groom promises his goodwill to the family is the bride returned.

In some countries, the flower girl and ring bearer are dressed as miniature versions of the bride and groom.

The Hispanic groom often wears a shirt that has been embroidered by the bride.

White roses are the flower of choice at Hispanic weddings.

Holland

Holland is populated by people from all over the world, many of whom have intermarried, and religions found here today run the gamut from Christian to Islam. Weddings are held Western-style, with extra emphasis on the theme of romance, which played an important role in old Dutch wedding traditions.

In times gone by, at a party held before the wedding, the bride and groom sat on elaborately decorated thrones surrounded by evergreens to show their enduring love for one another. At modern weddings today, Dutch families might still seat the bride and groom on thrones beneath a canopy of fragrant evergreens.

Traditional courting rituals centered on romantic gestures. An interested suitor would attach a flower or wreath to the door of a girl he wanted to pursue. If she discarded the wreath, he would venture further by leaving a bouquet of flowers and a card with his name. She would welcome these advances by placing a basket of flowers or candy with a love note inserted on her windowsill.

To seal an engagement, the father of the groom would give the bride a chatelaine—a silver chain from which hung a pair of scissors, a small knife in a leather case, a needle box, a pincushion, a scented ball, and a mirror—to represent all she would need as a wife.

In Broek, an engagement was celebrated when the couple sat on a bed in the presence of their parents and kissed and exchanged rings. The groom-to-be would then give his bride a large amount of money, which would be covered with a cloth on which her first name and the time of the betrothal were embroidered.

Dutch laws prohibited the shattering of an engagement. When such cases came to court, rings and love notes were often presented as evidence.

Wedding parties among commoners were held at inns and taverns, while the upper classes held their receptions at home, where rooms would be elaborately decorated with wax cupids and angels, flowers, garlands, and gold leaf. The "thrones" on which the bride and groom sat were likewise festooned with ribbons and paper ornaments.

Hungary

Although the Hungarian population is almost entirely Roman Catholic and Protestant, the communism that spread here in the early twentieth century encouraged atheism.

Before that time, the marriage vow was sealed with an exchange of scarves. The bride and groom would then have their hands tied together over a loaf of bread into which a twig was inserted. The twig represented the groom, the bread represented the bride, and together they formed a perfect union. The symbolic twig was also inserted into cakes and tarts and served to the guests.

In the modern ceremony, the bride gives the groom three or seven (both biblical numbers) handkerchiefs.

India

In India, where almost 90 percent of the population is Hindu, marriage is viewed as a religious duty whose purpose is to produce progeny who will continue the family line and be available to perform rites for those who have died. Young people have always been encouraged to avoid romantic relationships and leave the matchmaking to others.

While this attitude has been changing in recent years, even after an initial introduction, a prospective Indian couple still doesn't have much direct interaction before marriage. They may meet a few times, but ongoing communication takes place through the couple's parents or go-betweens.

Many families retain the services of a professional marriage broker, who is also a specialist in genealogy, to seek out good unions for their children.

In cities like New Delhi, elaborate processions wind through the streets as a bridegroom heads for his wedding on a white horse. Even families of modest means will incur enormous debts to provide lavish feasts and adequate dowries for their daughters.

The Hindu bride sports heavy necklaces and bracelets, earrings and nose rings, and noisy anklets (in India, each region practices its own style of bejeweling the bride), and she will have the profuse designs called Mehendi (see "Mehendi Wedding Customs," page 23) painted on her hands and feet.

A red canopy called a *mandapa* is erected for the ceremony and decorated with flowers.

During a Gujarati ceremony, the groom receives a special blessing known as a *saubbagyavati bhava,* which is whispered into his right ear by several married women.

At the close of the wedding ceremony, the groom's brother sprinkles flower petals on the bridal couple to ward off evil spirits.

During the reception, a coconut may be held over the couple's heads as they are circled three times by the guests. This is another way of banishing evil spirits.

Wedding bands are made of gold because it is said to last forever.

Indonesia

In Indonesia, almost the entire population is Muslim, so religion plays a primary role in marriage. The law requires not only that both civil and religious officiants preside at wedding ceremonies but that each person who is married register his or her religion with the Civil Registry Office; agnostics and atheists are not recognized.

Indonesian marriages are often arranged, but young people do have consultation rights. The process of arranging a union centers on a series of meetings: the "Acceptance of the Proposal Meeting," at which the bride price is set; the "Engagement Meeting," at which the wedding-day arrangements are determined; and the "Marriage Beforehand Meeting," where rice and palm sauce are shared and the bride price is forked over.

A Javanese Muslim custom is to have a father sit on a couch with both the bride and groom sitting in his lap. The bride's mother asks which one weighs more, and when the father responds that

> "When a man marries, he has fulfilled half of his religion, so let him fear Allah regarding the remaining half." — Mohammed

they weigh the same, it is an indication that the bride's parents will treat the newlyweds equally after they are married. Once thus blessed, the bride is secluded for six days.

Music at a wedding in Indonesia is likely to consist of an ensemble of chimes, drums, and gongs known as a *gamelan.*

On the island of Java, the reception takes place a week after the ceremony, to give the bride and groom a chance to become spiritually centered.

Ireland

The Irish wedding of yore included the entire community and was marked by robust partying and wild celebration. The festivities were kicked off by a race for a bottle of whiskey; the winner could kiss the bride first. The fun ended in the evening with the "bedding" of the couple and plenty of obscene teasing.

Today a couple wishing to marry in Ireland, where most weddings take place in the Roman Catholic Church, must show residence for at least 14 days in the district in which they wish to marry. Anyone under 21 needs a parent's consent to marry; young people under 16 may marry, but only with special consent from the High Court.

The bride and groom walk down the aisle together rather than with parents or sponsors.

The shamrock is often used in the floral displays and sometimes as a motif on the wedding stationery and as decoration on the cake.

The traditional Irish wedding ring features a claddagh. The heart held by two hands, with a crown, symbolizes love, faith, and honor (see sidebar about Irish claddagh wedding traditions, page 74).

Irish brides take no chances: for good luck, they mix English lavender into their bouquets, wear fine Irish lace at the hems of their wedding gowns, and carry a horseshoe for good measure.

Italy

In Italy, where the Western-style wedding originated, almost all weddings take place in the Roman Catholic Church. A large ribbon is hung on the door of the church to signify the spirit that binds the couple.

In the small villages of Italy, after the wedding Mass, the newly married couple walks through the town plaza, greeting their friends, relatives, and neighbors. There the villagers set up a saw-horse, a log, and a double-handled ripsaw. The newlyweds must saw the log apart with the prompting and cheering of the crowd. The ritual symbolizes the need for the man and woman to work together in all of life's tasks.

On the day of the wedding the bride is not supposed to wear any gold until after her wedding ring is placed on her finger lest she attract bad luck.

Old church traditions forbade marriage during Lent and Advent. Marriage was also avoided in the months of May and August. May was to be reserved for the veneration of the Virgin Mary, and August was thought to invite bad luck and sickness. Sunday marriages—except in the months just mentioned—were believed to be luckiest.

At a traditional wedding in the Veneto region of Italy, as the bride and groom walk to church, town residents present the bride with challenges. For example, they may put a broom on the ground and observe her reaction. If she notices it and picks it up to put it away, she is considered a good housekeeper. If she comes across a crying child, the hope is that she will lend comfort. If she gives money to a passing beggar, she has a kind heart.

In southern regions of Italy, the couple shatter a vase or glass into many pieces at the end of the wedding day. The number of pieces represents the number of years they'll be happily married to one another.

Italian folklore called for the groom to carry a piece of iron in his pocket for good luck, while the bride's veil protected her from evil spirits.

6 Italian Proverbs About Marriage

1. *Ne di Venere ne di Marte non si sposa ne si parte!* (Neither marry nor depart on the day of Venus or of Mars.)

2. *La buona moglie fa il buon marito.* (A good wife makes a good husband.)

3. *La moglie e' la chiave di casa.* (The wife is the key of the house.)

4. *La prima e' matrimonio, la seconda comagnia, la terza un'eresia.* (The first wife is marriage, the second company, the third heresy.)

5. *Chi non ha moglie non ha padrone.* (Who has no wife has no master.)

6. *Casa senza fimmina 'mpuvirisci.* (A house without a woman is poor.)

At some weddings, primarily in northern Italy, the best man cuts the groom's tie into little pieces that are then put on a tray and sold to the guests. The proceeds are given to the couple to help pay for the music.

In northern Italy, the groom brings the bridal bouquet to the wedding. Its color and style are kept a secret, since the flowers are to be a last-minute surprise. (Bridezillas in Italy must love this one!)

Jamaica

Formal weddings are a rarity in Jamaica since most unions take place out of wedlock. Since men are rarely able to fulfill the economic promises required of a bridegroom, "visiting relationships" in which men and woman have sexual relationships in the home of the woman's family are common and socially acceptable among all classes. When a marriage finally does take place, it is not uncommon for the illegitimate children to act as ushers and bridesmaids.

Japan

The predominant religion in Japan is Shinto, which means "the way of the gods." The traditional Japanese wedding ceremony is held in a Shinto shrine and is considered to be private, with only family and close friends present. Today brides and grooms who marry in this religious tradition truly embrace the idea of "something old, something new," as the traditional Shinto wedding rites as practiced in Japan have been influenced by modern Western thought.

In Japan, the marriage was traditionally arranged by a *nakodo*, or the original wedding planner. This individual not only facilitated the proposal, acceptance, and exchange of "gifts of happiness and fortune" between the families, but he or she also attended the wedding, often participating in the ceremony. Today only slightly more than 10 percent of Japanese families use a nakodo.

Two kinds of marriages take place in Japan today: *ren-ai*, which is a marriage based on love; and *mi-ai*, an arranged marriage, which today is voluntary. Ren-ai became much more widespread after World War II.

The Japanese wedding ceremony is conducted by a Shinto priest and consists primarily of a purification rite, the recitation of vows, and a ritual in which sake is shared (see sake ceremony section in "The Shinto Wedding," page 291).

The crane, which lives for 1,000 years, is a symbol of good luck and marital harmony. Cranes mate for life, and they build nests for their babies together. To show her aspiration for such a life, the Japanese bride folds 1,000 origami cranes before her wedding.

A Japanese bride may change her attire as often as two or three times during her wedding day. She may begin with the traditional kimono and end with a Western-style white dress. The kimono worn at a girl's wedding is traditionally a very expensive antique that is usually rented, not purchased.

Because ducks and geese represent fidelity, two ducks or a goose and gander sometimes accompany Japanese grooms as they proceed down the aisle.

In some ceremonies, the groom cracks a raw egg with his bare foot. Some say this is a prayer for fertility; others claim that it reminds the bride and groom that life and love are fragile.

Shukuji are special blessings offered to the bride and groom during the reception. Typically, these begin with grave pronouncements made by the elders in the families, but as the sake flows they become humorous and teasing in lighthearted attempts to embarrass the couple.

Korea

In the past, both Buddhist and Christian weddings have taken place in Korea, and most were arranged marriages that employed both matchmakers and fortunetellers. Only in recent decades have customs changed, with more and more young people finding their own mates. Those too busy for the job find mates online or through government-licensed marriage bureaus, which were established in 1988.

The financial responsibilities of the bride's family are many. They are expected to give substantial gifts to the couple—a home or a car—as well as Western clothing for the groom's entourage and jewelry for the bride's new mother-in-law. They must also pay for half of all the wedding costs.

Two Korean wedding traditions involve birds that mate for life—ducks and geese. The Korean groom used to travel to the home of his bride on the back of a white pony, bearing a goose,

A Korean wedding procession escorting the bride to the home of the groom, ca. 1919 LIBRARY OF CONGRESS

which symbolized fidelity. Nowadays they use symbolic wooden geese. In another tradition, a pair of wooden ducks, one symbolizing the bride and the other the groom, indicate whether the couple is happy or at odds: If the ducks face nose to nose, the couple is getting along. If they are tail to tail, the couple is fighting.

The ceremony includes a series of ancient rituals. A screen painted with peonies, symbols of beauty, affection, sex, and happiness, serves as a backdrop for the ceremony, and dots are applied to the bride's cheekbones to ward off evil. A photograph of the couple is taken in front of a traditional painting.

The bride wears a *chogori*, a short, long-sleeved jacket, and a *chima*, which is a full-length wraparound skirt. She may wear a white sash decorated with flowers or symbols of significance to the bride, as well as a crown or headpiece.

At the wedding, the bride and groom offer fruit and wine to their parents as a show of respect.

One of the most moving moments of the Korean ceremony is called *kunbere:* when the couple share wine from cups that are made of two halves of a gourd, the marriage is sealed; there are no spoken vows.

Korean women keep their maiden names after marriage.

Kuwait

The Kuwaiti government promotes marriage by presenting couples with a "wedding gift" in the amount of $13,000 (U.S.). Half of the money is a gift, to start their married life together on the right financial foot, and the other half is an interest-free loan. Both members of the couple must be Kuwaiti nationals; 90 percent of all marriages in Kuwait are between nationals.

Nonmarriage is considered a social problem and a threat to the traditional role of a woman as a wife and mother; it is socially undesirable for an unmarried Kuwaiti woman to live by herself. The goal of a social committee known as *Al-lajnat-al Othman al-Khairiya* (Al-Othman Committee for Social Welfare) is to encourage single women to marry, even as second wives of married men if necessary.

Macedonia

Each year in Macedonia, in an area called Galicnik, citizens host a traditional wedding that is intended to remind residents and visitors—who attend from all over the world—of the heritage of a country from which most young people today emigrate in search of better lives and more opportunities. The event is held at the beginning of July on St. Peter's Day, which was traditionally an especially lucky day for marriage. In fact, as many as 30 weddings are held on this day each year.

The weekend-long event begins on a Saturday afternoon as drums resound throughout the valley and some 7,000 spectators and participants gather for the event. The groom decorates a banner with flowers outside his family's house, and a rifle is thrown. His mother greets the family and relatives holding homemade bread and a jar and then proceeds to dance the *svekrvino oro* (mother-in-law's dance). In the evening, a torch-lit bridal procession lights the path to three fountains, where the bride fills jugs with water for the last time as an unmarried woman. The wedding dress is elaborately crafted in sterling silver and gold and is one of the most beautiful folk costumes in the world. One highlight of the weekend happens when the bride welcomes the groom on the balcony of her home as she looks through her wedding ring and declares, "Through this ring I behold you. Let me enter your heart."

Malaysia

In Malaysia, where Islam is the predominant religion, the bride and groom are treated as "king and queen for a day."

Until about three decades ago, over 50 percent of the Muslim women in Malaysia were married before they were 18, and over 99 percent of them were married by the time they'd reached their forties. The only socially acceptable reasons for not marrying were mental illness or physical deformity.

The *berinai* (henna application) ceremony is held prior to the wedding. The bride's palms and feet are decorated with the dye from the henna leaves.

Akad Nikah, the signing of the contract, is normally presided over by a *Kadhi*, a religious official of the Shariat Court. A small sum of money called the *Mas Kahwin* seals the contract.

The recent trend is to hold the solemnization in the mosque, as happened in the Prophet Muhammad's time.

Traditionally, each wedding guest is given a beautifully decorated hard-boiled egg, a symbol of fertility.

Morocco

Traditionally, the mostly Muslim weddings in Morocco were arranged; today young people have more of a say in who they marry.

A traditional wedding is expensive and impressive. The dowry is paid before a notary and is spent on the bride's trousseau and new furniture. The jewelry she receives must be made of gold (rings, bracelets, necklaces, and earrings).

The wedding day is marked by two separate receptions—one at the home of the bride's family and another at the groom's home. During the women's celebration, the bride is carried in a procession by her women friends. At the groom's party, music entertains the many guests. Late at night, the groom, accompanied by family and friends, makes his way to the bride's reception, where the celebration continues until the wee hours. Guests shower the newlyweds with dates, figs, and raisins, which symbolize fertility.

Some Moroccan weddings are a seven-day affair:

Day 1: A henna artist comes to the bride's house with antique jewelry that has been rented for the occasion. She styles the bride's hair and dresses her in finery, then decorates her hands and feet with elaborate designs.

Day 2: Female friends of the bride gather for a reception.

Day 3: Male friends take their turn at celebrating.

Day 4: A Muslim officiant comes to the bride's home and pronounces the couple man and wife. Only women and the groom attend this simple ceremony.

Days 5 and 6: Everyone comes together for a joyous celebration that features dancing and live music.

Day 7: In the final portion of the wedding, the bride, dressed in a style that Cleopatra might envy, is paraded about. When she is finally lowered from her "throne," the groom stands waiting.

Peru

The ancient Incas of Peru so valued the protection of bloodlines offered by marriage that men commonly married their sisters. Spinsters and bachelors were rare, and nuptials were often performed as group weddings, during which the young people of the village would line up waiting for the chief to pronounce them married. Couples who were actually in love would jockey for position at the front of the line.

In Peru today almost the entire population is Catholic, and most weddings are held in church. Wedding charms are attached with ribbons between the layers of the wedding cake. Before the cake is cut and served to the guests, each single woman pulls a string.

The one who pulls the ribbon with a ring on the end is the next one to marry within a year.

Philippines

In the only Asian nation that embraces Catholicism, brides often carry rosaries along with their bridal bouquets. Instead of a bouquet toss, some Filipina brides opt to offer the flowers to a favorite saint or to the image of the Virgin Mary at the church. Others might place the bouquet on the grave of a lost loved one.

The gold-coin tradition of the Hispanics (see "Wedding Customs Around the World," page 14) is also practiced in the Philippines.

Marrying couples have a few pairs of *ninongs* and *ninangs* (godparents) to stand as principal sponsors in the ceremony, much as they had during their baptisms.

Three special traditions are at the center of the Filipino wedding ceremony: a candle-lighting is facilitated by the godparents; the bride and groom are both covered with the bride's veil, symbolizing the union of two people "clothed" as one; and finally, the couple is connected with a silken rope (or string of flowers or links of coins) tied in a figure eight.

Newlyweds release a pair of white doves during the reception to signify a peaceful and harmonious marital relationship. During the reception, a bell-shaped basket hangs in the middle of the room. After the toast, the bride and groom pull on its ribbons to open a trapdoor from which two white doves emerge. If the birds fly up toward the heavens when they are released, the couple will have a successful life together.

Filipino wedding culture is fraught with superstition: rain is considered lucky if it falls on the wedding day; a bride who wears pearls (the "tears" of the oysters) on her wedding day will be miserable; siblings may not marry during the same year; the groom who is seated before his bride will be henpecked. The list goes on!

Poland

In Poland, where 90 percent of the population is Roman Catholic, people commonly believe that the success of a marriage depends on the lavishness and gaiety of the wedding celebration. Families often assume serious debts to pay for the festivities.

The night before a Polish girl hears her wedding bells, her mother and female relatives redo her customary single maidenly braid into two. This traditional wedding hairstyle symbolizes the new step the bride-to-be is taking into marriage.

North American Indian

Over 250 Native American tribes have inhabited the United States, and each has had its own religious and social customs. Before the colonization of America, most tribes practiced polygamy and most marriages were arranged. Bride price was an important aspect of the marriage transaction, and although marrying within bloodlines was not allowed, unions took place mostly within the clan. In the nineteenth and twentieth centuries, as North American Indians were forcibly assimilated into American culture, many traditional marriage practices disappeared.

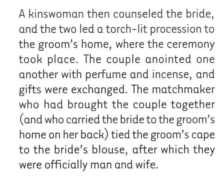

A Ute bridegroom, ca. 1906 LIBRARY OF CONGRESS

Aztec

The night before a traditional Aztec wedding, the bride was bathed, her hair was washed, and red feathers were attached to her arms and legs. The next day, wearing her best finery for the ceremony, she sat near a fire as well-wishers filed past. A kinswoman then counseled the bride, and the two led a torch-lit procession to the groom's home, where the ceremony took place. The couple anointed one another with perfume and incense, and gifts were exchanged. The matchmaker who had brought the couple together (and who carried the bride to the groom's home on her back) tied the groom's cape to the bride's blouse, after which they were officially man and wife.

Blackfoot

Marriages were arranged by families, sometimes without the knowledge of their children. An agreement was negotiated and followed by an exchange of gifts between the families and the payment of a bride price. Then the couple would simply begin life together, and they would be considered married. The bride would make pairs of moccasins for each male member of her husband's family. If she was lazy, her husband could send her back to her family. Men openly engaged in adultery, while women were expected to be faithful.

Cherokee

The Cherokees of North Carolina practiced trial marriages. Once a boy and girl had become attracted to one another, they were allowed to have sexual relations. But they were not allowed to live together until the boy had constructed a home for the couple and killed an animal to prove that he could provide for his wife. When this was done, the girl would prepare a special meal, and they were then considered to be married for one year. During this time, either could leave if unhappy. If they decided to stay together after the year was up, another binding ceremony took place.

Hopi

During the ceremony for an American Hopi wedding, the bride's hair was washed with yucca root shampoo. After the groom made a speech, a lock of his hair was tied together with a lock of the bride's hair, and they were pronounced man and wife. After the wedding, the bride's in-laws no longer spoke her name but called her *moewe*, which means daughter-in-law. (Hopi names are kept secret from outsiders and are revealed only on ceremonial occasions. State law requires Hopis to sign their American names on their marriage licenses.)

Navajo

The Navajo wedding took place in a hogan, a structure made of earth and branches. This would eventually become the temporary residence of the new couple. A fire blazed in the center of the hogan. The groom, carrying a saddle, en-

A Qagyuhl wedding party, ca. 1914 LIBRARY OF CONGRESS

tered the hogan with his entourage, after which the bride, carrying a basket of corn mush, entered with her family. Her mother remained behind, as it was considered taboo for the groom to see her. The officiant placed a water jug in front of the couple, and the bride used a gourd ladle to pour water over the groom's hands. Then she passed the gourd to the groom so that he could wash hers. The officiant scattered a small amount of corn pollen across the corn mush in the bride's basket and then circled the basket with pollen in a clockwise pattern. After making sure that the congregation approved of the marriage, the officiant twisted the basket in a half-turn, symbolizing the couple's attention to one another. The groom took a small amount of corn mush from the east side of the basket and fed it to the bride. Then the bride took corn mush from the north, south, west, and center of the basket, and once she had eaten it, the ceremony was over. After the ensuing celebration, the couple remained in the hogan for four days and nights.

On the way to church, the couple's way is blocked by children to whom the best man must pay a "toll."

The "money dance" is always popular at a traditional reception in Poland, as it is in many other parts of the world. Traditionally, the maid of honor wears an apron and collects the money given by the guests for their dance with the bride. After all the guests have danced with the bride, they form a tight circle around her, and the groom tries to break through the circle while the guests try hard to keep him out. Once he breaks through, he picks up his bride and carries her away from the wedding reception.

The sharing of bread, salt, and wine is an important feature of weddings in Poland. The bread represents the hope that the bride and groom will never go hungry. The salt is a reminder that life may be difficult at times, but that they will learn to cope. The wine symbolizes the desire that the couple will never go thirsty and that their lives will be filled with health and happiness.

During the *oczepiny* ceremony, the bride's veil is removed by her women friends as she enters the reception hall, signifying the end of her maidenhood. A funny hat is placed on the groom's head, representing the wish that the marriage will be full of happiness and laughter.

Quaker

Quakers believe that only God, not man, can join a bride and groom in matrimony. When a couple decide to marry, they declare their intentions at a town meeting, and a committee of citizens is then appointed to talk with them and make sure that they have properly prepared themselves for marriage: that they are able to make all the needed arrangements for the wedding ceremony; that they have sought out premarital counseling; and that they know how to acquire and file legal documents.

During the ceremony, which takes place in a Friends' meeting-house, the bride walks down the aisle unaccompanied, as it is believed that she belongs to no one but herself. During the ceremony, the couple recite a version of this simple vow: "In the presence of God and these our friends, I take thee to be my wedded wife (or husband), promising the Divine with assistance to be unto thee a loving and faithful husband (or wife) as long as we both shall live." No one pronounces them man and wife. Later, at a reception, each wedding guest signs the wedding certificate, which will be displayed prominently in the couple's home.

Polynesia

(SEE ALSO HAWAIIAN WEDDING CUSTOMS, PAGE 22)

Historically, Polynesian societies, inhabiting the Pacific Islands east of Micronesia, have embraced pleasure in lovemaking, and premarital sexual experimentation is encouraged. Among the lower classes, young people would become acquainted by gathering under moonlight for music and hula dancing.

When polygamy prevailed, marriages among the upper classes were often arranged before birth. While fidelity did not enter into the marriage vows, only certain types of extramarital relations were allowed. A husband was allowed to offer his wife to a visiting guest, and sleeping with his sisters-in-law was also permitted.

In Gambiers, a wedding begins with feasting and music, and the ceremony commences as the guests dance around lighted fires; eventually the bride appears. She steps into a circle of guests and dances suggestively before selected men. When she has won one over, she moves on to the next. At last she stands before her groom. They proceed to dance together passionately and then flee into the forest. When they reappear, they are married.

At one time on the Marquesas Islands, where European wedding customs are now embraced, a sexual rite was performed at the end of a wedding reception during which the bride, with her head resting on the groom's knee, would lie down and allow each of the males present to have sexual intercourse with her. When it was over, the groom would finally have sex with his bride. Then the bride's family would lie on the ground and create a human carpet for the couple to walk over.

Long ago at weddings in Tahiti, relatives stabbed their heads and faces with shark's teeth to promote bleeding, which expressed joy.

Russia

Although 65 percent of the population here is nonreligious, Russian Orthodoxy is the official religion. Under Communist rule (before the 1990s), weddings were held at grand public palaces where couples made state-witnessed vows of love to one another and loyal citizenry to the Communist government. Later, the entire wedding party would proceed to a national monument, where the bride would leave her bouquet.

In the Ukraine, just in case the marriage encounters rough spots, the bride and groom exact revenge on the matchmaker by burning an effigy of him or her at the ceremony.

On her wedding day, the Russian bride asks her parents for forgiveness for any offenses she may have caused. Her parents present the bride with bread and salt, in the hopes that she will never want for food.

During a religious ceremony in some parts of Russia, the best man holds a sacred icon and circles the bride three times counterclockwise while guests crack whips and make noise to scare away evil demons. The best man then kneels before the bride and scratches the ground with his knife so that all, including any remaining demons, may know that he is there to protect her.

After the ceremony, the party takes to the streets in a pageant that visits historic sites, leaving flowers on each, before they proceed to the reception.

At the reception, champagne glasses are thrown to the floor after the couple is toasted; if the glasses break, they will have happiness in their marriage.

To show their preference for their first child, the newlyweds tie to the front of their wedding car a doll for a girl and a toy bear if they would like a boy.

A loaf of bread, symbolizing health, long life, and prosperity, is bitten into during the ceremony by both the bride and the groom. It is said that whoever takes the biggest bite will wear the pants in the family.

Russian wedding guests receive—instead of give—wedding gifts.

In some parts of Russia, up until the nineteenth century, it was acceptable for a man to marry off his very young son to a young woman and then take her for his concubine. By the time the son came of age, his wife was middle-aged and already had children. The cycle then began all over again.

Scotland

Being a wedding guest in Scotland was once an expensive proposition indeed. Each guest was expected to bring his own food to the celebration, pay for the entertainment, and bring a gift as well. By the 1600s, weddings had become so elaborate that the clergy limited the number of wedding guests to 25 and placed a ban on music, dancing, and alcohol. These laws were commonly ignored.

A historical custom called "creeling" was once practiced in the Scottish Highlands. A large basket filled with rocks was tied to the groom's back, and he could escape his burden only with a kiss from the bride.

Today in Scotland, where church weddings are the norm, attire for the groom is just as important as the dress is for the bride. The groom proudly wears the kilt of his clan; the bride can wear a brooch fastened with a piece of this tartan, to symbolize her membership in her new family.

Bagpipe music is usually played at the entrance and during the recessional of the bridal party.

Scottish priests bless the newlyweds, their home, and their bed.

Scottish symbols are often incorporated into the theme of the wedding; thistle, tartan motifs, Robert Burns, and the Loch Ness Monster, for instance, can be found on wedding stationery, cakes, and decorations.

Scottish couples tip their hats to the Welsh tradition of spoons (see "Wales" on spooning, page 35) by presenting each of their mothers with silver serving spoons engraved with their initials and the wedding date.

Today Scots as young as 16 can marry without parental consent.

Originally symbols of Scottish clans, tartans are enjoying renewed popularity, and bridegrooms all over the world are now choosing kilts over tuxedos. The modern Rangers tartan, Celtic tartan, and Scottish Rugby Union tartan are all recognized by the Scottish Tartan Society. COURTESY OF DAVID DUNCAN, YOUR-KILT.COM

Marriage was serious business among the highly religious communities of Scotland; anyone who betrayed their wedding vows was made to stand in a barrel of cold water at the church door prior to a service. The wet and shivering culprit then joined the service and was further humiliated when the minister shared all the gory details of the indiscretion with the congregation.

Sri Lanka

Traditionally in the rural areas of Sri Lanka, marriages did not require a wedding ceremony or legal registration of the union. The man and the woman simply started living together, with the consent of their parents (who were usually related to one another). This type of marriage still survives, although the custom has been declining in recent years.

The highlight of a Hindu ceremony among the Tamils, who are descended from southern India, is the tying of a gold necklace on the bride. It contains three charms: a medallion inscribed with conch figures, a trident, and a ring, all of which together represent the Hindu holy trinity. Once the bride dons the necklace, she becomes the symbolic goddess of the home, and the groom is now her god.

The Sinhalese, who are descended from the Indo-Aryans of northern India, hold wedding ceremonies in a decorated structure called a *poruwa*. The ceremony is performed by the bride's uncle. During the ceremony, the fifth fingers of the marrying couple are tied together with gold cord, and water is poured over the knot to symbolize the sharing of their lives.

Except for some of the well-educated urban elite, the parents arrange all marriages, although their children may meet future spouses and veto a particularly unattractive marriage.

Sweden

Although a majority of Sweden's population is evangelical Lutheran, most weddings are secular, and almost 20 percent of unions are common-law, which is legally recognized. (Many Swedish weddings are instigated by the birth of a child.) This attitude can be traced to the early 1900s, when young men and women were free to date and enjoy premarital sex.

Before a Swedish wedding, the parents of the bride tuck money in her shoe so that she'll never do without—silver in the left (from Dad) and gold in the right (from Mom). The bride's shoes remain unfastened, to symbolize the wish for easy childbirth in the future.

The Swedish bridal crown is worn directly on the bride's head or over the veil and can consist of something as simple as a ribbon or (for historical authenticity) myrtle leaves. Only virgin brides may wear it.

Although the bride's father escorts her down the aisle in most cultures, in Sweden the bride and groom enter the church or venue together, and it is said that the first one to step over the threshold—or the one who says, "I do," the loudest—will dominate the relationship.

Singapore's Prime Minister Lee Kuan Yew must have been a romantic at heart. In the 1980s, concerned that young educated people did not have enough opportunities to find one another, he initiated boat trips and other events at which they could meet and mingle. Today matchmaking in Singapore is the province of the government, which runs one matchmaking agency for college graduates and another for the less educated.

Swedish wives wear three wedding rings: one for betrothal, one for marriage, and one for motherhood.

The groom is traditionally married in a shirt that the bride has made especially for the occasion. He never wears it again until he dies, and then he is buried in it.

Switzerland

Although the Swiss hold mostly traditional Catholic and Protestant weddings, they have a complicated list of days on which it is considered lucky to get married. Mondays in February are highly sought, as is the groom's birthday, unless it falls on the thirteenth of the month. The worst days are the bride's birthday; the second day of February, June, and November; and the first of December.

Junior bridesmaids carry colored hankies in a special Swiss tradition: guests may "buy" one of the handkerchiefs by contributing a dollar to the couple's "nest egg."

Thailand

In previous centuries the young Buddhist groom went to great lengths to prove himself before he could claim his bride. He had to live in the bride's home and work for her family for two years, and he had to spend several months attending a monastery, where he was instructed as a monk. Finally, he had to build the home in which he would raise his family (not too far from the in-laws, mind you). These prerequisites caused many young people to put off their nuptials. Thai society delayed marriage further with the traditional concept of *bunkhun*, which required both children to pay their parents a debt of gratitude before leaving their respective families. Men could fulfill the obligation by entering the monkhood temporarily, but daughters had to support their parents for a period or at least solicit a bride price. Even today weddings are often postponed until enough money for a formal ceremony has been saved.

Today's Thai wedding ceremony is unique in its complexity. In the Buddhist custom, the day begins with a monk's blessing at the home of the bride or the bridegroom, and the couple then proceeds to the registrar's office to legalize their marriage. A luncheon follows.

In the afternoon, both families witness the ritual known as *rodnam-sang*, in which the bride and groom sit close together on the floor (or small stage) with their hands held in *wai* style (as though praying to the Lord Buddha). Their hands are connected by a chain of flowers and then washed by an honored member of the wedding party.

The reception is held that evening. The joyous celebration includes a ritual in which the groom drinks a shot of whiskey for each of his friends. Given that the groom is likely to have as many as 50 friends present, it is understood that the wedding night may not necessarily be the one on which the marriage is consummated.

United Arab Emirates

Traditionally, Islamic parents believed, first and foremost, in the importance of preserving their social and economic heritage. The best way to do this was to keep it in the family, and so marrying cousins became the union of choice. Such a marriage ensured that neither family would be sullied by the bad reputation of the other; that disagreements would be settled easily among family members; and that monetary assets would stay in the family.

Among the Rwala Bedouins of Saudi Arabia, marriage was a quiet affair: a she-camel was killed as a sacrifice as the women pitched a special marital tent. Toward evening, the bride was taken to the tent by the male members of the groom's family. Once the bridegroom arrived, the party dispersed and the couple was married. For days after, the bride was not required to do any work, but her husband would continue to labor so he could purchase a trousseau of carpets, quilts, and clothing for his new wife.

In modern UAE, the setting of the wedding date marks the beginning of the bride's preparation for her wedding. Although the groom is also put through a series of preparations, the bride's are more elaborate and time-consuming. She is lavished with an assortment of traditional oils and perfumes from head to toe, and she is counseled by her elders. Traditionally, she is not seen for 40 days by anyone except family members as she rests at home in preparation for her wedding day.

During the week that precedes the wedding, traditional music and continuous singing and dancing take place, reflecting the joy shared by the bride's and groom's families.

At the *Laylat Al Henna* ("the night of the henna"), which takes place a few days before the wedding, the bride's hands and feet are decorated with henna. The men have their own celebration in the evening.

> "Wherever, in the history of civilization, woman has ceased to be an economic asset in marriage, marriage has decayed; and sometimes civilization has decayed with it."
>
> —Will Durant, *The Story of Civilization, Vol. 1*

The wedding celebration can go on for days, with various rites performed on each according to the region. The bride and groom are both adorned in native costumes and jewelry and often tour the village, encouraging a raucous entourage.

Uzbekistan

During Communist rule, when religion was banned, Muslim marriages would take place before sunrise so as to avoid the eyes of the police. It was also necessary to conceal the slaughter of livestock for the feast that followed.

In some rural areas of the country, couples practice a ritual in which the bride and groom crawl under a blanket and simulate the consummation of their marriage as others look on.

Wales

The Welsh often incorporate their national symbols in their weddings. Red dragons, leeks, and daffodils are used as decoration on wedding stationery, on the cake, in the bouquets, and even on the groom's tie or waistcoat. Florists sometimes use baby leeks and baby daffodils for boutonnieres.

"Spooning" comes from a Welsh tradition in which a suitor carved a spoon made from a single piece of wood for his beloved. If she wore it around her neck, they were engaged. The spoon could be carved into a variety of shapes, each with its own meaning: a heart said "I love you"; a key meant "you hold the key to my heart"; a wheel represented the man's promise to work hard; a bell signified wedding bells; and beads said "I want a child for every bead."

The Welsh bride includes myrtle, the flower of love, in her bouquet and hands out cuttings to single bridesmaids for their luck in romance.

African Wedding Customs

African wedding traditions are rich in color and symbolism and reflect the hundreds of cultures found there. While the customs may be diverse and mysterious to some, an underlying theme can be identified among African weddings. More than elsewhere, weddings on this continent are intended to unite families, not just individuals. Parents and siblings often play key roles in the ceremonies, and even the sharing of spouses is intended to strengthen families.

Ankole
Slim girls were considered unfit for bearing royal sons, so those girls in whom the king showed interest were force-fed with milk until they were so heavy they could barely walk.

Ghana
At some ceremonies, a priest sips palm wine from a cup and then offers it to the groom, who then hides among the crowd. The bride must sip from the cup as well—but first she must find the groom.

> *The art of braiding is common all over Africa, and men and women there have their hair finely braided in honor of their wedding day. To "set" the braiding, the hairdo is often covered with a mixture of ochre and animal fat.*

Kenya
Among the Maasai people of Kenya, women are given in marriage to men who are much older and with whom they are entirely unacquainted. To prepare for the wedding, the bride packs all her belongings and is dressed in her finest jewelry. At the marriage ceremony, the father of the bride spits on the bride's head and breasts as a blessing, and she then goes off with her husband, never looking back, lest she turn to stone. Weddings can be especially sad here when the bride, often as young as 13, fears leaving her home and facing life with a stranger.

The Swahili of Kenya bathe brides in sandalwood oils, remove all the hair below her neck, and tattoo henna designs on her limbs. A women elder, or *somo*, gives instructions to the bride on how to please her husband. Sometimes the somo even hides under the marriage bed in case help is needed!

Among the Samburu tribe, great importance is given to the preparation of gifts by the bridegroom (two goatskins, two copper earrings, a container for milk, a sheep). The actual ceremony is concluded when a bull enters a hut guarded by the bride's mother and is killed.

During the Samburu ritual of crossing sticks, now practiced at many African-American weddings, the bride and groom hold sticks that are crossed against one another. The ceremony symbolizes the hope that the relationship between the couple will deepen and that it will maintain the strength and natural life force of trees.

Madagascar
Once a traditional marriage ceremony is completed, the groom kills a cow and the guests all partake of a drink consisting of blood and water. If the couple are cousins, they perform a separate ritual to nullify the incest taboo. It is only weeks later that the bride goes to her husband's village to consummate the marriage. Once the groom is sure that his bride will continue to reside with him, he presents a gift to the bride's family of a cow. If he can afford it, a herd of 30 to 100 cattle is expected.

Maasai
Among the Maasai, the father of the bride sprays milk on his daughter to invoke fertility.

Nambia
Among the Himba, the groom and members of his family kidnap the bride before the ceremony and decorate her in an *ekori*, a marriage headdress made of leather. When the bride arrives at her husband's new home, his relatives tell her what her responsibilities as his wife will be, and they show her their acceptance by anointing her with butterfat from cows.

An African-American wedding, ca. 1908 LIBRARY OF CONGRESS

At one time, the marriage payment consisted of four or more head of cattle, some chickens, and a cow if the girl was a virgin.

Ndebele

The weddings of the Ndebele of South Africa are celebrated in three stages, the last of which can take several years. The first stage is negotiation of the payment for the bride, or *lobola*, which is paid in installments of money and livestock. A two-week sequestration of the bride is the second stage, during which time other women teach the bride how to be a good wife. The third stage is completed only when the bride has her first child.

Niger

The Wodabee of Niger court their cousins for marriage. The male cousins wear powerful amulets that are said to heighten desirability. If two cousins pursue the same girl, the girl chooses one, and the other man is welcomed into the home of the couple; if the bride consents, he may even share her bed.

Muslim men in Nigeria are expected to be polygamous—they can (and do) marry up to four wives.

Namwanga

A highly respected person representing the groom's interests known as a *katawa mpango* negotiates the engagement. When the girl receives a formal proposal, called an *insalamu*, from the katawa mpango, she brings it to her grandmother, who then notifies the rest of the family.

When the groom first comes to visit the bride's family, he brings with him a hoe, which is a symbol of the earth, cultivation, and fertilization. He also carries white beads and a small amount of money, which are placed on a small plate and covered. The groom is grilled with questions by the girl's family. If the family does not accept the young man, he takes back the hoe, and the family keeps the beads and money. If the answer is yes, marriage payments are immediately negotiated.

The Nile

Along the Nile, if a man wishes to see his sons well married, he must have numerous sheep, goats, and donkeys. When marriage negotiations are under way, the father of the bride will insist that each of her close relatives be given livestock.

Instead of sending out wedding invitations and expecting gifts in return, the groom makes the rounds of relatives in hopes of collecting contributions for his bridal herd.

On the wedding day, the groom arrives at the bride's homestead wearing a handsome leopard skin draped over his cowhide cape—and nothing else.

The Nilotes

These devoted nudists consider clay, ash, feathers, sandals, and a necklace ample dress for any occasion. At her wedding, the bride wears these plus the beaded apron and half-skirt of the unmarried girl.

Rwanda

Although the traditional Rwandan wedding unites not just the bride and groom but their families as well, the parents of the bride are not permitted to attend the wedding. Instead, the bride is accompanied at the ceremony by an aunt or another close female family member. The groom's father officiates at the wedding with a simple pronouncement. On the wedding night, someone is designated to check the marital bed to make sure the bride is a virgin. If she is not, the marriage can be voided. If she refuses to have intercourse with the groom, she may be forced into it.

South Africa

Before a ceremony begins, the bride's family, seated on one side of the church, and the groom's, seated on the other side, sing insulting songs to one another. "Your son is too poor to marry our daughter," sings the bride's family, and the other side responds: "You treat your daughter so badly, but now she will be treated like a queen." These "hymns" become increasingly insulting as the rite continues.

Sudan

Following a wedding ceremony, dancers shower the bride and groom with flowers to ensure a fragrant future for the couple. A sawer, made of turmeric rice, coins, and candy, is thrown at the couple. Rice is a symbol of prosperity, and the yellow of the turmeric symbolizes everlasting love. The coins remind the couple to share their wealth with the less fortunate, and the candy bestows sweetness and fragrance upon their marriage. Seven candles are lit representing the direction the couple should follow to bring about a happy married life. A betel nut set near the couple is a reminder that different customs should not spoil a harmonious marriage.

In a portion of the wedding ceremony called *sungkem*, the bride and groom kiss the knees of their parents as a way of asking forgiveness for their transgressions and of promising continued respect. This is done in front of a gargoyle fountain, whose waters symbolize the continuous flow of parental love.

Among the Neur people of southern Sudan, the groom must pay 20 to 40 cattle as a bride price, and the marriage is considered complete only after the wife has borne two children. If the wife bears only one child and the husband asks for a divorce, he may also be awarded the cattle and/or the first child.

Among the Rashaayda people of Sudan, a wedding is at least a two-day affair, with everyone congregating in the bride's family camp to feast and socialize. The wedding reception is considered a primary venue for competition. Young men and women perform in many different ways to garner prestige and impress the opposite sex. On the first day, they compete to butcher animals as rapidly as possible. On the second day, young men engage in a camel race, in singing, and in sword-dancing competitions, while young women dance.

In one competition, the young men form two facing lines and each steps forward, one at a time, to twirl his sword around in time with the music. The more talented he is, the longer he is allowed to perform. Then the women emerge from the tents dressed in their finery and dance between the lines in turn. The best receive prizes,

Among the Zande of Central Africa, a younger brother was allowed to have sexual relations with his older brother's wife, whom he would inherit when his brother died.

and these are then passed to the bride and groom.

Throughout Sudan, if a husband dies, his family must provide a brother to the widow, and any children born to the brother are considered the children of the deceased husband.

Yoruba

The custom of pouring a libation seems to have origins in Yoruba but is widespread in many forms in other cultures and has become part of many African-American wedding ceremonies. The libation is a blessing performed by an officiant who pours an alcoholic spirit onto the ground (or into a vessel, to be poured onto the ground later) and invokes the name of the couple and their ancestors while praying for their good fortune.

Zaire

Among the Woyo people, a young woman is given a set of carved pot lids by her mother when she marries and moves to her husband's home. Each of the lids is carved with an image that illustrates a proverb about marital relationships. If a husband abuses his wife in some way, or if the wife is unhappy, she serves the husband's supper in a bowl that is covered with a lid decorated with the appropriate proverb. She can make her complaints public by using this lid when her husband brings his friends home for dinner.

Jumping the Broom

Attend a modern African-American wedding and, despite its European trappings, you're liable to witness a ritual in which the bride and groom leap over a decorated broom into their new lives. The practice itself goes back to the days of slavery, when marriage was illegal for African Americans. The broom was considered a spiritual symbol of sweeping life clean; it developed as a marriage rite in the United States and was sometimes attended by slave masters and their wives.

Once slavery was abolished and formal marriage was legal for all, the practice all but disappeared. Most black Americans were glad to see it go, as they saw the broom as a horrific reminder of their days in slavery.

Some form of marital broom-jumping was practiced in other cultures as well—Gypsies, the Welsh, and Wiccans among them.

In 1976, Alex Haley's *Roots* inspired some communities to revive the practice, not as a nod to slavery but as a celebration of the spirit of Africa. The ritual caught on, and for many African-American couples today, "jumping the broom" is synonymous with "tying the knot." It is said that whoever jumps higher over the broom will rule the household.

The wedding broom is a symbol of the devotion with which African slaves re-created a solemn ritual under the most adverse conditions imaginable. Today decorative brooms are commonly used in African-American ceremonies. COURTESY OF MARLOW GATES, FRIENDSWOODBROOMS.COM

Mass Weddings

Westerners raise their eyebrows at the idea of group weddings, but in fact, historians suspect that the first marital unions took this form, and they were common for a long time in early Inca society. Although they had pretty much been left to antiquity, they were revived by the Rev. Sun Myung Moon during the 1960s in what came to be called "Moonie weddings."

On February 14, 2004, 40 blushing nude brides and 40 courageous nude grooms wed under tropical skies in SuperClubs' Hedonism III Resort in Jamaica at the third annual World's Largest Nude Wedding event.

- The Rev. Sun Myung Moon, a Korean evangelist and the founder of the Unification Church, developed a "blessing ceremony" designed specifically for mass weddings. The blessing, which is considered by the church the most significant and central ceremony in a person's life, was first given to 36 couples in Seoul, South Korea, in 1961. Many of the couples had never met prior to their wedding.

- On July 1, 1982, Moon held his first truly public mass wedding in Madison Square Garden in New York City; 2,075 couples were married.

- By 1995, "Moonie" marriages had reached huge proportions. More than 360,000 couples were married via satellite at 545 sites in over 100 countries. Moon and his wife, Hak Ja Han, matched thousands of these couples based on their sex, age, and nationality as well as their photos. American couples paid $2,000 each, and Japanese couples paid $29,000 for this honor.

- On February 13, 2000, more than 450,000 couples took part in a mass wedding ceremony. Conducted by Moon, the ceremony took place in the Seoul Olympic Stadium in South Korea. In the stadium itself, 10,000 couples who had never seen each other prior to the ceremony were married, while another 20,000 couples in attendance rededicated their marriage vows. Meanwhile, some 420,000 couples from around the world, including North Korea, were wed via the Internet and satellite television.

- On September 14, 2002, 500 followers of Moon who had only just met declared "we do" in a ceremony held in New York's Manhattan Center. The ceremony was broadcast live over the Internet to

The Oneida Community

One of the most interesting experiments in wedding history occurred when John Humphrey Noyes founded the Oneida Community in upstate New York in 1848. Noyes taught his followers that they were all free of sin and that it was impossible for them to sin at all. He also believed that relationships between men and women had largely deteriorated, and he aspired to a society in which males and females had equal voice. Thus, the traditional marriage, which Noyes and his followers viewed as an expression of jealousy and exclusiveness, was replaced with "complex marriage," which amounted to sexual communalism and shared parenting. In theory, every male in the community was married to every female in the community. The group flourished for some time but was disbanded by 1881. Similarly, the Kerista Community in San Francisco practiced group marriage from 1971 until 1991.

Science fiction often depicts group marriage as a feature of future societies. Robert A. Heinlein treats the subject in Stranger in a Strange Land, Friday, Time Enough for Love, *and* The Moon Is a Harsh Mistress. *Joe Haldeman describes group marriages in his 1981 novel* Worlds, *and the subject is briefly addressed in the 1989 novel* Star Trek: The Lost Years *by J. M. Dillard.*

Take Our Daughter — Please!

MarryOurDaughter.com sounded like a good idea at first. Why not use the Internet to marry off teen daughters, especially those who are starting to outlive their welcome at home? The site was actually a joke, but thousands of harried parents soon tried pawning off their daughters by registering on the site. Here are a few of the teens who were not, sadly for their parents, for sale:

1. Hailey is a rising star on her way up. She's already been in local billboard ads and has modeled for national catalogues. Her dream is to break into the movies and TV and she's looking for a husband who lives in the Southwest and will help her achieve her dream.

2. Anna R. has been living with foster families since she was 5 and is a bit rough around the edges but is basically a good girl. When she turns 18 she will age out of the foster system and will have to move out and is looking for a kind and caring man to look after her needs while she looks after his.

3. Courtney's grandmother married at 13, her mother married at 13, and Courtney has decided she wants to keep the tradition going. She would prefer to stay close to her large extended southern family and loves farm or at least rural life.

locations in Los Angeles, Chicago, Detroit, and 145 other countries where couples gathered to be married by Moon. A rabbi, an imam, a Christian pastor, and an American Indian kicked off the two-hour wedding event with their own blessings. Moon then recited the wedding vows in Korean. All together, Moon's church has raised a total of $1.3 billion staging these mass weddings.

• On November 21, 2006, South Korean cult founder Jung Myung Seok held a mass wedding of more than 300 Japanese members. Modeled after those held by South Korea's Unification Church, the wedding was largely an attempt to increase the cult's membership. Seok conducted interviews with the prospective brides and sexually assaulted some of them. Seok was later indicted on rape charges.

• On July 7, 2007 (07/07/07), a mass wedding was held in Kuala Lumpur, Malaysia, at the Buddhist temple Maha Vihara. The chief high priest, the Most Venerable K Sri Dhammaratana Maha Nayaka Thera, initiated the event to coincide with Malaysia's fiftieth anniversary of independence. Each of the 50 couples were married by one of the 50 monks assigned to participate in the ceremonies. Malay, Chinese, and Indian musicians accompanied the processional. The three best-dressed couples at registration day walked away with prizes.

December 12, 2006, marked the day of the highest number of simultaneous weddings held underground. The Datong Coal Group in China's Shanxi Province held wedding ceremonies for 10 of its miners and their fiancées. The ceremonies were conducted in a pit shaft 1,000 feet underground.

The Mail-Order Bride

The concept of the mail-order bride is thought to have begun with the early American settlers, men who could hardly have been expected to find suitable brides in the wilderness. Today the mail-order bride business is an international industry that employs the Internet to reach an unprecedented number of clients. Here is a brief history of the practice.

Those early American settlers who couldn't find local women to marry began writing letters to women in Europe with the hopes of finding suitable wives who would travel to the New World to share their lives. The Virginia Company of London, for instance, transported several ships with mail-order brides to Jamestown, Virginia, in 1619 as payment for tobacco they had received from the colonies. Unfortunately, an Indian uprising in 1622 caused the death of one-third of the settlers and the demise of their colony.

During World War II, lonely American soldiers would often write love letters to women they had never met before hoping to find a life companion.

The mail-order bride concept gained popularity again during the early 1980s. Men in Western countries wanted to expand their prospects by extending their search for wives outside their own country, especially in Asia. Around the same time, Asian women, primarily from Thailand and the Philippines, began advertising themselves as mail-order brides. The idea that Western men were "buying" Asian women arose at this time.

Two stereotypes were at play here. The Western man expects the Asian woman to be obedient, soft-spoken, submissive, and devoted. The Asian woman expects her new husband to be an easygoing, responsible individual who will treat her with kindness and respect.

The advent of the Internet in the 1990s allowed men to meet a wider number and variety of women. Introductions were arranged more quickly and were more enjoyable. Affluent men in particular now gained an advantage in obtaining a bride.

With the fall of communism, a completely new source of mail-order brides was created. Russian women seeking a better life for themselves and for their children began listing themselves on various Internet sites seeking men with a steady job and bright future. This trend continues today. It is estimated that there are now over 500,000 websites for mail-order brides, including one called The Mail-Order Bride Warehouse. Men who list themselves on the Internet are sometimes referred to as mail-order husbands. The future of the mail-order bride system is now primarily Internet-based.

Although the industry has flourished, there is evidence that many women who arrive in the United States as mail-order brides are disrespected, abused, and exploited. Studies have shown that the rate of spousal abuse among some immigrant women is as high as 75 percent. The International Marriage Broker Regulation Act of 2005, intended to remedy the situation, requires men to reveal their arrests or convictions for violent crimes prior to obtaining a mail-order bride.

A History of Gay Marriage

We're grateful to Dr. Rictor Norton, author of several books on gay history and literature, including *Mother Clap's Molly House* and *The Myth of the Modern Homosexual*, for the following history.

One of the most passionate sociopolitical debates of recent history concerns the subject of gay marriage. The religious, social, and economic effects that these unions have on society have irked many but given others a chance to experience marital bliss and benefit from the financial benefits that marriage offers. Despite current societal frowning, men seem to have frequently married one another throughout history. In fact, in some societies marriages between gay men were officially recognized by the state, as in ancient Sparta and on the Dorian island of Thera.

Much later, in second-century Rome, conjugal contracts between men of about the same age were ridiculed but legally binding. Such marriages were blessed by pagan religions, particularly sects of the Mother Goddess Cybele (imported from Asia Minor). At the ceremony, the bridal party consisted entirely of men, who entered the temple and decked each other with "gay fillets round the forehead . . . and strings of orient pearls." They lit a torch in honor of the goddess and sacrificed a pregnant swine. One man would get up and choose a husband for himself, and then dance himself into a frenzy. He would then drink deeply from a goblet in the shape of a large penis,

fling the goblet away, and strip off his clothes, at which point the two men were considered to be married.

The "bride" was a transvestite only for the duration of this ceremony, for in a deeply religious sense he had temporarily become the goddess at these holy rites. After the ceremony the other men would pair up among themselves to celebrate multiple nuptials by having group sex. The following day the names of all the pairs would be registered in legal records as formal marriages.

Many ancient writers, such as Strabo and Athenaeus, wrote that the Gauls and Celts commonly practiced homosexuality. Aristotle wrote that the Celts "openly held in honor passionate friendship between males." Diodorus Siculus wrote that, "although the Gauls have lovely women, they scarcely pay attention to them, but strangely crave male embraces." Eusebius of Caesarea wrote: "Among the Gauls, the young men marry each other with complete freedom. In doing this, they do not incur any reproach or blame, since this is done according to custom amongst them." Bardaisan of Edessa wrote that "in the countries of the north—in the lands of the Germans and those of their neighbors—handsome young men assume the role of wives towards other men, and they celebrate marriage feasts."

The Mollies

Eighteenth-century England found gay men marrying but without legal sanction. London in the 1720s contained approximately 40 "molly houses," disorderly pubs or coffeehouses where gay men socialized, singing bawdy songs and dancing country dances while some played the fiddle. Many of these gay clubs had a "marrying room" or "chapel" where, according to witnesses, "they would go out by couples into another room on the same floor, to be married, as they called it, and when they came back they would tell what they had been doing." These marriages were not monogamous, and 18-year-old Ned Courtney was "helped to two or three husbands" in the marrying room of the Royal Oak at the corner of St James' Square, Pall Mall. Molly marriages didn't have the blessing of any church until the 1810s, when the Rev. John Church officiated as the "chaplain" at male gay marriages at the Swan in Vere Street.

> "If we see gay marriage … as an emblem of variety and freedom manifest in love, we can understand why the Right feels compelled to crush it. And we can see why the Left must defend it, if only for its potential as a radical act."
> — E. J. Graff, *What Is Marriage For?*

American Indians

Across the waters, gay marriages existed among the American Indians, particularly the Sioux and the Cheyenne. In most such unions, one of the two men was a berdache, a transvestite—medicine man who wore men's clothes only when he joined a war party, where he cared for the wounded. Typically the berdaches either got married to the loafers of the village or became the second or third "wife" of the chieftain. Usually their husbands were more ridiculed than they themselves were, not because of homosexuality, which Indians generally tolerated, but because such husbands usually abandoned their economic status in society and allowed the berdache to do all the work to create the model household.

Same-Sex Marriage: A Timeline

In November 2003, the Massachusetts Supreme Judicial Court ignited a nationwide debate over same-sex marriage when it ruled that the state could not "deny the protections, benefits and obligations conferred by civil marriage to two individuals of the same sex who wish to marry." The ensuing battle has included fights in Congress over a federal marriage amendment that would define marriage as the union of a man and a woman; a spate of same-sex wedding ceremonies (in some cases in violation of state laws); and the passage of numerous state constitutional amendments banning gay marriage. In May 2008, California became the first state to follow in the steps of Massachusetts when the California Supreme Court struck down a statewide ban on same-sex marriage. As the debate rages on, the American religious community remains deeply divided over the issue.

Here is a year-by-year account of laws in the United States regarding this issue, courtesy of Barbara Rosewicz and the Pew Forum on Religion.

May 1993 Hawaii Supreme Court rules that the state must show a compelling reason to ban same-sex marriage and orders a lower court to hear a case seeking the right of same-sex couples to marry.

March 1995 Utah Gov. Mike Leavitt (R) signs into law the first state "defense of marriage" statute, which stipulates that Utah does not have to recognize out-of-state marriages that violate state public policy.

September 1996 President Bill Clinton signs into law the federal Defense of Marriage Act (DOMA), which upholds states' rights to ban same-sex marriages and to refuse to recognize such marriages performed elsewhere.

February 1998 An Alaska Superior Court judge rules that same-sex couples have a constitutional right to marry but stays the decision pending appeals to the state Supreme Court.

November 1998 Hawaii voters approve a state constitutional amendment reserving to the Legislature the right to define marriage. Alaska voters approve a constitutional amendment banning same-sex marriage.

September 1999 The Alaska Supreme Court rules that same-sex couples cannot seek the right to marry under the state constitution in light of the 1998 constitutional amendment banning same-sex marriage.

December 1999 The Vermont Supreme Court rules that the state constitution guarantees same-sex couples the same rights to marriage as heterosexual couples. However, the court leaves it up to the Legislature to decide how to provide marriage rights and benefits to same-sex couples.

April 2000 Vermont Gov. Howard Dean (D) signs a civil union bill, making Vermont the first state to legally recognize same-sex couples.

November 2000 Nebraska voters approve a constitutional ban on same-sex marriage.

2001 Seven same-sex Massachusetts couples file a lawsuit after being denied marriage licenses. In *Goodridge et al. v. Department of Public Health,* the couples seek the right to marry.

November 2002 Nevada voters give final approval to a constitutional ban on same-sex marriage. Voters first approved the ban in 2000, but state law required a majority vote in two consecutive election years to amend the constitution.

November 18, 2003 Massachusetts Supreme Judicial Court, the state's highest court, rules that the state constitution guarantees equal marriage rights for same-sex couples.

January 12, 2004 New Jersey Gov. James McGreevey (D) signs a domestic partnership law granting same-sex couples certain rights, such as hospital visits.

February 2004 Massachusetts Supreme Judicial Court reaffirms its decision and specifies that only marriage rights—not civil unions—provide equal protection under the state constitution. The Massachusetts Legislature holds a constitutional convention to consider amending the state constitution to limit marriage to one man and one woman. The measure fails to pass. San Francisco Mayor Gavin Newsom authorizes city officials to issue marriage licenses to same-sex couples.

February–March 2004 County clerks in Sandoval, New Mexico, issue licenses to 26 same-sex couples before courts intervene. Mayor Jason West of New Paltz, New York, begins officiating

same-sex marriages, and commissioners in Multnomah County (Portland), Oregon, issue marriage licenses to same-sex couples. President Bush announces support for a federal constitutional amendment banning same-sex marriage.

March 2004 The California Supreme Court orders a halt to San Francisco same-sex marriages. The Massachusetts Legislature votes to amend the state constitution to ban same-sex marriage but allow civil unions. The Legislature must approve the measure again by 2006 before the amendment can go to a statewide vote.

May 17, 2004 Massachusetts begins marrying same-sex couples.

August–November 2004 Voters in 13 states—Missouri, Louisiana, Arkansas, Georgia, Kentucky, Michigan, Mississippi, Montana, North Dakota, Ohio, Oklahoma, Oregon, and Utah—approve constitutional amendments banning same-sex marriage.

December 2004 The Montana Supreme Court rules that the gay and lesbian partners of Montana University employees have the same right to health insurance benefits as their heterosexual counterparts.

Invitees to a January 2006 wedding in Koh Chang, Thailand, were taken aback by the wedding invitation card, which announced the nuptials of bridegroom Yeuifa Meelaap and two brides: Vassana Uysap and Jenny Saibua. The wedding invitation for a threesome was in itself unusual, but all the more so because the groom was also a woman.

April 2005 Kansas voters approve a constitutional amendment banning same-sex marriage.

April 14, 2005 Oregon's Supreme Court nullifies nearly 3,000 marriage licenses issued to same-sex couples in 2004 in violation of state law.

April 20, 2005 Connecticut Gov. M. Jodi Rell (R) signs a bill authorizing civil unions for same-sex couples, effective October 1.

May 2005 Federal judge strikes down a Nebraska constitutional amendment denying marriage rights to same-sex couples.

June 2005 The California Supreme Court lets stand a new law creating a domestic partners' registry for same-sex couples.

August 2005 The California Supreme Court issues a first-of-its-kind ruling recognizing the coparenting rights of same-sex couples.

September 2005 The California State Assembly approves a Senate-passed bill to legalize same-sex marriage, but Gov. Arnold Schwarzenegger (R) vetoes it. The Massachusetts Legislature defeats a proposal at the second constitutional convention to amend the state constitution to ban same-sex marriages but allow civil unions.

October 2005 The Alaska Supreme Court rules that state and local governments must offer the same benefits to employees' same-sex partners that they do to spouses.

November 2005 The Washington State Supreme Court recognizes the coparenting rights of same-sex couples. Texas voters approve a constitutional amendment banning same-sex marriage. Maine voters reject an attempt to repeal a state law prohibiting discrimination based on sexual orientation.

March 2006 The Massachusetts Supreme Judicial Court upholds a 1913 state law banning out-of-state couples from marrying in Massachusetts if the marriage is illegal in their home state.

June 2006 Alabama voters approve a constitutional amendment banning same-sex marriage.

July 6, 2006 The New York Court of Appeals, the state's highest court, rules that the state constitution does not guarantee same-sex couples equal access to the rights and privileges of marriage.

July 2006 The Georgia Supreme Court reinstates a constitutional ban against same-sex marriage that had been thrown out by a lower court on procedural grounds.

July 12, 2006 A Connecticut judge rules that banning same-sex marriage does not violate same-sex couples' constitutional rights because the state's new civil union law provides similar protections.

July 28, 2006 The Washington State Supreme Court rules that the state constitution does not guarantee same-sex couples equal access to the rights and privileges of marriage.

October 25, 2006 The New Jersey Supreme Court rules that the state constitution guarantees same-sex couples all of the legal benefits of marriage but stops short of legalizing same-sex marriage.

November 7, 2006 Voters in seven states—Idaho, Colorado, South Dakota, South Carolina, Tennessee, Virginia, and Wisconsin—approve constitutional amendments banning same-sex marriage. Arizona becomes the first state to reject at the ballot box a state constitutional amendment banning gay marriage and other benefits for unmarried couples.

December 2006 New Jersey Gov. Jon Corzine (D), in the wake of a court order, signs a bill permitting same-sex couples to enter into civil unions, granting the same state benefits conferred on married couples.

February 2007 A Michigan appeals court rules that the state's ban on gay marriage prohibits state and local governments and public universities from offering health benefits to partners in same-sex relationships.

February 19, 2007 New Jersey begins accepting applications for civil unions.

February 21, 2007 Rhode Island Attorney General Patrick C. Lynch issues a legal opinion advising the state to recognize same-sex marriages performed in Massachusetts.

April 22, 2007 Washington Gov. Christine Gregoire (D) signs a bill creating same-sex domestic partnerships, starting July 22, 2007. The law also applies to senior heterosexual couples.

May 9, 2007 Oregon Gov. Ted Kulongoski (D) signs a bill creating same-sex domestic partnerships, starting January 1, 2008.

May 31, 2007 New Hampshire Gov. John Lynch (D) signs a bill creating same-sex civil unions.

June 14, 2007 Massachusetts lawmakers uphold the state's court-imposed gay marriage law, protecting it from a constitutional ban for at least five years.

September 18, 2007 Maryland's highest court overturns a lower court decision, ruling that same-sex couples do not have a constitutional right to marry.

March 4, 2008 The California Supreme Court hears oral arguments in a case determining whether the state's domestic partnership law adequately protects the equal rights of gay couples. The Washington State Legislature approves a bill expanding the rights conveyed under the state's 2007 domestic partnership law.

May 15, 2008 The California Supreme Court, in a 4–3 decision, rules that the state constitution guarantees same-sex couples the right to marry.

"There was one time of the year which was held in Raveloe to be especially suitable for a wedding. It was when the great lilacs and the alburnums in the old-fashioned gardens showed their golden and purple wealth above the lichen-tinted walls, and when there were calves still young enough to want bucketfuls of fragrant milk. People were not so busy then as they must become when the full cheese-making and mowing had set in; and besides, it was a time when a light bridal dress could be worn with comfort and seen to advantage."

—FROM GEORGE ELIOT, *SILAS MARNER*

12 Superstitions to Foretell a Marriage

1. Take a nine-pea peapod and suspend it over the doorway using a white thread. If the next person who enters by the same door is not a member of the family and is unmarried, then your wedding will take place in not more than a year's time.

2. When you hear a cuckoo for the first time in the year, say aloud: "Cuckoo, Cuckoo, answer me true, this question that I'm asking you; I beg that truly you'll tell me, in how many years I'll married be." The number of times the cuckoo replies represents the number of years that will elapse before you marry.

3. Take a photograph of the one you love and hold before it a ring on the end of a thread. Be careful to keep your hand still. If the ring moves in a circle, you will marry the person in the picture soon and will lead a life of bliss; if the ring moves to and fro, it is unlikely you will marry him. Should the ring not move at all, you are likely to remain single.

4. On the Eve of St. Agnes (the night before January 21), take a row of pins and pull them out, one after the other. Then stick a pin in your sleeve and you will dream of the one you will marry.

5. If you find a four-leaf clover, put it in your right shoe, and the next bachelor you meet will become your husband.

6. This ceremony must be practiced on the first night of the new moon. Open wide the windows of your bedroom and sit down on the windowsill, gazing with unblinking eyes at the moon and at the same time repeating softly and slowly the following incantation: "All hail, Selene, all hail to thee! I prithee, good moon, reveal to me this night to whom I'll wedded be." During the night you will dream of your future husband.

7. Take a small piece of wedding cake, pass it three times through a wedding ring, and then lay the cake under your pillow. In your dreams that night your future husband will appear to you.

8. Place a small piece of wedding cake under your pillow and put a borrowed wedding ring on the third finger of your left hand. Before you retire to bed arrange the shoes that you have worn that day in the shape of a T. Then your future husband will appear to you in your dreams.

9. If you eat a salted herring just before going to bed, your future husband will appear to you in a dream, carrying a cup of water with which to quench your thirst.

10. If you sleep on daisy roots (or a pullet's first egg, or the feathers of mourning doves), you will dream of your spouse.

11. To foretell the vocation of your future spouse, take a walk early on Valentine's Day morning and take note of the first bird you see. If it is a dove, you will marry a fortunate man, a sparrow a humble man, a bluebird a poor man, a robin a seaman, a goldfinch a rich man.

12. If you hold a candle in front of a mirror while eating an apple and combing your hair, your future husband will appear.

Good Fortunes as told by Tea or Coffee Grounds.

Ring –

A Happy Marriage

Copyrighted 1907 by Fred C. Lounsbury

Vintage postcard depicting the good fortune that could be foretold by tea or coffee grounds
AUTHORS' COLLECTION

13 More Wedding Superstitions

1. The first gift the bride opens should be the first gift she uses.

2. Seeing a rainbow, having the sun shine, meeting a black cat, and meeting a chimney sweep are all considered good omens on your wedding day.

3. Bad omens on your wedding day include seeing a pig, a hare, a lizard running across the road, or an open grave.

4. Meeting a nun or a monk on your wedding day is believed to foretell barrenness.

5. If the groom drops the wedding band during the ceremony, the marriage is doomed.

6. The new bride must enter her home by the main door and must not trip or fall. (Thus the origin of the custom of carrying the bride over the threshold.)

7. The spouse who goes to sleep first on the wedding day will be the first to die.

8. For good luck, marry on the upswing of the clock—that is, on the half-hour. For instance, at 2:30 the hands of the clock are on their way up, not down, as they are at 2:00.

9. Even today it is considered extremely unlucky for the bride and groom to see each other on the wedding morning before they meet in the church.

10. It was once considered bad luck for the bridal procession or ceremony to include the parents of the wedding couple. The worst of all omens is for the bride to encounter a funeral or even to catch sight of one from a distance.

11. Before the advent of cars, the bridal carriage was always drawn by gray horses if these could be obtained. It is still thought to be lucky for the bride or groom to encounter a gray horse on the way to church.

12. No matter the color, if the horses refused to start, either on the way to the wedding or on the trip back, it was considered a bad omen. In an easily understood transition, the modern car inherited this superstition: a breakdown or difficulty in starting is now an unlucky omen.

13. In some areas of England, it was thought unlucky until fairly recently for a bridal procession to pass through a lych gate (the north door of a church), which was normally used for funerals; wedding and baptismal parties always entered by the south or west doors. A superstition peculiar to Suffolk is recorded in the *Suffolk Garland,* published in 1818, as one of the beliefs still flourishing at that date:

No bridal procession ever passed over Gold Bridge on its way to or from the church. To do so would be extremely unlucky, and a marriage so begun would be unlikely to bring happiness.

Old English wisdom clearly dictates the best days for marriage:

Monday for health
Tuesday for wealth
Wednesday best of all
Thursday for losses
Friday for crosses
Saturday for no luck at all

Certain days and seasons have been thought to be unlucky for marriages. One of these is the month of May, which is still often avoided by modern brides. Nearly 2,000 years ago, Plutarch inquired why the men of Rome did not take wives in May, then answered his own question: May was the month when offerings were made to the dead and mourning was worn. As for the rest of the calendar:

Married when the year is new, he'll be loving, kind, and true.
When February birds do mate, you wed nor dread your fate.
If you wed when March winds blow, joy and sorrow both you'll know.
Marry in April when you can, joy for maiden and for man.
Marry in the month of May, and you'll surely rue the day.
Marry when June roses grow, over land and sea you'll go.
Those who in July do wed, must labor for their daily bread.
Whoever wed in August be, many a change is sure to see.
Marry in September's shrine, your living will be rich and fine.
If in October you do marry, love will come but riches tarry.
If you wed in bleak November, only joys will come, remember.
When December snows fall fast, marry and true love will last.

New Year's Eve is the Scots' favorite wedding day because by the time the next day rolls around the couple will already be enjoying their second year of wedded bliss.

The Origin of "Something Old, Something New . . ."

Brides have been honoring the tradition of wearing an old item, a new item, a borrowed item, and a blue item during their wedding for centuries. Although wearing these items is supposed to symbolize good luck for the bride, they also give the bride an opportunity to express her admiration for a few special people in her life on her special day. The rhyme itself dates back to the Victorian era. Mike Milton of WeddingFlorist.co.uk explains the origins of this popular refrain:

1. "Something old" is meant to represent the link with the bride's own family and the past. It is symbolic of continuity. To symbolize this link, brides may choose to wear a piece of jewelry, or they may select something from the mother's or grandmother's wedding gown. Other items that may be chosen include a handkerchief, a scarf, or a piece of lace.

2. "Something new" represents good luck and success and the bride's hopes for a bright future in her new married life. The wedding gown is often chosen as the new item but it can be anything that is purchased new for the wedding, such as the wedding flowers or the wedding rings. Wearing a new item on your wedding day conveys the message that you and your husband are creating a new union that will endure forever.

3. "Something borrowed" lets the bride know that friends and family will be there for her on the special day and in the future when help is needed. It is especially important that the "borrowed" item come from a happily married woman, who thereby lends the bride some of her own marital happiness to carry into the new marriage. Anything can be borrowed, but the item must be returned afterward.

4. "Something blue" in ancient times was the symbol of faithfulness, purity, and loyalty. Often couples wore blue bands on the border of their wedding attire to denote love, modesty, and fidelity. Blue garters are commonly used today to fulfill the requirement.

5. "A sixpence in her shoe"—the item so often deleted from American custom—refers to a coin worth six pennies that was minted in Britain between 1551 and 1967. The sixpence was not only symbolic of wealth but was also intended to bring the bride happiness throughout her married life.

Why Do They Do That?

6 MORE TRADITIONS EXPLAINED

Although there are other explanations for each of the traditions listed here, the ones offered are the generally accepted origins of these common wedding practices.

1. **Carrying the bride over the threshold** It is said that when brides were abducted, they were allowed to return home if their feet touched the ground before they were safely inside their new abode. Roman brides were instructed to at least pretend to be hesitant to give up their virginity by refusing to enter the bridal chamber unless they were carried. In China, a bride demonstrated her commitment to her new duties as she was carried over a pan of charcoal positioned at the doorway to her new home. In many areas of the world it is seen as a sign of bad luck for the bride to enter her new home through anything but the main door or to fall before she reaches the hearth of her new home. Thus, the bride is carried over the threshold.

2. **Tying shoes to the bumper of the getaway car** Shoes have been tokens of ownership since the days of the early Egyptians, who included a pair of sandals whenever they traded goods to seal the deal. It

In Greece, it was customary for a groom to present his bride with a new pair of shoes.

was logical, then, that the father of a bride would give the groom a pair of shoes to acknowledge their exchange. Even in Anglo-Saxon times, the groom often struck the heel of the bride's shoe to signify his new status over her. The custom seems to have roots in both these practices. Adding tin cans to the shoes harkens back to the ancient practice of banging pots and making joyful noises to mark the end of the wedding reception and/or to ward off evil spirits as the couple went out into the world.

3. **Throwing rice** Since early Roman times, some grain—usually wheat, which symbolized fertility—has been associated with the wedding ceremony. The bride carried a sheaf of wheat instead of a bouquet, or she wore a garland of it in her hair. As the couple left their wedding reception, guests threw grains of wheat at them, and girls clambered for the grains that fell on them, in the belief that the grains would bring them good luck in their own marriages. Rice, too, has been included in marriage ceremonies and is believed to be symbolic of fertility and prosperity. In some cultures, the act of supping together on rice bound a couple in matrimony. In other areas, cakes of rice were offered to the deities in return for the safekeeping of the bride and groom. Throwing rice or grains at the couple is a way to wish them a lifetime of blessings.

4. **Keeping the groom from seeing the bride before the ceremony** This custom is a throwback to the days when all marriages were arranged. The fear was that if a bad first impression was made, either the bride or groom would try to back out. What better explanation for the young couple than to be told, simply, that seeing each other would be "bad luck"?

5. **Throwing the garter and the bouquet** In French tradition, the practice of tossing the bridal bouquet stemmed from the fourteenth-century notion that it was lucky to get a fragment of the bride's clothing. In those days, the bride was treated poorly. Guests would grab at her wedding dress in order to tear off pieces for good luck. Objecting to this wanton de-

struction of a dress they most certainly hoped to wear again, brides searched for an alternative, and thus began the custom of throwing personal articles, such as the bouquet or the garter, to the guests. Other sources describe the garter as representing the virginal girdle. When the groom removed the garter, he was, in essence,

demonstrating publicly that the bride was relinquishing her virginal status. Another source explains that in medieval times it was traditional for wedding guests to accompany the newlywed couple to their bed chamber after the ceremony and that in following this practice guests became more and more rowdy, to the extent that some even attempted to disrobe the new bride or "take liberties" with her. To keep the other men at bay, the groom would distract them by tossing the bride's garter at them.

6. **Dressing the bridesmaids identically** The ancients may have feared the evil spirits, but they didn't put too much stock in their intelligence. They reasoned that if all the bridesmaids dressed exactly like the bride, the spirits would be unable to find the bride and ruin her happiness. At many Victorian weddings, bridesmaids dressed in white and wore short veils to camouflage the bride. Late in the nineteenth century, anodyne dyes opened a world of possibilities for women of fashion, and white became reserved for the bride exclusively.

In the fourteenth century, on a wedding night, guests would follow the newlyweds to their bedroom, wait until they undressed, steal their stockings, and then "fling" the stockings at the couple. The first person to hit the bride or groom on the head would supposedly be the next person to marry.

7 Centuries of British Bridal Gowns

Along with baptism and burial, marriage is one of the three great public occasions in a person's life, and the only one at which the principals can fully appreciate the glory of their central role. So it's no wonder that for the bride, at least, the wedding dress has been at the center of her concerns. Here is Elizabeth Davies' history of the bridal gown.

Something Old . . .

Throughout history, women have tried to make their wedding dresses special, to suit the festive occasion, to make the beautiful bride more beautiful and the not so beautiful at least splendid to look at. At the top of the scale, royal princesses have always tried to be most princesslike on their wedding days. In medieval times, when royal marriages were of great political importance and used to seal alliances between countries, it was necessary for the young bride to look magnificent to uphold the prestige of her country, to impress the bridegroom's people with her own nation's apparent wealth, and, if possible, to outdo anything they could have afforded. Her jewelry might well have been the topic of prolonged negotiation, as part of her dowry.

To this end, brides have used as much material as they possibly could, of the most costly kinds, like velvet, damask silk, satin, fur, and fabrics woven with gold and silver thread. In days when all fabrics were hand-spun, hand-woven, and hand-dyed and economical use of it was the norm, bridal skirts would nevertheless be gathered and full, the sleeves would sweep the floor, and trains would fall behind to a length of several yards. Colors would be rich too—only the wealthy could afford expensive red, purple, and true black dyes, which were much harder to acquire than natural vegetable-based shades. Additionally, the dress would be sewn with precious gems—diamonds, rubies, sapphires, emeralds, and pearls—so the bride would glitter and flash in the sunlight. In some cases, the gown would be so thickly encrusted with jewels that the fabric beneath was hidden. In the fifteenth century, when Margaret of Flanders was married, her dress was so heavy that she had to be carried into the church by two gentlemen attendants.

With the advent of constitutional monarchy, royal marriages were of dynastic rather than national importance, but a princess going, or from, overseas would still wish to impress her new country. This sometimes backfired when an outfit in the height of current style at her own court might not be so admired elsewhere. This happened to poor Catherine of Braganza at her wedding to Charles II of Britain in 1662, when her pink farthingale was castigated as dowdy, and her hairstyle as peculiar.

Of course, not many brides were princesses, and most could not afford such expense. But in order to look special, a bride would usually try to copy the dress of a woman of a higher social class than herself. A noblewoman would do her best with gems and fur trimmings. A well-to-do middle-class woman would aspire to velvet or silk fabrics, and because she could not usually afford mink or sable, she would wear fox or rabbit fur to impress her friends. The poor bride's dress would be of linen or fine wool, instead of the usual coarse homespun, and she would use as much fabric as she could; her dress would most likely become her Sunday best after the wedding.

The superstitions that grew up around weddings hardly overlooked the bride's dress; its colors were assigned meanings. White, or a variation of white, was always a favorite and symbolized a girl's virginity and innocence in the face of her imminent change of state. But it was not a practical shade for most purposes, and it was not always the favorite choice. Blue, with its associations with the Virgin Mary, was another strong symbol of purity, which also traditionally symbolized fidelity and eternal love (hence the popularity of the sapphire in engagement rings). Brides who wore blue believed their husbands would always be true to them, so even if the gown itself was not blue, "something blue" was at least included in the bridal ensemble.

Pink was a popular color, considered most suitable for a May wedding. It is flattering to most complexions and associated with girlhood, although some superstitions held it to be unlucky: "Marry in pink and your fortunes will sink"!

Among the unpopular shades was green. This was considered the fairies' color, and it was bad luck to call the attention of the little folk to oneself during a time of transition. Also linked with the lushness of verdant foliage, it was believed that the green wedding dress would invite rain on the big day.

Harkening back to the days of homespun garments, any natural shade of brown or beige was considered very rustic. "Marry in brown, you will live out of town" implied that the bride would be a "hick" and never make good in the city.

The bright shade of yellow has had varied popularity. In the eighteenth century, it was the trendy color for a while; previously it had been associated with heathens and non-Christians and was considered an unholy shade to wear in church.

For brides of the lower classes, an extremely common shade of wedding gown was gray, because it was such a useful color to reuse as Sunday best, being considered eminently respectable. In Victorian times, it became associated with girls in domestic service, as they would often be provided with a new gray dress each year by their employer. Its deeper

GODEY'S FASHIONS FOR DECEMBER 1861.

Illustration from *Godey's Lady's Book,* December 1861 LIBRARY OF CONGRESS

shade of black was of course banned, for its association with death and mourning. In fact, it was considered such a bad omen that in some places even the guests were not allowed to wear it, and a recent widow might change her mourning for a red gown for the day, in deference to the bride.

Something New . . .

The traditional wedding garb as we know it today first appeared in the late eighteenth century. With the introduction of machine-made fabrics, cheap muslins imported from India, and styles inspired by the classical world, by 1800 the white dress and a veil were definitely in. As usual with fashion, it began in London, spread to other cities and towns, and eventually to rural areas. But it was not until Queen Victoria chose white silk and Honiton

lace for her wedding gown in 1840 that the style became permanently entrenched in the minds of Western brides. Though brides continued to wed in gowns of different colors, white was now set as the color of choice for proper weddings. In 1849, *Godey's Lady's Book*, the arbiter of etiquette, declared: "Custom has decided that white is the most fitting hue, whatever may be the material. It is an emblem of the purity and innocence of girlhood, and the unsullied heart she now yields to the chosen one."

In the nineteenth century, even a bride who wore white would expect to wear her dress again. For the season of her "bride visits," when she would do the rounds of family, friends, and acquaintances as a newly married woman, she would wear her bridal gown, with the train and flowers removed. An affluent bride would then adapt the bodice of the outfit (which was often made separately)

A wedding gown from the 1890s *(left)* and one from 1940 *(right)* BOTH COURTESY OF VINTAGEWEDDING.COM

and retrim it for evening wear for another season. Queen Victoria herself removed the lace overskirt from her dress and frequently used it again; she wore it over a black silk gown for her Diamond Jubilee celebrations over 50 years later. In fact, it was not until the 1930s that the "tradition" of the once-only wedding dress took hold in America.

The Industrial Revolution of the 1890s brought about more change. The advent of the department store meant that almost every woman could realize her dream of being married in a brand-new wedding dress. Not only was the white dress gaining popularity, but the perception was that it had always been so. According to an 1890 issue of the *Ladies' Home Journal*, "That from times immemorial the bride's gown has been white." Although white became the rule, some brides, especially the frontier brides, were the exceptions, as they wore dresses that were more practical and could be worn after the wedding.

The Twentieth Century

Until the 1920s, wedding dresses were always in the style of the moment, if more elaborately decorated than usual and more modest than the most daring fashion. In that decade, however, there was a revolution in women's clothing, and hemlines for ordinary wear rose from the shoe to well above the knee. At first, wedding styles followed suit when Coco Chanel, one of the most powerful forces in the fashion industry, introduced the short wedding dress; it was a white knee-length dress worn with a long train. But as skirts grew ever more abbreviated, they became unsuitable for a church service, and many brides reverted to full-length wedding gowns.

After the "Roaring Twenties" came the depression of the thirties, and the times were characterized by yet more changes in fashion. Waistlines returned to their natural position and became more defined, and hemlines dropped back below the knee, though they were never to reach the floor again for daywear. Instead of the boyish look, women emphasized their shape again. The boyish look of the "flappers" was replaced by more shapely styles; bias-cut gowns now hugged the female figure.

The white wedding dress virtually disappeared during the Second World War. Clothes rationing was introduced in 1941, when fashion almost ceased to exist. A few made brave efforts with parachute silk, while others wore gowns borrowed from relatives, but most brides wore their uniforms if they were in the service and simple suits if they weren't.

In Scotland, a bride preserves her wedding dress so that she can be buried in it.

After the war ended, rationing was still in force in England, yet no one expected Princess Elizabeth to skimp on her wedding gown. Clothing coupons poured into Buckingham Palace in 1947 from loyal citizens wanting to see her at her best at her marriage to Philip Mountbatten in Westminster Abbey. Consequently, her gown was sumptuous, with embroidery and beading decorating the flowing satin and a long train and silk net veil. The sweetheart neckline and wide shoulders followed a predominant style of the decade, which was soon to give way, in the late forties, to Dior's stunning "new look."

With narrow shoulders, nipped waist, and wide skirts, Christian Dior's revolution in bridal gowns was embraced by society both high and low.

During the 1950s, a typical dress of the decade was of "ballerina" length and made with a removable jacket bodice; it would have a tight sleeve with cuff pointed over the hand and would be worn over a low-cut underdress with a circular skirt held out by stiff petticoats. Many women wore variations on this look and had the underdress dyed a new color afterwards to wear as a cocktail dress. Brocade and lace gradually superseded satin almost universally for wedding gowns. To counterbalance the bouffant skirts, veils, which had previously been usually square, worn folded diagonally with the point at the back and sides, now became circular and waist-length, usually attached to a coronet-style headdress.

The early sixties showed little change on the bridal front. Girls still wore circular skirts supported by crinolines, tight sleeves, and short veils. The only real change was that the veils became more bouffant, to match the back-combed hairstyles then in vogue. By the middle years of the decade, however, the influence of the "Swinging Sixties" designs of Mary Quant and company were beginning to alter even the bridal profile. Waistlines dropped, and straight, shift-style dresses came into vogue. Along with the narrower line returned the train and the long "cathedral" veil, so named because only brides married in cathedrals had previously worn them. The shift soon proved too shapeless for wedding fashion and evolved into the empire line, with the waist tight under the bust. Influenced by mainstream design, some girls abandoned veils in favor of floral bonnets or floppy hats. This development continued into the next decade, when hooded dresses and "Juliet" caps worn with or without a veil also became popular headgear.

Sleeves were the big feature of seventies dresses. The shape of the dress itself moved gradually from the narrow, high-waisted empire line of the late 1960s to the more flared princess line, with little or no train, and the waist gradually fell to its natural position by 1980. Pinafore styles were very popular, whether they were actually two-layered or just suggested the effect with a contrasting sleeve and bib front.

Just as Victoria had influenced the brides of her era, the Princess of Wales' extravagant skirt and huge sleeves proved the style icon of the 1980s. After the restrained outlines of the previous decade, every bride now wanted a fairy-tale crinoline and tiara just like Diana. Brides sought out full skirts gathered at the waist and big sleeves to the elbow, with flounces and bows and lace embellishments. There was a surge in popularity for taffeta and silk. However, it soon became clear that what looked wonderful on a 5'10" slender princess did not always suit short Miss Average. So when, in 1986, Sarah Ferguson modified the look to suit her fuller figure, with a low waistline, pointed at front and back, and flare as well as gathering in her satin skirts, other brides soon followed her, and this set the style that was to prevail for the next few years.

It is generally considered unlucky for the bride to make her own dress, and even professional dressmakers rarely do so. It is still more unlucky for her to put on her full bridal array too soon, particularly if she sees herself in the mirror. When the dress is being fitted, it should be put on in sections, never all at once, and if possible, it should not be completely finished before the actual day. When this proves entirely impractical, a short length of hem should be left unsewn, so that a few stitches can be put in at the very last moment.

By the 1990s, applied embroidery and beading, on a fairly stiffly sculpted satin corseted bodice, with prominent sleeves, had become very much the norm. A variation was introduced with off-the-shoulder designs derived from mid- or late-Victorian evening wear. As the decade progressed, a variety of skirt choices became available. The wide skirt stayed popular, but then a variant with a very dropped waist, to below the hip, and then flared, was often seen. Gradually, more fluid materials began to appear alongside the stiffly appliquéd fabrics, and narrower profiles returned. As the nineties progressed, bridal wear imitated a new development in daywear fashion: shift dresses made by layering a fine fabric over a lining for an ethereal effect were introduced. The softer, more relaxed look epitomized romance and suggested a more touchable bride. This small revolution heralded a new century.

The Twenty-first Century

As wedding fashion continues to evolve separately from the general vogue, people have felt freer to allow their imaginations full rein, and some wedding parties are not so much in "best" dress as fancy dress as themed and fantasy costumes become more and more common. In these "anything goes" times, today's bride can feel free to draw on a previous historical style or invent her own. And when in doubt, she can always choose the proverbial midground: something old and something new.

The Art of Dressing a Bride

From the Ladies' Home Journal, *March 1894*

Of all people in the world the French are the ones who most positively combine sentiment and frocks. The rich lace, the costly jewel, the much-trimmed gown never belongs to the unmarried woman until she has passed youth. Even on the very day of her wedding, the French girl, while she is essentially a bride, always has in her costume the suggestion of youth and innocence. The material especially dedicated to the bride is white satin, heavy and lustrous; occasionally some caprice of fashion may show itself on one of these gowns, as has the band of sable around the edge this winter. But the artist in dress disapproves of any such departure from regulation rules, the first one of which is that the bride shall be all in white. White silk, white crepe, white cloth, and some of the very thin stuffs are occasionally chosen for the wedding gown, but personally I can fully sympathize with the girl who chooses fewer frocks in her trousseau, yet elects that on her wedding day she

Dressing the bride, ca. 1907
LIBRARY OF CONGRESS

shall really look what she is, a bride. With her white gown come the white tulle veil and the orange blossoms.

There are some things that a bride must remember: her bodice must be high in the neck; her sleeves reach quite to her wrists, and her gown must fall in full, unbroken folds that show the richness of the material, and there must not be even a suggestion of such frivolities as frills or ribbons of any kind. The design for a white satin wedding dress . . . is that approved by the greatest and most artistic of dressmakers. It has about it not only the air of girlishness that should be there, but, by the disposition of the rich material, makes prominent the elegance of toilette that will be permitted to the young matron.

> "Some things came from Mme. Flotov for me to try on: I felt so funny putting on such smart undergarments and nightgowns, don't be shocked my mentioning them."
> — From a letter to the future Czar Nicholas Romanov from the future Czarina Alexandra

The Meaning of the Wedding Veil in 11 Cultures

Throughout history, the wedding veil has symbolized various things among different peoples. Nevertheless, the actual origin of the wedding veil is unclear. Some historians believe that it harkens back to the image of a man capturing his bride and throwing a blanket over her head before whisking her away. Another theory suggests that during times when arranged marriages were more common, a groom would not be given the opportunity to see his intended before the ceremony, lest he back out of the deal. A different theory has it that the veil was worn to protect the bride from evil spirits. Whatever its origins, it is commonly believed that the veil predates the wedding dress itself by at least four centuries.

Ancient Greece and Rome In both Greece and Rome, the veil was a complete head-to-toe covering intended to ward off evil spirits and to represent the subordination of a woman to a man. In Greece the veil was yellow, and in Rome it was red. Both these colors represented fire and were meant to ward off demons. By the fourth century B.C., sheer translucent veils were the fashion at both Greek and Roman weddings.

The Near East In the Near East, the veil served to protect against the wind and desert sun as well as to preserve the modesty of women in a time when the use of force was the rule of law. A woman covered her face so that her husband wouldn't be killed for her beauty.

Eastern cultures In some Eastern cultures, the veil protected the bride from evil spirits, but in Morocco and ancient India the veil was used to protect others from the bride. Today the veil is thought to shield the bride from unwanted suitors.

Japan Until the end of the Edo period in 1867, brides wore a headdress called a *tsuno kakushi.* Although this was not technically a veil, it served the function of veiling feelings of jealousy, ego, and selfishness, attributes that were not to be displayed at a wedding. The tsuno kakushi, along with the *wataboshi* (a hood), was designed to hide the bride's face from everyone except the groom and is still used in traditional Japanese weddings.

China The Chinese did not use a veil; instead, they held a sacred umbrella over the bride's head to shield her from evil spirits that might be watching from the heavens.

Judaism Prior to the Jewish wedding ceremony, the groom places a veil over the bride's head. The veil symbolizes modesty and imparts the lesson that regardless of how beautiful the bride is, her soul and character are of utmost importance. The importance of the veil being sheer goes back to biblical times and the marriage of Jacob to Leah. Instead of marrying his beloved Rachel, Jacob was tricked into marrying Leah, whose opaque veil prevented Jacob from seeing her face.

Christianity The use of a veil in Christian wedding ceremonies originated in ancient Rome, although the bridal veil is mentioned in Genesis. Early Christians absorbed the Roman custom that required brides to wear their veils from the moment of their betrothal until the conclusion of the wedding.

> "[Rebekah] said to the servant, 'Who is that man, walking in the field to meet us?' The servant said, 'It is my master.' So she took her veil and covered herself."
> — Genesis 24:65 (English Standard Version)

(The veils of nuns likewise denoted the constancy of their consecration as "brides" of Christ and were signs of their chastity.)

Europe Christian soldiers returning from the Crusades during medieval times introduced the veil to European culture. Arabian music, science, and art all came to influence the splintered states of Europe, and as the later crusaders returned from the East with wealth and riches, the veil came to symbolize modesty and virginity. Only first-time brides wore a veil. The groom's lifting of the veil signified his acceptance of the bride. He unwrapped his bride as he took possession of her.

Italy In northern Italy, the bride wore a bridal veil to conceal her from evil spirits, though tearing the veil was considered good luck.

Russia In Russia, it was forbidden for the groom to see the bride prior to the marriage for fear that this would lead to a variety of misfortunes and even untimely death. The newlyweds touched each other only through the veil.

Poland At a Polish wedding, everyone forms a circle around the bride, a traditional folk song, "Twelve Angels," is played, and it is during this ritual that the bride is allowed to transfer her veil. The bride's mother removes it, symbolizing the bride's new womanhood, and places it on the head of the maid of honor, who in turn passes the veil to the bridesmaids and the flower girl. Each who participates represents an angel bestowing gifts on the couple.

Veils first came into fashion in the American colonies after Nelly Curtis wore one at her wedding to George Washington's aide, Maj. Lawrence Lewis. Lewis saw his bride standing behind a filmy curtain and commented on the beauty of the image.

Handfasting: Tying the Knot

During a handfasting ritual, the hands of the bride and groom are literally tied together to represent their commitment to one another. The custom (which may have been a precursor to today's practice of shaking hands over a contract) dates back to a time when marriage was still a civil affair. Even after marriage became a function of the church, handfasting continued to be a popular ritual among those who could not afford more elaborate weddings. Said to have originated in the British Isles, it was still legal in Scotland until 1939.

The details of the procedure are as varied as the cultures that have adopted it. In some regions, handfasting constituted not a marriage, but a trial-run engagement, typically lasting a year and a day, during which carnal relations were often allowed. On the last day of the trial period, the couple would repeat their vows, this time for eternity.

Today handfasting is integrated into many wedding ceremonies. It is an important part of the Wiccan celebration (see page 313), and it is popular at gay and lesbian weddings and ceremonies. It is also practiced by couples who find personal meaning in the ritual or who simply want to acknowledge the ancient custom. As with many other wedding traditions, handfasting is sometimes adapted to accommodate modern circumstances. A nice use of the ceremony is to tie the hands of the bride and groom together with children from previous marriages, thus symbolizing the formation of a new family.

Pre-Wedding and Engagement Traditions Around the World

While an engagement period has been common to many cultures and absent in some, it was the romantic Victorians of the 1800s who, at least for Westerners, crafted an entire society around the time preceding a wedding. By this point in time, most cultures had agreed that such a period was of benefit: it gave the couple a chance to get to know one another, and it prepared them for society and their future duty to the community. However varied engagement and pre-wedding rituals might seem, common threads do exist: an engagement is usually cause for celebration; family members are asked to approve the union; accompanied by female members of the community, brides are specially prepared for the event; and the engagement sets off a string of gift exchanges and promises of future support, usually by the groom. Many cultures employ the use of go-betweens, and these respected individuals are often part of the pre-wedding festivities. Finally, whether in the form of tossing wheat onto the wedding bed or presenting the bride with a sprig of seaweed, good wishes for brides and grooms have always first and foremost included the hope for fertility.

We're grateful to Diane Ferraro of Robbins Brothers for the following account.

Africa

The Yorubans of Nigeria visit a priest before they marry for a spiritual reading to determine whether their ancestors approve of the union. If they don't, the couple must perform appeasement rituals, such as lighting candles, before they are allowed to marry.

In Nigeria and other areas of Africa, in a ritual called the fattening of the bride, a young woman is encouraged to put on weight before her wedding, which will make her fertile and more attractive to her husband.

Armenia

Before the days of communism, when religious and local customs had not yet been abolished, an engagement was celebrated with a ceremony that closely resembled the wedding itself. The couple took vows before a priest. She wore a veil, and together they lit candles, after which the young man's mother presented the bride-to-be with a ring. The union was binding, and if either party chose to abandon it, the other family would receive amends.

Austria

In the past, the groom sent his friends or family to offer a proposal of marriage to the family of the bride-to-be. If they encountered goats, pigeons, or wolves on the path to the house, they believed they would have good fortune in the marriage.

Bohemia

It is a traditional Bohemian wedding custom for the couple getting married to give each other specific wedding presents. The groom gives his bride a rosary, a prayer book, a fur hat, and a wedding ring. To protect his wife's chastity, he also gives her a girdle with three keys. The bride gives her groom a shirt that has been sewn with gold thread and colorful silks and a wedding band.

Brazil

Long ago in Brazil, a man would have to prove himself a suitable husband by taming an unbridled donkey in a ritual called *bumba-meu-boi*.

Czechoslovakia

It's tough for a bride in Czechoslovakia to not get the hint: the night before the wedding day, an infant is laid on the bed of the couple, representing hope that the couple will produce children.

Denmark

The progressive Danes traditionally have tolerated premarital sex for a couple who are betrothed and even invented a temporary marriage—sealed by a clasping of hands called handfasting (see page 59)—to legitimize it. Couples are allowed to enter into trial marriages that last for a year and a day. Many then simply "forget" to marry until a baby is born.

England

During the Middle Ages, the groom had to kidnap his bride in order to marry her. Because the bride was very valuable to her family (she helped take care of the farm and the household chores), the groom would often pay his debt by offering the family gold rings to pay for the hired help to replace their daughter.

If you plan to propose on one knee, you'll be honoring a custom that goes back to medieval times, when a knight would bend his knee to show his respect for his master and mistress.

The British practice of bundling was happily accepted by young couples when it was introduced to New England communities in the nineteenth century. It involved giving the couple permission to spend one night together in bed, wearing underclothes and separated by a wooden plank.

Finland

A proposal is considered a private affair. But once it's out of the way, not one but two raucous parties ensue. The groom's party usually takes place in one of the country's massive saunas, and at the bachelorette party the bride is likely to be dressed in a costume and encouraged to kiss and sing to passing strangers.

On an evening before a wedding in Finland, groups of women or men, headed respectively by either the bride or groom, take to the streets. The leader in each case, often masked and perhaps even only partly clothed, amuses his or her friends by handing out hastily scribbled advice on life to passersby.

Germany

A celebration called the *Polarabend* is held the night before a wedding in Germany. After a meal and a ceremony rehearsal, a short play, operetta, or charade portraying the imagined future of the couple is presented. The evening ends with the smashing of pottery and the bride sweeping up the broken shards.

Holland

Because Dutch law made engagements legally binding, traditions involving courtship were widely practiced. During the 1600s, a young man could attach a flower or wreath to the door of the woman he sought to pursue. If the flower or wreath was discarded, the suitor took this as a sign of accep-

China

In ancient times, a negotiator communicated between the parents of the bride and groom-to-be. The family of the groom gave the negotiator gifts and a proposal request to present to the prospective bride's family. If the girl's family accepted, they gave a document to the negotiator that contained the girl's date and hour of birth. The document was then placed on an altar for three days, and if no harm came to either family, an astrologer looked at the birth dates of the bride and groom-to-be to determine that the marriage union would be successful. It was only after these steps were taken that the families would investigate each other's backgrounds, position in the community, education, and appearance. Then a decision would be made to proceed with the marriage.

Strict traditionalists followed the ritual of "the Three Letters," which were issued by the groom. The Request Letter verified the contract; the Gift Letter included a list of the gifts that would be exchanged; and the Wedding Letter was given on the day of the marriage, confirming all.

A traditional Chinese bride is taken to her new home amid much fanfare and well-wishing. She is carried in a sedan chair, her face is covered with a red veil, and a red umbrella hides her from the eyes of heaven. The noisemaking and banging of pots and pans on the part of the wedding party is intended to scare off evil spirits. The bride carries an apple for peace and harmony and may toss her fan to the crowd signifying that she is leaving her childhood home forever.

A new bed is always installed in the couple's home on the day before the wedding. Children are invited into the room to provide an omen of fertility. The bed is scattered with fruit, which the children are allowed to take. In an alternative version of this ritual, the guests follow the married couple to their bedchamber and continue to party to "chase away demons." The groom may take a sip of wine from a "flesh cup" and then pass the wine in his mouth to the mouth of the bride. Bawdy jokes are told and songs are sung, and the entourage is sometimes encouraged to remain for as long as three days, just to make sure the demons do not return.

To prepare for the ceremony, the bride takes a grapefruit-scented bath, and her hair is specially styled by a woman who is considered to be lucky.

At a special dinner with the bride's family, the groom is served an egg. His breaking of the yolk symbolizes the breaking of the bride's ties with her family.

Astrology is commonly consulted for planning many aspects of the Chinese wedding. The female attendants, for instance, are chosen according to whose horoscope animals are compatible with the groom's.

tance; then he left a tied bouquet with a card bearing his name. If the advances were welcomed, the girl would write a love note and put it in a basket with candies or flowers, which she would set on her windowsill.

India

In India, an astrologist is commonly consulted to see if a couple is a good match. If they are, the astrologist will even pick the day for the ceremony—for an extra charge, of course.

> Long ago, a wife in India was not allowed to speak to her husband outside of their sleeping quarters until her mother-in-law died.

On the day before the wedding, the *Ghari Puja* is held. The priest comes to the couple's new home and performs a blessing. The bride grinds wheat, and the groom offers the priest a handful of the ground wheat to symbolize that though his life is changing, he will always remain charitable and help those less fortunate than himself. The bride and groom wear old clothing, which is torn by their friends to symbolize the end of their old life.

On the afternoon before a wedding in India, female friends gather and the bride's hands and feet are painted with a henna paste. The paste is allowed to dry and is then washed off. The remaining stain remains for days. It is said that the darker the stain, the stronger the love between the bride and groom. After the ceremony, the bride does not leave her house until it is time to go to the wedding.

Before a wedding in India, the sisters and female relatives and friends of the groom visit the bride-to-be and bring her small gifts. The ritual is designed to acquaint the bride with the important people in the groom's life.

Ireland

The Irish celebrate an impending wedding by kidnapping the bride, dressing her in bizarre clothing, covering her with flour, and wheeling her around in a wheelbarrow. Funny people, those Irish!

Japan

Starting in the fifteenth century, Japanese marriages were arranged by a go-between called a *nakado*. This trusted individual arranged for the engagement and the rituals that followed an acceptance. A betrothal period called *yui-no* involved a gift exchange between the groom and bride-to-be. The bride-to-be was presented with a sash, or *obi*, that represented virtue. Then a skirt called a *hakama*, representing fidelity, was given to the groom. In all, up to nine gifts were exchanged that represented fortune and happiness.

Today engagement gifts in Japan communicate meanings. The groom may give his bride white linen thread, anticipating the fact that they will grow old together, or seaweed, to foretell fertility.

Judaism

At a Sabbath service before the wedding, the groom is called to the Torah and given a special blessing in a ritual known as the *aufruf*. He is then showered with nuts, raisins, and candy in the hopes that he will have a sweet future. After the aufruf, a kiddush reception is held at which a special prayer is said over wine.

It is customary for the bride and groom to visit the graves of departed parents before the wedding.

Before her wedding, the Jewish bride (and sometimes the groom as well) takes a ritual bath called a *mikvah* during which she purifies herself in preparation for her life as a woman. The Jewish Orthodox bride is then secluded so that she cannot see her groom before the wedding.

Korea

In the past, when a man in Korea wanted to ask for a girl's hand in marriage, he would ride a white pony to her home, where he would present her family with a pair of geese as his promise to be faithful for life.

Unlike Western engagements, in which the groom seeks approval from the bride's parents before proposing, a Korean bride must first be introduced to the groom's family before she is accepted as his bride-to-be. Instead of throwing rice at the happy couple outside the church, the groom's father may throw red dates, symbolic of fertility, at his new daughter-in-law.

Astrologers are commonly consulted to determine the compatibility of the engaged couple.

On the evening before the wedding, the bride is visited by the

A wedding party in Israel, 2006 AUTHORS' COLLECTION

Moroccan costumes—Ali Baba style—and they carry the bride and groom around the room, showering them with sweets, well-wishing, and spirited music.

Five days before the wedding, a mattress, blankets, and other necessities are carried into the bridal chamber. The bride is given a bath by her female wedding attendants, called *negassa*, who closely supervise. They apply elaborate henna designs on her hands and feet and then dress her in wedding finery. She is then placed behind a curtain, symbolizing her transition to a new life.

Native Americans

The Cheyenne practiced a "blanket proposal": a young man would stand outside a girl's tepee wrapped in a blanket. When she came out, he would embrace her. If she allowed the embrace, they were engaged.

A Hopi woman would feed cornmeal cakes known as *piki* to the man she loved. If he took a bite, an engagement celebration ensued at which everyone ate piki and the couple exchanged rings made from horn. Today the groom and bride each wash their hands to cleanse themselves of past loves. The bride wears a dress that features traditional colors of white, blue, yellow, and black, each pointing to one of the four corners of the earth. The black points north, yellow points west, blue points south, and white points east.

groom's friends, who beat drums and dance. They then present her with a *hahm*, a box filled with presents from the groom's family. In the box, she's liable to find stalks of ripe millet (a symbol of fertility), gold jewelry, and silks.

Latvia

Brides and grooms have it easy in Latvia—they simply choose a favorite married couple, who must arrange the wedding for them.

Morocco

During the engagement period, the prospective groom continually sends his bride-to-be gifts of cloth, gowns, and perfume on feast days.

Middle Eastern Jews, especially those from Morocco, celebrate an engagement with a colorful celebration known as a *henna* (pronounced "cheena") that can take place anywhere from several months to just a week before the wedding. Henna is applied to the bride's hands in an intricate design that sometimes includes the name of her betrothed. The wedding party dresses in traditional

The Philippines

Traditionally, a woman who found a spear thrown at the front of her house was officially engaged.

Today, when a man wants to marry, his parents bring gifts to the girl's home and make promises of further substantial contributions. The groom's parents pay for everything in the Philippines, including the wedding.

Among the Tagalogs, weddings are held during the waxing of the moon, a symbol of fortune and growth.

Camels being used to carry the bridal party to an Egyptian wedding, ca. 1910
LIBRARY OF CONGRESS

Polynesia

In some societies, men must prove their prowess before they are allowed to marry. In Taumotuas, the young man does so by wrestling with sharks. A suitor from Pendercost must dive from a 90-foot tower toward the ground in a bungee-type feat. In Gambiers, the new groom paddles his bride to a distant shore in his canoe.

Quaker

If a Quaker couple wants to marry, they must make a formal request to the congregation, who then appoint a marriage committee to determine whether the union is suitable.

Scotland

Before a Scottish wedding, a shower, called a spree, is held so that the bride can open the wedding gifts surrounded by everyone who has sent a gift. Even the groom attends. At this shower, the bride is dressed up in a veil made from an ordinary household object (a tablecloth or a shower curtain), and she is given a plastic baby doll and a plastic toilet or container. The party walks through town singing songs. The bride can exchange kisses for money, which is placed in the toilet or container.

Sikh

The Sikh wedding follows only days after a marriage proposal. Once the engagement is official, the groom's parents tie a knot in a piece of string every day for five days. At the wedding, they present the bride's parents with the string.

On the night before her wedding, a bride and her friends gather to celebrate, and they decorate a wall with five handprints, for good luck.

Tanzania

The Chagga people of Tanzania don't believe that the bride should diet before her big day. Three months before the wedding, she is taken to a "fattening hut," where she must remain, doing no work and feasting on the milk, bananas, sheep fat, butter, and other cooked foods sent by the groom.

Poland

In Krakow, parents seeking a husband for an eligible daughter would paint their house blue.

To seal an engagement, a couple sips vodka from a single glass.

In a handfasting engagement ceremony before the wedding, guests gather around the couple as their hands are tied together with a silk scarf over a loaf of bread. They eat beans dipped in wine, and after the bride and groom both sip some wine, the rest is poured onto the ground. The best man (*swat*) and maid of honor (*swata*) pray that the union will be blessed.

Before the wedding, the Polish bride's traditional maidenly braids are undone by her bridesmaids in a custom called *rospleciny* that marks the bride's new womanhood.

Wedding Night Rituals Around the World

Wedding night celebrations vary from culture to culture. Some of these customs are charming, while others are downright cruel and archaic, at least by Western standards. Common here is the idea that the marrying couple are first blessed with wishes for fertility and long life and then—at least good-naturedly—tormented.

China
Elegantly designed candles shaped like a phoenix and dragon are placed in the bridal chamber to ward off evil spirits. The couple drink wine from goblets tied together with a scarlet red sash while they both have their arms intertwined. The bride then is given half-raw dumplings that she must eat to ensure a prosperous life.

Greece
Newly married couples once shared an unpartitioned bedroom with the groom's parents, and they had to ask for permission to have sexual relations.

India
The wedding night is referred to as the *Suhag Raat* ("first time"). The couple's bedroom is adorned with colorful flowers. Sweets, perfumes, and drinks are provided for the bride and groom by their families, along with an idol of Krishna presented by the bride's mother.

Islam
When an Islamic bride enters the bedroom, the groom removes her shoes and washes her feet. He then sprinkles water around the room. Next he prays, asking his bride to do so as well. Before the couple go to bed, the groom puts his hand on his forehead and prays again. Sex on the first night is neither compulsory nor forbidden.

Japan
The wife is carried over the threshold by the groom in order to prevent her from tripping and bringing bad luck to the marriage. Because chastity is re-garded as sacred, various friends and neighbors are assigned the task of remaining in the bedchamber and actually witnessing the consummation of the marriage.

Nestorians
A wedding night custom practiced by members of the Assyrian Church of the East involves the bridegroom kicking his wife and then commanding her to remove her shoes as a declaration of her submission.

Polynesia
In the Polynesian islands, it was once customary for the bride to have sex with all the male guests before the groom did. Tribesmen felt that they were entitled, since the groom was going to sleep with her for the rest of her life.

Scotland
In ancient Gaelic culture, it was traditional for close friends and family to practice a version of chiverie. The couple would spend

France
Chiverie is a wedding night prank in which the newlyweds' friends bang pots and pans, ring bells, and blare horns in an attempt to disturb the consummation of the marriage. The bride and groom are expected to appear in their wedding clothes and provide treats for their tormentors. Chiverie has been an extremely popular ritual, one often carried to extremes. It is still practiced in many forms throughout the world. In America, for instance, it's known as shivaree.

The Bridal Trousseau

The tradition of the bride's trousseau can be traced back to the earliest times, when marriage often meant that a young girl was leaving her home forever. To prepare her for life, she was given gifts of linens, clothing, and household items, and even from a young age she was encouraged to stitch her own contributions to her trousseau. The more affluent the bride's family, the more extravagant the trousseau, which could include everything from brooms and quilts to ball gowns and jewelry. The Victorians created a short-lived custom called the Trousseau Tea, at which the bride's possessions were put on display for visiting gawkers. The practice was considered pretentious and disappeared quickly, although the tradition of displaying wedding gifts remained popular up through the twentieth century.

their first night together in a hay barn. Close friends of the bride would dress her for bed and invite every male who attended the wedding to kiss her good-night. When the couple was finally left alone, the revelers would gather outside the barn and create a further racket. The couple was finally left alone once the revelers were too drunk or exhausted to continue.

For good luck, the newlyweds would often sprinkle water on the bed to "cleanse" it.

5 Important Dates in the History of Brides Magazine

1934 The mother of all bridal magazines is first published as a free pamphlet, published quarterly, entitled "So You're Going to Be Married: A Magazine for Brides." It was created by Agnes Foster Wright,

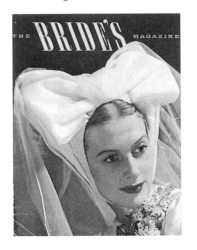

a prominent interior designer who was married to the editor of *House and Garden.*

1949 Following in the footsteps of *Modern Bride,* which is first released this year and which promises a more contemporary approach to weddings, *Brides* magazine hits the newsstands.

1959 The magazine is purchased by Condé Nast, joining the mainstream magazine lineup.

1960 The magazine now carries some $2 million in ads in each issue and has a circulation of 220,000. In its new status as arbiter of all things wedding, the magazine works with retailers to create contests and help shape taste.

2000 The 1,271-page spring issue makes the *Guinness Book of World Records* as the largest magazine ever produced.

> "The bridal magazines have been so constitutive of the wedding industry, and have served so unwaveringly to further its interests, that it is fair to say there would be no wedding industry without them."
>
> — Rebecca Mead, *One Perfect Day*

A History of the Wedding Invitation

We are grateful to MyExpression.com for this detailed and fascinating look at wedding invitations over the ages.

Announcing impending nuptials has been a part of weddings since people first began tying the knot, although the form in which invitations have been issued has changed vastly over the years.

Prior to the invention of the printing press in 1447, wedding invitations were announced by town criers, men who were responsible for walking through their cities and verbally proclaiming in a loud voice the news of the day to a population that was largely illiterate. In some cultures, friends of the engaged couple went door to door with the good news, and in some parts of Germany a male friend of the family was designated to be the "wedding inviter." Adorned with flowers and ribbons, he would invite people to the wedding by hitting a stick against their door.

The first written invitations were a luxury created for the wealthy nobility of Europe. They were crafted by hand by monks who were skilled in calligraphy, and the affair was extremely costly in those pre-photocopying days. Most of these invitations also included the family's coat of arms, or crest, a practice still in use today in some circles.

After Johannes Gutenberg invented the printing press in 1447, literacy rates began to rise, and printed invitations became more common. But early printing techniques produced only a stamped image that could be easily smudged. While the technique was useful for broadsides, the look was disappointing for a formal wedding invitation.

Another invention changed that forever. In 1642, Ludwig von Siegen created metal-plate engraving. With this method, an artisan would carve a message in reverse onto a metal plate. The results were much more beautiful and stylish, and engraved invitations became a common trapping of the upper-class wedding.

The ink still smudged a bit, though, and to stem the problem, a piece of tissue paper was placed over the printed surface of the invitation, a practice that is still in use today, however needlessly.

In 1605, the first newspapers began to be printed. Not long after, couples began announcing their upcoming weddings in those newspapers as an easy way to spread the word. These announcements didn't replace invitations, they just made the weddings that much more public.

The next revolution in invitation history was heralded by Alois Senefelder's invention in 1796 of lithography, a process in which chemicals were used to create images. Now a crisp printing without the time constraints of engraving metal plates became possible.

Despite all of the innovations of the Industrial Revolution, most wedding invitations were still delivered by hand and on horseback, as the postal system, still in its infancy, was notoriously unreliable. Given its often grimy journey, the invitation required protection, and so the envelope was placed inside yet another envelope.

When the invitation was delivered, it would be handed to a servant who would remove the actual invitation from the outer envelope in order to bring it to the head of the household. The practice is still in use, however needlessly; the ecologically minded bride wisely discards it.

At a time when many guests might have been invited to a church wedding but not to the reception, which was reserved for close family and friends, the Victorians popularized an element known as reception cards—these were essentially invitations given to select ceremony guests who were being asked to come to the reception as well. Modern brides and grooms sometimes send reception cards if the wedding and reception are not taking place at the same location.

Public weddings gave rise to the first wedding crashers, and to stem their advances, some families would include a small card, often including a specific pew number for seating, which was to be presented to an usher at the ceremony. Without the card, the person would not be allowed to enter.

The invitation industry changed little after the development of lithography until World War II, after which household incomes began to increase dramatically. Now the middle class had the means to imitate the lifestyles of those in the top rungs of wealth in their countries. That imitation became common in weddings and, in particular, in wedding invitations. Fine wedding stationery became de rigueur, and with its popularity there rose a blinding array of questions about how exactly they were to be worded. Along came society figures such as Amy Vanderbilt and Emily Post, who were ever-ready to tutor the common folk in the ways of the wealthy. Their teachings haunt us to this day.

The refinement of a technique known as photothermography in the 1960s further revolutionized the invitation industry. Using heat to create raised-ink lettering on paper, thermography, which had been around since the nineteenth century, could now be used to create the same beautiful invitations as engraving but at a fraction of the cost. It made invitations more affordable for average families.

The current state of the wedding invitation industry has less to do with technological advances than it does with changing attitudes. As weddings remain a chance to advertise one's worth, the range of available possibilities has grown to include hundreds of varieties of handmade papers, delicate ribbons, and even the dried flowers that were so central to weddings of old. Invitations can now be sent via tubes and boxes and may include elegantly presented photographs. At the other end of the spectrum, do-it-yourself and online stationers have made elegant invitations possible for even the most frugal bride.

A Brief History of the Bridal Bouquet

We suspect that flowers or herbs have been used in weddings since the beginning of time, although the actual first recorded use of wedding flowers dates back only to the ancient Greeks. Flowers and plants were used to make a crown for the bride to wear and were considered a gift of nature. Often, the bridesmaids would make posies (small bouquets) for each guest to wear as a symbol of thanks from the bride. Garlands and wreaths, worn by both the groom and bride, were also popular.

• Bridal flowers were originally made of herbs and bulbs of garlic, which were said to have a magical power to ward off any evil spirits that might plague the future. Different herbs had different meanings. Dill was the herb of lust. As flowers replaced bulbs of garlic, these too were assigned meanings (see "Flowers and Their Meanings," page 69).

• By the time Queen Victoria married Prince Albert in the midnineteenth century, flowers had all but completely replaced herbs, although the edible flowers Victoria included in her bouquet—marigolds, for instance—might very well have been a reference to the herbs that had once been used. Victoria's bouquet was also notable for its shape. Up until this time, bouquets were mostly free-style—flowers gathered with ribbons. But when Victoria opted for a posy—a small round bouquet of tightly wrapped flowers that could be held in one hand—it became the rage, as did all things Victoria.

• At the beginning of the twentieth century, the conspicuous consumption practiced by the new middle class led to the abandonment of the simply posy for elaborate bouquets that included a great variety of flow-

ers and bows, and the ribbons that adorned them often hung to the floor. It was during this time that the floral industry began to grow by leaps and bounds as florists were able to craft more intricate designs with new materials. Hollywood showcased such extravagant spectacles, introducing creative new designs—crescent- or ring-shaped bouquets—in its high-profile weddings.

• It wasn't until the 1960s and 1970s, when hippies popularized "roots" weddings, that bridal bouquets started returning to their natural roots. Now simple designs replaced elaborate creations and less became more. Brides chose single flowers for their bouquets instead of an assortment of buds, and color began taking over. Wreaths worn atop the bridal veil reappeared, recalling the earliest use of wedding flowers.

• The modern bride's bouquet can take almost any form, from a sheaf of long-stemmed calla lilies to a hand-tied bouquet featuring rhinestones and pearls. Or it can be absent altogether. As brides continue to think "outside the bunch," we can only imagine that new designs will be on the horizon before long.

Flowers and Their Meanings

The practice of assigning meaning to flowers goes back to man's very first appreciation of nature's blossoms. Mystical qualities and symbolism were assigned to each of the varieties, and messages were often communicated by bouquets in which each flower had been as carefully chosen as a word. The Victorians popularized "florigraphy"—"the language of flowers."

We're grateful to Rose Smith of WedThemes.com, author of the e-book *How to Create a Beautiful Medieval Wedding,* for this version of the list.

Flower Name	Meaning
Acacia	Friendship
Acorn	Life, immortality
Allium	Unity
Alyssum	Incomparable worth
Amaryllis	Pride, beauty
Ambrosia	Reciprocated love
Angelica	Inspiration
Apple blossom	Preference
Arbutus	Thee only do I love
Arum lily	Ardor
Aster	Variety
Bachelor's button	Celibacy, hope
Bluebell	Humility
Bridal Rose	Happy love
Buttercup	Riches, childishness
Camellia (red)	You are a flame in my heart
Carnation (pink)	I'll never forget you
Carnation (red)	My heart aches for you
Carnation (white)	Innocence
China rose	Ever new beauty
Chrysanthemum (red)	I love you
Chrysanthemum (white)	Truth

Flower Name	Meaning
Chrysanthemum (yellow)	Sighted love
Clover	Good luck
Coreopsis	Always cheerful
Cosmos	Modesty
Crocus	Youthful gladness
Dahlia	Dignity, elegance
Daisy	Innocent
Daisy (garden)	Sentiments shared
Dandelion	Faithfulness, happiness
Dogwood	Love undiminished
Fern	Magic, fascination
Gardenia	Secret love
Gladiolus	Sincerity
Heather (lavender)	Admiration
Heather (white)	Protection, wishes come true
Hibiscus	Delicate beauty
Holly	Domestic happiness, festivity
Hollyhock	Ambition
Honeysuckle	Country beauty
Hyacinth (blue)	Constancy
Hyacinth (purple)	Please forgive me
Hyacinth (red/pink)	Playful
Hyacinth (white)	Loveliness
Iris	A message for you
Ivy	Wedded love
Jonquil (daffodil)	Desire
Lady's slipper	Flighty
Lavender	Devotion, cautious
Lilac (purple)	First love
Lilac (white)	Youth
Lily (day)	Coquetry
Lily (tiger)	Wealth, pride
Lily (white)	Purity, virginity
Lily of the valley	Increased happiness, sweetness
Magnolia	Love of nature, nobility
Marjoram	Blushes, mirth
Mint	Virtue

Flower Name	Meaning
Mistletoe	Affection
Monkshood	Chivalry
Morning glory	Affection
Moss	Charity, maternal love
Myrtle	Love, home
Narcissus	Egotism
Oleander	Caution
Orange blossom	Purity, eternal love, marriage
Orange flower	Chastity
Orchid	Love, beauty
Pansy	Thoughts, consideration
Peach blossoms	I am your captive
Peony	Happy life
Petunia	Resentment, anger
Phlox	Our souls are united
Poppy (red)	Pleasure
Poppy (yellow)	Wealth, success
Primrose	I can't live without you
Purple clove	Husbandry, thrift
Queen Anne's lace	Haven
Ranunculus	Radiant with charm
Rhododendron	Danger
Rose (bridal)	Happy love
Rose (dark crimson)	Mourning
Rose (dark pink)	Thank you
Rose (peach)	Enthusiasm, desire
Rose (red)	I love you
Rose (pink)	Perfect, you're lovely
Rose (white)	Innocence, secrecy
Rose (wild)	Simplicity
Rose (yellow)	Joy, friendship, jealousy
Rosebuds (red)	Purity
Rosebuds (white)	Youth
Rosemary	Sweet remembrance
Sage	Domestic virtue
Star of Bethlehem	Purity
Statice	Sympathy, remembrance

Flower Name	Meaning
Stephanotis	Happiness in marriage
Stock	Lasting love
Sunflower	Adoration
Sweet William	Gallantry, bravery
Thyme	Activity
Tuberose	Illicit pleasures
Tulip (red)	Believe in me
Tulip (variegated)	Beautiful eyes
Tulip (yellow)	Hopeless love
Veronica	Fidelity
Violet (blue)	Watchfulness, I'll always be true
Violet (purple)	Faithfulness
Violet (white)	Let's take a chance
Water lily	Purity of heart
Wheat	Friendliness, fertility
White rosebud	Awakening love
Zinnia (magenta)	Lasting affection
Zinnia (mixed)	Thinking of an absent friend
Zinnia (scarlet)	Constancy
Zinnia (white)	Goodness
Zinnia (yellow)	Daily remembrance

To Gather Orange Blossoms:
Brides and the Orange Blossom Legend

During her 30 years as a wedding entrepreneur, Cornelia Powell has worked with thousands of women—brides as well as their mothers, grandmothers, sisters, and friends—and she tells their heartwarming stories in her online magazine, Weddings of Grace (www.WeddingsOfGrace.com). We found her history of orange blossoms most enlightening.

Through the centuries, brides have always worn some form of headdress for their wedding ceremony. Of all bridal customs and traditions, wearing flowers or greenery in the hair—formed into a circlet, wreath, or some other fanciful concoction—seems to best represent the bridal legend. In varied world cultures, flowers and herbs have been chosen for the bride to use for sensible as well as sentimental reasons. Ancient evergreens, like rosemary and myrtle, were highly prized for their fragrance and herbal influences. Roses were selected not only for their beauty and scent, but they were also thought to be the flower of Venus, goddess of love. In India and other Eastern lands, aromatic jasmine has been worn to help enliven the bride's sensuous nature.

Depending on the season, romantic country maids of old wound wildflowers into a wreath for their bridal headdress, or in winter would gild small branches of leaves and wheat, then shape them into a golden coronet. Even royal brides sometimes chose something botanical and pastoral, putting aside their crown jewels and precious metal tiaras.

Orange Blossoms Come West

The delicate white orange blossom became associated with brides ages ago, through mythological legend ("It is said that Juno, Roman goddess of marriage, gave these fragrant blossoms to Jupiter on their wedding day"), as well as being tracked throughout history. One story goes that incorporating orange blossoms into the bride's costume originated in ancient China where they were emblems of purity, chastity, and innocence. Other reports state that "five hundred years before the birth of Christ, Saracen brides in what is now Syria held sprigs of orange blossoms to ensure fruitful marriages." Like many of our Western practices and customs, orange blossoms come into the picture from the Exotic East.

"There are few trees, it is said, so prolific as the orange. . . ." According to the book *Wedding Customs and Folklore,* "The orange tree, simultaneously bearing golden fruit, sweet-scented white flowers and leaves—typifying fertility through this abundance—is a traditional ingredient in love charms and marriage luck." (And it can also be said that there are few bridal customs that don't have their origin based in some way on wishes for fertility for the wedding couple.)

Tracking the route of the orange blossom legend from the East, it appears that during the time of the Crusades, the association of brides and orange blossoms was brought from the Mediterranean regions first to Spain, then to France, then to England in the early 1800s. At the time, the orangerie—a special greenhouse or conservatory—became the custom for fashionable European homes in order to winter citrus trees and other exotic botanicals.

The Legend Spreads

By then, many enchanting stories had spread throughout the continent of maidens entwining fresh orange blossoms into a bridal wreath for their hair. Due especially for the taste of flower-language during the nineteenth century, the influence became so indoctrinated into the culture that the phrase "to gather orange blossoms" took the meaning "to look for a wife."

When the fragrant orange blossoms were in short supply, or in northern climates where citrus fruits did not flourish, wax replicas were used instead. However, explains English author Ann Monsarrat in her book *And The Bride Wore . . . The Story of the White Wedding,* " . . . in the reports of some weddings 'real orange blossoms' are specified, and journalists at grand nuptials occasionally vowed that the air was heavy with the scent of these flowers, but that might have been over-enthusiasm or over-writing."

American brides became enthralled with orange blossoms as well—or at least the wax replicas. Ann Monsarrat found this account: "Miss Mary Hellen, a badly-behaved young lady who trifled with the affections of all three sons of President John Quincy Adams before settling for the middle one, wore orange blossoms for her White House wedding in Washington in the winter of 1828, when, according to her cousin and bridesmaid, Abigail Adams, she 'looked very handsome in white satin, orange blossoms and pearls' . . ."

In the early 1800s, as the fashion changed into softer, less-structured dress, floral headdresses made a "comeback," which helped usher in the appeal of the simple, natural beauty of orange blossoms. The nineteenth-century bride—more from following fashion than from following symbolic rituals—even decorated her gown with this ancient symbol of fertility. When Queen Victoria chose to wear "a substantial wreath, undiluted by jewels, feathers, or any other bloom," for her 1840 wedding to her beloved Albert, the de rigueur floral theme for the era of "Victorian brides" (and beyond) was indeed set.

> "In a glimmer of gems and a sheen of white,
> With the orange wreath on her snowy brow."
> — "The Bride Flown" (nineteenth century)

According to Ann Monsarrat, the very influential etiquette journals of the nineteenth century dictated that every bride include the blossoms in her wedding. This was so carefully obeyed that by the 1870s one of the powerful arbiters of good taste in England, John Cordy Jeaffreson, was begging for a change from the all-white headdresses, stating that "not one lovely girl in a thousand could wear without disadvantage the solely yellow-white orange-flowers." And it seems that "he also found the connection between orange blossoms and fertility extremely distasteful."

Even French couturiers of the nineteenth and early twentieth centuries got into the act. Historian Carol McD. Wallace explains that when the couture designers shipped a custom order to a bride during this time, a supply of ready-to-wear wax orange blossoms was packed in the box with the gown.

And the Legend Continues

The luminous wax replicas of these exquisite folkloric flowers continued to be used to "fulfill the demands of tradition" well into the 1950s, often nestled among other blossoms or tucked into a tiara. When Jacqueline Kennedy married Aristotle Onassis in 1968, they were crowned with orange blossoms in the traditional Greek style, and even today delicate wax replica orange blossoms are still treasured by new generations of brides, as they promulgate the mysterious romance of the orange blossom.

The wedding ring, which in some non-European marriage ceremonies is absent altogether, has in Britain and most parts of Europe so deep a significance that its loss or breaking foreshadows the destruction of the marriage through the death of the husband, the loss of his affection, or some other disaster. It is usually considered unlucky to remove it once it has been put on in church. If it falls off or is accidentally removed, then the husband must replace it in order to avert the threatened evil. In some areas, it is thought safe to take the ring off after the birth of the first child, but not before.

With This Ring

The wedding ring is fraught with symbolism. It is said that early man would capture a woman and encircle her wrists and ankles with chains to prevent her from escaping, and one ancient practice was to circle the bride's body with a rope, which would both keep her from evil spirits and bind her to her groom.

Among the ancient Romans, it was customary, in the absence of banks and similar places of safe deposit, for valuables to be kept in a strongbox, and the key, for the sake of security, was attached to a ring and worn on the finger. It was not presented to the bride during the actual ceremony, however, but after she had been lifted over the threshold of her new home. The presentation of the key denoted the confidence placed in her by her husband and was a token that henceforth she should share all that he possessed.

Although in past generations women wore wedding bands much more commonly than men did, the double-ring ceremony became popular during the twentieth century. Rather than having its beginnings in ancient practice, or being symbolic of anything at all, the double-ring movement began as a marketing campaign by the American jewelry industry in the late nineteenth century. By the late 1940s, 80 percent of all weddings were double-ring ceremonies. Today modern ring sets in the United States are often marketed as a three-piece set: the man's wedding band, the woman's engagement ring, and a slender band that is mounted to the engagement ring before the wedding, converting it into a single, permanent wedding ring.

Here is a brief history of wedding rings:

• Betrothal or engagement rings were as common among early Romans and Egyptians as they are today. One of the earliest and prettiest forms was the gimmal ring, once used by the Anglo-Saxons and probably derived from the French or Normans. It consisted of two or three links, fastened on a hinge and joined in one ring. Sometimes when the two flat sides and the central ribbon joined, there were male and female hands to clasp at the union. A heart above these signified love, fidelity, and union. At the betrothal, the man and woman were often linked by a finger in each end of the three-hooped chain, and then, severing them, each kept the part held, and the witness the third. A gimmal ring of nine interlaced loops still exists, often with verses engraved on the inner surface.

• Throughout other cultures, the engagement ring has taken various forms. Jewish jewelers, for instance, created shimmering gold gem-studded towers that represented ancient temples and were so tall (one or two inches high) and elaborate as to be entirely unwearable.

• The first wedding rings appeared in Egypt more than 5,000 years ago and were worn on the index finger. To the Egyptians, a circle, having no beginning or end, signified eternity. Thousands of these rings have been unearthed at Pompeii, buried and preserved by the lava flow.

• In the third century B.C., Greek physicians believed that the "vein of love" ran from the third finger (not counting the thumb) directly to the heart, and so that became the logical finger for a wedding ring.

• Legend states that Mary and Joseph used a wedding ring, probably made of onyx or

---

3 Reasons for Wearing the Wedding Ring on the Fourth Finger of the Left Hand

1. The most practical is the Roman explanation that this finger best protects the valuable ring. The left hand is used less than the right; therefore the ring belongs to the left. And of the fingers on the left hand, the fourth is the only one that cannot easily be extended except in the company of another.

2. Early Egyptians believed that a vein ran from the fourth finger of the left hand directly to the heart. Since the heart controlled both life and love, this finger was the most honored.

3. To impress the seriousness of the ceremony upon the bride and groom, the Christian Church lectured that the thumb and the first two fingers of the hand stood, respectively, for the Father, the Son, and the Holy Ghost and that the fourth stood for the earthly love of man for woman.

The Language of the Ring

The Victorians gave meaning to everything: the way in which a woman held her fan, the flowers chosen for a special event, and even the way in which rings were worn. Thus, the marriage-minded could depend on these meanings to determine the availability of any man or woman.

If a man wanted to find a wife, he would wear a ring on the index finger of his left hand.

If he was engaged, he would wear it on the middle finger of the left hand.

If he was married, he wore it on the third finger of his left hand (the ring finger).

If he was a confirmed bachelor, he wore his ring on the pinky of his left hand.

If a woman was open to an engagement, she wore her ring on the index finger of her left hand.

If she was engaged, her ring would be on the middle finger of the left hand.

If she was married, she wore her ring on the ring finger of the left hand.

If she never wanted to be married at all, she wore her ring on the pinky of her left hand.

amethyst. It is said to have been discovered in A.D. 996 and that it held certain curative powers.

- In the time of Pliny, around A.D. 40, an iron ring was sent as a pledge to an intended bride. The ring was set with stones, the hardness and durability of both iron and stone signifying the perpetuity of the contract. Also found were nuptial rings made from brass, copper, and gold.

- Mary of Burgundy became the first bride-to-be to receive a diamond engagement ring, on August 17, 1477. Maximilian of Austria, her betrothed, fearing rejection, heeded counsel that the diamond would impress her.

- In the fourteenth and fifteenth centuries, it became common for romantic rhymes called poesies to be engraved in betrothal rings. The ring given by St. Louis, king of France, to his wife contained the sentiment: "Beyond this ring, there is no love."

- By the seventeenth century, diamond engagement rings were all the rage in Europe, among the upper classes at least, and a bride's status was greatly reduced without one.

- The Irish have long believed that it is bad luck or even illegal to be married with a ring made of anything but gold.

- Although a ring is absolutely necessary in a Church of England marriage, it may be of any metal, and of any size.

- In Iceland, the betrothal and the marriage were both confirmed by money, and the ring seemed to have little to do with the transaction. It was used there but could hardly have been thought of as a finger-ring, being variously made of bone, jet,

stone, gold, and silver so wide as to allow the palm of the hand to be passed through it. At the ceremony, the bridegroom would pass four fingers and his palm through one of these rings, so receiving the hand of his bride.

- Meaningless rings of rushes were once used in England to delude girls into mock marriages. In 1217, lawmakers put a stop to the sport by declaring the rush-ring contract legal. As one writer of the time put it: "Twas a good worlde, when such simplicitie was used, sayes the old women of our time; when a ring of a rush would tie as much love as a gimmon of golde."

Irish claddagh wedding tradition originates from a seventeenth-century tale about a man in ancient Galway. He was soon to become wed but was taken prisoner by roving sailors and forced into labor in a foreign land. During that time, he taught himself the art of jewelry-making. Upon his return to his homeland, he found that his maiden had never married, and in his happiness he fashioned the now famous claddagh wedding band. The ring depicts a heart held by two hands with a crown over it. Today it is worn by many "lassies," according to this code:

On the right hand, crown in, heart out:
The wearer is available for romance.

On the right hand, crown out, heart in:
The lass is spoken for.

On the left hand, heart in, crown out:
She is happily married forevermore.

In 1886, Tiffany introduced its signature diamond solitaire ring, with the stone raised on prongs. This was the first ring to allow the light to shine through the diamond, making it appear larger than it was.

"The form of the ring being circular, that is, round, and without end, importeth this much, that mutual love and hearty affection should roundly flow from one to the other, as in a circle, and that continually for ever."
— Henry Swinburne, *Treatise of Spousals*, 1686

Toward the end of the twentieth century, as inventive couples sought unique wedding rings, some chose to have them tattooed onto their fingers. Designs range from simple bands to Celtic designs and the spouse's name spelled in elaborate letters. If you choose this route, bear in mind that such tats can be almost impossible to remove, and their placement on the finger can mean a long healing period and a blurred image in the end. Proceed with caution.

Wedding Quilts

Quilts have always played an important role in American social history. Over the years their designs were carefully executed by women who today can be considered true historians. Quilts tell the stories of families, of events, even of slavery. So it should come as no surprise that quilts have found a place in wedding tradition.

During the nineteenth century, a girl could not marry until she had made thirteen quilts—twelve for everyday use plus a special one known as the bridal quilt, which would be used on special occasions. Once the bridal quilt was completed, the pattern was destroyed, since it was considered to belong exclusively to the couple for whom it had been created.

Friends were allowed to help make the quilts at the commonly held quilting bees, but the bridal quilt had to be completed by the bride herself on the night before her wedding. Girls would begin making their quilts upon their betrothal or engagement, and woe to the lazy girl who did not have her quilts done on time.

Many bridal quilts are on display in museums today; most contain elaborately stitched motifs of birds, flowers, vines, wedding rings, and cottages, depicting the dreams of their hopeful young creators.

A History of Wedding Cakes

The history of the wedding cake goes back as far as the Roman Empire, well before the concept of elaborately icing a cake was invented. Through the years, the wedding cake has become the focus of a variety of customs and traditions, some of which have survived through time.

We've long abandoned, for instance, the custom of breaking the cake over the bride's head, a ritual that symbolized the breaking of the bride's virginal state and the subsequent dominance of the groom over her.

• In medieval England, cakes were described as breads that were flour-based foods and included no sweetening. No accounts tell of a special type of cake appearing at wedding ceremonies. There are, however, references to a custom of stacking small sweet buns in a large pile in front of the newlyweds.

• First appearing in the middle of the seventeenth century and continuing to be popular well into the early nineteenth century was a dish called the bride's pie. Whatever the pie was filled with—sweetbreads, mincemeat, or mutton—the main "ingredient" was a glass ring. An old adage claimed that the woman who found the ring would be the next to be married. Bride's pies were by no means universally found at weddings, but there are accounts of these being featured as a centerpiece at less affluent ceremonies.

• By the late nineteenth century, wedding cakes had become wildly popular, and the use of the bride's pie disappeared. Early cakes were simple, single-tiered plum cakes, with some varia-

tions. It was a while before the first multi-tiered wedding cake of today appeared in all its glory.

• The notion of sleeping with a piece of cake underneath one's pillow dates back to the seventeenth century. Legend has it that a person would dream of their future spouse if a piece of wedding cake was placed under their pillow. In the late eighteenth century, this notion led to the curious tradition in which brides would pass tiny crumbs of cake through their rings and then distribute them to guests who could, in turn, place them under their pillows.

• Traditionally wedding cakes have been white, which denotes purity. Previous to Victorian times, most wedding cakes were also white, but not because of the symbolism. Using the color white for icing had a more pragmatic basis. Ingredients were very difficult to come by, especially those required for icing, including the finest refined sugar. Thus, a white wedding cake became a symbol of affluence.

• The traditional cake-cutting ceremony symbolizes the first task that bride and groom perform jointly as husband and wife. The first piece of cake is cut by the bride with the "help" of the groom. This task originally was delegated exclusively to the bride. It was she who cut the cake and she who distributed servings to the guests. But as the number of wedding guests grew, so did the size of the wedding cake, making the distribution process impossible for the bride to undertake on her own. Cake cutting became more difficult with early multi-tiered cakes, and the ritual turned into a joint project. After the cake-cutting ceremony, the couple proceed to feed one another from the first slice. This provides another lovely piece of symbolism, the mutual commitment of bride and groom to provide for one another.

A Piece for Good Luck

• The first slice of wedding cake must always be cut by the bride; otherwise the marriage will be childless.

• When the rest of the cake has been cut up, all present must eat a little. To refuse is very unlucky, both for the bridal pair and for the guest concerned.

• If the bride keeps a portion of her wedding cake, her groom will remain faithful.

• The groom's cake is a tradition that was prevalent in early American ceremonies but seems to have fallen from favor in most contemporary weddings. The groom's cake was usually dark (e.g., chocolate) to contrast with the bride's cake. The origin of the groom's cake is unclear; some believe it was to be served by the groom, with a glass of wine, to the bridesmaids. Others believe it was to be saved and subsequently shared with friends after the honeymoon. The tradition seems to have survived primarily in the southern United States.

• The once-simple wedding cake eventually evolved into a multi-tiered extravaganza largely reserved for English royalty. Pillars as decoration existed long before multi-tiered cakes appeared, so it was a natural progression for cake bakers to try using pillars as a way to support the upper tiers.

In parts of England, a plate of cake was flung over the new wife's head as she returned from the church and omens were read from the way the plate broke. The more pieces there were, the happier the marriage would be. In some places, the number of broken bits indicated the number of children. If the plate remained intact, it was a bad sign, and usually some quick-witted person stamped on it with all possible speed to avert the evil omen.

To Make a Rich Cake

The colonial wedding cake was a thick, rich spice cake that included alcohol, dried fruit, and nuts; it was more like a fruitcake than the spun-sugar confection common today. This recipe comes from a 1747 "cookery-book," *The Art of Cookery Made Plain and Easy* by Hannah Glasse:

Take four Pound of Flour well dried and sifted, seven Pound of Currants washed and rubb'd, six Pound of the best fresh Butter, two Pound of Jordan Almonds blanched, and beaten with Orange Flower Water and Sack till they are fine, then take four Pound of Eggs, put half the Whites away, three Pound of double refin'd Sugar beaten and sifted, a quarter of an Ounce of Mace, the same of Cloves and Cinnamon, three large Nutmegs, all beaten fine, a little Ginger, half a Pint of Sack, half a Pint of right French Brandy, Sweetmeats to your liking, they must be Orange, Lemon, and Citron. Work your Butter to a Cream with your Hands before any of your Ingredients are in, then put in your Sugar, mix it well together; let your Eggs be well beat, and strain'd thro' a Sieve, work in your Almonds first, then put in your Eggs, beat them all together till they look white and thick, then put in your Sack and Brandy and Spices, and shake your Flour in by Degrees, and when your Oven is ready, put in your Currants and Sweetmeats as you put it in your hoop; it will take four Hours baking in a quick Oven, you must keep it beaten with your Hand all the while you are mixing of it, and when your Currants are well wash'd and clean'd, let them be kept before the Fire, so that they may go warm into your Cake. This Quantity will bake best in two Hoops.

[To ice the cake,] take two Pound double refin'd Sugar, beat and sift it very fine, and likewise beat and sift a little Starch and mix with it, then beat six Whites of Eggs to Froth, and put to it some Gum-Water, the Gum must be steep'd in Orange-flower-water, then mix and beat all these together two Hours, and put it on your Cake; when it is baked, set it in the Oven again to harden a quarter of an Hour, take great Care it is not discolour'd. When it is drawn, ice it over the Top and Sides, take two Pound of double refin'd Sugar beat and sifted, and the Whites of three Eggs beat to a Froth, with three or four Spoonfuls of Orange-flower-water, and three Grains of Musk and Amber grease together; put all these in a Stone Mortar, and beat these till it is as white as Snow, and with a Brush or Bundle of Feathers, spread it all over the Cake, and put it in the Oven to dry; but take Care the Oven does not discolour it. When it is cold paper it, and it will keep good five or six Weeks.

Wedding Cakes Around the World

The cake is not always white, and it's not always multi-tiered, but it always makes for an exciting focal point at any wedding.

• On the Caribbean islands of St. Lucia, Haiti, and Granada, a dark dried-fruit confection known as black cake is served for dessert.

• The cake at a Danish wedding, called the *overflødighedshorn*, consists of a lavishly decorated cornucopia covered with medallions of marzipan and filled with candies and miniature cakes.

• The wedding cake at a traditional Egyptian wedding can consist of as many as ten tiers. It is lowered from an opening in the ceiling.

• The traditional English wedding cake is a fruitcake, and the top tier is called the "christening cake," which is saved for the baptism of the couple's first child. The cake is typically made of raisins, ground almonds, and cherries and topped with marzipan candies.

• In lieu of a traditional wedding cake, the French choose a tall cone of caramel-coated cream puffs called *croque-en-bouche* ("crisp in the mouth"), or croquembouche.

• The wedding receptions of the French West Indies are likely to feature a traditional rum-flavored wedding cake that is hidden from guests with a fine white tablecloth. Wedding guests must pay for a lucky peek.

• An Irish wedding cake is usually a rich fruitcake covered with white icing. The top tier is an Irish whiskey cake.

• The Japanese serve Western-style wedding cakes in addition to sweet buns filled with rainbow-colored miniature buns that underscore the hope for many children for the couple.

Above left: A modern cake that suggests wedding cakes of old, designed by Carrie's Cakes of Utah COURTESY OF CARRIE BIGGERS/PEPPER NIX PHOTOGRAPHY

Above right: The French *croquembouche* is often decorated with delicate spun-sugar designs. COURTESY OF CARRIE BIGGERS/PEPPER NIX PHOTOGRAPHY

• In Norway, and in other parts of Scandinavia, *brudlaupskling,* a wedding cake made of bread, dates back to the days when white flour was rare on Norwegian farms and foods containing it were greatly admired. The bread is topped with a mixture of cheese, cream, and syrup, then folded over and cut into small squares. Today the traditional Norwegian cake is the *kransekake,* made of almond paste and shaped in the form of rings. The bride and groom keep the top layer for themselves and then break—rather than cut—the rest of the cake for their guests.

• The traditional Scottish wedding cake consists of two tiers of brandy-flavored fruitcake. The cake is baked at the time of the couple's engagement. Only one tier is eaten at the wedding celebration, while the other is saved to celebrate the birth of the couple's firstborn.

• In the West Indies, the traditional rum-flavored wedding cake is kept covered by a white cloth until it is time for it to be cut, possibly to protect it from the heat. In the meantime, guests "bribe" the couple for a sneak peek at the rum-soaked fruitcake.

Beyond Cake

Nuptials and celebrating have always gone hand in hand, and few celebrations are complete without some form of feasting. In some areas of the world, the very act of sharing food signifies the union of a couple, and in others, symbolism is served up with the wedding meal itself.

- During a wedding ceremony in **Afghanistan**, the males in the bridal party drink a ceremonial container of sugar-water, symbolizing that the couple should always be sweet to one another.

- A coconut cake with papaya or mango filling adds an **African** flavor to the menu.

- At an **Armenian** wedding, the bride's mother may place a *lavash* (flatbread) on her daughter's head to symbolize the bride's role as the "breadmaker" who sustains the couple.

- The **Aztec** ceremony ends with "tamale rites," during which the bride's mother places four spoonfuls of tamale and sauce into the mouths of the bride and groom.

- Every aspect of the **Chinese** wedding is fraught with symbolism. As the number four is considered to be lucky in Chinese culture, many courses consist of four dishes. A cold dish of poultry, meats, nuts, jellyfish, and abalone represents the phoenix and dragon, symbols of the bride and groom. Yu fish is served because the name suggests abundance and prosperity. Foods that  are red (the good-luck color), like lobster and pork, lend themselves to the décor, and long noodles echo the wish for a long life for the couple. *Lian zi*, a dessert made of honey and lotus seeds, is a popular wedding confection.

- **Dutch** wedding meals traditionally include a sweetmeat called "bridal sugar" and a spiced wine called "bride's tears."

- *Krunsaka*, a traditional wedding treat in **Iceland**, consists of almond-flavored iced pastry rings piled into a hollow cone that is then filled with white chocolate candies.

- In **Iran**, a cone of molded sugar is grated over the heads of the bride and groom to signify "sweet wishes" for the future.

- Honey mead is served at **Irish** weddings to protect the bride from fairies who may come to kidnap her.

- In **Italy**, wedding guests look forward to *wanda*: bow ties of fried dough dipped in sugar that symbolize the union.

- The symbolism inherent in any well-planned **Japanese** ceremony is evident in the menu. Tai fish is a favorite because the word *tai* is a homonym for the word for "lucky," and clams are served because the two shells hinged together are a reminder of the couple's union. Purple, the color of love, is represented with plums, and lobster is served for its color and its reputation for being a symbol of prayer and long life. For favors, Japanese hosts send their guests home with traditional *kohaku manjyu,* stuffed pastry buns presented in a special red box.

- At **Jewish** weddings, a special blessing called the *motzi* is said over a loaf of challah bread.

- In **Korea**, the long noodles known as *kook soo sang* that are served at weddings symbolize the wish for a long, happy life for the couple. Mandatory foods for a Korean wedding reception include *jung jong*, a sake that everyone must drink; *yakshik*, a ball of sweet rice rolled in raisins and nuts; and *dok*, a rice cake filled with bean paste. The Korean couple share three spoonfuls of rice, which represents the meals they will share for the rest of their lives. They pour a Korean liquor made of rice into two cups that have been made from the same gourd. This symbolizes the union of their souls.

- A soft, white, crumbly, closed horseshoe–shaped butter cookie called *ghoraibi* is often served at **Lebanese** weddings. The bride and groom serve the white (for the bride's purity) cookies themselves to their guests. The single pistachio on the cookie represents the bride's tiara.

- At a **Lithuanian** reception, the couple are given the "elements of life": bread and salt, so as never to hungry, and wine and honey for everything good in their life together.

- Couples in the **Philippines** eat from the same plate after their ceremony to signify their new shared commitment.

- The *syska* is a special **Polish** wedding bread baked in the shapes of flowers, animals, or pinecones.

- *Koloch* is a poppy seed–filled pastry served at **Slovakian** weddings.

A Brief History of Wedding Photography

According to San Francisco–based wedding photographer Joseph Kohn, the history of wedding photography begins in the early 1840s, a time when photography had very little commercial use but the idea of creating memories of the wedding day had already been born.

• Wedding photography was studio-based for more than a century, owing mainly to equipment limitations. In the 1800s, there were no paper photographs, no multiple photographs, no albums. There was only a daguerreotype portrait on a tiny copper sheet.

• At the beginning of the twentieth century, the production of color photographs became possible, but the process was too unreliable for professional photography. Colors shifted and faded after a short period of time, taking memories with them. While technology led to the invention of new materials used for producing photography film and better chemistry to process it, wedding photography techniques remained the same until the end of World War II.

• The idea of capturing the event itself was born during the "wedding boom" after World War II. For photographers, this surge created profitable opportunities for shooting weddings without a contract, or "on speculation." Using their new portable roll film–based cameras and compact flashbulb lighting, photographers would show up at a wedding, photograph it, and then try to sell the photos to the bride and groom. Some of these photographers had been trained in the military, but most were amateurs who were fascinated by the new portable cameras. Despite the poor quality of these early pictures, these photographers created competition and forced the studio photographers to start working on location.

• A dynamic change in the photo industry occurred in the 1930s with the introduction of the 35mm Leica camera, which made it possible for a number of photos to be taken in quick succession. This gave rise to the photojournalistic, or documentary, style. Now the wedding could be photographed as it unfolded.

• As the camera technology of the 1950s and 1960s put cheap, dependable cameras in the hands of just about everyone, the documentation of weddings took on a more relaxed feel, which is reflected still in the most popular styles today.

• With the invention of digital photography, new creative opportunities emerged. Digital cameras allow deeper coverage of the event, providing opportunities for a virtually unlimited number of photographs to be taken as well as great design opportunities. While traditional film photography is still widely used, it is obvious that the future belongs to digital photography.

The photojournalistic approach to wedding photography documents every moment of the big day. COURTESY OF GARDENSTATEPHOTO.COM

Jordan Almonds and Weddings

Since the sixteenth century, wedding favors have played a special role in weddings across a wide range of cultures. They were initially an extravagance at celebrations hosted by the European upper classes, who could afford to provide elaborate gifts for their guests, many of whom might have traveled great distances to be present at the nuptials. The early wedding favors were small fancy boxes known by their French name of *bonbonieres*. They were fashioned of crystal, porcelain, or gold and often encrusted with precious stones. The delicate boxes were meant to hold bonbons or other confectionery delicacies at a time when sugar was quite expensive.

Brides of modest means could mimic the practice by gifting their guests with elegantly wrapped packages of almonds, which had been commonly given as wedding gifts for more than a millennium; their bitter and sweet properties were said to symbolize the life of the couple, and the almonds harkened back to a thirteenth-century wedding confection known as confetti: candied fruit coated with honey. The introduction of sugar cane into the European kitchen made candy coating possible and produced the lovely pastel treats we know today as Jordan almonds, also commonly known, like their thirteenth-century counterpart, as confetti. These became a wedding staple; elegantly wrapped in lace and ribbon, they made perfect party favors.

Historically, Jordan almonds appeared in a variety of cultures, each of which contributed its own twist to the custom. In the Middle East, the bride provided five almonds to represent fertility, longevity, wealth, health, and happiness, and at Greek weddings the almonds were given in odd numbers, symbolizing the fact that the couple would always be undivided.

Today Jordan almonds provide one of the most common and meaningful wedding favors. They're available in myriad colors and can even be custom-dyed to match the meticulous bride's color scheme.

Many cultures share the tradition of distributing candy to wedding guests as a way of celebrating the sweetness that life has to offer. Italians distribute chocolate confections known as Amorini hearts, and the Danish hand out "chocolate lentils." The Dutch distribute Goelitz mints, and in France you might leave the nuptials with delicate, mint-filled, blue and white seashells.

"With gay music and noisy laughter and merriment, the bridal procession passed into the yard . . . the doors were thrown wide open and soon like a swelling tide the crowd rolled through the house, and the lofty halls shook with the hum and din of the festivity. The hall was decorated for the occasion with fresh leaves and birch branches, for birch is the bride of the trees. . . . The seats of honour, of course, belonged to the bride and bridegroom, and they having taken their places, the master of ceremonies urged the guests to the tables and arranged them in their proper order in accordance with their relative dignity or their relationship or acquaintance with the bride."

— From *Gunnar, A Tale of Norse Life*
by Hjalmar Hjörth Boyesen

160 Years of British Royal Weddings

Royal weddings are always eagerly anticipated, and millions of people around the world are fascinated by the pageantry of these lavish spectacles. These weddings have created traditions that the world has quickly mimicked, and they have defined wedding splendor. Nevertheless, even royal brides have not been able to escape the tiny annoyances that plague every bride: Princess Elizabeth's bouquet, which had been sitting in a refrigerator, could not be located until the last minute, and Princess Michael of Kent tore the hem of her dress as she arrived for her wedding reception. Bridezillas take note: these annoyances may have hindered the brides, but the monarchies survived all the same.

Here are some memorable British royal weddings of the past 160 years.

Queen Victoria and Prince Albert

On February 10, 1840, Queen Victoria married Prince Albert of Saxe-Coburg-Gotha in an event that changed the face of weddings forever. Albert was reputed to be extremely handsome and irresistible to the Queen. In her journal, the Queen described her feelings for Albert, referring to him as "an angel."

They were wed in the Chapel Royal at St. James' Palace. Twelve bridesmaids attended the Queen, and each one was awarded a gold brooch personally designed by Prince Albert. The Queen designed the bridesmaids' white dresses to match her own wedding gown. It was at this wedding that the white wedding dress first gained popularity.

Princess Alice and Prince Louis

Princess Alice, second daughter of Queen Victoria, married Prince Louis, later Grand Duke of Hesse, in 1862. The wedding was nearly called off because Alice's father, Prince Albert, had recently died of typhoid fever.

The wedding did, however, proceed at the insistence of the Queen. The ceremony and reception were both conducted in an extremely subdued and somber fashion. Almost everyone was dressed in black, the Queen and several of Alice's siblings wept throughout the service, and even the recently widowed Archbishop of Canterbury, performing the ceremony, was in tears.

Princess Alexandra and Prince Albert Edward

Queen Victoria's son, Albert Edward, Prince of Wales, married Princess Alexandra of Denmark, the daughter of Prince Christian and Princess Louisa of Denmark, on March 10, 1863. The wedding took

Illustration, ca. 1868, of the wedding of Mary Stuart, Queen of Scots, to Henry Darnley **LIBRARY OF CONGRESS**

place in St. George's Chapel and was officiated by the Archbishop of Canterbury, the Bishop of London, the Bishop of Winchester, the Bishop of Chester, and the Dean of Windsor.

The Princess was not the royal family's first choice for Albert, but the political climate at the time made her the most suitable choice.

Alexandra's wedding gown was decorated with swags of artificial orange blossoms and foliage to match the floral circlet on her head. The Princess's arrival in London was greeted by huge crowds and an address by Alfred Lord Tennyson:

Alexandra!
Saxon and Norman and Dane are we,
But all of us Danes in our welcome of thee,
Alexandra!

Lady Elizabeth Bowes-Lyon and Prince Albert

Lady Elizabeth Bowes-Lyon, the future Queen Mother, married Prince Albert, Duke of York, on April 26, 1923, at Westminster Abbey.

Prince Albert met Elizabeth Bowes-Lyon at a ball, and by the end of the evening he had fallen in love with her. But she did not share his feelings. Over the next couple of years, Albert proposed to Elizabeth twice using intermediaries and was refused both times. It wasn't until three years later that he got up the nerve (he had a stammer that made him extremely self-conscious) and decided to propose face to face. This time she accepted.

This was the first royal wedding to be captured on film. A number of ornately decorated wedding cakes were created for the occasion, including one that was 9 feet high and weighed 800 pounds.

Elizabeth placed her bridal bouquet at the Tomb of the Unknown Warrior on the day of the ceremony, a practice that has been continued by every royal bride to this day.

Queen Elizabeth and Prince Philip

Queen Elizabeth II was only 13 years old when she met Prince Philip of Greece for the first time. She was instantly smitten and stayed devoted to him throughout her teen years. They were married on November 20, 1947. Philip gave up his Greek citizenship and title and adopted the surname Mountbatten in order to marry her.

During the ceremony, Philip gave Elizabeth a band of Welsh gold to wear alongside her engagement ring. The diamond used for the engagement ring had once been set into a tiara belonging to Philip's mother.

Elizabeth wore an embroidered white satin wedding dress adorned with garlands of pearl orange blossom, syringa, and white rose of York. These were skillfully combined with flowing lines of wheat ears, the symbol of fertility, and worked in pearl and diamante.

Many felt that an elaborate and luxurious wedding was improper considering how hard British citizens were struggling in

Britain's Princess Elizabeth leaving Westminster Abbey in London with her husband, the Duke of Edinburgh, after their wedding on November 20, 1947 AP IMAGES

the aftermath of World War II, but it was finally decided that a national celebration was just what the country needed. Winston Churchill described the occasion as a "bright ray of color on the hard gray road we have to travel." The wedding feast at Buckingham Palace immediately after the wedding was attended by 150 guests.

The priests stood stoled in their pomp, the sworded
    chiefs in theirs,
And so, the collared knights, and so, the civil ministers,
And so the waiting lords and dames—and little pages
    best
At holding trains—and legates so, from countries east
    and west. . . .
And when between the quick and dead, the young, fair
    queen had vowed,
The living shouted "May she live! Victoria, live!" aloud.
And as the loyal shouts went up, true spirits prayed
    between,
"The blessings happy monarchs have, be thine, O
    crowned queen!". . . .
She vows to love who vowed to rule—(the chosen at her
    side)
Let none say, God preserve the queen! —but rather,
    Bless the bride!

—From Elizabeth Barrett Browning, "Crowned and Wedded,"
written upon the marriage of Queen Victoria

Princess Margaret and Antony Armstrong-Jones

Princess Margaret, the younger sister of Her Majesty Queen Elizabeth II, married photographer Antony Armstrong-Jones at Westminster Abbey on May 6, 1960, at the first royal wedding to be televised. Over 2,000 guests and millions of TV viewers witnessed the ceremony.

Margaret's wedding gown, a Norman Hartnell creation, was white silk organza with a cinched waist. Her hair was adorned with a tiara to which a cathedral-length veil of silk organza was attached. The Princess carried a cascading bouquet of orchids.

Katherine Worsley and the Duke of Kent

The Duke of Kent, fourth son of George V and Mary of Teck, married Katherine Worsley (known simply as Kate), the daughter of Sir William Worsley, on June 8, 1961, in York Minster. Katherine's gown, with its 15-foot train, was created by John Cavanaugh, the same designer who had created Princess Marian's wedding dress.

The wedding was a simple affair with only a small honor guard. Nevertheless, it took nearly 50 television cameras to broadcast the occasion, after which the couple proceeded to spend the first part of their honeymoon at the estate of the Queen Mother in Scotland.

Princess Anne and Mark Phillips

Princess Anne married Mark Phillips, a lieutenant in the 1st Queen's Dragoon Guards, on November 14, 1973. It was just the second time in 200 years that a member of the British royal family married a commoner. The couple met through their mutual interest in horse riding and were British eventing teammates.

The marriage was broadcast around the world, with an estimated audience of 100 million, and celebrated as a national holiday. Following the ceremony, the couple appeared on the balcony of Buckingham Palace and waved to the crowds below. After an overnight stay in Richmond Park, Princess Anne and her husband departed for their honeymoon in Barbados and a cruise in the Atlantic and Pacific Oceans.

The Princess Royal, as Anne was now known, and Mark Phillips were formally divorced in April 1992, but they have remained friends and continue to run horse trials together.

Lady Diana Spencer and Prince Charles

An estimated 750 million television viewers watched as Prince Charles and Lady Diana Spencer were wed at St. Paul's Cathedral on July 29, 1981. In attendance at the ceremony were 3,500 guests. Prince Charles had proposed to the 19-year-old Diana in the nursery of Windsor Castle after knowing her for less than a year.

Britons marked the occasion as a national holiday. The Archbishop of Canterbury remarked that the ceremony was "the stuff of which fairy tales is made." Diana became the first Englishwoman to marry an heir to the throne in over 300 years.

After the ceremony, the now Prince and Princess of Wales appeared on the balcony of Buckingham Palace and blew kisses to the crowd.

A traditional royal wedding breakfast was then held for 120 family guests, after which the newlyweds left on their honeymoon. (For more information about the event see "Charles and Diana: Another 'Wedding of the Century,'" page 104.)

Sarah Ferguson and Prince Andrew

On July 23, 1986, Prince Andrew, the Duke of York, married Sarah Ferguson in Westminster Abbey. Two thousand guests were invited to attend the ceremony, and 500 million television viewers worldwide watched the event.

Sarah's Victorian-style gown was made of cream-colored silk embroidered throughout. The dress was decorated with thistles and flowers and the bridal family coat of arms.

Following the ceremony, Andrew and Sarah, whom Britons would later affectionately refer to as "Fergie," appeared on the balcony of Buckingham Palace for a playful first kiss in front of a throng of well-wishers below.

The Queen bestowed them with the titles Duke and Duchess of York.

Although the couple had known each other since childhood, their romance did not blossom until Princess Diana brought them together at a party.

Princess Anne and Commander Timothy Laurence

On December 14, 1992, only eight months after Princess Anne's divorce from Mark Phillips, she married Commander Timothy Laurence, whom she had met while on a tour of duty on the Royal Yacht *Britannia*.

Because the Church of England forbids the remarriage of divorcees but the Church of Scotland does not, Anne married her second husband at Crathie Kirk, by the Queen's Balmoral estate. Anne wore a white suit and white blossoms in her hair, and Commander Laurence was attired in an elegant Royal Navy uniform.

Approximately 500 locals and 150 journalists stood along the road for hours before the ceremony to catch a glimpse of the royal family.

The marriage made Anne the first British royal since Henry VIII to divorce and remarry.

Sophie Rhys-Jones and Prince Edward

Prince Edward and Sophie Rhys-Jones were married on June 19, 1999, in St. George's Chapel, Windsor Castle. Royals traditionally married in either Westminster Abbey or St. Paul's Cathedral, but the couple wished to have a low-key wedding with a relaxed tone. Edward did not wear military dress, and all the guests were asked to dress informally. The Prince gave Sophie a delicate three-diamond engagement ring, and a reception was held for over 500 guests.

The couple had met in 1994 and announced their engagement following a five-year courtship. Sophie had been surprised by Prince Edward's proposal and described it as follows: "I was slightly stunned for a minute, and then I finally realized I should actually answer the question, so I said, 'Yes'; I said 'Yes, please.'"

Camilla Parker Bowles and Prince Charles

Camilla Parker Bowles and Prince Charles were married on April 9, 2005, at Windsor Castle in a civil service followed by religious prayer. The couple first met at a polo match in 1970, before either had married, and they maintained a close and sometimes intimate relationship prior to their engagement, despite the fact that Charles was married to Diana Spencer. Diana publicly blamed Camilla's affair with Charles for the failure of her own marriage.

Charles presented Camilla with a ring that belonged to his grandmother, the Queen Mother. It was a platinum ring with a central, emerald cut diamond, with three diamond baguettes on each side.

The civil service was attended by only 20 people, including Prince Harry, Prince Andrew, Prince Edward and his wife Sophie, Princess Anne and her husband Timothy Laurence, Major Bruce Shand, and Laura Parker Bowles. Over 800 guests attended the blessing ceremony in Windsor Castle at which the couple pledged faithfulness to each other.

Camilla wore a regal golden feather headpiece accented with Swarovski crystals that matched her Robinson Valentine light blue coat dress.

Queen Elizabeth did not attend the civil service, stating that she did not wish to overshadow the event, although some suggested that, because of the Queen's religious beliefs, which forbid her to attend a civil wedding, it was an intentional snub. The Queen did attend the religious service, conducted by the Archbishop of Canterbury and the Dean of Windsork, at St. George's Chapel, and afterward she hosted a reception at Windsor Castle.

Princes William and Harry decorated the getaway car with multi-colored balloons and the words "Just Married."

> "When a man opens a car door for his wife, it's either a new car or a new wife."
>
> — Prince Philip

Chapter 2

The Culture of Weddings

Even when we're not having them ourselves, weddings seem to be part of our general consciousness. From the Barbie brides that have been occupying little girls' toy chests since 1959 to our daily obsession with royal and celebrity weddings, the subject has found its way into almost every corner of our culture. This chapter celebrates our fascination with all things nuptial.

The most elaborate weddings ever staged are described here, along with the weirdest, the wackiest, and the most wonderful. Here you'll find the most unusual wedding gifts on record, from the shawl that Mahatma Gandhi knitted for Queen Elizabeth to the vegetable garden that Henry David Thoreau planted on the occasion of the wedding of his friend Nathanial Hawthorne, as well as accounts of the over-the-top weddings of the rich and famous. Here too you'll meet the folks who used the occasion of their marriage to break world records: the Tennessee couple who renewed their vows an astounding 83 times, the oldest bridesmaid ever (105!), and the bride whose train fell just short of a mile.

Because our fascination with weddings extends beyond the here and now to the fictional and the artistic, this chapter also covers the weddings we have come to celebrate in art and literature. Shakespeare on weddings, the weddings depicted in fine art and classical literature, a Hollywood wedding tradition that goes back to the earliest films—all shed light on the many forms that weddings have taken as well as our interpretation of their importance.

Thus, this chapter serves as a general survey of the complex and ever-changing culture we have created around the subject of weddings. Taken all together—with its sentiment and spectacle, its history and humor—Planet Wedding is a place both rich in history and far-reaching in its appeal.

Vintage postcard by Eugene Hartung, ca. 1900 AUTHORS' COLLECTION

Kids on Dating and Marriage

• "You got to find somebody who likes the same stuff. Like, if you like sports, she should like it that you like sports, and she should keep the chips and dip coming."—Alan, age 10

• "No person really decides before they grow up who they're going to marry. God decides it all way before, and you get to find out later who you're stuck with."—Kirsten, age 10

• "No age is good to get married at. You got to be a fool to get married."—Freddie, age 6

• "I'm never going to have sex with my wife. I don't want to be all grossed out."—Theodore, age 6

A grandmother overheard her five-year-old granddaughter playing "wedding." The vows went like this:

"You have the right to remain silent, anything you say may be held against you, you have the right to have an attorney present. You may kiss the bride."

• "Single is better, for the simple reason that I wouldn't want to change no diapers. Of course, if I did get married, I'd just phone my mother and have her come over for some coffee and diaper changing."—Kirsten, age 10

• "It's better for girls to be single but not for boys. Boys need someone to clean up after them."—Anita, age 9

• "Tell your wife that she looks pretty, even if she looks like a truck."—Ricky, age 10, on how to make a marriage work

• "If you want to last with your man, you should wear a lot of sexy clothes, especially underwear that is red and maybe has a few diamonds on it."—Lori, age 8

• "When somebody's been dating for a while, the boy might propose to the girl. He says to her, 'I'll take you for a whole life, or at least until we have kids and get divorced, but you got to do one particular thing for me.' Then she says yes, but she's wondering what the thing is and whether it's naughty or not. She can't wait to find out."—Anita, age 9

• "You flip a nickel, and heads means you stay with him and tails means you try the next one."—Kelly, age 9

• "My mother says to look for a man who is kind. . . . That's what I'll do. . . . I'll find somebody who's kinda tall and handsome."—Carolyn, age 8

• "Once I'm done with kindergarten, I'm going to find me a wife."—Bert, age 5

• "On the first date, they just tell each other lies, and that usually gets them interested enough to go for a second date."—Martin, age 10

• "Many daters just eat pork chops and French fries and talk about love."—Craig, age 9

• "Never kiss in front of other people. It's a big embarrassing thing if anybody sees you. . . . If nobody sees you, I might be willing to try it with a handsome boy, but just for a few hours."—Kally, age 9

• "It gives me a headache to think about that stuff. I'm just a kid. I don't need that kind of trouble."—Will, age 7

• "Love is when Mommy gives Daddy the best piece of chicken."—Elaine, age 5

• "Love is when my mommy makes coffee for my daddy, and she takes a sip before giving it to him to make sure the taste is okay."—Danny, age 7

Einstein's Theory of Marriage

Noble Prize–winning scientist Albert Einstein married his cousin, Elsa Lowenthal, after his first marriage went sour in 1919. Einstein stated that he was drawn to Elsa because she had a rather ample bosom, and he claimed that the attraction a man feels to large breasts is far stronger than any DNA connection. This has come to be known as Einstein's Theory of Relative Titty.

Kissing Cousins

Of the 26 U.S. states that permit first-cousin marriages, many have special requirements. In Wisconsin and Utah, for instance, cousins can get married only if they promise not to have children. In Maine, the marriage can go forward, but only after the related couple has had genetic testing. All European nations permit marriage between first cousins. Historically, 80 percent of all marriages worldwide took place between cousins; today the figure is closer to 20 percent.

The percentage of marriages that take place between first cousins in the following countries are:

India: 15 percent

Turkey: 22 percent

Kuwait: 35 percent

Israeli Arabs: 32.5 percent

United Arab Emirates: 54 percent

Saudi Arabia: 55 percent

Oman: 56 percent

On December 12, 1957, rocker Jerry Lee Lewis married his third cousin, 13-year-old Myra Gale Brown. It was said that she still believed in Santa Claus.

12 Weird Wedding Laws

In Saudi Arabia, there is a law that states that a woman may divorce her husband if he does not keep her supplied with coffee. Sound strange? Some equally bizarre wedding laws are in effect, as of this writing, right here in the United States.

1. In Oblong, Illinois, it's punishable by law to make love while hunting or fishing on your wedding day.

2. In Kentucky, it is illegal to remarry the same man four times.

3. In Truro, Louisiana, a would-be groom must prove himself manly prior to marriage by hunting and killing six blackbirds or three cows.

4. In Pennsylvania, ministers are forbidden from performing marriages when either the bride or the groom is drunk.

5. In the state of Washington, there is a law against having sex with a virgin under any circumstances, including the wedding night.

6. In Alabama, a man can't seduce "a chaste woman by means of temptation, deception, arts, flattery, or a promise of marriage."

7. In Kansas, a wife may successfully file for divorce on the grounds that her husband mistreated her mother.

8. In Bellingham, Washington, it is illegal for a woman to take more than three steps backward while dancing. Watch your steps at the reception!

9. A state law in Illinois mandates that all bachelors should be called master, not mister, when addressed by their female counterparts.

10. In most American states, the law does not consider a wedding ring an asset in a bankruptcy procedure. This means that creditors can't seize your ring.

11. Thanks to a typographical error, even toddlers can marry in Arkansas, with parental consent. The legislation was intended to establish 18 as the minimum age to marry; pregnant teens under that age could marry with parental consent. But an extraneous "not" in the bill caused it to read that anyone who is not pregnant can marry if the parents allow it. As of this writing, the mistake will not be corrected until the Legislature reconvenes in 2009.

12. In Montana, a couple can get married without either of them attending. It's called a double-proxy wedding.

How to Propose in 35 Languages

Don't worry about not being able to pronounce these proposals correctly; the engagement ring—assuming the proposal is accompanied by one—will speak volumes.

1. Afrikaans: *Sal jy met my trou?*

2. Arabic: *Tahib tajawazini?*

3. Bosnian: *Hoces li se udati za mene?*

4. Catalan: *Vols casar-te amb mi?*

5. Chinese: *Chin Ja Gay Wu Hao Ma?*

6. Czech: *Chces si me vzít za zenu?*

7. Danish: *Vil du gifte dig med mig?*

8. Dutch: *Zult u me huwen?*

9. Finnish: *Tuletko vaimokseni?*

10. French: *M'épouserez-vous?*

11. Gaelic Irish: *An bpósfaidh tú mé?*

12. Gaelic Scottish: *Am pòs thu mi?*

13. German: *Heiraten Sie mich?*

14. Hebrew: *Ha-iim Ti-Na'as-ii Li?*

15. Hindi: *Tum Mujhse Shaadi Karogi?*

16. Hungarian: *Hozzám jössz feleségül?*

17. Italian: *Vuoi sposarmi?*

18. Japanese: *Kekkon shiyou?* or *Mahou no kotoba?*

19. Nepali: *Timi masanga biha garchau?*

20. Norwegian: *Vil De gifter seg med meg?*

21. Persian: *Aya baham ezdevaj mikoni?*

22. Polish: *Wyjdziesz za mnie?*

23. Portuguese: *Você casar-me-á?* or *Queres casar comigo?*

24. Pushto: *Ghwaa'ri chi maa sara waada wuk'rea?*

25. Russian: *Ty vydesh zah menya?*

26. Slovak: *Chcel by si si ma vziat?*

27. Slovene: *Bi se poroèil z mano?*

28. Spanish: *¿Usted me casará?*

29. Swedish: *Vill du gifta dig med mig?*

30. Tagalog: *Pakakasalan mo ba ako?*

31. Tamil: *Ennai thirumanam saeivaya?*

32. Telugu: *Nuvvu Nannu Pelli Chesukuntaava?*

33. Turkish: *Benimle evlenir misin?*

34. Urdu: *Kiya tum mujh say shaadi karo gee?*

35. Yiddish: *Vilstu mit mir khasene hobn?*

10 Famous Proposals

Though the origin of the tradition of proposing on bended knee is unknown, historians note that kneeling is common in a number of ceremonial situations, such as entering a church, praying, and receiving honors at the hands of kings and queens. Thus proposing on bended knee has become a sign of respect and admiration. Today, only about 60 percent of engagements begin with this chivalrous gesture, while others attempt to set the mood using their own devices. Here are some of the most memorable marriage proposals.

1. In 1761, when infamous philanderer Casanova approached the mother of a 17-year-old girl he wished to marry, the woman fainted dead away. As luck would have it, she had had an affair with him 20 years prior.

2. Famed Russian writer Fyodor Dostoevsky could not bring himself to propose to much-younger Anna Grigorevna Snitkina, so he began writing a novel about a tormented, middle-aged writer who had fallen in love with a young girl. When Anna suggested a happy ending for the story, Fyodor realized that his proposal had been accepted. They were married the next year, in 1866.

3. Pioneering psychoanalyst Sigmund Freud was immediately smitten upon meeting Martha Bernays in 1881, but courage escaped him. Before long, her family moved away and Sigmund could only send letters to his beloved. Much later he finally asked if he could address her by the less-formal German pronoun *du* instead of *sie*. When she agreed, he knew they would eventually marry.

4. F. Scott Fitzgerald proposed to Zelda Sayre by sending her his grandmother's engagement ring with this message: "Darling, I love you so much, much, much that it hurts every minute I'm without you." Soon thereafter they eloped.

5. U.S. President Lyndon Baines Johnson didn't believe in dragging things out. He proposed to Claudia Alta Taylor (aka Lady Bird) on the first day they met. It took him only ten weeks to prove that he meant business, eventually convincing her to marry him the same day they became officially engaged.

6. Desi Arnaz and Lucille Ball were making a film together in 1940 when Desi overheard an interview in which Lucy listed all the reasons she would never marry Desi. Outraged, Desi approached Lucy after the reporter left and announced that they would get married the next day. They did.

7. Coretta Scott was in Boston studying to become a concert soloist when she went out on a blind date with Martin Luther King Jr. Coretta hadn't been looking forward to the event; how much fun could a Baptist minister be, after all? But they realized they had a common devotion to civil rights, and when Martin proposed on that first date in 1952, Coretta accepted.

8. Jacqueline Bouvier's romance with John F. Kennedy began when he was a young congressman from Massachusetts and she was a reporter for the *Washington Times Herald*. They dated for a while, and one day, when Jackie was in London covering the coronation of Queen Elizabeth II, she received a telegram from Jack that read: "Article's excellent but you are missed." She soon returned home to a formal marriage proposal and a diamond and emerald ring.

9. Grover Asmus proposed to actress Donna Reed every day for three years until she finally relented.

10. Prince Charles had been seeing Lady Diana Spencer for less than a year before he popped the question on February 6, 1981. According to Diana, "He said, 'Will you marry me?' and I laughed. I remember thinking, 'This is a joke,' and I said, 'Yeah, okay,' and laughed. He was deadly serious. He said, 'You do realize that one day you will be queen.' And a voice said to me inside, 'You won't be queen, but you'll have a tough role.' So I said, 'Yes.' I said, 'I love you so much, I love you so much.' He said, 'Whatever love means.'"

The World's Longest Marriage Proposal

On February 14, 2006, Cameron Kelly presented his girlfriend, Angie Kreimer, with a Valentine's gift that consisted of a 113-page marriage proposal. The self-published paperback book, entitled *50 Reasons Why You Should Marry Me . . . and 51 Reasons Why I Should Marry You,* contained 101 pages of text and 44 color photographs. Angie's one-word reply after reading the book was "Yes." You can buy the book at Lulu.com.

4 Historic Marriage Proposals

1. "By revolving in my mind the contents of your last letters, I have put myself into great agony, not knowing how to interpret them, whether to my disadvantage (as I understood some others) or not. I beseech you earnestly to let me know your real mind as to the love between us two. It is needful for me to obtain this answer from you, having been for a whole year wounded with the dart of love and not yet assured whether I shall succeed in finding a place in your heart and affections. This uncertainty has hindered me of late from declaring you my mistress . . . lest it should prove that you only entertain an ordinary regard for me. But if you please to do the true duty of a trusted and loyal mistress and to give yourself heart and person to me, who will be, as I have been, your most loyal servant (if your rigor does not forbid me), I promise you that not only the name shall be given you but also that I will take you for my mistress, cutting off all others that are on competition with you, out of my thought and affections, and serving you only."

— Henry VIII's proposal to Anne Boleyn, who accepted the proposal, only to be beheaded by her "loyal servant" just three years into their marriage.

2. "Dear Cousin: The striking qualities which enhance your person have inspired in us the desire to serve and honor you. We are requesting the Emperor, your respected father, to entrust to us the happiness of Your Imperial Highness. May we be permitted to hope that you will receive graciously the feelings which impel us to take this step? May we harbor the flattering hope that you will agree to this marriage not only because of filial obedience and duty? If your Imperial Highness has but the slightest affection for us, we will cultivate this feeling with the greatest pains, and make it our supreme task ever to seek your happiness in every respect. In this way we fondly hope to win your complete affection some day. That is our most fervent wish, and we beg Your Imperial Highness to be favorably inclined to us."

— Napoleon to Archduchess Maria Louisa of Austria after divorcing Josephine, who had been unable to give him an heir. Maria Louisa did not love Napoleon, but she married him anyway and bore him an heir, a young boy who died in childhood. After Napoleon's death in 1721, she married again.

3. "I have commenced two letters to send you before this, both of which displeased me before I got half done and so I tore them up. The first I thought was not serious enough, and the second was on the other extreme. I shall send this, turn out as it may. This thing of living in Springfield is rather dull business, after all; at least it is so to me. I am quite as lonesome here as I ever was anywhere in my life. I have been spoken to by but one woman since I have been here, and should not have been by her if she could have avoided it. I've never been to church yet, and probably shall not be soon. I stay away because I am conscious I should not know how to behave myself. I am often thinking about what we said about your coming to live at Springfield. I am afraid you would not be satisfied. There is a great deal of flourishing about in carriages here, which would be your doom to see without sharing it. You would have to be poor, without the means of hiding your poverty. Do you believe you could bear that patiently? Whatever woman may cast her lot with mine, should any ever do so, it is my intention to do all in my power to make her happy and contented; and there is nothing I can imagine that would make me more unhappy than to fail in the effort."

— Abraham Lincoln to Mary Owens, May 7, 1837

4. "Summon all the courage of your heart in order not to be shocked by the question I shall put to you: Will you marry me? I love you and feel as if you belong to me already. Not a word about the suddenness of my affection. At least there is no guilt in it, and therefore nothing need be excused. But what I should like to know is whether you feel the same: that we have never been strangers to each other, not for a moment! Do you not also believe that, united, we could become freer and better than separate—excelsior? Will you risk going with me—as with one who struggles valiantly for liberation and progress on all the paths of life and thought? Now be frank with me and keep nothing back."

— Friedrich Nietzsche, philosopher whose superman theory did not help him sound less like Superman than like Clark Kent, proposing to Mathilde Trampedach in 1876. She turned him down and married a friend of his instead.

> "When marrying, ask yourself this question: Do you believe that you will be able to converse well with this person into your old age? Everything else in marriage is transitory."
>
> — Friedrich Nietzsche

5 Wedding Urban Legends

1. **The In-law from Hell** At a young couple's wedding, the father of the bride left an envelope containing tip money to pay for all in the pocket of his jacket, which he removed at some point. When he returned for his jacket, he discovered that the envelope and cash were missing. The next day, when the family gathered to watch the wedding video, they were horrified to see the groom's father in the background, clearly taking the envelope. The marriage was annulled.

2. **Bride-and-Seek** During a wedding reception, the bride, the groom, and their friends decided to play a drunken game of hide-and-seek. When the groom was "it," he managed to find everyone except his new wife. After hours of searching, he finally suspected that she had changed her mind about marrying him. He went home and never heard from her again.

A few years later, a cleaning lady dusted off an old trunk in the attic of the building where the reception had taken place. Out of curiosity, she opened it and discovered the decomposed body of the missing bride, who had apparently become locked in the trunk she'd chosen to hide in. Her face was frozen in a scream.

3. **Robin Hood, Not!** An engaged couple saw the film *Robin Hood—Prince of Thieves.* They fell in love with the theme song, "Everything I Do, I Do It for You," and decided that it would be their wedding song. On the day of the wedding the groom requested that the organist play the Robin Hood theme instead of the usual wedding march. The processional began as the organist launched into the highly inappropriate "Robin Hood, Robin Hood, Riding Through the Glen" theme from the late-1950s television series *The Adventures of Robin Hood.*

4. **Picture This** At a large and lavish wedding, the groom rose to make a toast. He thanked all the guests for coming and announced that he had a special gift envelope taped to the bottom of everyone's chair. The guests were horrified when they opened their "gifts" only to discover 8-by-10 photos of the bride having sex with the best man. The groom had been suspicious of them and had hired an investigator, who took the photo. He then thanked the father of the bride for the $50,000 wedding, turned to his wife, and said, "Hasta la vista, baby." The marriage was annulled two days later.

5. **A Killer Dress** A young woman of modest means bought a used wedding dress in a pawn shop. It had previously belonged to a deceased woman whose family had her buried in it but later decided they needed the money and had the dress removed.

The new bride was elated and wore the dress with pride on her wedding day. But during the reception, things took a turn. The bride began to feel faint and nauseous, and she soon died on the spot. It was later discovered that she had been asphyxiated by the embalming fluid that had been used on the cadaver and that had seeped into the dress.

When Barbie Met Ken: 19 Bridal Barbies

Barbie took her first trip down the aisle in 1959 in an ensemble that was commemorated some 30 years later. In fact, Barbie has been married numerous times, each time emphasizing for her young fans the promise of the white wedding. Separately sold accessories and toys and even a child-size Barbie wedding gown available in toddler sizes have served as helpful texts for bridezillas in training. Here are some highlights of Barbie's many wedding celebrations.

1. **Wedding Party Barbie, 1989** Barbie renews her vows in this porcelain reproduction of the 1959 Wedding Day doll. She has the same face makeup she wore 30 years before, along with the same gown and flowers. This Barbie wears the famous blond ponytail.

2. **Star Lily Bride Barbie, 1995** Around this time, Mattel introduced a line of Barbies that celebrated the romance of flowers. Here Barbie embraces lilies in a white brocade gown accented with Austrian crystals. She carries a bouquet of lilies, of course.

3. **Romantic Rose Bride Barbie, 1996** This porcelain, limited-edition Barbie is as graceful and lovely as the flower she's named for, with her lavish, appliquéd rose-dotted dress and rosette-accentuated train. The gown suggests antique lace and swirls gently around her ivory, satin skirt. Her hair is styled in a demure upsweep, and she carries a bouquet of roses.

4. **Blushing Orchid Bride Barbie, 1997** Here comes Barbie in a creation that celebrates the orchid. Her soft blush satin gown has a train of sparkling tulle edged in ribbon. Iridescent lace covers the bodice, which dramatically tapers into long petals that simulate an orchid. This porcelain special edition doll is decorated with tiny pearls on Barbie's gloves and bouquet.

5. **Wedding Day Barbie, 1997** This is a vinyl reproduction of a 1960s Barbie wearing a gown of white flocked tulle and a sprinkling of glitter over a satin lining. The bodice has a sweetheart neckline with white netting under a full skirt. Her accessories include "something old" (her mother's "pearl" necklace), "something new" (white heels), "something borrowed" (white gloves), and "something blue" (her garter).

6. **Vera Wang Bride Barbie, 1998** In 1998, Mattel began commissioning famous bridal designers to address Barbie's nuptials. Here the contemporary chic look that is the hallmark of Vera Wang's bridal creations has Barbie taking her vows amid elegance and sophistication. The gown features velvety black piping, black bows, and faux pearl buttons. The dress itself is ivory, made of duchess silk satin with Vera Wang's signature sheer illusion netting on the shoulders and sleeves. Finishing touches include a bouquet of red roses, a tulle underskirt, stockings, and a lace garter.

7. **Elizabeth Taylor in *Father of the Bride* Barbie, 2000** Commemorating the life and career of Elizabeth Taylor, this Barbie appears as the bride in the classic film *Father of the Bride.* She wears a re-creation of the glamorous satin and lace wedding gown from the movie, with a fitted lace and satin bodice complemented by a full satin skirt, split in front to reveal a delicate lace underskirt. Her floor-length tulle veil has scalloped lace trimming, and she holds a bouquet of white flowers tied in a satin ribbon.

8. **Millennium Wedding Barbie, 2000** Now Barbie walks down the aisle in a strapless white bridal gown with a lace-trimmed bodice and voluminous skirt. Her sheer overskirt is trimmed in bands of satin, and she has

faux pearl earrings and a necklace that complement the gown perfectly. A sheer veil, long white gloves, and a bouquet complete the look.

9. **Romantic Wedding Barbie, 2001** She says, "I do," in an ensemble that combines traditional bridal motifs with modern-day elements. Her off-white gown is set off with a soft yellow floral design, and her veil is accented with pink and yellow flowers. She wears a faux pearl necklace and ring.

10. **Maria Therese Bride Barbie, 2002** Barbie is the epitome of matrimonial elegance in a dress created especially for her by bridal designer Maria Therese. She is dressed in a satin gown covered in organza and trimmed in satin; the V-shaped back has tailored bows and faux pearl buttons. She sports a midlength veil accented with a tailored bow at the center, a petticoat, pantyhose, a delicate bouquet of flowers, and a blue garter. Faux pearl drop earrings, ruby red lips, and a sleek upswept bun provide the finishing touches.

11. **Sophisticated Wedding Barbie, 2002** She wears a floor-length gown with a satin bodice and a slim skirt of ivory jacquard with a matching train. Her hair is styled into an elegant upsweep, and her long veil has a pale pink bow at the crown. She carries a bouquet of lilies.

12. **Badgley Mischka Bride Barbie, 2004** This Barbie bride is resplendent in a gown that features iridescent beading, rhinestones, and delicate embroidery. The fitted bodice sits above a full skirt of satin-faced silk organza covering a taffeta underskirt. Crystal chandelier earrings with filigree details, a solitaire rhinestone ring, a white headband, a white velvet evening bag, and pearl-white high heel shoes complete the ensemble.

13. **David's Bridal Unforgettable Barbie, 2004** For the marriage of Mattel and David's Bridal, Barbie wears a gown with a white glitter-print satiny bodice and a full, glittery tulle skirt. Her "dowry" includes a tulle veil with a faux rhinestone tiara attached, a faux rhinestone necklace, silvery earrings, a red bouquet, white charmeuse gloves, and white high heel shoes.

14. **David's Bridal Eternal Barbie, 2005** When Mattel and David's Bridal renewed their vows, Barbie wore a contemporary gown featuring a glitter-print top and white satin dress and a veil whose faux pearl details are repeated in the bride's jewelry. A red rose bouquet with white ribbons lends a final air of romance.

15. **Carolina Herrera Bride Barbie, 2005** Famed bridal designer Carolina Herrera dresses Barbie in an elegant beaded gown with ecru corded lace on her big day. The bodice is crisscrossed with satin-edged organza ribbon, and the veil of off-white tulle is edged with lace and embellished with faux pearls. The ribbons on her shoes represent "something blue," and her rose bouquet completes the romantic look.

16. **Couture Confection Bride Barbie, 2006** Famed designed Bob Mackie created a bridal Barbie as part of Mattel's Gold Label Collection. She wears a fantasy wedding gown that evokes spun sugar and petit fours. With sparkling Swarovski crystal earrings, this is Barbie at her most glamorous.

17. **Monique Lhuillier Bride Barbie, 2006** Famous bridal designer Monique Lhuillier has Barbie walking down the aisle in a sophisticated interpretation of the modern bride, in a gown featuring a white silk lace bodice above a tulle A-line pleated skirt. A blue satin sash with rhinestone floral brooch accents the waist, and the ends of her wrap are decorated with faux pearls and tiny silvery sequins. Her accoutrements include "diamond" stud earrings and ring, and her undergarments include an off-white garter with blue ribbon detail.

18. **Reem Acra Bride Barbie, 2007** Reem Acra, one of the leading ladies of luxury bridal wear, dresses Barbie in a chic, romantic satiny gown adorned with the designer's signature beading and embroidery and a detailed, extra-long train. This Barbie comes with "pearl" studs and a tiara accenting her sleek updo.

19. **Romance Barbie, 2007** Inspired by an exclusive David's Bridal design, this Barbie's ethereal strapless gown features a lace bodice and a full tufted skirt. She wears a silvery tiara and sports a faux rose bouquet.

6 of the World's Most Elaborate Weddings

WOULDYOU?
GO THE LIMIT

1. **Attila the Hun and Il-dico** (A.D. 453) Not content with the even dozen he already had, the barbarian Attila took a young girl named Ildico for his thirteenth wife. Their wedding was attended by royalty of every nation under the domain.

Thousands of gallons of booze and whole herds of sheep served as refreshment for the affair. The wedding feast lasted for days, but on the morning after finally taking his 16-year-old bride to bed, the 50-something warlord was found dead.

2. **Margaret of York and Charles the Bold** (1468) The celebrations surrounding this marriage constituted one of the undisputed pinnacles in the history of the Court of Burgundy and truly became the "marriage of the century." The ceremony took place in the Church of Notre-Dame at Damme, near Bruges.

The most famous knights in Europe competed in a contest called "the Tournament of the Golden Tree," which lasted for days. The celebratory parades, the streets lined with tapestries hanging from windows, the music, feasting, and jewels were all so lavish that the proud citizens of Bruges to this day reenact the event annually for tourists.

3. **Prince Rainier of Monaco and Grace Kelly** (April 19, 1956) On April 18, 1956, the film star Grace Kelly married Prince Rainier in a civil ceremony in the palace's throne room. The following morning they were remarried at the Cathedral of St. Nicholas. The ceremony was attended by over 600 of the world's richest and most famous people, including diplomats, heads of state, and film stars such as Frank Sinatra, Cary Grant, Ava Gardner, and Gloria Swanson. The Bishop of Monaco performed the ceremony.

After the ceremony, the couple rode through the streets of Monaco in a cream-and-black Rolls convertible—a gift from the citizens of Monaco.

4. **Muhammad and Salama of Dubai** (1981) The wedding of Sheikh Muhammad to Princess Salama lasted seven days. The ceremony was held in a stadium especially built for the occasion and was attended by 20,000 guests. Rashid bin Sayid al-Maktoum, the groom's father and sheikh of Dubai, shelled out over $44.5 million (the equivalent of $100 million in today's dollars) for the festivities. This wedding is listed in the *Guinness Book of World Records* as the most expensive wedding ever held—as of 1981. Read on.

5. **The Mittal Affair** (2004) The Mittal Affair, the world's most expensive wedding on record, took place on June 22, 2004. Lakshmi Mittal, an Indian steel magnate, spared no expense for the wedding of his daughter Vanisha Mittal to Amit Bhatia. The ceremony was the culmination of a six-day event held at a seventeenth-century French chateau. The engagement ceremony had been held at the Palace of Versailles two days earlier. As part of the wedding celebration, Mittal hosted a "Bollywood Night" that featured performances by Indian superstars Rani Mukerji and Shahrukh Khan. The estimated cost was $70 million.

6. **Donald Trump and Melania Knauss** (2005) Live performances by Billy Joel, Tony Bennett, and Paul Anka, 10,000 flowers, 45 chefs, and a 200-pound Grand Marnier cake were only some of the highlights of Donald Trump's marriage to Slovenian model Melania Knauss. The ceremony, conducted at Trump's 18-acre estate in Palm Beach, Florida, was attended by the likes of Bill Clinton and Shaquille O'Neal. Melania's wedding gown, which she modeled on the cover of *Vogue,* was adorned with 1,500 rhinestones. The dress weighed 60 pounds.

> "There wasn't a wet eye in the place."
> — Julie Baumgold, writer, on the wedding of Donald and Marla Trump

Bridal Attire Across the Globe

In the United States, the white dress is standard wedding attire, but brides from different cultures around the world choose to don various other distinctive looks for their special day. Traditional wedding attire ranges in style, color, fabric, and decoration from country to country. Sarah Stefanson and WeddingFashion.Suite101.com provide this summary of bridal attire across the globe.

Both the Maasai bride and groom wear tanned-hide capes. The beadwork on the capes represents the wealth of the couple as well as their skills as artisans. COURTESY OF WAKE FOREST UNIVERSITY MUSEUM OF ANTHROPOLOGY/TEN THOUSAND VILLAGES

African

A traditional African bridal outfit consists of items made from matching fabric in bright, cheerful colors, including a headpiece called a *gele*, a wrap skirt called an *iro*, a shawl called an *iborum*, and a blouse called a *buba*.

American Indian

For an American Indian wedding ceremony, the bride wears a long dress covered in beading and finished with fringes. Colors representing north, south, east, and west are included in the garment.

Chinese

The most essential element for Chinese wedding attire and decorations is the color red. The color means good luck in Chinese culture, so everything from the dress to the lanterns is red. Traditionally, a one-piece dress called *Qi Pao*, featuring intricate designs in gold and silver, is worn in northern China. In southern China, the bride usually wears a *Qun Gua*, a *Kwa*, or a *Cheongsam*, which are two-piece outfits decorated with a golden phoenix or dragon. When arranged marriages were still the norm in China, the bride would wear a red veil during the ceremony and her face wouldn't be revealed until the wedding night.

Hispanic

The Hispanic bride wears a slim dress and may choose to wear a bolero jacket over it. Alternatively, she may wear a flamenco-style dress. A mantilla veil is a remnant of Spanish influence that has become standard for Mexican and Latin American brides. A Hispanic bride often pays homage to her ancestors by wearing a dress passed down from her mother and grandmother, represent-

Grooms of the Mapuche Indians of central Chile and lower Argentina wear woolen headbands that contain a host of symbols. The brides adorn themselves with silver, as they do for all important occasions. COURTESY OF WAKE FOREST UNIVERSITY MUSEUM OF ANTHROPOLOGY/TEN THOUSAND VILLAGES

Japanese

In Japan, a bride wears a colorful kimono with a hood to her ceremony. The hood, called a *tsuno kakushi,* shows that she is obedient to her new husband. She changes into another kimono once the ceremony is finished. Both garments are made into bedding after the wedding, which will be passed down to future generations.

Korean

During the Korean wedding ceremony called *Pae Baek,* customary Korean clothes are worn with additional robes and headdresses. Bright colors are important in Korean wedding attire, to inspire the brightness of spirit that is required at such a special event. The bride's outfit, or *hanbok,* is based around a long, high-waisted skirt that wraps around the body. She also wears a long-sleeved short jacket with two ribbons tied in a bow.

ing the pride she has in her family. She sews ribbons of yellow, blue, and red into the lingerie she wears under her wedding dress, which symbolize the food, money, and passion that she hopes to attract to her marriage. Pearls are never part of a Hispanic bride's outfit since they are thought to bring future tears and grief to the marriage.

India

The traditional wedding attire of Hindu brides usually consists of saris in red and white, colors symbolizing fertility, wealth, and purity. In the days leading up to the ceremony, the bride's female family members paint her hands and feet with henna in elaborate patterns. This decoration is called *mehendi.*

Irish

In Ireland, blue is a lucky color, so the bride often wears a blue dress. She avoids wearing green, however, as this color is thought to attract the attention of the meddlesome fairy folk. While many a bride would have a fit if her dress were torn on her wedding day, the Irish bride would consider it a sign of good luck.

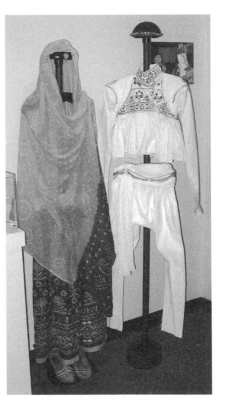

Scottish

A Scottish wedding dress prominently features tartan, in ribbons trimming a white dress, in a shawl around the shoulders, or in a sash around the waist. The dress may also have embroidered Celtic knotwork symbolizing eternal love. The groom may pin a piece of his tartan to the bride's outfit, representing her joining his clan.

Wedding costumes for a Javanese bride and groom bear a strong resemblance, symbolizing unity. The bridal headdress, with its crownlike design and mirrors, invokes the beauty of a goddess. The groom's belt includes a sheath for his traditional dagger, an important symbol of his manhood and class. COURTESY OF WAKE FOREST UNIVERSITY MUSEUM OF ANTHROPOLOGY/TEN THOUSAND VILLAGES

"And the wedding guests assembled,
Clad in all their richest raiment,
Robes of fur and belts of wampum,
Splendid with their paint and plumage,
Beautiful with beads and tassels."

— From Henry Wadsworth Longfellow, *The Song of Hiawatha*

A Bollywood Wedding

On April 23, 2007, Abhishek Bachchan and Aishwarya Rai, one of Bollywood's best-known screen couples, married in a traditional Hindu wedding. The emerald-eyed bride, Rai, is a former Miss World, and Bachchan, the groom, belongs to Indian film royalty as the son of India's best-known actor, Amitabh Bachchan. Indian media often liken the couple to the Hollywood celebrity duo Brad Pitt and Angelina Jolie.

The celebration had all of India spellbound and sent its celebrity-obsessed media into a frenzy, even though the Bachchans tried to keep the event strictly private and low-key, owing to the illness of the groom's grandmother. The subdued wedding was a great letdown for fans who were expecting a more elaborate event.

Abhishek wore a long Indian tunic, a silver-colored turban, and a veil of flowers on his face as he rode on a decorated mare into his residence, Prateeksha, in Jalsa, Mumbai, where his bride-to-be waited. Aishwarya wore a traditional hand-embroidered sari with intricate gold work on her wedding day, by her favorite designer, Neeta Lulla.

The ceremony was conducted in a huge, flower-filled, air-conditioned tent encircled by gold curtains in the garden adjoining the Bachchan family home, where Abhishek and Aishwarya exchanged wedding vows to the sound of trumpets, drums, and clanging cymbals.

The marriage was blessed by priests who chanted hymns from ancient Indian scriptures amid the blowing of conch shells and ululation. The wedding ceremony was the culmination of three days of festivities.

Hundreds of fans lined the roads leading to the marriage venue. Many slept on the pavement outside to be close to the couple. Crowds of fans jumped over media barricades to catch a glimpse of the Bachchans and their celebrity guests.

Over 400 private security personnel, as well as members of the Mumbai police, managed traffic and kept the enthusiastic fans at bay.

The King Takes a Wife

Elvis and Priscilla Presley, May 1, 1967 KOBAL COLLECTION

The 1994 wedding between Lisa Marie Presley and Michael Jackson in the Dominican Republic was shrouded in secrecy. Many felt that the wedding was just a masquerade, a ploy to improve Jackson's public image.

When asked by the media if they had sex, the couple replied, "Yes, yes, yes," and stated that they were deeply in love.

The couple divorced 18 months after they married, on grounds of irreconcilable differences.

Elvis and Priscilla Ann Beaulieu met in 1959 at a party in Elvis's off-base residence in West Germany during his stint in the U.S. Army. Although she was only 14 when they first met, Elvis was captivated.

In 1963, Elvis, "the King of Rock and Roll," persuaded the reluctant Beaulieu family to allow Priscilla, by then age 18, to live with his father, Vernon Presley, and stepmother, Dee Presley, in his Memphis, Tennessee, home, Graceland.

Priscilla married Elvis on May 1, 1967, in a private civil ceremony among a small group of family and friends at the Aladdin Hotel in Las Vegas. She was 21 years old. Elvis was dressed in a black brocade silk tuxedo, and she in a full-length white chiffon dress with a 6-foot satin train. Her ring had a 3-carat diamond and 20 smaller ones. The reception following the ceremony featured a 5-foot cake, breakfast for 100, and a strolling string trio. The couple's first dance was reported to have been to Elvis's "Love Me Tender." The maid of honor was Michelle Beaulieu, a cousin, and best men were Marty Lacker and Joe Esposito, members of Elvis's entourage. The couple had a four-day honeymoon in Palm Springs.

Later on that month the couple had a second wedding reception in Graceland's trophy room for friends and family who were not at the Las Vegas wedding.

Unfortunately, the marriage lasted only six years. Priscilla grew tired of Elvis's demanding work schedule and constant travel and hated his inner circle of friends, known as "the Memphis Mafia." On February 1, 1968, the couple had a daughter, Lisa Marie, whose questionable marriage to Michael Jackson on May 26, 1994, made headlines of its own.

"I got gaps; you got gaps; we fill each other's gaps."
— Rocky

10 Unforgettable Wedding Gifts

1. Queen Elizabeth received a shawl from Mahatma Gandhi that he had knit himself.

2. For the wedding of Nathaniel Hawthorne and Sophia Peabody, their good friend Henry David Thoreau planted a vegetable garden at their home in Concord, Massachusetts.

3. A tear-shaped La Peregrina Pearl, discovered by a slave in the Gulf of Panama in the 1500s, was given to Queen Mary Tudor of England by Spain's Prince Philip II. It was later acquired by Richard Burton and incorporated into a Cartier-designed ruby-and-diamond necklace for Elizabeth Taylor. It was considered to be priceless.

4. Princess Kalina of Bulgaria and Kitin Munoz, the Spanish explorer, received an embroidered dress and an "enormous sheep bell" from a Bulgarian cosmetics company.

5. For a wedding gift, vampire-slaying bride Sarah Michelle Gellar gave her groom, Freddie Prinze Jr., a Molly Ringwald—autographed copy of the film Pretty in Pink.

6. Sophie Rhys-Jones received a priceless Asprey & Garrard black-and-white pearl necklace with matching earrings from her royal husband Prince Edward.

7. Sir Andrew Lloyd Webber loaned his personal chef, Paul Lengronne, to Posh Spice Girl Victoria Adams and David Beckham for their honeymoon.

8. Prince Rainier gave Grace Kelly the yacht *Deo Juvante II* as a wedding gift.

9. Internationally acclaimed singer Jennifer Holliday presented Jeffrey L. Newman, CEO of the Gay Financial Network website, and Jeffrey W. Purker, an accomplished men's accessories designer, with a live presentation of a direct-from-the-heart repertoire of songs on the occasion of their wedding.

10. Burt Prelutsky, whose screenwriting credits include *M*A*S*H* and *The Mary Tyler Moore Show,* sprang for two $10 Target gift certificates for Nicolas Cage and Lisa Marie Presley.

Sheet music cover for "General Tom Thumb's Grand Wedding March," composed by E. Mack and respectfully dedicated to "General Tom Thumb and Lady," 1863 LIBRARY OF CONGRESS

Tom Thumb's Wedding

The real "General" Tom Thumb was a 2'11" midget named Charles Stratton, born in 1838 in Connecticut. At age four, he became an entertainer with the Ringling Brothers Barnum and Bailey Circus, and in 1863 he married a dwarf named Lavinia Warren at a spectacular ceremony at Grace Church in New York City. A reception followed at the Metropolitan Hotel, where the newly married couple stood atop a grand piano to greet some 2,000 guests. The event was highly publicized and lavish, and Barnum was heavily criticized not only for filling his pockets with the proceeds but also for making a spectacle of what had been, until then, a private concern.

But most Americans adored the spectacle, and its details were front-page news. An extensive article in the *New York Times* of February 11, 1863, headlined "The Loving Lilliputians," noted that a stretch of Broadway for several blocks was "literally crowded, if not packed, with an eager and expectant populace."

8 Televised Weddings

These weddings were nothing like the nasty nuptials that can be seen on any given episode of The Jerry Springer Show, but they were spectacles just the same.

1. **Prince Rainier and Grace Kelly** The royal couple officially married in a civil ceremony on April 18, 1956. The religious ceremony, held the following day, was billed as "the Wedding of the Century." The event was seen by over 30 million television viewers.

2. **Patrick Nugent and Luci Baines Johnson** The wedding of President Lyndon Baines Johnson's daughter on August 6, 1966, was televised by all three major networks. The ceremony, held at Washington's Roman Catholic Shrine of the Immaculate Conception, attracted protesters who were angered that the President's daughter chose to be married on the anniversary of the atomic bombing of Japan.

3. **Tiny Tim and Miss Vicki** On December 17, 1969, the marriage ceremony between famed performer Tiny Tim and Victoria Mae Budinger, known as "Miss Vicki," took place on *The Tonight Show with Johnny Carson*. The odd couple were joined together in matrimony as a publicity stunt. It became the very first televised wedding on nighttime television. Tiny Tim, known for his recording of "Tiptoe Through the Tulips," and Miss Vicki were married for eight years and had a daughter named Tulip.

4. **Wayne and Victoria Chew** One of the most widely watched noncelebrity weddings took place during Dick Clark's *New Year's Rockin' Eve* in 1985, when Wayne and Victoria were married during a live telecast in Times Square in New York City. They have been married over 22 years.

5. **Darva Conger and Rick Rockwell** Darva, a nurse, was one of 50 single female contestants invited to participate in the reality show *Who Wants to Marry a Multi-Millionaire?* and vie to capture the heart of millionaire Rick Rockwell. Darva agreed to marry Rick, and the wedding was then televised live. Conger filed for an annulment after the honeymoon, during which the couple failed to consummate their marriage. Turns out Rockwell was not exactly as rich as he claimed to be.

6. **Lt. David Kozminski and Jeannie Rhoads** This couple was married on *Good Morning America* on May 1, 2003, on a segment called "Operation Instant Wedding." Producers of the show heard that David and his fiancée had postponed their nuptials twice because of David's 10-month deployment aboard the USS *Abraham Lincoln,* and they wanted to help the couple finally tie the knot. The wedding took place in a hangar bay.

7. **Rob Sarofeen and Louise Fullerton** Rob and Louise were married live on ABC's *Live with Regis and Kelly* in 2005. The couple's wedding day had been postponed because Rob, a quadriplegic, had been hospitalized several times. The show, which invites couples who haven't been able to wed because of unforeseen obstacles, chose the most romantic day of the year—Valentine's Day—to televise the ceremony.

8. **Siti Nurhaliza binti Tarudin and Datuk Khalid** The wedding ceremony of multiple award—winning Malaysian pop singer and songwriter Tarudin, the most popular Malaysian singer of all time, and businessman Datuk Khalid was televised live and seen by more than 2 million viewers. The reception was held on August 28, 2006, at the Kuala Lumpur Convention Centre (KLCC) and was televised to 6.3 million viewers nationwide.

Highlights of Grace Kelly's Wedding to Prince Rainier

It has been estimated that over 30 million viewers watched the wedding of film icon Grace Kelly to Prince Rainier of Monaco on live television—a significant viewership at that time. The wedding took place on April 19, 1956, and was described by Robert Lacey, one of Kelly's biographers, as "the first modern event to generate media overkill." Here are the highlights of that fairy-tale wedding.

• Hollywood film star Grace Kelly was 25 years old when she first met Monaco's Prince Rainier. Renowned for her beauty as well as her acting skills, Kelly had appeared in *High Noon* and the Alfred Hitchcock thrillers *Rear Window* and *Dial M for Murder.* She had received an Oscar nomination in 1953 for her work in the film *Mogambo.*

• Kelly was in the South of France attending the Cannes Film Festival in 1955 and had a photo shoot scheduled with the Prince of Monaco, whom she had never met. The shoot conflicted with a hair appointment, and Grace nearly blew off the meeting until an old boyfriend told her, "Grace, you can't possibly do that. He's a reigning prince!" After the photo shoot, they visited the Prince's gardens and small zoo, and the rest is wedding history.

• In December 1955, the Prince presented Grace with a 10.47-carat emerald cut diamond and two baguette diamonds mounted in platinum after proposing marriage. She wore the ring as her character's engagement ring in the 1956 film *High Society.*

• Grace and her 65-member wedding party arrived in Monaco on the ocean liner the USS *Constitution* on April 4, 1956. (Air travel at the time was not readily available.)

• The couple were married on April 18, 1956, in a civil ceremony held in the palace's baroque throne room. Kelly wore a pale pink taffeta gown with cream-colored Alençon lace, white kid gloves, and a Juliet cap. Rainier wore a black morning coat, striped trousers, a white vest, and a gray tie. The couple exchanged their vows in French.

Grace Kelly and Prince Rainier tied the knot on April 19, 1956.
KOBAL COLLECTION

• Later that day Rainier and his bride held a reception for the 3,000 citizens of Monaco, giving each guest the opportunity to meet Grace and shake her hand.

• The couple had a religious ceremony the following day in St. Nicholas Cathedral, Monaco, in what was commonly referred to as "the Wedding of the Century." The service began at 9:30 A.M. and was attended by over 600 guests. In accordance with Monaco tradition, Grace was the first to walk down the aisle, escorted by her father, and the Prince was last to walk down the aisle; he wore a Napoleonic military-style uniform that he himself designed. The flowers decorating the altar and church included white hydrangeas, lilies, and snapdragons. Famous guests included Aristotle Onassis, Gloria Swanson, Ava Gardner, Cary Grant, Aga Khan, and David Niven, as well as heads of state and diplomats. It has been rumored that Grace herself hated every moment of her wedding.

• Grace's wedding gown, a gift from MGM Studios, was designed by the studio's head costume designer, Helen Rose. It was a high-necked dress constructed of 450 yards of Brussels rose point lace and silk taffeta. The veil was embroidered with orange blossoms and pearls. She carried a lily-of-the-valley bouquet and a small Bible.

• Seven hundred guests attended a reception in the Palace Court of Honor. The bride and groom cut the six-tier wedding cake with the Prince's sword.

• The couple honeymooned aboard Prince Rainer's yacht *Deo Juvante II.*

Charles and Diana: Another "Wedding of the Century"

On Wednesday, July 29, 1981, at 11:00 A.M., in London's St. Paul's Cathedral, 32-year-old Charles, the Prince of Wales and heir to the British throne, wed Lady Diana Spencer, age 20. A congregation of 3,500 gathered beneath the soaring painted dome of the cathedral to witness the ceremony, which was broadcast to a worldwide audience of 750 million. In a time of recession, high unemployment, and chronic rioting, the fairy-tale romance of Charles and Di and the grand pageantry that, by binding them in holy matrimony, secured the future of the British monarchy was a much-needed diversion.

- On the eve of the wedding, 101 celebratory bonfires were lighted throughout the United Kingdom, and a dazzling display of pyrotechnics was set off in Hyde Park. London's buses were painted with festive bows, and the royal crest of the Prince of Wales, created using 4,500 pots of blooming plants, adorned the wedding route.

- Lady Diana traveled to St. Paul's in a glass coach.

- The magnificent wedding cake cost $6,000.

- The bride's gown, created by Mayfair designers David and Elizabeth Emanuel, was made from 40 yards of silk taffeta, 100 yards of crinoline, some old Carrick-macross lace that once belonged to Queen Mary, and thousands of mother-of-pearl sequins. A small 18-karat gold horseshoe was tucked into the billowing skirts for good luck.

- The Archbishop of Canterbury, Dr. Robert Runcie, led the traditional Church of England service, aided by clergymen of various denominations. The ceremony itself went off without a hitch—almost. Diana's nervousness was evident when she mixed up the Prince's names—calling him Philip Charles Arthur George, rather than Charles Philip. Charles, in the full dress uniform of a naval commander, flubbed his vows a bit also, referring to "thy goods" rather than "my worldly goods." New Zealander Kiri Te Kanawa, the Royal Opera's soprano sensation, sang an anthem by Handel, accompanied by 95 musicians selected from three orchestras.

- In attendance were First Lady Nancy Reagan, the King and Queen of Sweden, and Queen Beatrix of the Netherlands. (The Spanish king, Juan Carlos, chose not to attend to protest the decision by the newlyweds to begin their honeymoon cruise aboard the royal yacht *Britannia* in Gibraltar, a British colony long claimed by Spain.) Also attending was Sir Dawda Jawara, Gambia's president, who learned from the Foreign Office that he had been driven from power by a coup launched during his absence. In all, more than a dozen presidents, 15 Commonwealth heads of state, and 9 members of reigning royal families were among the VIPs present at the wedding.

- Security was stiff: bobbies were posted every six feet along the processional route taken by the Prince and Princess from St. Paul's to Buckingham Palace. Spectators who had paid $390 apiece for a prime view from office windows overlooking the route had to clear police security and wear an ID badge. Charles and Diana made the 22-minute journey in an open 1902 State Postillion Landau flanked by a mounted detachment of the Sovereign's Escort and cheered by the two million onlookers who lined the way.

- After gracing the crowd of well-wishers with a kiss on the balcony of Buckingham Palace, the couple sat for a wedding portrait by Lord Snowdon. At the traditional royal wedding breakfast that

"Amid all England's troubles, the monarchy endures, and around the world people will wonder why and many will criticize it as an expensive, useless anachronism. But the faces of the people in the streets and the pomp and tradition of the ceremony provided the answer that this is the British way; that Britain will carry on through bad times and good as it has for centuries."

—*Philadelphia Inquirer*

Princess Diana and Prince Charles on their wedding day, London, July 29, 1981 AP PHOTO/PA POOL

Facing: The Arms of Lady Diana Spencer AUTHORS' COLLECTION

followed, 120 guests dined on gold plates filled with brill in lobster sauce, chicken breasts garnished with lamb mousse, and strawberries with Cornish cream washed down with claret and port. The groom used his ceremonial sword to cut the first slice of a five-tiered wedding cake adorned with emblems from his naval days and sugar doves and topped with a garden of confectionery roses, lilies of the valley, fuchsias, and orchids accenting an ornamental "C" and "D."

• A "Just Married" sign attached to their carriage by Princes Andrew and Edward raised smiles as the couple were driven over Westminster Bridge to get the train to Romsey in Hampshire to begin their honeymoon.

• A slice of Princess Diana's wedding cake was auctioned on eBay with the "Buy It Now" price of $2,749.

• Diana ordered a spare wedding dress, which went on display at Madame Tussauds in London. This exact replica sold for more than £100,000 at a celebrity memorabilia show at the Proud Gallery Camden in London.

• David and Elizabeth Emanuel, the designers of Diana's gown, published a limited edition gift book, *A Dress for Diana,* costing $2,430. Each book contains a piece of the fabric from which the dress was made.

• Diana's gown, complete with train, diamond tiara, shoes, and parasol, has been on exhibit at the Western Reserve Historical Society, the Florida International Museum, the Houston Museum of Natural Science, and the Dayton Art Institute. The gown was also exhibited in Sydney, Australia, in September 2007.

• The Princess Diana wedding package offered by the Princess Wedding Chapel in Las Vegas, Nevada, is priced at $599.

> "You really have to admire the British. They have class. Even as police were battling rioters in Liverpool for the third straight night and British army bomb experts were disarming a 400-pound explosive planted by the Irish Republican Army in Northern Ireland, Britons celebrated the continuity of their history with the wedding of the century. The marriage of Lady Diana Spencer to Prince Charles, the Prince of Wales . . . did more to revive the glorious aura of symbols and myths surrounding British royalty than any other event of recent times."
> —*Baltimore Sun*

7 Infamous Bachelor Parties

It's known as a stag party in the United Kingdom, Ireland, Canada, and New Zealand; as a bulls party in South Africa; as bucks night in Australia; and as bachelor's eve in Nigeria. Its origins go back to fifth-century Sparta, where soldiers would toast one another on the eve of a wedding. Absent of female guests, the parties would inevitably take a raucous turn, and bachelor parties today are still typically associated with drinking, carousing, and, of course, the Stripper. The idea has been to give the groom a chance to sow whatever wild oats he has left on his last night of freedom. Thanks to David Boyer, author of the entertaining cultural history Bachelor Party Confidential, for this list of notorious bachelor parties.

1. Clinton Barnum Seeley, 1896 Capt. George Chapman raided the high-society stag party of P. T. Barnum's nephew after his precinct received a tip that the famous burlesque performer Little Egypt would be performing naked. Those involved denied that anything untoward occurred and cried police misconduct. Chapman was put on trial, and the public was shocked as party details emerged, including the groping of young women, the exposing of genitals, and the presence of syringes. Chapman was exonerated; Little Egypt went on to become a legend.

2. Jimmy Stewart, 1949 Jimmy Stewart held his bachelor party at the legendary Hollywood hangout Chasen's. The highlight of the televised affair was two midgets, dressed only in diapers, popping out of a silver serving dish.

3. Thomas Bruderman, 2003 The bachelor bacchanal for this Fidelity Investments trader incorporated a dwarf, a private jet and yacht, two prostitutes, and several suites at South Beach's Delano Hotel and cost in excess of $100,000. Two years after Bruderman's last hurrah, the Securities and Exchange Commission launched an investigation of the party.

4. Sean Sullivan, 2004 Their comeback was cemented with a very public walk down the aisle, but former newlyweds Jessica Simpson and Nick Lachey hit a snag after tabloids claimed that Nick was getting a little grabby with porn star Jessica Jaymes, who was performing at Sullivan's bachelor party in the Hollywood Hills. All concerned denied that anything untoward occurred at the time; the pop pair split two years later.

5. Mario Lopez, 2004 The actor best known for his portrayal of Slater on Saved by the Bell allegedly cheated on his bride-to-be, former Miss Teen USA Ali Landry, at his bachelor party in Acapulco. The C-list couple went on with their nuptials and allowed Oprah Winfrey's crew to film the whole thing for a never-to-be-aired segment. Two weeks later, Landry filed for an annulment.

6. Paris Latsis, 2005 Instant replay: Paris Hilton dumped her fiancé Paris Latsis after learning that the Greek shipping heir cheated on her at his bachelor party. In a televised interview with Extra, she advised all grooms-to-be, "Don't cheat on her at your bachelor party. It's gross what you guys do at those parties. . . . Whoever I marry is not going to have a bachelor party."

7. Elton John and David Furnish, 2005 Sir Elton and his filmmaker hubby made headlines with their star-studded stag party in London featuring topless waiters wearing black ties and riding boots; pop luminaries, including Ozzy Osbourne, were in attendance, and there was a video message from Bill Clinton.

---

9 Slang Words for "Wife"

1. Old lady
2. Better half
3. Old ball and chain
4. She who must be obeyed
5. Little woman
6. Old boiler
7. Trouble and strife
8. Bread knife
9. Sheila

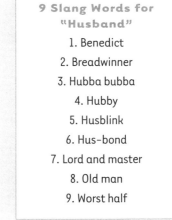

9 Slang Words for "Husband"

1. Benedict
2. Breadwinner
3. Hubba bubba
4. Hubby
5. Husblink
6. Hus-bond
7. Lord and master
8. Old man
9. Worst half

Diamond Rings: The Bigger the Better

When it comes to engagement rings, most status-conscious couples agree, "the bigger, the better," and celebs are no exception. Privacy issues prevented us from being able to determine the exact amount paid for the rings listed here, but we did our very best to come as close as possible to their real value.

1. Paris Hilton was given a choice of two engagement rings by her former fiancé Paris Latsis. The first was a 24-carat emerald cut diamond ring worth approximately $4.5 million; the second was a 15-carat white diamond ring valued at $2.1 million. She opted for the 24-carat model. The ring was put up for auction after the five-month engagement ended.

2. One of the most expensive engagement rings (according to Donald Trump) is the one he presented to his third wife, Slovenian model Melania Knauss. The ring, a 12-carat flawless emerald cut diamond set in platinum, was purchased at the House of Graff in New York and is valued at approximately $1.5 million—$125,000 per carat. Trump claims to have paid over $3 million for the ring. But other reports suggest that the actual price of the ring was closer to $500,000.

3. Brad Pitt designed the platinum engagement ring and wedding bands for his marriage to Jennifer Aniston. Brad's ring, embedded with 10 diamonds, is inscribed with "Jen 2000," and Jennifer's ring, embedded with 20 diamonds, is inscribed "Brad 2000." Prices were not available.

4. Aristotle Onassis presented Jacqueline Kennedy with a 40-carat diamond engagement ring. The ring was put up for auction in 1996 and sold for a staggering $2.6 million, making it one of the most expensive engagement rings in history.

5. Michael Douglas gave Catherine Zeta-Jones an antique-designed 10-carat marquise cut diamond engagement ring worth an estimated $2 million.

6. The ring that Tom Cruise presented to Katie Holmes was an Edwardian-style oval-shaped diamond ring that reportedly set him back $1.5 million.

7. The 6.1-carat pink diamond ring that Ben Affleck presented to Jennifer Lopez was a Harry Winston creation valued at $1.2 million. The ring was reacquired by Winston for resale when the relationship ended.

8. Camilla Parker Bowles's 8-carat heirloom ring has a classic traditional emerald cut with three stair-stepped/bar-set-tapered baguettes on each side. A commoner with deep pockets could purchase a similar ring for $250,000, but the fact that the ring belonged to the Queen Mother raises its value to $1 million.

9. The engagement ring that Prince Charles presented to Diana Spencer was a large oval sapphire surrounded by 14 brilliant cut diamonds. The ring, which Diana gave to her son Prince William, was valued at approximately $85,000.

10. Singer and actress Brandy was presented with an 11.5-carat ring by her fiancé Quentin Richards. The ring, valued at $1 million, was created by jeweler Jason Arasheben and was completed just half an hour before Quentin proposed.

11. Actor Charlie Sheen purchased an enormous radiant cut yellow diamond for his fiancée Brooke Mueller. The ring is valued at over $550,000.

12. The engagement ring that Ben Affleck gave actress Jennifer Garner set him back $500,000.

13. When Tony Parker decided to propose to Eva Longoria, he commissioned famed jeweler Jean Dousset to create an original emerald cut diamond ring. The estimated value is over $500,000.

14. Richard Burton presented Elizabeth Taylor with a 69-carat pear-shaped Harry Winston stone. Liz decided it was a bit too large as a ring and had it made into a necklace. She later sold the necklace for $500,000 and used the proceeds to help fund a hospital in Botswana.

15. Pop singer Seal gave his fiancée Heidi Klum a 10-carat yellow diamond valued at $150,000. He chose an elongated shape to complement Heidi's long fingers.

16. Christina Aguilera became engaged to Jordan Bratman after he presented her with a $54,000 20-carat diamond engagement ring designed by jeweler Stephen Webster.

17. Britney Spears has two engagement rings. She bought one for herself before her wedding to Kevin Federline—a $40,000 4-carat cushion cut diamond ring with a platinum pave setting. She received the second one from Kevin nine months after they were married.

18. Actor Harry Hamlin presented Nicolette Sheridan with a round center diamond set in a melee diamond wreath that cost $22,000.

6 White House Weddings

1. Maria Hester Monroe James Monroe's daughter, Maria, was the first child of a president to marry in the White House. Her wedding to Samuel L. Gouverneur, held in 1820, was restricted to family members only.

2. Grover Cleveland The wedding of Grover Cleveland to 21-year-old Frances Folsom took place in 1886. Cleveland became the first and only president to marry in the White House. Frances, the youngest first lady in history, was beautiful, charming, and extremely popular. She gave birth to their daughter Esther in the president's bedroom in the northwest area of the second floor. Esther was the only child ever to be born in the White House.

3. Ellen "Nellie" Wrenshall Grant Nellie was the third child and only daughter of President Ulysses S. Grant and Julia Boggs Dent. She married Englishman Algernon Charles Frederick Sartoris, the son of opera singer Adelaide Kemble, on May 21, 1874, in the East Room.

4. Alice Roosevelt Teddy Roosevelt's daughter married Nicholas Longworth, a Republican congressman from Ohio, on February 17, 1906, in the East Room. Their wedding was the most talked about social event of the Roosevelt years. The wedding breakfast consisted of two breakfasts held simultaneously—one small one for the bridal party and another 700-person extravaganza held in the Blue Room.

5. Lynda Bird Johnson In 1967, Lyndon Johnson's daughter, Lynda Bird, married White House military aide Capt. Charles Robb. The wedding took place in the East Room. Their wedding photo was taken beneath a painting of George Washington.

6. Tricia Nixon Richard Nixon's daughter Tricia married Edward Cox on June 12, 1971. The ceremony, attended by more than 400 guests, took place in the Rose Garden and was the first outdoor wedding held at the White House. The reception was held in the East Room.

Above: George Washington's marriage to Martha Custis, painting by Junius Brutus Stearns, ca. 1854; President Richard Nixon escorting his daughter Tricia down the aisle, June 12, 1971

Opposite page: Rutherford B. Hayes and his wife on their wedding day, December 30, 1852; The White House wedding of Mr. A.C.F. Sartoris and Miss Nellie Grant, newspaper illustration by Henry Ogden, 1874; Alice Roosevelt Longworth on her wedding day, February 17, 1906 ALL COURTESY OF LIBRARY OF CONGRESS

Hillary and Bill Clinton's Love Story

Although they both attended the same civil liberties class at Yale Law School, it wasn't until they ran into each other at the library that they first spoke. Hillary and Bill began eyeing each other while seated at different tables, and there was definitely an attraction between them. Hillary, age 27, made the first move and introduced herself. Bill, age 29, apparently was so flustered that he forgot his name.

They went on a European vacation together after graduation. Bill proposed marriage. Hillary refused, but Bill wouldn't take no for an answer and proposed numerous times after that.

They were on their way to the airport one day when they spotted a small brick house for sale. She admired the house but gave it no more thought. When she returned from her trip, Bill informed her that he had bought the house and he proposed again. This time Hillary accepted.

They were married on October 11, 1975, in a small ceremony held in their new home. Hillary wore an off-the-rack cotton wedding dress. Only 15 people attended the ceremony, but the reception, held in the backyard, was attended by a few hundred of their friends. They honeymooned in Acapulco.

"The sheer numbers from that day are staggering: seven hundred guests at the church, an additional five hundred attending the reception, two dozen wedding attendants, fifty yards of silk taffeta for her gown, scores of bottles of vintage champagne."

— Jay Mulvaney

ON THE MARRIAGE OF JOHN FITZGERALD KENNEDY AND JACQUELINE LEE BOUVIER, WHICH WAS ATTENDED BY FIVE U.S. SENATORS, THE SPEAKER OF THE HOUSE OF REPRESENTATIVES, TWENTY CONGRESSMEN, AND NOTABLES INCLUDING ADLAI STEVENSON, NANCY LADY ASTOR, ACTRESS MARION DAVIES, SUPREME COURT JUSTICE WILLIAM O. DOUGLAS, ALICE ROOSEVELT LONGWORTH, AND ALAN JAY LERNER, ON SEPTEMBER 12, 1953, IN *KENNEDY WEDDINGS: A FAMILY ALBUM* (1999)

"Only two things are necessary to keep one's wife happy. One is to let her think she is having her own way. The other, to let her have it."

— Lyndon B. Johnson

The Ballad of John and Yoko

Ron Schaumburg, author of the best-selling *Growing Up with the Beatles* (1976) and more than a dozen other titles, gives us this account of the romance between John Lennon and Yoko.

John Lennon and Yoko Ono transformed their wedding—like everything in their lives—into a social, political, and artistic statement. The ceremony itself, held on the island of Gibraltar on March 20, 1969, was simple and private. Both bride and groom wore all white: she, a miniskirt, knee-length boots, and floppy hat; he, a turtleneck, jacket, and sneakers.

Elton John's Wedding

On December 21, 2005, Sir Elton John, 58, married his long-time partner, Canadian filmmaker David Furnish, 43, in a civil ceremony conducted at Windsor Guildhall, the same venue used by Prince Charles and Camilla Parker Bowles for their nuptials.

Elton and Furnish had been living together for nearly 12 years. The marriage took place on the first day civil partnerships became legal in England and Wales. Seven hundred other gay couples were married the same day.

Only a handful of guests were allowed to witness the actual nuptials, but the couple's black-and-white spaniel, Arthur, was a privileged guest. Attendees at the reception party included David Beckham, Sting, Rod Stewart, Elvis Costello, Donatella Versace, Claudia Schiffer, James Blunt, Ringo Starr, Sharon Stone, Elizabeth Hurley, Cilla Black, and Lulu.

The reception, which set the couple back $1.75 million, featured 19,000 red roses and an original Ben & Jerry's wedding cake topped by two tin soldier figures supporting guardsman-style helmets.

It is rumored that the couple turned down an $11 million offer to have the wedding recorded for British television. Elton stated that "our relationship doesn't come with a price tag."

Their spur-of-the-moment decision to marry was, in part, a response to the wedding a mere eight days before of his musical partner (and rival) Paul McCartney to Linda Eastman. Knowing their marriage would generate worldwide publicity, John and Yoko turned their honeymoon in Amsterdam into a media event. During their week-long "bed-in" for peace, they were besieged by reporters, filmmakers, and curious onlookers wondering just what this famous couple—who'd earlier released the notorious *Two Virgins* album, the cover of which showed them, well, uncovered—might get up to.

Madly in love and fired up by the experience, John dashed off a song—"The Ballad of John and Yoko"—whose controversial lyrics told the saga of their multinational wedding, honeymoon, and subsequent media circus. John wanted to record and release the tune as quickly as possible, like a kind of musical news item. The only other Beatle available for the session was Paul, still a bit of a newlywed himself. John sang and played lead and rhythm guitars; Paul added vocal harmonies and played bass, drums, piano, and maracas. They knocked out the record in a few hours and released it (credited to The Beatles, though only half the group performed) a few weeks later.

More vinyl soon followed: In late spring, the anthem "Give Peace a Chance," recorded during another bed-in as part of their extended honeymoon in a Montreal hotel, made it into *Billboard*'s top 20. And in October the duo provided die-hard fans with a souvenir recording, cleverly titled *Wedding Album.* Side one of the LP featured the loving couple muttering each other's names in every tone of voice conceivable (and some not-so-conceivable). Side two was a sound collage, including snippets of peace interviews conducted during the Amsterdam event. The elaborate packaging—more interesting, in many ways, than the recording itself—reflected the wedding's black-and-white color scheme. Included in the box were a copy of the wedding license, a booklet of photos, a postcard, and even a slice of the wedding cake (photographically reproduced, of course).

For a wedding to leave a more indelible mark on the cultural landscape than that of John and Yoko would be hard to . . . imagine.

In a Church Where a Wedding Has Been: Four Beatles Marriages

Thanks again to Ron Schaumburg, our resident Beatles expert.

1. **John married Cynthia Powell in Liverpool on August 23, 1962.** (Cyn was pregnant at the time; their son Julian was born eight months later, in April 1963.) Paul was best man. The reception was a lunch at a nearby café, paid for by their manager, Brian Epstein. The couple were "toasted" with glasses of water. John spent his wedding night playing a gig with the band. Coincidentally that same day, the Liverpool music newspaper *Mersey Beat* announced a Beatle divorce, of sorts: to the dismay of many of their fans, Ringo Starr had officially replaced Pete Best as the group's drummer. John and Cynthia themselves divorced on November 8, 1968.

John's second marriage was to Japanese artist Yoko Ono in Gibraltar on March 20, 1969. They had met in late 1966 during one of her exhibits at a London gallery. He was charmed by her avant-garde style; the story has it that she'd never heard of him. In 1968 they became inseparable. His insistence that she join him in the recording studio alienated the other Beatles and contributed mightily to their breakup. Knowing that their wedding and honeymoon would attract global attention, they turned it into a multimedia advertising campaign for peace. Their son Sean was born in 1975; he would follow in his father's musical footsteps.

2. **Ringo Starr tied the knot with Liverpudlian hairdresser Maureen Cox on February 11, 1965.** She'd been a Beatle fan during their days playing at the Cavern. The wedding was in London, with Brian Epstein as best man. She, too, was pregnant at the time; son Zak was born in September of that year. The couple had two more children, a boy, Jason, and a girl, Lee. Ringo's post–Beatles breakup alcoholism led to the couple's divorce in 1975. Maureen died of leukemia in 1994.

During and after his Beatle years, Ringo pursued his interest in acting, and it was on the set of the prehistoric comedy *Caveman* that he met statuesque actress Barbara Bach, who had been a "Bond girl" in *The Spy Who Loved Me.* They were married in a civil court in London on April 27, 1981, in a ceremony led by the same man who'd conducted the event for Paul so many years before. Their marriage was strengthened by their mutual passage through drug and alcohol rehabilitation. Barbara and the other Beatle wives, Linda McCartney, Olivia Harrison, and Yoko Ono, became active together in various charities.

3. **George married Patti Boyd on January 21, 1966.** She was a model and actress; the two had met two years earlier during the filming of *A Hard Day's Night.* Such were her charms that George apparently proposed to her on the spot. She also charmed George's friend and fellow guitar god Eric Clapton; their affair inspired Clapton to write the rock classic "Layla." The Harrisons, childless, divorced on June 9, 1977. (Patti married Clapton in 1979; they divorced nine years later.)

George wasn't alone for long; his only child, Dhani, was born in August 1978, and on September 2 of that year George married the mother, Olivia Trinidad Arias. It was a very private affair; only Olivia's parents were present. Olivia, a Latina from Los Angeles, had been a secretary at A&M Records, George's label at the time. She made news in 1999 when she fended off a knife-wielding intruder in their home in Hawaii by bashing him over the head with a lamp (and saving George's life in the process). After George's death from cancer in 2002, Olivia produced the memorial "Concert for George," in which Dhani—the very image of his father—played guitar.

4. **The last Beatle bachelor to succumb to domesticity was Paul, who married Linda Eastman in London on March 12, 1969.** The daughter of an American lawyer, Linda had penetrated the inner circles of rock's royalty as a photographer. They met backstage at a concert in May 1967, just two weeks before the album *Sgt. Pepper's Lonely Hearts Club Band* was to change the course of music history. As a member of his band Wings, she performed on his records and in concerts. Paul later boasted that he and Linda never spent a night apart (except, perhaps, for the ten days he spent in a Japanese jail, busted on a charge of marijuana possession). They had three children: Mary; Stella, today a noted fashion designer; and James. Linda died of breast cancer on April 17, 1998.

Paul met Heather Mills, a onetime model and activist, at a 1999 charity event, where the formal Beatle donated money to her cause. They soon became an item (and tabloid fodder) and married at a castle in Ireland on June 11, 2002. Their marriage was controversial from the beginning, as Heather endured hostile charges of "gold-digging" from Paul's family, his fans, and the press. They had a daughter, Beatrice, in 2003. A protracted and public divorce procedure finally ended in 2008, with the court awarding the former Lady Mills-McCartney a whopping $48.6 million settlement. It seems to be true—money can't buy you love.

19 Luminaries of the Wedding World

1. Preston Bailey Panamanian-born Preston Bailey was raised in a tropical paradise that had a profound influence on his sense of style. Bailey left Panama in 1968 at the age of 19 and started his career in design as a fashion model. By 1980, he was doing floral decorations in New York in the homes of his Fifth Avenue clients, drawing on his homeland's vibrant colors and natural beauty for inspiration. Bailey's exotic sense of style has been the force behind the weddings of many top pop icons, including Donald Trump, Uma Thurman, Liza Minnelli, and Donna Karan. With more than 20 years at the helm of Preston Bailey Entertainment Design, he sets the bar for event designers worldwide. Bailey's incredible collection of inspirational photos and ideas for brides and grooms were published in his book *Preston Bailey's Fantasy Weddings* (2004).

> "The weddings that are my favorites are the ones that have something personal for my clients. [At one recent wedding I did] guests arrived at an organic farm. They walked down this long pasture and there were photos of the bride and groom hanging in the trees. There were wind chimes ringing in the distance. We called that their "memory lane," and it went all the way down to the ceremony, which was in the round." — Sasha Souza

2. David Beahm Primarily known for his bold floral designs, Beahm has become one of the premier wedding designers in the world. His background in art and theater has enabled him to employ visually compelling elements in his wedding designs. Beahm's reputation as a wedding designer was sealed after he created a $3 million wedding for Catherine Zeta-Jones and Michael Douglas at New York's Plaza Hotel. Beahm was also chosen to be Marshall Field's wedding expert. He has appeared on numerous talk shows, and his work has been featured in countless magazines and newspapers.

3. Marcy Blum Marcy Blum is a world-renowned event planner whose weddings stimulate the senses. *Modern Bride* chose her as its "Trendsetter of the Year" in 2006, and *New York* magazine named her its first (and only) "Best Wedding Planner" in 2007. Her clients have included Kevin Bacon and Kyra Sedgwick, Salman Rushdie and Padma Lakshmi, Billy Joel and Katie Lee, the Rockefeller family, and Regis and Joy Philbin. Blum is the author of *Wedding Kit for Dummies* (2000) and *Wedding Planning for Dummies* (2004), and she has contributed articles to *InStyle Weddings, Town and Country, Modern Bride,* and *New York.* She has also hosted segments on *Oprah, The Today Show, Good Morning America, Live! With Regis and Kelly, Dateline,* and *Top Chef.*

4. Colin Cowie Zambian-born Colin Cowie is recognized around the world as one of the leading arbiters of style. He is the author of *Colin Cowie for the Bride* (2000), *Cowie for the Groom* (2000), *Colin Cowie Weddings* (2004), and *Colin Cowie's Extraordinary Weddings: From a Glimmer of an Idea to a Legendary Event by Colin Cowie* (2007).

For five years Cowie hosted his own television series, *Everyday Elegance with Colin Cowie,* on the Women's Entertainment Network. Today he appears regularly as a popular lifestyle consultant on *The CBS Early Show* and *Oprah.*

Jerry Seinfeld, Jenny McCarthy, Sela Ward, Don Henley, Kelsey Grammer, Kenny G., Lisa Kudrow, Sugar Ray Leonard, Paula Abdul, and Hugh Hefner are among Cowie's clients.

5. Kate Edmonds New York City planner Kate Edmonds is the owner of Kate Edmonds Corporate and Private Events Ltd., a Manhattan-based corporate and private event production and wedding design firm that has been planning parties in the United States, the United Kingdom, Canada, and Australia since 1986. She has been a guest on numerous radio and television programs throughout the country. Edmonds has been featured as an event designer on Bridezilla and Metro Television. She has been profiled in *InStyle, New York, Brides,* the *New York Post, Hampton Style, Modern Bride, Quest,* the *Observer, Newsday,* the *British Daily Mirror,* and the *New York Times* style section.

6. Jo Gartin Gartin is a Los Angeles–based wedding specialist who got into the wedding planning business after getting fed up with the outrageous prices she was quoted for her own wedding. She occasionally teams up with renowned fashion designer Monique Lhuillier to style and personalize Lhuillier's most-sought-after gowns, giving each bride a look all her own. She is the author of *Jo Gartin's Weddings: An Inspiring Guide for the Stylish Bride* (2005), and she has planned events for Courteney Cox, Brooke Shields,

Molly Shannon, Tim Allen, and Taye Diggs. Gartin serves as *Vogue*'s in-house planning expert and is a regular contributor to *InStyle*.

7. Sarah Haywood   Haywood is Britain's premier wedding planner and the author of Britain's top-selling bridal books, *Wedding Bible* (2007) and *Wedding Bible Planner* (2007). Considered one of the most influential people in the British wedding industry, she is the founder and managing director of the inspirational Wedding Bible Company.

Sarah regularly appears on TV and radio in the United Kingdom and abroad as "the Wedding Doctor." She is regularly quoted in wedding and lifestyle publications and in the broadsheet and tabloid press, and her weddings are featured in bridal and celebrity magazines. She brings her reputation for excellence to her current position as the official wedding planner for Visit Scotland.

8. Harriette Rose Katz   Harriette Rose Katz Events/Gourmet Advisory Services was established more than 25 years ago and is one of America's leading wedding planners. Celebrity wedding clients have included William Baldwin and Chynna Phillips, and Donny Deutsch. Katz is known within the industry as a trendsetter and is one of today's most respected event designers. She was named the "Number One Wedding Planner in Manhattan" by *New York Metro* and is quoted frequently in leading lifestyle publications, including the *New York Times, Quest, Modern Bride, InStyle, Brides, People,* the *Daily News,* the *New York Post,* and *The Robb Report.* Her expertise was documented on the Discovery Channel on a show about the ultimate wedding.

Katz has also served as president and chief operating officer of the Confrérie de la Chaîne des Rôtisseurs, one of the world's most prestigious food and wine organizations, which originated in France in 1248. She has received that organization's Gold Star of Excellence.

9. Romona Keveza   After receiving a university degree in fine arts and business, Romona Keveza opened specialty stores in Canada and Washington, D.C., selling designer ready-to-wear to high-profile clients, including Jacqueline Kennedy Onassis. Her success in this business led her to create a line of couture bridal gowns, many of which have appeared on the covers of magazines such as *Town and Country,* the *United Kingdom's Brides, Elegant Bride, Manhattan Bride,* and *The Knot.* Her work has also been featured in *InStyle, Martha Stewart Weddings, Modern Bride,* and *Bridal Guide,* as well as in many other publications. Keveza is a three-time winner of the prestigious Couture Bridal Award for "Classic Designer of the Year."

> "A wedding is many things. Foremost, it is a rite of passage, an end and a beginning, a fulfillment and a promise."
> — Martha Stewart

10. Abigail Kirsch   Abigail Kirsch has been providing culinary excellence in wedding catering for over 30 years. She has been the tristate (New York, New Jersey, and Connecticut) region's most trusted caterer and wedding planner, having orchestrated thousands of weddings.

Trained at the Culinary Institute of America and Le Cordon Bleu in Paris, she is the current president of the New York chapter of Les Dames d'Escoffier. She is the coauthor of *The Bride and Groom's First Cookbook* (1996).

11. Sharon Naylor   Sharon Naylor is the author of more than 30 wedding planning books, including *The Complete Outdoor Wedding Planner, The New Honeymoon Planner, How to Plan an Elegant Wedding in Six Months or Less, The Ultimate Bridal Shower Idea Book,* and *How to Have an Elegant Wedding for $10,000 or Less.* She is a member of the highly prestigious Association of Bridal Consultants (ABC) and is currently the wedding Q&A specialist at NJWedding.com and PashWeddings.com. She has been featured in *Wedding Bells* magazine, *Ritz Carlton Weddings, InStyle Weddings, Bride and Groom,* and *Vows.*

Naylor has been a guest on numerous television programs and has been featured on *The View*'s website. Her podcast "Here Come the Moms" appears on WeddingPodcastNetwork.com.

12. Jenny Packham   This British designer was honored as "Hollywood Style Designer of the Year 2006" and "British Bridal Dress Designer of the Year 2007." Some of her high-profile clients have included Mary J. Blige, Alicia Keys, Keira Knightley, Nelly Furtado, Eva Longoria, Sarah Jessica Parker, and Beyonce. Packham's designs have appeared in the films *The Devil Wears Prada, Casino Royale,* and *Die Another Day,* as well as on television's *Sex and the City.*

13. Claire Pettibone   This Los Angeles–based designer has been featured in *InStyle Weddings, Brides, Inside Weddings, Bridal Guide,* and many other magazines. Her gowns combine a vintage look with a modern feel. She designed a gown for the bride of Joey Fatone of 'N Sync and the gown for Jessica's on-air wedding to Dr. Diamond on *Beverly Hills 90210.*

14. Sasha Souza Sasha Souza Events was founded in 1995, specializing in full-service wedding and event design. Today Souza is a renowned bridal consultant and a distinguished member of the Association of Bridal Consultants. Her clients include Amy Acker and James Carpinello, "Ferocious" Fernando Vargas (world champion boxer), mega-producer Todd Wagner, and actress Dayna Devon.

In 2004, Souza was honored by *Modern Bride* magazine as one of the top 25 trendsetters in the wedding industry. She is also a member of the *Modern Bride* advisory panel and has been a featured event planner on the Style Network TV show *Whose Wedding Is It, Anyway?*

15. Martha Stewart Since 1987, when *Martha Stewart Weddings* was first published, the doyenne of design has represented the crème de la crème in weddings. And you can't copy her stuff: Martha's weddings are often punctuated with flowers that she has grown herself and one-of-a-kind antique table accessories. (She grows the strawberries for her own strawberry butter.) Yet through her books, TV shows, magazines, and general media presence, she inspires wedding design for everything from a backyard barbecue to a party for 200 aboard a yacht—and she's done them both. Nobody does it better.

16. Pnina Tornai Tornai is one of Israel's leading bridal wear designers and the creator of a unique corset that is said to give the wearer the best figure possible. All her gowns are handmade and feature the finest European materials. A favorite dress designer among Israeli celebrities, Tornai has expanded her business to include clients in New York, Los Angeles, Miami, and Cyprus.

17. David Tutera Award-winning design expert David Tutera is a world-famous trendsetter and leading creative force in the wedding and party planning industry. In Manhattan, he has planned events for J-Lo, the Rolling Stones, Elton John, and Al Gore, among others. Tutera also has his own TV show, *The Party Planner,* on the Discovery Home Channel.

Tutera was honored in 2006 by *Modern Bride* magazine as one of the "Top 25 Trendsetters of the Year." He is also a contributing expert on TV's *The View* and was the creative force behind Star Jones's wedding.

In January 2007, the Disney Corporation hired Tutera to design a new line of celebrity-style weddings for its resorts. The results were Disney's Couture Wedding Collection by David Tutera, which offers brides a choice between the "Whimsical Garden," "Cocktail Soiree," "Classic Elegance," and "Simply Chic" weddings.

18. Sylvia Weinstock Known as "the Queen of Cakes" and "the Leonardo da Vinci of Cake Design," Sylvia Weinstock's creations are designed and created according to the exact specifications of her clients, who include Donald Trump, Mariah Carey, Whitney Houston, Michael Douglas, Liza Minnelli, Bryant Gumbel, and the Saudi royal family. Weinstock creates more than 500 cakes a year. She's done a Leaning Tower of Pisa, a bust of Picasso, and cakes that are as tall as 12 feet and feed as many as 5,000 people. She is the author of *Sweet Celebrations: The Art of Decorating Beautiful Cakes* (1999).

19. Mindy Weiss Weiss is one of the most sought-after event planners and lifestyle experts in the United States. Known for her creative and unusual ideas, she has a bubbly personality and calm demeanor that have made her the top choice for celebrities. She has created weddings for Trista and Ryan of *The Bachelorette* TV show, Shaunie and Shaquille O'Neal, Jessica Simpson and Nick Lachey, Gwen Stefani and Gavin Rossdale, Jackie and Adam Sandler, and Heidi Klum and Seal.

In May 2005, *Modern Bride* voted Weiss one of its "Top 25 Trendsetters." She is also the style expert for Weddingchannel.com and has been featured on a variety of television shows and networks, including *Dr. Phil, E!, Entertainment Tonight, MTV, The Today Show,* and the Learning Channel.

Mindy and her events have been featured in *Brides, Elegant Bride, InStyle, InStyle Weddings,* the *Los Angeles Times, L.A. Confidential, Martha Stewart, Modern Bride,* the *New York Times, O, the Oprah* magazine, *People, Real Simple, Town and Country, U.S. Weekly,* and the *Wall Street Journal.*

18 Prenups of the Rich and Famous

1. **John Jacob Astor** was among the world's wealthiest men in his day. At age 47, the divorced Astor married an 18-year-old girl named Madeleine. Both were onboard the *Titanic* when it went down. Astor died, but Madeleine escaped in a life raft. Astor had established a prenup agreement with Madeleine to protect his children's inheritance. Madeleine received only $1.7 million, although that was still a great amount of money at the time.

2. **Jacqueline Bouvier Kennedy** married Greek shipping tycoon **Aristotle Onassis** on October 20, 1968. The couple remained married until Onassis's death in 1975. After Jackie's lawyers contested the prenuptial agreement between them, she was awarded $26 million in an out-of-court settlement.

3. After **Donald** and **Ivana Trump** announced their plans to divorce, they ended up in court battling over their prenup. Ivana was awarded $14 million in cash, $350,000 in annual alimony, and $300,000 per year for the support of their three children. She was also awarded their 45-room mansion in Greenwich, Connecticut, and their apartment in Trump Plaza. As part of the settlement, Ivana agreed not to discuss her life with Donald without his permission.

4. Hotelier **Leona Helmsley**, also known as "the Queen of Mean," was accused of violating the terms of her prenuptial agreement and trying to gain control of her husband's estate by selling off nearly $2 billion of his real estate holdings.

5. Actor **William Hurt**'s second wife, **Heidi Henderson**, specified in their prenuptial agreement that Hurt, a recovering alcoholic, would have his alimony payments increased if he relapsed into his drinking habit.

6. Seventy-seven-year-old Washington Redskins owner **Jack Kent Cooke** married 37-year-old **Marlena Remallo Chalmers**, but Marlena's subsequent behavior embarrassed him and Cooke wrote her out of his will. Their prenup agreement protected his nearly $900 million estate. Marlena had to settle for a mere $20 million.

7. *Playboy* publisher **Hugh Hefner** and **Kimberly Conrad** signed a prenup before they strutted down the aisle on July 1, 1989. As of this writing, Hef, age 80, is planning another marriage to 27-year-old Holly Madison and is planning another prenup. This will be Hef's third marriage.

The Ultimate May-December Romance

In May 2006, **Muhamad Noor Che Musa,** a 33-year-old man from northern Malaysia, married **Wook Kundor, 104.** It was his first marriage and her 21st. According to *The Star,* a Malaysian-language newspaper, the groom insisted that he had found peace and contentment when they first met, and that their love eventually blossomed out of friendship and respect. Musa felt compassion for Wook because she was poor, had no children, and was all alone.

The report did not say whether any of Wook's previous 20 husbands were still alive.

5 of the World's Longest Marriages

1. The longest marriage ever recorded was between Sit Temulji Nairman and his wife Lady Nariman, who were married at the age of 5. The marriage lasted for 86 years.

2. According to the *Guinness Book of World Records,* the title of the world's longest marriage goes to Liu Yung-yang, 103, and his wife Yang Wan, 102, from Taoyuan, northern Taiwan. They were married in April 1917 and remained married for 85 years.

3. According to *The Farmer's Almanac,* the record-breaking duo was a New England couple. Lazarus Rowe and Molly Webber married in 1743 when both were 18. Their marriage lasted 86 years.

4. One of the world's longest marriages was between Percy Arrowsmith, age 105, and his wife Florence, age 100. The British couple celebrated their 80th anniversary on June 1, 2005. The Arrowsmiths also hold the record of the oldest combined ages of a married couple. Percy claimed that the secret to his long marriage were two phrases: "Yes, dear," and "I'm sorry."

5. In 2006, 104-year-old Huang Fu and his 100-year-old wife Gan claimed that they had been married for 83 years. The Chinese couple married when Huang was 21 and Gan was 17.

8. **Michael Douglas** and **Catherine Zeta-Jones** signed a detailed prenuptial agreement after he was forced to pay $40 million as a financial settlement to his ex-wife Diandra.

9. Argentinean bombshell **Shakira** is making her fiancé, Argentine lawyer **Antonio de la Rua**, sign a prenuptial agreement renouncing his right to any of her fortune if they divorce. The couple, at the time of this writing, are still engaged but have not as yet wed.

10. Before **Britney Spears** married her now ex-husband **Kevin Federline**, she had her lawyers draw up a prenuptial agreement that reportedly awards him only $300,000 of her estimated $100 million in assets in case of divorce.

11. Tennis ace **Andre Agassi** and actress **Brooke Shields** took two years to work out their prenup agreement after announcing their engagement. The marriage lasted for just about that same length of time. Agassi also had a prenup drawn up before his second marriage to former Wimbledon champ **Steffi Graf**.

12. Famed film director **Steven Spielberg** and actress **Amy Irving** met in 1979 and were married in 1985. When Spielberg left Irving to marry actress **Kate Capshaw**, Irving's attorneys had the prenup thrown out, and Irving was awarded a staggering $100 million.

13. **John F. Kennedy Jr.** dated **Madonna**, **Cindy Crawford**, and **Daryl Hannah** before marrying **Carolyn Bessette**. The couple had a prenup agreement before their marriage on September 21, 1996. Tragically, the couple died in a plane crash in 1999.

14. In 2006, Revlon chairman and billionaire **Ronald Perelman** and actress **Ellen Barkin** made headlines when they put money before love by agreeing to a prenup. When their marriage ended, Barkin was awarded $40 million.

15. **Tom Cruise** and **Katie Holmes** signed a prenuptial agreement that ensures that Katie will receive $3 million a year for 11 years should the couple divorce.

16. **Brad Pitt** and **Angelina Jolie** settled on a $200 million prenup that will secure the future of their six children (as of this writing) and lays down the division of their real estate.

17. **Nicole Kidman** and **Keith Urban** finalized a prenup agreement in which Kidman agreed to pay Urban $600,000 for every year the couple stays married. Reports are that she is worth somewhere in the neighborhood of $150 million. The agreement also stipulates that if Urban begins using cocaine or drinks excessively, the prenup is void.

18. **Eric Benet Jordan**, the estranged husband of Oscar-winning film actress **Halle Berry**, challenged their prenuptial agreement in court and was awarded a $4 million home. In addition, Berry agreed to pay Eric $20,000 a month in support and will pay for his legal fees.

5 of the World's Oldest Newlywed Couples

1. On February 2, 2002, François Fernandez, a 96-year-old widower, and Madeleine Francineau, a 94-year-old divorcée, became the world's oldest newlyweds when they were married in Clapiers, France. The couple had met five years earlier when Madeleine asked François to repair her garlic press. François said he would do so in exchange for a kiss. The ceremony took place in the nursing home in which they were living. They hold the *Guinness Book of World Records* title as the world's oldest newlyweds.

2. On May 27, 2007, Harold Bentzien, age 100, and Madonna Marshall, age 81, became the oldest couple to tie the knot in San Diego's history. One of the flower girls was Harold's great-granddaughter, and one of Madonna's middle-aged sons gave her away at the altar.

3. Felicja Kubacka and Jozef Mucha were born on the same day, in the same month, in the same year. They met in a community home in Zielona Gora, Poland. They fell in love and were married at age 90, becoming Poland's oldest newlyweds.

4. Hugues Cuénod, the world's oldest living tenor, was 105 when he and his partner, Alfred Augustin, 64, a retired Swiss civil servant, were married in a civil ceremony after Swiss law changed to allow same-sex unions.

5. When 96-year-old Raymond Robson married 90-year-old Faye Webber, they became one of the world's oldest couples to tie the knot. They had met at a residential home in Berkshire, England, in 2006. Although Raymond could not get down on one knee, Faye was thrilled by the proposal and accepted immediately. The wedding was attended by 120 guests, including 16 grandchildren and great-grandchildren.

The Bridezilla Hall of Fame

The Bridezilla Hall of Fame is "the product of a bridal magazine overdose on an otherwise boring day at the office," says Bridezilla.com editor in chief Jade Nirvana Ingmire. This rousing postfeminist list is but a taste of the tongue-in-chic wedding advice offered on the website.

• **Beatrix Kiddo in Quentin Tarantino's *Kill Bill*** This bride's got killer instincts, and we don't blame her. How could we not feel sympathy for someone whose cold killing spree is aimed at those who allegedly killed her baby, almost killed her, and got blood on her ultra-expensive wedding dress?

• **The Bride of Chucky** Topping our list of the most misunderstood brides of all time is definitely the Bride of Chucky. She brings Chucky back to life. He totally blows her off. Despite being brutally rebuffed by the evil Chucky, this cute little doll is surprisingly mild in her retaliation. The Bride of Chucky, like so many bridezillas, is not a devil but just a woman driven by desperate love, now doomed unfairly as a villain for all eternity.

• ***Jane Eyre*'s Bertha Mason, aka "the Mad Woman in the Attic"** Bertha married Mr. Rochester in good faith. He locked her in the attic and "took up" with the nanny. This would-be bridezilla is described in the book as notably beautiful and kind enough to leave her family and the lure of tropical drinks in the West Indies to come romp with Mr. Rochester for all eternity in his mildewed, drafty Victorian manor. Hardly a fair trade if you ask us!

• **Lady Macbeth** Despite the fact that her husband is the one who commits all the murders at her mere constructive suggestion, Lady Macbeth is blamed and hated by all. Sure, Lady Macbeth gets portrayed as a cruel dominatrix, bridezilla of all bridezillas, but deep down she is just a good ole housewife, concerned with her inability to remove tough stains and get a good night's sleep. I mean, how many women do you know who are so dedicated to good housekeeping they would commit suicide over their inability to get "out damn spots"?

• **Jack Spratt's Wife** She wanted Big Macs, he wanted broccoli. No wonder she was upset. We've all heard of the poor Ms. Spratt, who lived on Atkins and was doomed to a cellulite existence while her spry husband of the gazelle-like metabolism was perfectly happy on a permanent diet of lean foods. We seek to clear poor Lady Spratt's name by saying she was probably just suffering from food cravings, and the cruel Jack should have had the common decency to engage in sympathy eating, which is in fact the very definition of true love.

• ***Great Expectation*'s Miss Havisham** Everyone says she is a mental case, but really she is just highly monogamous. Okay, so this misunderstood bride keeps her cobwebbed wedding cake out and won't take down any of her decorations after she's left at the altar. Some people think this is raving mad. We think it's romantic. And while people think she was loony for flitting around in a faded wedding dress, we know she was really just a forerunner of the "you-can-wear-it-again" movement. The real villain is the guy who jilted her on her wedding day.

• **Camilla Parker Bowles** She saw him first! Okay, we are as big a Lady Di fan as anyone else, but poor Camilla really did get the shaft. Elegant and graceful, Camilla demurely waited another 25 years before marrying Charles. Congrats to Camilla for redefining the bridezilla "other woman" stereotype. You are most misunderstood indeed!

• **Ursula the Sea Witch in *The Little Mermaid*** She's just using her assets to catch her man. Ariel wanted Eric and would do anything to get to him. So would Ursula. Eventually, both women deceive and disguise themselves in order to try and win the prince's love. So what if Ursula just happens to be better at it than the dim-witted, utensil-impaired Ariel? For the simple crime of impersonating a more beautiful woman to marry the handsome prince Eric, Ursula is not only jilted at the altar, her lover harpoons her through the heart.

> "Whatever you may look like, marry a man your own age — as your beauty fades, so will his eyesight."
>
> — Phyllis Diller

A History of Weddings in Las Vegas

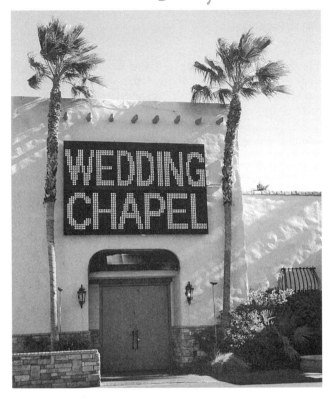

- In 1931, Nevada was a large patch of dry desert land with one of the smallest resident-per-acre ratios in the country. Prohibition was in full swing, and police in the two main centers of population, Reno and Las Vegas, were cracking down on the speakeasies. At that time, ranching and the railroads were two of the largest industries in the state, and railroads were fast losing ground to the automobile.

- That year, however, the Nevada state legislature relegalized gambling (it had been outlawed in 1910, though underground clubs continued to operate) and relaxed the state marriage and divorce laws, dramatically altering the future of Nevada in general and the town of Las Vegas in particular. The new laws changed the residency requirements for divorce from three months to six weeks and allowed a couple to marry with nothing more than the payment of a license fee—no waiting time, no blood tests.

- Around the city of Reno, locals began to open "divorce ranches"—renting accommodations to people waiting to establish residency to get a quickie divorce. Famous fighter Jack Dempsey divorced his wife Estelle Taylor in Nevada that year. And while Reno became the place to end a marriage, Las Vegas became the place to begin one. The combination of Nevada's romantic last-of-the-Old-West atmosphere, legalized gambling, and easy marriage and divorce laws was irresistible to another relatively new American phenomenon—the Hollywood celebrity.

- In December of 1931, two of Hollywood's hottest properties were married in Las Vegas in a hush-hush late-night ceremony. The judge was sworn to secrecy because the bride-to-be, silent film star Clara Bow, was on the verge of a nervous breakdown from enduring years of relentless media pursuit.

- The little desert oasis of Las Vegas grew in popularity, especially after prohibition was repealed at the end of 1933. Then, in the 1940s, two small chapels were built near the Fremont Street area. These chapels were located for convenience and designed for quick, quaint, quiet weddings. The Wee Kirk O' the Heather is today the oldest continually running wedding chapel in Las Vegas, having opened its doors in 1940. The Little Chapel of the West, opened in 1942, has seen perhaps the largest number of celebrity weddings in Las Vegas history.

- In June of 1931, the deputy county clerk recorded that a record 117 marriage license applications had been processed that month. Today the marriage license bureau often processes that many applications in a single day. Today Las Vegas is the destination of choice for kitschy couples both famous and not. Few marriages, however, endure like that of Clara Bow and Rex Bell. The couple remained married until Bell's death in 1963, while he was running for governor of Nevada.

> "There's only one way to have a happy marriage, and as soon as I learn what it is I'll get married again."
> — Clint Eastwood

37 Celebrity Vegas Weddings

Almost 120,000 souls get hitched in Las Vegas annually, and it's no surprise that some of our favorite celebs are part of that big love-in. Thanks to Vegas.com, the most comprehensive website on the subject, for this list.

1. **Pamela Anderson and Rick Salomon, October 6, 2007** Former *Baywatch* babe Pamela Anderson slipped away from her role as Hans Klok's magician's assistant at Planet Hollywood to wed the other star of Paris Hilton's sex tape, Rick Salomon, in one of the private villas at the Mirage Hotel and Casino. The courtship was brief, involving poker debts and "sexual favors," according to the 40-year-old *Playboy* Playmate and mother of two. The marriage was also brief, ending in an annulment just two months later, with both parties citing fraud as the reason.

2. **Kevin Dillon and Jane Stuart, April 22, 2006** Even Hollywood stars can't resist an Elvis Presley impersonator at their wedding. *Entourage* star Kevin Dillon married model-actress Jane Stuart in a Vegas Wedding Chapel ceremony that included several serenades by "Elvis." That day, Dillon also had his own "entourage" present—costar Jerry Ferrara was Dillon's best man, while fellow cast member Kevin Connolly walked Stuart down the aisle.

3. **Nicky Hilton and Todd Andrew Meister, August 15, 2004** Fashion designer Nicky Hilton wed money manager Todd Andrew Meister at the Vegas Wedding Chapel at 2:30 A.M. Tabloid princess Paris Hilton and gal-pal actress Bijou Phillips were present to witness the early-morning ceremony. It was reported that Paris's dog Tinkerbell wore a tiara and carried the ring pillow. The marriage ended after less than two months.

4. **Leah Remini and Angelo Pagan, July 19, 2003** After dating her real *King of Queens* sweetheart for seven (lucky) years, funny gal Leah Remini wed actor Angelo Pagan at Bellagio Hotel's beautiful poolside. VH1's *(Inside)Out* filmed a documentary of the event.

5. **Angelina Jolie and Billy Bob Thornton, May 5, 2000** With a visible "Billy Bob" tattoo on her upper arm, Angelina Jolie wed *Pushing Tin* costar Billy Bob Thornton in a 20-minute ceremony at the Little Church of the West. The couple were known to wear vials of each other's blood around their necks, and both wore blue jeans for the ceremony.

6. **Dennis Rodman and Carmen Electra, November 15, 1998** Colorful Chicago Bulls basketball star Dennis Rodman married *Baywatch* actress Carmen Electra, whose real name is Tara Patrick, at A Little Chapel of the Flowers. Rodman reportedly tried to have the marriage annulled, claiming he was drunk at the ceremony; Electra countered that Rodman's comments had been taken out of context and that they were truly in love. Whatever the case, the couple divorced five months later.

7. **Mark Consuelos and Kelly Ripa, May 1, 1996** Will it last? Tune in tomorrow. When both were stars on *All My Children,* Mark Consuelos and Kelly Ripa married in a touching ceremony at what the couple refer to as the "Chapel of Cheese" (the actual name escapes them).

8. **Rich Little and Jeannette Markey, October 29, 1994** Master impressionist Rich Little married Jeannette Markey at the MGM Grand Hotel and Casino.

9. **Richard Gere and Cindy Crawford, December 12, 1991** Actor Richard Gere married supermodel Cindy Crawford in 1991, beginning a whirlwind, four-year media campaign that went something like this: no, Richard is not gay. They divorced in 1995.

10. **Michael Jordan and Juanita Vanoy, September 2, 1989** Basketball legend Michael Jordan wed Juanita Vanoy in Vegas in 1989.

11. **Jon Bon Jovi and Dorothea Hurley, April 29, 1989** He may give love a bad name on paper, but not in practice. In 1989, fluffy-hair rock star and budding actor Jon Bon Jovi married Dorothea Hurley at the Graceland Wedding Chapel.

12. **Lorenzo Lamas and Kathleen Kinmont Smith, January 21, 1989** Following in his father's footsteps (his parents had tied the knot here in 1954), Lorenzo Lamas wed Kathleen Kinmont Smith at the Graceland Wedding Chapel.

13. **Dudley Moore and Brogan Lane, February 21, 1988** Dudley "Arthur" Moore married makeup artist Brogan Lane at Little Church of the West.

> "I'm the only man who has a marriage license made out, 'To Whom It May Concern.'"
> — Mickey Rooney

14. **Bob Geldof and Paula Yates, June 21, 1986** Shortly after his *Live Aid* support efforts for Ethiopia—a crusade that earned him a knighthood—former Boomtown Rats singer Bob Geldof wed Paula Yates at the Little Church of the West.

15. **Robert Goulet and Vera Chochorovska Novak, 1982** After their ceremony, the newlyweds rode in a horse-drawn surrey down the Strip. The reception was held at the Dunes Hotel and Casino and was attended by 1,200 guests, some of whom could even pronounce the bride's middle name.

16. **David Cassidy and Kay Lenz, April 1977** Singer and former teen heartthrob David Cassidy and actress Kay Lenz were married at the Little Church of the West.

17. **Wayne Newton and Elaine Okamura, June 1968** Wayne Newton, 26, married former airline stewardess Elaine Okamura at the Flamingo Hotel.

18. **Leslie Ann Warren and Jon Peters, May 1967** Actress Leslie Ann Warren married her hairdresser, Jon Peters, at the Sahara Hotel and Casino. Warren would go on to be a successful film star, and Peters became a successful producer, pulling the purse strings on *Rain Man,* Tim Burton's *Batman,* the Barbra Streisand remake of *A Star Is Born,* and others.

19. **Ann-Margret and Roger Smith, May 1967** Ann-Margret of *Viva Las Vegas* fame and Roger Smith, who starred in television's *77 Sunset Strip,* were married by District Judge John Mowbray at the Riviera. The hotel's manager and the public relations director served as witnesses to the wedding.

20. **Elvis Presley and Priscilla Ann Beaulieu, May 1, 1967** Elvis Presley, 32, reportedly the highest-paid entertainer in the world, married Priscilla Ann Beaulieu, 21, at Milton Prell's Aladdin Hotel. It was the first marriage for both. The couple was wed in a quiet ceremony that was attended by a few relatives and close friends, and an elaborate banquet followed. An estimated 100 guests attended the reception. State Supreme Court Justice David Zenoff performed the eight-minute ceremony.

21. **Xavier Cugat and Charo, August 7, 1966** Latin music king Xavier Cugat and singer Charo were the first couple to exchange vows at Caesar's Palace. Cugat had discovered Charo—whose birth name is María Rosario Pilar Martínez Molina Baeza—performing in Spain in a production of *Night of the Iguana.* She went on to bring a little "coochie, coochie" into the lives of millions.

22. **Frank Sinatra and Mia Farrow, July 19, 1966** Ol' Blue Eyes had as sure a way with the "dolls" as he had with ballads. Frank Sinatra married actress Mia Farrow at the Sands, practically Sinatra's second home for the better part of a decade. They divorced in 1968.

23. **Judy Garland and Mark Herron, 1965** Actress and singer Judy Garland married Mark Herron at the Little Church of the West, then located just over the rainbow.

24. **Jane Fonda and Roger Vadim, August 14, 1965** Jane Fonda and director-producer Roger Vadim were married in Vegas. The reception was held at the Dunes.

25. **Betty White and Allen Ludden, 1963** *Golden Girl* actress Betty White married Allen Ludden, host of television's *Password* and *Liar's Club,* at the Sands Hotel and Casino.

26. **Mary Tyler Moore and Grant Tinker, 1962** Mary Tyler Moore married then-NBC vice president Grant Tinker, a full eight years before Tinker and Moore produced *The Mary Tyler Moore Show* on CBS and Moore turned the world on with her smile.

27. **Billy Martin and Gretchen Winkler, 1959** Under an arch knitted from Louisville Sluggers, Cleveland Indian second baseman and eventual New York Yankees manager and whipping boy Billy Martin married Gretchen Winkler at the Desert Inn. George Steinbrenner wasn't at the reception, thank God.

28. **Paul Newman and Joanne Woodward, January 29, 1958** Movie stars Paul Newman and Joanne Woodward were married at the El Rancho Hotel and Casino. They remained married for 50 years, until Newman's death in 2008. Said Newman of his professional collaborations with his wife: "You should see us when we get back to the bedroom."

29. **Steve Lawrence and Eydie Gorme, December 29, 1957** Steve Lawrence and Eydie Gorme were married at the home of Beldon Katleman in Las Vegas. Katleman was then the owner of the El Rancho Hotel and Casino. Steve and Eydie continue to perform to packed houses as a husband-and-wife team.

30. **Carol Channing and Charles Lowe, July 1956** Broadway star Carol Channing married Las Vegas advertising and television executive Charles Lowe at a ceremony in Boulder City.

31. **Joan Crawford and Alfred Steele, May 1955** Clothes-hanger fetishist Joan Crawford and Alfred Steele, then chairman of the board of Pepsi-Cola, were married at the Flamingo Hotel and Casino.

32. **Fernando Lamas and Arlene Dahl, June 1954** Fernando Lamas and Arlene Dahl were married at the Little Church of the West. They divorced in 1960; nine years later, he married water-logged actress Esther Williams.

33. **Kirk Douglas and Anne Buydens, May 28, 1954** He was Spartacus, he was Vincent Van Gogh, he was master harpooner Ned Land—but all he wanted was to be loved. Kirk Douglas married Parisian Anne Buydens at the Sahara, and they remain married to this day.

34. **Dick Haymes and Rita Hayworth, September 24, 1953** The Sands Hotel and Casino was host to the wedding of singer Dick Haymes and Hollywood actress Rita Hayworth. They were married two years, then divorced. Previous to that, Hayworth had been married to Prince Ali Khan and Orson Welles.

35. **Zsa Zsa Gabor and George Sanders, 1949** Dahling, Zsa Zsa Gabor married actor George Sanders—best known today as the voice of the murderous tiger Shere Khan in Disney's *Jungle Book*—at the Little Church of the West.

36. **Mickey Rooney and Betty Jane Rase, 1944** One should hope he got a buy-one-get-one-free coupon or something. Mickey "Let's Put on a Show" Rooney married Betty Jane Rase at Little Church of the West. He would visit the church six more times, each time with a different blushing bride: Martha Vickers in 1949, Elaine Mahnken in 1952, Barbara Ann Thompson in 1958, Marge Lane in 1967, Carolyn Hockett in 1969, and January Chamberlin in 1978.

37. **Betty Grable and Harry James, 1943** Actress and original "pinup girl" Betty Grable married bandleader-trumpeter Harry James at the Little Church of the West.

8 Celebrity Couples Who Got Married in Las Vegas's Graceland Chapel

The Graceland Chapel, a simple Las Vegas wedding locale, has become an internationally celebrated wedding site. It's the home of the original Elvis wedding, and countless celebrity couples have walked down its aisle. If "Loving You" is more appealing than the traditional wedding march, visit gracelandchapel.com. The chapel is located at 619 Las Vegas Boulevard South, Las Vegas, Nevada 89101. Call 800-824-5732 or, in Las Vegas, 382-0091.

You'll be following in these footsteps.

1. Rocker Jon Bon Jovi
2. Ritchie Scarlet of the Ace Frehley rock band
3. Country music star Billy Ray Cyrus
4. Aaron Neville of the R&B-soul Neville Brothers band
5. Blane and Robert Trump
6. Roger Glover of the rock band Deep Purple
7. Late-night television talk-show host Jay Leno
8. The authors of this book, who renewed their vows at the chapel on the occasion of their 25th wedding anniversary

Graceland Wedding Chapel COURTESY OF THE GRACELAND WEDDING CHAPEL

7 Big Weddings, 7 Big Divorces

Here's proof that the perfect wedding doesn't necessarily lead to the perfect marriage.

1. **Mariah Carey and Tommy Mottola** In 1993, Mariah Carey married the head of Sony Music, Tommy Mottola. The wedding, held at Manhattan's St. Thomas Episcopal Church, was a large-scale affair with luminaries such as Barbra Streisand, Bruce Springsteen, Robert De Niro, and Billy Joel in attendance. The wedding was reputed to have set Mottola back $500,000.

The couple separated in 1997 and were divorced a year later.

2. **Eddie Murphy and Nicole Mitchell** Eddie and Nicole were married on March 18, 1993, at the Grand Ballroom of the Plaza Hotel in New York City. Quincy Jones, Stevie Wonder, James Brown, Queen Latifah, Sugar Ray Leonard, Bill Murray, Prince, Chris Rock, and Donald Trump were among the 500 guests in attendance. It has been reported that the Plaza's Grand Ballroom was recarpeted in white for the $1.5 million affair.

The couple split in August 2005 and divorced in April 2006.

3. **Liza Minnelli and David Gest** The wedding of Liza Minnelli to David Gest took place on March 16, 2002, and was held at Manhattan's Marble Collegiate Church. Pop legend Michael Jackson escorted longtime friend Elizabeth Taylor to this glitzy affair. Taylor was Minnelli's matron of honor, and Jackson was Gest's best man. The star-studded gala featured performances by Al Green, Luther Vandross, the Pointer Sisters, Dionne Warwick, Ashford and Simpson, and Little Anthony and the Imperials. The wedding was reputed to have cost $3.5 million.

The couple split 16 months later.

4. **Marc Anthony and Dayanara Torres** The couple was originally married in Las Vegas on May 9, 2000, in a simple ceremony attended by just a few friends and family. However, when they renewed their vows in San Juan, Puerto Rico, on December 7, 2002, no expense was spared. During the reception, which had a Moroccan theme, a seven-course feast was served. 'N Sync's Lance Bass and Backstreet Boy Howie D performed. The wedding reputedly cost $500,000.

The couple separated in October 2003 and were divorced in 2004. Mark married Jennifer Lopez just a few days after the divorce was finalized.

5. **Jennifer Aniston and Brad Pitt** The couple married on July 29, 2000, at TV producer Marcy Carsey's Malibu mansion. Cameron Diaz, Courteney Cox, and Matthew Perry were among the 200 guests present. The wedding, which set the couple back $1 million, featured 50,000 flowers, a gospel choir, four bands, and fireworks. Lobster and champagne were in abundance, and Pitt reportedly shelled out an additional $100,000 for security. The couple divorced five years later in 2005.

6. **Paul McCartney and Heather Mills** The wedding between music legend Paul McCartney and Heather Mills took place on June 11, 2002, at St. Salvador's Church in Monaghan, Ireland. Approximately 300 guests, including Ringo Starr, Elton John, and Eric Clapton, attended the Indian-themed party, which featured dancers in authentic Indian dress and a vegetarian feast. Fireworks topped off the night. The wedding set Paul back $3 million.

In 2008 the British courts awarded Heather Mills a divorce settlement of $48.6 million.

7. **Tori Spelling and Charlie Shanian** Spelling and Shanian were wed on July 3, 2004. They had an outdoor wedding on the grounds of Aaron Spelling's estate. The food at the reception was prepared by renowned chef Wolfgang Puck. Over 400 guests, including Bob Newhart, Jason Priestly, and Joan Collins, attended the $1 million affair. A canopy of white balloons was used to prevent paparazzi and circling helicopters from intruding on the wedding.

The couple were legally divorced in 2006.

> "Love: a temporary insanity, curable by marriage."
> — Ambrose Bierce

> "Always get married early in the morning. That way, if it doesn't work out, you haven't wasted a whole day."
> — Mickey Rooney

When Oprah Met Deepak: 23 Unions That Never Were

1. If Oprah Winfrey married Deepak Chopra, she'd be Oprah Chopra.

2. If Yoko Ono married Sonny Bono, she'd be Yoko Ono Bono.

3. If Dolly Parton married Salvador Dali, she'd be Dolly Dali.

4. If Bo Derek married Don Ho, she'd be Bo Ho.

5. If Cher married U2's Bono, she'd be Cher.

6. If Ella Fitzgerald married Darth Vader, she'd be Ella Vader.

7. If Boog Powell married Felipe Alou, he'd be Boog Alou.

8. If Cat Stevens married Snoop Doggy Dogg, he'd be Cat Doggy Dogg.

Celebrities with the Most Marriages

And the award for the most marriages goes to . . .

1. **Zsa Zsa Gabor**, film star and television celebrity: married 9 times

2. **Elizabeth Taylor**, actress: married 8 times

3. **Lana Turner**, actress: married 8 times

4. **Joseph Stephen Crane**, actor and restaurateur: married 8 times

5. **Artie Shaw**, jazz musician and composer: married 8 times

6. **Mickey Rooney**, film legend: married 8 times

7. **Robert Evans**, film producer: married 7 times

8. **Jerry Lee Lewis**, rock 'n' roll legend: married 6 times

9. **Billy Bob Thornton**, actor: married 5 times

10. **Joan Collins**, actress and author: married 5 times

11. **Geena Davis**, actress: married 5 times

12. **William Shatner**, film and television star: married 4 times

13. **Liza Minnelli**, star of the Broadway stage and films: married 4 times

9. If Olivia Newton-John married Wayne Newton, then divorced him to marry Elton John, she'd be Olivia Newton-John Newton John.

10. If Sondra Locke married Elliott Ness, then divorced him to marry Herman Munster, she'd become Sondra Locke Ness Munster.

11. If Javier Lopez married Keiko the whale, and Edith Piaf married Rose Tu, the elephant, they would be Javier Keiko and Edith Tu.

12. If Bea Arthur married Sting, she'd be Bea Sting.

13. If Tuesday Weld married Hal March III, she'd be Tuesday March 3.

14. If Liv Ullman married Judge Lance Ito, then divorced him and married Jerry Mathers, she'd be Liv Ito Beaver.

15. If Snoop Doggy Dogg married Winnie the Pooh, he'd be Snoop Doggy Dogg Pooh.

16. If G. Gordon Liddy married Boutros-Boutros Ghali, then divorced him to marry Kenny G., he'd be G. Ghali G.

17. Nog (related to Quark on *Star Trek: Deep Space Nine*) has no other name, so he uses it twice when getting a marriage license. If he married Howard Hughes, and then Pamela Dare, he'd be Nog Nog Hughes Dare.

18. If Belle from *Beauty and the Beast* married Sgt. Pepper, she'd be Belle Pepper.

19. If Whoopie Goldberg married Peter Cushing, she'd be Whoopie Cushing.

20. If Jack Handy (*Saturday Night Live* writer) married Andy Capp, then married Jack Paar, then moved on to Stephen King, he'd be Jack Handy Capp Paar King.

21. If Woody Allen married Natalie Wood, divorced her and married Gregory Peck, divorced him and married Ben Hur, he'd be Woody Wood Peck Hur.

22. If Ivana Trump married, in succession, Orson Bean, King Oscar (of Norway), Louis B. Mayer, and Norbert Wiener (mathematician), she would then be Ivana Bean Oscar Mayer Wiener.

23. If Wanda Landowska married Howard Hughes, then divorced him and married Henry Kissinger, she'd be Wanda Hughes Kissinger now.

64 Celebrity Wedding Dates

1. Film legend **Elizabeth Taylor** and hotel heir **Nicky Hilton**: May 6, 1950

2. **Marilyn Monroe** and baseball legend **Joe DiMaggio**: January 14, 1954

3. **Marilyn Monroe** and playwright **Arthur Miller**: June 29, 1956, and July 1, 1956, civil and religious ceremonies, respectively

4. **Johnny Cash** and **June Carter**: March 1, 1968

5. President **George W. Bush** and **Laura Welch**: November 5, 1977

6. Comedian **Jeff Foxworthy** and **Pamela Gregg**: September 18, 1985

7. Actor **Arnold "The Governator" Schwarzenegger** and TV broadcaster **Maria Shriver**: May, 1986

8. Actors **Demi Moore** and **Bruce Willis**: November 21, 1987

9. **Elizabeth Taylor** and **Larry Fortensky**: October, 1991

10. Musician **Sting** and **Trudie Styler**: August 22, 1992

11. Actress **Jane Fonda** and media mogul **Ted Turner**: December 21, 1992

12. Film star **Julia Roberts** and country singer **Lyle Lovett**: June 27, 1993

13. Real estate mogul **Donald Trump** and former model **Marla Maples**: December 20, 1993

14. **Michael "King of Pop" Jackson** and **Lisa Marie Presley**, daughter of Elvis, the "King of Rock": May 26, 1994

15. **Michael Jackson** and former nurse **Debbie Rowe**: November 14, 1996

16. **Paula Abdul** and sportswear designer **Brad Beckerman**: February 2, 1997

17. Singer-actress **Jennifer Lopez** and chef **Ojani Noa**: February 22, 1997

18. Actress **Brooke Shields** and tennis ace **Andre Agassi**: April 19, 1997

19. Actors **Sarah Jessica Parker** and **Matthew Broderick**: May 19, 1997

20. Actor **Macaulay Culkin** and actress **Rachel Miner**: June 21, 1998

21. Singer-actress-director **Barbra Streisand** and actor **James Brolin**: July 1, 1998

22. Singer **Posh Spice** (**Victoria Adams**) and soccer star **David Beckham**: July 4, 1999

23. Actors **Courteney Cox** and **David Arquette**: June 12, 1999

24. Pop superstar-actress **Madonna** and filmmaker **Guy Ritchie**: New Year's Eve 2000

25. Actors **Angelina Jolie** and **Billy Bob Thornton**: May 5, 2000

26. Actors **Jennifer Aniston** and **Brad Pitt**: July 29, 2000

27. Actress-singer **Liza Minnelli** and **David Gest**: March 16, 2002

28. Rock/pop legend **Paul McCartney** and **Heather Mills**: June 11, 2002

29. Actress **Julia Roberts** and **Danny Moder**: July 4, 2002

30. **Lisa Marie Presley** and **Nicolas Cage**: August 12, 2002

31. Actors **Sarah Michelle Gellar** and **Freddie Prinze Jr.**: September 1, 2002

32. Rock stars **Gwen Stefani** and **Gavin Rossdale**: September 14, 2002

33. Singers **Jessica Simpson** and **Nick Lachey**: October 26, 2002

34. Rock legend **Ozzy Osbourne** and TV personality **Sharon Arden**: December 31, 2002

35. Actor-director **Edward Burns** and model **Christy Turlington**: June, 2003

36. Comic **Adam Sandler** and actress-model **Jackie Titone**: June 22, 2003

37. Rock star **Melissa Etheridge** and **Tammy Lynn Michaels**: August, 2003

38. Actress **Carmen Electra** and rocker **Dave Navarro**: November 22, 2003

39. **Trisha "The Bachelorette" Rehn** and fireman **Ryan Sutter**: December 6, 2003

40. **Mary J. Blige** and record producer **Kendu Isaacs**: December 7, 2003

41. Opera star **Luciano Pavarotti** and **Nicoletta Mantovani**: December 13, 2003

42. Singer-actress **Jennifer Lopez** and singer-actor **Marc Anthony**: June 5, 2004

43. Songwriting and singing legend **Billy Joel** and **Katie Lee**: October 2, 2004

44. Pop star **Britney Spears** and dancer **Kevin Federline**: September 18, 2004

45. Television personality **Star Jones** and banker **Al Reynolds**: November 13, 2004

46. Survivor contestants **Amber Brkich** and **Rob Mariano**: April 16, 2005

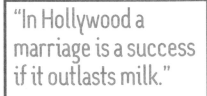

"In Hollywood a marriage is a success if it outlasts milk."

— Rita Rudner

47. Supermodel Heidi Klum and pop singer Seal: May 10, 2005

48. Actor Robert Downey Jr. and film producer Susan Levin: August 27, 2005

49. Oscar-winning actress Renée Zellweger and country crooner Kenny Chesney: May 9, 2005

50. Songstress Christina Aguilera and Jordan Bratman: November 19, 2005

51. Actor Matt Damon and Luciana Bozan: December 9, 2005

52. Country music superstars Garth Brooks and Trisha Yearwood: December 10, 2005

53. Elton John and David Furnish: December 21, 2005

54. Rocker Pink and motocross star Carey Hart: January 7, 2006

55. Tori Spelling and Dean McDermott: May 7, 2006

56. Actors Neve Campbell and John Light: May 5, 2007

57. Spice Girl Melanie Brown and Stephen Belafonte: June 6, 2007

58. Singing legend Tony Bennett and Susan Crow: June 21, 2007

59. Actress Eva Longoria and basketball star Tony Parker: July 7, 2007

60. Actor-author Steve Martin and writer Anne Springfield: July 28, 2007

61. Singer Usher and Tameka Foster: August 3, 2007

62. Actor Tobey Maguire and Jennifer Meyer: September 3, 2007

63. Actress Pamela Anderson and Paris Hilton's ex, Rick Salomon: October 6, 2007

64. Comedian/TV host Ellen DeGeneres and Portia de Rossi: August 16, 2008

Celebrity Couples with the Shortest Marriages

For some Hollywood types, getting married is easier than collecting a paycheck. The hard part seems to be staying married. It has been estimated that a celebrity marriage has only a 35 percent chance of success. Here are some couples whose fires fizzled fast.

1. Rudolph Valentino and Jean Acker: 6 hours

2. Zsa Zsa Gabor and Felipe de Alba: 1 day

3. Robin Givens and Svetozar Marinkovic: 1 day

4. Britney Spears and Jason Allen Alexander: 55 hours

5. Dennis Hopper and Michelle Phillips: 8 days

6. Cher and Gregg Allman: 9 days

7. Robert Evans and Catherine Oxenberg: 12 days

8. Eddie Murphy and Tracey Edmonds: 2 weeks

9. Darva Conger and Rick Rockwell: 3 weeks

10. Drew Barrymore and Jeremy Thomas: 29 days

11. Ernest Borgnine and Ethel Merman: 32 days

12. R. Kelly and Aaliyah: 3 months

13. Nicolas Cage and Lisa Marie Presley: 3 months, 15 days

14. Janet Jackson and James DeBarge: 4 months

15. Charlie Sheen and Donna Peele: 4 months, 24 days

16. Shannen Doherty and Ashley Hamilton: 5 months

17. Carmen Electra and Dennis Rodman: 5 months

18. Drew Barrymore and Tom Green: 5 months

19. Axl Rose and Erin Everly: 7 months

20. Elizabeth Taylor and Nicky Hilton: 8 months

21. Jennifer Lopez and Cris Judd: 8 months

22. Blink 182 drummer Travis Barker and Melissa Kennedy: 9 months

23. Jim Carrey and Lauren Holly: 9 months

24. Shannen Doherty and Richard Salomon: 9 months

25. Alyssa Milano and Cinjun Tate: 10 months, 19 days

26. Helen Hunt and Hank Azaria: 11 months

27. Mike Tyson and Robin Givens: 12 months

28. Jennifer Lopez and Ojani Noa: 13 months

29. Paula Abdul and Brad Beckerman: 17 months

30. Lisa Marie Presley and Michael Jackson: 20 months

31. Julia Roberts and Lyle Lovett: 21 months

A Wedding Dress Auction on eBay

Larry Star made eBay history when he auctioned off his ex-wife's wedding dress. Star, who said he had no idea his auction would get so much attention, started the bidding at $1. "I'm selling it hoping to get enough money for maybe a couple of Mariners tickets and some beer," he said in the auction description.

According to an eBay spokesman, this auction broke all records for the number of views, with over 6 million hits in all. The winning bid was $3,850.

13 Wedding Record Holders

1. **The Largest Wedding Banquet** On September 7, 1995, Jayalalitha Jayaram, Bollywood star and former chief minister of Tamil Nadu, India, paid for a luncheon for over 150,000 guests at the wedding of her foster son, V. N. Sudhakaran, in the state capital of Chennai, India.

2. **The Largest Underwater Wedding** On March 26, 2005, Stuart and Misty Rex set the record for the largest underwater wedding ceremony at the McMurtrey Aquatic Center in Bakersfield, California. The wedding was attended by 208 guest-divers.

3. **The World's Largest Wedding Cake** A wedding cake measuring 17 feet tall and weighing 15,032 pounds was created for the New England Bridal Showcase at Mohegan Sun Casino on February 8, 2007. This 7-tiered cake was almost 3 times the weight of the previous record holder. The cake was vanilla-flavored, and the ingredients included: 10,000 pounds of batter and nearly 5,000 pounds of frosting. The cake, which was assembled by chef Lynn Mansel and a team of 57 chefs and pastry artisans, could have fed 60,000 people.

4. **The Longest Wedding Dress Train** The longest wedding dress train in history was created by Andreas Evstratiou for her bridal shop Green Leaf in Cyprus. The dress was completed on February 18, 2007, with the train measuring slightly over 4,468 feet—just 832 feet short of a mile!

5. **The Most Marriage Vows Renewals by the Same Couple** Tennessee couple Lauren and David Blair hold the distinction of having had the most vow renewals. They married each other for the 83rd time on August 16, 2004, at the Lighthouse Lounge at the Boardwalk Hotel and Casino in Las Vegas. The couple first tied the knot in 1984. Coming in second are Richard and Carole Roble, a pair of New Yorkers, and Ralph and Patsy Martin from Arizona. Both of these couples have taken their vows 55 times, and both couples have chosen to renew their vows in a variety of locations, including all 50 states.

6. **The "World Record Wedding Video Event"** In January 2006, the Sacramento Professional Videographers Association and the Wedding and Event Videographers Association created the "World Record Wedding Video Event" to set a new world record for the

number of cameras used to professionally videotape an actual wedding ceremony. More than 100 cameras were used to film a wedding that took place at the Library Galleria in Sacramento, California, on February 15, 2006.

7. **The World's Largest Wedding Vow Renewal** On February 10, 2008, the Carnegie Museum of Art and Natural History in Pittsburgh, Pennsylvania, hosted a *Guinness Book of World Records* attempt called "Re-Union: The World's Largest Wedding Vow Renewal Ceremony." A cake and champagne reception was held after the ceremony, which was attended by 750 couples.

8. **The World's Tallest Man Gets Married** On July 12, 2007, Bao Zishun, the world's tallest man, married a woman who was just two-thirds his height in a traditional ceremony in Mongolia. The record-breaking 8-footer is a Mongolian farmer who met his bride, Xia Shujian, after sending advertisements around the world. Xia comes up to her husband's elbow when they stand side by side. The ceremony, which took place at the tomb of Kublai Khan, was attended by more than 2,000 guests.

9. **The Largest Wedding Dress** On June 23, 2006, Carly O'Brien of Gloucester, England, wore a wedding gown that was so large and wide that it had to be literally squeezed down the aisle. The gown was 8 feet wide and 60 feet long, and it weighed 350 pounds. It took nine and a half hours to get Carly into the gown and 20 guests to help force it to the altar. "Carly wanted a bigger and better wedding gown than English *Glamour* model Jordan André, and she got it."

10. **The World's Oldest Bridesmaid** On March 31, 2007, Edith Guillford, born on October 12, 1901, served as a bridesmaid at the wedding of a British couple. Edith was 105 and a half years old at the time.

11. **The Most Expensive Wedding Bouquet** Valued at $125,000, a wedding bouquet made of red and white gemstones is the most expensive ever created. Displayed at Ruby Plaza on Vietnam's Le Ngoc Han Street, this over-the-top nosegay consists of 9 diamonds, a star-shaped ruby, and 90 other gemstones.

12. **The World's Longest Engagement** Octavio Guillen and Adriana Martinez hold the record for the world's longest engagement. They were betrothed in their native country of Mexico in 1902 but did not tie the knot until 1969, 67 years later. They were both 15 years old when they got engaged and 82 when they finally got hitched. We guess Octavio finally ran out of excuses.

13. **The World's Shortest Engagement** The shortest engagement lasted only 25 minutes. A fellow named James and his girlfriend dated for one year, each promising to save themselves for their wedding night. James proposed marriage, and his girlfriend accepted. He then accompanied her to a routine doctor's appointment and learned that she was pregnant. 'Nuff said.

3 of the Most Expensive Wedding Gowns in History

The average bride spends anywhere from $500 to $12,000 on her wedding gown, with $800 representing the norm. Here are some gowns that broke the bank.

1. A collaboration between Martin Katz Jewelers and Renée Strauss, a bridal couture designer, resulted in the creation of a wedding gown that incorporated 150 carats of diamonds and was worth **$12 million**. The dress, known as "the Diamond Wedding Gown," was displayed at the bridal show held at the Ritz-Carlton Hotel on Rodeo Drive in Marina Del Rey, California, on February 26, 2006. It was the most expensive wedding gown in history at that time.

2. In January 2007, Japanese designer Yumi Katsura created a wedding gown valued at **¥1 billion ($10 million)**. The dress was made using silk-satin and was decorated with 1,000 pearls, a green 8.8-carat diamond emblem, and a 5-carat white gold diamond, of which there are only two in existence.

3. On February 18, 2007, another "Diamond Wedding Gown" with an estimated worth of **$19 million** went on display at the "Spectacular Bridal Show" held at the Ritz-Carlton in Marina del Rey, California. The gown was a collaboration between Kazanjian Brothers, who supplied the jewels, and Simin Haute Couture, a custom bridal and high-fashion salon that designed the dress. The gown included priceless diamonds and was created specifically for the show.

8 People Who Married Animals

If you're starting to think that Rameau would look cute in a tux, visit Marryyourpet.com. They claim to offer the simplest to the brashest and most vulgar wedding ceremonies imaginable. The marriage contract includes a clause preventing abuse of the animal and conjugal rights. Here are eight couples who did it the hard way.

Vintage postcard by Alfred Mainzer, ca. 1900 AUTHORS' COLLECTION

1. Roman emperor Caligula not only married his **horse** Incitatus but, in an act of defiance against the state, appointed it to the Roman Senate.

2. In June 2003, nine-year-old Karnamoni Handsa, resident of a small town in India, was formally married to a **dog** to ward off a bad omen, as was "evidenced" by a malpositioned tooth protruding from her upper gum. Her tribe considered this a bad sign and encouraged her to marry the dog. Over 100 guests attended the nuptials. The girl was given the option of remarrying a human upon reaching adulthood.

3. In December 2003, a fellow from Missouri appeared on *The Jerry Springer Show* along with his 22-year-old **mare**, Pixel. He admitted to living and sleeping with his horse and also announced that they were married. The episode was never aired, as it was deemed too racy even for Springer, but it was later aired on BBC television as a documentary called *I Married a Horse*.

4. In April 2005, a five-year-old Indian girl was married to a **dog** that lived in her village. It was believed that the marriage would prevent the girl from being attacked by man-eating tigers. The groom seemed perplexed during the ceremony, but the bride's family was very pleased.

5. In February 2004, a 75-year-old Nepalese man married a **dog**, following a local custom of his Tharu community.

6. In December 2005, Sharon Tendler, a 41-year-old British woman, became unofficially married to a male **dolphin** named Cindy. The wedding, held in Eilat, Israel, was a real treat for Cindy: he was fed fish during the ceremony.

7. In February 2006, a Sudanese man was caught having sex with a neighbor's **goat** and was ordered by the village council of elders to pay the neighbor a dowry of $50 and marry the animal. The marriage didn't last, however, as the goat died shortly afterward. (We suspect foul play.)

8. In June 2006, an Indian woman married a **cobra snake** with whom she had fallen in love. The traditional Hindu wedding was attended by over 2,000 guests.

They'll Never Forget Their Vows

Two **elephants** named Grand and Candy were married on December 15, 2007, in the Yerevan zoo, located in the Armenian capital of Yerevan, while hundreds of guests and well-wishers looked on. Candy, the bride, had been the star of Moscow's Animal Theater but gave up her career to be with the man she loved. The zoo built special living quarters to house the newlyweds.

5 Doggie-Style Weddings

"Do you, Pookie, take Darla as your lawfully wedded wife? Do you promise to play nice, share your toys, and keep her safe from the postman? Do you, Darla, promise to honor and love Pookie, to never fight over the food bowl, and never complain about going for a walk in the rain, for as long as you both shall live?"

Take a couple of pampered pooches, add elaborate wedding attire, a dog-food cake, a wedding ring attached to a decorative collar, an outdoor venue, vows, and some wacky humans, and you've got yourself a canine wedding.

The American Kennel Club confirms that 18 percent of dog owners have included (or would include) their dog in their wedding ceremony. Los Angeles wedding planners claim that this number is higher and that 30 percent of their weddings involve dogs.

Here are some actual doggie-style nuptials.

1. In 2005, actress Pamela Anderson and her now ex-hubby Kid Rock held a wedding for her pet Chihuahua, Luca (the groom), to Star (the bride), Pam's golden retriever. The canine couple were married on a Malibu beach in California amid bridal bouquets of flowers and a flood of doggie wedding gifts.

2. In September 2006, the bride, an eight-month-old pooch named Muffin, and her fiancé, a two-and-a-half-year-old dog named Timmy, were married in London's famed Harrods department store. Muffin was a vision in white satin, with a lace hood and a train. Timmy wore a black silk cloak and a magenta bow tie. The couple departed in a horse-drawn carriage. The wedding set the couple's "parents" back $7,000.

3. On July 27, 2006, a Bernese mountain dog named Buck and a collie-beagle-basset mix named Peaches were married at the Vanadium Woods Retirement Village in Bridgeville, Pennsylvania. The bride wore a white satin gown and a tulle veil. The groom's natural black-and-white coat served as his tux. He did, however, wear a bow tie. Fifty humans were in attendance at this pet-friendly gathering.

4. An upscale shopping center in Littleton, Colorado, held a mass canine wedding on May 19, 2007, as a fundraising event supporting the Denver Dumb Friends League. More than 356 dogs were married, shattering the record for the largest canine wedding in history, according to the *Guinness Book of World Records*. The ceremony was called "Bow Wow Vows." Single dogs were invited to attend a doggie speed-dating event, and several couples emerged and were also married.

5. On Valentine's Day 2007, nine canine couples were married in a Hong Kong shopping mall. The pups were dressed in tuxedos, gowns, and veils. The event was intended to raise awareness and funds to help support local animal charities.

For a mere $5,000, Harrods of London will host a proper doggie wedding. The price includes designer outfits for both the bride and the groom, a dog-friendly wedding cake, and a champagne reception for 20 human guests. Also included is a luxury honeymoon at the exclusive Paw Seasons Dog Hotel in Kent. For an additional $2,000, the couple can leave the reception in a horse-drawn carriage complete with a "Just Married" sign attached.

Weddings in 11 Works of Classic Literature

In the opening chapter of *The Good Earth* by Pearl Buck, the peasant farmer Wang Lung purchases a slave as a bride for a paltry sum and brings her to his home. After a small celebration at which O-Lan, the long-suffering wife in the story, is not even present, the two are considered to be married. Years later, when Wang Lung has become a rich landlord, the wedding of his son is a lavish affair for which the bride is specially prepared, and the celebration takes the form of an elaborate reception.

Comparing the two events tells us much about marriages in Chinese culture, just as similar descriptions in other great works of literature give us valuable insight into the nature and customs surrounding weddings throughout history. Although they are taken from works of fiction, the following accounts tell us a great deal about how weddings took place in times gone by.

1. *Bracebridge Hall* by Washington Irving (1822) The day passed off with great rustic rejoicing. Tables were spread under the trees in the park, where all the peasantry of the neighborhood were regaled with roast beef and plum-pudding, and oceans of ale. . . . Loads of bridecake were distributed. The young ladies were all busy in passing morsels of it through the wedding ring to dream on.

2. "The Wedding Knell" by Nathaniel Hawthorne (1837) The clumsy wheels of several old-fashioned coaches were heard, and the gentlemen and ladies composing the bridal party came through the church door with the sudden and gladsome effect of a burst of sunshine. The whole group, except the principal figure, was made up of youth and gayety. As they streamed up the broad aisle, while the pews and pillars seemed to brighten on either side, their steps were as buoyant as if they mistook the church for a ball-room, and were ready to dance hand in hand to the altar. So brilliant was the spectacle that few took notice of a singular phenomenon that had marked its entrance. At the moment when the bride's foot touched the threshold the bell swung heavily in the tower above her, and sent forth its deepest knell. The vibrations died away and returned with prolonged solemnity, as she entered the body of the church.

"Good heavens! what an omen," whispered a young lady to her lover.

3. *Jane Eyre* by Charlotte Brontë (1847) "The marriage cannot go on; I declare the existence of an impediment."

The clergyman looked up at the speaker, and stood mute; the clerk did the same; Mr. Rochester moved slightly, as though the earth had rolled under his feet: taking a firmer footing, and not turning his head or eyes, he said, "Proceed."

Profound silence fell when he uttered that word, with deep but low intonation. Presently Mr. Wood said, "I cannot proceed without some investigation into what has been asserted, and evidence of its truth or falsehood.". . . Mr. Wood seemed at a loss.

"What is the nature of the impediment?" he asked. . . . The speaker came forward and leaned on the rails. He continued, uttering each word distinctly, calmly, steadily, but not loudly,—

"It simply consists of the existence of a previous marriage; Mr. Rochester has a wife now living."

4. *David Copperfield* by Charles Dickens (1850) The church is calm enough, I am sure; but it might be a steam-powered loom in full action, for any sedative effect it has on me. I am too far gone for that.

The rest is all a more or less incoherent dream.

A dream of them coming in with Dora; of the pew-opener arranging us . . . before the altar rails . . . of the clergyman and clerk approaching . . . of Miss Lavinia, who acts as a semi-auxiliary bridesmaid, being the first to cry . . . of our kneeling down together, side by side . . . of my walking proudly and lovingly down the aisle with my sweet wife upon my arm.

5. *Madame Bovary* by Gustave Flaubert (1857) They went on foot, and as soon as the ceremony at the church was over they trudged back again. The procession, at first keeping well together, resembled a colored scarf as it undulated through the countryside, winding slowly along the narrow footpath through the green cornfields. But before long it began to straggle, and broke up into separate groups that loitered on the way to gossip. The fiddler went on ahead, the top of his fiddle all bedecked with streamers; after him walked the bridegroom and his bride, the relations and friends following in what order they pleased. Last of all came the children, who amused themselves by plucking little sprays of oats, or had a little game all to themselves, when no one was looking.

6. "The Courtship of Miles Standish" by Henry Wordsworth Longfellow (1858)

> This was the wedding morn of Priscilla
> the Puritan maiden.
> Friends were assembled together; the Elder and
> Magistrate also
> Graced the scene with their presence, and stood like
> the law and the Gospel,
> One with the sanction of earth, and one with the
> blessing of heaven.
> Simple and brief was the wedding, as that of Ruth and
> of Boaz.
> Softly the youth and the maiden repeated the words of
> betrothal,

> Taking each other for husband and wife in the
> Magistrate's presence,
> After the Puritan way, and the laudable custom of
> Holland.

7. *Adam Bede* by George Eliot (1859) I envy them all the sight they had when the marriage was fairly ended and Adam led Dinah out of church. She was not in black this morning, for her Aunt Poyser would by no means allow such a risk of incurring bad luck, and had herself made a present of the wedding dress, made all of gray, though in the usual Quaker form, for on this point Dinah could not give way. So the lily face looked out with sweet gravity from under a gray Quaker bonnet, neither smiling nor blushing, but with lips trembling a little under the weight of solemn feelings. Adam, as he pressed her arm to his side, walked with his old erectness and his head thrown rather backward as if to face all the world better. But it was not because he was particularly proud this morning, as is the wont of bridegrooms, for his happiness was of a kind that had little reference to men's opinion of it. There was a tinge of sadness in his deep joy; Dinah knew it, and did not feel aggrieved.

8. *Silas Marner* by George Eliot (1861) There was one time of the year which was held in Raveloe to be especially suitable for a wedding. It was when the great lilacs and the alburnums in the old-fashioned gardens showed their golden and purple wealth above the lichen-tinted walls, and when there were calves still young enough to want bucketfuls of fragrant milk. People were not so busy then as they must become when the full cheese-making and mowing had set in; and besides, it was a time when a light bridal dress could be worn with comfort and seen to advantage.

9. *Little Women* by Louisa May Alcott (1868) Meg looked very like a rose herself, for all that was best and sweetest in heart and soul seemed to bloom into her face that day, making it fair and tender, with a charm more beautiful than beauty. Neither silk, lace, nor orange flowers would she have. I don't want a fash-

ionable wedding, but only those about me whom I love, and to them I wish to look and be my familiar self.

So she made her wedding gown herself, sewing into it the tender hopes and innocent romances of a girlish heart. Her sisters braided up her pretty hair, and the only ornaments she wore were the lilies of the valley, which "her John" liked best of all the flowers that grew.

"You do look just like our own dear Meg, only so very sweet and lovely that I should hug you if it wouldn't crumple your dress," cried Amy, surveying her with delight when all was done.

"Then I am satisfied. But please hug and kiss me, everyone, and don't mind my dress. I want a great many crumples of this sort put into it today." And Meg opened her arms to her sisters, who clung about her with April faces for a minute, feeling that the new love had not changed the old.

10. *Gunnar, A Tale of Norse Life* by Hjalmar Hjörth Boyesen (1874) With gay music and noisy laughter and merriment, the bridal procession passed into the yard, where from the steps of the mansion they were greeted by the master of ceremonies in a high-flown speech of congratulation. The doors were then thrown wide open and soon like a swelling tide the crowd rolled through the house, and the lofty halls shook with the hum and din of the festivity. For at such times the Norsemen are in their lustiest mood. . . . The . . . hall . . . was decorated for the occasion with fresh leaves and birch branches, for birch is the bride of the trees. . . . The seats of honor, of course, belonged to the bride and bridegroom, and they having taken their places, the master of ceremonies urged the guests to the tables and arranged them in their proper order in accordance with their relative dignity or their relationship or acquaintance with the bride.

11. *The Good Earth* by Pearl Buck (1931) The two sat down side by side, shy and in silence of each other, and the wife of Wang Lung's uncle came in fat and important with the occasion, bearing two bowls of hot wine, and the two drank separately, and then mixed the wine of the two bowls and drank again, thus signifying that the two were now one, and they ate rice and mingled the rice and this signified that their life was now one, and thus they were wed.

Now the maid that was to be wed must not of course be seen by the young man and Lotus took her into the inner court to prepare her for marriage . . . they washed her clean from head to foot, and bound her feet freshly with white cloth under her new stockings, and Lotus rubbed into her flesh some fragrant almond oil of her own. Then they dressed her in garments she had brought from her home; white flowered silk next to her sweet virgin flesh and then a light coat of sheep's wool of the finest and most curly kind, and then the red satin garments of marriage. And they rubbed lime upon her forehead and with a string tied skillfully they pulled out the hairs of her virginity, the fringe over her brow, and they made her forehead high and smooth and square for her new estate. Then they painted her with powder and with red paint and with a brush they drew out in two long slender lines her eyebrows, and they set upon her head the bride's crown and the beaded veil, and upon her small feet they put shoes, embroidered, and they painted her fingertips and scented the palms of her hands, and thus they prepared her for marriage.

"A good marriage is one which allows for change and growth in the individuals and in the way they express their love." —Pearl S. Buck

ISTOCKPHOTO.COM

"Here Comes the Bride"

Richard Wagner composed the piece popularly known as the "Bridal Chorus" in 1848 as a passage in his opera *Lohengrin*. Many opera critics have deemed the "Bridal Chorus" the weakest part of this opera. The chorus begins singing the piece as the hero, Lohengrin, along with his new bride, Elsa, enter their bridal chamber. Attendants then help them disrobe for their wedding night. Because this scene is overtly sexual in nature, some religious sects have objected to using the "Bridal Chorus" as a wedding march.

The "Bridal Chorus" was used as the wedding march at the royal wedding of Princess Victoria, the daughter of Queen Victoria, to Prince Frederick William of Prussia in 1858 and has been popular ever since. In fact, even during World War II, when Wagner's heroic works were so identified with Nazi Germany that his operas were rarely produced by the Allies, English-speaking countries retained the "Bridal Chorus" as a wedding march.

Most people are familiar with the lyric "Here comes the bride, all dressed in white," but the actual lyrics, as far as we can gather, are unavailable. Here are some alternative and humorous lyrics that have been suggested over the years.

Here comes the bride,
The groom is roped and tied.
Soon he'll be branded
On his quaking hide.

Here comes the bride
All fat and wide
Doesn't she wiggle
From side to side

Here comes the groom
Riding on a broom
He saw her behind
And changed his mind
And swept out the room

Here comes the bride,
All dressed in white.
Stepped on a turtle,
And down came her girdle.

Here comes the bride
All dressed in white
Slipped on a banana peel
And went for a ride.

Here comes the bride
Tall, fat, and wide
I might have said
She was good in bed
But then I would have lied

Here comes the bride,
What's she trying to hide?
There's something in the oven,
Is it mother's pride?

Here comes the bride,
All dressed in white,
Sweetly, serenely, in the soft
glowing light.
Lovely to see, marching to
thee,
Sweet love united for eternity.

14 Wedding Scenes Depicted in Fine Art

1. *The Wedding of Peleus and Thetis*, a vase painting by Sophilos, ca. 590 B.C., is the earliest-known depiction of the god Dionysus. He is seen walking barefoot in a wedding procession wearing a clay-colored tunic and a classic himation cloak.

2. *The Arnolfini Marriage* was painted by Jan van Eyck in 1434. It is a portrait of Giovanni di Nicolao Arnolfini and his wife, done in oil on wood. Entire books have been written about this fascinating work of art.

3. *The Wedding Feast* by Sandro Botticelli, ca. 1483, is one part of a four-panel piece representing the Boccacio story of Nastagio degli Onesti. In this panel, we see a wedding feast under imposing Renaissance arches. Servers are carrying trays of food while eager guests look on.

4. Famed Venetian artist Paolo Veronese created works of grand proportion and vivid colors. His most famous painting, *The Wedding at Cana*, completed in 1563, is now on display in the Louvre Museum in Paris. The artist included himself and fellow artists Titian and Tintoretto as three of the attendees in this massive work.

5. *Wedding Dance* was painted by Flemish artist Pieter Brueghel the Elder in 1566. It depicts a lively outdoor peasant wedding celebration. Most of the guests are enjoying themselves, but in the lower left-hand corner we can see a mysterious figure with his back turned toward the revelers.

6. *Samson Propounding the Riddle at the Wedding Feast* by Rembrandt van Ryn, ca. 1633 to 1639, was painted during a very happy period in the artist's life, as reflected in the use of rich color and the dramatic action of the figures.

7. *Wedding Breakfast of Empress Maria Theresa of Austria and Francis of Lorraine* by Martin II Mytens, ca. 1736, portrays a wedding breakfast in the tradition of the French high baroque and was commissioned by Maria Theresa. It is on display at the National Museum in Stockholm, Sweden.

8. *Signing the Register* by British artist Edmund Blair Leighton, ca. late 1800s, an oil on canvas, is an example of his medieval scenes depicting couples in domestic settings. We see the bride in her wedding dress signing the wedding register while the groom and their families look on. The painting is on display at the Bristol City Museum and Art Gallery in Bristol, England.

9. *The Wedding Party*, ca. 1905, is one of Henri Rousseau's most famous works. The people in the painting are unidentifiable with the exception of Rousseau himself, who is positioned just behind and to the right of the bride. The painting can be viewed at the Musée de l'Orangerie in Paris.

10. *Russian Wedding* by Marc Chagall, ca. 1909, depicting a wedding processional, was painted as oil on jute and is part of the E. G. Bührle Collection in Zurich, Switzerland.

The Wedding by Fernand Leger, 1910
AUTHORS' COLLECTION

Wedding Dance by Pieter Brueghel the Elder, ca. 1566 AUTHORS' COLLECTION

11. *The Wedding* by cubist pioneer Fernand Leger, ca. 1910, an oil on canvas, is on display at the Georges Pompidou Center in Paris. It is a fine example of early cubist art.

12. *The Wedding Candles* by Marc Chagall, ca. 1945, is one of his most famous works. It is a remarkable oil painting with exceptional use of color, detail, and brush strokes. The painting depicts a typical Russian-Jewish village scene.

13. *Bella's Wedding* by Marc Chagall (date unknown) is one of several paintings in which Chagall's wife Bella is the central figure.

14. *The Wedding* by art nouveau and art deco master Erté (aka Romain de Tirtoff) is a magnificent bronze sculpture that was created in 1986. Two women in elegant wedding attire and splendid body jewelry are seen holding hands.

The Story of The Arnolfini Marriage

The Arnolfini Marriage is considered by many to be the most recognizable and popular of all wedding or betrothal paintings ever created. The artist, Jan van Eyck (ca. 1385–1441), was the official court painter of the House of Bruges in Belgium. Nowhere is his mastery of oil painting more evident than in this portrait of Giovanni di Nicolao Arnolfini, a merchant from Lucca, and his bride, Giovanna Cenami. The painting depicts a solemn moment in the couple's lives, as we see the young woman holding her betrothed's hand as a representation of their union.

Both the year the painting was created, 1434, and Van Eyck's signature appear on the back wall of the room. Van Eyck's reflection in a mirror leads historians to believe that he was a witness at the wedding.

The Arnolfini Marriage by Jan van Eyck, 1434
AUTHORS' COLLECTION

34 Great Wedding Movies

Weddings have always been wonderful backdrops for romantic comedies or dramas. Listed here are some of the very best.

David Copperfield marries the beautiful but naive Dora Spenlow in the 1935 film *David Copperfield*, directed by George Cukor. KOBAL COLLECTION/MGM

1. *Father of the Bride* (1950) The 1991 remake of this film starring Steve Martin is excellent, but the original version starring Spencer Tracy and Elizabeth Taylor is far better. Stanley Banks loves his daughter, but his life is thrown into emotional and financial chaos when she tells him she's engaged. The movie is a classic, often admired for its endearing depiction of the relationship between father and daughter.

2. *The Catered Affair* (1956) This drama stars Bette Davis as a poor woman who goes into hock trying to throw her daughter (Debbie Reynolds) the wedding she never had, a "catered affair." Plans for the wedding, which is to take place just a week after the engagement is announced, wreak havoc on the family.

3. *The Graduate* (1967) Ben, played by Dustin Hoffman, is a recent college grad. He is seduced by the wife of his father's business partner, the infamous Mrs. Robinson (Anne Bancroft), then later meets and falls in love with Mrs. Robinson's daughter, Elaine. When Ben crashes Elaine's wedding to another man, they flee together, hopping a bus and riding off into the Los Angeles sunset.

4. *Lovers and Other Strangers* (1970) A series of comedic subplots come together during a family's preparation for a wedding. The bride's father struggles to placate his teary-eyed mistress while keeping his wife happy; the bride's sister has a nonexistent sex life and battles her husband both verbally and physically; and the groom's father waxes poetic.

5. *Fiddler on the Roof* (1971) Norman Jewison's adaptation of the long-running Broadway musical gave new life to the story of Tevye the Jewish milkman whose love of tradition is challenged not only by the czar's minions in the Ukraine, but also by his daughters, who spurn the marriages arranged for them and choose, instead, their own partners. The wedding scenes here depict both the joy and sadness of the characters and the times.

6. *Plaza Suite* (1971) Based on Neil Simon's hit Broadway play, this film is a trilogy of comic episodes set in a suite at New York City's famed Plaza Hotel. In one segment, a man and his wife deal with their daughter's wedding day jitters after she locks herself in the hotel bathroom and refuses to come out. Walter Matthau is unforgettable as the exasperated father of the bride.

Spencer Tracy makes it down the aisle—kicking and screaming all the way—in *Father of the Bride*, 1950. KOBAL COLLECTION/MGM

Dustin Hoffman and Katharine Ross make their getaway in *The Graduate*, 1967. KOBAL COLLECTION/EMBASSY

7. *A Wedding* (1978)   Director Robert Altman's *A Wedding* begins with a wedding ceremony during which Muffin and her philandering boyfriend Dino are read their vows by an over-the-hill and clueless bishop. This classic spoof of modern-day weddings boasts a stressed-out wedding coordinator, a pesky photographer, a grandmother who is lucky if she'll make it through the day alive, and a fumbling behind-the-scenes staff.

8. *Betsy's Wedding* (1990)   Betsy is getting married. The wedding plans trigger an outrageous series of battles between the bride's and groom's parents over the size and style of the affair. The parents prevail, and the couple's wishes for a small, intimate service are defeated.

9. *Father of the Bride* (1991)   In this wonderful update of the much-loved Hollywood classic, George Banks (Steve Martin) has a hard time letting go of his daughter when she unexpectedly announces her plans to wed. Martin Short is dazzling as the off-the-wall wedding consultant Franck.

10. *Four Weddings and a Funeral* (1994)   It all starts out when the dapper Brit Charles (Hugh Grant) and the charming American Carrie (Andie MacDowell) meet at a wedding. He, a confirmed bachelor, falls for her and begins to think that commitment might not be such a bad thing. A popular film that examines love and marriage against a backdrop of the stages of life.

11. *Muriel's Wedding* (1995)   Misfit Muriel (Toni Collette) dreams about getting married. When she and her free-spirited friend Rhoda (Rachel Griffiths) leave their small hometown in Australia and head for the big city, Muriel meets and falls for a hunky sports hero looking for Aussie citizenship. Their path to the altar has plenty of surprising twists.

12. *In and Out* (1997)   Howard Brackett's (Kevin Kline) ridiculously long engagement to Emily (Joan Cusack) becomes suspect. Howard is unintentionally outed by Hollywood heartthrob Cameron Drake (Matt Dillon). Can Howard actually be gay? Attracting the interest of TV reporter Peter Malloy (Tom Selleck) complicates Howard's plans in a comedy that underscores the importance of knowing who you really are before you "take the plunge."

13. *My Best Friend's Wedding* (1997)   Julianne Potter (Julia Roberts) panics when she receives word that her longtime platonic pal, Michael (Dermot Mulroney), is finally getting married. She sets out to sabotage the wedding and makes one last unsuccessful play for Michael's affections.

14. *That Old Feeling* (1997)   Ex-spouses Lilly (Bette Midler) and Dan (Dennis Farina) reunite at their daughter's wedding, 14 years after their nasty divorce. Family and friends brace themselves for an all-out war. Sure enough, the couple threaten to ruin the event—by reuniting. Their on-again, off-again shenanigans make for a lively script.

15. *The Wedding Singer* (1998)   The wedding singer (Adam Sandler) and the waitress (Drew Barrymore) first meet at a wedding, then again as Barrymore is making plans for her own marriage to a philandering idiot. Sandler learns about the two-timing jerk, which works out perfectly as he himself is secretly in love with Barrymore.

16. *The Best Man* (1999)   Harper Stewart (Taye Diggs) is scheduled to be best man at his friend's wedding. The problem is that an advance copy of his kiss-and-tell, semi-autobiographical novel, which has been selected by Oprah's Book Club, is making the rounds of the bridal party. Now Harper's friends are about to find out what he really thinks of them.

17. *Runaway Bride* (1999)   Commitment-challenged bride-to-be Maggie Carpenter (Julia Roberts) has already left three men standing at the altar. The sexy newspaper columnist who seeks out her story, Ike Graham (Richard Gere), gets more than just the scoop when, in the end, the bride hangs up her running shoes.

La famiglia, from *The Godfather,* 1972 KOBAL COLLECTION/PARAMOUNT

"Someday—and that day may never come—I'll call upon you to do a service for me. But until that day, accept this justice as gift on my daughter's wedding day."

—Don Corleone in *The Godfather* (1972)

18. *Meet the Parents* (2000) Gaylord Focker (Ben Stiller) must ask his girlfriend's overprotective ex-CIA agent father (Robert De Niro) for permission to marry his daughter, and it proves to be a formidable task. Gaylord eventually is admitted into the father's "circle of trust" despite the fact that he almost single-handedly ruins his future sister-in-law's wedding.

19. *The Wedding Planner* (2001) Ultra-rich Fran Donolly hires Mary Fiore (Jennifer Lopez), San Francisco's premier wedding planner, to stage her wedding. While planning Fran's nuptials, Mary meets and falls in love with Steve, a handsome pediatrician (Matthew McConaughey). All is well until Mary finally meets Fran's fiancé—Steve.

20. *Monsoon Wedding* (2001) As monsoon rains loom in this romantic and often comedic drama set in New Delhi, Lalit Verma and his extended family reunite for the last-minute arranged marriage of his daughter Aiditi. Five stories emerge and intersect as the preparations proceed, revealing the different aspects of love and boundaries between people of different classes.

21. *My Big Fat Greek Wedding* (2002) In this comedy, adapted from Nia Vardalos's one-woman off-Broadway show, a Greek American woman, Toula, played by Vardalos, meets and falls in love with a schoolteacher, Ian, who is a customer at her family's restaurant. But Ian is not Greek, and Toula's parents are horrified when he pops the question. The road of acceptance is long—and fairly hilarious.

22. *American Wedding* (2003) In this final chapter of the *American Pie* trilogy, Jim and his girl, the former band geek, are engaged to be married, and their road to the altar is predictably rocky. "The Stiffmeister" and Finch vie for the affections of Michelle's younger sister, Jim's grandmother objects to the wedding because Michelle is not Jewish, Jim's father continues to function as a well-intentioned embarrassment, and Stiffler's badly timed surprise bachelor party are just some of the obstacles that stand in the way of the nuptials.

23. *The In-Laws* (2003) While preparing for his daughter's wedding, dentist Sheldon Kornpett (Alan Arkin) meets Vince Ricardo (Peter Falk), the groom's father, a manic fellow who claims to be a CIA agent. Vince enlists the reluctant Sheldon into a series of chases and misadventures that lead from New York to a banana republic in South America. They do manage to make it to the wedding on time—but not in a way that anyone expects.

24. *Bend It Like Beckham* (2003) In this charming comedy, Jess, an Indian girl born in England, dreams of becoming a soccer star just like her idol, British soccer sensation David Beckham. Against the backdrop of preparations for her sister's impending traditional marriage, Jess must battle her family's stereotypes and expectations.

25. *The Princess Diaries 2: Royal Engagement* (2004) Teen ugly duckling Mia learns that she is the princess of Genovia. In order to become the country's ruler and retain her family's 500-year heritage, Mia must marry. Uninterested in the man who has been selected for her, she falls for the very man who is vying with her for the throne.

26. *The Wedding Banquet* (2004) A gay New Yorker stages a marriage of convenience with a young woman in order to placate his traditional Taiwanese family, but the wedding becomes a major inconvenience when his parents fly in for the ceremony and begin planning an enormous traditional wedding feast.

27. *Monster-in-Law* **(2005)** Charlie Cantilini (Jennifer Lopez) has finally met her "Mr. Right," Dr. Kevin Fields (Michael Vartan). In a tour-de-force comedic performance, Jane Fonda plays Kevin's overbearing and contentious mother, who will stop at nothing to break them up. Charlie's final words to her tormentor are ones that brides and their MOBs should take to heart.

28. *Confetti* **(2005)** In this British "mockumentary," a bridal magazine called Confetti holds a contest in which three anxious couples, aided by wedding planners, compete to win a prize for most original wedding concept. One couple opts for a Busby Berkeley–style musical, another chooses a tennis theme with dancing ball boys, and the final pair settles on a "naturist" wedding in which the couple are to be wed in a fig-leaf ceremony.

29. *Bride and Prejudice* **(2005)** In this musical based on Jane Austen's classic novel *Pride and Prejudice,* the Bakhsi family is celebrating the arrival of British-born Mr. Balraj, who may be the perfect spouse for one of the Bakhsis' four unmarried daughters. Lalita is chosen but refuses to marry someone who has been handpicked for her, believing that true love is waiting for her. This movie combines the wit of Austen with the song and dance of Bollywood.

30. *Tim Burton's Corpse Bride* **(2005)** Set in nineteenth-century Europe, this animated tale centers on Victor, a young man who is whisked away to the underworld and wed to a mysterious "Corpse Bride," while his real bride, Victoria, waits grieving in the land of the living. Victor finds the Land of the Dead fascinating, but he wants only to return to his true love.

The corpse bride and groom from the 2005 film KOBAL COLLECTION/ WARNER BROS.

Carrie and Big finally tie the knot in the *Sex and the City* movie, 2008. *From left:* Cynthia Nixon, Kristin Davis, Sarah Jessica Parker, Kim Cattrall KOBAL COLLECTION/NEW LINE CINEMA/CRAIG BLANKENHORN

31. *Imagine Me and You* **(2006)** Rachel finds herself in love on her wedding day, but not with the groom. During the ceremony, she catches the eye of Luce, the female wedding florist, and realizes that Heck, her new husband, isn't the one for her after all and that Luce may very well be. But Rachel will never know unless she and Luce spend some "quality" time together. They do, and what follows is a romantic, funny, and often poignant journey.

32. *I Now Pronounce You Chuck and Larry* **(2007)** Chuck Levine and Larry Valentine are both firefighters and best of friends. Larry is a widower with two small children. Chuck is single. Larry asks Chuck to become his domestic partner in order to cut some red tape that would allow him to claim his kids as his pension beneficiaries. Chuck agrees to the deception, and he and Larry head for Niagara Falls to get married. Chuck and Larry must now fumble through a charade of domestic bliss under one roof.

33. *27 Dresses* **(2008)** The film centers on Jane (Katherine Heigl), an idealistic, romantic, and completely selfless woman, a perennial bridal attendant whose own happy ending is nowhere in sight. When her younger sister Tess captures the heart of Jane's secret crush, Jane begins to reexamine her "always a bridesmaid" lifestyle.

34. *Made of Honor* **(2008)** Tom (Patrick Dempsey) realizes that he's in love with his best friend Hannah (Michelle Monaghan) a little too late. She's already engaged and wants him to be her "maid of honor" at the wedding.

13 Honeymoon Movies

1. *Honeymoon in Bali* (1939) Bill (Fred MacMurray) is madly in love with Gail, a hardheaded businesswoman, in this classic love triangle film. He'll do whatever it takes to win her heart. But as soon as he thinks they're connecting, she leaves for a trip to Nassau. While she is gone, Bill reconsiders their relationship and opts to marry his boss's daughter. Gail, suddenly realizing her mistake, follows them to Bali.

2. *Once Upon a Honeymoon* (1942) Set during World War II, *Once Upon a Honeymoon* stars Ginger Rogers as a burlesque queen from New York who passes herself off as a socialite from Philadelphia. She is about to marry an Austrian baron who she thinks is saving countries but in fact is helping Adolf Hitler conquer them. Their honeymoon is spent traveling around in the countries that Hitler is about to invade. Cary Grant is the news commentator sent to interview her to find out what the baron is up to.

3. *The Ghost and the Guest* (1943) In this screwball comedy, Webster and Jackie are newlyweds who arrive at an old spooky country house for their honeymoon. They are horrified when a coffin arrives carrying the body of the former owner. By the time police arrive, the body has disappeared. The situation becomes even more complicated when the suspicious next-of-kin of "the deceased" arrive to claim the body while a gang of jewel thieves show up hot on the trail of a fortune in diamonds hidden in the house.

4. *Niagara* (1953) Marilyn Monroe plays Rose, a femme fatale, in this pseudo-Hitchcock thriller. Rose, on her honeymoon with her disturbed husband (Joseph Cotton), torments him and drives him deeper into total insanity while enlisting the help of her mysterious lover to do him in.

5. *The Long, Long Trailer* (1954) Lucille Ball and Desi Arnaz play newlyweds Tacy and Nicky Collini. Nicky wants to save up for a house, but Tacy convinces him that touring the country in a 40-foot trailer would be a great way to spend their honeymoon. The couple have several disastrous adventures while traveling: Tacy's awkward attempt to cook dinner in a moving trailer and a cliffhanging ride through the mountains are truly hilarious.

6. *Honeymoon of Horror* (1964) Lilli has just married her perfect man, a charismatic artist named Emile, and they are off to his countryside mansion for their honeymoon. But when Emile's former flame shows up and Emile's disturbed brother falls for Lilli, the honeymoon turns into a nightmare.

7. *Hatchet for the Honeymoon* (1969) John Harrington runs an exclusive fashion salon specializing in wedding attire for women. He's a haunted man on a mission. Impelled to kill women after dressing them in bridal gowns, he embarks on a spree of homicides in order to learn the truth about his own mother's mysterious death.

8. *The Heartbreak Kid* (1972) Three days into his honeymoon, Jewish Lenny is bedazzled by WASP goddess Kelly and soon realizes that he's married the wrong woman. He wants Kelly and is willing to do almost anything to have her, including leaving his new wife. Kelly brings Lenny home to meet her family and soon learns that they hate everything about him.

9. *10* (1979) Writer-director Blake Edwards's celebration of la dolce vita stars Dudley Moore as successful but discontented songwriter George Webber, who becomes obsessed after getting a glimpse of the stunning Jenny Miles (Bo Derek in her film debut) as she's en route to say, "I do." He stalks the honeymooning newly-

Film poster, 1958 KOBAL COLLECTION/PARAMOUNT

weds all the way to Acapulco, where, after saving the life of Jenny's new husband, George gets the perfect reward.

10. *Haunted Honeymoon* (1986) Larry Abbot (Gene Wilder) is a radio actor in search of love. When he finds it, Abbot and his new fiancée, Vickie Pearle, visit his Aunt Kate (Dom DeLuise) in her big, old mansion in the country. Rather than the fun, quiet family weekend they anticipated, Larry and Vickie soon realize they're in for a fright when Kate mentions something about a werewolf on the loose.

11. *Honeymoon In Vegas* (1990) Betsy (Sarah Jessica Parker) is the long-suffering fiancée of her commitment-challenged boyfriend, Jack Singer (Nicolas Cage). They go to Las Vegas to finally tie the knot, but Jack is suckered into a "friendly" but crooked poker game and loses Betsy to mobster Tommy Korman (James Caan). After Jack agrees to "lend" Betsy to Tommy for the weekend in order to satisfy the debt, Tommy takes Betsy to Hawaii and woos her, while Jack tries desperately to find her and win her back.

12. *Just Married* (2003) It's love at first sight when Tom Leezak, a traffic reporter, and wealthy Sarah McNerney meet in this romantic comedy. They marry despite the objections of Sarah's family and set off for their Italian honeymoon. But when Sarah's ex-boyfriend shows up and tries to win her back, the happy couple experience the honeymoon from hell.

13. *Zombie Honeymoon* (2004) Danny and Denise are happy, loving newlyweds on their way to their honeymoon when Danny is attacked and bitten by a zombie and starts slowly becoming one himself. Sure, marriage is all about adjustment, but can the couple cope with Danny's new condition?

9 Monster Brides in Film

1. *Bride of Frankenstein* (1935) This sequel to the original *Frankenstein* film (1931) is regarded as one of the greatest horror films of all time. Dr. Frankenstein and evil Dr. Pretorius bring the monster's bride to life. Elsa Lanchester plays the bride, and her hairstyle would become famous for its electric look. Lanchester also portrays Mary Shelley, the author of the novel.

2. *Bride of the Gorilla* (1951) Burr is a plantation owner who changes into a gorilla and terrorizes his wife, baffling the local authorities. Lon Chaney Jr., as the jungle police commissioner, plays the good guy for a change.

3. *Bride of the Monster* aka *Bride of the Atom* (1955) Horror icon Bela Lugosi (Dracula) appears in his last starring role as Dr. Eric Vornoff, who, with his crazed man-beast servant, is conducting flesh-burning radiation experiments in an attempt to create a legion of atomic supermen. When a newspaperwoman gets too inquisitive for her own good, Vornoff takes steps to protect his research. Produced and directed by cult filmmaker Ed Wood Jr., the film features many of his regular players.

4. *The Bride and the Beast* aka *Queen of the Gorillas* (1957) Big-game hunter Dan (Lance Fuller) brings his new bride Laura (Charlotte Austin) home to the jungle, where she realizes, to her dismay, that in a past life she was queen of the gorillas and now must resist the urge to run into the wilderness to meet her former tribe. As she learns more about her past, she finds herself strangely attracted to the camp's pet gorilla in this horror gem penned by director Ed Wood Jr.

5. *The Brides of Dracula* (1960) Van Helsing (Peter Cushing) hunts down his nighttime nemesis, Dracula, in none other than a school for girls.

6. *The Brides of Fu Manchu* (1966) Starring Christopher Lee as Fu Manchu, who has imprisoned 12 beautiful girls in his North African headquarters. Each is related to an influential figure whose collaboration Fu Manchu hopes to gain to further his plan to dominate the world.

7. *Brides of Blood* aka *Brides of Death, Grave Desires, Island of Living Horror,* and *Terror on Blood Island* (1968) The indigenous chiefs of Blood Island are kidnapping young virgins who will be sacrificed to the chiefs' god. When scientists learn of the intended sacrifice, they battle the chiefs and "the Evil One" in order to save them and the world.

8. *Bride of Re-Animator* aka *Re-Animator 2* (1990) Drs. West and Cain are experimenting again. But this time, instead of reanimating corpses, they've decided to create new life—in the form of a beautiful companion (from spare body parts, of course) for Dr. West.

9. *Bride of Chucky* (1998) The soul of killer Charles Lee Ray still inhabits the diminutive devil doll, and when his old flame Tiffany (Jennifer Tilly) finds him, he turns her into a doll as well. Together, the happy couple sets out on a terrifying spree.

14 TV Wedding Shows

TV and weddings have always enjoyed a happy marriage. Who can forget Rhoda's famous 1974 subway ride—in full wedding regalia—after Phyllis forgot about her on her wedding day? Or the magic that was Luke and Laura as they wed in 1981 nuptials that were attended by some 20 million TV viewers? Today TV wedding programs abound, some offering help and suggestions, while others simply celebrate the 'zillas of our time. Here are some current offerings. (Exact days and times of broadcast change often; check your local listings.)

1. *Bridezillas* (WE) follows the adventures of various control freaks as they plan their weddings, wreaking havoc on their loved ones every step of the way. Meet Alicia, who insists on a toe check of all members of the wedding party just before the ceremony; and Michelle, who defines her perfect wedding as a day on which "nothing goes wrong, money is not an object, and everyone acts like they worship the ground that I walk on."

> "That was the tradition in TV. When your ratings went down, you turned it into a wedding. We got Fonzie married, we got Richie married, we got Mork married. We almost got Laverne married. We got Shirley married. Brides and sweeps weeks go together."
>
> —TV producer Garry Marshall, producer of *Runaway Bride*, on the use of weddings to boost ratings

2. *Buff Brides* (Discovery Channel's FitTV) follows 20 brides for 3 to 4 months before their wedding dates as they slim down and tone up to look their best in their wedding dresses. Film crews track their progress as they work to meet specific goals, and the brides share their emotional highs and lows as they rush to get gowns fitted, invitations mailed, and flowers ordered.

3. *Bulging Brides* (WE) features a dream team of fitness experts who help selected overweight brides go from flab to fab just in time for their weddings. In one episode, a bride bemoans her fiancé, who can eat anything and stay thin, while she struggles to lose weight a few weeks before her wedding.

4. *For Better or for Worse* (TLC) is a reality show in which couples turn over their wedding preparations to a team of family and friends who have only seven days, a meager $5,000 budget, and a wedding planner they've never met to help them plan for the couple's big day. The fun is watching the team clash with the planner on the theme, the budget, and the timeline and still pull off a halfway decent wedding.

5. *Getting Married* (WE) covers weddings from A to Z, including trends, celebrity interviews, expert tips and ideas, surveys, and plenty of information about destination weddings and honeymoons. The show is produced in conjunction with Get Married.com.

6. *I Propose* (Style) follows grooms as they hem and haw their way toward popping the question. A treasure hunt, a tailgate party, and a ride on the Goodyear blimp all make for creative backdrops. Film crews catch every stuttering, sweaty-palmed moment.

7. *Married Away* (Style) features two different couples each week experiencing the perils and pitfalls of destination weddings. In one episode, a Washington, D.C., couple plan a wedding on the Grenadines' Canouan Island, and a New Jersey bride hopes her groom can return from England in time for their wedding in Savannah, Georgia.

8. *My Big Fat Fabulous Wedding* (VH1) goes behind the scenes of the most extravagant nuptials in America. With film crews in tow, average couples (if "average" refers to those who spend $450,000 on décor alone) tackle the tough decisions and sky-high spending that goes into creating the most amazing million-dollar weddings ever.

9. *Platinum Weddings* (WE) features the breathtaking design and irresistible romance of over-the-top weddings. Planning a dream wedding on a fixed budget is never easy, but these brides-to-be have millions, so the sky's the limit. Peonies flown in from Paris and one-of-a-kind couture gowns are the order of the day for these moneyed marriages.

Friends' Monica and Chandler overcame major hurdles on their way down the aisle, but they finally get married in the episode called "The One with Chandler and Monica's Wedding," which first aired on May 17, 2001. KOBAL COLLECTION/WARNER BROS. TV/BRIGHT/KAUFFMAN/CRANE PRO

10. *The Real Wedding Crashers* (NBC) is a reality show in which wedding couples team up with wedding-crasher actors who stage practical jokes and fake disasters, all to ensure that guests never forget the event. One groom is convinced that he has ruined the wedding dress; another is arrested just hours before the event.

The improvisational actors keep the gags going until the bride and groom finally reveal all to their speechless guests.

11. *Rich Bride Poor Bride* (WE) follows a different couple and their wedding planner each week in their quest to execute a dream wedding. Drama results when costs collide with expectations and each decision affects the couple emotionally. Will they make it to the altar on budget? Will they make it to the altar at all?

12. *Say Yes to the Dress* (TLC) reveals the inner workings of the world's premier bridal salon, Kleinfeld Bridal in New York City. Part fashion show, part bridal story, part family therapy, the show uncovers the hurdles every staff member faces in trying to satisfy brides on what they perceive to be the single most important day of their lives.

13. *A Wedding Story* (TLC), another reality show, also follows couples who are planning weddings, but these are couples from all walks of life, of different religions and ethnicities, and their nuptials are just as varied. The focus here is on the people more than on the planning.

14. *Whose Wedding Is It, Anyway?* (Style) focuses on wedding planners as they attempt to capture the individuality and personal style of each of the couples they work with. The superhuman efforts of the planners will humble even the most fervent bridezillas.

Tony 'n' Tina's Wedding

Tony 'n' Tina's Wedding is the longest-running comedy in off-Broadway history. The show, which opened on February 14, 1988, was the creation of Mark Nasser and Nancy Cassaro (the original Tony 'n' Tina).

During the show, the audience is shuttled back and forth between fantasy and reality by being called on to play the roles of Tony 'n' Tina's family members and friends. The price of admission to this all-inclusive evening of entertainment is in lieu of a gift to the happy couple and includes the show, dancing, and dinner (although menus vary depending on the venue).

In the show's first commercial production, the wedding ceremony took place at St. John's Church in Greenwich Village, New York. It now plays in over 100 cities worldwide.

Chapter 3
The Wedding Planner

Without a doubt, what separates today's brides from all those who have preceded them down the aisle is the number of options they have available to them. Weddings have changed. Gone is the idea of the virginal bride who arrives at her nuptials directly from childhood, and the notion that all weddings should take one particular form even within a particular community has all but fallen by the wayside. Today wedding details are limited only by your imagination, and the maze of choices is enough to test the mettle of the most experienced wedding planner.

This chapter, then, is intended to serve as a map for the bride who must negotiate a path around thousands of choices, not to mention the beckoning promises of the vendors who dominate this industry with their seductive ways and tempting wares.

We have assumed two things about today's bride. First off, she's probably a busy gal, with perhaps a job and a household of her own. So we've scoured books, magazines, and the Internet for the most authoritative information available. We further assume that if the bride in question is clever enough to have landed a groom, she won't need the kind of fluff and filler found in most wedding guides. So we've presented the information here in a concise format that is easy both to peruse and to use.

While we've concentrated on the essentials in this chapter, we couldn't resist a few side trips. Most modern weddings take the white form, but more and more creative souls are exploring off-the-beaten-aisle weddings. So if you've always dreamed of getting married in midair, or thousands of feet below the earth, or while enjoying a ride on the world's tallest roller coaster, this chapter can get you there. Other choices reflect a new societal awareness: here's a guide for the eco-friendly bride in search of a green wedding, along with plenty of tips for handling the myriad challenges of the blended and multi-faith weddings that are so common today.

The media depict today's bride as an out-of-control child who will stop at nothing to obtain her heart's desire and who is far more interested in her wedding than in her marriage. We disagree. The many brides we spoke with were mature young women who entered this new stage of life with maturity and commitment. In fact, we believe that the "bridezilla" phenomenon has been foisted on us by the media and by vendors who have everything to gain from the foolhardiness of women in love. You can plan a wedding without breaking the bank, and you can enjoy the process. And you can use this period in your life to set a good example for those who will follow by staying focused and calm and by always letting those around you know how grateful you are for their help. This chapter tells you how.

The Bride's Brain AUTHORS' COLLECTION

6 Things the Wedding Industry Doesn't Want You to Know

Weddings are big business, and if the industry has its way, future growth will exceed anything we can even imagine today. At the time of this writing, Americans spent some $161 billion a year on weddings, plus another $83 billion in postnuptial expenses. It is no accident that the average cost of a wedding—$28,000—has more than doubled since 1990, but is rather part of a plot—yes, a plot—to separate the bride-to-be and her family from as much money as possible, even beyond what they can afford.

It's been going on for decades, and it involves every aspect of the industry—from those who do all they can to convince brides that marriage without a big white wedding will be risky, to the vendors who have invented "traditions" in order to sell their trappings, to the folks who charge $50 apiece for unity candles that can easily be assembled with materials purchased at any dollar store. Hollywood has helped by dazzling audiences with the opulence of film weddings and by shamelessly promoting invented traditions.

The savvy bride focuses on the essence of the wedding and makes her choices intelligently, with her eyes open and with an understanding of the traditions for which she is opting.

In 1969 a feminist group called Women's International Terrorist Conspiracy from Hell (WITCH) staged a protest at New York's First Bridal Fair, releasing mice on the convention floor, staging a mock wedding, and challenging panelists by asserting that marriage was the province of the oppressed woman.

No one would try to deny today's bride the dream wedding that is available to her. But the savvy bride focuses on the essence of the wedding and makes her choices intelligently, with her eyes open and with an understanding of the traditions for which she is opting. She stays within her budget despite the offers of goods and services bombarding her daily, and she avoids falling into the bridezilla mind-set, even though she is encouraged to do just that everywhere she turns. Above all she understands that the perfect wedding does not guarantee the perfect marriage.

1. During the early part of the twentieth century, most weddings were still modest, private rituals. But as the middle class grew, so did the wedding industry, and a push was made to separate people from their money. Jewelers, florists, fashion designers, and retailers all conspired to sell their wares in such a way as to make consumers believe that they were respecting old traditions when in fact the double-ring ceremony, gift registries, and the bridal salon were all invented by the industry for the single purpose of making more money.

2. In 1938 the De Beers Company, which was responsible for most of the diamonds imported into the United States, hired the well-known advertising firm N. W. Ayer to address lagging sales. The tactics that the ad agency came up with included selling brides on the idea of diamonds as a "timeless tradition," which they were not, and convincing brides that despite the pressures of the times (conspicuous consumption was especially discouraged during the war years, and in fact women were being asked to donate their diamonds for the war effort), sporting a diamond expressed prog-

ress, affluence, and even democracy itself. While a man was off at war, advertisers suggested, a diamond token of love bestowed on the finger of the girl he loved would somehow make the separation less painful. Suddenly men were encouraged to wear "traditional" wedding bands (which had heretofore been rare and whose sudden appearance confounded clergymen everywhere), which just happened to contain about three times more gold than the average woman's wedding band. (In 1926 there was a failed attempt to sell men's engagement rings, which had been worn briefly in the nineteenth century; such "modern expressions of ancient customs" caught on sometimes, but not always.) Expensive platinum was encouraged over gold (platinum was said to better enhance the diamond), and De Beers suggested to retailers that they might have better luck with grooms of modest means if they extended credit to them. And when Francis Gerety invented one of the most successful advertising slogans of all time in 1948—"A diamond is forever"—she was paid in cold, hard cash.

3. It's well known that little girls are targeted for white weddings at the very earliest ages. Toys, costumes, television, and dolls especially give them a head start on the conspicuous consumption to which the wedding industry hopes they will aspire. Even their involvement as flower children instills in them the idea that someday they too will walk down the aisle at their own opulent nuptials. But the trend became much more methodical in the 1950s when World War II ended and soldiers returned home. The new prosperity that gripped America was not lost on the wedding industry. As the average marriage age dropped, the younger bride was targeted—with ads in *Seventeen* magazine, for instance, which had

> "If the bride gets married in a justice of the peace's office, it seems too quick and easy and not too important. But if the bride and her family go to a lot of trouble arranging a big wedding — and her father has paid a lot of money for it — she'll think twice about running home to Mother after the first tiff."
>
> — Priscilla Kidder (of Priscilla of Boston), 1970

never before carried ads for diamond rings, silverware, and the trappings of new brides. No longer satisfied with selling their wares to a onetime customer (the divorce rate was still low back then), companies pursued what they called "the customer for life." Girls graduating from high school would typically receive invitations to shows and fairs at which they could sample goods; the Lane furniture company produced thousands of miniature cedar "hope chests" that were given away free so that girls would remember the name "Lane" when it came time to buy the real thing. "They're never too young to start" may easily have been a motto of the wedding industry.

4. One of the biggest winners in the bridal industry sweepstakes has been the magazines, which carry millions of dollars worth of advertising in their glossy pages. *Brides* magazine kicked it off in 1934 and quickly came to be perceived as the bride's bible. Its throne was challenged in 1948 by the short-lived *Wedding Belle,* and in 1949 by *Modern Bride,* which addressed the "forward-thinking bride." True, all of these magazines carried editorials on subjects like wedding etiquette, but it was the advertisers who shaped content by influencing the accoutrements recommended by the writers and who even took it one step further by teaming up with magazine staffs to institute market research and help shape tastes. Magazine advertising, which was a $862 million industry in 1914, had grown to almost $3 billion in 1929. By 1940 over 40 pages of advertising preceded the contents page of *Brides,* and by 1960 each issue carried $2 million worth of advertising. In June 1952, a bride appeared on the cover of *Life* magazine in support of an article entitled "The Wedding Business," which cited the "profits from the U.S. sentiment of brides at the unsentimental rate of $3 billion a year." Astonishingly, the article celebrated rather than condemned conspicuous wedding consumption. With *Life*'s blessing, wedding consumption was becoming inextricably entwined with the American Dream.

5. Before 1910, shopping for bridal ensembles was a mail-order business dominated by Montgomery Ward and Sears. Shortly thereafter, when department stores began opening their doors, managers looked upon brides with dollar signs in their eyes. Here was the dream customer—one who was in the market potentially for just about everything they sold—and they had much to gain from promoting bridal consumerism. Gift-giving had traditionally been a personal, private gesture that was left to the discretion of the giver, but Marshall Field changed all that in 1924 by opening

After the wedding comes the home-making, when the young wife has often her first experience with those problems that make the weal or woe of the new home. As cleanliness takes a high place in the qualities that bring comfort and welfare, soap must be had. There is one soap that is always satisfactory because always pure. She may try others said to be just as good, but perfect comfort will come only with Ivory Soap — it is the standard.

Woe to the bride who fails to recognize the importance of Ivory soap, claims a magazine ad ca. 1900.

the first North American centralized gift registry in its stores and quickly following up by offering that service exclusively to brides. By 1929 more than half the department stores had started a gift registry. Not only was giving a gift to the bridal pair becoming a requirement (it was not always so), but guests were being told exactly what to give. The idea was sold to brides under the pretense of convenience—using a gift registry would do away with multiple toasters and too many sets of towels. What the stores were really doing, however, was selling more merchandise. Now brides who could not afford china and silver were being encouraged to register for these items, as well as a host of others, having been made to believe that these fine wares were the proper accoutrements of the new bride. "If you don't get your silver now, you may never get it," warned Amy Vanderbilt in 1952. Some retailers worked directly with bridal consultants to promote merchandise. The lavish window displays featuring elaborate bridal tableaux at stores like Wanamaker, Marshall Field, Altman's, Lord and Taylor, and Strawbridge and Clothier helped underscore the message to the passing public.

6. In 1855 a church deacon at Grace Church in New York City took it upon himself to offer general wedding advice to couples marrying in his church. He called himself "an undertaker of weddings," a job title that had changed to "master of ceremonies" by 1870. In 1925 the *Saturday Evening Post* reported on the growing number of "purveyors of the bride," and by 1930 bridal consulting had become a full-fledged occupation for women (with the occasional Franck here and there). In 1951 forward-thinking Jerry Connor, a jeweler by trade, established the National Bridal Service, which

was the first organization to train bridal consultants. The power of this group cannot be underestimated. Working with retailers and manufacturers, Connor's students were taught to promote products, legitimize new rituals, push ideas that benefited the industry, and generally be the best possible advertising for the wedding industry. Their job was to encourage brides to overcome any resistance they might have to the lavish wedding. At fairs and conventions, consultants were introduced to new wares and told exactly how brides might be convinced to purchase the items. "If you can get inside the bride's head, if you can dream what she is dreaming," Connor told an audience of bridal consultants, "you are no longer a worker charging an hourly rate. You are selling dreams, and you can charge anything." When consultants once complained that brides simply refused to adopt the new "bridal purse" that was to be carried throughout the wedding, they were told to "try harder." While bridal consultants in recent decades have become much more independent, it is always wise to inquire as to what partnerships or conflicts of interest may exist.

> "Sweetheart, I don't really care.... I just get 'em down the aisle." — Colin Cowie, FAMED BRIDAL DESIGNER, WHEN ASKED ABOUT THE SUCCESS OF THE MARRIAGES FOR WHICH HE HAS ARRANGED WEDDINGS, QUOTED IN *REBECCA MEAD, ONE PERFECT DAY* (2007)

Consider your Husband

..... WHEN YOU BUY YOUR TROUSSEAU SHEETS!

What! *Men* have ideas about sheets? Young lady, what a lot you have to learn! Just pick out any happily married couple you know, and ask Mrs. what her Mr. says about sheets.

You'll find that men have a horror of flimsy sheets. They're nervous if a sheet looks so flimsy that a yank might split it.

So, be good to your husband and make his bed with Pequots from the very start. Pequots are handsome, rich-looking sheets with a firm, strong body. To a man, this means comfort.

To you, that firm Pequot weave will mean luxury. A trim, smart look on the bed. A smooth surface that washing won't "fuzz up" ...that stays crisp in use...keeping "clean-sheet freshness" for days.

Best of all, Pequot strength means *wear*. Years of wear. You'll celebrate many wedding anniversaries before you think of replacing Pequots...another way to make a husband grateful! Pequot Mills, Salem, Massachusetts.

PEQUOT
SHEETS AND PILLOW CASES

Hints to New Homemakers...

1. *You'll get longer wear* if you have six sheets per bed and three cases per pillow. Rotate them in use.
2. *Not certain* how to tell quality? Every Pequot sheet bears a *guarantee* to exceed U. S. Government standards.
3. *"Efficient* as a filing system" your husband will say when he sees Pequot's projecting size tabs. At a glance, they help you select the right sheet from your linen shelf.
4. *Men like* plenty of foot room. Get 108-inch sheets (torn size)

and have plenty to tuck under at the foot...and plenty to turn back at top, saving your pretty new blankets.
5. *Extra strength* is furnished by Pequot's exclusive double tape selvage. Smart and handsome in appearance, too.

Cinderella Dreams:
The Allure of the Lavish Wedding

Cele Otnes is a professor of business and marketing at the University of Illinois at Urbana-Champaign. Her work focuses on ritualistic consumption—in particular, how and why consumers devote seemingly unbounded resources of time, energy, and money to occasions such as holidays, weddings, and other celebratory events. She is the author, with Elizabeth Pleck, of *Cinderella Dreams: The Allure of the Lavish Wedding* (2003). She writes:

Lavish weddings are the product of an industry—from advertising for De Beers diamonds, to the emergence and current state of wedding-oriented retailing, to the growth and evolution of the honeymoon industry and the ways Hollywood and other cultural producers have communicated the desire for, or resistance of, lavish weddings. Understanding this enables consumers to gain both an historical and a current understanding of the intricacies of the wedding industry, and of the benefits and drawbacks of living in a consumer culture in general.

Previous research on the meaning of the wedding typically argues that lavish weddings are primarily ways for families to either communicate their current social prestige or to attempt to elevate their status. Others suggest that the lavish wedding is intended to reward a woman for the sacrifices she will make for her husband. Here are some findings that shed additional light on the subject.

1. Weddings are celebrations both of our love of consumption, and of the consumption goods specifically designed to celebrate our culture's fascination with love—such as luxurious food, drink, attire, and travel.

Most Popular Wedding Months

June: 10.8 percent	December: 7.8 percent
August: 10.2 percent	November: 7.4 percent
May: 9.8 percent	April: 7.4 percent
July: 9.7 percent	February: 7.0 percent
September: 9.6 percent	March: 6.1 percent
October: 9.4 percent	January: 4.7 percent

No Laughing Matter

In January 2007, a bride in Austria jokingly answered "No" instead of "Yes" when asked if she wanted to marry her husband-to-be. The officiant promptly broke off the ceremony. Not even the bride's tears could reverse the decision, and the couple had to wait two and a half months before they could try it again.

2. Weddings, as well as engagements and honeymoons, allow consumers to inject magic into their lives. For women especially, but increasingly for men as well, weddings provide a way to bring the Cinderella myth, and all it implies, to life, even if just for a short time.

3. A wedding allows us to participate in a ritual that "freezes time," so that we might remember ourselves through photographs, videos, and other memory-capturing artifacts as youthful, beautiful celebrities within our own social circle. Moreover, the memories created by weddings allow us to link to the memories of other weddings within our own social networks.

4. The ethic that may lead many consumers to buy used cars or homes, or take a vacation at a local lake resort rather than a trip to Europe, is typically tossed out of the window when a wedding is being planned. This is because the complex of businesses that profit from lavish weddings has successfully reconceptualized the lavish wedding not just as a rite, but also as right for citizens in consumer cultures. As such, consumers have been given cultural permission to indulge in perfection-oriented consumption in this context, without the guilt hangover that might normally accompany a spending binge.

Cities with the Most Weddings

In 2002, New Orleans, Louisiana, proudly boasted over 36,000 weddings annually, and it would have appeared on this list were it not for Hurricane Katrina's devastation of the city in 2005.

1. Istanbul, Turkey: 166,000 weddings per year

2. Las Vegas, Nevada: 114,000 weddings per year

3. Gatlinburg, Tennessee: 42,000 weddings per year

Weddings by the Numbers

These statistics on weddings in the United States were gathered from the National Association of Wedding Ministers, the Bridal Association of America's Wedding Report, the Wedding Market Database, and other sources.

Annual sales income generated by the wedding industry: $50 billion

Average number of weddings performed annually in the United States: 2.4 million

Length of planning time for the average wedding: 7 to 12 months

Percentage of grooms who propose with ring in hand: 85 percent

Average size of engagement diamonds: 1.4 carats

Average cost of engagement rings: $4,976

Most popular diamond shapes: round (43 percent) and princess cut (31 percent)

Most popular engagement ring setting: white gold (39 percent)

Length of average engagement: 17 months

Number of first-time brides who receive a diamond engagement ring: 75 percent

Number of repeat brides who receive a diamond engagement ring: 67 percent

Number of couples who hire a wedding consultant: 45 percent

Number of weddings that include ethnic customs: 15 percent

Average number of wedding guests: 173

Age of the average bride: 26

Age of the average groom: 28

Median age for remarriage for women: 34

Median age for remarriage for men: 37

Number of weddings that take place in the summer: 35 percent

Number of weddings that take place in the spring: 29 percent

Number of weddings that take place in the fall: 23 percent

Number of weddings that take place in the winter: 13 percent

Number of engagements that take place between December and February: 30 percent

Number of winter weddings that take place during Christmas: 11 percent

Number of weddings that are destination events: 12 percent

Number of weddings that take place outdoors: 35 percent

Number of weddings that take place in a church: 53 percent

Number of weddings that take place in a hotel or country club: 22 percent

Length of average honeymoon: 7 days

17 Reasons Why Men Get Married

Jean Sanders Torrey, a "love expert," gives classes at the Learning Annex in New York City and has been featured on the "Ask the Expert" segments of Fox TV. She is the author of *Why Men Marry and Why Men Don't*. Here are the most common reasons men choose to marry, according to Torrey.

1. **Love:** Nothing makes a man more vulnerable than that fantastic euphoric feeling of being bewitchingly weak in the knees and crazy in love. He's incurably hooked, floating on clouds, clicking his heels, humming a love song, and dancing down the aisle vowing to love happily ever after.

2. **Lust:** When a man is deeply in lust, his testosterone is raging. Hormones run amuck, and this helpless man is enslaved by an uncontrollable primal passion to possess his woman. He pounds his chest, bays at the moon, and craves to capture her, drag her to his cave, and sate his sexual appetite through all eternity.

3. **Trophy wife:** This show-off, self-proclaimed trophy winner gets to wear his extraordinary prize—often purchased at an exorbitant prenuptial price—of a beautiful and usually much younger second or third wife on his arm. He basks in the covetous cordiality of his cronies.

4. **Companionship:** It's a lot more fun to laugh out loud at *I Love Lucy* reruns with shared Chinese take-out. Besides, with two you get egg roll.

5. **Peer pressure:** He's a widower who was married most of his long life. His and her women friends are on a mission to find an appropriate wife for him before an inappropriate one finds him. They want him safely married sooner rather than later.

6. **Fitting in:** He's one of the few single men left in his social circle and just doesn't fit in with the scheme of things. The wives arrange blind dates for him or flirt with him. The men keep an eye on their wives and are secretly envious of his freedom.

7. **Religion:** At long last, he's given up his sinning ways, seen the light, settled down, and done the right thing, by God.

8. **Social status:** If he's in a lower class of society and lacking in prominence but she is socially well situated, slammed doors may swing open by simply saying, "I do."

9. **Pressure in business matters:** In business a fetching spouse is a professional asset and will definitely give you a leg up on the corporate ladder. Financially speaking, when a man marries for money, he is often considered to have a good head for business. He can certainly make dear old Mom and Dad happy and thereby satisfy his family's wishes.

10. **For spite:** Once in a while, a rakish rogue plays rebound relay. He has a mean streak and wants to get married just to make a former wife or girlfriend jealous.

11. **Caretaker:** He is helpless and wants to be pampered, pleased, placated, and petted. And the poor darling needs someone to sort his socks, ski equipment, and sedatives, too.

12. **Fear of illness:** A macho man can quickly be reduced to a frightened little boy by an imagined or real malady, and the fear of being helpless or alone has prompted many a man to revive his priorities and promptly propose.

13. **Fear of death:** A life-threatening disease or a tragic accident can cause a confirmed bachelor to reexamine his life choices and even exchange hurried marriage vows while he is still bed-ridden.

14. **Likes being married:** He enjoys playing house, likes being a husband, and likes the idea of a wife. It's a feel-good habit with him. If this marriage fizzles and fails, he won't be discouraged, he'll just get married again.

15. **Wants a housekeeper/hostess/social director:** Experience has taught him that good help is expensive, hard to find, and difficult to keep. So he does one-stop shopping and marries the perfect candidate for the position . . . after interviewing many contenders, of course.

16. **Familial duty:** The union of families has long been used for power, prestige, and possession. He may propose marriage in order to strengthen the ties between the two families.

17. **Financial merger:** Money marries money, and the sum total makes more money, or at least lives a lovely lifestyle while trying. As somebody's mother once said, "It's just as easy to fall in love with a rich girl as a poor one."

Top Wedding Venues in 5 Major American Cities

Eventective.com is the Web's most complete online resource for meeting and event space. With more than one million visitors a month, Eventective offers the most comprehensive range of wedding venues, from museums and resorts to galleries and banquet facilities. Here is its list of the top wedding venues in five major cities in the United States.

Chicago

1. The Grand Ballroom
2. Galleria Marchetti
3. Germania Place
4. Studio 501
5. Great Hall of Café Brauer
6. Chicago Fine Arts Exchange
7. West Loop Studio
8. South Shore Cultural Center
9. Odyssey Cruises
10. Garden Weddings

Los Angeles

1. Park Plaza
2. Four Seasons Los Angeles at Beverly Hills
3. Los Angeles River Center and Gardens
4. City Club on Bunker Hill
5. MountainGate Country Club
6. Oviatt Penthouse
7. Hollywood Hotel
8. Silent Movie Theatre
9. University of California at Los Angeles (UCLA) Faculty Center
10. Golden Eagle Hospitality

Houston

1. Bella Terrazza
2. Groovey Grill Mansion
3. Magnolia Ballroom
4. Chateau Polonez
5. Houston Zoo
6. Always and Forever
7. Chateau Crystale
8. Alden Houston
9. Gardens Houston
10. Villa Ballrooms

New York

1. Broad Street Ballroom
2. Landmark on the Park
3. Tavern on the Green
4. Puck Building
5. Columbia University Faculty House
6. Central Park Boathouse
7. 21 Club
8. Omni Berkshire Place
9. Battery Gardens
10. 3 West Club

Miami

1. Zen House
2. Vizcaya Museum and Gardens
3. Fairchild Tropical Botanic Garden
4. Koubek Mansion and Gardens
5. Miami Shores Country Club
6. Coral Gables Venetian Pool
7. Fast Track Charters
8. Kovens Conference Center
9. Grand Salon Reception Hall
10. Birdside Banquet Hall

17 Recognized Wedding Officiants

Although a wide variety of individuals are permitted to perform wedding ceremonies, it is important to check local laws. In Colorado, for instance, couples can perform their own marriage, providing they have completed the necessary paperwork. It is widely believed that a ship's captain can perform a wedding ceremony, but this is in fact a myth and only happens on *The Love Boat*. Here is a list of recognized officiants:

1. Licensed minister or pastor of any denomination
2. Priest
3. Rabbi of any temple or congregation
4. Imam
5. Tribal chief (may perform only a Native American ceremony)
6. Pagan priestess or priest
7. Judge (current or retired)
8. Commissioned officer of the Salvation Army
9. Marriage commissioner (current or retired)
10. Magistrate
11. Notary public
12. Justice of the peace
13. Mayor
14. Governor
15. Clerk of the circuit court
16. Clerk or clerk-treasurer of a city or town
17. Legislator or constitutional officer

Still can't find an officiant? Visit UrdainMeNow.com to instantly become an ordained minister.

Wedding Day Numerology

Thousands of people have witnessed Elizabeth Joyce's incredible psychic powers on TV shows such as *Unsolved Mysteries, Beyond Chance,* and *The Psychic Detectives*. She is a frequent guest on radio shows across the country and the author of numerous articles and guided meditation recordings in addition to her book *Psychic Attack: Are You a Victim?* (2007). Elizabeth writes:

Numerology is the concept that all of life, known and unknown, is shaped by vibration and a specific creative moment of universal energy. As this energy moves and flows, it takes the shape of the wind, the sun, the ocean, the wedding dove, and all physical embodiments. From this flow and the energies describing it, you can interpret a life direction for your own individuality. You can see your purpose, your goals, and your obligations.

Your name and your date of birth represent a chemical formula which directs your karmic pathway and reveals your chosen purpose as you travel in this lifetime, including the cosmic influences on your wedding day. With every intake of breath you, too, belong to the cosmic universe and the heavenly spheres. These universal energies also affect your marriage, and the wedding day is as important as the decision to marry, the engagement ring, and the actual wedding vows.

One of the most important decisions regarding your wedding is the day and hour chosen to be married. We can often find our motives for marriage hidden carefully within our definition of love.

The date chosen for the wedding may determine the course your life together—as a couple—will take. The number of that day provides a key to the reasons we marry, and will open a doorway to help us understand how to obtain the happiness we seek as we begin to share our life, in every possible way, with our beloved.

To determine the numerology number of your wedding day, simply add the month, day, and year you will be, or have already been, married.

Example: Married: June 12, 2003 = 6 + 1 + 2 + 2 + 0 + 0 + 3 = 14

Continue to reduce the number 14 down to a single digit by adding 1 + 4.

Your Marriage Vibration Number = 5

Wedding numerology can supply the clues to what the special meaning of your wedding day holds for you, your partner, and your future together. The vibration of your special day will fall between Numbers 1 and 9. Below is a description of each day determined by the numerology.

Number 1: A Number 1 wedding day is ruled by the Sun. This day will place importance on what your disposition was together as a couple, as well as individually, prior to the marriage. The courtship was unforgettable, and perhaps a bit longer than most, and how you and your beloved met is quite a romantic story. Much like the hand of Fate. Choosing a Number 1 wedding day indicates that you are a very affectionate and loving couple. It shows a maturity with the marriage, and an ability to work through disagreements and upsets in a respectful manner. This loving couple is seeking total oneness with each other.

There is a strong desire within both of you for the marriage to succeed, even if there have been past failures. You both have tested each other quite thoroughly before the engagement was announced. You know each other's likes and dislikes very well, and that has been important, but remember that from this day forward you need to allow for the inevitability of change.

Number 1's Wedding Day Key to Success: Flexibility and understanding

Number 2: If you choose a Number 2 wedding day to be married, you will want either a very private or extremely public wedding. This is the number for eloping, and the Number 2 wedding day may need to be a marriage in secret. Your mother's advice will either be strongly accepted or rejected when making the wedding plans. There is no in-between. Emotional maturity of one of this couple may be lacking, but maturity is a valuable asset to the success of this union. Don't be surprised if everyone sheds a tear or two on this wedding day, for the ceremony will certainly have a sentimental quality.

The comforts of home will be stressed in a Number 2 marriage. You may have your apartment or home already set up, with one of you living in it, before the actual wedding. The Number 2 wedding day is ruled by the Moon, which represents womanhood and secrets, and the desire for a family may be a strong reason for this marriage. Also, the desire for a mate who can love the children of a previous marriage, and be someone who can be an understanding step-parent to them, may be a motive for a Number 2 wedding day.

If a pregnancy or these previous children are the only reason for the marriage, you may wish to reconsider your decision to marry.

Number 2's Wedding Day Key to Success: Being safe and being sure

Number 3: If you weren't joking when you said you'd marry only for the money, then you might find a Number 3 day an excellent choice for boosting your financial security through the luck of this partnership. You both may be overly concerned with what family and friends are thinking of your union, and also that your wedding has to be the biggest and the best. If you two expect too much, then this day should start off as a great big disappointment, with perhaps even a downpour of rain.

A Number 3 wedding day is ruled by Jupiter, so there may be many children born to this couple, as well as the possibility of multiple births, or extended family members living with you part of the time.

Number 3's Wedding Day Key to Success: Frugality and a willingness to expand your housing and your thinking

Number 4: If you both have been discussing and agreeing on all of the responsibilities of what marriage brings and have carefully weighed the pros and cons of married life, perhaps you will choose a Number 4 day to be married. The significance of a Number 4 wedding date is faithfulness until death do you part. This is a couple who can work together and accomplish goals that would otherwise seem impossible, such as running a business successfully together. Whatever it is, from buying a home to having your children, will be carefully timed and planned.

A touch of fate may have brought you and your beloved together. Somehow one partner fulfills the emotional needs of the other. Something thought missing in life is now found! A desire for security is another motivating factor with this marriage date. A Number 4 wedding day creates a marriage where it will be very important

to put down some roots, carry on the family name, and build a future. This is a Saturn-ruled marriage, and the couple will almost always choose to live near their parents or near the town where the bride grew up.

4's Wedding Day Key to Success: Oneness, watchfulness with money, an open heart, and joy

Number 5: If you have chosen a Number 5 as your wedding day, you may be putting the emphasis on how well you and your beloved communicate with each other. This will be an active marriage, and will need to fight monotony and boredom, so it will be wise to have some individual interests as well as ones shared. This is a marriage where each of you will need your space, your own workplace, and lots of alone time.

There will be quite a lot of traveling after this wedding, and each child born to the Number 5 marriage may be born in a different location. The Number 5 marriage is ruled by Mercury and signifies that possibly one mate will have to work to put the other one through college, law school, or medical school. In retirement this couple will remain active, with an interest in young people, to maintain a healthy outlook.

Number 5's Wedding Day Key to Success: Travel, change, surprises, and devotion to children and grandchildren

By U.S. presidential order, August 26, 1965, was the last day on which anyone could marry in order to improve their draft status, and 161 couples fled to Las Vegas in response. James Brennan, a minister there, performed 67 of the ceremonies, at $8 a pop. In her 1967 essay "Marrying Absurd," Joan Didion reported that one bride loaned her veil to six others and that the pastor, pressed to shrink the time each ceremony required, "got it down from five to three minutes. I could have married them en masse," he said, "but they're people, not cattle."

Lucky Sevens

Despite the caveats associated with the number seven, superstitious couples who subscribe to Las Vegas–style numerology, in which sevens are lucky, have gone to great lengths to secure triple sevens as their wedding date. Thus, on July 7, 2007 (7/7/07), some 38,000 couples tied the knot. That's more than three times the number of couples who normally get married on any Saturday in July. The Chapel of Flowers in Las Vegas, which normally hosts anywhere from 30 to 50 weddings on a Saturday, held 113 ceremonies on 7/7/07, and the Flamingo Las Vegas and the Venetian Resort Hotel Casino each held 77 weddings. The Ritz-Carlton offered a "Seven Ways of Wonderment" package that included posh accommodations and a tour of the Hoover Dam, one of the Seven Wonders of the World, for $7,707.

In 2008 the date to wed was August 8—triple eights—and although the rush to the altar was less frenzied, record numbers of couples chose this date known for bringing its own luck and good fortune. The Chinese believe that eight is a very lucky number, especially when associated with birth or wedding dates. (The opening ceremonies of the Olympic Games, held in Beijing, were staged on August 8, 2008.) As East meets West and our society encourages cultures to intertwine, many non-Chinese couples have adopted the significance of the numeral eight, especially in multiples, and decided that it is meaningful enough to be chosen as their wedding date.

Number 6: The blessings of Venus with all of her Love and Devotion fall on the Number 6 wedding day. Love, affection, peace, and happiness are the favors Venus may bestow. This does not mean that there is no challenge or that you are under some kind of magical charm. Responsibility, trust, and caring are a must for maintaining this wonderful beginning. This couple will be willing to work hard and long hours together, with lots of time for discussion and planning things out, because the marriage will become the utmost of importance in both lives.

Every effort will be made to patch up any quarrels, and the Number 6 marriage, as a Venus-ruled date, will be a good one for reconciliations. This also is a date of the couple's responsibility for an ailing parent in old age, as well as inheritance for maintaining one of the parents' home.

Number 6's Wedding Day Key to Success: Keeping an idealistic viewpoint and nurturing the love between you

Number 7: Watch out if you have chosen the Number 7 wedding date. Change, upsets, or a relocation of the reception hall may be in order. Though the Number 7 day represents upsets with plans, it may also represent being rescued at the very last minute. Ruled by Uranus, the Number 7 wedding day can represent lost plane tickets, accidents, a gown that doesn't fit, or the maid of honor showing up after the ceremony. Uranus also represents a fast and furious courtship, waking up in the morning and finding yourself married to a stranger, being stood up at the altar, as well as this partnership being an unwise decision. If there is happiness and love with this union, then perhaps one of the parents does not accept your intended as the proper mate, putting pressure and guilt on everyone.

This could be the wedding day of a mixed-race marriage, a Catholic-Protestant wedding, people of the same sex, or people of completely different backgrounds tying the knot.

Number 7's Wedding Day Key to Success: Freedom, flexibility, and sudden changes

Number 8: When choosing the Number 8 for your wedding day, you want to be compatible in every way with your partner, and sex will be a very important aspect to this relationship. This is the couple who, one enchanted evening, exchanged glances with each other across that crowded room and knew right away that they were meant for each other. Then they spent the next several weeks in bed, woke up one day, went to the Justice of the Peace, and were married. They will tell you that they felt married before the second glance on the first night they met. Once locked, they are inseparable.

The Number 8 wedding day is ruled by Mars and represents an excellent possibility for this couple to thrive in a business together as well as become a strong personal team. This may also be the marriage where one partner has to sacrifice for the other's career, with each partner admiring the courage of the other.

Number 8's Wedding Day Key to Success: Meeting challenges, occupation first, financial success, and servitude

Number 9: A Number 9 wedding day may indeed be one of secrecy, and another date of possible elopement, because the Number 9 wedding day is ruled by Neptune. The faith you were brought up in may be a very important factor to consider before this marriage takes place. This will be a very spiritual event, following all of the wedding rules of whatever faith is followed. One of this couple may practice medicine or perhaps may be handicapped. There is an overshadow of the Divine with this union, whether the couple being married are aware of it or not.

This is a marriage where there was a struggle to come together caused either by distance or by the strong objections of both families. It could be a marriage of different religions, where both choose to follow their religion of childhood, and may take a lot of working out. Also, one part of the duo may be quite wealthy while the other barely makes it financially, or they may be separated by a great age difference. Whatever the reasons for the objections to this wedding, both partners will find strength and solace with each other as they become of one house and hearth. If sacrifices have to be made of this union, and they usually do, they will be made with great love and devotion.

Number 9's Wedding Day Key to Success: Forever darling, loyalty, and an inner knowing of oneness

Age Requirements for Getting Married in the United States

Most states require that the bride and groom be at least 18 years old to marry legally, 16 with parental consent. Here are the exceptions:

Arizona: No statutory minimum. Those under 18 must have parental consent; those under 16 must receive the approval of a superior court judge as well as parental consent.

Arkansas: Age 18 for females, and 17 for males.

Georgia: Age 18; 15 with parental consent; 16 without parental consent if pregnancy is involved.

Hawaii: Age 18; 15 with parental consent.

Indiana: Age 18; 17 with parental consent.

Mississippi: Age 15 for females, and 17 for males; unlimited with parental consent.

Missouri: Age 18; 15 with parental consent.

Nebraska: Age 19; 17 with parental consent.

New Hampshire: Age 18, but as young as 14 for males and 13 for females with parental consent and under certain special circumstances.

Oregon: Age 18; 17 with parental consent.

Puerto Rico: Age 21; 18 with parental consent.

Texas: Age 18; 14 with parental consent; younger with judicial consent.

Utah: Age 18 for first marriage; 16 with parental consent; 14 with court approval or previous marriage.

Washington: Age 18; 17 with parental consent.

States That Recognize Common-Law Marriages

Most people are under the impression that once a couple has lived together for seven years they are legally married by common law. This is only partially true. Not all states recognize common-law marriages, and those that do generally have very specific requirements for such a union to be legal. Here is a list of these states and their requirements.

1. **Alabama:** The requirements for a common-law marriage are that each party have full mental capacity; that there be an agreement to be husband and wife; and that the marital relationship has been consummated.

2. **Colorado:** A common-law marriage may be established by proving cohabitation and a public reputation of being married.

3. **Georgia:** The union is recognized only if it was created before January 1, 1997.

4. **Idaho:** The union is recognized only if it was created before January 1, 1996.

5. **Iowa:** There must be a clear intent and agreement to be married, proof of continuous cohabitation, and public declarations that the parties are husband and wife.

6. **Kansas:** The couple must have the mental capacity to marry, agree to be married at the present time, and represent to the public that they are married.

7. **Montana:** The couple must have the capacity to consent to the marriage, have an agreement to be married, prove cohabitation, and have the reputation of being married.

8. **New Hampshire:** Common-law marriages are recognized for inheritance purposes only.

> Every state requires a license to legalize a marriage, and each state has its own laws regarding marriage licenses. Visit marriagelicense.com to determine your state's requirements.

9. **Ohio:** The union is recognized only if it was created before October 10, 1991.

10. **Oklahoma:** The couple must be mentally competent, agree to enter into a marriage relationship, and cohabit.

Exchanging McVows

In March 2006, coworkers Tyree Henderson and Trisha Lynn Esteppe tied the knot at the place where they worked, McDonald's, in Fairborn, Ohio. A traditional wedding ceremony was performed not far from the counter where customers continued to place orders for Big Macs and Chicken McNuggets.

11. **Pennsylvania:** The union is recognized only if it was created before January 1, 2005.

12. **Rhode Island:** The couple must have serious intent to be married and display conduct that leads to a reasonable belief by the community that they are married.

13. **South Carolina:** A common-law marriage is established if a man and woman intend for others to believe they are married.

14. **Texas:** The couple must sign a form provided by the county clerk. In addition, they must agree to be married, cohabit, and represent to others that they are married.

15. **Utah:** The couple must be capable of giving consent, intend to get married, cohabit, and have the reputation of being husband and wife.

16. **Washington, D.C.:** The couple must express an intention to be married and evidence of cohabitation.

5 Myths About Premarital Agreements

Between news coverage, soap operas, and family drama, we all have some preconceived notions about premarital agreements (also know as prenuptial agreements). Here are a few of the most common myths, debunked by Peace Talks Mediation Services, a divorce and custody mediation service in Los Angeles.

Myth 1: Prenuptial agreements are only for wealthy people. "My fiancé and I are not rich and so we don't need an agreement."

Fact: You may not be rich, but you definitely want to have a successful marriage. Having those honest discussions regarding how the two of you will approach finances will ensure that there won't be any surprises once you are married. You never want to actually need to enforce the premarital agreement, right? Talking about financial issues in advance will help ensure that you handle your finances with minimal conflict during your marriage as well as in the case of divorce.

Example: You may become rich in the future. Your education or ideas and talents may one day become more valuable than they are today. You need to think about how you'd want to handle the sale of a book, screenplay, or song; you may also need to think about how you'd handle the division of a business in the event of a divorce.

Example: Second and third marriages can often bring conflict between children from prior relationships and new spouses. Clear discussions about finances in a divorce or premature death situation help everyone avoid conflict later.

Myth 2: Prenuptial agreements are designed to simply protect the wealthier spouse and strip the other spouse of all of his or her rights. "I have no real assets, so why would I need a prenup?"

Fact: Prenuptial and premarital agreements should be designed to protect both spouses. Premarital agreements that are unfair and completely one-sided are probably not enforceable in court. By definition, the agreement must be fair. The basic requirements for premarital agreements to be enforceable are that the agreement must be signed voluntarily; it can't be unfair when it's signed; and each party needs to make a full disclosure of his or her assets and debts. Premarital agreements can be designed so that everyone's needs are met.

Example: With a premarital agreement, you will know in advance how your assets and debts would be handled in the event you do not stay married. You're negotiating the property settlement while

you're both in love with each other. You would not be at the mercy of your spouse's generosity or lack of generosity at the time of a divorce.

Example: If you end up needing your agreement to be enforced by the court, you'll be glad that you made it reasonable from the beginning (and therefore enforceable). For example, by providing a reasonable support structure for your spouse in the event of divorce, the premarital agreement defines the support's limits, terms, amount, and duration. If you left it up to a court, you would have no control over any of the terms.

Myth 3: Premarital agreements aren't romantic. "She'll think I'm not really committed."

Fact: Jessica Simpson didn't think they were romantic either. And there's nothing romantic about fighting about money once you're married because you never discussed how you'd handle your finances either. Clearly, premarital agreements are touchy subjects, but consider this quote from the Nolo Press book *Prenuptial Agreements: How to Write a Fair and Lasting Contract* (2004):

While a prenuptial agreement may not seem like a very romantic project, working together to consider and choose the terms of a prenup can actually strengthen your relationship. After all, marriage is a partnership in every sense of the word. Learning how to deal respectfully and constructively with each other about finances is a benefit in itself. So even if you conclude that you don't need a prenup, using this book can help you converse with each other about the important—and sometimes challenging—financial matters that are sure to arise in the course of your marriage.

When you marry, you make what you expect and hope will be a lifetime commitment to be there for each other in every way. Your prenup should support and reflect the spirit of partnership with which you approach your wedding vows.

Myth 4: Premarital agreements must deal with every issue that might come up in a divorce.

Fact: You can include as many issues or as few issues as you wish.

Because premarital agreements are private contracts, you can make them as detailed as you want.

Example: If the only thing you want your premarital agreement to accomplish is to protect your premarital property, you can limit your premarital agreement to that issue alone.

Example: If the only thing you want your premarital agreement to accomplish is to outline what would happen in the event of your death, in addition to a will or a trust, you can limit your premarital agreement to that issue alone.

Example: If you want your premarital agreement to cover almost every issue that might come up in a divorce except one or two issues (like spousal support, or contributions to a pension during the marriage, for example), then you can have the agreement cover everything except the issues you want to exclude.

Example: If you want your premarital agreement to cover every issue, you can do that too.

Myth 5: "If we don't get married, my live-in mate won't have any claims to my income or property."

Fact: You could risk your income or assets by living together without marrying. Palimony is a spousal support substitute for alimony or spousal support for people who are not married. Palimony claims are difficult to prove, but that doesn't stop some people from trying. Also, if you have an oral or written discussion about how you will own property, share income, assets, debts, and so forth, it's sometimes possible to make a claim that contract law applies (as opposed to family law) and that property should be divided even if it's only in one person's name, or only one person paid the bills. There are also real estate partition laws that can dictate how

A blank marriage certificate with spaces for pictures to be inserted, ca. 1869 **LIBRARY OF CONGRESS**

property is divided, and in some cases you can even force an involuntary sale at auction. If you are going to live together without getting married, you'll want a cohabitation agreement. It's better to decide who contributes to and owns property before you buy things rather than afterwards.

Example: Remember actor Lee Marvin (*The Dirty Dozen* and more than 60 other movies)? In the 1970s, his live-in girlfriend of 6 years, Michelle Triola, brought an action against him alleging that she and Lee Marvin entered into an oral agreement that during the time they lived together they would combine their efforts and earnings and share equally the property accumulated through their individual or combined efforts, and that Michelle would be his companion, homemaker, housekeeper, and cook and give up her career as an entertainer and singer. She further alleged that Lee Marvin agreed he would provide for all her financial support for the rest of her life.

After a couple of appeals, the court agreed with Michelle Triola. Lee Marvin had to pay her $104,000, which was quite a bit of money back in the 1970s. Worse still, you can imagine what he probably paid in attorney's fees to defend these claims. But that's only half the story: Michelle Triola Marvin also had an attorney who needed to be paid. Taken in this perspective, a premarital agreement or cohabitation agreement is a cost-effective way to handle this type of situation.

The truth is that a carefully crafted premarital or prenuptial agreement can cement your relationship, prompt you to have the hard discussions that engaged couples need to have, and ensure that your finances are handled the way you each intend in the event you were to divorce or pass away prematurely.

9 Reasons to Have a Small Wedding

You don't have to have an aisle runner; you don't even need an aisle. You don't have to have a white dress; you don't even have to wear white. You can pare it down and focus on the intimacy of the event. Intimate-Wedding.com gives us nine reasons to skip the frills.

1. You get to celebrate one of the biggest days of your life surrounded by people who love you. You'll feel more relaxed.

2. Because only close friends and family will be present, you'll get to spend time with each of your guests.

3. You can save thousands of dollars by having an intimate wedding, which means your nuptials won't put you or anyone else in debt.

4. You can splurge on special details. Some couples choose a small guest list not necessarily because their budgets are limited but because they can pull out all the stops and have a truly lavish—though small—wedding.

5. You have more options when choosing a venue. Since you won't need a large space to accommodate your guests, many doors will be open to you.

6. You will have more freedom to customize your wedding to your own tastes. A small wedding gives you the opportunity to get your creative juices flowing and make your wedding a unique reflection of the two of you. Your wedding will be more likely to be remembered in years to come.

7. You'll benefit the environment by dispensing with all those extra invitations and decorations.

8. You will defy a multibillion-dollar industry that methodically preys on the emotions and vulnerabilities of brides in order to extract as much money from them as is humanly possible.

9. By having a small wedding, you can devote more of your time and resources to what's really important: your marriage and your future.

> "Money has nothing to do with style.... You may feel compelled to do a black-tie affair, but if you're a casual person, there's nothing wrong with a party that's casual and elegant." — Colin Cowie

The Pros and Cons of Destination Weddings

To pull off a destination wedding, you need to keep everyone informed of your plans. (Here's where a wedding website comes in really handy; see "10 Things to Include on Your Wedding Website" on page 190.) In choosing a destination, check out the list that follows and surf the Internet for the zillions of other possibilities. Do remember that low prices are best had during low season, and if it's low season, there's a reason. Check out long-term weather patterns before you commit. Here are some reasons to do it and some reasons not to.

Pros	Cons
You'll save money . . .	but you won't get as many gifts.
You'll have an instant honeymoon . . .	without any kind of privacy whatsoever.
Someone else will handle most of the details . . .	and you'll have to give up control.
You can still have a party later for friends who could not attend . . .	but chances are there will still be hurt feelings somewhere.

23 Important Tips for Planning an Outdoor Wedding

Whether the setting is the beach in Puerto Vallarta, the local botanical garden, or your own backyard, outdoor weddings come with their own challenges. These tips will help.

1. Make sure guests know that the wedding will be an outdoor affair so they can dress appropriately. You can emphasize this on the map or directions card you enclose with the invitation.

2. Make sure there are adequate bathroom facilities, even if the wedding is being held at home. Rented latrines—these actually come in wedding models, complete with flush toilet and sink—might be appropriate.

3. Make sure the site has adequate electricity for the party you have planned. The musicians and photographers will depend on it.

4. Let all your vendors know that it's an outdoor affair. There may be extra setup charges, and you don't want to be surprised when you tally up the bill.

5. Be sure the photographer is familiar with the site and its particular challenges.

6. Have a plan B. You'll need a tent if it rains. Make sure the tent is big enough to accommodate all your guests. Allow 15 square feet per guest.

7. Even if it doesn't rain, make sure the area is not one that will get muddy or flood if it rains the day before.

8. Arrange for parking nearby.

9. If the wedding is in a residence, make sure the neighbors are aware of the event so that you can work out any objections to the crowd ahead of time and make sure that lawn mowers and noisy children don't interrupt your ceremony. Invite as many neighbors as possible to the wedding to garner cooperation.

10. Include citronella candles in your decorations to keep bugs at bay.

11. Place candles in hurricane lamps so that breezes won't get to them.

12. If the wedding is in a grassy area, set up a wooden dance floor for the reception. (The musicians may be able to help you with renting a floor.)

13. Plan the ceremony downwind—use tents or trees to block the wind.

14. Practice walking down the aisle before the ceremony, especially if you'll be traversing soft or rocky ground.

15. Set up seats so that your guests aren't facing the sun. Visit the venue the day before at the exact time of your ceremony to determine the position of the sun.

16. Use heavy tablecloths, cloth napkins with heavy napkin rings, and weighted vases and accessories to keep everything in place in a windy setting.

17. Use a pretty umbrella to protect the cake.

18. Use fondant or marzipan frosting for the cake; buttercream will melt outdoors.

19. Offer your guests a continuous supply of sparkling water to keep everyone hydrated.

20. If there's a chance of a chill in the air, rent portable outdoor heaters.

21. The bride will probably be most comfortable in a dress with a detachable train or none at all.

22. The groom should consider bringing an extra shirt or two to the event. Humidity together with inevitable jitters can wreak havoc on a man's clothing.

23. If the wedding is at home, make sure you've not only notified the neighbors but also secured whatever permits might be needed (check with the local police department). Make sure nothing else is going on that day, lest the "I do's" can't be heard over the noise of, say, roadwork going on just up the street.

12 Symbols of Life

In a wedding ceremony honoring African culture, the officiant may administer the 12 symbols of life, each representing the love and strength that brings two families together:

Wine: The mixing of the blood of the two families

Wheat: Fertility and the giving of life and land

Pepper: The heated times the families will have

Salt: Healing and preservation of the marriage

Bitter herbs: The growing pains of married life

Water: Purity and dissolution of bitterness

Spoon, pot: Healthy food that builds strong families

Broom: The cleanliness of health and well-being

Honey: The sweet love between a black man and woman

Spear: Protection of the sanctity of home and community

Shield: The honor and pride of the home

Bible or Koran: The symbol of God's truth and power

14 Ways to Incorporate Your African Heritage into Your Wedding

1. Opt for a traditional costume such as a tunic-style gown and a headdress made of African materials. Kente cloth, for instance, is popular.

2. Use African colors—red, green, and black—as your color scheme.

3. Choose invitations that include ethnic accents, such as natural papers with gold trim or dried greenery.

4. Have a gospel choir sing during the processional.

5. Have a drum beating softly during the ceremony.

6. Appoint a "warrior" instead of a best man. He will walk down the aisle ahead of the groom holding a shield in front of him to protect the bonding of the bride's and groom's families.

7. Ask the family members to share kola nuts after the ceremony.

8. As you stand at the altar, hold hands with your spouse as someone binds your wrists together with a long length of braided grass.

9. Perform the jumping-the-broom ritual after the formal ceremony and ask the officiant to explain its history and significance to your guests.

10. Hire dancers to perform traditional African dances during the reception.

11. Incorporate the thoughts and ideas of famous African Americans into your vows and speeches.

12. Write about your decision to honor your heritage in the wedding program and include the thoughts of those who have inspired you.

13. Include traditional African foods such as chicken, plantains, yams, and banana fritters in the menu.

14. Ask a jeweler to design wedding rings that incorporate African symbols and decorations.

How to Add Ethnic Accents to Your Wedding

Incorporating foreign customs or accessories into your wedding plans can go far in uniting families of different cultures and religions, or it can simply be your way of making a statement about your worldview. You can dedicate one pre-wedding event to a particular style or custom, or you can use foreign rituals and motifs in your

- Decorations
- Music
- Food
- Invitations
- Wedding program
- Clothing accessories
- Dances
- Ceremony blessings

Peruse the lists in chapter 1 to learn more about the brides in other countries who have walked down the aisle before you; they have lovely customs, and you may want to use some of them even if you have no connection to the culture in question. Be sure to describe your efforts and the meaning behind them in your wedding program. Here are some ways to feature foreign cultures in your wedding plans.

Buddhist: The bride carries a string of 21 ojuju beads, representing Buddha, the families, and the bride and groom.

Chinese: Use red flowers to symbolize luck, and to bring families together, incorporate the tea ceremony into your ceremony.

English: Before the wedding, assemble the wedding party and have them walk to the church together. Some musical accompaniment might be nice.

Filipino: Releasing two white doves at the end of the ceremony is a lovely way to honor this culture.

French: Forgo the wedding cake and opt instead for stacks of cream puffs filled with French pastry cream—called a croquembouche. These are becoming popular everywhere.

Greek: The bride wears a red or yellow veil, symbolizing fire, which keeps her safe from evil spirits.

Hispanic: White flowers will invoke Spanish culture. During the ceremony, the bride and groom have their hands loosely tied with a decorative rope to symbolize their union.

Indian: In a henna ceremony, the bride has her hands and feet painted with elaborate designs (or just one small one). The couple marries beneath a red canopy called a *mandapa*.

Irish: The bride (who might carry a horseshoe) and groom walk down the aisle together. Shamrocks figure prominently in the decorations.

Japanese: A sake-sharing ceremony unites the new family. The groom crushes a raw egg with his bare foot to symbolize the delicacy of the marriage bond. Origami cranes, perhaps hanging from branches, make appropriate decorations.

A "double-happiness" wedding cake COURTESY OF WEDDING STAR/
BRIDALPEOPLE.COM

Jewish: The groom steps on a glass at the end of the ceremony. Dancing the hora at the beginning of the reception brings guests together.

Korean: Ducks and geese—birds that mate for life—are often seen at these weddings.

Native American: Corn figures prominently in the menu. Decorations consist of a cornucopia of dried fruits and vegetables.

Scottish: The kilted groom kicks off the lively Highland fling dance. The poetry of Robert Burns punctuates the ceremony. And there are always bagpipes.

Ethnic cake toppers COURTESY OF WEDDING STAR/BRIDALPEOPLE.COM

Musical Accents

No matter what you've chosen for your musical lineup, adding these instruments to the ensemble will lend yet another ethnic accent to your wedding.

African	drums, kalimba
Celtic	bagpipes, flute
Chinese	lute
Indian	sitar
Italian	concertina
Jewish	klezmer
Mexican	guitar
Middle East	harp, flute
Polish	accordion
Russian	bulalaika, autoharp

15 Wacky Ways to Wed

1. While Skydiving Hundreds of couples have taken the plunge—literally—by skydiving their way into the future. Various packages, offered throughout the country, include a preacher who performs the ceremony as the aircraft climbs to jump altitude, a terra-firma reception, and a DVD of the event. The veil probably won't fit under the helmet, but who cares—couples who choose this venue are used to casting their fate to the wind.

2. On a Roller Coaster Experience the thrill of soaring through the air, your veil flailing in the wind, as you scream your vows on a roller coaster. Thousands of couples have started married life this way at places like Disneyland and Six Flags. In 1993, at Busch Gardens, 46 couples coasted into matrimony in one of the most unusual group weddings ever. "The bride just needs to make sure she straps on her veil extra tight," says the Rev. Cliffert Herring, who has been marrying couples on roller coasters since 1985. Most amusement parks host weddings on terra firma as well (see "Mass Weddings," page 40).

3. In a Hot-Air Balloon Hot-air balloonists have been traversing the skies since the eighteenth century. Today you can start the most romantic day of your life at sunrise and watch the excitement unfold as ribbons of fabric come to life and a hot-air balloon takes you above the earth. You can take your vows above valleys and rivers while you wave to the tiny "ants" on the ground. Such weddings, which evoke feelings of awe and wonder in everyone who witnesses them, have become fairly common today.

4. In a Cave If you prefer stalactites and stalagmites to cupids and confetti, consider going underground for your nuptials. There's a wooden pulpit and pews in the Crystal Wedding Chapel at Niagara Cave in Harmony, Minnesota; at Cumberland Caverns in McMinnville, Tennessee, the reception takes place below the earth beneath a three-quarter-ton crystal chandelier. In fact, you can take the rocky road to the altar in any number of cave attractions throughout the United States. Those who find such weddings a bit too tame often head for Moaning Cave in Vallecito, California: after donning jumpsuits and taking the plunge 180 feet into the cave's main chamber, the bridal pair greet their guests, who have descended a 100-foot spiral staircase to the reception area.

5. Underwater The vows may sound a bit garbled, and there's no telling when a barracuda might show up to crash the wedding, but getting married underwater seems to hold a special attraction for couples who choose to say their vows among family, friends, and fish. Australia's Great Barrier Reef has been a popular place for such weddings, and they are routinely held in Bali, Maui, and other exotic locations. Americans who choose stateside weddings have their pick of any number of Florida Keys underwater wedding services, including Jules' Undersea Lodge, "the world's only underwater hotel," in Key Largo. The kiss is a little tricky.

6. At the Largest Shopping Mall in the World Imagine being able to register for gifts at Macy's, pick up a wedding dress at Jessica McClintock's, choose wedding rings from Zale's, purchase all your bridal gear at a special wedding boutique, and get married—all in one day and all without ever leaving the shopping mall. Who

A wedding on high PHOTO BY MYLES ARONOWITZ/LUSHPHOTOGRAPHY.COM

Fish was the main course at this underwater wedding. COURTESY OF MARY SEID

would want to get married in a shopping mall? Over 5,000 couples who loved the charming little 70-seat Chapel of Love in the largest shopping mall in the world, the Mall of America in Bloomington, Indiana, which has been performing McWeddings since 1994. There's a photographer right on the premises, and after the ceremony guests can head over to Moose Mountain Adventure Golf for a green reception.

7. **Atop the Empire State Building** Bridezillas and groomzillas who think they're above it all might opt to marry against the backdrop of the New York City skyline, following in the footsteps of King Kong by ascending to the top of what may no longer be the tallest building in the world but which certainly remains one of the most legendary. Weddings on Valentine's Day have been a tradition at the Empire State Building since it was completed in

1933. Although private events are no longer accommodated, each year building management teams up with Condé Nast Bridal Media's Brides.com to invite couples to submit their love stories and state why they want to be married at the top of the Empire State Building. Fourteen couples are selected to exchange their vows atop the building on Valentine's Day, and they are each treated to the exclusive planning, fashion, and beauty help of Brides.com, along with gifts valued at $500. Entries are accepted until October 31 of each year, and winners are notified by November 19. Visit Brides.com for more information.

8. **In Front of a Bridge in Madison County** Roseman Bridge in Winterset, Madison County, Iowa, is the place where Robert Kincaid and Francesca Johnson's star-crossed romance was memorialized in Robert James Walker's best-selling novel *The Bridges of Madison County*. Since shortly after the book was published in 1992, tourists have been flocking to this tiny town with a population of just 4,500 to relive their favorite tearjerker. And inevitably, romantic-minded travelers have chosen to marry there. "Couples like the extent of the commitment that Robert and Francesca had to each other, that they found their soul mate," says Pat Nelson, an event planner whose quiet event business was swamped with requests for over 50 weddings after the movie was released in 1995. "They always want the minister to say what Robert says to Francesca: 'This kind of certainty comes once in a lifetime.'"

9. **In Birthday Suits!** Is the bride just too busy to find a dress? Does the groom abhor the idea of a tux? Do without. No one will notice what anyone's wearing at one of the many nude weddings that are held throughout the world, at resorts, on cruises, and in communities dedicated to the idea that less is more. "Couples who get married in the nude are closer to God," claims the Rev. Jo Ann Pessagno, a minister who has officiated at more than 80 nude ceremonies. The resort known as Hedonism III offers an annual "Group Nude Wedding" package that invites couples to wed en masse, and Nancy Tiemann, owner of Bare Necessities Tour and Travel, has seen a rise in the number of nude weddings, especially after the release of the 2005 film *Confetti* (see page 139), which features a nude wedding. No more hideous bridesmaid dresses!

10. **At the Ice Hotel, Quebec City, Canada** Imagine the ultimate fairy-tale wedding in a setting that sparkles with the majesty of ice-carved surroundings. The only hotel in the world that is reconstructed annually takes 15,000 tons of snow and 500 tons of ice. It hosts more than 65,000 visitors and 4,000 overnight stays each year, and yes, everything from the 80-seat chapel to the beds is

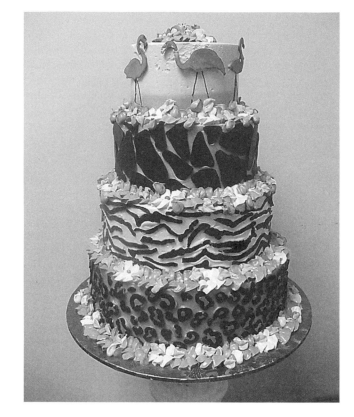

What's a wacky wedding without a wacky cake? COURTESY OF CARYN NASH, CARYNSCAKES.COM

made of ice. Since its creation, the Ice Hotel has hosted weddings for more than 150 couples from around the world. The sleigh ride through the wooded path, the spa facilities, and rental of fur capes are optional.

11. **In Outer Space** Over the next decade, Space Adventures' clients will fly on suborbital flights, on voyages that orbit Earth, and on historic expeditions that circumnavigate the moon. On dozens of different vehicles, space travelers will visit private space stations by boarding flights leaving from spaceports both on Earth and in space.

Space Adventures, which sent financier Dennis Tito on the first space tourism trip in 2001, has done global demographic research to assess the potential of its honeymoon tours. It estimates there are 500 to 1,000 people who can afford a $100 million ticket for the 10- to 21-day round trip, with a possible stopover at the Inter-

national Space Station. It is hoping to lift off a couple for a lunar rendezvous sometime soon.

12. **In a Tent** For the rugged at heart, consider Turtle Dreams B&B and Tipi Campground, where your reception can take place around a huge bonfire under the stars and your first night as a married couple is spent inside a spacious (27-foot-wide) traditional tipi.

13. **At Tori Spelling's House** The home of Tori Spelling and her husband Dean McDermott, Chateau la Rue in Fallbrook, California, offers couples a unique wedding experience amid hip, mod furnishings and country kitsch. The Oxygen network captures Tori and Dean's struggles in a reality TV show.

14. **In Outer Mongolia** Set amid the beauty of Mongolia's spectacular Gobi Desert, the largest in Asia, the eco-friendly Three Camel Lodge is a place where you can get married in a nomadic tent or have local artisans whip up something special in traditional Buddhist style (without any nails). The place offers a unique combination of adventure and sophistication, traditional style and full service, with expedition offerings that no wedding guest will soon forget.

15. **On Third Base** If you're the type who's thinking of postponing the wedding because you don't want to miss a big game, why not get married at a baseball field? Most large sports venues can accommodate special events, and getting married in a ballpark could turn your wedding day into a field of dreams. This kind of wedding is usually held on a nongame day or up to five hours before a game. Digital billboards will greet your guests, and what could be more fun than a wedding cake in the shape of the venue itself? Imagine getting married on home plate with your guests seated in the bleachers cheering you on. The views are always wonderful, and your wedding photos will be nothing if not unusual.

On March 11, 2006, Yankee Stadium in New York served as the wedding chapel for Ed Lucas, a blind radio baseball reporter, and Allison Pheifle, his legally blind fiancée. It was the first time a wedding took place on the actual baseball diamond.

13 Themed Las Vegas Weddings

Graceland Chapel's Reno (officiant at the wedding of the authors), with his real-life bride COURTESY OF THE GRACELAND WEDDING CHAPEL

Viva Las Vegas Weddings invites marrying couples to let their imaginations soar. Sure, Elvis weddings are fun, but Ron Decar, who has been operating the venue since the 1980s, has taken themed weddings a few steps further. Gangsters, pirates, ghosts, and bikers have all been in attendance at the weddings here, and if your special fantasy isn't on the menu, Decar will help you make it your wedding reality. Many packages include costume rentals, a video, and a live webcast of the ceremony, so just about anyone can "attend," and prices for all these themed possibilities are a fraction of the norm for a formal wedding (which is also offered at Viva Las Vegas Weddings). To find out more about the four different chapels available, visit VivaLasVegasWeddings.com.

Here are some of our favorite wedding themes:

1. **Intergalactic** Stardate: your wedding day. Presiding over your ceremony is the one and only Captain James T. Quirk, who is "beamed" into the chapel. Surrounded by live-size cutouts of your favorite space characters, you enter into your new life going where no spouse has gone before.

2. **James Bond** If you've always wanted to get married at Casino Royale, choose this package, which includes a 007 impersonator to perform the ceremony, a spectacular sports car entrance for the bride and groom, the dancing Bond Girls, and a special rendition of "Diamonds Are Forever." Lasers and fog abound, and friends who are unable to attend can watch the event live on the Internet via a special spycam.

3. **Egypt** Because your love is as timeless as the Pyramids, the chapel will be transformed with a golden sarcophagus, Pharaoh's treasures, hieroglyphic displays, theatrical lighting, and fog. The bride enters on Cleopatra's Throne, carried down the aisle by

An Egyptian-themed wedding at the Viva Las Vegas Wedding Chapel COURTESY OF VIVALASVEGASWEDDINGS.COM

slaves who attend to her every need, and a belly-dancing goddess performs for the groom's pleasure. King Tut presides over the ceremony as you bind your lives together in the eternal light of Ra, the Sun God.

4. **Harley Wedding** Here comes the biker bride! His and hers bikes are available for the trip down the aisle (some couples opt for one bike with the bride on the backseat), and fog lights and rock music add to the festivities. Get your motors runnin' as you ride into the sunset together as husband and wife.

5. **Woodstock** Fill your wedding with the classic music of Woodstock. Would you like Jimi Hendrix to perform the ceremony? How about Janis Joplin as your maid of honor? Impersonators are available, and they'll even sing three songs as part of the basic package. BYOA.

The Big Kahuna gets his Gidget. COURTESY OF VIVALASVEGASWEDDINGS.COM

A bridal bash at Dr. Frankenfurter's castle for a Rocky Horror wedding COURTESY OF VIVALASVEGASWEDDINGS.COM

6. **Rocky Horror Wedding** Star in your very own cult classic as Minister Frankenfurter is joined by Riff Raff, Magenta, Eddie, and the rest of the cast of the *Rocky Horror Picture Show*. Frankenfurter kicks off the festivities with "I'm Just a Sweet Transvestite" and launches into "There's a Light" as the unity candle is lit. The bride and groom may be dressed as Janet and Brad as they time-warp their way out of the chapel once the ceremony is over. Guests love this theme, but it's the pelvic thrust that really drives them insane.

7. **Viva du Cirque** As you light the flame of the unity candle, an aerial adagio will be performed high above your guests by a per-

Merlin officiates at a medieval-style wedding. COURTESY OF VIVALASVEGASWEDDINGS.COM

Skullcrusher. Sing along to sea shanties and chart a course for adventure on the high seas of marital bliss. It's a swashbuckling good time. Shiver me timbers—ye shall be wed!

10. **Beach Party** Beach balls, party gear, and a good old-fashioned clambake transform your wedding into a summertime extravaganza. The bride is escorted down the aisle on a surfboard, and a party-heart minister performs the ceremony. The music of the Beach Boys and beach movie clips provide plenty of nostalgia.

11. **Gangster** Welcome to la famigilia! It's the Jazz Age, a time of gangsters and molls, bootleggers and backroom deals. The Godfather will perform the ceremony in what appears to be a quaint Italian restaurant with checkered tablecloths, candles, and Chianti bottles, and he'll bless your union and remind you of the importance of loyalty to your new family. Buona fortuna!

12. **Camelot** Fill your wedding day with all the pageantry of King Arthur's Court. For the minister, choose Merlin the Magician or King Arthur himself. The bride and groom are king and queen for the day, with two Knights of the Round Table to herald their entrance amid medieval fanfare and all the wizardry and magic of the time.

13. **Gruesome Gatherings** Couples who prefer black roses to orange blossoms and ghouls to wedding guests can choose from among a number of spooktacular weddings at Viva Las Vegas Weddings. Possible officiants include Count Dracula, the Phantom, the Grim Reaper, or a vampire, and haunting music and fog provide atmosphere for a wedding that will haunt you forever. Spirits are always in attendance, but you can't see them.

forming duo whose movements symbolize the union of your two souls, their bodies intertwining in the mists overhead. Las Vegas drama at its best.

8. **Sigmund and Freud** These well-known Las Vegas maestros of magic, mystery, and machismo will confound you and your guests as they fill your ceremony with laughter, illusion, and a stuffed menagerie of wild animal friends. Watch closely as they make all your last-minute jitters about getting married disappear! Trapeze performers can be added for an additional fee.

9. **Pirates** All hands on deck as you take your plunge into wedded bliss with the smart-talking, knee-slapping humorous Captain

7 Great Las Vegas Wedding Chapels

The Rev. Dr. Aurore Leigh Barrett, an ordained minister, licensed wedding officiant, marriage counselor with over 20 years' experience in Las Vegas weddings, and the CEO of Weddings Las Vegas, rates the following chapels as offering the best bang for your wedding buck. For more information visit WeddingsLasVegas.com.

1. **A Special Memory Wedding Chapel** is owned by a family that has been in the wedding chapel business for over 35 years. In fact, the son, who now runs the chapel business, started out by stamping brochures when he was 4 years old. The family once owned the famous Candlelight Wedding Chapel, which was closed in 2004; the building was donated to the Clark County Heritage Museum, where it now sits. In 2005 the family purchased A Special Memory Wedding Chapel. President Ronald Reagan once attended a wedding here, and John Tesh and Connie Selleca renewed their vows at this pretty chapel. It's a lovely, New England–style, stand-alone building located between the Las Vegas Strip and downtown Las Vegas.

2. The **Graceland Wedding Chapel** has been in business for over 50 years, and it is the place to go if you want an "Elvis" wedding. You can even have a wedding with dueling Elvis impersonators. Jon Bon Jovi was married here, and in 2001 he held a concert in the chapel parking lot with 75 couples who renewed their vows with him and his wife!

3. **Little Church of the West** opened for business in 1942. The motif is the Old West. With an exterior of cedar and an interior of California redwood, the small chapel looks much the same today as it did when it was built. The chapel building has been moved four times and is now located at the south end of the Las Vegas Strip. In 1992, when the chapel turned 50 years old, it was elected to the National Registry of Historical Places.

4. **Little Chapel of the Flowers** is a small, white, stand-alone chapel located on Las Vegas Boulevard between the Las Vegas

What You Should Know About Getting Married in Las Vegas

To find out more about the legal aspects of the kitschiest weddings in the world, contact the Las Vegas Marriage License Bureau at 702-671-0600. (Read more about the history and lore of these weddings in chapter 2.) Here are the basics:

Cost: The license fee is $55 cash. No appointment is necessary.

Blood test: No blood test is required, and there is no waiting period after a license is issued.

Application: Both parties must appear at the Marriage License Bureau, 201 Clark Avenue. For faster service, you may download the marriage license application and have it filled out before you arrive at the Marriage License Bu-

reau. However, you may not submit the application online, and both the bride and groom must complete the application. Proper identification (in the form of a driver's license, a birth certificate, a passport, a military ID, or a resident alien card) must be presented for both parties.

Age requirements: Those under the age of 18 and over the age of 16 must have parental consent.

Marriage ceremonies: In order to have a legal marriage, a ceremony must be performed in the State of Nevada within one year from the date of issuance of the marriage license by any person licensed or authorized to perform ceremonies

in Nevada. The ceremony may be performed in any wedding chapel or church or by the Civil Marriage Commissioner. The marriage license must be obtained from the Marriage License Bureau and presented to the chapel prior to the ceremony. These marriages are recognized throughout the world.

Witness: There must be at least one additional witness other than the person performing the ceremony. All the chapels provide a witness free of charge.

Prior marriages: If you are divorced, the divorce must be final. You must know the month, year, city, and state in which the divorce became final.

Strip and downtown Las Vegas. There are actually three chapels located on this property. The chapel has been in the wedding business for 50 years and offers military discounts and renewal-of-vows specials to any couples originally married at the Little Chapel of the Flowers.

5. The **Little White Wedding Chapel** has been in business for almost 65 years. Its owner, Charlotte Richards, has been working in the Las Vegas wedding industry since the 1950s and has been featured on many television programs. Located between downtown and the Las Vegas Strip, there are five chapels on the grounds from which to choose. This chapel boasts many celebrity weddings, including Paul Newman/Joanne Woodward and Steve Lawrence/Eydie Gorme, and six of Mickey Rooney's eight weddings were celebrated here.

6. **Wee Kirk O' the Heather** has been operating since 1940 and was featured in the film *Intolerable Cruelty* with George Clooney and Catherine Zeta-Jones. The chapel is a small white building with a wrought-iron fence surrounding it, but everything from a simple ceremony to an elaborate spectacle can be accommodated.

7. **Viva Las Vegas** is the perfect setting for your over-the-top wedding. Costumes and theatrical effects are part of any of its themed packages. The "Elvis Blue Hawaii Wedding Package," with its lush tropical set and hula girls dancing to the "Hawaiian Wedding Song," is a popular choice. Camelot, pirates, exotic Egyptians, and Elvis are all on the menu here, with others.

The Rev. Barrett's Most Memorable Wedding Moments

1. The couple who worked in the circus and had a lion for a ring-bearer

2. The couple who insisted on being married at a drive-through window so that all their dogs could be present at the ceremony

3. The wedding that featured three dogs as maid of honor, best man, and flower girl

4. The drive-through wedding at which all the guests, crowded into a vintage roadster, were dressed as 1920s gangsters

5. The cross-dressing couple: she wore a tux, he wore the dress

6. The couple who showed up dressed as fairies from Midsummer Night's Dream

7. The Elvis wedding at which all the male guests were dressed as Elvis

8. The couple who showed up as Tina Turner and Ike, who told the bride he'd beat her if she didn't hurry down the aisle

9. The wedding at which the groom faked a seizure to get out of it

Marriage on the Rocks: 7 Weddings Set on Stone

Couples who are drawn to the strength and stability that rocks symbolize can make their choice among these stony sites:

1. Mount Rushmore, South Dakota, for the famous granite quartet (great photo ops)

2. Sedona, Arizona, where New Agers can marry amid the swirling waves of energy that emanate from the earth's surface

3. Sentinel Dome, Yosemite National Park, Yosemite, California, where a rounded, lunarlike expanse of granite rises up to 8,122 feet and offers a majestic 360-degree view of the breathtaking surroundings

4. Hawaii, Volcanoes National Park, where the lavalike landscape sets the mood for steamy romance

5. Crow Creek Mine, Girwood, Alaska, a 100-year-old mining camp where there are no modern amenities whatsoever and couples head down to the creek after the ceremony to pan for gold

6. Chimney Rock Park, Chimney Rock, North Carolina, a 535-million-year-old monolith where windswept weddings are held at 2,280 feet

7. Herbert Glacier in Juneau, Alaska, where the "aisle" is 8.5 miles long and can be traversed only by helicopter and where, because cold feet are the norm at the dozen or so weddings held here each year, the bride needn't bother with "something blue"

9 Outrageous Gay Weddings in the United Kingdom

Pink Weddings is the United Kingdom's first and most respected gay-owned, dedicated gay wedding company. It handles civil partnerships, marriages, commitment ceremonies, blessings, affirmations, and celebrations, the last of which can take a variety of shapes and forms.

Gino and Mike Meriano, founders of the company, were one of the first couples in the United Kingdom to form a civil partnership (legal gay marriage); the ceremony was televised live on the BBC.

For more information on gay weddings in the United Kingdom, visit PinkWeddings.biz.

Here are some of Pink's most famous (or infamous, depending on how you look at it) affairs.

1. **A Wedding with Pride** The wedding was held in the middle of a field with a tent for 300 people. The theme was "Pride," and the wedding was an experiment in rainbows. Musicians, dancers, and stilt walkers entertained the crowd, who basked in the abundance of balloons and streamers. Guests wore appropriate costumes.

2. **The Carnival Comes to Town** Held on the grounds of a seventeenth-century home, the ceremony was dignified and stylish, a quintessentially British wedding with Pimms (a gin-based beverage) for celebration drinks and a jazz band playing on the lawn.

But in the evening the atmosphere took a turn when everyone was asked to change into casual wear, and soon the grounds were transformed into a full-tilt carnival, rides and all, with drag queens dressed in black and white serving drinks and canapés while tribute acts (to Madonna and ABBA, among others) played onstage.

3. **Flying Time** What's a wedding without your own private jet? For this private party of ten, Pink flew all the guests to three different destinations in Europe. The couple took their vows on the plane while flying over Italy. They stopped for drinks and hors d'oeuvres in Italy, ate a full-course dinner in Spain, and partied till dawn in Prague.

4. **Who Needs a Venue?** With five pink stretch limos and one Daimler limo, the couple treated their guests to a tour of London like no other. The ceremony was stylish and took place near the London Bridge. From there it was on to afternoon tea at the Dorchester, then dinner at an exclusive members-only club, followed by a spot of gambling at the Ritz. It all led to the evening's final destination: the glitzy, glamorous Café de Paris.

5. **What Not to Wear** A couple who enjoy the country life decided to declare their love and commitment to one another by celebrating with a small group of friends atop a picturesque hill with a champagne picnic lunch—and no clothing. None of the guests wore a stitch.

6. **Murder Mystery and Most Haunted** Held in a Gothic castle, the wedding was a fantastic display of Old Elizabethan–style dress, complete with a piper, a joker, hog roasts, and crowns and thrones for the happy couple. The height of the event was the reenactment of scenes from the TV series *Most Haunted*, after which the wedding party was split into groups and invited to hunt for ghosts throughout the castle. A screaming good time was had by all.

7. **Fire and Ice** To transform a tent into a fantastic display of fire and ice, simply cover it with fake snow, surround it with ice sculptures featuring an amazing ice castle, and use glowing ice cubes in the cocktails. At least that's how Pink Weddings did it. Guests headed for dinner through a hallway in which ice seemed to be melting, and fire took over in the second room, which radiated with red lighting, flamethrowers, and centerpieces of glowing flames for that extra spark.

8. **BollyRouge** For this four-day affair, Pink Weddings created a full Bollywood set for a fantastic mix of Bollywood and the Moulin Rouge. Every feature of the venue, from the backdrops and displays to the dancers and music, celebrated the Orient. A film crew was brought in, and the whole wedding was filmed as a typical Bollywood movie. The wedding video was probably among the most amazing wedding videos ever.

9. **SOCO (Scene of Crime Officer) Meets CSI** At this unique wedding, all the guests were police, undercover cops, and inspectors. Also in attendance was a fake CSI crew, who set the stage for a murder mystery.

After the ceremony, guests arrived at a manor house for drinks and dinner and what was thought to be a night of celebrating. Instead, a mock murder took place. Using police skills and the props, the party was asked to figure out who killed the butler. The winner was given a seven-day trip to Las Vegas.

10 British Castle Weddings

CelticCastles.com is an award-winning online castle-booking company based in the heart of Yorkshire. The company now features more than 80 unique and diverse castle properties within its extensive portfolio across the United Kingdom, Ireland, and France. Here are some of its favorite wedding locales.

1. Ashford Castle, Ireland Situated on the west coast of Ireland, 30 minutes from Galway, Ashford's long history goes back to A.D. 1228, when it was originally built as a monastery. Today this wonderful castle with its imposing exterior and 350 acres of wooded parklands has become a renowned deluxe castle hotel with 83 individually designed bedrooms. Fly a hawk in the School of Falconry, take a picnic in the Walled Garden, or catch wild trout or salmon in one of the most famous fisheries in Ireland. Once the home of the Guinness family, Ashford was the chosen location for the film *The Quiet Man* and has also played host to President and Mrs. Reagan and, more recently, the wedding of James Bond (aka Pierce Brosnan) and Keely Shaye Smith.

2. Borthwick Castle, Scotland Borthwick is a tall, fifteenth-century castle on a north-facing slope in the rolling Borders countryside located just south of Edinburgh. Borthwick's sheer immensity was designed to intimidate, but what you see now represents less than half the original structure. Entering the gate from a tiny country road, one passes through twin 110-foot towers that extend from the dungeons to the battlements. During World War II, the castle was used as a secret storage space for the nation's official public records and national treasures.

Guests at Borthwick Castle always enjoy a tour through the castle's bedrooms, including the Queen's Bedchamber and the Red Room, which is covered with red flocked wallpaper. Legend has it that a young servant girl bore an illegitimate Borthwick son in this room. Mother and baby, potential threats to the title, were quickly put to the sword. The ghost of the young servant girl still wanders the stony spiral staircases of Borthwick, and even the most stalwart visitors admit to feeling invisible presences in the Great Hall.

3. Bovey Castle, England Originally built in 1906 as a private home and sporting estate, Bovey Castle is set within 368 square miles of the Dartmoor National Park, Devon, in southwest England. Its ceremonies are conducted in the Cathedral Room, with its vaulted ceiling, and two new alfresco areas: the Summer House and the Portico, positioned on the terrace with views of Dartmoor and the surrounding valleys.

Couples can enjoy a specially designed holistic spa, complete with saunas, steam rooms, hydrotherapy, exceptional treatment rooms, and gymnasium. The swimming pool, housed in the Orangery, opens onto the sun terrace. Trout and salmon fishing are on offer, plus sea fishing for mackerel and night fishing for sea trout.

Film buffs note that Bovey Castle served as the original Baskerville Hall in the 1939 movie *The Hound of the Baskervilles*, starring Basil Rathbone as Sherlock Holmes.

4. Castle Stuart, Scotland Castle Stuart is set on the Moray Firth in the Scottish Highlands, just a 20-minute drive from Loch Ness. Enter its portals and step back in time. Walk its battlements with Charles I before he lost his kingdom and his head, or with Bonnie Prince Charlie the night before his tragic defeat at nearby Culloden Moor. The castle is said to be haunted by 4 ghosts that are depicted in a series of 12 oil paintings now hanging in the main dining room.

A Ghostly Affair

In April 2007, Nigel and Jane Sleath, who held their nuptials at Scotland's most haunted hotel, were stunned when a mysterious green phantom crashed their wedding. The eerie figure appeared as photos were being taken at the cocktail bar at Airth Castle, Stirlingshire.

The best man who took the photo stated, "I took hundreds of photos, but this is the only one to capture something like this." The ghostly visitor appeared standing behind a chair.

The staff at the four-star venue reported many spooky sightings and goings-on over the years, but admitted that the haunting image at the wedding was the most remarkable they had ever seen.

Ireland's Dromoland Castle, built in the sixteenth century COURTESY OF DROMOLAND CASTLE

Julius Caesar and Peter the Great, has continued; barrel upon barrel of this vintage continues to age in the cellars of the castle.

Nearby Albi is known as "the City of the Arts" and is home to St. Cecile's Cathedral, built between the thirteenth and sixteenth centuries and a masterpiece of southern Gothic architecture. The old bridge over the River Tarn, built in the eleventh century, is one of the oldest in France.

6. **Comlongon Castle, Scotland** Comlongon Castle, near Gretna, is a restored, fourteenth-century medieval Scottish castle set on a private 120-acre estate. Thousands of couples have married there over the past 22 years. It is the only medieval castle in southern Scotland to offer religious, civil, and Celtic ceremonies.

Guests will delight in the displays of armor, weapons, and banners of medieval Scotland. The castle boasts opulent bedrooms with four-poster beds and Jacuzzis along with two award-winning oak-paneled restaurants for receptions.

7. **Culzean Castle, Scotland** Designed by famous Scottish architect Robert Adam, this storybook castle stands on a cliff with views across the sea to the mountains of the Island of Arran.

When the Kennedy/Anderson families of Scotland donated the castle to the National Trust for Scotland in 1945, they asked that the top floor be given to Gen. Dwight Eisenhower as a thank-you from the people of Scotland. Ike stayed at the castle in 1946 and returned three more times when he enjoyed its gardens, woodland, and seashore.

The castle was used as the ancestral home of Lord Summerisle (played by Christopher Lee) in the 1973 film *The Wicker Man*. Today weddings here may include pipe bands and Highland dancers.

8. **Dalhousie Castle, Scotland** Dalhousie Castle is a thirteenth-century fortress with acres of forest, parkland, and riverbanks. King Edward I stayed here on his way to meet Sir William Wallace at the Battle of Falkirk in 1298. In 1400, Sir Alexander Ramsay

Guests can enjoy clay-pigeon shooting, fishing, and guided tours, and they can help themselves to the snooker table, chess, darts, and board games in the drawing room/billiard room. More than anything, Castle Stuart offers intimacy: it has accommodations for only 16 guests.

Complimentary Highland dancers and the release of white fantail doves are part of the wedding package here.

5. **Château de Mercues, France** The chateau has existed in one form or another since about A.D. 650 and was home for centuries to the bishops of Cahors. In its present incarnation, this luxury hotel features fairy-tale turrets and towers that have been converted into guest rooms, some with stone walls and exposed timbers, others more refined, with fabric-covered walls and ornate antique wardrobes.

The tradition of the Cahors wines, so admired by the likes of

withstood a six-month siege at Dalhousie by English forces led by King Henry IV. Since then, earls of Dalhousie have taken an active part in British political and military leadership.

The castle's bedrooms are decorated in Scottish fabrics such as tweed, tartan, and twill. Guests enjoy the Aqueous Spa, the library's extensive collection of books, drinks from the secret bar next to an open fire, and dining in the ancient barrel-vaulted dungeon. With Edinburgh only seven miles away, this popular wedding locale should be booked well in advance.

Rosslyn Chapel, only five miles from Dalhousie Castle, was recently featured in the film *The Da Vinci Code* as a possible resting place of the Holy Grail.

9. **Dromoland Castle, Ireland** Dromoland Castle was built in the sixteenth century and was once the royal seat of the O'Brien clan, direct descendants of the High King Brian Boru. Dromoland features landscaped gardens, winding staircases, and sumptuous guest rooms. Woodcarvings, stone statuary, hand-carved paneling, and fine antique furnishings abound.

On the castle's 375-acre estate, guests can hunt, fish, ride horseback, play tennis, and enjoy archery, clay-pigeon shooting, swimming, and moutain biking.

The castle's wine cellar holds a selection of over 600 vintages from around the world, and the castle's expert sommelier ensures that a wide range of wines are available for tasting.

10. **Lumley Castle, England** Named for its original creator, Sir Ralph Lumley, the castle has stood for more than 600 years. It is surrounded by beautiful parklands overlooking the River Wear and is a monument to a bygone age of chivalry and honor.

Each of its bedchambers is uniquely decorated and full of medieval character. The castle is filled with historical artifacts

The dining room at Lumley Castle in Scotland COURTESY OF LUMLEY CASTLE

and possesses a strong atmosphere of history and intrigue.

As with any historic location, Lumley Castle has its resident ghost. Lady Lily Lumley, the wife of Sir Ralph, is said to walk the corridors of her former home, where she was murdered by local priests before her body was dumped in the well, which you can still see today. In 2005, the touring Australian cricket team was said to have been haunted during their stay at Lumley Castle.

Today the medieval atmosphere is enhanced by the staff, who dress in period costume.

4 Western Weddings

Before the Apacheland Movie Ranch in Gold Canyon, Arizona, burned down in 2003, it was home to TV's *Death Valley Days* and *Maverick,* not to mention hundreds of wedding ceremonies. These were all executed with the dramatic flair for which the place was known. Typically, a ceremony was interrupted by a "varmint" intent on kidnapping the "little filly" and making off with her on horseback. But the pistol-equipped groom would whip it out and shoot the guy "dead," after which the nervous preacher would commence with the ceremony. In fact, Apacheland offered a menu of dramas from which hundreds of wedding couples chose their nuptial backdrops. We mourn the loss of Apacheland, but happily report that western weddings are still to be had throughout the United States. Here are a few current offerings for those in search of a real shotgun wedding.

1. At the Boot Hill Museum, Dodge City, Kansas, the stagecoach is a popular spot for saying, "I do." Prairie dress is available for rental.

2. Old Trail Town, Cody, Wyoming, looks like a ghost town but is actually a collection of historic buildings that were lovingly brought here from abandoned hills throughout Wyoming. The 1890 Rivers Saloon, with original flooring and authentic bullet holes, is a popular setting for weddings.

3. Knott's Berry Farm, Buena Park, California, offers both traditional weddings and weddings with Old West atmosphere, complete with stagecoaches and mock robberies.

4. The Union Hotel in Santa Barbara, California, offers couples a chance to wed in an authentic historic setting that was once a stagecoach stop in the 1880s. Johnny Cash and Buck Owens used to hang out here before they became famous, and this is where Paul McCartney and Michael Jackson filmed the video for "Say, Say, Say," but that's another theme altogether. . . .

A Real Cinderella Wedding

Walk down an aisle flanked by 800 blooming rosebushes as music from *Sleeping Beauty* wafts through the air and your personal "fairy godplanner" stands by to grant your every wish. Conclude the ceremony with greetings from your favorite storybook characters while spectacular fireworks light up the night. This is the magic of Disney's "Fairy Tale Weddings."

Since 1955, Disneyland in Anaheim, California, and Disney World in Orlando, Florida, have been offering weddings for anywhere from 2 to 1,200 guests, and each year couples flock to these two venues to take their vows in the shadow of Sleeping Beauty's Castle. Proposing at Cinderella's Royal Table Restaurant has become so popular that the restaurant now offers a special engagement package complete with a server who presents the engagement ring in a glass slipper lying on a bed of rose petals, and the bridal salon offers a line of gowns inspired by Disney characters (think Cinderella, not Minnie).

Various sites are available, including the Disneyland Hotel Rose Garden, where Cinderella's horse-drawn crystal coach delivers the bride and, for an extra charge, Mickey and Minnie show up to greet guests, each of whom receives a free Mickey Mouse ear hat as a wedding favor. At the end of the event, everyone goes home and lives happily ever after. Just don't try to get that in writing.

When Money Is No Object

Ice sculptures make for memorable photos and can be carved to almost any specifications. These examples were created by Steven R. Berkshire of Ice Impressions. **COURTESY OF ICE-IMPRESSIONS.COM**

Here are some budget-busting ideas from Lisa Akers, author of *The Wedding Theme Workbook* and *The Wedding Consultant in a Box.*

1. Buy two dresses—one for the ceremony, the other for the reception.

2. Book a full gospel choir for the church.

3. Go crazy with flowers—string them from chandeliers, tie them to chairs, tuck them into mirrors, bracket the bandstand with them, and top every surface in sight.

4. Commission an artist to make a hand-painted aisle runner.

5. Release 500 doves outside the church doors.

6. Rent limousines to get everyone—guests and wedding party—to the reception and back home again.

7. Serve a caviar course.

8. Have your baker create miniature wedding cakes for each guest to take home.

9. Pour champagne (the really good stuff) from dusk until dawn.

10. Landscape the grounds with your favorite flower, or in an all-white color scheme.

11. Hire a fleet of horse-drawn carriages and take everyone for a ride.

12. Fly in that blues band you loved from your vacation in New Orleans.

13. Ask your photographer to take a picture of each guest, then send silver-framed prints to each one, along with your thank-you note.

14. Buy linens for the reception tables and have them monogrammed with your names or initials.

15. Get a plane to sky-write your names and the date over the reception site.

16. Put on a fireworks display.

17. Buy out an entire floor of your wedding night hotel—the party can go on until the wee hours.

18. Rent something outrageous—a classic Airstream trailer or a helicopter—for a dramatic getaway.

19. Charter a plane and take everyone along on the honeymoon.

20. All of the above!

The 54 Strangest Places People Have Gotten Married

1. In a hospital room
2. At an ATM
3. At the town dump
4. In a subway tunnel
5. On a ferryboat
6. During a hockey game
7. At a White Castle restaurant
8. In an elevator
9. In a funeral parlor
10. In a zoo
11. In a helicopter
12. In a cemetery
13. At the finish line at a racetrack
14. In a grocery store
15. Via cell phones
16. During halftime at a pro football game
17. In a strip club
18. On John Deere tractors
19. In a bowling alley
20. At a Wal-Mart
21. In a fire station
22. On a Colorado mountaintop with a horse and sleigh
23. At a pig roast in the bride's backyard
24. In a super-stretch limo
25. On top of the Empire State Building in New York City
26. In a gasoline station bathroom
27. In a shopping mall
28. In a movie theater

29. In an airport
30. In Howe Caverns
31. On a covered bridge in Madison County, Iowa
32. At the Charmin Restrooms in Times Square, New York City
33. At the top of a roller coaster
34. In a brewery
35. In a mine
36. On top of a mountain
37. In a Winnebago
38. In a spaceship
39. In a boxing ring
40. On a bus

41. On an archery range
42. On a Ferris wheel
43. In the woods
44. In a recycled wedding chapel
45. In a shark tank
46. On the wreck of a sunken ship
47. In the middle of a desert
48. At a bullfight
49. In a hot-air balloon
50. At a funeral
51. In a barn
52. In a library
53. In a college dorm
54. At a pre—football game tailgate party

Buff Brides

Forget the Mao suits of a generation ago. Actually, forget about any clothes at all. Naked wedding photos are the hot new trend among young couples in once deeply conservative China.

Even in Anhui, a largely rural province in the east, many newlyweds are having their pictures taken in the nude, to the fury of their parents' generation.

Dead Set on Marriage

On October 27, 2007, Tina Milhoane and Robert Seifer exchanged vows at the entrance to the 7 Floors of Hell Haunted House's outdoor cemetery in Berea, Ohio. Well-wishing zombie and witch guests looked on as the couple tied the knot. The groom made his entrance in a hearse, emerging from a coffin carried by six pallbearers. The ceremony was conducted by a minister dressed as the Grim Reaper, who read "The Lord's Prayer" from a scroll clutched in a bony-gloved hand.

How to Have a Green Wedding

"People are making purchasing decisions based on environmental concerns," says Gerald Prolman, the founder of Organic Bouquet.com, an online organic florist whose sales have doubled since 2001. "Whether it's food or cotton or flowers, people are asking questions: How are farmworkers treated? Who produced the product? How is the environment affected in that process?"

Your green wedding will tell your guests how committed you are to a sustainable lifestyle. Here are some ideas for making Mother Nature an honored guest at your nuptials.

1. Buy a man-made diamond instead of one that has been mined, probably with human and ecological sacrifice. The synthetics that are available today are amazing and have fooled even the most knowledgeable professionals. If you prefer the real thing, insist on a diamond mined in a peaceful country like Canada or Australia. In any event, opt for a diamond certified as "conflict-free" under the Kimberl Process, an ongoing effort to reform diamond mining in Africa.

2. Use recycled or handmade paper and vegetable or soy-based inks for invitations, table cards, napkins, programs, and thank-you notes, but try to keep your use of paper to a minimum. Avoid papers that are metallic or plastic-coated and therefore difficult to recycle. Don't use double envelopes or tissue for your invitations, and request that RSVPs be handled online. Stay away from oversized invitations for which fewer trees have suffered (and which won't require additional postage). Recycle all unused paper products after the event.

3. Create a wedding website with all the information guests will need about the event—locations, directions, and day-of arrangements—so that the information doesn't have to be printed out for each guest.

Invite Mother Nature to your wedding by presenting your guests with their very own wildflower gardens as wedding favors and suggest that they plant your wedding invitations. BotanicalPaperWorks.com is just one of the many sources of seeded paper—handmade paper embedded with flower seeds—that can be placed under soil to produce perennial wedding memories for you and your guests.

11 Eco-Friendly Favors

1. An 11-watt compact fluorescent lightbulb. Each guest who replaces one 50-watt incandescent bulb with the one you provide will save 685 pounds of carbon dioxide.

2. Packets of seeds

3. Gourmet organic chocolates or another organic or local food item

4. Attractive bags of fresh or dried organic herbs

5. Seeds in a commemorative container

6. Reusable cloth tote bags

7. A small plant

8. Natural soaps

9. Soy or beeswax candles

10. A downloadable playlist of your favorite songs

11. A small charitable donation made in each guest's name

4. Have your wedding outdoors, where guests can be reminded of the importance of making environmentally sound decisions every day.

5. Choose a setting for your wedding that's convenient to the most guests to minimize travel impacts, and minimize or eliminate the distance between them. Use only hybrid rental cars for transportation.

6. Choose eco-friendly wedding attire. Synthetic fabrics are cheaper, but polyester is petroleum-based. Cotton is a better choice, but even so, the average cotton suit uses an average of 5.8

pounds of pesticides per acre. The most environmentally friendly cotton is certified organic in its natural color or tinted with gentle natural vegetable dyes.

7. Have your wedding dress made of hemp, mon. Or choose organic cotton or silk, and donate the gown to charity when you're done with it.

8. Use green in your color scheme. Mint green can be paired with a variety of colors, and deep greens, with gold and red, can provide a colorful backdrop for the autumn wedding. Plus, we checked, and there are no laws against green wedding gowns.

9. Wear borrowed or pre-owned wedding attire.

10. Accentuate natural beauty with all-natural makeup.

11. Use potted plants and shrubs as decorations.

12. Use silk and dried flowers. If you must use live blooms, choose flowers that have been grown on organic farms. Include wildflowers in your arrangements.

13. Decorate with branches, dried grasses, grains, greens, berries, or live plants. Potted or dried arrangements can double as favors.

14. Choose beeswax or soy-based candles over those made with paraffin, a petroleum byproduct.

15. Throw biodegradable confetti or organic rose petals instead of rice.

16. Don't use paper plates or plastic utensils. If you must use these, make sure they are recycled after the event. If you can't afford real flatware, rent it.

17. Choose organic and free-range ingredients for your menu. Or go vegan.

18. Choose a cake made with yogurt instead of butter; honey, not sugar; and egg whites only (no yolks).

19. Seek out cruelty-free meats and wild rather than farmed fish.

20. Avoid single-use cameras. Instead, ask friends with digi-cams to share their photos with all the guests online in a free Flickr group or Snapfish group room you set up for your wedding.

21. Include a short essay in your wedding program letting guests know the lengths to which you have gone to create your green wedding, and let them know you'll happily act as a consultant for anyone who has similar plans.

22. Have guests throw birdseed instead of rice, but be sure the seed is for plants native to the area. Throwing standard birdseed mix in a nature preserve or national park, for instance, can damage the ecosystem. Wildflower seeds, flower petals, and bubbles blown from little bottles make fine alternatives.

23. Register with an eco-friendly charity for donations instead of gifts. Or register only with stores that offer local, fair-trade, handmade, organic, or other eco-friendly products like Branch, Gaiam, Greenfeet, GreenSage, Ten Thousand Villages, or UncommonGoods.

18 Wedding Acronyms

1. BIL: brother-in-law
2. BM: bridesmaid
3. DFH: dear future husband
4. DH: dear husband
5. FFIL: future father-in-law
6. FH: future husband
7. FMIL: future mother-in-law
8. FOB: father of the bride
9. FSD: future stepdaughter
10. FSS: future stepson
11. FW: future wife
12. GM: grooms man
13. MOB: mother of the bride
14. MOH: maid of honor
15. NWR: not wedding-related
16. SIL: sister-in-law
17. SO: significant other
18. STD: save the date

Here Comes the Bride — Again!

Second weddings are different from first weddings. Experience brings more mature brides and grooms to the altar, and there's a sense that the wedding is not nearly as important as the marriage. These ceremonies often involve children as the new blended family comes together, and there's a special etiquette involved as well. Whereas second weddings were once mostly quiet affairs, often not even announced until the ceremony had taken place, today's second- and third-timers are more inclined to shout it from the rooftops and celebrate the occasion in high style. After all, although the bride and groom may each have been married before, this is a first wedding for them as a couple. Here's what you need to know about second-wedding planning:

1. **How big should your second wedding be?** These weddings are usually less formal and lavish than first weddings, but today anything goes. Especially if one member of the couple hasn't been married before, it's quite common to go all out.

2. **How should the invitation be worded?** Mature couples issue invitations in their own names, especially if they are paying for the wedding. If the couple is younger and one of them has been married before, the invitation may be issued by the bride's parents or whoever is hosting the wedding.

3. **What about pre-wedding parties?** The encore bride usually dispenses with engagement parties and showers. If you do choose to have such an event, infuse it with a theme or make it a no-gifts outing (to the theater or a sporting event, for instance) that everyone will enjoy.

4. **What kind of dress does the second-time bride wear?** Second-timers were once encouraged to avoid white and wear a simple pastel-colored suit. These days, when white no longer represents purity, a wedding gown is acceptable, although mature brides tend toward simpler styles.

5. **Who should be included in the wedding party?** Remarrying couples often dispense with bridesmaids and ushers, opting instead to include children and stepchildren in the bridal party. Older children can even accompany their parents down the aisle.

6. **Should announcements be sent?** If it's a small wedding limited to family and close friends, an announcement should be sent to those who will not be included among the wedding guests. If it's a large wedding, you might still want to send announcements to business acquaintances, especially if there's a name change involved.

7. **How are engagement rings selected for a second marriage?** Diamonds are always appropriate, but three-stone settings, with a diamond in the center and perhaps two other stones flanking it, are a popular choice for second-time couples.

8. **Who pays for the second wedding?** If the bride hasn't been married before, her parents are expected to pay for the wedding. Otherwise, the couple should bear the expense. Still, it's not unusual for both families to contribute.

9. **What about gifts?** If, like many remarrying couples, households have already been established and there really isn't room for one more fondue pot, consider forgoing gifts altogether (your invitation can state "no gifts, please"). Or think about requesting donations for a charity (see "20 Unusual Wedding Registries," page 191).

10. **Are prenups important in a second marriage?** Prenups are especially important for second marriages, not only because each partner may be coming to the marriage with great assets, but also because they may want to ensure that their children from another marriage will be the direct recipients of the assets they brought into the marriage in the event of their death. Without a prenup, state laws will apply.

11 Ways to Preserve Your Sanity While Planning a Wedding

1. **Get organized.** Organization is the key to everything, especially saving money. Start early. Choose your method—online, ring binder, or fancy-schmancy hardcover book (does anyone really want to lug these around?)—and keep your system up to date at all times.

2. **Give yourself time.** You can't plan a cathedral wedding in a month. But in a year? No problem. If you need to get the event planned quickly, however, be realistic about what's possible.

3. **Don't buy into the wedding hype.** Skip back to the beginning of this chapter and read "6 Things the Wedding Industry Doesn't Want You to Know." Remember that wedding vendors are carefully trained in capturing their prey.

4. **Divide the work into smaller jobs.** Listing the various jobs involved will help you see that planning a wedding is not really a big job at all—it's thousands of little ones! No matter how long the list is, seeing it all broken down will help you to get started. Take baby steps, at least in the beginning.

5. **Assemble your team.** Whether they're in the bridal party or not, list those who will be helping with any aspects of the wedding. Be clear about what their responsibilities are, and get them to communicate with each other. Make sure that everyone is clear on who is paying for what. Delegate!

6. **Everything is negotiable.** The caterer can find some way to make sure that the hors d'oeuvres alone don't cost more than the honeymoon, and cousin Betsy will leave Pumpkin—her darling pit bull—at home just this once if you pay for a sitter. When all seems lost, seek alternative routes. There always are some, and sometimes you just have to know how to ask.

7. **Make careful choices.** There will always be choices. Pick one and stick to it. Changing your mind about a color scheme, for instance, can cost lots of money once you've ordered paper goods and decorations. Think carefully before you finalize anything.

8. **Stick to your budget.** If the florist is too expensive, keep shopping. If the baker tells you that these days a nice wedding cake runs about $4,000, don't believe her. No matter who's paying for the wedding, it's in everyone's best interest to stick to the original plan.

9. **Keep records of everything.** You'll be able to compare estimates, review lists of services, and expose liars if you have easy access to every contract, receipt, and list that has been given to you.

10. **Thank your helpers.** That doesn't mean just handing them each a token gift after the event. Stay in touch with them and let them know often that you appreciate their continued support. Show interest in the events going on in their lives.

11. **Take care of you.** Whether you're the bride, the groom, the MOG, or the MOB, keep it all in perspective and don't let the wedding overshadow the marriage. Relax when you can, and don't give up nonwedding activities; they keep you whole.

How Bridal Consultants Charge for Services

Today American couples spend over $2 billion annually on wedding planners and consultants. To make sure your dollars are well spent, read everything you sign and make sure you understand it. Be sure that the contract includes all the details you have discussed. The fee will probably be due in thirds: one-third on signing of a contract, one-third when half the details are completed, and one-third on completion of all duties to be performed. Beware of the coordinator whose services are free—kickbacks and commissions are at play here, and you will never know if you're really getting the most for your money. Here are some ways in which the charges are calculated:

1. A percentage of the overall budget, usually 10 or 15 percent

2. A per-guest fee

3. A flat rate determined by the estimated number of hours that will be needed

4. An hourly rate starting at around $40 an hour

Brides Beware: Top 9 Wedding Rip-offs

When it comes to weddings, sentiment can get expensive. Don't fall for every monogrammed napkin or heart-shaped swizzle stick you see, despite the industry's attempt to separate you from every last penny you can borrow. Here are some of the tricks they will employ.

1. **Cake-cutting fees:** Some hotels and reception halls charge as much as $2 per guest just to cut them a slice of the wedding cake. This can add up to as much as an additional $200. You may also be charged for the opening of wine bottles, known as the "cork fee."

2. **The phony band demo tape:** Some unscrupulous bands actually go so far as to hire studio musicians to record their demo tape or video. You may think you're getting Earth, Wind, and Fire but wind up with Taylor Hicks on acid. Always ask for a live audition.

3. **Disintegrating bridesmaids' dresses:** Don't be surprised if those $200 bridesmaid dresses start falling apart during the reception. They're made of cheap polyester fabric, and much of the detailing is simply glued on, while hems and seams are often left unfinished. These dresses were made to be worn only once. (After all, how would the bridesmaid boutiques survive if we all started sharing dresses?)

4. **Punch at champagne prices:** Some hotels and reception halls can charge as much as $40 per gallon of fruit punch and call it champagne. You don't even get to keep the punch bowl.

5. **Pimping your ride:** You may think driving to impress will help you achieve the worldly air that will make wedding vendors less likely to try to pull the wool over your eyes, but the opposite is actually true. Some wedding vendors hike up their prices based on how nice your car is. The bottom line: when it comes to weddings, your stylish wheels can work against you. Leave the Beamer in the garage and borrow your nephew's 10-speed to get real bargains.

6. **Lucky for whom?** Sometimes it's the little items that can add up. At some bridal shops, you'll find accessories with sky-high price tags—such as faux pearls at real-pearl prices and "lucky" pennies for $5 each.

7. **A picture's worth a thousand cuss words:** If you hire a professional photo studio, ask for a guarantee that the veteran you interviewed is the one doing the actual wedding photo shoot, lest you end up with the photo intern and his Polaroid on your big day. Make sure you get what you see.

8. **The most expensive cardboard in the world:** Be wary of any companies that offer "cleaning and preservation" for your wedding gown and then provide you with a $250 cardboard box.

9. **Name-change scam:** After you're married, expect official-looking mail from companies offering to change your name with the Social Security Administration and other federal agencies for just a $15 fee. Download the form for free from the Social Security Administration's website.

Wedding Consultants 101

While wedding consultants come in all shapes and sizes, they generally fall into five categories, as described here by the Massachusetts Wedding Guide, an online wedding planning service. Note that these titles are often used interchangeably.

1. **Independent Bridal Consultant** This person works directly with the bride and groom in helping them plan any or all aspects of their wedding. They do not work for a specific vendor, and they can perform a range of services or just a chosen few.

2. **Bridal Consultant** Bridal consultants work for a specific vendor (such as a consultant at a flower shop or a consultant at a photography studio) and help with general wedding arrangements.

3. **Wedding Coordinator** This person is an on-site consultant who coordinates the wedding activities (rehearsals and ceremony procedures, etc.) at a wedding venue.

4. **Church Wedding Coordinator** This person works with the church to make sure that the church rules and regulations are being followed.

5. **Wedding Day Coordinator** This person conducts rehearsals and wedding day activities and does not coordinate the initial planning.

You Need a Bridal Consultant If . . .

According to the Association for Wedding Professionals International, the number of wedding consultants and planners increased dramatically after the release of the 2001 film *The Wedding Planner*, which starred Jennifer Lopez. The trend has led many community colleges to offer wedding planner certification courses. Today roughly half of all couples opt for a consultant.

The average wedding can take up to 150 hours to organize. A bridal consultant (aka wedding coordinator or wedding planner) is a mediator, a money manager, a shopping and travel consultant, and more. Hiring one will cost you in the neighborhood of 10 to 15 percent of your entire budget—more if you want swans flown in from the Riviera. Find competent consultants by asking friends for referrals, browsing online, or consulting the Association of Bridal Consultants at bridalassn.com. You want a consultant who is calm, communicative, and creative without being overbearing. Do you need one? You do if . . .

1. You are pressed for time and don't have the 150 hours it takes to plan the average wedding. You don't have the wherewithal to find vendors, let alone deal with the traps and small print of their contracts. Is cropping and retouching included in the photographer's fee? Are you being charged a per-slice cake-cutting fee? If these details don't sound like a great way to spend all your spare time for about a year, you should consider a bridal consultant.

2. You know how much you want to spend but have no idea how to budget the money. A consultant will advise you, for instance, that flowers should cost no more than 10 percent of your total budget. A consultant who has good relationships with vendors will also get you the best prices.

3. You are planning a destination wedding, or you do not live in the city where the wedding will take place. How will you know who the best local vendors are? What logistical problems might the wedding site pose? Who will arrange for the transportation of the guests? The Association for Wedding Professionals International can help you find consultants almost anywhere in the world (visit afwpi.com).

4. You want to be a guest at your own wedding. You don't want to be bothered with day-of details like helping blind Aunt Bertha to her table, calming rambunctious ring-bearers, or handling the ladies' room emergencies that will undoubtedly arise. Does the chef know which guests will require kosher meals? Your wedding planner will take care of it and also ensure that photographers, musicians, and florists don't get in each other's way. All you'll have to do is show up and get married.

5. You really haven't had much experience with weddings, and this one poses some cross-cultural challenges. How should invitations be worded? When should they be sent? Are save-the-date cards necessary? What is the proper etiquette for ensuring that all members of all families feel welcome at the wedding?

6. You've always dreamed of getting married in a castle, while bungee-jumping, underwater, or on skis. A good wedding consultant can make it happen. (A great wedding consultant will check the length of the bungee cords before the ceremony begins.)

Don't Hire a Wedding Coordinator If . . .

1. You're a control freak and the idea of someone else deciding the contents of the ladies' room courtesy basket makes you break out in hives.

2. You have the time and willingness to oversee what will probably be one of the most spectacular days of your life.

3. You have tons of referrals by friends and for the most part know exactly which vendors you want to hire.

4. You have the time to take advantage of the many Internet resources and guidebooks available.

5. You want a simple wedding free of all the expensive options that can detract from the true meaning of the event; you're just going for the basics.

6. You didn't love Franck.

If you think wedding coordinators are overpaid, why not become one? Numerous online courses offer accreditation, and it's a great way to utilize all that you learn in the course of planning a wedding.

"If someone comes to me and says, 'I want the perfect wedding,' I'll tell her she's come to the wrong man. Things are always going wrong — that's why you need a professional."

— COLIN COWIE

Choosing a Wedding Consultant

You want to be able to communicate easily with your wedding planner, and you don't want to be bullied into anything. Here are five questions to ask:

1. Will this person respect my budget and help me avoid things I can't afford?

2. Does he have good rapport with the top suppliers and will he be able to negotiate discounts with them on my behalf?

3. Will she be there on the wedding day to oversee the event?

4. Does he seem like the type who will remain calm under pressure?

5. Does she carry personal liability and professional indemnity insurance?

How to Get a Free Wedding

Tom Anderson and his bride-to-be Sabrina Root took advertising to a higher level when they sold advertising space to pay for their August 1999 wedding.

A total of 24 companies were more than happy to provide the couple with their $34,000 Philadelphia wedding and honeymoon suite in Cancun, Mexico. In exchange, the couple agreed to have the name of each sponsor printed on the invitations, thank-you notes, placement cards, and scrolls that appeared at each dinner table. The groom also agreed to mention each sponsor by name after his first toast.

The idea for the corporate wedding occurred to Tom when he realized that the struggling company he was working for often traded services for goods. Tom now owns two websites, SponsoredWedding.com and WeddingSponsors.com, both of which direct visitors to a large number of wedding products and services.

By the way, the groom spent his own money for the engagement ring, and the bride bought her own dress. Big spenders!

See also "3 Ways to Get a Free Honeymoon," page 324.

10 Things to Include on Your Wedding Website

Having a website dedicated to the wedding gives you a chance to communicate with everyone accurately and to retain a record of every single conversation. Especially useful if you're planning a destination wedding, the website can keep everyone apprised of logistics as they develop. Audiovisual postings can keep your website lively and give your guests a chance to share your progress as the event draws closer. Note that it is seriously impolite to make mention of your gift registry on your website.

Here are some things you can post on your site:

1. The story of how you met and why you decided to marry

2. Background information on both the bride and groom so that all can become familiar with the new family member

3. If this is a multi-faith wedding, information on rituals that may be observed at the wedding, as well as words to traditional songs that may be sung

4. Information on appropriate dress

5. Everything your guests need to know about travel and accommodations, including events that may be planned before and after the ceremony

6. Information for out-of-towners (who will be especially appreciative) about transportation (including maps and tour bus schedules), shopping, and dining in the immediate area where the wedding is taking place

7. Updates on guest responses (family members may be excited to hear that Aunt Vildechaya is flying in from the Ukraine!)

8. Wedding news (you won the honeymoon raffle at the bridal show!)

9. Photos of you and your intended, as children, on your first dates, etc.

10. Your thanks for all the continued support you are getting from everyone

I Now Pronounce You—Online!
Top 13 Wedding Planning Websites

You can purchase any of a number of elegant wedding planning books and then lug them around for a year or so, or you can buy a $3 loose-leaf notebook and about $3 worth of paper and dividers, which also gets the job done. But doing it online makes the most sense of all, and there are tons of websites that are there to help you.

E-planning your wedding today is a snap on the Internet. The comprehensive sites listed here will assist you in every aspect of wedding planning and will host your personal wedding website as well, all for free. (Some sites charge as much as $10 a month for the same service; avoid them.) You'll be able to keep track of everything from guest responses to florists you hate, and you'll get suggestions for everything that comes up along the way. These resources also offer a wealth of choices: gay and lesbian weddings, lavish weddings, destination weddings, alternative weddings, and green wedding resources can all be found on these websites. When shopping for a wedding planning website, be wary of the ones that charge fees or are time-consuming to navigate. Know also that although most of what you read on these sites is well meaning and sounds sincere, any site that takes advertising (and they all do) is in business.

1. GreenEleganceWeddings.com focuses on eco-friendly wedding tips for couples who want to leave a small green footprint when they get married. GreenEleganceWeddings.com also offers wedding contests and green wedding news.

2. TheKnot.com is a huge wedding planning website that also hosts sibling sites, such as DestinationWeddings.com and Chinese Weddings.com. On TheKnot.com, you can set up your own person-

alized wedding to-do list, and there's an active forum for both brides and grooms.

3. WeddingChannel.com has the answers to all your wedding planning questions and offers tools such as checklists and budget calculators.

4. Indiebride.com isn't afraid to deconstruct the bridal beast and gives couples plenty of license to think outside the wedding cake.

5. InStyleWeddings.com is a classy, celebrity-studded Internet resource that can help you plan a dream wedding. Even if you can't afford the lavish events they encourage, you can pick up some fine ideas here.

6. FrugalBride.com will offset the splash of InStyleWeddings .com with a bulletin board filled with ideas and opinions from other brides, frugal wedding crafts, and budget-tracking worksheets.

7. WeddingSolutions.com is a wedding planning website that offers celebrity wedding news and gossip, wedding resources, and wedding advice. WeddingSolutions.com is an adjunct of *Bridal Guide* magazine.

8. GayWeddings.com answers a variety of questions about the details and etiquette for a same-sex marriage. There's a wedding boutique here and links to gay and lesbian wedding resources.

9. DestinationWeddings.com focuses on weddings in exotic locations but also includes ideas for honeymoons closer to home. Lots of ideas here and guidelines for handling logistics.

10. BridalNetwork.ca is a wedding directory that brings together bridal websites across Canada and the United States, showcasing vendors from all over the world. BridalNetwork.ca is a great way to surf everything wedding from dance instructors to wedding cakes.

11. OffbeatBride.com is a blog that offers "taffeta-free alternatives for independent brides," with plenty of smart suggestions for planning a wedding while maintaining your sanity. Good ideas here on what to skip.

12. EZWeddingPlanning.com is a customized planning tool that will enable you to organize and execute your wedding on plan and on budget. It's the perfect way to keep track of the vendors you've been talking to, details about each of your guests, and your gift registry. Free seating software and other similar resources can all be found here.

13. YourWeddingPlace.com has tons of tips and lists in addition to their wedding-planning downloadable software. Their resources cover everything from how to spend money on things you don't need to how to borrow the money you'll need to pay for these.

20 Unusual Wedding Registries

Many couples who marry these days have already maintained their own household, either together or on their own. They already have too many blenders, chafing dishes, linens, and china. If you fall into this category, here are some unique gifts for which couples have registered.

1. Video games

2. Cars

3. Motorcycles

4. Paintings and art objects

5. Landscaping

6. Home entertainment centers

7. Furniture

8. Honeymoons

9. Contributions to a down payment toward a home

10. Season tickets to sporting events or the theater

11. Books, especially if the couple is still in school

12. Scuba diving lessons

13. Cooking lessons

14. Computers

15. Accessories for the wedding itself, such as decorations, a guest register, and even the bride's accoutrements

16. Wine

17. Works of art

18. Dance lessons

19. Central heating

20. Favorite charities

The Pros and Cons of Eloping

Once it was all about running away in the middle of the night, small suitcase in tow. Modern elopements are about seeking out exciting and adventurous alternatives to the traditional wedding. Couples who plan to elope should do their research and familiarize themselves with the marriage requirements of their destination location.

I love my lad but oh you ladder

Vintage postcard, ca. 1914 AUTHORS' COLLECTION

Pros

1. Saving money While the cost of the average wedding is $28,000, it's not impossible to spend 10 times that amount on a luxury event. Resorts and tourism organizations, recognizing the growing trend of elopement, now offer package wedding deals that include plenty of extras, like a free bridal consultant and officiant. By combining the wedding locale and the honeymoon, an eloping couple can have a lovely wedding experience for as little as $5,000, or even less if they opt for a domestic location or a foreign country with a good monetary exchange rate.

2. Saving time A conventional wedding can take a year or more to plan. An elopement can be planned in a matter of weeks or even days. The couple has more time for themselves and can relieve their families of the work that weddings require.

3. Preserving your sanity The pressure, the deadlines, and the endless decisions involved in planning a wedding can stress out even master multi-taskers and have a serious impact on relationships, work, and your very sanity. Eloping gives the couple a chance to have a more intimate marriage, with their attention focused on one another, where it should be.

4. Adventure and romance The sense of spontaneity can be exhilarating, and keeping your destination a secret ensures privacy, intimacy, and an experience that only the two of you will share.

5. Avoiding complications If this is a second marriage that involves the blending of families, it's likely to bring with it a number of awkward situations. Should exes be included in the festivities? What about estranged grandparents and stepkids? Eloping allows you to sidestep these issues entirely.

Poster for a play by John Drew, ca. 1896 LIBRARY OF CONGRESS

1. **Logistical risks** Planning an elopement to a far-off destination can result in unforeseen complications. It may, for instance, be difficult to obtain a marriage license in a foreign country, and if the chosen resort doesn't have a wedding planner on staff, the couple will have to make all the arrangements themselves.

2. **Excluding family and friends** Excluding family and friends from a wedding can backfire on the couple—big-time. Prospective guests who have been looking forward to the event might vent hurt feelings and carry grudges for a long time to come. (It's a good idea to think about having a wedding reception for them all once you have returned from the honeymoon.)

3. **Planning a wedding is doable** While the myriad details that go into even a modest wedding can be overwhelming, resources abound: consultants and planners will execute everything from the entire event to just the part you're dreading, and Internet tools now make guest lists and schedules a snap. While the emphasis throughout *Planet Wedding* may seem to be on excess, modest weddings can be made more memorable than the most lavish events with a little ingenuity and plenty of heart.

4. **Avoiding the rush** Many elopements take place soon after two people meet and fall in love but before they have really had enough time to get to know each other. While the marriage may work out, rushing things could end in disaster. The engagement period is more than just a time to plan details and rush from one appointment to another: it is also a time for the bride and groom to learn to function together as a unit in preparation for the challenges that life will no doubt present.

5. **"Regrets, I've had a few . . ."** Missing out on the formal wedding experience, with its excitement, ritual, and drama, may be something you regret in the future.

18 Tips for the Pregnant Bride

A MaternityBride.com survey of bridal shop owners indicated that one in six brides is pregnant. In decades past, the pregnant bride was cause for scandal, and wedding ceremonies were typically hushed-up and private, hidden from the raised eyebrows of society. According to *Brides* magazine editor-in-chief Millie Martini Bratten, "Today we see so many celebrities who are . . . pregnant at the altar . . . so it's something people are talking about openly." Pregnant brides now beam from the covers of the tabloids, and more and more designers are catering to this new market for their wares. Here are some tips for those who chose to put the horse before the cart.

1. Ask yourself if you are truly up to the many hours of planning—often stressful—at this time. Yes, it's possible to plan a wedding in just a matter of weeks, but can you handle the pressure? If you're determined to make your commitment before the baby arrives keep it simple.

2. Decide early on whether you're going to hide the pregnancy during the wedding or use the event to celebrate two joyous occasions at once. Let your bridesmaids and guests know what choice you have made. If you're flaunting it, ask your maid of honor to throw a bridal/baby shower. If members of your family are making the situation difficult, talk to them before the wedding and ask that they put aside their issues for this one day.

3. Shop on the Internet to save time and energy. Visit websites and make phone calls before you visit local wedding shops.

4. Save money any way you can; you're looking at lots of expenses down the line. Be practical by registering only for items you really need.

5. Get help. Make lists of all the tasks your wedding will entail, and create a team of friends who are willing to take them on. Or hire a wedding planner.

6. Let the bridesmaids choose their own dresses. Delegate tasks and decisions to those bridesmaids who are closest to you and most likely to make the same choices you would.

7. Choose the officiant who will preside over your ceremony and meet with him or her to discuss any religious conflicts.

8. Yes, you can wear white.

9. If you are working with a dressmaker for your wedding gown, choose a style that will accommodate last-minute alterations: lacing ties that can be loosened, tabs in the back that can be tightened or loosened as the growing waistline demands, a flowing style to which panels can be added. Empire waists are popular among pregnant brides (think Gwyneth Paltrow in Emma) for their elegance and romance.

10. Don't limit your dress shopping to wedding gown sources. Most major designers offer maternity formalwear that is both stylish and appropriate, and in this day and age of anything goes, you can choose any color you like.

11. Your fingers will probably swell during the pregnancy, but if this hasn't happened yet, get fitted for a ring as soon as possible. You might want to use a fake larger ring for the ceremony or borrow one from a friend. If you're buying a ring when you're already into your later months, choose a ring style that can be altered later on.

12. Talk to your photographer about your pregnancy and let him or her know how you want your pictures to look. If you want to play down the pregnancy, suggest that photos be taken from high angles.

13. Insist on comfort. Choose undergarments that allow you to breathe and move around freely. Stay away from itchy lace and restricting elastic. Don't try to squeeze yourself into styles that just don't fit.

14. If the ceremony is to be very long, ask the officiant to have you and the groom seated for at least part of it.

15. If reception rituals (raising the bride and groom in chairs during frenzied dancing, for instance) pose a hazard, let the wedding attendants know these will be avoided.

16. Make sure your maid of honor keeps your champagne flute filled—with ginger ale. If nausea is an issue for you, ask the chef to have on hand anything you have been handling well.

17. Choose a spa honeymoon that will give you a chance to relax between one big day and the next, preferably one close to home.

18. Wear shoes with a low, chunky heel, but don't buy them until just before the wedding, as your feet are likely to swell. If you must buy them early, buy them in two sizes—one larger than you normally wear—and return the unworn pair after the wedding. Or buy a pair of fancy heels for the wedding and good old Keds or even thongs (hot-glue a few silk flower buds to each) for the reception.

How to Cancel or Postpone a Wedding

Weddings are usually postponed or canceled for sad reasons, and the task of notifying everyone can be most daunting. On the other hand, the sooner everyone has been notified, the sooner everyone can move on with their lives. Here are some guidelines:

Spreading the News

You don't have to give everyone the gory details of the breakup or postponement, but you do want to notify everyone as soon as possible, especially those who may need to cancel travel arrangements, which often have deadlines for refunds. In a concise way, explain why the wedding is being postponed, such as "the bride's illness," "a death in the family," "by mutual decision," or simply "a change of plans." If the wedding hasn't been announced and no invitations have been issued, the process is fairly simple. If invitations have already gone out, you can send out simple cards along the lines of:

Due to a family illness, the wedding of Jennifer Aniston and Donald Trump will not take place on October 14 as originally planned.

A new wedding date will be announced as soon as possible.

Or, If you already know the new date:

Mr. and Mrs. Simon Cherry announce that the wedding of their daughter Miss Olivia Cherry to Mr. Thomas Right, which was postponed, will now take place on December 20, 2004, at the Scranton Club.

If invitations have already been sent, each guest must be contacted personally to explain the situation. If the task is too emotional for the bride, friends and family should help with the calls.

If the wedding is being canceled after invitations have gone out, simple cards can be sent to all guests:

Mr. and Mrs. John Arial announce that the marriage of their daughter Precious to Mr. Wrong will not take place as scheduled.

While many people may ask you why you are canceling, an explanation is not required.

Vendors

Vendors should be contacted as soon as possible. If you've purchased wedding insurance, you're in good shape, although most policies don't have a "cold-feet" clause. Otherwise, be prepared to lose at least some of your deposits. Contact vendors first by phone, then follow up in writing. Check your contracts for cancellation policies that entitle you to a return of at least a portion of your deposit if you pull out by a certain date. The closer you are to the wedding, the less likely you are to get anything back.

Canceling the Honeymoon

We know of one bride who took her best friend on a cruise after she was left at the altar, and the change of scenery went far in helping her get over the loss. But if you decide to cancel, know that your ability to recoup any expenses, particularly for airfare or cruise tickets, depends largely on what kind of ticket you bought and the cancellation policy of the airline or cruise line. Even trip insurance usually applies only to cases of illness or natural disaster, not a change of heart.

The Dress

If your dress was a special order, it's unlikely that you'll get any sort of refund. But do contact the dressmaker as soon as possible to see what options are available to you. If it's still early, can production be stopped? Can the dress be resold at the next store sale? If not, the dress can be sold on eBay or through a consignment shop or donated to a charity for the tax deduction. Know, too, that a talented dressmaker might be able to restyle the dress and even dye it for further use.

Returning Gifts

All gifts should be returned along with a thank-you note. If you've already used some items or if the gift was monogrammed, you can keep these, but send thank-you notes and explain why you are not returning the gift.

What About the Ring?

It's generally agreed that if the ring was a family heirloom, it should go back to the family it came from, no matter who called off the wedding, for any reason. But in the case of a newly purchased ring, opinions vary. Dear Abby believes firmly that the ring should always go back to the giver, no matter who called it off, but her sister, the late Ann Landers, held that the ring should go back to the giver only if the receiver of the ring is the one to call off the wedding. If the giver of the ring is the one who calls off the wedding, then the receiver may opt to keep it, sell it, or return it. We believe that Miss Manners has the last word on the subject: she maintains that the ring is a symbol of the union that was to be and should be returned, though she admits that it nevertheless remains a symbol if a perturbed bride "ran over it with her van, melted it down, or threw it away."

Everyone seems to agree that if the couple bought the ring together, they should decide jointly what to do with it.

25 Things That Can Go Wrong at the Wedding and How to Prevent Them

1. The bridal shop where you ordered your dress goes out of business two weeks before you are supposed to pick up your gown. *Solution:* Stick to reputable bridal shops that are established and popular.

2. The gown is lost or damaged beyond repair just days before the event. *Solution:* Order all your accoutrements in plenty of time to replace them if things go awry.

3. After you have ordered your bridal gown, you see it at another store—for 20 percent less than you paid. *Solution:* Do your homework before you shop.

4. The bridesmaids' dresses don't fit any of the bridesmaids, at least two of them aren't the exact color of the others, or, in spite of how much you paid for them, faulty zippers and uneven hemlines show off poor workmanship. *Solution:* Know that sizing for wedding wear is different from regular sizes. All bridesmaids should be specially fitted, and dresses should be picked up early enough so that there is time for alterations if necessary.

5. The flowers wilt just moments before your outdoor ceremony. *Solution:* Even DIY weddings need consultation with professionals for some aspects. Research the heartiest wedding flower varieties for the area where the wedding is taking place, especially in the case of destination weddings.

6. You need only 5 more invitations, but the minimum order is 25 and they're costing $7.50 apiece. *Solution:* Figure on an extra 20 percent when you place the original order. It's better to have extras.

7. There are typos in the invitation. It's the stationer's fault, but he's still going to need another three weeks to reprint, and that totally thwarts your timetable. *Solution:* Check all proofs carefully and ask others in your family to give them a fresh eye as well. Sign a copy of the approved version. Order early to leave time for such a disaster.

8. The invitations are finally addressed and mailed, but now they've all been returned for additional postage. *Solution:* Take a sample invitation to the post office before you stamp them all to make sure they have proper postage.

9. Some invitations are lost in the mail, and you can never convince some of those people that they really were invited. *Solution:* Double- and triple-check your address list, and call people you may not have seen in a few years to make sure you have the right address.

10. The caterer verbally promised to throw in chair coverings for free, but the day before the wedding he doesn't recall a thing about it. *Solution:* Get everything in writing. No exceptions.

11. The band, which came highly recommended by the catering hall, is a disaster. *Solution:* A vendor who is recommended by another vendor may be getting a kickback. Sample the wares of all vendors before you commit.

12. The catering hall surcharges—for uncorking wine bottles, for rest room attendants, for cutting the cake (a dollar a slice!), for a built-in gratuity—and throws in an extra service fee on top of all that has been contracted. The total is staggering! *Solution:* Read the contract and feel free to question and negotiate any items that you deem inappropriate, even if you're told, "Everyone pays that—it's standard."

13. The ballroom promised for the reception is under construction, and you are being moved to the smaller one—the one with the funny smell. *Solution:* Your contract should stipulate at least a partial refund for any services that are not delivered as promised.

14. The hors d'oeuvres taste just like those frozen ones you served at your last barbeque. *Solution:* You should be allowed to taste anything that will be served at the wedding beforehand.

15. A week before the wedding the caterer informs you that food prices have gone up and there will be an extra charge for the sushi bar. *Solution:* Your contract should stipulate that prices are locked in as of the day of the signing of the contract.

16. The celebrity photographer never shows up, but he does send an assistant—someone you've never met who seems to have no clue about how to carry out the copious instructions you have written out. *Solution:* Be careful about bait-and-switch routines, for photography services as well as musicians and others; your

contract should include the names of the people who will be working at the event.

17. You thought the photographer would automatically airbrush away the fly that landed on your nose a moment before the ceremony ended; you were wrong. *Solution:* Find out what services are not included in your photography contract. Airbrushing, cropping, and color correction should be part of the deal.

18. You printed out all your pictures on an ink-jet printer, and now, just six months after your wedding, they are fading. *Solution:* Know what you're doing when you take on DIY wedding tasks. Ink-jet color fades. Even if you're not using a professional, you may want to consult with one before the event.

19. You planned an e-wedding and are now receiving enough spam to feed a small country for decades. *Solution:* Set up a special e-mail address for wedding correspondence, then cancel the address after the wedding.

20. The cake tastes like sandpaper. *Solution:* Many wedding cakes taste like sandpaper; taste before you buy.

21. The twin flower girls were adorable—until they ran into the kitchen and caused the cake to collapse only three hours before the reception. *Solution:* Don't have the cake delivered until just before the event; accidents happen.

22. The DVD the photographer delivered won't work on your DVD player. *Solution:* Make sure you and your videographer discuss the technology beforehand. As DVD technology develops, this problem will become more common.

23. The photographer never took any pictures of the cake-cutting or the groom's family—who happened to be paying for the photography. *Solution:* The photographer should have a complete list of all your "must-have" pix, and someone should check with him or her halfway through the event to make sure that all bases are being covered.

24. The videographer never mentioned the surcharges for extra microphones and lighting, which the venue said it would supply. *Solution:* Read the contract carefully before you sign. If surcharges are mentioned, find out what they are likely to be.

25. The videographer was running behind, so he stayed an extra half-hour to finish up, and now the venue is claiming the wedding went overtime. *Solution:* Don't assume that because everyone is smiling at you, everything is all right. They may be smiling because they are thinking of ways to spend the extra money you are going to have to pay them. Assess surcharges ahead of time.

The wedding day was fast approaching. Everything was ready, and nothing could dampen Jennifer's excitement, not even her parents' nasty divorce. Her mother, Sheila, had finally found the perfect dress to wear and would be the best-dressed mother of the bride ever!

A week later, Jennifer was horrified to learn that her young new stepmother, Barbie, had purchased the same dress. She asked Barbie to exchange the dress, but Barbie refused. "Absolutely not! I'm going to wear this dress. I'll look like a million bucks in it!"

Jennifer told her mother, who graciously replied, "Never mind, dear. I'll get another dress. After all, it's your special day, not hers."

Two weeks later, Jennifer and her mother went shopping and found another dress. When they stopped for lunch, Jennifer asked her mother, "What are you going to do with the first dress? Maybe you should return it. You don't have any place to wear it." Sheila grinned and replied, "Of course I do, dear! I'm wearing it to the rehearsal dinner!"

10 Ways to Avoid the BS: Preventing the Bridezilla Syndrome

Gina Romanello (GinaRomanello.com), the author of *Chicken Soup for the Bride's Soul,* which brings comfort and enlightenment to stressed brides, writes:

In the fast-paced world of wedding planning, stress levels are high; immune systems are low; and over the course of the past 20 years, brides have contracted what has become a bridal epidemic of our time.

This broadening illness has been commonly termed "Bridezilla Syndrome" or "BS."

A contagious condition, Bridezilla Syndrome has become more prominent and has plagued today's busy, wedding-planning woman. Symptoms include recurring mood spells, bouts with selfishness, signs of controlling behavior, and feelings of meticulousness.

Symptoms are recognized most often by the fiancé and maid of honor, and are completely undetectable by the actual victim. In some cases, a bridal party member, having had too much alcohol to drink, has confronted the Bridezilla. Most often, an emotional breakdown of the victim follows. In a survey of 100 maids of honor, an alarming 85 percent said they avoided confrontation with the victim for fear it would only aggravate the illness.

Bridezillas seem to have been unfairly blamed for their actions, for which some believe they have no control. In fact, it's been clinically proven that a Bridezilla actually does have feelings—feelings of selfishness, insecurity, anxiousness, and stress!

A survey of healthy brides who successfully planned their weddings without contracting the disease was conducted, and the results showed commonalities of the actions performed to avoid the disorder. Doctors, psychologists, and wedding planners strongly suggest the following preventative therapy:

1. **Maintain a perspective.** Remind yourself that the wedding is only one day in your life. When things get out of control, close your eyes and think of the reason you are planning this wedding in the first place. It's not about the wedding; it's about marriage.

2. **Especially if you're naturally a control freak, don't exclude your groom by assuming he doesn't want to help.** Ask him what he'd like to take responsibility for, and then let him. [If, like many grooms,

he declines your offer, be gracious. See "9 Ways to Involve the Groom," page 216.]

3. **Know that no matter how many demands you make or how much money you spend, you will never be in total control of your wedding.** Life just isn't like that. Expect some surprises and deal with them graciously.

4. **Delegate, delegate, delegate.** Allow trusted friends to make some decisions on your behalf, and accept the results. Know how to ask for help.

5. **Don't sweat the small stuff.** No one really cares if the invitation has two envelopes or if the table linens are not the exact shade of the bridesmaid's dresses. Save your energy for the biggies.

6. **Treat the people you cherish with love.** You want the day to be memorable, but what, exactly, do you want it to be remembered for? The wedding is one day; your family and friends are forever. Try to ensure that the memories they take away from the event will be just as lovely as yours.

7. **Allow others to vent.** Ask your fiancé, family, and bridesmaids to tell you when you're going off the deep end. Listen to what they have to say and remember that this time is stressful for them too.

8. **Take the heat.** If you've stepped on toes and ruffled feathers, take time to make amends. Then reevaluate your behavior and make changes as needed.

9. **Do something for yourself every day that doesn't involve the wedding.** You'll be able to think more clearly if you step back for a while every day and concentrate on your life, not your wedding. Yoga classes, good books, and helping others are great antidotes for BS.

10. **Know that there is an end in sight.** BS is not a terminal illness. In fact, in most cases, the bride has been known to be miraculously cured once she has returned from her honeymoon. Doctors and psychologists theorize that the change in altitude from flying coupled with excessive levels of the "love hormone" oxytocin counteracts the disease by boosting the immune system, thus eliminating symptoms.

How to Tell if You're a Bridezilla

With 27 years of experience in the wedding business, Rose Giffen, the owner of Rosann's Bridal in Greentown, Ohio, and operator of BeachBride2Be.com, offers advice to brides who want real, truthful, and useful wedding information with a bit of humor thrown in. Here's Rose's Bridezilla test. Take it at your own risk by answering these questions honestly.

1. Is the wedding all about me?

2. Do I feel entitled to special treatment from everyone because I'm getting married?

3. Do I obsess about every detail of the wedding and have trouble making decisions? Am I changing my mind and second-guessing every decision I make?

4. Do I talk about my wedding 24/7?

5. Do I spend hours online chatting and comparing notes with other brides I don't even know?

6. Are my friends avoiding me because "it's all about me"?

7. Is my fiancé sick of hearing about the wedding?

8. Am I focusing on the wedding instead of the marriage?

9. Am I having temper tantrums and anxiety attacks?

10. Do I expect perfection in every aspect of my wedding?

11. Do I expect a huge shower, a bachelorette party, and a fancy rehearsal dinner?

12. Am I in the "gimme gimme I want good gifts" mode?

13. Do I spend hours looking at my online wedding registry to see what's been purchased?

14. Am I lashing out at my mother, fiancé, bridesmaids, and friends?

15. Am I bossing around the wedding party? The staff at the bridal salon? The reception coordinator?

16. Do I demand to have everything my own way?

17. Am I dictating hairstyles, manicures, and even pedicures for my bridesmaids?

18. Am I dictating orders to the groomsmen?

19. Am I complaining about my bridesmaids to everyone who will listen?

20. Has any member of the wedding party stepped down due to my behavior?

21. Am I competing just to make my wedding bigger/better than that of a cousin or a friend?

22. Has my fiancé been making excuses to people about me?

23. Have I been arguing with everyone about everything?

Scoring

If you answer yes to 5 or fewer questions: You are not a Bridezilla. Some wedding anxiety is normal. You need to step back and relax with your fiancé. Take a few days off from wedding planning. Take a deep breath; it will all work out fine. Nothing is perfect, and no one will be the wiser if something goes wrong.

If you answer yes to 6 to 10 questions: You are on your way to becoming a Bridezilla. It's time to reevaluate this wedding and marriage. Are you in love with your fiancé or in love with the idea of getting married? Time to get a grip and a clue and relax a bit. It's a wedding; it's about the two of you. The rest is just a party.

If you answer yes to 11 or more questions: You are a full-blown Bridezilla. Time for a major attitude adjustment and amends to everyone you've alienated during the planning process. Do you really want to get married? What is making you so unhappy? Work on what's really bothering you and the rest will fall into place. No one wants to be a Bridezilla, and no one wants to be around a Bridezilla. Don't let it happen to you. Take a deep breath and reassess your priorities.

How to Tell if You Are a Momzilla

MOBzillas and MOGzillas can ruin it for everyone by insisting on supervising every aspect of the wedding. Take Rose Giffen's Momzilla Test and check your behavior.

1. Is this wedding the focus of my life?

2. Do I speak of the wedding as "my" wedding?

3. Do I spend every waking moment working on wedding plans?

4. Do I insist on the last word on every decision?

5. Have I been arguing with the bride and groom about the wedding?

6. Is there contention between myself and the person my child is marrying?

7. Do I argue with my own husband over the wedding plans?

8. Have I voiced my opinion that my daughter or son could have done better in choosing a partner?

9. Do I curb spending on the wedding except when it's something I want?

10. Have I tried to influence the bride by manipulating her into second-guessing her decisions?

11. Did I insist on the wedding location?

12. Did I make it my business to pick out the invitations?

13. Was I overbearing when we shopped for the bride's dress? Did I make her try on dresses she hated? Did I respect her final decision?

14. Did I bore the bridal salon staff—and anyone else who would listen—with a detailed description of my own wedding?

15. Did I criticize the bride by telling her she needs to lose weight, change her makeup, or choose a new hairstyle? (Add 10 points to your score automatically if you made the bride cry in the bridal salon.)

16. Did I insist the bride wear my veil, just to save money?

17. Did I take it upon myself to help choose the bridesmaids' dresses, and did I insist on accompanying them when they shopped?

18. Have I insulted any of the vendors by telling them I could do their job better than they could?

19. Did I insist on elaborate floral displays and then complain to the florist about the cost?

20. Did I tell the DJ that I wanted to go over the playlist with him after the bride and groom already approved it?

21. Did I base the menu on my own personal preferences rather than that of the bride and groom?

22. Have I commandeered the guest list?

23. Do I insist on inviting all my friends just because I'm paying for the wedding? (If these are friends who don't even know the couple, automatically add 5 points to your score.)

24. Do I expect to be invited to the bachelorette party?

25. Do I spend hours on the Internet "just getting ideas"?

Scoring

If you answer yes to 5 or fewer questions: Normal wedding stress between a bride and her mom. Congratulations, you are not a Momzilla. Most moms have some amount of input into the wedding, and it's normal to have some differences of opinion. And yes, most moms and daughters argue at some point over the wedding.

If you answer yes to 6 to 10 questions: You are a Momzilla in training. Tread very carefully, Mom. You are on thin ice. This isn't your wedding. Take a chill pill and bite your tongue. It will all work out, and it will be a wonderful wedding for the loving couple.

If you answer yes to 11 questions or more: Momzilla! It's time to step back and readjust your attitude. Step way back. Get a hobby, get a job, get a life. Find out why you are so obsessed with the wedding. Then back off and apologize to your daughter or son before permanent damage is done to your relationship. Relax and enjoy the wedding. Your relationship with your adult child is more important than any party. And the party is not important in the big scheme of things; the marriage is what really counts.

> "Shut up and wear beige."
> — Good advice to mothers of brides and grooms

Premarital Counseling: Considerations in Preparing for Marriage

Angela Holloway is a licensed marriage and family therapist in southern California and the author of *The Bipolar Bear Family: When a Parent Has Bipolar Disorder*. Her wide-ranging expertise includes relationship issues, and we are grateful to her for the following advice.

Premarital counseling can help damage-proof a relationship, especially for couples at risk. How does this counseling help? What should you consider before marriage?

As divorce rates continue to rise in the United States, more and more couples are approaching marriage with increasing caution. While Americans are still opting for marriage, many are looking for opportunities to damage-proof their relationships before they say "I do." Premarital counseling is just one approach couples are taking.

What Is Premarital Counseling?

Premarital counseling, like any couples counseling, is usually facilitated by a skilled family therapist (and sometimes members of the clergy). The function of premarital counseling is twofold:

• To assist couples in developing skills to navigate their way through marriage successfully
• To identify (and if possible resolve) areas of difference between couples that may become a source of conflict later

Many professionals performing premarital counseling will use assessment tools to help identify these potential difficulties. Perhaps the most commonly used instrument is the PreMarital Inventory (PMI), available to clinicians and clergy through Intercommunications Publishing. The PMI addresses the following areas, all common discussion grounds in premarital counseling:

• Interests and activities
• Role expectations
• Personal adjustment
• Interpersonal communication
• Religion and philosophy
• Marriage expectations
• Family issues
• Finances
• Children (and parenting)
• Sexuality

When Should a Couple Seek Premarital Counseling?

The basis for the following criteria has been suggested by the California Association for Marriage Family Therapists:

• When you are young and have never been married (some states, such as California, require by law that individuals under the age of 18 complete premarital counseling before the wedding)
• When one partner is "commitment-phobic"
• When a couple cannot resolve significant issues (if a couple has disagreements regarding money, parenting, household responsibility, work, sex, etc., the time to resolve them is before marriage)
• When one or both partners have a previously failed marriage and want to avoid repeating the same mistakes

Additional reasons to enter premarital counseling may include:

• Difficulty handling conflict: no marriage tool box is complete (nor can any marriage survive) without strong conflict resolution skills.
• History of childhood abuse or domestic violence: Abuse, unfortunately, has been correlated with higher rates of divorce. It is important to seek help from a trained professional to learn alternatives to patterns that have resulted from emotional or physical abuse, or to heal from the hindrances of sexual abuse before marriage.

Other Considerations in Preparing for Marriage

Don't fall for the classic marriage myths: analyzing the myths of marriage before you say "I do" can be good preventative medicine.

Educate yourself on marriage in general. Browse the Internet or your local bookstore for information on marriage and relationships.

If blending families, couples may want to prepare for the transition by following the "Help for Blended Families Steps to Success" as well as developing a parenting plan.

Marriage and family can be among life's greatest assets. If we strive to protect assets that mean less to us than our loved ones, why not explore the issues ahead of time to "damage-proof" the precious gift of marriage?

7 Antiquated Rules of Wedding Etiquette

The iconographic image of the demure virgin clinging to the arm of her groom has become outdated, and thankfully, so have many of the formalities that gave white weddings of yore their cookie-cutter uniformity. Here, according to Elise MacAdam, author of *Something New: Wedding Etiquette for Rule Breakers, Traditionalists, and Everyone in Between,* are some notions that have either fallen by the wayside or been seriously challenged.

1. The age-old bouquet toss was limited to bridesmaids only, which meant not only that bridesmaids had to be single (because whoever catches the bride's bouquet is supposed to be the next one to marry), but that all single women who weren't in the wedding party were left on the sidelines.

2. Classical superstition warned against having the bride-to-be participate in her wedding rehearsal. Instead of walking through, she would have a friend or relative take her place while she supervised, so that her first trip down the aisle would (presumably) be her last.

3. Wedding registries are completely commonplace today, but in the not-too-distant past, they were considered utterly obnoxious and demanding. Some people still feel this way, and it remains in poor form to include any gift requests or registry information in one's wedding invitation.

4. Today, it seems, anything goes when it comes to the kinds of presents engaged people may give each other, but it used to be extremely bad form for a woman to accept certain types of presents from her future husband, including: cars, fur coats (though a small stole could be acceptable), and clothing.

5. In many circles in the nineteenth century, it was considered presumptuous to give wedding presents that were too intimate, too useful, or too deeply connected to the workings of someone's house (if blenders had existed, they would not have been welcome gifts). Instead, slightly more formal offerings of art and books were suggested, and often people were encouraged not to give anything at all.

6. It used to be considered bad form and bad luck to congratulate the bride, especially when talking to her on the receiving line. (In many parts of the United States, this taboo lives on.) The reason for this is that it creates the impression that the bride is terribly calculating and needs to be praised on her success at snaring a husband or that she should consider herself lucky to be married at all. To be on the safe side, one would congratulate the groom and give one's best wishes to the bride.

7. Friends and relatives who could not attend a wedding were once expected to send telegrams to be read at the reception. Reading them during the toasts fell to the best man. The bride and groom were also expected to write notes thanking and acknowledging the telegrams.

6 More Rules You Can Break

1. The engagement ring doesn't have to be a diamond. It doesn't even have to be a ring: an engagement pendant or bracelet can be even more meaningful, especially for a second or third wedding. Then again, there needn't be any exchange of gifts at all except those that come from the heart.

2. Rules as to who pays for what are fuzzy at best. Today those who are best equipped to pick up the tab, or those who are incurring most of it, pay for the wedding.

3. Formal, heavy-on-the-paper invitations are becoming a thing of the past. Only recently has less become more, and now, less formal invitations with RSVP postcards and fewer inserts are viewed as green rather than skimpy.

4. The standard wedding procession is now far more democratic. Anyone can walk anyone else down the aisle, and get this—you don't have to have bridesmaids!

5. Pre-engagement parties are no longer structured events: they take various forms now and rarely adhere to a particular schedule of parties. Many bachelor and bachelorette events are co-ed these days, and they often involve a full day of sports or entertainment activities.

6. Standard vows are being replaced with the homegrown variety. Bring your own, and if you want to throw in a joke or two, hey, that's entertainment.

13 Rude Wedding Guests and How to Handle Them

The pressure that comes with wedding planning doesn't take its toll just on the hosts; all the excitement often brings out the worst in guests as well. Let these people get to you and you fall into one of the worst traps the experience has to offer. Set boundaries but remain flexible; let those around you know that you have a very specific idea of how you want the day to go, but remember that as a host or hostess, it is your job to accommodate guests and let them know you value their presence and good wishes. Here are some common faux pas and ideas for handling them.

1. **They don't respond to the invitation on time.** It's rude, but this oversight occurs. Don't read too much into it; just get on the phone and let the culprits know that you must have a final guest list in order to plan your wedding properly. If these invitees haven't made up their minds, suggest that they take another day to think about it. If you still don't get a response, send them a note saying how disappointed you are that they won't be sharing your big day. You can communicate via e-mail or ask a diplomatic bridesmaid to step up.
How to avoid the problem: Send out timely save-the-date cards.

2. **They get involved from day one.** It seems that there is always someone on the guest list who fancies themselves a wedding planner, and they have no qualms about sharing their "wisdom" with you, from how the guest list should be handled to your seating arrangement. They'll even go so far as to criticize the choices you have made. Try to listen to all the opinions you are being offered and remember that they are being given in the spirit of helpfulness. Some people do this because it's their way of reliving what might have been the biggest day of their life. They want your day to be just as wonderful. Smile gratefully and then do it your way.
How to avoid the problem: Tell them that the decisions have already been made.

3. **They assume they may bring a date or their children.** Cousin Rose can't get a babysitter, and Aunt Lindsay would love to show off her new beau. If you're lucky, they'll indicate these circumstances on the RSVP card, but brace yourself for getting some of this information in the course of casual conversation. Don't stand for it, especially if these additions are likely to ruffle the feathers of guests who have already accepted your cutbacks. Let them know that your budget or space is at a premium and that you hope they won't mind coming solo. In the case of small children, explain that you do not have provisions for watching them. This should be especially understandable if the wedding is in the evening. You might have to make an exception for an out-of-town guest who may, for instance, be breast-feeding an infant. If that's the case, take some time to explain to other young parents that there were extenuating circumstances in this one case.
How to avoid the problem: Stay in close communication with potential troublemakers.

4. **They regift or give you something awful that you can't possibly use.** The most considerate guests will stick to your registry or give you cash. The worst of the lot will send you something you can't even imagine ever using, or worse, rewrap a set of pink flowered sheets for a bed size you don't even own. You can't return these items, and asking for store information will only insult them and lead to a more uncomfortable situation. The best you can do here is to unload the stuff by donating it to a charity or offering it to someone in need. Don't even think about continuing the cycle by passing it along to the next unwitting bride. What goes around comes around. If you suspect that the gift is returnable, talk to the giver politely about obtaining a receipt; explain that you just don't have room for the item or that it's not the look that you and your honey are shooting for. Always send a polite thank-you note for any gift you have received.
How to avoid the problem: Register at a variety of stores so that those guests who want to send you something unusual will at least have some guidance. Remember to include some inexpensive choices.

5. **They show up late or not at all.** There you are, making your way down the aisle, and there's Uncle Stanley, drifting in late, waving hello to all and disrupting your big moment. Be gracious, know that the instant will pass, and hope that he won't get caught on the video.
How to avoid the problem: Start the ceremony some 15 minutes after the stated time, thereby giving latecomers a little leeway. Have at least one and possibly two ushers stationed at the back of the room to run interference. Latecomers should

> *John and his fiancée Jill were a modern couple:*
> *they were quite realistic about the state of*
> *marriage these days. They met with the minister*
> *of the church to discuss their marriage vows.*
>
> *"Pastor," said Jill, "we wonder if we could make a*
> *change in the wording of our ceremony."*
>
> *"Yes, Jill," replied the pastor, "it is sometimes*
> *done. What do you have in mind?"*
>
> *"Well," said Jill, "we'd like to alter the 'until death*
> *do us part' section to read, 'substantial penalty*
> *for early withdrawal.'"*

stand in the back until the processional has made its way to the altar, and then they can quietly take seats in the back.

There's not much you can do about the no-shows whose dinners still must be paid for. Don't fret about this during the wedding reception; your bad mood will be reflected in your photos, and you will be giving these rude guests more attention than they deserve.

Chances are, you will be given a reasonable explanation in due time.

6. **They give unexpected speeches or inappropriate toasts.** Weddings and alcohol can do funny things to people. That story about you running naked through the family picnic at age three might have been cute at some point in time, but it's not a visual you want invoked at your wedding, and—sheesh!—does this story have to go on forever? Deal with it; know that guests will take all this with a grain of salt, and your stock will go up for handling the situation gracefully.

How to avoid the problem: Have an emcee who knows when to step in, either by thanking the guest for his remarks and ushering him out of the spotlight or by signaling the band to resume playing. If you know that Uncle Al always tells the same embarrassing joke at every family wedding, talk to him before the event and beg him to abstain just this once.

7. **They request songs.** From the time you were a child, you dreamed of a white wedding, a beautiful wedding cake, a candlelit ceremony—and no Chicken Dance. But there it is, and there

are all your guests lining up for the fun. There's nothing you can do to stop the mayhem, and having to be urged by all to join in is just making it worse. Gracious hosts relent, knowing that modern editing techniques will save the day and there'll be no sign of this nonsense on the video. You can just make the gesture of joining in and then feign fatigue or a need to get off your feet.

How to avoid the problem: Let your bandleader or DJ know ahead of time that you want to stick with your own set list and that any suggestions from guests must be cleared by you ahead of time.

8. **Young people party hearty—a little too hearty.** While their parents are off socializing during the cocktail hour, young guests might view this as the best time of all to break every rule in the book—from boozing it up to men's room antics and generally rude behavior. Don't even try to deal with it. Have a bridesmaid or usher ask the parents to handle their own kids; they can do it more effectively than anyone.

How to avoid the problem: Ask the bartenders to be especially careful around sneaky youngsters and to feel free to card your guests if they are in doubt. Don't invite young guests who have a reputation for this sort of behavior. If they must be included, ask someone to keep an eye out for trouble. Or talk to the parents before the event and explain that an incident would ruin your day—could they please read their kids the riot act before the event?

9. **They assume the marrying couple will act as their travel agent.** You have enough details on your list to last a lifetime. You don't really have time to seek out vegetarian restaurants for out-of-towners, pick up theater tickets, or draw maps to point out the best shopping areas.

How to avoid the problem: Your bridesmaids should be helping you with some of this, but to make sure all the pertinent information is distributed properly, include it on your wedding website (see "10 Things to Include on Your Wedding Website," page 190) and make sure that all special-needs guests understand that you will not be acting as full-time concierge. You might assign bridesmaids to each of the high-maintenance guests, who should be contacted a week before the event to ask if they have everything they need.

10. **They dress inappropriately.** It's possible that at the last minute one of your bridesmaids will decide that a bright pink rose in her hair will show off the gold specks in her eyes, even though none of the other bridesmaids is wearing one, and it's possible that those who are culturally challenged might decide to wear jeans to your black-tie affair. Ask the rude bridesmaid to dispense with the

rose at least for the photos; grin and bear the misdressed culprit. A wedding is no time to employ fashion police. Know that wedding guests dress differently in various cultures. In Israel, for example, casual clothing is acceptable for even the most formal affair. **How to avoid the problem:** Stress your dress code on your wedding website and provide appropriate shopping information. The friend with the rebellious sense of fashion might not make the best choice for a bridesmaid.

11. **They disregard your seating arrangements.** Some may call before the event and demand to be seated as close to (or as far away from) certain other guests as possible. Others may simply toss their table cards in the wastebasket and plop themselves down wherever they are comfortable—even going so far as to take the seat of another guest who now has nowhere to sit. If you're lucky enough to hear of the plan before the event, you can at least assure the guest that you will make every effort to accommodate him but that you hope he'll honor your final decision. In the latter event, hope that your wedding planner or a member of the wedding party will step in and politely ask for the seat. **How to avoid the problem:** Try to anticipate such instances and take them into account when preparing the seating arrangement. Divorced couples and stepfamilies will have issues; think these through before you finalize your plan. If you have been forced to seat someone at a table with strangers, make sure someone takes the time to introduce him to his tablemates and explain why he was seated there in the first place ("Everyone at your table is in the music business too; you all have a lot in common").

12. **Everyone's a photographer!** Just as he's about to place the ring on your finger—flash!—a blinding light from Cousin Sara's camera ruins the moment. Some guests assume that because they own a camera, it is appropriate to bring it to the wedding, and then they take it upon themselves to document the entire event, regardless of the fact that they may be jostling your $400-an-hour pro for the best shot. Or worse, they become art directors, distracting your appointed photographer and dragging him over to the table to get a shot of "Mortimer and the kids." **How to avoid the problem:** Make it clear to your photographer that he is under your direction and no one else's. See "Photography Tips" (pages 271–72) to make sure you end the day with the photos you've hoped for. Appoint someone to stand at the back of the room during the ceremony and ask would-be paparazzi to limit their photos to the reception only. They should explain that the photographer you have hired prefers to work alone.

13. **They don't bring a gift.** They didn't send one before the event, they brought nothing with them to the reception, and even weeks after the flowers have wilted, there's no gift in sight. To complicate matters, you're not sure how the thank-you card should be worded. If there's a good chance that these people couldn't afford a gift (perhaps they spent a small fortune to travel to your wedding), be grateful for their presence and ignore the rudeness of not even presenting you with a small, inexpensive present. If you suspect an oversight, you might call and explain that after the event you came across two gifts without attached cards, and you wonder if either of these was theirs. Most likely, you will be given a reasonable explanation.

How to avoid the problem: Remember that you have already received one of the most important gifts life has to offer—the promise of loving arms around you for the rest of your life—and that no silver service or pewter urn could ever take its place.

3 Ways to Find Bridal Shows

1. The Great Bridal Expo holds approximately 40 shows each year at various locations throughout the United States. Attendees find almost anything they might need for their wedding, honeymoon, and new home, all in one convenient location. Exhibitions and exhibitors include bakeries, bridal fashions, bridesmaid dresses, cakes, catering, ceremony locations, DJs, entertainment, favors, house and home, invitations, jewelry, music, officiants, party rentals, photography, reception locations, tuxedos, videography, wedding coordinators, wedding insurers, and more. Visit Great BridalExpo.com for more information and to find the locations nearest you.

2. On Wedalert.com, you can link to a number of bridal show sites in California, Connecticut, Delaware, Florida, Georgia, Maine, Maryland, Massachusetts, New Hampshire, New Jersey, New York, North Carolina, Pennsylvania, Rhode Island, South Carolina, Vermont, Virginia, and Washington, D.C.

3. Onewed.com, a comprehensive and user-friendly online wedding planning resource, offers a comprehensive list of bridal shows and expos across the country and enables you to link to many of them.

A Deadly Combination: Your Wedding and Your Job

Patricia Lee of weddingexpress.com provides the following advice about how to combine wedding planning with your other full-time job.

Planning a wedding can be a full-time task on its own. For most women, it becomes a second job to the one they already have. Time management becomes quite difficult, and you try to figure out how to get everything done while still doing well at work. So how do you do both? It can be difficult, but you can do it.

1. Work around your job. Plan appointments before and after work and on weekends. If you commute, use the time to plan and read contracts and make calls on your cell phone. Squeeze in calls during your lunch or coffee breaks. Online services offer quick access to information, so use downtime to gather information. Just make sure you don't ignore your duties.

2. Inform your boss and staff of your plans. Let them know if you'll be out of the office for any extended periods in advance. They'll be impressed with your sense of organization and appreciate your consideration.

> "I have yet to hear a man ask for advice on how to combine marriage and a career."
> — Gloria Steinem

3. The most hectic times of wedding planning occur at the beginning and the end of the process. Always try to be organized and prepared for crunch times. If you make checklists and follow them, you will probably be able to complete all your tasks on time. If you miss a few meetings or show up late, make up for the lost time when you're able. Let your coworkers know you appreciate their understanding.

4. Consider hiring a bridal consultant. Make sure it's someone you can trust with good decisions, but retain final approval over all. Let them do what they do best so you can do what you do best.

5. Be sensitive about wedding talk at work, especially if not all your coworkers are invited to the wedding. If you can, talk to those who are being excluded and explain your budgetary or space limitations. If you have a small enough work environment, it may be easier to just invite everyone. If that's not possible, treat everyone

to a special lunch at some point as a way of making up for any stress your wedding has placed on others.

6. Your wedding is a very important event in your life, but your paycheck is just as important. Both affect your future and how you will be living. Be wise in the time you spend planning your wedding and always consider the quality of your work. If you remain on task, you can successfully plan a beautiful wedding while also getting your work done.

All About Bridal Registries

When the first bridal registry appeared in 1901 at a store called China Hall in Rochester, Minnesota, society was outraged. While the plan purported to eliminate duplicate gifts and make life easier for all, some claimed it was an outright demand for a gift, a rude gesture not at all in keeping with the social etiquette of the time.

It took almost 100 years, but today the bridal registry is accepted readily by wedding guests who are pleased to be able to give gifts that are truly wanted. Of course, there's no law against buying a gift outside the registry, just as there's no law against displaying ugly candelabras only when the giver visits.

• Register for gifts right after the engagement is announced.

• Do some homework before you actually register with stores. Look around for those with the best prices and the widest range of choices. Make your decisions together using online resources before you register.

• Make sure you and your honey register together and agree on all your choices, and choose some items that you may each enjoy separately (fishing tackle, certain books). Don't rush through the process.

• Do not make any mention of a registry when extending invitations of any kind unless you are asking for a charitable donation instead of a gift, in which case this can be mentioned on the invitation. News of your registry should travel via family members and bridal attendants. There are conflicting opinions as to whether it's polite to mention a gift registry on your wedding website. We believe guests will appreciate the information if it's stated modestly.

• Register with at least two stores (and not more than four) to give people price-range choices.

• Keep tabs on the registry every few weeks to make sure you haven't changed your mind about the items you've chosen.

• Keep a list of the gifts you get so that your thank-you cards can include details.

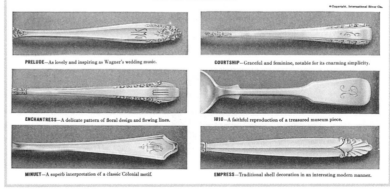

Choose your silver

AS YOU CHOOSE YOUR HUSBAND

IN CHOOSING A HUSBAND for keeps, naturally you recognize these two "musts"! He must have that intangible quality called "character." And he must be a man of whom you never tire.

Keep those same things in mind when you make *another* lifetime choice—the choice of your *silver*—and we believe you'll decide on the sterling that's made by International.

For International Sterling has a character that only a century's "know-how" in fine silver-smithing can produce. It brings a great silver tradition into your home. And, as the years pass, your International Sterling becomes a part of your family background. Associations cluster around it—and you value it far beyond price.

See International Sterling at your leading jeweler's. You'll marvel at its exquisite beauty—and at its moderate price!

Complete place settings—knife, fork, salad fork, teaspoon, cream soup spoon, and butter spreader—from $16.75. Complete 36-piece service for six, from $100. *And your jeweler will gladly arrange a convenient budget payment plan.*

International Sterling
Master craftsmen for five generations*

*Copyright, International Silver Co.

PRELUDE—As lovely and inspiring as Wagner's wedding music.

COURTSHIP—Graceful and feminine, notable for its charming simplicity.

ENCHANTRESS—A delicate pattern of floral design and flowing lines.

1810—A faithful reproduction of a treasured museum piece.

MINUET—A superb interpretation of a classic Colonial motif.

EMPRESS—Traditional shell decoration in an interesting modern manner.

Favorite Bible Verses for Wedding Ceremonies

If you're going to incorporate Bible verses into your ceremony, take the time to read and think about the passages. Your understanding of them will enhance the event for you and for those around you. Deborah Spence and GlassLady.com provided the following list of biblical excerpts.

The Old Testament

- Genesis 1:27–28a, 31a—God's good and gracious work in creating man and woman for each other
- Ruth 1:16—The devotion of Ruth to a new family
- Song of Solomon 2:10–14, 16a—The lover arrives in spring to call for his bride
- Song of Solomon 8:6–7—A bride beseeches her lover to be faithful
- Isaiah 26:3–4—Trust in God
- Isaiah 43:1–7—Our redemption by God and God's presence and love in our lives
- Isaiah 55:10–13—God's word feeds and nurtures us
- Isaiah 61:10–62:3—Our certain salvation and a new status
- Psalm 19—A psalm praising God as creator
- Psalm 34:8—Verse 8 of this psalm of Thanksgiving is particularly nice for weddings that include Holy Communion
- Psalm 98:1a, 4–6—A psalm of praise
- Psalm 100—A psalm of praise
- Psalm 119—The longest in the Bible, the entire psalm is a reflection on God's laws, with verses 1–16 reflecting on walking always in God's way
- Psalm 127—A home built by God
- Psalm 128—The blessings of lives led by God

The Apocrypha

- Tobit 8:5–9—Tobias and Sarah praise God and acknowledge Him as the creator who ordained marriage. Tobias prays for mercy and prays that God will allow him and Sarah to grow old together.

The Gospels

- Matthew 5:1–10—The famous Beatitudes, which proclaim God's favor to those who try to live by God's law (see Luke 6:17–49 for a shorter account of the Sermon on the Mount that also includes a few other verses found elsewhere in Matthew)
- Matthew 7:24–27—A metaphor on establishing your home on a foundation in God
- Matthew 22:35–40—The greatest commandment of love and the many ways it applies to life
- Mark 2:18–22—Christ as the bridegroom and His followers as the bride
- Mark 10:42–45—It is better to serve than to be served
- John 2:1–11—The wedding at Cana where Christ performs his first miracle of turning water into wine
- John 3:16—The famous "For God so loved the world . . ."
- John 14:6—"I am the way, the truth, and the life . . ."
- John 15:9–17—An admonition to love one another and a reminder of Christ's sacrificial love for us

The New Testament

- Romans 12:9–18—The Christian's duty to love and all that is encompassed by that duty: hope, patience, prayer, compassion, and more (be sure to compare this passage to the 13th chapter of I Corinthians)
- I Corinthians 13—Perhaps the most famous of all wedding Bible verses, this chapter defines the ultimate gift of the Spirit: love
- I Corinthians 14:1—"Make love your aim" in all you do (verses 2–5 go on to discuss the superior gift of prophecy rather than speaking in tongues)
- I Corinthians 16:14—Be certain that everything you do is motivated by love
- II Corinthians 5:14–17—Through Christ's sacrificial love, we have become new creations
- Ephesians 2:4–10—God's gracious love for us saves us through faith
- Ephesians 4:25–5:2—Be loving and forgiving, speaking only good and imitating Christ ("do not let the sun go down on your anger")
- Ephesians 5:21–33—This passage depicting the Christian home is difficult for some because it deals with "submission theology." However, the general thought is mutual submission. Understand it from an early church point of view.

> "He who finds a wife finds what is good."
> — Proverbs 18:22

- Philippians 2:1–5—Guard against selfishness; be humble and serve others
- Philippians 4:4–9—Rejoice and don't be anxious; live honorably and justly, and God's peace will be a part of your lives
- Colossians 3:12–17—The Christian life lived in love and harmony; do all in Christ's name
- Colossians 3:18–20—More submission theology with the admonition to husbands to love their wives
- I John 3:1—"See what love the Father has given us"
- I John 3:16—Christ's example of sacrificial love
- I John 3:18–24—Believe in Christ, and keep His commandments by loving one another
- I John 4:7—Love each other because love comes from God
- I John 4:16–19—God loves us; if we live in love, it serves as a sign that God lives in us, and we are capable of love only because God loved us first

7 Sources of Inspiration for Writing Your Wedding Vows

1. The lyrics to a favorite song
2. A passage from a poem or a book
3. Biblical passages
4. A famous quotation
5. An important date in wedding history (see chapter 1)
6. A proverb
7. A line from a movie

How to Write Your Own Vows

Writing your own vows is not as hard as it sounds—not if you take the time to recall why you took this step in the first place, to remember when you first discovered that you were in love, and to think about the impact on your life now that you have found your other half. Here's a guide to the process.

1. Start by reading the traditional vows for the type of wedding you're having—Catholic, Jewish, etc. Read the words carefully and think about whether they express your feelings. If they do, you may want to use them and just add a sentence or two to personalize the moment ("And I promise to go skydiving with you anytime you choose").

2. Decide together whether you want to say the same vows or if each of you will say something different. If one of you is less comfortable with the writing process, simultaneous vows are probably best.

3. Next, gather ideas. There are zillions of vows all over the Internet, and there are excellent books on the subject as well. But the number of choices available is liable to make your head spin. You can keep your vows more personal by drawing inspiration from a poem you both love, a song, a movie, a passage from the Bible, or a famous quotation. Then think about how this relates to your relationship. What made you fall in love? What are you looking forward to most? How will your spouse add value to your life? Jot down your ideas.

4. Write the vows by listing the essential points you want to make and then arranging them in some kind of order, perhaps chronologically. For instance, you might want to be sure to cover three points: one about the past, one about what you are feeling at this moment, and one about the future you anticipate. In any event, you want your vows to have a beginning, a middle, and an end. Edit them down once you're done and take out any extraneous words.

5. Write your vows on paper and practice them a few times, but not so often that you start to sound like you're giving a memorized speech. Your vows should be spoken from the heart. Still, reading them from a piece of paper at the ceremony, where jitters can play all sorts of tricks on you, won't make them less meaningful.

6. Be sure to show your vows to your officiant in order to determine whether they are acceptable from a religious standpoint. This will also give your officiant a chance to get to know you as a couple.

7. The most important aspect of your wedding vows is your promise to live by them. Remember them and consider repeating them to one another on every wedding anniversary.

6 Tips for Planning the Multi-Faith Wedding Ceremony

Joyce Gioia is a multi-faith minister who specializes in bonding couples from diverse religious and cultural backgrounds. Fluent in numerous languages, Joyce delights in creating ceremonies that are unique and balanced reflections of the couple's backgrounds. For a free candle ceremony, access her website at www.multifaithweddings.com. We're grateful to Joyce for this helpful list.

With the growing diversity in our society, it is not surprising that more and more couples are marrying outside of their faith. Marrying someone not of your religious or cultural background can sometimes be challenging. However, bridging the gap can be very rewarding. Here are some tips and tactics for avoiding the pitfalls and obstacles of the multi-faith wedding.

1. Don't be afraid to talk about your preferences with each other before you meet with a member of the clergy. You'll save time and effort and be able to present a consistent message that your officiant will appreciate.

2. If you are not choosing one religion for the ceremony but want representation from both sides, you have two choices: one is to find someone who will deliver a balanced ceremony with equal parts from both sides; the other is to have two members of the clergy, each representing his or her own religious background.

3. When you meet with your potential officiant, she or he should be able to review the ceremony with you. Hearing the ceremony will allow you to ensure for yourself that you are both okay with everything that is in it. (If your chosen clergy is a family priest or pastor, they may not want to review the ceremony with you. Press for this opportunity.)

4. If one of you is not happy with some aspect of the ceremony, tell your officiant. As a multi-faith minister, I always want my couples to be happy with their ceremony. Don't be afraid to ask for what you want.

5. Involve the families, particularly when there is a new blended family that includes young children. This inclusive attitude works

very well with the new in-laws as well. In almost every ceremony I ever conducted, I included a wine or honey (honoring Islam, because it prohibits alcohol) ceremony. After the couple shares the wine, I invite the new in-laws to share the wine too. This helps the parents to feel included, and it lets them know that their support is important to you.

6. If you are marrying someone from a different culture, take the time to research the wedding rites and customs they practice. This will give you a better understanding of some of the rituals you may be performing, and you'll get major brownie points for the effort (see "How to Add Ethnic Accents to Your Wedding," page 166).

What Your Color Choice Really Means

Erica Tevis of LittleThingsWeddingFavors.com writes: Color and the choices we make regarding the use of it reflect our personalities and convey meaning to wedding guests. Your color choices may be based on personal preferences, a particular theme, or a seasonal palette. However you make the choice, your color scheme will affect the atmosphere at your wedding. Here are some of the most common color schemes and what they communicate.

White: Brides have been wearing white since the Victorian times, and it is now the traditional color for wedding dresses. To the human eye, the color white is brilliant and bright. It's no wonder that wearing it on your wedding day will make you stand out. White symbolizes purity, cleanliness, and innocence.

Ivory: Ivory, like white, represents quiet, pleasantness with a touch of luster. Ivory is a soft, neutral color that has a touch of earthiness of brown hues. It carries the same pureness, softness, and cleanliness of white but is slightly richer, a touch warmer. This is a great color choice for spring or fall brides, as the traditional seasonal colors complement ivory.

Gold: Gold is a precious metal and is associated with wealth and prosperity. Gold is eye-catching and lends richness and warmth to your color palette. Add a golden glow to an earthy palette of browns, oranges, or greens to emphasize their brilliance. Red, burgundy, and purple are warmed with hints of gold. It's a wonderful accent color for fall weddings, and a traditional hue.

Silver: Silver, especially bright silver, is cool like gray, but lively and playful. It is sleek and modern while still adding the feeling of riches. Silver accents to your wedding will add glamour and make your day sparkle. Silver pairs nicely with almost any other color. Use silver with cool shades of blue for winter weddings. Silver is also a lovely addition to a black-and-white theme, enhancing the colors without detracting from them.

Black: A conservative color, black goes with almost any color, except very dark ones. It's sexy and sophisticated, modern and elegant. Black can communicate opulence and grandeur, and it works year-round

Which White?

In 2006, Justin Alexander was the proud recipient of the Debi Award for "Distinctive Newcomer" in the bridal gown industry. The gowns in his collection show special attention to details and historical references. Here is Alexander's guide to choosing from among the many versions of white you'll come across when shopping for bridal gowns.

Whites can easily be divided into four distinct colors:

Stark white: The brightest, crispest white you can find.

Silk, diamond, or natural white: A shade off of stark white that may be hard to differentiate from stark white in photos. "Eighty percent of the population looks best in a soft, diamond-white wedding dress, which isn't as chalky as a white-white," explains dress designer Melissa Sweet. "When in doubt, buy diamond white."

Ivory: Also referred to as "eggshell" or "candlelight." Some ivory wedding dresses have yellow undertones, making them look creamy; some are just a "quiet" white.

Rum or champagne: A white with pink undertones that looks nearly white in photos.

The key to finding your shade? Knowing your skin tone.

If your skin is fair: You'll look best in yellow-ivories and warmer natural colors. You should probably steer clear of stark white, though—it may wash you out.

If your skin is medium with pink undertones: Opt for creamier colors.

If your skin is medium with yellow undertones: Try diamond whites or champagne.

If your skin is dark: Lucky you—most shades of white will complement your skin. If you have yellow or olive undertones, yellow-ivory wedding dresses may not be best for you. Stark white is a good choice for you.

Red: Red is an extremely strong, passionate color. As a stimulant, red is the hottest of the warm colors, and it can make your blood boil or your passion ignite. In some cultures, red denotes purity, joy, and celebration. In China, red is the color of happiness, prosperity, and good luck. It's a wonderful color for Christmas and Valentine weddings, and the deeper shades, like burgundy, are great in the fall.

Pink: Pink is the softer, sweeter side of red. It is a delicate color that symbolizes abundance, compassion, and love. Pink roses symbolize grace, gentleness, and joy. Pale pinks are wonderful for spring weddings, and vibrant pinks are lovely in summer. It can be warmed with gold or cooled when paired with silver.

Orange: Brides who choose orange are spontaneous, bold, daring, and trendy. Orange is inspirational and stimulating, yet warm and inviting. It is said that people who love life love orange. Orange is also the color of transition, which can symbolize your new life together. Orange is versatile for weddings: choose a soft Creamsicle shade for spring, tangerine for summer, or burnt orange for fall.

Yellow: Yellow is the color of sunshine. It denotes happiness and joy and is a symbol of hope and courage. Alone, the warmth of yellow makes an impact, and it complements many other colors well when used as an accent. Very pale yellows work for spring weddings, lemon yellows are lovely for a citrus summer theme, and dark mustard yellows make fall weddings come alive.

Green: Green shades symbolize life, growth, fertility, health, and the environment. With both a warming effect like yellow and a cooling effect like blue, green is a balanced, harmonized color. Down-to-earth brides may be drawn to green, which can be used year-round by varying the shades. Think crisp bright green for summer weddings, olive green for fall, and emerald shades for winter.

Blue: Blue is tranquil, calm, peaceful, honest, trusting, and faithful. It is said to bring love and luck to weddings, and in many cultures it is believed to ward off bad spirits. Pastel blues work well in spring; sky, aqua, or turquoise blues are great for summer. Deep royal blues and navy work well for fall and winter events.

Purple: Often associated with royalty and spirituality, purple is a mysterious color with both warm and cool properties. Deep or bright purples suggest riches and wealth, while lighter purples are more romantic and delicate. Purple in your wedding can also symbolize dignity, value, tolerance, and togetherness. Lavenders and lilacs are wonderful for spring and summer weddings. Deep purples and eggplant are marvelous for fall and winter.

Brown: Brown is a down-to-earth, natural, neutral color. It is a warm color that represents wholesomeness, dependability, friendliness, and steadfastness. Use shades of brown to represent the warmth and honesty of your marriage. Taupe, beige, or cream make lovely spring and summer colors, and chocolate brown is currently trendy for fall and winter. Brown is lovely paired with an ivory wedding gown; gold, copper, and rust accents add warmth and dimension to brown.

Wedding Gown Fabrics

Batiste: Lightweight, sheer, delicate fabric in a plain weave. Similar to cotton, but thicker

Brocade: Heavy material with a pattern

Chiffon: Lightweight, flowing, sheer woven fabric with a soft drape

Crepe: Lightweight fabric with a wrinkled surface

Damask: Medium-weight fabric with a pattern formed by weaving

Dupioni: Thick, heavy, 100 percent silk

Gazar: Sheer, stiff, linen-like fabric similar to organza

Organdy: Stiffer semi-sheer fabric

Organza: Sheer fabric similar to tulle but heavier

Peau de soie: A medium to heavy, drapeable fabric with a satin weave and de-lustered finish

Polyester: Man-made fabric often blended with silks or made to mimic a certain type of fabric

Rayon: Similar to polyester but more elastic

Satin: Smooth and heavy fabric typically used for wedding gowns; comes in silk or polyester

Shantung: Nubby, rough-textured fabric with lines

Silk: A soft, lustrous fabric that is the most popular for wedding dresses

Taffeta: Crisp, rustling fabric

Tulle: Stiff netting similar to organza but stiffer and coarser

Pre-Wedding Parties

Just about every culture has its own pre-wedding festivities, some of which are fraught with meaning and ritual; others are simply intended to celebrate the lucky pair. But those traditions are being challenged today. The wedding shower consisting of 12 women sipping daiquiris and snacking on watercress sandwiches has morphed into anything from a spa day to a Las Vegas spree (see "The New Bridal Shower," page 214). And while the strip-club bachelor party doesn't seem to be any less popular than it was decades ago, some forgo it altogether for a co-ed (and tamer) night out.

Here are six excuses to party even before she dons the dress.

1. **The Engagement Party** The first of the celebrations, held just after the couple has become engaged, was traditionally held to formally announce the betrothal and to introduce the new couple to society. The need to announce the couple as such has become much less important in recent times, and the engagement party has been further eclipsed by the celebrations that follow. Still, many couples have them. The engagement party is usually hosted by the bride's family, and guests are limited to close friends and family.

2. **The Wedding Shower** Traditionally, this was the "biggie," the gathering where female—and only female—friends and family members showered the bride with gifts and through games and girl talk got into the spirit of the event. Held at least two weeks before the wedding, showers were sometimes staged as surprise parties (like she wasn't expecting it) and hosted by the maid of honor. Today shower rules are being bent right and left: men can have showers for a groom, showers can be co-ed, they can be limited to just a few people (in the case of expensive excursions), or they can be done away with altogether. Themed showers, where all the gifts address one area of need, such as the kitchen, are popular with brides who already have most of their household goods in place.

> *Married in white, you have chosen right.*
> *Married in gray, you will go far away.*
> *Married in black, you will wish yourself back.*
> *Married in red, you will wish yourself dead.*
> *Married in green, ashamed to be seen.*
> *Married in blue, you will always be true.*
> *Married in pearl, you will live in a whirl.*
> *Married in yellow, ashamed of your fellow.*
> *Married in brown, you will live in the town.*
> *Married in pink, your spirit will sink.*
> —Traditional English rhyme

3. **The Bachelor Party** The bachelor party has a bad rap, sometimes well deserved, sometimes not. It's traditionally thrown by the best man or the brother of the groom just a few days before the wedding and attended by males only. It often consists of a night of bar- (and/or strip club) hopping, or it can take place at one such location. The bachelor party is known for the liquor consumed and the resulting raucous behavior. (We recommend using limos if alcohol is the theme for the party and leaving all cameras at home. What happens at the bachelor party stays at the bachelor party.)

4. **The Bachelorette Party** Hey—girls just want to have fun, and this new addition to the pre-wedding parties is a chance for them to go out for just as much fun as the boys might be having. It follows the wedding shower and is usually hosted by the maid of honor or the bride's sister. The evening can take place in a variety of locations or just one, and the event invites creativity. Anything goes!

5. **The Bridesmaids Party** This can be held any time after the bridesmaids have been asked and they have accepted. It's hosted by the bride, and it's her chance to thank the girls for all they do. It can consist of a special brunch or other event, or it can be a dinner held right after the final bridesmaids' dress fittings. With so many attendants spread around the globe today, the party might be held just a day or two before the wedding, when all have gathered together.

6. **The Rehearsal Dinner** Even if there's no rehearsal on the night before the wedding, this party is key in bringing families together and making sure that everyone is on the same page for the next day's event. If there are hurt feelings or disagreements among family members, they should be put aside by this time. The party is traditionally hosted by the groom's family, but today it's handled by those who are best able to do it. It can consist of an informal at-home get-together or a formal sit-down dinner. Family members, clergy, and those who have traveled long distances to attend the wedding should be invited.

The New Bridal Shower

In centuries past, as a young bride left the community for her unknown future, her friends would gather to lend moral support and help prepare her for her new role in life. This bonding experience eventually became something of a ritual, and toward the end of the nineteenth century, just as weddings were starting to become big business, gift-giving started to become popular at these events. At some point a creative hostess decided to gather these presents in a parasol and then open it over the bride's head, thus "showering" her with gifts.

Soon the bridal shower became standard practice among brides. The bride's attendants would gather for parlor games and pre-wedding festivities hosted by the maid of honor, usually a few weeks before the wedding. The experience gave the bride a chance to strengthen old ties and form new ones with the female members of her new family.

Traditional wedding showers are still the norm—the party is held in a restaurant or at the home of the hostess, and gifts often follow a theme: kitchen accessories, lingerie, and household items are common. But more and more modern brides are opting for gatherings that reflect the common interests of the bride and her entourage. Here are some alternatives to the traditional "hen party":

1. A party at which wedding paraphernalia is supplied and guests spend the time making decorations and assembling programs

2. A scrapbooking event at which guests can share memories of past weddings

3. A wine-tasting event held at a local winery

4. A flower-arranging event, where a professional florist can instruct the guests on this useful art

5. A cooking class or cake-decorating class set up especially for the party

6. A theater outing

7. A spa outing

8. A makeup instruction party

9. A good old-fashioned sleepover, complete with manicures, pedicures, bad movies, and junk food

10. A day of volunteering services to the needy (such as preparing food or preparing clothing for donation)

11. A one-day cruise

12. A sexy lingerie party where a supplier of such items brings samples and guests are allowed to try them on for possible purchase

13. A swimming party (skinny-dipping or otherwise) if you have access to a pool

14. A karaoke night

15. A night out dancing

16. A bowling party

If you buy your wedding gown at Kleinfeld's in New York City, don't forget to visit the store's Exact Replica Miniature Wedding Gown Department, where you can order an exact miniature replica of your wedding gown, which stands 18 to 20 inches tall. In creating these precious little miracles, Kleinfeld's expert sewers and beaders treat each one as if it were a bride's real wedding dress. Prices start at $500 for the simplest designs.

Superstition dictates that the person who gives the third gift opened at a bridal shower will soon have a baby.

11 Games to Play at Wedding Showers

If the traditional all-girl bridal shower is your fare, here are some games to play that help get everyone in the marrying mood.

1. What's the Good Word? Each guest receives a clothespin as she arrives, along with this explanation: "If you catch someone saying the words 'bride' or 'wedding,' you can take her clothespin." At the end of the shower, the guest with the most clothespins wins a small favor or gift.

2. Who Wants to Be the Bride? Create a Who Wants to Be a Millionaire? game using 15 questions about the bride and the groom that will lead to stories about the future couple. Organize the questions from easy to difficult. Give each guest a chance to be a contestant.

3. Pass the Box Gift-wrap a small "prize" with about 10 layers of different wrapping papers. Play some music while passing the box around from guest to guest. When the music stops, the guest left holding the box unwraps the first layer of wrapping paper. Then the music starts again and the box is passed. Every time the music stops, another layer is removed until someone finally unwraps the very last layer—and the prize is won.

4. The Wedding Dress Game The guests are divided up into several groups, each of which is given a roll of toilet paper. The teams must create a wedding dress using only the toilet paper. One member of the team becomes the model and the rest decorate. Give them about 10 to 15 minutes to create the dress. The bride will judge the results and declare a winner. Make sure to have the camera ready for this one.

5. Penny for Your Thoughts Have ready two pennies from the same year for each of the guests. When guests arrive, they are given one penny and the other penny is placed in a jar. When all the guests have arrived, the bride-to-be selects a penny from the jar, and the person with the penny with that corresponding year tells a little about herself, how she knows the bride, and maybe a story about her. After everyone has spoken, the bride-to-be puts her pennies back into the jar and selects one to win a prize.

6. Pass the Carrot Provide a long carrot that each guest has to pass to the person beside her—between her knees! Every time someone drops the carrot, cut off about an inch of it. When the carrot is so small that it can't be passed anymore, the person who has it at the end without dropping it wins.

7. Guess the Spice Buy 10 or more different spices in new containers and cover the outsides of the containers so that the name of the spice cannot be read. On each container, write the first name of a guest. During the shower, give each guest a sheet of paper with the guests' names listed and a space next to each for adding the name of a spice. Each guest has to try to identify the spices, and the one who guesses correctly most often gets to keep all the spices.

8. Bake Us a Cake Set up a table with all the ingredients for baking a cake (flour, sugar, eggs, etc.), then add a few extra ingredients that don't belong—baking soda (often confused with baking powder), spices, oil, etc. Also supply all the tools for mixing and baking the cake. The bride is then told she must make a cake, from scratch. She is not allowed to use a cookbook or get help from friends. Do this at the beginning of the event so that the cake will be done when the bride is finished opening gifts. When the cake is taken out of the oven for her to taste-test, make sure the camera is ready when she takes her first bite.

9. White Stuff Fill sandwich bags with the following cooking items: flour, sugar, salt, baking powder, baking soda, powdered sugar, cornstarch, cream of tartar, powdered milk, unflavored gelatin, and Bisquick. Number each bag and keep a list of the contents of each. Guests are allowed to feel and look at the bag but not open it, and they have to guess what is in each bag. The person with the most correct answers wins a prize.

10. The Tray Game A tray full of various items related to a theme such as cooking is brought out with a towel over it covering the contents of the tray. The tray is uncovered and placed in the center of the room. The guests have exactly two minutes to look over the tray. The tray can be rotated so that it can be seen from other angles but touching is not allowed. The tray is then covered, and everyone is handed a sheet of paper on which they must list as many items as they can remember.

11. Who Knows the Bride and Groom? Prepare copies of a list of 10 or 15 questions about the bride and groom. Hand these out to the guests and ask them to provide answers for each question. The bride is then asked to answer each question, and the guest with the most correct answers wins a prize.

9 Ways to Involve the Groom

Blake Kritzberg is the proprietor of Just-Wedding-Favors .com, where you can find unusual, affordable wedding favor ideas and a free wedding screen-saver. She writes:

Imagine that your fiancé has told you he's going to draft a dream team in his fantasy football league, and it's going to cost him $50K to participate. Now imagine that he's told you your help is supremely important to him. You'd be a little hesitant to give opinions, right? Some of your ideas might sound feeble, even to your own ears. Hopefully he'd welcome your thoughts, however odd it felt for you to venture them. Now imagine your fiancé feels kind of like that when it comes to the wedding.

What to do? Here are nine ways to involve him without increasing both of your stress loads:

1. **Delegate areas that have a prayer of interesting him.** The worst thing you can do is expect him to match your 10 to 20 years of feminine wisdom on the relative merits of buttercream versus fondant. So ask him to help you in areas in which he may have some interest or expertise. He probably won't get excited about selecting the cake frosting, selecting the wedding colors or floral arrangements, or choosing the wrapping for the favors. Then there are the tasks fraught with hazards: choosing the photographer and finalizing seating arrangements; these involve too many details and variables that you'll want to address. On the other hand, he might enjoy selecting the DJ or the band and choosing the song list, setting up and maintaining your wedding website, researching charities if you choose to donate instead of giving out favors, and arranging for transportation. Ask him to be completely in charge of choosing and purchasing the groomsmen's gifts (but keep an eye open for a sudden fascination with bobble-heads).

2. **If you ask him to help you choose vendors and styles, narrow down the choices first, then be prepared to live with his decisions.** It's a jungle of options out there, enough to give the most natural-born party planner pause. So if you want his opinion on photographers, invites, flowers, or cakes, do some research first and give him three or four choices. At times, it'll feel so good to share the load that you'll be tempted to drag him into the butter-

cream debate despite your better instincts. At these times, take a deep breath, count to 10, and call your mother or your maid of honor.

3. **Ask him directly for help.** Let him know how important his input is to you, and that you can't do it without him. Guys like to

The way to his heart is through his cake! The groom's cake traditionally reflects his special interests. **COURTESY OF CARYN NASH,** CARYNSCAKES.COM

be needed. Your frank request for help may be enough to pull him out of his comfort zone and onto your team.

4. **Don't bring him in too early.** Treat your fiancé as a pinch hitter. Sure, you may be fully aware that you can shave 5K off your costs by starting your favor crafts and reservations 18 months ahead of time. But if he's like most guys, the wedding won't become real to him until it draws closer. Expect him to jump in about 6 months before the actual ceremony and break into a (relative) frenzy of activity about one month in advance.

5. **Try the art director/production staff approach.** If you think your guy wants to help but feels uncomfortable around all that lace and tulle, have him handle finances and logistics: making the payments, picking up the food or décor, handling the rentals, doing online comparison shopping, or reserving the hotels and reception halls. These are all jobs that will take a load off your shoulders, while freeing up time for the aesthetic stuff you probably enjoy and he doesn't.

6. **Let him know what's involved.** Share your calendars, lists, and schedules with him so he can choose the events he wants to attend. Encourage him to make his own lists. At the very least, he'll be far more supportive when he sees what you're going through.

7. **Weave his family heritage/ethnicity/traditions into the ceremony.** Where are his parents from? Are there special ethnic rituals that they may be looking forward to? Ask his parents about their wedding, and ask yourself if there are elements you might incorporate in your own. Ask to see their wedding album and think about using some old world traditions in your ceremony.

8. **Talk about something besides the wedding.** Guys aren't the only ones who complain about brides-to-be talking of nothing but upcoming nuptials. Anyone can get overwhelmed by all the wedding chatter. Spend time on activities that have nothing to do with the wedding and try to recapture the moments that made you want to get married in the first place. Especially if you live together, you might institute the rule of no wedding talk after 10:00 P.M.

9. **Check your subtext for hidden meanings.** Are you taking out your frustrations on him? Don't. Listen to yourself and ask yourself if your tone may have become bossy or sarcastic. When you ask for his opinion, take his answer seriously. When you give him ownership of a task, don't second-guess his decisions.

Top 10 Rules for the Ideal Bachelor Party

VegasVIP.com is Las Vegas's premier destination management company specializing in group event planning of every type imaginable. If you can dream it, VegasVIP can make it happen. Here are some tips for making sure that the groom's last night of freedom is remembered positively by all.

1. **Arrange for transportation.** Let's face it, there's gonna be some drinking, and we all want everyone to get around safely. Hired transportation will ensure that everyone makes it to the wedding.

2. **Select a date no less than three days before the wedding.** Leave plenty of time between the party and the wedding for hangovers to subside.

3. **Start planning the event at least a month out.** This gives enough time for most of the attendees to clear their calendar or make appropriate arrangements.

4. **Share the cost evenly or at least fairly.** Plan out all of the expected expenses, add 20 percent for incidentals, and divide it among the attendees.

5. **It's the last supper—make it good.** A good dinner will prepare everyone for the evening's alcohol consumption.

6. **A strip club is a safe bet.** Private in-room entertainment is always nice but can end up being more expensive and lacks the overall ambience of a well-equipped gentlemen's club.

"We Do!"

More and more modern couples are taking a "we" approach to wedding planning. Some stores are now offering "groom registries" that make it possible to add fishing equipment and grilling tools to the wish list. Similarly, showers and bachelor parties are being replaced by co-ed celebrations.

7. **Choose the final party group wisely.** Sure, the soon-to-be-father-in-law and bride's older brother can come to the dinner, then maybe the first bar stop, but make sure the final group of guys are trustworthy before the debauchery begins.

8. **No photos, please.** If anything risqué is planned, leave the cameras behind. No one wants to see these floating around the Internet at a later date.

9. **Keep the daytime drinking to a minimum.** If daytime activities are planned before the big night, go easy on the booze. This will ensure more guys, especially the bachelor, make it through the night's festivities.

10. **Keep it simple.** Sure, the idea of a party that consists of stopping at three bars, two nightclubs, and every strip club within a 100-mile radius sounds great, but keeping 12 guys on the same page to accomplish all of this will prove to be quite a challenge. Better to keep it down to a limited number of locations.

A Groom's Planning Tips

Even if you're from Mars and she's from Venus, the bride and groom need to be on the same page where wedding planning is concerned. That's pretty difficult considering how different your responsibilities are—and the degree to which those of the groom pale in comparison to those of the bride. "Always keep in mind," we're reminded by the website FrugalBride.com, "that your fiancée has been dreaming about being a bride and playing 'dress up' bride since she was a little girl." And now that she's found her Prince Charming, she expects all her dreams to come true. That may not be realistic, but you do need to step up nevertheless. Here are some tips from FrugalBride.com on handling the rough spots.

1. **She talks about the wedding 24/7!** If you want to play it safe, just sit there and listen. Offer your ideas and advice. She'll never fully understand why this wedding isn't as big a deal to you as it is to her. Don't even try to explain.

2. **All the questions!** Your fiancée will be coming up to you and asking you questions about the music, the wedding theme, the flowers, and the colors. Don't feel bad if you don't know what she's talking about. Ask her to explain; she'll like that you care.

3. **Who's wedding is it, anyway?** As the groom, know that you're actually planning two weddings: the one your fiancée wants and the one your mother envisions. You're going to feel like a referee. It's your responsibility to handle your family, not hers, and vice versa. If you're smart, you'll stay on your bride's good side; she's the one you're gonna have to live with.

4. **Ideas are coming from left and right.** You can gracefully accept ideas and then privately place them in your "circular file." Choose your arguments carefully and use these mantras:

"I'll talk to [bride's name] about it."
"[Bride's name] has everything under control."
"I think [bride's name] took care of that already."

4. **Your fiancée gets a gift.** Some couples choose to exchange gifts with each other before they get married. This could take place at a dinner together where you're alone or at the rehearsal dinner, when you give your wedding party their gifts. Put some thought into the gift because you can bet she's put plenty into yours. Traditionally, this gift is something that will last forever, like jewelry.

5. **About stag night . . .** Whatever you do, don't have your stag party the night before the wedding. Plan it for the weekend before. You're already gonna feel weird when you wake up the morning of the "last day of your single life"; you don't need a liter of scotch trying to tackle its way back out the way it went in. Then again, if you can't remember it all the next day, maybe it's for the best.

6. **The rehearsal dinner** You and your family are responsible for organizing the rehearsal dinner. Here's what you need to know:

• Try to make it a small intimate affair for close friends and family. If you are having a very small wedding, forgo this event altogether.
• Be sure to determine the budget for the rehearsal dinner and keep to it.
• To save money, you could plan a barbecue at home or a casual buffet dinner at your favorite restaurant.
• There should be no haggling about who attends the rehearsal dinner. The general list is you, your bride, both sets of parents, the wedding party, and any other family members who may not be in the wedding party. Beyond that, you are not required to invite anyone else, although it's always nice to include out-of-towners.
• Small invitations are generally good etiquette for the rehearsal dinner and should be prepared by the groom's family.
• This dinner is held generally on the evening of the rehearsal, but nothing is written in stone.
• If you keep the dinner party small, everyone can sit at the same table and interact.
• It is generally known that the couple takes this opportunity to toast and thank everyone who has put work into helping them with the wedding preparations. Be sure to address a few words to your parents.

117 Things for the Groom to Do Before the Wedding

Are you having enough trouble just remembering to get your groomsmen gifts? Well, it turns out that before you make it to the altar, you have a much longer list of things to accomplish than just that. Groomstand.com compiled this exhaustive to-do list for grooms by asking everyone from single guys to married women for their advice on what grooms need to do before they get married. Get to it!

1. Get your finances in order.

2. Have a bachelor party.

3. Buy new underwear.

4. Go to Las Vegas.

5. Buy a house.

6. Travel to Europe.

7. Get a prenup.

8. See her without makeup.

9. Take a good long look at why you are getting married and be able to know why.

10. Make sure you're financially ready—SAVE, SAVE, SAVE!

11. Throw away all traces of past relationships.

12. Get premarital counseling.

13. Reassure friends that they will remain important and spend time with them.

14. Pick at least one planning task and be involved and enthusiastic.

15. Make sure you have a decent job.

16. Make sure you have a place for both of you to live that will be big enough.

17. Do something really, really nice for the future mother-in-law. Call it "insurance."

18. If you haven't already, a guy might want to get going to a strip club out of his system in case the wife doesn't approve.

19. If you're sexually a bit curious, visit a gay bar to check out those feelings before taking the plunge.

20. Get in shape.

21. Plan and pay for an adventurous honeymoon.

22. Get plastered and then sleep as late as you want.

23. Fart whenever and wherever you want without being jabbed in the rib cage.

24. Lock out all the channels on the cable service that do not have sports on them.

25. One more night out with the guys.

26. Get rid of all your porn.

27. Order and pay for all the tuxes.

28. Discuss money with your spouse.

29. Get a marriage license.

30. Decide where you will live.

31. Insure the wedding rings.

32. Do a cake tasting; she'll like that.

33. Make sure she's the one.

34. Relax!

35. Get acquainted with your bride's parents and friends.

36. Tell her all the truth about your past relationships and your health, if you have any health problems.

37. Go on a road trip.

38. Clean out the basement.

39. Get rid of all old girlfriend pictures.

40. Evaluate life plans and goals/future plans.

41. Go away for a weekend by yourself for your last real alone time.

42. Define the chores and who does what.

43. Seriously diet.

44. Pick out your tux.

45. Call your mom.

46. Secure your hotel reservation for the wedding night.

47. Decide what type of birth control you are going to use before the wedding night.

48. Go over health insurance information, legal papers, and will.

49. Buy a wedding ring.

50. Choose a best man.

51. Pay off as much credit card debt and student loans as possible.

52. Become well liked by her family and friends.

53. Hang out with your boys.

54. Talk about kids.

55. Talk about future finances.

56. Talk about family.

57. Go diving.

58. Go skydiving.

59. Go scuba diving.

60. Begin pulling away from the friends you tend to spend most of your time with because you will need the additional time with your new spouse for a healthy solid marriage.

61. Find out if your fiancée has any debt that you may be inheriting by marrying her.

62. Find out if she is on any medication for a mental illness or has ever been hospitalized for a mental disorder.

63. Start thinking like a married person. Singles can be very self-centered because they are used to living by themselves, eating by themselves, choosing what they want to watch on TV, and when they want to go to bed. Marriage means you will need to take into consideration the other person's wants, desires, and needs. So you might as well start practicing early.

64. Cook dinner for the future in-laws.

65. Listen to everyone if they are all saying you should not marry this woman, even if you have already sent out invitations and made other financial commitments.

66. Go on a camping trip with your prospective bride, one without electricity or water, and in a location where cell phones don't work, then see how well you get along.

67. Revisit all of the sports you like to personally do, or watch and see if she minds you playing or watching them.

68. Write a list with her about pros and cons of marriage and see how you two match up.

69. Meet with the officiant.

70. Buy a special wedding day gift for your new spouse.

71. Prepare your vows.

72. Buy a motorbike.

73. Discuss future career, education, and moving plans.

74. Get life insurance.

75. Buy something you really want.

76. Discuss religion of kids with future spouse, if relevant.

77. Discuss who will be paying for wedding, if relevant.

78. Do all those activities your future partner loathes, in excess.

79. Make sure that ALL of your previous relationships have closure so that none of your former girlfriends come back to haunt you later.

80. Watch as much football as you can . . . you know you ain't going to once she owns "half" the remote.

81. Start a joint checking account.

82. Listen to everything she tells you about the wedding arrangements, or else, no wedding.

83. Have a one-on-one talk with her parents.

84. Make sure you're sexually compatible before dedicating the rest of your life to her.

85. Prepare a speech . . . don't wing it.

86. Agree that you will be combining your finances when you are married—the number one cause of divorce in North America is money fights and money problems.

87. Learn how to clean house.

88. Remind your buddies not to prank-call your phone number while drunk in the early morning anymore.

89. Select your groomsmen.

90. See at least one more naked woman.

91. Give her your list of wedding invitees immediately and don't add to or subtract from it—ever.

92. Talk to married friends about their experiences—find out what to expect in marriage.

93. Keep focused on each other so that you keep your sanity.

94. Go to financial counseling together.

95. Set a monthly budget.

96. Live together to try it out.

97. Buy your groomsmen gifts.

98. Pay off the ring.

99. Embark on a difficult project together.

100. Play all the video games you own again.

101. Make sure your rings fit each other BEFORE going to the altar.

102. Think once.

103. Think twice.

104. Think thrice.

105. Change your cell phone number so ex-girlfriends don't call you.

106. Go by yourself to the movies.

107. Dance with a stranger.

108. Go out on dates—it's important during this stressful time!

109. Pick out which of your things you're willing to get rid of and which you've got to keep. It's a partnership, you won't get to keep everything she hates, but if you're smart, you don't have to get rid of all of it.

110. Make peace with an old girlfriend.

111. Practice taking care of a baby for a day.

112. Find out how the other person deals with having a bad day.

113. Get a lap dance.

114. Book flowers to be delivered on the day of the wedding to your bride-to-be. While you're at it, order some for both moms too.

115. Clean up your wardrobe and your life to make a place for her.

116. Approve whatever cake she picked out for the wedding.

117. Spend an entire day on the couch in your pajamas.

7 Ways to Save Money on the Ring

1. It doesn't have to be a diamond. Birthstone gems and man-made diamonds are becoming more and more popular, and a white topaz can stand in for a diamond.

2. The most expensive diamond purchased in the year 2005 was bought for a fraction of its retail cost at Costco of all places. Don't forget that the wholesale clubs also carry jewelry—for the bride and others.

3. Fourteen-karat gold is harder and wears better than 18- or 24-karat gold.

4. Attend estate sales and visit antique stores for vintage wedding rings.

5. Insure the ring if it costs more than $1,000. The extra money you spend will be well worth it if the ring is lost or stolen.

6. If there's an heirloom ring in the family, use it instead of buying a new ring. If the vintage piece isn't to the bride's taste, have the stone placed in a new setting.

7. Don't forget to bring the rings to the ceremony. (We know this is not a money-saving tip, but we just can't stress this enough.)

Symbols of Happiness

"She who receives the bride's bouquet will next be happily wed, they say."

Lovely Orange Blossoms, age old symbol of tender sentiment and devotion are also the mark of quality in Engagement and Wedding Rings by Traub.

Long known for their beauty, quality and value, these beautiful creations are recommended by dependable jewelers everywhere.

Ask them for "Orange Blossoms," Traub's helpful book for Brides

Genuine "Orange Blossom"
ENGAGEMENT AND WEDDING RINGS

RINGS: COPYRIGHT © 2008 BY JUPITER IMAGES CORP; ADVERTISEMENT: AUTHORS' COLLECTION

9 Most Common Mistakes People Make When Buying Diamonds

According to Genesis Diamonds, "the official jeweler to the Tennessee Titans football team," these are the most common errors men make when purchasing a diamond. To learn more, visit GenesisDiamonds.com.

1. **Making the wrong assumptions about diamond quality** Assuming that all diamonds of the same color and clarity are equal is a common mistake. How a diamond is cut determines its beauty and brilliance. Just because a diamond possesses a high grade of color and clarity, beauty won't be guaranteed. Poor cutting can render a diamond lifeless and dull. Careful selection and comparisons are necessary in selecting a diamond of value. That's where a professional can educate you to the differences and help balance out the proportions, color, clarity, and size with budgetary considerations. Remember that cutting alone can make a difference by as much as 50 percent in price for a specific color and clarity grade.

2. **Buying on price point or a discount** Although comparison shopping in order to find the best value is a great idea, the lowest-priced diamond of a given grade is often the one with the worst cut. The smart choice would be based on a careful evaluation of the 4 Cs (cut, color, clarity, and carat weight) and a true understanding of how the price was calculated. You will often find that prices at the retail level may vary greatly depending on the jewelry store where the diamond is sold. Just because a diamond is discounted doesn't make it a good deal.

3. **Assuming a diamond can be purchased without professional guidance** The right expertise is critical to make that choice. It is very difficult for the average consumer to analyze a diamond as painstakingly as a trained gemologist. Your selection should be made from a reputable and established store.

4. **Making a decision without having the right selection to choose from** A good selection makes it easy to compare many diamonds of different qualities without the hassle of going from one place to another to make comparisons. Don't let a seller convince you to buy a diamond from his limited selection. Find a dealer who has a large collection instead.

5. **Buying a diamond on the Internet** Finding companies that sell diamonds on the Internet is easy. You may feel that these companies are able to sell you a diamond for less money than a traditional "brick-and-mortar" jewelry store—but that's rarely the case. The finest stones aren't available from these stores. In fact, they don't even stock diamonds; they gather readily available diamond databases from other companies and post these offerings on their site. In other words, they neither own nor have ever seen the diamonds that they are offering to you, and in most cases the diamond won't even be available when you give them a deposit.

6. **Not getting the proper guarantees and customer service** A good deal includes features such as a choice of a free 14-carat yellow or white gold presentation mounting for the diamond; free lifetime ring sizing; free certification and insurance appraisals; free maintenance inspections; free cleaning and polishing; a lifetime upgrade policy without the limitations imposed by other jewelers (some policies require that an upgrade purchase be as much as twice the value of the original stone); a full 30-day money-back return policy; and 90-day price protection.

Wedding Ring Saves Man's Life

On December 1, 2007, two robbers entered an antique shop in Jackson, Mississippi. When the proprietor, Donnie Register, had his back turned, the men pulled out guns. When one of the robbers aimed his gun at Register's head, he immediately assumed a defensive posture by placing his left hand over the side of his face. A shot was fired, hitting Register's gold wedding band. The ring deflected the bullet, thus saving Register's life. Register now has one more reason to be thankful that he's married.

7. **Assuming that a diamond with a laboratory report is automatically a good diamond** Just because the diamond is "certified," you still need a trained adviser to evaluate all of its characteristics. Labs can and do make errors in evaluations; a trained expert can help you avoid this pitfall.

8. **Believing that an appraisal is a grading report** Men often make the mistake of assuming that an appraisal is a report of diamond quality. A diamond quality report can be issued only from an accredited gemological laboratory such as GIA (Gemological Institute of America), EGL (European Gemological Laboratory), or the AGS (American Gem Society). These reports provide an independent analysis of diamond characteristics and do not place a value on a diamond.

   An appraisal is typically used for establishing a replacement value on an item of jewelry for insurance purposes, but can also be used for other purposes as well. These are usually done by the seller of the item and represent the opinion of the seller. You are relying on only the word of the seller when purchasing a diamond without the independent grading report.

9. **Buying from a family friend or chain store** If you feel compelled to purchase a diamond from a friend or relative, you must prepare yourself to pay extra for the privilege. Your buying price is determined by the seller's cost and profit margin. The best place to buy a diamond is from a seller whose cost is low and who is willing to sell at a low profit margin. Chain stores have high profit margins, as do most Internet sellers. When you buy from family members and friends, you will find that you are paying not only for the diamond but also for the emotional investment that the person might have made in the stone. Haggling over the price can seriously ruin a friendship; better to buy from a jeweler.

> "I think men who have a pierced ear are better prepared for marriage. They've experienced pain and bought jewelry."
>
> — Rita Rudner

5 Books to Help You Deal with Your In-Laws

1. *Toxic In-Laws: Loving Strategies for Protecting Your Marriage* by Susan Forward, PhD (2002) This book draws on real-life voices and stories of both women and men struggling to free themselves from frustrating, hurtful, and infuriating relationships with their toxic in-laws. Dr. Forward offers you highly effective communication and behavioral techniques for getting through to partners who won't or can't stand up to their parents and lays out accessible and practical ways to reclaim your marriage from your in-laws.

2. *When Difficult Relatives Happen to Good People: Surviving Your Family and Keeping Your Sanity* by Leonard Felder (2005) Using a combination of psychology and spirituality, Felder shows us that we can learn to live with our annoying and difficult relatives—not by trying to change them but by determining what triggers certain behavior patterns and findings ways to achieve acceptance and compromise with them.

3. *Mothers-In-Law Do Everything Wrong: MILDEW* by Liz Bluper and Renee Plastique (2004) The playful acronym (MILDEW) was created as a secret code word to allow the authors of this book to talk about their mother-in-law problems within earshot of their husbands. From the all-too-revealing quiz for the mother-in-law to the laugh-out-loud war stories, to the "hey that really might work" strategies, this book is both informative and amusing.

4. *The Daughter-in-Law's Survival Guide: Everything You Need to Know About Relating to Your Mother-in-Law* by Eden Unger Bowditch and Aviva Samet (2002) Find solutions for handling boundary issues, criticism, child-rearing disputes, and nonsupportive partners. The book teaches women to identify and analyze relationships, change thinking and behavior patterns that feed a dysfunctional dynamic, overcome chronic areas of conflict, and prevent new battles from breaking out.

5. *The Mother-in-Law Dance: Can Two Women Love the Same Man and Still Get Along?* by Annie Chapman (2004) The author believes that a mother-in-law and daughter-in-law can become friends. Through thoughtful ideas, real-life insights, humorous advice, and biblical wisdom, this book puts them on a joyful journey to a better relationship.

Divorced Parents at Your Wedding: 8 Tips

Warring parents at a wedding can wreak serious havoc on everyone's nerves. Weddings, it seems, tend to open old wounds, and divorcés who might have avoided one another for decades are suddenly thrust into a spotlight—together, no less. Amid the challenges of including your divorced parents in your wedding, remember this simple fact: they are still your parents. Consider these solutions to common problems.

1. **"I'm not going if he(she) is going!"** In cases where the divorce was especially bitter, either parent may resent the attendance of the former spouse. Regardless of their past, both parents should be willing to set aside their differences for this special occasion. If you (the bride or groom) need to remind them of that fact, so be it. Of course, it is advisable to take a diplomatic approach in voicing your concerns. If you're willing to address the situation in a calm, mature manner, perhaps your parents will be more likely to respond in kind. If it's a matter of one parent not wanting to attend if the other's new spouse or significant other will be present, you may have to decide to limit the invitation to your parents only. This is a delicate situation, especially if you're closer to your stepparent than your actual parent. Talk the situation over with your fiancé and wedding officiant; perhaps a trusted family member can step in on your behalf.

2. **Who pays for what?** There are two options here. The parents can pay for personal items (wedding dress, flowers, limousine), and the couple can pay for the services that will be enjoyed by everyone (the reception site, catering, DJ). This way neither parent needs to worry about "their" money being used to the benefit of their ex. Another option is to open a bank account into which the parents can make deposits. The money is used at the couple's discretion, and nobody knows whose money paid for what. Of course, if the groom's parents (or one of your parents who might be considerably better off than the other) are willing to pick up the tab, there's no problem.

3. **How should the invitation be worded?** This is a tricky one. Basically the invitation should reflect who's contributing the most and/or who raised you. If both parents have contributed equally, the invitation should say: "Ms. Jane Smith, Mr. John Smith cordially invite you." Notice the word "and" is not used—the comma shows there are several "hosts" but indicates they are not hosting the wedding together.

4. **Who gives away the bride?** Unless the bride's father had minimal contact with her during her life, he gets the privilege of walking her down the aisle. If her stepfather essentially raised her, the honor should be his. If she's close to both, they can walk her down the aisle together—a departure from normal etiquette that will underscore how very much you are loved by both.

5. **Where should they sit?** If the parents get along, they both sit in the first-row pew. If they don't, the mother sits in the first row and the father sits in the second. Or you can seat them both in the first pew but separated by other relatives. For the reception, again, if the parents get along, they both sit at the parents' table. If they don't, they can each sit at and host separate tables.

6. **What happens in the receiving line?** Whoever is hosting the wedding stands in the receiving line. If both parents are hosting but they don't want to stand beside each other, then they should line up as follows: bride's mother, her new husband, groom's mother, groom's father, bride's father, and so on.

7. **"What do I do about the first dance since I'm close to both my dad and stepdad?"** Don't have an announced father-daughter dance, but be sure to dance with both men sometime during the evening. If you do want to have the dance, let both fathers know ahead of time of your decision and how you want the dance handled. You could dance with one for half the dance and the other for the rest.

8. **What about the photographs?** If former spouses choose not to be photographed together, explain the situation to the photographer and make sure he or she knows who's who at the wedding. You can, of course, pose for separate portraits with each. There's no need to include a parent's casual date in the photos.

In-Laws and Outlaws: 8 Ways to Cope

Payal Mirchandani, a retired Toronto, Canada, wedding planner, writes: In-laws come in different shapes and sizes: some are supportive and respect the marital boundaries; others act like it is your duty to serve their needs. Especially if your marriage combines cultures, it's important to take the time to understand what you are being asked for and why. Your mother-in-law's behavior may be based on thousands of years of tradition. A bride who keeps an open mind ensures smooth sailing for her future family.

1. First and foremost, accept that your in-laws are not your parents. They aren't likely to have the same ways of doing things or the same sets of rules as your parents did. Compromise on differences that are less important and negotiate those that are more essential.

2. Realize and accept that you can't change others; you can only change your reaction to them. Build better relationships with your in-laws by recognizing your role in any conflicts.

3. Think of your in-laws as a potential resource to expand your support network. Get to know them by spending time with them. Listen to them, and create a reciprocal relationship where they can get to know you. Find out what their special talents are and ask them to share these with you.

4. Create a separate relationship from your spouse with your in-laws. Go shopping with your mother-in-law; invite both in-laws to a private lunch. Let them get to know you as a person in your own right.

5. If you are experiencing conflicts with your in-laws, talking to your spouse to get her opinion is a good thing; asking her to continually act as a go-between is not fair. You are signing on for a lifelong relationship with your in-laws; learn to deal with them in a pleasant way.

6. Host a formal event to meet the in-laws. Serve food that you have cooked yourself. Let them know that you have talents to share with them.

7. Don't live with your in-laws unless it's absolutely necessary. If this situation is unavoidable, make sure that you have open lines of communication. It might be helpful to have a heart-to-heart with your in-laws explaining your likes, dislikes, and personal boundaries, and give them an opportunity to do so as well. This will go far toward avoiding any misunderstandings.

8. Be complimentary to your in-laws by paying public and private tribute where appropriate. Let your family know that you respect these people and you sincerely hope that they will too. If children from a previous marriage are part of the picture, make sure they are involved in your new extended family.

IT IS WITH DEEPEST REGRETS THAT YOU ARE INVITED TO THE WEDDING BETWEEN MY PERFECT SON,

The Lawyer

AND SOME

Two-Bit Whore

WHOSE NAME DOESN'T MATTER

THE BIGGEST MISTAKE HE'S EVER MADE
WILL TAKE PLACE AT

7 p.m. on Saturday, June 8th

AND WILL BE ANNULLED AS SOON AS HE COMES
TO HIS SENSES.
THE DREADED CEREMONY WILL BE FOLLOWED BY DINNER,
WHERE FISH WILL BE SERVED BECAUSE WHAT'S-HER-NAME
IS HIGHLY ALLERGIC.

14 Rules for Fighting Fair

There's nothing wrong with a good all-out fight once in a while to clear the air. Fighting also gives partners a chance to say what's on their minds and to raise issues that may have been ignored. Besides, kissing and making up is always great fun. But you need ground rules to ensure that the conflict results in constructive change on which you both agree. Together, read this list provided by longevity.com and agree that you will both adhere to it. Review it occasionally. And visit longevity.com for more sound information on turning the happiness you experienced on your wedding day into a lifetime of joy.

1. **Silence is a relationship killer . . . you need to FIGHT.** Studies show that couples who fight have a stronger relationship and marriage. An old axiom says, "The dirtiest fighter is the one who refuses to fight at all." Someone who doesn't want to rock the boat and skirts the issues to avoid conflict ultimately damages the relationship. Fighting can actually get us through a conflict to a level of greater intimacy. So don't be afraid to fight for your relationship—it's the best thing you can do.

2. **Be nice.** Remember that you are trying to grow together. Often we learned unhealthy or unfair ways of fighting from parents or from our culture. Break the cycle and know that if both of you don't win, no one wins. If your partner's feelings have been hurt, tell him or her you are sorry before you launch into a defense. Acknowledge your partner's feelings even if you never intended to be hurtful.

3. **Do not involve other people.** The argument is between the two of you. Young couples make the mistake of involving friends or parents (usually mothers). The damage comes later in several forms: (1) A parent will more than likely remember the issue long after a couple has forgotten it. (2) The respect and perception once held by a parent for a child's spouse will decline. (3) A couple may feel uncomfortable facing the parent even after an incident has been resolved. (4) A parent's natural reaction is to protect a child, and this reaction may cause further damage to the relationship.

4. **No name-calling.** Calling a spouse a name such as "stupid" simply backs that person away from a fight. Don't label your partner. Explain how your partner's actions make you feel. Someone can do something rude without being labeled rude. Limit your criticism to the action that made you mad. Use "I" statements ("I don't like it when you leave your clothes lying around") instead of "you" statements ("You are such a slob!").

5. **Don't bring up an issue once it's been settled.** The past is the past. It is irrelevant and merely a way to smear your partner. It is okay to go back to learn, but not to get something on your spouse.

> "All married couples should learn the art of battle as they should learn the art of making love. Good battle is objective and honest — never vicious or cruel. Good battle is healthy and constructive, and brings to a marriage the principle of equal partnership."
> — Ann Landers

6. **Stick to the subject.** Stay focused. Find the issue and don't bring in other issues just to prove your point. When he comes home later and she feels taken for granted or unloved, deal with feelings to make the real issue apparent.

7. **Don't hit below the belt.** Don't throw your partner's weaknesses in his or her face. You may win the argument but lose more than you gain. On the other hand, don't be too sensitive to what your spouse says.

8. **Don't interrupt.** Even if you know what your partner is about to say, let him or her say it. Listen attentively and try not to respond defensively.

9. **Don't assume anything.** You may think you know what your

> "It is sometimes essential for a husband and a wife to quarrel — they get to know each other better."
> — Goethe

partner was thinking when he or she left you stranded at the bus stop for an hour, but perhaps you don't. Wait for an explanation before you fly off the handle.

10. **Watch your words.** Don't make statements using the words "never" or "always." Remember that words can sting long after a fight has ended. Even if you didn't mean the awful thing you said, the memory of it can hurt for a long time. Choose your language carefully.

11. **Don't go to bed angry.** Finish the fight. Dragging a fight out is as life-draining as avoiding a fight. Unresolved anger can destroy intimacy.

12. **Maintain a sense of humor.** Laughter is sometimes the best medicine. It's good to be able to laugh at yourselves, but don't laugh at or make fun of your spouse.

13. **Take a time-out if you need it.** If you want to back off for a while and rethink your position, or if you just need to gather your thoughts, let your partner know you need a time-out and tell him or her when you'll be ready to resume the discussion. Don't just storm out.

14. **Hold hands and look into each other's eyes.** Being in contact with each other, rather than turning your backs, is hard to do when you're mad, but it takes the focus from the issue and places it where it belongs—on the most important person in your life.

Who Pays for What?

While tradition once dictated how wedding costs should be handled, all bets are off today, when those who can most easily afford the expenses usually bear them. Thus, the information here should be used solely as a general guide.

The bride typically pays for:

- The wedding ring for the groom
  - Gifts for the attendants
  - Accommodation for out-of-town attendants
  - A wedding gift for the groom
  - The flower child's outfit and accessories

The groom typically pays for:
  - The bride's rings, including the engagement ring
  - The honeymoon
  - A wedding gift for the bride
  - The marriage license
- The groomsmen's gifts
- Accommodation for out-of-town groomsmen
- Flowers for the bride
- The going-away corsage
- Corsages for the mothers
- The boutonnieres for the men in the wedding party
- The gloves, ties, and accessories for the men in the wedding party
- The officiant's fee

The bride's family typically pays for:
- The costs of the reception
- The bride's wedding attire/trousseau
- Invitations, announcements, and thank-you notes
- The seating assignment chart, napkins, and mailing costs
- The photographer
- The videographer
- Ceremony costs
- Flowers and accessories for the bridesmaids, flower girl, and ring-bearer
- Transportation for the bridal party on the wedding day from the ceremony to the reception
- All gratuities for all services

The groom's family typically pays for:
- Clothing for the wedding
- Travel and lodging expenses
- The rehearsal dinner
- A wedding gift for the newlyweds

The attendants typically pay for:
- Their wedding clothes
- Their travel expenses
- A wedding gift for the newlyweds

Wedding Insurance

The venue goes out of business three months before the big day and you have lost your deposit. The limo driver never shows and you need to book another at the last minute—at twice the original cost. The groom announces that he is being shipped overseas—on the day of the wedding. A sudden ice storm prevents travel within 50 miles of your wedding site, and none of your deposits are refundable. Such nightmares can and do occur, and although you can't avoid them entirely, you can protect the deposits you have paid for services by purchasing wedding insurance. Even stolen or lost wedding gifts can be covered. Wedding insurance can cost anywhere from $150 to $600, and especially if your wedding budget represents a lifetime of savings, it can be well worth the expenditure, even if all it does is allow you to sleep better during the months and weeks before the event. Here's what you need to know:

• You may already be covered. Check with the venues and services you are hiring to find out what insurance they already carry. Your homeowner's policy may offer some coverage as well. Policies vary, and you don't want to pay for something you already have. Talk to your insurance agent to determine the kind of policy that is right for you. If you already have a homeowner's policy, try to arrange for wedding insurance through the same company.

• While some companies won't allow you to insure your wedding expenditures more than a year in advance of the event, you should try to purchase the policy as soon as you start laying down big bucks.

• A comprehensive policy will cover all problems, including those having to do with the wedding site, the vendors, and even bad weather and illness that may threaten the wedding. Each of these is covered for a different amount, and there will be a different deductible in each case. Compare the policies available to you and choose the one that most closely matches your needs.

• Policies vary a great deal. Some but not all cover loss or damage to the engagement and wedding rings, while others don't. A few policies will pay to have the event restaged for photographs if the photographer never showed, even going so far as to pay for another cake, new flowers, a new photographer, and transportation of the key players to the re-shoot. None of the policies we've seen cover cold feet or a change of heart.

• Don't overlook personal liability and medical insurance. Anyone who is injured at your wedding, be it a guest or a vendor, may have a shot at your nest egg. Check the venue contract and policies you may have to see if protection is already in place.

From *Brides* magazine, 1940 AUTHORS' COLLECTION

• Don't buy separate travel insurance to protect your honeymoon if your wedding insurance policy already covers it. Similarly, your auto insurance may cover accidents that occur in rented cars. If no such protection already exists, talk to the travel agent who books your honeymoon to make sure you are covered in case of postponement or cancellation.

Wedding Budget Breakdown

This is a standard breakdown of expenses showing the portion of your budget that should be allotted to each kind. The figures are based on the averages of numerous weddings of various types. Of course, if you're lucky enough to be able to save money on one category (say, Uncle Albert is handling the photography), you can apply it to another. These are general figures and should be adjusted according to your own priorities.

1. Reception (including food): 50 percent
2. Photography/video: 10 percent
3. Flowers: 10 percent
4. Entertainment: 10 percent
5. Attire: 10 percent
6. Invitations: 2 percent
7. Everything else, including the cake, transportation, and gifts: 8 percent

Wedding Expenses

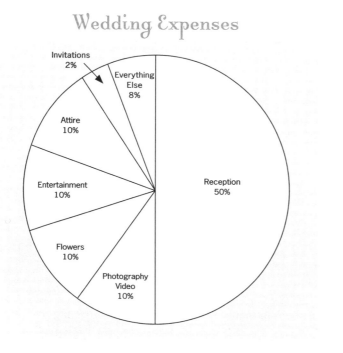

- Invitations 2%
- Everything Else 8%
- Attire 10%
- Entertainment 10%
- Flowers 10%
- Reception 50%
- Photography Video 10%

Tips for Handling Wedding Professionals

The consultants, the florists, the photographers, and the musicians are after your money. Sure, they smile and glad-hand you, but in the end it's a business, and no matter how personal the service they offer, you need to handle all the details professionally.

1. Rely on personal recommendations for the vendors you interview. Websites, four-color brochures, and press releases won't tell you the whole story. The experiences of your friends will be much more reliable. Once you have chosen a vendor, check with the Better Business Bureau to find out if any complaints have been filed.

2. Shop around. No matter how pressed for time you are, no matter how perfect a fit that first one seems to be, shop around. Even if you stick with your original choice, you'll know that it was the right one.

3. Be firm about your needs, your preferences, and especially your budget. If you are told that wedding flowers cannot be arranged for the amount you have allotted, find another florist. The truth is that true professionals can find a way to work within almost any budget.

4. Negotiate. See "How to Bargain Like a Pro," page 231.

5. Get it in writing. Your contract should include all the final details (see "What Every Contract Should Include," page 234) so that there is never any question as to what you have actually purchased.

6. Get receipts for all payments and deposits.

7. Never hesitate to ask questions.

How to Bargain Like a Pro

The vendors you'll come across while planning a wedding are among the most hardened hawks out there. Here are some strategies for making sure you get the best deal possible.

1. Nothing is set in stone. Even if "everyone pays that much" or "there are no substitutions on our packages," don't be shy about proposing a deal on your own terms. The worst that can happen is that you'll be turned down.

2. Start low. Never feel guilty offering what seems to be a ridiculously low price; after all, many merchants automatically quote prices that are several times more than they expect to get. Your starting price should be no more than one-third to one-half the asking price.

3. Use your poker face. The less your face betrays your interest in the item or the service, the better. Coming back again and again to admire a venue is a good way to ensure that you'll overpay. Stay cool, and don't be afraid to point out flaws in whatever is being offered to you.

4. Do your homework. Find out before you go shopping how much the item is actually worth. Have a target price in mind before you begin haggling, and think in terms of a maximum price to keep from going over budget.

5. Be prepared to commit to the purchase once your target price is approved. Have your checkbook ready; don't give the vendor too much time to rethink his position.

6. Play "good cop/bad cop." Bring a friend (or the groom) with you and ask that person to appear to discourage you from the purchase. If you seem reluctant, the price might go down. Try to bring someone who has experience shopping for this particular item.

7. Refuse any vendor who bargains rudely or who doesn't seem to respect your position. Such an attitude may be indicative of the kind of service this vendor delivers.

8. Let the vendor know you have options. Make it clear that you're shopping around and that you have every intention of staying within your budget. Get competing estimates in writing and bring these with you when you shop.

9. Just say no. If the vendor isn't budging, be prepared to walk. Thank the vendor for his or her time and walk away. The price may plummet at that point.

10. Don't haggle just for the fun of it. Once you engage in bargaining, be prepared to make the purchase once your terms have been met. Declining an item after you have finally gotten your way is considered rude.

7 Ways to Turn Your Wedding into a Time of Giving

What better way can there be to bless your wedding day than to share your happiness with others? Here are some ways in which your wedding can touch the lives of people in need.

1. For those who have everything, and especially for second and third weddings, ask your guests to donate to one (or several) of your favorite charities, or one of their own, in lieu of a gift. Direct them to justgive.org, where you can register for the charity of your choice.

2. Forgo cute, useless favors and instead print cards indicating that a donation has been made in the name of each guest.

3. Arrange to have leftover food transported to a local homeless shelter.

4. The day after the wedding, have the flowers sent to a nursing home or women's shelter.

5. Donate your dress to a charity that will put it to good use (see "6 Ways to Donate Your Wedding Gown," page 318, and "3 Charities That Seek Out Donations of Bridesmaids' Dresses," page 319).

6. Set up a special fund for a family in need, a local community effort, or your school alma mater and ask guests to make donations in lieu of gifts.

7. Donate duplicate wedding gifts to appropriate charities rather than return them.

Don't forget to take the proper tax deductions for all your charitable donations.

48 Tips for Saving Money on Just About Everything

See also our separate lists on how to save money on wedding venues (page 232), invitations (page 242), wedding attire (page 248), food and beverages (page 236), transportation (page 281), flowers (page 264), favors (page 269), decorations and accessories (page 263), cake (page 269), photography (page 273), and entertainment (page 280).

1. Buy the current edition of *Bridal Bargains* by Denise Fields. It's in its eighth edition as of this writing, and we're hoping the series lives happily ever after. Even if you have money to burn, the book will help you get the most out of every dollar you spend.

2. Read "How to Bargain Like a Pro," page 231.

3. Rethink the old standard:

Something old,
Something new,
Everything borrowed . . .

4. Check with the Better Business Bureau for existing complaints before you hire vendors.

5. The word *wedding* used in conjunction with any other word like *shoes, flowers,* and *dresses* automatically doubles the price of the item. For instance, you'll find that "wedding shoes" cost more than shoes that are simply white, and especially in summer months it's possible to find beautiful white dresses that can serve as elegant wedding gowns.

6. A talented seamstress can decorate the gown—adding a removable train, for instance. So when you initially inquire about prices, don't tell the vendor it's for a wedding—say it's for an anniversary or retirement party. You'll be quoted prices 10 to 30 percent lower than what you'd be charged for a wedding dress.

7. Enlist the help of local Boy Scout and Girl Scout troops, local choirs, and other community organizations for all sorts of help.

8. Make the logistics of coordinating vendors much easier by using ones who have worked together before.

9. Start by hiring the one vendor you know and trust, and rely on recommendations from there.

10. If you don't own it, borrow it. If you can't borrow it, rent it. If you can't rent it, you don't need it.

11. If you need blood tests, get them done at a free clinic in your area.

12. Choose your vendors as far in advance as possible so that when negotiating you can let them know you have plenty of time for other options.

13. Have the wedding at an off-peak time of year, or even a non-standard time of day. Consider, for instance, a brunch wedding. The most inexpensive time to get married is on a Sunday in winter.

14. If your family is scattered across the globe, hold the wedding at a time when they are already gathered for another event—a family reunion or even another wedding.

15. Ask friends to step in for professionals.

16. If the wedding is formal, keep events like showers and rehearsal dinners relaxed and informal. A barbecue, a pizza party, or a potluck dinner can take the edge off stressful preparations for a more elaborate event.

How to Save Money on Wedding Venues

1. Choose a public setting, like a park, a museum, or a library—a beautiful place that requires almost no decorations.

2. Find out if the local college has a facility you might use.

3. Have the reception in the church or synagogue in which the ceremony will take place, if possible. You'll save tons on transportation, decorations, and more.

4. Have the wedding in a small town, where prices are far cheaper than those you'll find in a big city.

17. Combine events: there's no law against having a combination bridal shower and bachelor party.

18. If a package deal includes something you don't need, try to trade it for something you do want. Don't be shy about counteroffering your own package deal.

19. When comparing prices among vendors, you'll find yourself dealing in apples and oranges, since most quotes will include certain packages and services that might not be included in another. To find out which vendors are the least expensive, ask for prices on some basic items (a dozen roses, for instance, if you're dealing with florists) and use those quotes to compare pricing.

20. When choosing vendors, consider using newcomers to the industry who need your business in order to attract other customers. Use your promise of referrals as a bartering tool.

21. Know that even if you bring in your own vendors for such things as decorations and other services offered by the wedding venue, you will probably be charged an "administration" fee. Keep this in mind when negotiating.

22. It's polite to feed your vendors—or at least those who remain throughout the evening, such as the photographers and musicians. But you can order sandwiches or simple meals for them; they don't necessarily have to eat the same food as the guests.

23. Even if you pay all expenses for, say, 20 guests, a small destination wedding can save you tons of money.

24. Don't get married around April 15. Your gifts are liable to reflect budgets that have been stretched by tax season.

25. Are you a professional of some sort? Consider bartering for services.

26. When you sign contracts, often a year in advance, you need to make sure that the price is being locked in and that there won't be increases, for example, on food items.

27. Make sure you know what you're paying for and what you're not paying for. Find out how much extra will be charged if the reception runs overtime. You might be in for a shock.

28. Hire professionals for only part of the duties. A wedding planner can be hired to simply point you in the right direction, and photographers don't have to stay for the entire event. Don't pay for services you don't need.

Wedding Vendors to Avoid

1. Yes men—the type who seem to have no problems with anything you suggest and who don't seem to be thwarted at all by your budget restrictions. If it seems too good to be true, it is.

2. The vendors who seem to have their own agenda. They've done "tons of weddings" and insist that their way is best, no matter what your ideas are.

3. If the vendor won't talk about money, there's a reason. This person will confuse you about final charges and is loath to give out straight answers. He or she is hiding something—stay away.

4. The vendor who is too busy to return your calls and answer your questions probably won't have time to do it your way in the end. You should be able to communicate about details with any kind of wedding vendor.

5. The photographer who sends his assistant, the bandleader who is busy that night but will send others to perform, and the florist who promises hydrangeas but tells you at the last minute that they're out of season—all these vendors are pulling the old bait-and-switch. Avoid them.

29. Charge as many of the fees as possible to your credit card. You can stock up on cash-back benefits or mileage for the honeymoon. This will also make it easier to challenge charges if you have questions later on.

30. Don't buy an expensive wedding planner book. Most likely, half the pages won't be applicable to your event, and you can create a much more user-friendly version on your own.

31. Make sure that all rented items are returned promptly to avoid overcharges.

32. Keep receipts for everything you buy, especially for cash payments to vendors. Leave nothing to your memory—or anyone else's, no matter how much you trust them.

33. Use items that you can sell on eBay when the wedding is over—the gown, the centerpieces, and even the bridesmaids' dresses can all be recycled.

34. Avoid printed matchbooks and napkins. They're passé and useless.

35. The fewer people you hire, the less you will pay and the fewer tips you'll have to worry about. Hire a caterer who is willing to supply everything from the food and decorations to dinnerware, tablecloths, and chair coverings.

What Every Contract Should Include

You should understand every word of a vendor's contract. If you don't, it's because something is wrong with the contract, not you. Consult a lawyer or someone with experience if anything is confusing or "sounds weird."

1. The date and time of the service to be delivered

2. The exact fee for the service

3. The time at which the fee or portions of it will be due

4. A description of the service to be delivered

5. The names of the people who will perform the principal services (will the head photographer be taking the pictures or will he be sending an assistant?) and the number of people who will perform other services (how many bartenders, servers, etc.?)

6. The cancellation/refund policy

7. The number of guests you are paying for (including dinners for service people if you have agreed to that)

8. All verbal agreements, even if they must be last-minute, initialed (by both you and the vendor) additions

9. All the details of the service you are purchasing

For instance, a catering contract should include every dish that is being served, the type of liquor that has been requested (regular or premium—and exactly which brands the vendor considers premium), and any extras that have been ordered. A limousine contract should indicate the number of people who will be transported, where and when they are being picked up, and the number of hours for which the limo is being rented.

36. Check out the wholesale clubs (Costco, Sam's, BJ's) for appetizers, liquor, favors, and decorations.

37. Make your own wedding programs.

38. Find other brides in your area who are getting married around the same time (find them online; make contact when you meet them while shopping) and suggest that you share expensive items.

39. Keep the bridal party small. You don't have to have a ring-bearer or a flower girl. You don't even need bridesmaids.

40. Check out European magazines and websites for ideas. The wedding industry is far less frenzied outside the United States, and you're liable to find simple, practical, but timeless ideas for everything from the bridal gown to the favors.

41. Beware of consultation fees. Vendors who are after your business have no business charging for an initial interview. When vendors demand such payment, move on; they'll probably have other equally unfair practices as well.

42. Refuse to negotiate with anyone but the owner or manager of any business. Underlings don't have authority.

43. If you get married in a religious setting, your payment to the church or synagogue is tax-deductible. The same goes for payment to a religious officiant.

44. Announce the wedding only in newspapers that run wedding notices for free.

45. Skip the wedding software. The hundreds of details they include can easily slow you down.

46. Try to keep as much of your communications online as possible. Network with vendors, members of the wedding party, and guests this way to keep phoning to a minimum. You'll also have a record of all communications.

47. Avoid delivery fees by getting friends to pitch in. Check your contracts to find out what delivery fees might have been included in the price of the item. Try to get free delivery when you are negotiating.

48. Ask a friend to teach you and your honey to dance instead of signing up for an expensive package at a dance school. Or rent a video.

16 Questions to Ask Before You Book a Venue

Whether you're getting married at the local zoo, a movie theater, or the Ritz, you need to choose a venue carefully. Before you lock down a wedding location, make sure you and your sweetie have agreed on the style and financial considerations. The best referrals are of the personal sort; if you've had a chance to attend a wedding at a venue you're interested in, you're way ahead of the game. Here are questions to ask, no matter where you wind up.

1. Is the place large enough? Will it accommodate your guests, a dance floor, and space for a band or DJ?

2. How does the space look? Does it make you happy to be there? Is it so stark that you'll have to spend more on decorations? What vibes are you getting from the place?

3. Is parking available and nearby?

4. Is the coatroom ample and available?

5. How many other events might be taking place on the premises at the same time, and what provisions will there be for your privacy? Will staff be stretched too thin? Will there be room for everyone to park?

6. Is the dressing room large enough, and will there be a bridal attendant to assist?

7. Will you be allowed to bring in your own vendors, or do you have to use "their people"? If outside vendors are allowed, will you have to pay a charge for this privilege?

8. Can you bring in your own liquor (thereby saving a bundle) or must you use theirs?

9. How are the acoustics?

10. Is the place clean? Ask to use the bathrooms, and check the entranceways and hallways. Does the place smell nice?

11. Is there ample lighting and electricity to accommodate your musicians and photographers? If not, will they work with these vendors to make the needed alterations?

12. Can you afford it?

13. Are they on the up-and-up? Check with the Better Business Bureau to find out if any complaints have been filed. The venue should be willing to put all its promises in writing and to ask for no more than 50 percent up front. Find out about overtime fees and any extra charges that might come up.

14. Does the venue carry liability insurance in case someone is injured?

15. How pleasant is the staff? Will someone handle your wedding from the beginning of the contract to the day of the event, or will you be shuffled around from one individual to another? The venue should share your enthusiasm for the event; will its staff cooperate with your special requests?

16. Is security an issue?

26 Ways to Save Money on Food and Beverages

If you're having the wedding at home or bringing the food to the venue, visit lotsofinfo.tripod.com/weddinghelp.html for guidelines on feeding large groups.

1. Keep entrée choices down to two of the least expensive options.

2. Go heavy on the appetizers and keep the main meal down to just a few courses.

3. Serve food with expensive ingredients (shrimp, lobster) for appetizers and keep dinner simple.

4. Serve dinner buffet-style.

5. Don't overlook the catering services that many supermarkets offer. Bring your own appetizers to a catered dinner to cut down on food expenses. Wholesale clubs such as Sam's and Costco offer choice hors d'oeuvres.

6. Substitute less expensive cuts of meat in beef entrées.

7. Opt for ethnic foods (Mexican, Indian, Chinese), which are often cheaper.

8. Instead of food stations, have servers walk the floor with trays of hors d'oeuvres. Portions are much more easily controlled this way. You might want to use this method for the more expensive appetizers only.

9. Shorten the cocktail hour to 45 minutes instead of an hour.

10. Offer a vegetarian entrée choice, not only to save money but to accommodate what is probably a good portion of your guests.

11. Use expensive ingredients only minimally: shrimp toast instead of shrimp, lobster bisque instead of lobster tails.

Some say it's okay to have a cash bar for at least part of the reception. We are not among them. The only time it is acceptable to do this is if the reception is in a restaurant. Even then, the bar should be free for at least part of the event.

12. Avoid labor-intensive hors d'oeuvres.

13. You don't have to serve an appetizer with dinner if you're having a cocktail hour.

14. Choose between soup and salad; you don't need both.

15. "White glove" and table service cost more than dishes served family-style.

16. Don't serve premium liquor. Stick to the basics and think about offering an attractive signature cocktail for those with more exotic tastes.

17. Serve punch.

18. If you're skimping on hard liquor, make up for it by offering flavored coffees, a selection of microbrewed beers, or a special drink such as margaritas and fruit coladas.

19. Close the bar during the reception and simply place bottles of both red and white wine on the tables.

20. Instead of purchasing liquor through the reception hall, buy it wholesale from a local supplier, who will probably give you a volume discount and allow you to return unopened bottles.

21. Close the bar after a few hours and serve only wine after that.

22. If you don't know much about the subject, research the Internet and ask friends for the names of good inexpensive wines.

23. Serve only wine and beer, with champagne for the toast.

24. Skip the champagne for the toasts.

25. Buy champagne on New Year's Eve, when it's least expensive. Store it properly until the wedding—at 55 degrees Fahrenheit; don't refrigerate until the day of the event.

26. Buy magnums (twice the size of regular bottles). You'll save money on the wine by buying in a larger volume, not to mention the unconscionable corking fees that catering halls charge.

Feeding the Masses

Catering a wedding is a lot simpler if the food is to be provided by the venue you've chosen, and that's how it's most often handled. If you do choose an outside caterer, make sure the venue manager approves of the arrangement. Try to choose a caterer who has had a pleasant working experience with your venue in the past. Here are some questions to ask before the first canapé is served:

1. If you're using an outside caterer, who will supply the table settings?

2. Will the venue facilities be sufficient for whatever on-site food preparation might be necessary?

3. How many servers will there be?

4. What type of liquor will be used? What premium liquors are available?

5. Will the venue be able to provide the kosher, vegetarian, and other special meals you might need?

6. What is the payment schedule?

7. When does the final headcount have to be submitted?

8. Do you have to pay full price for children? (What is the age cutoff here?)

9. Are gratuities included in the price?

10. What is the cancellation/refund policy?

11. Is liability insurance in place?

Serving Styles

There are several alternatives for serving up the wedding feast, and one or more of them may be used in conjunction.

1. **Buffet:** Food is placed in one or more areas and guests serve themselves.

2. **Food stations:** Food is freshly prepared at various tables and guests visit these as they wish.

3. **Cocktails:** Servers walk around the room with trays of hors d'oeuvres.

4. **Seated meal:** Guests are seated at tables and food is served to them.

When Do We Eat?

Breakfast	9:00 A.M.–11:00 A.M.
Brunch	11:00 A.M.–12:00 P.M.
Lunch	12:30 P.M.–3:30 P.M.
Cocktails	5:00 P.M.–7:00 P.M.
Dinner	9:00 P.M.–10:30 P.M.
Midnight snack	11:00 P.M.–1:00 A.M.

You Are Cordially Invited . . .

Invitations should be just that—inviting. Whether they consist of nine-piece stationery ensembles or a simple announcement card, these guidelines will help you avoid common pitfalls.

1. Know the difference in the types of printing available (see "A Menu of Printing Techniques," page 238) so that you know what to expect. Each of the choices gives your invitation a different look, and each will affect your finances in a different way.

2. To find reliable stationers, consult friends. You have your choice of commercial printers, Internet companies, department stores, mail-order catalogs, and independent dealers, many of whom work from small home businesses. Insist on working with someone who is willing to explore your choices with you and who has enough experience to advise you as to the materials that work best together. You should be able to look at tons of samples, both in the books they'll show you and online.

3. Before you finalize the wording of the invitation, have other family members take a look to make sure no one has been slighted or ignored.

4. Read printed proofs as opposed to an online representation. Things look different on paper.

5. Buy 20 percent more invitations than you need, so you'll be prepared for the inevitable last-minute additions. Order extra envelopes in case there are mistakes in addressing.

6. If you want your thank-you cards to match the invitations, order everything at the same time to ensure that the printing technique and paper stock are all identical.

A Menu of Printing Techniques

Engraved: The most formal and the most expensive. You can feel the raised printing under your fingers.

Thermography: It has the raised feel of engraving, but it's not as sharp. It's cheaper than engraving and widely accepted today as the best alternative to it.

Offset printing: It's the most common form of printing for books and magazines. The printing is flat, and although it's "low-end," offset printing can manage images and complicated artwork that engraved and thermographic techniques can't.

Trends in Wedding Invitations

1. Save-the-date messages are being sent out via e-mail.

2. Save-the-date magnets are proving extremely useful.

3. Many couples, equipped with home printers and lots of imagination, are making their own invitations, choosing papers from the large array available (thanks in part to the scrapbook set) and the many DIY programs available.

4. Seal-and-send invitations, with a detachable postcard that works as a reply card, are becoming very popular with those who seek to save money on postage. Return postage is not included, and guests are invited to reply via e-mail.

5. Growing environmental consciousness has led to attempts to cut down on the amount of paper used. Protective tissues are now rarely used, and the double envelope is on the wane. The eco-friendly bride and groom are insisting on recycled paper.

6. Despite GPSs (global positioning systems), maps have become de rigueur.

7. Traditional, formal white invitations are still quite popular, but so are modern designs with bold colors, relaxed typefaces, and dramatic ribbons.

8. More and more invitations are reflecting the theme or season of the event.

9. Traditional calligraphy, either handwritten or computer-generated, still remains the addressing method of choice.

At Stamps.com, you can create postage stamps with your own photo and sentiment. Or you can visit sites such as ArtisticPostage.com and choose from a variety of wedding stamps to which you can add your own message.

More and more brides and grooms are printing address and return labels on their home computers—to the chagrin of the trendsetters, who consider this approach a faux pas.

Wedding Fonts

You've finally chosen the style, the colors, the paper, and even the wording that everyone can agree on. You've decided that you want a nice, elegant script typeface for your invitations. But there are so many of them, and they are clearly not all created equal. And what about those other typefaces? Will they do a better job of communicating the spirit of the event?

Steven Brower, an award-winning graphic designer and writer, has won two National Magazine Awards for General Excellence and has work in the permanent collection of the Smithsonian Institute. He teaches design at the School of Visual Arts in New York and at other colleges. Here are his guidelines for choosing a typeface from the thousands that are available.

1. Script faces, most commonly used for invitations, were created in the seventeenth and eighteenth centuries to mimic handwriting. When used on invitations, the moods they evoke are at once familiarity and stylishness. There are several to choose from, such as the popular contemporary revivals Snell Roundhouse and Kuenstler Script. Both come in various weights and will add a touch of elegance and sophistication to your invitation. These delicate faces should not be confused with the 1950s sign painting—influenced faces such as Brush Script, Kaufmann, and Mistral.

2. Script faces are designed to be displayed in upper and lower case. Nothing is more woeful than an invitation that displays a script face set in all caps, rendering it utterly illegible. Also, the point size of the type is paramount, as setting it too small may cause the thin strokes to drop out, or it may be hard to read. Point sizes should always be taken into consideration. Setting your type too large or too small may defeat your intended purpose. Unfortunately there are no catchall rules for type, as no two faces are exactly the same size despite being the same point size. Therefore you should examine printouts of the faces you are considering, displayed at the size you intend. (Do not approve proofs online; type looks different when it is printed on paper.)

3. If you are so inclined, you may consider a classic serif face as an alternative. While still traditional and elegant, these faces might better reflect your individuality. Some faces to consider are:

Bodoni
Designed in 1798, this face adds sophisticated elegance to any design.

Caslon
This simple yet beautiful face designed in 1734 is easy on the eyes.

Garamond
Although created circa 1540, the face is still one of the most legible and easy to print of faces.

Goudy Old Style
A face from the early twentieth century, it possesses the elegance of Bodoni and the legibility of Garamond or Caslon.

4. If you're looking for something modern and bold and want a contemporary approach, you might consider a sans serif face. Some to consider:

Franklin Gothic
Named after Benjamin Franklin and created in 1902, this typeface comes in a variety of weights and styles, including a condensed version that can be helpful if names are long and you have lots of copy.

Futura
Paul Renner's 1920s face adds a nice Bauhaus/jazz age feel to anything it touches.

Gill Sans
Designed in England in the 1920s, its asymmetrical design possesses a playful feel, especially in the bolder weights.

News Gothic

Solid, clean, dependable, as the name implies.

Trade Gothic

Both in its condensed and "regular" form, this is the typeface of choice for many designers who want type that is legible yet stylish.

5. In designing wedding invitations, there are also faces to avoid because of their utilitarian design: Times, Times New Roman, Arial, and Helvetica are fine for business letters, annual reports, and signage, but will add little style or individuality to your design.

6. If you decide to get creative and mix typefaces, it is recommended that you not use more than two. Using more will draw attention to the fonts and away from the content. A combination of script and sans serif, or serif and sans serif would be best.

7. Since there are thousands of typefaces, choosing yours can seem daunting, but it can be fun. It is the final "cross" on the "t" and "dot" on the "i," an opportunity to make a statement about yourselves as a couple, to let folks know in advance the type of affair they will be attending and can look forward to. Along with the movie, the photo album, and wedding presents, your invitation will be a keepsake, one that you will treasure.

7 Ways to Cut the Guest List

Be vicious. Lay down a rule and stick to it. If third cousins aren't being invited and you make even one exception, that will no doubt annoy the others. If you can't cut the guest list, consider eliminating the martini bar. Whatever you do, do it consistently, and be open with those who aren't on your list about how much you regret not being able to invite everyone. Here are some of the people who can be left off of your guest list:

1. Coworkers who are not really connected to the bride or groom at all

2. Youngsters under a certain age, say, 12 or 16 (if the event is in the evening, don't even think of inviting the little ones)

3. People you haven't talked to in over a year

4. Dates for single guests, unless the date is obviously the guest's significant other or fiancé or a member of your wedding party wants to bring a date

5. Distant relatives

6. Exes and steps, especially if they are no longer involved in family affairs

7. People you hardly know—imagine opening your wedding album in five years and not recognizing half your guests!

3 Disadvantages of DIY Invitations

The wedding invitation is everyone's introduction to the big event. It sets the stage by establishing a level of formality and communicating the spirit of the wedding. Your wedding plans can be hectic enough without taking on a task that requires time, talent, money, and patience. Unless you're an experienced graphic designer, we suggest that you leave the invitation to the pros, who know the ins and outs of paper, ink, and how they affect one another. Here are some other drawbacks of doing your own invitations:

1. It can be expensive. You'll need plenty of ink cartridges, which don't come cheap. Fine paper is also pricey, especially when you add up the various pieces you'll need for RSVP cards and directions.

2. It can take a lot of time. Finding the right card stock and cutting it to your specifications, downloading fonts, and familiarizing yourself with a program you may not have used before can take more time than you have. And if you haven't worked with layout before, you'll find it can be troublesome. The results can be amateurish and not at all what you envisioned.

3. You'll need a truly fine printer, and most home printers are not up to the job. The texture of the paper may affect the print quality, some invitations are liable to print lighter as your ink cartridge runs out, and the ink may smudge.

21 Ways to Save Money on Invitations

1. Limit the guest list to immediate family and very close friends. Let others know that this will be a small affair and that you are sorry you cannot include everyone. Evaluate business relationships honestly before you invite your entire staff to the wedding.

2. Have a B-list. These are people who will take the places of those on your A-list who decline. Just be sure to get invitations to these people as far in advance as possible so they don't know they were on the B-list.

3. Forget about the upscale wedding invitations that cost $25 apiece. You can find gorgeous ensembles online, and if you ask for samples before you order anything, it'll be just like ordering from an expensive stationer.

4. Don't be manipulated by pushy relatives into inviting guests you don't want. Stick to your guns.

5. You don't have to invite distant friends and relatives just because they invited you to their wedding, especially if your wedding is a smaller affair.

6. Don't invite single friends to bring escorts unless you know the couple might be following in your footsteps before too long.

7. Don't order the invitations too early. Details of the wedding are liable to change, and you might have to reprint them.

8. Your thank-you cards don't have to match your invitations; there are many less expensive ways to show your appreciation. For instance, ask your photographer to come up with an inexpensive photo card—guests will appreciate the memento.

9. If one of your bridesmaids has an especially beautiful handwriting, ask her to address the invitations instead of using an expensive calligrapher. (Be sure to express your appreciation to your talented friend.)

10. When ordering invitations, stick to the exact colors and materials of the samples shown; changes cost extra, and those charges can run very high.

11. Don't use double envelopes for your invitations.

12. Use thermography instead of engraved printing. It's the most popular, and although you can tell it's thermography, it will cost a fraction of its expensive counterpart.

13. Choose invitations that won't require exorbitant postage.

14. Handle responses online or use postcards.

15. Bypass addressing envelopes by hand calligraphy and have them computer-printed instead.

16. Include directions with the invitations only for those guests who really need them.

17. Order at least 15 percent more invitations than you think you need. If you make errors and waste some, remember that it would cost a lot more to initiate a new printing, not to mention the time it would take to get additional invitations ordered this way.

18. Send save-the-date cards only if you fear that out-of-towners and busy guests will truly need the heads-up. If most of your guests are close friends and family who are aware of your plans, the cards aren't necessary. Helpful bridesmaids and word of mouth should cover it.

19. Churches and synagogues often offer printing services as a fundraising effort. Order from them and expect a deep discount.

20. Instead of having your return address printed on the outside envelopes, buy an embosser.

21. The more colors you use on your invitations, the higher the printing price. Try to stick to one color only.

They won't attend, but if you invite celebrities to your wedding, you may wind up with a letter that will make an interesting addition to your album of wedding memorabilia. Check official websites for addresses and send your invitation at least eight weeks prior to the event. Here are addresses for inviting the President of the United States and the Queen of England to your wedding.

The Honorable _____
and Mrs. _____
The White House
Greetings Office Room 39
1600 Pennsylvania Avenue
Washington, DC 20500

The Secretary to Her Majesty
Queen Elizabeth II of England
Buckingham Palace
London, England
SW1A 1AA

How to Choose a Wedding Gown

Terrica Skaggs, a former model and chief wedding designer with the Georgia wedding consulting firm of Once Upon Your Wedding, writes:

You've been dreaming about your wedding gown since you dressed your first Barbie, but now that the time to choose has arrived, you find yourself drowning in endless possibilities. Where to begin? At the beginning.

Choosing the Style

There are many things to consider when choosing the perfect gown—color, your complexion, size, style, and the formality of your event. The last is something many brides fail to take into account, and it's an important consideration. That long-sleeved crushed velvet dress would be lovely in December but totally inappropriate for a summer wedding, and an ultra-formal gown would overpower a Sunday brunch garden wedding.

The first step in all of this is a big dose of reality. Take your measurements. Are you short, tall, pear-shaped, or thin? Be honest with yourself. While the gowns you see online, in magazines, and in books are gorgeous, you can't possibly know how they will look when you try them on. Those glossy images you're seeing involved a lot of airbrushing, tape, invisible corsets, and more.

Take a look. If you are:

Top-heavy: You need to create an illusion of balance and length. Choose a full, billowing skirt with plenty of adornments and an elongated bodice. Avoid any extra ornamentation on the bodice. It will draw too much attention to your chest. The same goes for low necklines, full sleeves, and empire-style dresses.

Short: Steer clear of any design that will accentuate your stature. Instead, create an illusion of height with an empire waistline. High necklines and trim along the neck and shoulders also look fabulous on your frame. If you are going formal, try short sleeves with long gloves.

Pear-shaped: If you are narrow in the torso and fuller in the hips and thighs, shoot for a bodice that is textured and bejeweled. You are the opposite of our top-heavy bride, so you need to bring attention to the bodice and away from the waistline and below. Accentuate the waist in a simple skirt instead.

Tall: Try the high-fashion look of tiers and flounces to balance your height. Look for bodices with low, ornamented necklines.

Full-figured: Avoid the frills and flounces. Instead, opt for a princess-style gown that will skim the body. Necklines with a V or U shape are best, especially when accompanied by an A-line skirt.

Thin: You also look great in princess-style gowns or gowns with a Basque waist and full skirt. Bloused bodices with a gathered skirt are also great options for you.

Never, ever put a deposit down or pay for a gown when you have not confirmed the date of the wedding. Brides with rose-colored glasses sometimes start buying gowns at the mere mention of marriage. You don't have a budget, you don't know the month of the wedding, and you haven't agreed on an approach to the wedding with your intended. All of these decisions will affect the kind of dress you buy, so hold off, lest you wind up in a high-neck brocade and taffeta gown — at your beach wedding.

Never, ever crash-diet or buy a gown sizes smaller with the expectation of losing weight. It is far easier to take a gown in than it is to have it let out if you don't meet your goal.

Choosing the Color

Once you confirm your shape, the next task is to consider your complexion. It is important, even if you intend to tan, to understand that your hues will determine what will flatter your appearance best, both live and in photos. Darker-complexioned brides and those with dark hair look best in crisp, bright whites. Blondes and redheads are stunning in creamy and silk whites. This is also true for porcelain-skinned brunettes. If you would like to throw in a bit of color to your dress, look for those with undertones of pink or coral—they flatter all brides.

How Formal Should It Be?

If the wedding is formal to ultra-formal: Your gown should be cut from a rich fabric (silk chiffon in the summer, satin in the winter). You may choose a full skirt with a train. (Remember, the longer the aisle, the longer the train.)

If the wedding is semiformal: Your gown should at least be full-length or your train should sweep the floor. For this type of occasion, bare shoulders and taffeta-type skirts are considered acceptable.

If the wedding is informal: You have the most choices without restrictions or provisos. You can look for anything from a ballerina- or floor-length-type skirt to a dressy suit. Some designers make beautiful prom dresses that can pass as wedding gowns. Your possibilities are endless.

Putting It All Together

Once you have a fairly good idea of what it is you're shopping for, you can browse thousands of dresses without ever leaving your chair by searching online to further narrow down your choices. Explore the websites of the top designers, and don't forget to take a look at what eBay has to offer. You never know. . . . In the meantime, once you set out to shop, whether you're headed to a bridal salon, a department store, or a vintage clothing emporium, consider these tips:

Get a salesperson to help you. These people know their stock, and they've had experience with just about every size and shape bride you can imagine. Take advantage of their wisdom. Be open to their suggestions, even if you think you know exactly what you want; you can, of course, reject their ideas at any point.

Bring an honest friend with you. Another pair of eyes can help prevent a disaster. Ask this person to be brutally honest about her opinion of the dresses you try on.

Bring accessories. A strapless bra, a bustier, hose, and shoes with the approximate-height heel you think you'll be wearing will give you a better idea of exactly how your dress will look.

Don't buy until you're ready. Don't be pressured into putting down a deposit until you are absolutely sure of the purchase. Don't be shy about letting salespeople know you are still shopping around or that you just haven't made up your mind.

Wedding Gown Sleeves

Our thanks to OurMarriage.com for this guide to sleeves.

1. **Bishop sleeves** are fuller in the lower forearm and gathered with a wide cuff at the wrist.

2. **Capped fitted sleeves** are very short sleeves just cupping the shoulder.

3. **Dolman sleeves** produce a capelike effect, extending from large armholes, and are often fitted at the wrist.

4. **Gigot (leg-of-mutton) sleeves** are loose, full sleeves rounded from the shoulder to just below the elbow, then shaped to the arm, often ending in a point at the wrist.

5. **Illusion fitted sleeves** can be long or short and are slender sleeves that follow the shape of the arm. Made from illusion net, they are often encrusted with heavily beaded and sequined appliqués.

6. **Melon sleeves** appear as a highly exaggerated puff, rounded from the shoulder to the elbow.

7. **Renaissance sleeves** have a slightly gathered puff at the shoulder, then taper down the arm to a point ending just below the wrist on the hand. They are usually made in satin and encrusted with appliqués of beads and sequins.

8. **Short sleeves** are fitted sleeves that fall just short of midway between the shoulder and the elbow. Short sleeves are slightly longer than cap sleeves.

9. **Tapered sleeves** are slightly gathered at the shoulder, with little fullness, and taper down the arm to the wrist.

10. **Three-quarter sleeves** most often are fitted sleeves that end slightly below the elbow.

Wedding Dress Silhouettes

The "silhouette" refers to the shape of the dress, most notably the skirt. This is one of the key elements of a dress (along with the neckline) that will help determine the type of dress that best suits your style and is most flattering to the shape of your body.

A-Line

This silhouette features a flared-out skirt from the waist down to your feet, creating an "A" shape. The design consists of vertical seams running from the waist or shoulders down to the bottom of the skirt. This is one of the more popular shapes because it is flattering to most body types. It's recommended for petite figures because it can make a shorter bride appear taller and for full-figured brides hoping to de-emphasize their hips. The A-line, however, is not recommended for brides with a thick waist, as the hourglass shape accentuates your waist.

- Recommended for: A petite, full, or short-waisted figure
- Not recommended for: A thick-waisted or hourglass figure

Basque Waist

This style is characterized by a low V- or U-shaped waistline that begins several inches below the waist. This shape is great for taller brides who are looking to create an hourglass appearance with the low waistline. Petite brides may want to consider other shapes, as this style may make them look even shorter.

- Recommended for: Taller brides, those with large hips, and those with an hourglass or pear-shaped figure
- Not recommended for: A petite figure

Ball Gown

The ball gown is the most traditional and formal of all shapes. This style of skirt is best suited for the bride in search of a classic and elegant look. The ball gown is characterized by a fitted bodice and a waistline that leads to a full skirt. This dress is a great choice for brides who are medium to tall in height and for those who wish to hide large hips. This shape is not recommended for petite brides, as the full skirt can overwhelm or take away from the small bride's appearance.

- Recommended for: A thin, full, or pear-shaped figure, and brides who are medium to tall in height
- Not recommended for: A petite figure

Empire

This style features a high waistline that stems from the bust and falls to a slender skirt. An A-line skirt is also popular with this style. The empire style is best suited for brides with a small bust and a slim figure. The shape can give the impression of increased height, and for those with a thicker waist, it can de-emphasize the area.

- Recommended for: A petite or thick-waist figure
- Not recommended for: An hourglass, curvy, full, or pear-shaped figure

Mermaid

This style contours to your body (similar to the sheath style), but flares out at the bottom. The skirt has a distinctive diagonal cut. For a bride wanting to accentuate her curvaceous figure, this dress is ideal.

- Recommended for: An hourglass figure
- Not recommended for: A full figure

Sheath

This style is very form-fitting, following the contours of your body very closely. A sheath dress features a straight skirt with no waist. It is highly recommended for brides with a tall, well-proportioned (thin) figure.

- Recommended for: A thin or petite figure
- Not recommended for: A pear-shaped or full figure

> "When I design a wedding dress with a bustle, it has to be one the bride can dance in. I love the idea that something is practical and still looks great."
>
> —Vera Wang

Wedding Gown Necklines

Our thanks to OurMarriage.com for this guide to necklines.

1. **Bateau (boat) neckline:** A neckline that softly follows the curve of the collarbone, high in both the front and back, opening wide at the sides and ending in shoulder seams

2. **Contessa neckline:** An off-the-shoulder gown attached to sleeves cut about three inches below the shoulder and forming a continuous line across the neckline and the arms

3. **Halter neckline:** A deeply sleeveless gown, often displayed with a high choke neck

4. **Illusion high neckline:** A gown with a yoke of sheer net and an often ornately decorated satin band that fits snugly on the neck to create a choker effect

5. **Off-the-shoulder neckline:** A neckline that lies gently hovering across the top of the bust line, with shoulders either uncovered or visible through a sheer yoke of net or organza, with a high collar

6. **Open sweetheart back yoke:** A heart-shaped opening, often fringed with beads; also known as a keyhole back

7. **Portrait neckline:** A shawl collar that wraps the shoulders

8. **Queen Anne neckline:** A high rising collar at the back of the neckline, cupping the sides of the neck, then sculpting low across the chest to outline a bare yoke

9. **Sabrina neckline:** A high scoop neck

10. **Scoop neckline:** A softly curved line gently sloping downward across the bodice

11. **Square neckline:** An open yoke in the form of a half-square

12. **Sweetheart neckline:** A graceful, open yoke shaped like the top half of a heart (one of the most popular necklines)

13. **Tank top bodice:** A sleeveless gown with a scoop neck

14. **U-scalloped neckline:** An open yoke in the shape of a U, embellished with scalloped lace appliqués

15. **V-neck line:** An open yoke coming to a V shape midway down the bodice

16. **Wedding band neckline:** A gown with a yoke that is either open or of sheer net with an ornate band fitting snugly on the neck, creating a choker effect

> "Today people want to be free to wear what they like, in any combination they like, to be confined by no rules, and to set their own standards — yet they all end up looking exactly the same."
> — Carolina Herrera

It's Not Just a Dress: 7 Hidden Costs

Vintage photo, ca. 1905 **LIBRARY OF CONGRESS**

When you budget an amount for a wedding dress, bear in mind that the "little extras" listed here can add up to more than the dress.

1. Fitting fees
2. Alterations
3. Storage fees
4. Delivery
5. Pressing
6. Cleaning
7. Preservation

The 5 Wedding Gown Train Lengths

Crystal Unrau, a wedding planner and the owner of Chrys Cross Bridal, an online bridal salon that specializes in creating dream wedding gowns on a budget, writes:

We all know what a wedding train is from when we were girls and tied bath towels to our waists as we waltzed "down the aisle." In fact, we were mimicking royalty of ages gone by, who commonly wore trains, topped by their crowns, of course, for formal events. The longer the train, the higher up on the food chain was the wearer. During the nineteenth century, the length of the train often corresponded to the societal position of the bride, and all opted for either the tiara (think crown) or a garland type of headdress. Queen Victoria's 18-foot train and Princess Diana's 25-foot creation were both trendsetters in their time.

Today trains are entirely optional. They are often abandoned altogether for informal or garden weddings, or even for semiformal ceremonies. There are five standard train lengths, and they are often used in combination (a royal train or a chapel-length train for a ceremony, for instance, and a sweeping train or none at all for the reception). Here's a short course in "trainspeak."

1. **Sweeping train:** This is the shortest of the trains and is also called a brush train because it just brushes the floor. Usually, the back hem is only a few inches lower than the front hem. It is perfect for an elegant informal or semiformal wedding gown. It provides the elegance of a train without too much added fabric in the way.

2. **Chapel-length train:** This is currently the most common train because it has the elegance of a full train but is still not overly cumbersome. A chapel train is generally 1⅓ yards or 4 feet from the waistline. This is perfect for a semiformal wedding gown but could be used for a formal or informal wedding gown as well.

3. **Semi-cathedral-length train:** A semi-cathedral is about halfway between chapel and cathedral length. Perfect for a semiformal or formal wedding gown.

4. **Cathedral-length train:** This is a popular choice for a formal affair or for that fairy-tale look. A cathedral train is generally 2½ yards or 7½ feet from the waistline and is usually used for a formal wedding. These gowns often come with a bustling option or a removable train to allow for better movement on the dance floor.

5. **Royal train:** Remember Princess Diana's wedding gown? This is one of those trains that is still out the door when you reach the altar. If your dream is to have a Princess Di train, this is it. Also called a monarch train, it generally falls 9 feet from the waistline and is used for only the most formal weddings.

30 Ways to Save Money on Wedding Attire

A Flushing Bride: Katrina Chalifoux, of Rockford, Illinois, wiped away the competition in the fourth annual Toilet Paper Wedding Dress Contest, held in New York City in the "odditorium" of Ripley's Believe It or Not. The dress is made entirely of toilet paper, tape, and glue. **COURTESY OF CHEAP-CHIC-WEDDINGS.COM**

1. Get your dress on eBay, Craigslist, or some other Internet site. There are zillions there, in every style imaginable. Just remember that cleaning a wedding dress can cost as much as $250, and alterations can be expensive as well. Only fools rush in.

2. You can save as much as 50 percent off retail by buying a gown directly from the manufacturer over the Internet. The dresses that can be purchased from China, where most dresses are made anyway, look amazing. (For more information, visit bluecatalog.com, 1koo.com, or juliusbridal.com.) But be ready for possible problems. Alterations will be needed (sizes in wedding dresses vary greatly), and there's a good chance that you'll be stuck with whatever arrives in the mail—whether or not it's exactly what you ordered. If there are problems, you can complain to the Better Business Bureau, but if the dress never shows, you'll be stuck, and it's hard to enforce consumer rights from halfway across the globe. Proceed with caution.

3. Order the bridesmaids' dresses from the same source as the wedding gown and negotiate a package deal for all.

4. Buy discontinued styles.

5. When shopping for matching wedding accessories, bring color and fabric swatches with you to avoid expensive mistakes. Don't guess at colors.

6. Hit the bridal shows. You'll get discounts and helpful hints as to what's available in your area. Plus the door prizes can be amazing: free high-end housewares, free bridal consultations, and even free honeymoons.

7. Wear decorated ballet slippers instead of expensive wedding shoes.

8. If you keep the wedding less formal, your bridesmaids can wear less expensive short dresses instead of gowns.

9. A talented dressmaker can copy anything.

10. Do you really need bridesmaids' dresses? Go for a black-and-white color scheme and have each bridesmaid wear her favorite black dress. Your friends will appreciate your thoughtfulness and flexibility.

11. Forgo silk and satin for less expensive polyester gowns that don't wrinkle.

12. Ring-bearers and flower children can wear their Sunday best.

13. Order a dress that can be altered and dyed for later use.

14. Avoid last-minute alterations by wearing the correct under-garments and shoes to your fittings. Don't crash-diet or pig out days before the wedding.

15. Make your own veil. You can buy kits online or at craft stores, or you can let your imagination guide you; it's not rocket science.

16. Skip the veil altogether.

17. Don't wear gloves.

18. If the dress you have your heart set on is wildly expensive, find out if it can be made in a cheaper fabric.

19. Buy a sample dress off the rack for a fraction of the original price. Just remember to take alteration and cleaning fees into account when you figure out the true cost of the dress.

20. Don't overlook vintage clothing shops for bridal attire, for both men and women.

21. Don't miss Filene's annual bridal sale. It's amazing! (See "The Running of the Brides," page 250.)

22. Keep it simple. The more beading and decoration on your gown, the higher the price tag.

23. Especially around holiday time, bridal shops tend to hold sales and you may be able to pick up a designer gown for as little as $100. Call local shops to find out when these sales are being held.

24. Shop for bridesmaids' dresses around prom time, when beautiful gowns and dresses can be purchased more cheaply.

25. Use baby's breath or fresh blooms instead of expensive wedding hair accessories.

26. Use someone who does both hair and makeup instead of hiring two people for these jobs. Or ask friends to handle these chores.

27. The groom doesn't need to rent shoes if he already has a nice pair that match his tux. Same goes for the bride. No one sees the shoes.

28. Look online for tux rental coupons; you'll find tons.

29. Rent all tuxedos in the same place to take advantage of group discounts.

30. If it's a destination wedding, save money on late charges by renting the tux from a chain that will allow you to return it to any of its locations.

The Parachute Wedding Gown

In a 1947 wedding, a bride wore a wedding dress made out of the parachute that had saved the groom's life during World War II. Major Claude Hensinger, a B-29 pilot out on a mission, bailed out of his plane to safety after its engine caught fire. The parachute he used provided him with both warmth and shelter until he was rescued. Hensinger kept his lucky parachute and presented it to his fiancée Ruth when he proposed marriage. It is now on exhibit at the Smithsonian Museum in Washington, D.C.

The parachute dress was a copy of one worn in the film *Gone with the Wind,* a huge hit at the time. COURTESY OF NATIONAL MUSEUM OF AMERICAN HISTORY, SMITHSONIAN INSTITUTION, BEHRING CENTER

7 Ways to Tell if It's a Quality Gown

The fact is, whether you pay $500 or $5,000 for the dress, you are buying something that was made to be worn only once. (How else would the wedding industry survive?) But a poorly made dress at any price can ruin the day, not to mention the photos. Here are some shopping tips.

1. **Beads:** They should be sewed on, not glued on.

2. **Embroidery:** The stitches should not cause the fabric to buckle; it should lie flat.

3. **Seams:** There should be no visible threads or stitches.

4. **Lining:** The dress should be completely lined, with no unfinished seams.

5. **Fabric:** It should have some weight to it; cheap fabrics feel like you can tear them like paper. The fabric should feel comfortable on your skin, not scratchy.

6. **Hem:** There should be some sort of scalloped edge at the bottom of the dress, as opposed to a simple straight-stitch hem.

7. **Buttons:** A row of tiny buttons is preferable to a zipper. If buttons have been sewn on to hide the zipper, they should not make the dress more bulky.

The Running of the Brides: Filene's Annual Bridal Gown Event

Filene's Basement is known for its bargains on everything from fashions to home goods, but the store may be most famous for its annual "Bridal Gown Event," when brides-to-be can save hundreds and even thousands of dollars on designer wedding gowns.

The event often brings out the worst in shoppers (and brides), but by its end, new friendships have often been formed as the brides share stories and bond with one another. In some families Filene's has become a bridal tradition, and in others it is simply de rigueur for saving bucks. As one bride put it, "If we get a gown here, we can invite twenty more people to the wedding." Her fiancé had other ideas for the savings, like extending the honeymoon.

The sale is held in selected Filene's Basement stores once a year (twice a year in Boston) and is fraught with frenzy. The day of the sale, brides-to-be and their helpers line up early, and when the doors open, they run full speed toward the racks. In less than 60 seconds, the racks are stripped bare. (Store employees have to hold on to the fixtures so they don't topple.) The women grab whatever gowns they can, haul them off to a corner, strip down to their underwear, and start trying on dresses.

Once they have determined what they are looking for, a unique process begins minutes later as the trading begins. A bride "shops" any gowns she has rejected to other brides, who often appear in groups or with helpers, looking for fresh merchandise. This can get complex—one trade can involve multiple transactions. For instance, bride #1 wants a gown that bride #2 has, so she offers a gown in trade; #2 has her eye on a gown being held by bride #3, so she sends bride #1 to negotiate with bride #3. Often you'll see helpers making their way through the crowd holding signs with messages like "Size 10–12 in Ivory" or "Simple Size 20 Wanted."

Every dress, no matter what size, style, or color it is, gets bartered for another as each bride tries to find the gown of her dreams at a cut-rate price. Each sale features anywhere from 1,300 to 2,500 designer gowns, and they are priced from $249 to $699, marked down from $900 to $9,000 each. Filene's buyers travel the world to obtain dresses that come from a variety of sources and have become available for a variety of reasons—canceled orders, postponed weddings, small shops needing to make space for new gowns, and so on.

To find out when the next sale will be held, e-mail Pat.boudrot@ filenesbasement.com or just visit filenesbasement.com.

9 Foundation Garments to Enhance a Wedding Dress

In addition to Photoshop, the bride with the appetite from hell has many tools at her disposal for looking good in her wedding gown. Here are nine more:

1. **Bodysuit:** This leotard-like garment may or may not have snaps at the crotch and is usually form-fitting and sleeved, although some are sleeveless and cut like a tank top.

2. **Brassiere:** The bra is considered a foundation garment, as well as an undergarment, because of its role in shaping the wearer's figure. It can be worn to support and enhance breast shape during everyday activities. The bra may also be worn to observe modesty or to present a certain image of femininity.

3. **Corset:** This is a garment worn to mold and shape the bride's torso into the desired shape for aesthetic purposes. Genuine corsets are usually made by a corset maker and ideally should be fitted for the individual wearer.

4. **Control brief:** A control brief is a type of panty girdle with longer legs and a higher waist, normally worn by a woman to lift and shape her buttocks while flattening her stomach.

5. **Garter belt:** This is a woman's undergarment consisting of an elastic piece of cloth worn around the waist to which garters are attached to hold up stockings. It is the precursor of pantyhose. Garter belts continue to be sold because many women find them more comfortable than girdles or pantyhose, not to mention their sex appeal.

6. **Girdle:** The word *girdle* originally meant a belt. Most commonly used as a form of women's foundation wear, it replaced the corset in popularity. Some girdles include a brassiere and thus become functionally equivalent to a corset. But since they don't use boning, they don't produce the constricted waistline that Victorian-era corsets do.

7. **Body briefer:** A body briefer is a garment similar to the girdle but provides more comprehensive coverage and firmer shaping. A body briefer is similar in form to a leotard but is made with heavier elasticated fabric and may contain wires to give additional support. Women who use this item want comprehensive reshaping of most of the body, especially the breasts, and flattening of the stomach.

8. **Corsellette:** A corsellette is a one-piece brassiere and girdle. This foundation garment sometimes has lace in front or in the back. From 1975 on, Maidenform and other mainstream lingerie and undergarment manufacturers have sold corselettes as "control slips."

9. **Control camisole:** This tank-top style of undergarment offers medium control of the bust, tummy, and waist in a modern silhouette that looks like a camisole. Many have built-in bras. Control camisoles are sleek and lightweight and can create a defined silhouette under clothing. They are the most casual of all shaping garments and the easiest to wear, covering the torso from above the chest to at or below the waist.

How to Knit Your Own Wedding Dress

This knitting pattern is provided by Linda Daniels, the owner of Northampton Wools, located at 11 Pleasant St., Northampton, MA 01060, 413-586-4331.

Finished size: 34" bust circumference (easily stretches to 36")

Yarn
- Berroco Zen (60% nylon, 40% cotton; 110 yd): off-white, 4 skeins
- Karabella Lace Mohair (61% kid mohair, 8% wool, 31% polyester; 540 yd): #201 white, 14 skeins

Needles
- Size 9: straight, 16", 24"; circular (cir) 47"
- Size 10½: 16" cir

Adjust needle sizes if necessary to obtain the correct gauge

Notions
- Tapestry needle
- Marker (m)
- Sewing needle and thread
- Size I/9 or J/10 crochet hook
- 1½ yd bridal gown trim
- Vogue Accessories, pattern 7009, for satin flowers
- About ¾ yd off-white satin ribbon
- 3 yd off-white tulle for underskirt (optional)

Gauge Bodice
16 sts and 20 rows = 4" with both yarns held tog on size 9 needles

Skirt
No specific gauge; very, very loosely knitted on size 9 needles. (Note: The stitches will appear uneven and netlike—the looser the better.)

Bodice Back and Front
(Make 2) With both yarns held tog and size 9 needles, CO 24 sts. (Note: To make a larger size, CO more sts.) Work in St st, inc 1 st each end of needle every row 18 times—60 sts; piece should measure 3" from beg. Work even for 1".

Dec 1 st each end of needle every 3rd row 4 times—52 sts rem. Work even for 1". Inc 1 st each end of needle every other row 8 times—68 sts. Work even if necessary until piece measures 13" from beg, ending with a WS row. Shape armholes: BO 5 sts at beg of next 2 rows—58 sts rem. Dec 1 st each end of every other row 4 times—50 sts rem. Work even until armholes measure 5", ending with a WS row.

Shape Neck
(RS) K10, join new yarn and BO center 30 sts, knit to end—10 sts rem each side. Working each side separately, inc 1 st at each armhole edge every row 10 times—20 sts each side. BO all sts.

Bodice Finishing
With yarn threaded on a tapestry needle, sew side seams. Back collar: Starting at shoulder point with right side facing, pick up and knit 72 sts around neck. Beg with a knit row, work in St st, inc 1 st at beg and end of even knit row 4 times—80 sts. Work even for 2½". BO all sts loosely.

Front Collar
Work as back collar. Sew collars tog along shaped sides. (Note: Points of front and back do not necessarily meet, but are joined by collar seam.) Fold collar to right side and tack down to front and back.

Flowers
Cut lengths of Zen, 6"–8" long. Using sewing needle and thread, gather the lengths into small floral shapes and attach to collar, spaced about 1" apart.

Skirt
With a single strand of mohair and size 10½ needle, loosely CO 150 sts. Do not join. Change to size 9 16" cir needle and knit 1 row. Place marker and join, being careful not to twist sts. Working very loosely, work St st until piece measures 2".

Work incs as foll, changing to progressively longer cir needles as needed. Increase Rnd: *K1, yo; rep from *—300 sts. Work even in St st for 2". Rep inc rnd—600 sts. Work St st for 3". Rep inc rnd—1,200 sts. Work St st for 6". Rep inc rnd—2,400 sts. Work St st for 12". Rep inc rnd—4,800 sts. Work even in St st until piece measures about 37" from beg or desired total length, when stretched (as will happen naturally when the skirt is worn).

With crochet hook and using the crochet method, BO loosely as foll: *Insert hook into first st kwise, wrap yarn around hook, and pull through loop as you let the st slide off the needle, wrap yarn around hook, and pull through another loop. Insert hook into next st, pull through loop (2 loops on hook), wrap yarn around hook, and pull through both loops on hook. Rep from * until all sts have been bound off.

Finishing

Hang skirt in closet for a few days to allow it to stretch, helping it by pulling on it now and then. With sewing needle and thread, stitch skirt to bodice. Cover seam with purchased bridal trim. If desired, follow Vogue pattern for flowers and attach to back seamline with needle and thread. Cut lengths of Zen for streamers. If desired, sew off-white tulle to inside seam for underskirt.

This knitted wedding dress was crafted by five people and worn only once. COURTESY OF LINDA DANIELS, NORTHAMPTON WOOLS

3 Ways to Dress the 'Maids

The days of the ugly bridesmaids' dresses seem to be behind us, thankfully, and the forward-thinking bride takes pride in the range of people with whom she surrounds herself. Watching the tall lanky one, the short plump one, and the pregnant one all walking down the aisle together, we remember that, like love, friendship is blind. Be sure to thank your bridesmaids in your wedding speech or ask another speaker to acknowledge them.

Here are three ways to make sure they're all smiling for the photographs.

1. Let them be themselves. Consider choosing a color palette and letting them come up with their own approaches. Or go with black and let them each wear a new dress or one they already own. One clever bride whose bridesmaids were scattered across the globe purchased fabric and mailed some to each. The result was something of an international fashion show, with each bridesmaid proud of the creation she had designed herself. Matching wraps, fastened by jeweled brooches (which can make thoughtful, useful gifts), can complete the ensembles.

2. Invite them to contribute ideas. You don't have to choose the fashions they prefer, but you can hear them out and make choices accordingly.

3. Choose a basic color like black, white, gold, or silver for their shoes and let them wear their own.

CHARLOTTE: I don't want to disappoint you, but I've decided not to have bridesmaids.
MIRANDA: Woohoo!
CARRIE: Hallelujah!
—*Sex and the City*

Wedding Headpieces and Veils

The type of hairstyle, veil, and gown you choose and your personal taste will determine the type of headpiece you should wear.

The Headpiece

A headpiece can give your ensemble a finished look, but it's not altogether necessary. Alternative choices include a decorative bow, combs, barrettes, garlands, a wide-brimmed sun hat, or even a single fresh flower tucked behind the ear. Headpieces come in a variety of styles:

Half-hat: This is exactly what it sounds like. It covers half of the head or less.

Toque: A toque is small, tight-fitting hat.

Tiara: Perfect for the "princess" look, this delicately decorated crown rests high on the head. A tiara is wonderful because it works with any design of gown and most any type of hairstyle. A crystal tiara portrays an elegant look.

Wreath: Ornamented with flowers, this headpiece sits on top of the head or at the forehead. A wreath complements short hair nicely.

Juliet cap: This jeweled hat fits snugly on the crown.

Upturned picture hat: This hat has a brim that angles up one side.

The Veil

Headpieces can be worn with or without a veil. If you do choose a veil, it should be appropriate to your dress and the formality of the wedding. Try veils on when you are wearing the dress and practice moving around in them. It makes sense to use a detachable veil so that the headpiece can still be worn during the reception.

In choosing a veil, consider the detailing of your dress. The veil should accentuate and be proportional to the dress, not detract from it. Your veil length should be cut just above or below any focal point on your dress. For example, don't choose a veil that ends right where your bodice begins. This will visually cut you in half. If you have a sharply defined waistline, don't choose a veil that ends right at the waistline.

If you are shorter than 5'4", you should select an elbow-length veil. If you are taller than 5'7", you should select a fingertip-length veil (36" long). If you are in between, you could go with either length depending on your personal taste.

The color of the veil should match the dress as closely as possible. If there is any color variation between the dress and your veil, you always want to choose a veil that is a shade lighter (versus a shade darker) than your gown.

Veils come in three basic lengths:

Elbow-length (approximately 30" long): The most popular length, the elbow veil is generally used for gowns without a train and will enhance

formal weddings. The veil extends onto the floor at least 6 inches past the train for a dramatic look. A cathedral-length veil looks best when worn with a cathedral- or semi-cathedral-length gown. Know that these can be difficult to maneuver, and a fingertip-length veil will look just as lovely with a chapel- or cathedral-length gown.

Veils also come in single- and two-ply:

One-tier veils: These are lovely with any dress and do not include a blusher, which is a shoulder-length layer of the veil that is worn over the face. One-tier veils work for the bride who wants a minimal, less formal, but chic look. It's elegant and a nice choice for the bride who wants to wear a veil in the back of the head—to accentuate an updo hairstyle, for instance.

Two-tier veils: The two-tier veil adds a touch of drama to the bridal ensemble. It's suitable for nearly all dresses but looks especially nice with a semiformal or formal gown; two-tier veils do have blushers. They are also fuller and frame a face beautifully. They work well with any hairstyle.

any detailing at or around the waist. It also complements a gown with a full skirt (ending below a low back and above the start of the skirt). The elbow-length veil is mostly worn for formal and semiformal weddings.

Fingertip-length (approximately 36" long): The fingertip veil falls right at the fingertips of the bride if her hands are at her side. It can be worn with any full-length gown but is not recommended for gowns with a train. This veil is used for formal and semiformal weddings.

Cathedral-length (floor-length): Cathedral veils are worn only for

> "Bad bridesmaids are everywhere. We are getting our hair twisted in unflattering updos with wispy ringlets framing our faces, and pulling on control-top panties in eighty degree heat. We are trying to rent stretch Hummers in towns so small they don't even have a Starbucks, and taking calligraphy classes so we can help the bride personally pen 250 invitations. Some of us are contemplating stepping down altogether. Others will soon hit the dance floor in strapless dresses, praying that their breasts will be restrained as they hop their way through another embarrassing rendition of the Chicken Dance."
>
> — Siri Agrell, Bad Bridesmaid

If the Shoe Fits: All About Bridal Shoes

The wrong shoes can ruin a wedding day, and even the barefoot bride needs to take certain considerations into account when planning wedding day attire. On the other hand, bridal shoes don't have to be expensive; footwear is one of those categories in which you can easily save money by keeping things simple. For one thing, don't buy "wedding shoes." Buy white shoes at anything but a bridal boutique and save a bundle. And then follow these tips for guaranteed happy feet.

- Avoid bridal boutiques. As you probably know by now, any item described with the words "bridal" or "wedding" costs almost double what you should be paying. Most large department stores have a good selection of white and dyeable shoes.

- Know that if you are wearing a floor-length wedding dress, there is a good chance that no one will see your shoes. (Think about it: do you remember the kind of shoes the bride wore at the last wedding you attended?) Keep it real.

- That said, although bridal slippers will do in most instances, heels offer a posture boost and elongate your silhouette. Short, stout brides should wear the highest heel in which they are comfortable.

- Choose shoes that you can dye and wear again. If you choose to re-dye them, choose an unusual color to match or complement a special outfit. Then dye them black and wear them forever.

- Don't settle for anything less than comfortable shoes. Three-inch heels will elongate your legs, but will they stand up (literally) to the hours of posing for photos and greeting guests, not to mention your trip (make that "journey") down the aisle? If the shoes are tight and you are told that they will stretch, don't believe it; keep shopping. Choose the heel height you normally wear; this is not the day to try out stilettos or a style you've never worn before. Wider heels offer more support and protect your ankles and feet while walking and dancing. Don't overlook old-fashioned "granny boots" as a possible choice; they have heels but offer plenty of support and can enhance the look of an old-fashioned bridal ensemble.

- Keep the style simple. Shoes with lots of decoration are more likely to catch the hem of your dress.

- Buy your shoes early enough so that you can bring them to your first dress fitting to avoid expensive alterations later on.

- Shop for wedding shoes toward the end of the day, when your feet are the most swollen.

- The three main fabrics for bridal shoes are silk, satin, and peau de soie. Choose the one that best matches the fabric of your dress. Be sure to bring a fabric swatch with you when you go shopping; the many shades of white can get quite confusing after a time. For the best possible match, have dyeable shoes custom-matched to your gown.

- If your dress calls for it, consider metal-colored shoes such as gold, silver, or bronze.

Seeing Red

Who says shoes have to match the dress? Bold brides have lately been seen sporting red shoes under their traditional white ensembles. What better way to acknowledge that life and love are full of surprises?

- If you're wearing slingbacks or any other style that exposes part of your feet, be sure to get that all-important pedicure before the big day.

- Break your shoes in before you wear them on your wedding day. Wear them inside and outdoors and scuff the bottoms so you don't slip. If they feel a bit large, experiment with foam cushions until you get a perfect fit. Bring a variety of these pads with you the day of the wedding; all that extra adrenaline can affect your shoe size.

- If you opt for two pairs of shoes—something stylish and fancy for the ceremony and a more comfortable pair for the reception—make sure they both have the same heel height. Brides often choose lower heels or kick off their shoes altogether at some point, causing their dresses to trail on the floor.

- The beach bride need do little more than buy a pair of rubber flip-flops and embellish them with silk flowers or rhinestones. The groom can go with a black pair decorated with small carnations.

A Groom's Wedding Wear Glossary

Ascot: A broad-neck scarf looped under the chin and fastened with a tie tack or stickpin; should be worn with a wing-collar shirt

Cutaway morning coat, or cutaway coat: A long coat that tapers from a waistline button to one broad tail in back

Designer: Fashion formalwear uniquely designed by the top menswear names, such as Calvin Klein, After Six, Fumagelli, Geoffrey Beene, Giorgio Bissoni, Neil Allyn, and Manzoni

Dinner jacket: A formal, standard-length evening jacket with a notched or shawl collar

Director's suit: Similar to a business jacket; worn for a daytime formal wedding only

Four-in-hand tie: A knotted tie that hangs vertically, similar to a business suit tie, and can be fastened with a tie tack; should be worn with a spread collar

Full dress tails or tailcoat: Short in front and long in back, the black coat for the most formal occasions

Regular coat: The formal coat length that extends to the second knuckle, worn at daytime or evening events

Spencer coat: An open coat without buttons, cut right at the waistline

Stroller: A daytime formal coat with a regular cut but no satin lapel, worn with contrasting vest and a four-in-hand tie

Tails: High-end formal dress coat with a cosmetic vent in the back of the coat, creating the rear tails; reserved for ultra-formal evening events

Tuxedo: The standard formal coat length, with either single- or double-breasted satin lapels; suitable for almost all formal occasions (including weddings), proms, and tux-required events ("Tuxedo" is commonly used to describe all men's formal wear)

Vintage or classic: Outdated styles that are no longer manufactured but are still classic formalwear

Waistcoat/Eton jacket/spencer: A coat that is tight-fitting, ends at the waist, and is worn at evening functions with matching or contrasting trousers

How to Choose a Tuxedo to Match Your Body Type

MassachusettsWeddingGuide.com, an online planning resource, offers these tips for choosing the right tuxedo for any build.

1. **The tall and thin groom** can wear just about any type of tuxedo or suit. He can also wear just about any color and style. If the groom is very thin, he can try a double-breasted jacket. This will give him a little extra padding in the chest area. If he wants to look broader in the shoulders, he can ask for more padding. A pleated shirt will also look great on a thin groom.

2. **The short and thin groom** should not wear double-breasted jackets. He'll end up looking lost in it. A three-button jacket with pleated trousers or tuxedo pants is a great look for this build.

3. **The tall and broad groom** should also stay away from the double-breasted jacket. It will just make him look more husky. He should also avoid pleated shirts. And if he's had a few too many brewskies lately, he should wear a vest rather than a cummerbund, which would draw attention to his waistline; the vest, on the other hand, will hide it.

4. **The short and broad groom** should wear a single-breasted jacket. A one- or two-button jacket that closes near the waistline is a perfect choice. Once again, if he has a large waistline, he should wear a vest rather than a cummerbund. Padded shoulders will also draw attention away from the waistline up to the shoulders.

A Groom's Guide to Formalwear

We're grateful to Minsky Tux of Richardson, Texas, for this chart of men's formalwear for weddings and other good times.

Traditional	Groom	Ushers and Junior Groomsmen	Fathers	Guests	Ring Bearer
Very Formal Evening	Black full dress (tailcoat) with white wing collar pique formal shirt, white pique vest and bow. Shoes: patent. May wear sprig from the bride's bouquet as boutonniere.	Identical to groom, with different boutonniere.	Identical to groom, with different boutonniere.	May wear tuxedos, or if you specify "White Tie" on invitations, guest should wear full dress identical to groom.	Identical to groom/groomsmen.
Formal Evening	Black tuxedo, white pleated formal shirt, bow tie, vest or cummerbund to match tuxedo lapels. White dinner jacket with formal trousers for summer or tropical climate.	Same as groom, perhaps with different boutonniere.	Same as ushers.	Should be formally dressed. Specify "Black Tie" on invitations.	Identical to groom/groomsmen.
Very Formal Daytime	Cutaway coat, grey striped trousers, grey vest, ascot, or striped four-in-hand tie. Optional top hat, spats, grey gloves. Shoes: patent.	Similar to groom in style, with possible variation in tie or shirt.	Same as groom, or same as ushers.	You may suggest "Traditional Morning Attire" on invitations, if you would like your guests to be formally dressed. They would then choose formalwear similar to the groom's.	Identical to groom/groomsmen.
Semi-Formal Daytime	Grey stroller, with striped trousers, pearl grey vest, four-in-hand tie with white pleated formal shirt. Optional: homburg gloves.	Identical to groom, perhaps with different boutonniere.	Same as groom, or same as ushers.	Formalwear optional.	Identical to groom/groomsmen.

Contemporary	Groom	Ushers and Junior Groomsmen	Fathers	Guests	Ring Bearer
Very Formal Evening	Black full dress (tailcoat), white or other color tailcoat acceptable. Shirt coordinates with tailcoat, tie and vest match tailcoat in color, except if wearing black full-dress wear white wing collar pique shirt with white pique vest and bow. Shoes: patent.	Similar to groom in style. Most formal: identical tailcoat suits.	Same as groom, or same as ushers, or in classic tuxedo.	Formalwear similar to groom. For an elegant mood, specify "Black Tie" on invitation; guests will wear black tuxedos.	Same as groom/groomsmen.
Semi-Formal Evening	Tuxedo or tailcoat, in range of colors—dark for fall and winter, pastels for spring and summer, white for any time of year. Shirt white or coordinate with tuxedo in color, may be pleated or flat. Shoes: patent	Formalwear similar to groom in style; however, if groom chooses a tailcoat ushers can wear similar-color tuxedos. Shirts white or coordinate with tuxedos in color, ties and vests match tuxedos.	Similar to ushers, or in classic black tuxedo.	Formalwear optional. For an elegant evening, specify "Black Tie" on invitations.	Same as groom/groomsmen.
Very Formal Daytime	Updated cutaway usually grey, with striped or matching trousers, white shirt, striped tie or ascot; or tuxedo in conservative colors, dark for winter or all grey cutaway outfit with wing or fold collar formal shirt and striped grey ascot or four-in-hand tie.	Similar to groom in style, or can wear matching stroller coats with striped or matching trousers. Usually same color as groom.	Same as groom, or same as ushers, or in classic tuxedo.	Formalwear optional.	Same as groom/groomsmen.
Formal Evening	Tuxedo or tailcoat, in range of colors, dark for winter, white and pastels for spring and summer or tropical climate. Updated stroller coat, with striped trousers.	Similar to groom, coordinated in color.	Either similar to the male attendants or formalwear of own choice.	Formalwear optional.	Same as groom/groomsmen.
Second and Later Weddings	Formalwear appropriate to time of year, time of day, and style of the bride and her attendants.	Similar to groom, coordinated in color.	Same as groom or same as ushers.	Similar to groom. Specify on invitations if you want your guests to dress formally.	Same as groom/groomsmen.

If the invitation says "White Tie" or "Full Dress"

It's a very special occasion. A debutante dance, a diplomatic ball or reception, a Mardi Gras ball; an important fundraising dinner. You'll be dashing—and proper, too—in traditional full dress: A freshly laundered white wing collar pique shirt, crisp white pique vest, white pique tie, classic black trousers with the formal satin stripe, traditional black tailcoat just covering the vest, black patent shoes.

If the invitation says "Black Tie" or "Black Tie Invited"

You'll want to dress correctly, in a smart, comfortable tuxedo, cut almost like your newest business suit. The traditional black, worn with white shirt and vest (or cummerbund) in black or dark shades), and a black tie or tie matching the cummerbund; and patent shoes. Worn to any festive event after six in the evening, to which the women will be wearing formal clothes. Formalwear specialists who are members of the International Formalwear Association can show you the latest formal attire appropriate for "Black Tie" events.

A cummerbund should always be worn with the pleats facing upward.

How a Tuxedo Should Fit

The key to looking good in your tuxedo is the fit; even the most expensive tux can look shabby if it doesn't fall just so. Whether you're renting one, buying one off the rack, or having one made especially for you, a good tailor is imperative. Ask friends for recommendations. Give yourself plenty of lead time too; tuxes are big business, especially around prom time, and alterations take time. These guidelines will give you a crisp, tailored look no matter where you got the tux.

The Jacket

Regardless of style, the jacket should always fit comfortably—especially around the neck and shoulders—and be easily buttoned. It's a good idea to sit down with the jacket fully buttoned to make sure it still feels comfortable. The shoulders of the jacket should fit so that the sleeves fall in a clean unbroken line. The chest and shoulders should be roomy enough to allow you to lift your arms comfortably without pulling the front of the jacket open or stretching across the back. The jacket sleeve should end where the thumb meets the wrist and expose about a half-inch of the shirt's cuff. The bottom hem of the jacket should cover the butt, and the vent shouldn't pull open, even if you have your hands in your pockets. If you are wearing tails, they should line up with the back of your knee.

The Pants

The trousers should button comfortably so that there's no chance of popping a button when you sit. Many trousers have adjustable waistbands, which allow for a better fit. Trousers should be worn at the waist, and the pant crease should fall naturally in an unbroken line. The bottom of the trou-

sers should brush the shoe tops and then fall slightly to just above the laces of the shoe. Flat-front pants are generally more slimming than their pleated counterparts.

The Shirt

The shirt should fit comfortably around the neck, shoulders, and waist. Cuffs should be one-quarter to one-half inch below the jacket sleeve. The collar should lie flat on the back and sides of the neck without any gaps or bulges.

The Vest

If you opt for a vest, it should fall just over the trouser waistband, hiding the slide adjustments. Vests usually have straps on the side and should be adjusted for a perfect fit. The vest should fit comfortably across the chest, even when buttoned.

Shoes

They don't have to be shiny, but they do have to be black, unless you're going for the anti-groom look, in which case psychedelic-patterned high tops will do just fine. The fact is that there's a good chance no one will ever see your shoes. Try to get her to let you wear your own if you have a pair that's somewhat appropriate.

Cummerbund

The wide, pleated fabric belt should be worn around the waist with pleats facing upward. (Picture ushers in theaters sticking ticket stubs into them.)

Socks

A pair of colorful socks is an effective way to put some originality into your outfit without making a spectacle of yourself.

Jewelry

Cuff links are always appropriate at a formal affair. If the shirt requires studs instead of buttons, the studs should match the cuff links.

The 3 Types of Jacket Collars

1. **Notched:** A triangular indentation marks the place where the collar meets the lapel (informal)

2. **Peaked:** A V-shaped lapel juts up where the collar meets the lapel (formal)

3. **Shawl:** No notch or triangle, just a smooth round line from the collar down the lapel

The 4 Types of Shirt Collars

1. **Wing collar:** A standing collar with the points pressed to stick out horizontally, like wings

2. **Lay-down (or turn-down or point) collar:** A full collar, similar to a regular business shirt collar, that accommodates different types of ties

3. **Spread:** Like the lay-down collar, but with the points spread wider apart

4. **Mandarin:** A collar made of a plain band, as seen on Nehru jackets

The 4 Basic Tie Types

1. **Necktie:** The standard tie, in black silk; works for a formal event

2. **Bowtie:** The classic, in black or white; works for a super-formal event

3. **Ascot:** A wide tie worn folded over and fastened with a stickpin or tie tack; for highly formal events

4. **Bolo:** A string tie, held together with a brooch; works only if you are a direct descendant of John Wayne

> "All through the recorded past, men, too, have been preoccupied with fashion and body adornment. For centuries, the groom was grandly enrobed in silks, satins, velvets, and brocades, every bit as sumptuous as the bride's."
> — Arlene Hamilton Stewart,
> *A Bride's Book of Wedding Traditions* (1995)

A white dinner jacket from the 1950s COURTESY OF VINTAGEWEDDING.COM

Crossing Color Lines

Black or gray formalwear offers timeless elegance, but to add a touch of color, accent your look with a colored vest, pocket square, or cummerbund. White tuxedos are mostly appropriate for tropical climates; it is best to avoid them. Pastel-colored tuxedos are starting to make a comeback but can easily lead to a "what was I thinking" moment years from now. Of course, check with the bride before you make a color choice that clashes with hers.

How to Choose the Right Wedding Bouquet

Liztiany Zakaria of Flower-Arrangement-Advisor.com writes:

First, it helps to know a few basics. Wedding bouquets come in three basic styles: cascade, round or posy, and hand-tied.

As its name suggests, the cascade bouquet is shaped like a waterfall, with more flowers on top and some flowers flowing downwards. It's mixed with some greenery for a natural look.

The round bouquet is, of course, round in shape. It typically contains much less greenery and many more flowers. The flowers can be of one or several kinds, as long as the color balance is intact.

The hand-tied wedding bouquet, which is gaining popularity these days, is more casual than the other two styles. It's composed of a bunch of flowers tied together with a ribbon, with the stems revealed.

How do you know which bouquet style is best for you?

Your selection depends on three things:

1. Your body size
2. Your wedding gown style
3. The look that you want

If you're self-conscious about your appearance on your wedding day, choosing the right wedding bouquet style can enhance the way you look and probably hide some figure imperfections.

Let's say you want to look slimmer on the big day. In that case, you would probably choose a cascade bouquet, because of the shape's flattering effects. A cascade bouquet is roundish at the top and pointed at the bottom, which works to slim your silhouette.

If you're a tall, slender person, consider a cascade bouquet or a

A classic round bouquet of roses COURTESY OF GARDENSTATEPHOTO.COM

hand-tied bouquet. If you choose a round bouquet, you may find it makes you look even taller. Add a pair of wedding heels, and suddenly you're two inches taller.

A bride-to-be with generous hips should choose a cascading or hand-tied bouquet, but not a round bouquet, which will emphasize the hips.

If you like a garden look or a casual look, no other wedding bouquet will do but the hand-tied bouquet. The casual flowers will look like you hand-picked them fresh from the garden, and you'll look natural and unaffected.

If you have a petite body, choose a round bouquet, which will balance your body.

> "Each society, each culture from time immemorial, has used flowers to interpret the deepest of human emotions. The love of flowers is universal. From the college professor to the primitive savage, all make space in their lives for flowers' symbolic and decorative purposes."
> — Bill Hixson,
> *A History of Weddings, Tradition, Bouquets*

A Glossary of Floral Terms

TYBinc.com provides the following definitions of floral terms:

Boutonniere: A tiny flower arrangement usually worn on the lapel of a man's jacket.

Candelabra: A floral centerpiece created at the base, neck, or top of a multi-armed candelabra. Such a centerpiece is usually trimmed with flowing greens or ribbons, depending on the wedding's style.

Cascade: A waterfall-like spill of blooms, often composed of ivy and long-stemmed flowers, that is wired to fall gracefully over the bride's hands.

Chuppah: A wedding canopy decorated with flowers that is an integral part of the traditional Jewish ceremony.

Classic bouquet: A dense bunch of blooms that can be anchored in a bouquet holder, wired, or hand-tied.

Composite: A handmade creation in which different petals or buds are wired together on a single stem to create the illusion of a giant flower.

Corsage: A single bloom (or small cluster of blooms) arranged against a lace or tulle doily and/or accented with ribbon. Corsages come in pin-on, wrist, and hand-held styles and are typically worn by mothers and grandmothers. Orchids and gardenias are popular choices for corsages.

Crescent: Bouquet composed of one full flower and a flowering stem, often orchids, wired together to form a slender handle that can be held in one hand. Designed as either a full crescent—a half-circle with a central flower and blossoms emanating from two sides—or a semi-crescent, which has only one trailing stem.

Dais: The centerpiece at the head table (where bride and groom are seated), which drapes to the front of the table for visual effect.

Fish bowl: Low centerpiece style that consists of flowers clustered in a glass bowl.

10 Ways to Save Money on Decorations and Accessories

1. Ask one of the bridesmaids to assemble a courtesy basket for the ladies' room instead of paying for the expensive one that will be offered by the banquet hall (see "14 Things to Put in the Courtesy Basket," page 300).

2. Buy tons of inexpensive tulle (it comes in various grades, and you don't need the expensive stuff) at a florist supply shop and use it everywhere—as table covers, in sashes to decorate chairs, gathered in bunches to decorate the aisle. Don't forget to save some to make your own veil (although you'll want a finer tulle for that).

3. You don't have to decorate aisles and pews. All eyes will be on the bride no matter what you create. Skip the fancy aisle runner if the floor is carpeted.

4. Tiny white lights can make the most mundane room romantic. Buy them on sale right after Christmas.

5. Haunt dollar stores for decorations, cake plates, paper goods, and candles.

6. If another wedding is taking place the day before yours at the same venue, find out if you can use their flowers and decorations. (Offer to pay something toward the original price.)

7. Ask your bridesmaid to throw you a "working" shower. Each guest brings supplies, and everyone can pitch in to help prepare favors, table cards, programs, and decorations.

8. You don't really need wedding programs. They have been made fashionable in recent years by people who have way too much time on their hands.

9. Skip the leather guest book or ask for one as a gift.

10. Rented glassware can be cheaper (and greener) than plastic. Check prices before you decide which to use.

Garland: Elaborately woven rope or strand arrangement, typically used to adorn pews and doorways. A garland can also be paraded down the aisle by two or three young attendants.

Growing garden: Centerpiece featuring abstract wildflowers. The composition is airy and less full than other designs. Lisianthus, hollyhock, rambling roses, digitalis, and smilax are well suited to this arrangement style.

Ikebana: Japanese-style flower arrangements that are aesthetically in unison with space, size, earth, and air.

Nosegays: Small, round bouquets, approximately 16 to 18 inches in diameter, composed of densely packed round flowers, greenery, and occasionally herbs. Nosegays are wired or tied together.

Oasis: Special foam used in flower arrangements. Oasis fits in a bouquet holder and retains water like a sponge, hydrating flowers for extended time periods.

Pomander: A bloom-covered ball suspended from a ribbon. Ideal for child attendants.

Posies: Smaller than nosegays but similar in design, posies often include extras like ribbons or silk flowers. Perfect for little hands.

Presentation: Also known as the pageant bouquet, this is a bunch of long-stemmed flowers cradled in the bride's arms.

Taped and wired: Arranging technique for bouquets, boutonnieres, headpieces, and wreaths. The head of a flower is cut from the stem and attached to a wire, which is then wrapped with floral tape. Taped and wired flowers are more easily maneuvered into shapes and styles.

Topiary: Flowers or foliage trimmed into geometric shapes, often resembling miniature trees or animals.

Tossing: This copy of the bridal bouquet is used solely for the bouquet toss ritual.

Trellis: A woven wooden frame used as a screen or support for climbing plants and flowers.

Tussy mussy: From the Victorian era, a posy carried in a small, metallic, hand-held vase. Today the term is often used in reference to the holder itself.

Wreath: A ring of flowers or other decorative materials that can function as centerpiece, headpiece, or door hanger.

> "The more candles you use, the more glamorous and younger everyone looks."
> — Colin Cowie

14 Ways to Save Money on Flowers

1. Choose flowers that are in season, preferably from local growers. They'll be more expensive if they have to be flown in.

2. Ask your florist for a price comparison chart for reference.

3. Consider alternatives to flowers (see "16 Alternatives to Traditional Centerpieces," page 267).

4. Substitute gorgeous single, long-stemmed blossoms for the bouquets carried by the members of the wedding party.

5. Use combinations of silk and dried flowers with live blooms.

6. Recycle the flowers: once the ceremony is over, the flowers used for the altar can be moved to the reception room.

7. Rent potted flowers and plants for key spots instead of decorating them with flowers. Consider using silk flowers, which can be rented, for the ceremony.

8. Decorate a simple white candle with faux pearls and gems instead of buying an expensive unity candle. Ask an especially crafty member of the wedding party to do this.

9. Flowers cost more in February; Valentine's Day drives up their cost.

10. Use expensive flowers as accents and surround them with more reasonably priced blooms. Be generous with the use of greenery, which can be enhanced with tiny white lights.

11. If flower petals are being scattered, use silk ones that will be less slippery than the real thing and cost less. Plus, they won't stain.

12. Use the bridesmaids' bouquets as centerpieces once the ceremony is over.

13. Is there a horticultural school near you? Does the local college offer such a course? They may be able to handle your wedding flowers at a deep discount.

14. Buy flowers wholesale on the Internet and have friends arrange them. The savings are enormous; you can buy 200 roses, for instance, for under $300, and many wholesale sources offer wedding packages.

Planning Your Wedding Flowers

Of all the aspects of wedding planning, choosing flowers seems to be the least stressful, perhaps because just shopping for them and seeing them in all their glory—with their vibrant colors and delicate scents—brings us close to the soothing effect of Mother Nature. Your wedding flowers play a huge role in creating the atmosphere for your wedding, and creative choices go a long way toward personalizing the event. You want them to be beautiful, but you want them to say something about you as well. How to do it best? Step by step:

1. Once you have shopped around for a florist (do shop around —prices vary greatly), arrange an appointment for a wedding consultation. This is best done at least six months prior to the wedding date. Most consultations for wedding flowers take between one and two hours, so be sure to allow enough time in your schedule. Prepare for the consultation by gathering pictures from bridal magazines of wedding flowers that appeal to you. Have a list of some of your favorite flowers as well as some that you don't especially care for. This will make your florist's job easier when suggesting bouquets and other floral decorations. Bring pictures of the bridal gown and the bridesmaids' dresses, as well as a sample of the fabrics being used in those dresses. In many cases, it is the color of the bridesmaids' dresses that determines the palette of colors to be used in the wedding flowers. Also, bring along a picture of the wedding cake if possible. This will help in planning flowers or other decorations for the cake and the wedding cake table.

2. Make a list of all the members of the wedding party. Besides the bride and groom, this list should include the maid of honor, the other bridesmaids, the best man, the other groomsmen, the flower girl, and the ring-bearer, if any. Also list the parents, the grandparents, and any stepparents of both the bride and the groom, as well as any special honored guests. Include additional ushers and anyone who may be singing or reading at the wedding ceremony.

3. Obtain a floor plan of the site for both the wedding ceremony and the wedding reception. Make note of any unique architectural features, as well as colors and style of décor. Know what kinds of banquet equipment, such as tables and linens, are available at the wedding reception facility, and have the names of the staff people with whom you've spoken. Make a list of the flowers you will need, choosing from this list:

- The altar
- Columns and candelabra flanking the altar or creating a backdrop for the ceremony
- Archway or canopy
- The podium or lectern
- For Jewish weddings, the chuppah
- The ends of the pews or the aisle itself
- Communion rails
- Window ledges
- Entry vestibule
- Doors leading into the sanctuary
- The guest-book table
- Stair rails outside the entrance
- Entry area
- Place-card table
- Buffet table centerpieces
- Guest seating table arrangements
- Head table design
- Stage décor
- Wedding cake and cake table
- Restrooms
- Any unsightly areas that you may want to hide

Some of the Most Expensive Flowers	Inexpensive Flowers
Amaryllis	Even these low-end choices can look elegant in the right container or arrangement.
Anemone	
Delphinium	
French tulip	Carnation
Gardenia	Chrysanthemum
Gloriosa lily	Dahlia
Hydrangea	Daisy
Larkspur	Gerbera daisy
Lilac	Gladiolus
Lily (Oriental, Asiatic)	Ivy (which symbolizes wedding bliss)
Orchid	
Parrot tulip	Lady's mantle
Peony	Peruvian lily
Ranunculus	Queen Anne's lace
Rose	Stock
Sweet pea	Tulips (if they're in season)
Tuberose	
Viburnum	Zinnia

A word to horticulturalists who want to grow their own: don't. It's almost impossible to produce blooms as perfect as those that are available commercially, and homegrown varieties simply won't stand up to the rigors of formal arrangements, especially if they are being transported or preserved for any period. If you're a talented flower arranger and really want to do this on your own, buy the flowers wholesale on the Internet. You'll still save a bundle.

4. At the wedding flower consultation, ask to see photos of the florist's work, especially any that were taken at the venue you've chosen. Explain the feeling or mood you would like to create for the ceremony and the reception. Will it be dramatic and sophisticated? Elegant and romantic? Casual and upbeat? Does the venue present any particular challenges? (Do you want to hide unsightly areas?) Let the florist know what your budget is. If possible, bring copies of the wedding policies for each venue for reference. All of this information will guide your florist in making suggestions for the wedding flowers. Ask lots of questions:

• What flowers will be in season when your wedding takes place?

• If your budget is on the small side, how you can maximize your options?

• What are some less expensive alternatives to blooms beyond your price range?

• What are the hottest floral trends of the moment? Why do they work or not work?

• What is the most innovative concept the florist has recently brought to a design project?

• Which flowers are best for your wedding season? If you're marrying in the summertime, what are some hot weather no-no's?

• Has the florist done weddings at your ceremony or reception site before?

• Will the florist just drop off the flowers to your wedding or spend time at the site, setting up and making sure everything is in order? You'll pay more for a full-service florist, but you'll get what you pay for.

• How many weddings will the florist do on the same day or weekend as yours? You'll want to know that your florist won't be rushed on the day-of.

• Does the florist offer rental items—vases, potted plants, arches, trellises, candelabras, urns—or must you contact a rental company?

• Does the florist preserve bouquets after weddings? If this is something you want to do, plan for it before the wedding to ensure that your bouquet can be preserved directly afterward.

5. Shortly after your appointment, you should receive a written proposal, and there's a good chance it will be for more than you said you wanted to spend (duh). If you're shopping early enough, you still have time to look elsewhere. But if you have your heart set on this florist and you think you've made a pleasant connection, work with the florist to see how you can shave some of the cost (see "14 Ways to Save Money on Flowers," page 264) and consider a different approach to decorating the wedding. Can you live with a bare entryway, given that guests probably won't be spending more than a moment or two in the area? Can the same effect be achieved with a less costly flower? Work with your florist toward a viable solution. A talented florist can make even the most modest blooms go a long way.

As you can see, planning the flowers for a wedding is no simple undertaking. But it doesn't have to be difficult. With adequate preparation and a little forethought, combined with the expertise of a talented professional florist, the planning process can be as smooth as a silk wedding dress, and you will have created the kind of beautiful memories that last a lifetime.

Birth Month Flowers	
January	Carnation
February	Violet
March	Daffodil
April	Sweet pea
May	Lily of the valley
June	Rose
July	Larkspur
August	Gladiolus
September	Aster
October	Calendula
November	Chrysanthemum
December	Narcissus

7 Ways to Choose Flowers

1. If you've always had a favorite flower, here's your chance to surround yourself with it, providing it's in season.

2. Choose your favorite color and then go for the flowers in season.

3. Pick flowers that have special meanings: for instance, red if you want to honor the Chinese tradition, or magnolias for the southern belle.

4. Choose the flower with your favorite fragrance.

5. If there's a theme to the wedding, the flowers can address it: wildflowers for the medieval wedding, poinsettias and holly for a Christmas event.

6. Choose the flower of your birth month.

7. Consider allergies—maybe you don't want to use flowers at all!

How to Decorate Chairs

You can rent chair back covers online for under $2, sash included, from www.ChairCoversOnline.com (800-260-1030). But beware of shipping costs. You might be better off paying a local vendor a few dollars more if they pick up and deliver.

Or you can choose one of these inexpensive alternatives:

1. Make your own chair covers from dyed or stenciled pillowcases.

2. Decorate the chair with inexpensive strings of pearls or colored beads, Mardi Gras style.

3. Tie a tulle sash around the back of the chair and fasten it with a small silk wired flower.

4. Hang tassels or paper wedding bells from the corners of the backs of the chairs.

5. Wrap favors in colorful bags and attach them to the chairs with matching ribbon.

16 Alternatives to Traditional Centerpieces

1. Assign a different flower to each table and have the appropriate blooms on each.

2. Determine themes for your tables—famous works of art, favorite movies, local landmarks—and decorate each table with photos and memorabilia from these.

3. Rent statues of lovers from a local prop store. Each one can be different, and they can be draped with ivy garlands.

4. A large round goldfish bowl, with a little tulle decoration, can house pretty goldfish, which become favors (parceled out in plastic bags or miniature aquariums) at the end of the event.

5. Fill large bowls with floating candles.

6. Edible arrangements—everything from veggie bouquets and fruit sculptures to gingerbread houses for a holiday wedding—are all the rage. You'll find tons of ideas on the Internet, or check out Edible Arrangements, which now has hundreds of stores across the country.

7. Set out baskets heaped with bread and rolls or raw vegetables.

8. Hang colorful candies with ribbons on a potted shrub.

9. Fill large glass canisters or giant martini glasses, which can be found at florist supply shops, with penny candy. Each table can feature a different candy, and these can be ladled into individual bags as favors when the party's over.

10. Arrange origami sculptures on spray-painted branches, and send guests home with them as favors.

11. Put out bowls filled with fruit, dried flowers, penny candy, acorns, or anything else you can think of. (And they don't all have to be alike.)

12. Light candles of varying heights.

13. Decorate candelabras with ivy garlands.

14. Arrange framed personal photos.

15. Arrange balloons.

16. Your dessert platters can double as centerpieces. Individual cakes can be placed on each table in lieu of a wedding cake, or stacks of cupcakes can be set out in addition to cake or dessert. (Check out elegantcheesecakes.com, located in San Francisco, for one-of-a-kind cheesecake sculptures.)

A Wedding Cake Glossary

Our thanks to TYBinc.com for this sweet glossary:

Anniversary cake: A smaller version of the wedding cake to be enjoyed on a couple's first anniversary.

Backup cake: An undecorated sheet cake of the same flavor as your wedding cake, kept in the kitchen and used to serve a very large guest list after your display cake is used up.

Buttercream icing: The classic icing, made of butter, confectionery sugar, and milk. It is inexpensive and versatile in texture.

Centerpiece cake: A specialty cake that takes the place of flowers as your table decorations.

Chocolate ganache: A thick, delectable icing made of chocolate and heavy cream.

Croquembouche: A specialty wedding cake formed with profiteroles (cream puffs) filled with hazelnut pastry cream, dipped in hot caramel, and placed on top of one another.

Groom's cake: A smaller version of the wedding cake or one that reflects the groom's interests. Usually served at the engagement party or the rehearsal dinner.

Marzipan: Almond paste mixed with egg white and sugar; used for sculpting.

Raised tiers: Layers are separated by columns to make the cake appear taller.

Rolled fondant: This icing is made of gelatin, confectionery sugar, and water. It has a beautiful porcelain finish suitable for beading or tiny flowers, but is extremely sensitive to high temperatures.

Royal icing: Sugar and egg white mixture piped through a bag to create flowers and other decorations that are allowed to dry and then placed individually on the cake.

Solid cake: Cake layers are held together with icing as opposed to filling.

Tiers: Cakes that are stacked on top of one another to create a multi-layered cake.

Torted cakes: Cakes that are layered with mousse or fruit preserves.

Trompe l'oeil: Made of square layers instead of round ones, this specialty cake can be decorated with ribbon and wrapping paper to look like a pile of gifts. The perfect Christmas wedding cake!

Chidi Ogbuta's childhood dream of having a doll made in her likeness finally came true on September 22, 2007, when she and her husband, Innocent, renewed their vows. Chidi chose to celebrate the occasion by ordering a life-size wedding cake made in her own image. The six-layered cake, which took more than five weeks to make, stood five feet tall and was an exact replica of the bride in her wedding gown. The head, arms, and body were made of polymer clay, and the edible portion was butterscotch. The cake fed more than 500 guests. **COURTESY OF UCHE OGBONNA**

19 Ways to Save Money on Cake

1. Wedding cakes can be custom-ordered, or you can choose a standard style offered by the baker. The latter is much cheaper.

2. Go with a baker who doesn't necessarily specialize in wedding cakes.

3. Is there a culinary school near you? You might get a great deal on a cake if those classes are in session.

4. Register for the cake or ask a relative to present it as a gift.

5. Don't use the caterer's cake. He gets it from a supplier and marks up the already exorbitant price. Look for one on your own.

6. The most expensive aspect of decorating a wedding cake is getting the frosting smooth on the sides of the layers. If you ask for the sides to be covered in nuts, sprinkles, or cake crumbs, you can save a bundle.

This creation from Carrie's Cakes of Atlanta, Georgia, utilizes a variety of techniques and materials. **COURTESY OF CARRIE BIGGERS/PEPPER NIX PHOTOGRAPHY**

7. Don't get a wedding cake. Instead, cover the cake table with three or four gorgeous single-tier cakes decorated with fresh flowers.

8. Borrow the cake topper or ask for one as a gift.

9. Beautifully stacked cupcakes can substitute for a cake. Platters of them can double as centerpieces.

10. Rent a fake cake. There will be one real slice for you to cut, but the rest will be foam. Serve inexpensive sheet cake for dessert.

11. Skip the cake and offer a dessert buffet.

8 Ways to Save Money on Favors

Let's face it: most wedding favors are useless. Sure, people might go home and actually use the candle, and the sweet treats will no doubt be enjoyed on the ride home. But does anyone actually need these? Probably not, but they are still a standard element of wedding fare. Here are some ways to save.

1. Make a large donation to a charity in the names of your guests instead of buying favors. Leave cards on the tables indicating that you have done this.

2. Rent life-size cardboard cutouts of famous lovers and invite your guests to have their (Polaroid) photos taken with them instead of handing out favors.

3. Think about the businesses with which your close friends are connected. Can they help arrange special discounts for you? A friend in publishing might be able to help you purchase books for favors; your hairdresser might have access to beauty products; almost anyone who works in retail can get a store discount.

4. Don't buy expensive bags or boxes for favors. Wrap them in tulle or organza. Or put them in inexpensive paper shopping bags, each decorated with a small flower and thank-you note.

5. You might give out favors to each family instead of each guest, especially if the gift is something like a set of coasters or a frame.

6. Fill wedding cake treat boxes with slices of wedding cake to use as favors.

7. Give out copies of your favorite book. If you buy these on a nonreturnable basis directly from the publisher's special sales department, you might get as much as 50 percent off.

8. Some clever videographers can edit the film of your ceremony at the event while the reception is taking place and have finished CDs by the end of the evening to give out as favors.

Craftsman Eric Harshbarger created the ultimate wedding cake money-saver. His cake, made entirely of LEGO bricks, is 15 inches in diameter (at the largest tier). The cake is a traditional white with a yellow interior, and "slices" of the cake can actually be removed. It "feeds" 124. **COURTESY OF ERIC HARSHBARGER,** ERICHARSHBARGER.ORG

The Most Expensive Wedding Cake

On October 17, 2006, the world's most expensive wedding cake went on display at the Luxury Brands Bridal Show on Rodeo Drive in Beverly Hills, California. The cake, adorned with priceless diamonds and not meant for human consumption, ironically contained the finest ingredients. The cake was the result of a team effort by Mimi So Jewelers and cake designer Nahid of La Patisserie Artistique. Valued at a whopping $20 million, the cake was guarded by a team of uniformed security guards during the event.

12. Edible fruit arrangements can make fascinating centerpieces, and they double as an additional dessert course.

13. Use a small wedding cake for cutting and serve sheet cake (or something else entirely—ice cream and cookies, for instance) for dessert.

14. Skip the real cake; create your own by stacking cake-slice-shaped boxes into a giant cake shape. Fill each box with candy and treats. Your "cake" will double as favors.

15. When choosing a cake size and figuring out the per-slice cake-cutting charges, remember that approximately 10 percent of your guests will pass on the cake.

16. Stacked layers are cheaper than pillared layers and are more modern.

17. Fondant is more expensive than cream frosting, plus it's inedible. (But it does make for some gorgeous cake designs that can't be achieved without it.)

18. Skip the groom's cake—or bake it yourself.

19. If you insist on using a fancy cake cutter for that first slice, register for it.

Photography Tips

The guests will depart, the flowers will fade, and the dress will go on sale on eBay. But you'll keep your wedding photos forever, and that makes them one of the most important elements of the planning process. Here are some tips from Patrick Rice of PRFisheye.com:

1. Don't choose a photographer based on price alone. There will always be someone who will offer to take your wedding photos for a very low cost. In wedding photography as in many other aspects of life, you get what you pay for.

2. Start your search for a photographer by asking friends and family for referrals. Word of mouth is always the best and most honest form of advertising in any field. If your friends were happy with their photographer, look at their albums. If you like what you see, you will probably be happy with that studio as well. After getting referrals, check out photographer websites—you can view the work of hundreds of fine photographers in a short time. But don't choose a photographer strictly from what you see on a website. The sample photos you see online can help you eliminate some photographers you don't want to work with, but you still need to get up close and personal to determine whether the individual's personality meshes with your own and if you generally feel as though you are in good hands.

3. Determine whether the photo package is for a defined number of hours or for the entire wedding day. Many studios offer "all day" (get them to define the term "all day") coverage, which begins with the bride's preparations and extends through the end of the reception. The photographer should be willing to put this in writing along with all other details: the number (and names) of the photographers who will actually be taking pictures, how many pictures he'll be taking, how many proofs you will see, etc.

4. Talk to the photographer about his or her photographic style; is it traditional, photojournalistic, or a combination of both? Some older studios may have a very entrenched traditional style and may like to control the posing and lighting to create technically perfect photographs. Newer photographers who are almost exclusively photojournalistic in their approach and rarely pose a photo have gained popularity lately. Know that these photographers rely heavily on black-and-white photography for effect; if you prefer color, let them know. The vast majority of experienced wedding photographers are capable of creating both traditional and photojournalistic images to meet the needs of any couple, but these

How to Find a Photographer Anywhere in the World

Leading the way in wedding photojournalism, the Wedding Photo Journalist Association (WPJA) represents the most discriminating talent around the world technically, creatively, and visually. Qualified members have industry-leading standards, skills, and business integrity. The WPJA sponsors educational programs, including seminars, conventions, and workshops geared toward the wedding photojournalist. It also hosts wedding photojournalism contests, judged by top working photojournalists and news photo editors. Most importantly, the WPJA can assist destination brides in finding dependable photographers throughout the world.

styles are vastly different, and you need to agree on an approach to style.

5. Find out if the photographer belongs to any professional photographic association. As in so many professions, photographers' trade associations are a way for its members to stay current with the latest trends, styles, and techniques through continued education. These photographic associations meet on a monthly or yearly basis and give their membership the opportunity to network with other professional photographers.

6. Ask the photographer for professional credentials. There are numerous associate's, bachelor's, and master's degree programs available to photographers as well as certification. Photographers who have achieved these levels of education and/or been certified by a state or national association have proven that they are the best in the field. Remember, anyone with a camera can call himself a professional photographer. But not everyone will have a photographic degree or certification.

7. Make sure the photographer is aware of the lighting and electrical resources at the wedding venue. Photos might be difficult if

you've opted for a candlelight ceremony, and if the event is out-doors, special extension cables might be needed.

8. Introduce the photographer to as many close family members as possible, so he or she will know who to ask if there is a question. Plus, the familiarity might result in some special shots.

9. Very important: make a list of your "must-have" photos and give copies of the list to the photographer and videographer and their assistants as well as one or two people who are willing to check throughout the evening to see that all bases are being covered.

10. When you look at wedding albums, you're looking at collections of the photographer's very best work. These pictures have been retouched and have enjoyed the best photo processing available. Some of them haven't even been taken by the photographer you are thinking of hiring. So what you see is not necessarily what you're getting. Ask to look at real albums of recent events. Make

sure that at least a certain amount of retouching and cropping is included in the price of the package you choose.

11. Find out how the photos are being printed. You want "archival quality" printing, not ink-jet printing, which can fade after a few short years.

12. Delay the purchase of prints. Right after the wedding, you'll want to freeze every single moment in time. In a few short months, you'll come to see things in a slightly different perspective.

13. When you choose photos for your album, try to arrange them so that they tell the story of the day, from beginning to end. Mix photo sizes on facing pages to show ambiance, on the one hand, and detail, on the other. Let some photos "bleed" off the page while leaving others framed by white space. Think about adding mementos of the day to the album.

14. Make sure you own the copyright to the photos. Buy the proofs if you can.

Our Best Makeup Tip

Whether you opt for a professional makeup artist (highly recommended) or rely on your own abilities, it's a good idea to plan a dry run before the wedding. Apply the makeup you plan to wear (or have the pro do it), and then have yourself photographed at a local photo shop. You don't have to wear the dress, but it would be helpful if you wore your hair in the style you've picked out for the wedding. You won't be able to duplicate the conditions under which you'll be photographed at the wedding, and your photographer will have access to plenty of tricks to eliminate troublesome variables. But you will get a good idea of the look you're going to achieve. You might want to rethink the purple eye shadow. (Actually, that's our best makeup tip.)

4 Reasons Not to Go on a Diet Before Your Wedding

1. There's a good chance your dress won't fit properly on the day of your wedding.

2. You don't need the extra stress.

3. He loves you just the way you are.

4. One word: Photoshop.

24 Ways to Save Money on Photography

1. Go for a photography/videography package, which will cost less than hiring vendors for these services separately.

2. Go heavy on the black-and-white shots, which are less expensive than the color and in the end make for the most classic photos.

3. If you want to use more photos than the album specs allow, ask the photographer to put more photos on each page rather than adding to the page count, which is more expensive.

4. Avoid the gimmicky shots—your image superimposed over a close-up of the ring. They cost more and look cheesy for the most part.

5. Don't sign up for low-cost albums with irresistible prices. They often include as few as 20 photos, which won't be nearly enough to record all the faces and memories you'll want to preserve in your wedding album. The photographer will count on you to upgrade the album later on—at inflated per-photo prices. The more expensive albums with more pages might be a better value.

6. Limit the photography to just the ceremony and the first few hours of the reception. Friends can photograph the more intimate moments—the bride getting dressed, the bride and groom leaving for their honeymoon.

7. Place disposable cameras on the tables and ask guests to capture those special moments that professional photographers always miss. Just know that many of the shots will be wasted.

8. Ask friends to bring their digital cameras; ask specific people to cover certain aspects of the festivities so that they don't all assume that others are handling, for instance, the cake-cutting ceremony.

9. Have large-group photos taken so you can order copies of fewer prints when friends ask for them.

10. In negotiating a package, try to get the photographer to agree to a mini–photo shoot of the engagement party or another pre-wedding event. It will give you both a chance to determine the best ways to work together.

11. If you purchase film at a local photo shop, try to negotiate a bulk rate that includes developing.

12. Before you buy the disposable cameras you've chosen, check online for coupons. Just Google the brand together with the word *coupon*.

13. Rent a photo booth—the kind they have at amusement parks!

14. Limit the lavishness of the photo albums you order. One of the most beautiful albums we've seen was a miniature (just five inches square) of the same album ordered for the bride and groom. Proud parents will appreciate being able to tote these around for showing off, and they can borrow the larger counterpart from time to time.

15. Don't opt for high-definition; it costs more and just isn't worth it.

16. Hire a photographer who will give you the negatives and allow you to have inexpensive prints made at a local photo shop. You'll be able to get all the retouching and cropping done at a fraction of the cost.

17. Don't order paper proofs of your photos; request them online.

18. Order the bride and groom's wedding album from the photographer, but create your own albums for the individual families. Offer to lend your wedding album out for weeks at a time so others can enjoy it.

19. Hire a videographer who will give you the raw film, and then edit it yourself.

20. Ask two or three friends to shoot video footage at the wedding, then have a professional edit these together to make one master film.

21. Ask the videographer to bring only one camera instead of the two or more they usually use.

22. Talk to your videographer about the ways in which he can cut down on editing time. A pro will be able to do an "in-camera" edit, which will save you money.

23. Save money on your video by incorporating stock footage into your final film. If you're having a destination wedding in Hawaii, for instance, you can buy stock film that will offer far better coverage than your photographer will be able to manage.

24. Use iMovie instead of hiring a videographer.

19 Tips for Looking Good in Photographs

In a recent survey of customers conducted by Fujifilm, it was determined that 73 percent of women and 50 percent of men are uncomfortable in front of a camera. The biggest fears are that flaws will be visible and that the best images won't be captured. Being photographed on what you've come to think of as the biggest day of your life doesn't help to minimize the fear.

Ideally, you'll be working with a professional photographer who will guide you toward the best portraits. But if you're left to your own devices, here are some tips for getting the most bang out of your photo buck.

1. Study photographs of yourself that you like. Determine what makes them look good: Is your head turned a special way? Is the angle particularly flattering? Does the lighting show off your best features? Show these to your photographer and ask him or her to use these as guidelines.

2. Practice smiling. Take different photos of yourself with various smiles to determine which works best. (Don't smile just because a photographer tells you to.) If you have a toothy grin, smile with your mouth closed.

3. Think of something pleasant while you are being photographed. If you have issues, put them aside for now.

4. Practice your poses in the mirror until you find the ones you like best. (Include some goofy ones; they'll bring humor to your wedding album.)

5. But don't be shy about instigating some action shots. When you see the photographer approaching, do something—pick up a flower or some other object; take someone's hand and talk to them; peruse some nearby literature, or just pretend to. Allow the photography to capture who you really are.

6. If you're standing for a photo, stand with one foot slightly back; this is a model's trick for centering the spine. Keep your shoulders back and stand tall.

7. Turn your gaze to the side of the lens a little to avoid red-eye.

8. If you're scared of blinking at the flash, close your eyes just before the shot and then open them as the shot is being taken.

9. If you're heavy, stand slightly behind the people with whom you are being photographed.

10. If you have a large nose, avoid profiles.

11. If you're wearing glasses, tilt your chin down a little to avoid lens glare.

12. If you have a double chin, tilt your head up a little.

13. Photos taken from a lower angle can minimize a groom's bald spot.

14. Avoid direct sunlight, which will accentuate your features. Opt for indirect lighting.

15. Keep hair out of your face.

16. Easy on the lip liner, and keep lipstick colors soft. Dark colors will appear darker in your photos.

17. Avoid sparkly powders and eye shadows; they'll be exaggerated in photos.

18. Blot your face often with a tissue or dab on some face powder to avoid shiny or sweaty spots on your face.

19. If you wake up on the morning of the wedding with a pimple or blemish, cover it up. Trying to remove it can make matters far worse.

Choose a Videographer Who . . .

- Has solid experience
- Will show up at your wedding, as opposed to sending assistants
- Includes all details—titles, montages, music—in the package you are being offered and is willing to put it all in writing
- Is willing to stay overtime if necessary (for a fee)
- Carries liability insurance
- Has reasonable cancellation and guarantee policies

How to Choose a Videographer

Lisa Robinson, the founder of award-winning Crystal Clear Video Productions in Lehigh Valley, Pennsylvania, has been producing cinematic-style wedding videos since 2001. Here's what Lisa has to say about choosing a competent videographer:

Photographs are great, but they reflect only moments in time. A wedding video, on the other hand, can capture the mood, feelings, and emotions of the event, and it often features the special interactions that exist among family and guests.

Choosing the right wedding videographer can be confusing. Below is some advice to clear away the confusion, compliments of WeddingApproved.com.

1. If you are basing your choice solely on price, you may be in for a huge disappointment when your wedding video arrives. Most people are unaware of the time and effort that good wedding videographers spend on filming and editing a video. In most cases, prices will reflect their achievements. A good wedding videographer will spend up to 15 weeks to complete your video. The editing process is lengthy and involved; it can take up to one hour to edit just two to five minutes of footage. Here, especially, you get what you pay for.

2. Choose a wedding videographer who uses only professional "3-chip" cameras for the best picture quality. Make sure that the person you hire uses more than one camera to ensure that nothing is missed on your day; having more than one camera will make for a more interesting wedding video. Having multiple angles, especially during the ceremony, allows the editor to transition between two or more different shots. The result is beautiful.

3. Your wedding videographer should be someone who is personable and friendly. He or she should be flexible and willing to listen and consider all of your ideas and needs. Ask as many questions as you can about their process to determine if this person has the right temperament for you.

4. In addition to watching a demo video, it is always a good idea to view a full-length video taken by your prospective wedding videographer. Usually only the best shots are used in a demo video. The emotional impact is much more prevalent in a demo because it is shorter in length. You'll want to watch a full-length video to see if it is just as impressive.

5. If your wedding videographer is creative, he or she will know how to tell your story via the editing process. When you look at sample videos, ask yourself if you feel as if you have come to know the family. What does the video say about the bride and groom? Does it include a range of emotions as well as a variety of situations? Look for subtleties and details when you view previous work.

6. Make sure that your wedding videographer uses wireless microphones to capture every word that is spoken during the ceremony.

7. An experienced wedding videographer will know how to direct the people who are being photographed. Most footage of your day will consist of candid moments, but a real professional knows how to gently direct these for the best possible results. Most importantly, he or she will do this without bullying the guests or making them feel stiff and uncomfortable by getting in their way and giving them cause to feel self-conscious.

The Lowdown on High Def

High-definition (HD) videography employs the latest technology to provide you with the very best possible picture and sound quality. The picture that most of us are used to seeing on our TV has at most 480 visible lines of detail, whereas HD video or TV has as many as 1,080. The resulting image is sharper and clearer than anything you've seen before. If you don't own an (expensive) high-definition TV and an even pricier Blu-ray disc player, you won't get the total benefit of HD technology. Many wedding photographers don't even offer it. If you do choose the HD option, make sure that the disc you receive is compatible with your own equipment. On the one hand, you may want to spring for HD videography in anticipation of a future upgrade. On the other, you might want to spend those extra bucks on something else.

The Most Popular Wedding Songs

DiscJockeys.com, an online directory of entertainment services, has provided us with the following lists of the top wedding songs as requested by brides and grooms around the country. For more information, visit DiscJockeys.com.

PRELUDE

(played prior to the ceremony, while guests are arriving)

1. "Moonlight Sonata" (Beethoven)
2. "Isn't It Romantic" (Glenn Miller)
3. "Water Music" (Handel)
4. "Ave Maria" (Schubert/Gounod)
5. "The Four Seasons" (Vivaldi)
6. "Greensleeves" (traditional)
7. "Rhapsody in Blue" (Gershwin)
8. "God Only Knows" (The Beach Boys)
9. "As Time Goes By (A Kiss Is Just a Kiss)" (Tony Bennett)
10. "Arioso" (Bach)
11. "Ode to Joy" from the Ninth Symphony (Beethoven)
12. "Brandenburg Concerto No. 2" (Bach)
13. "Gloria" (Vivaldi)
14. "Unchained Melody" (The Righteous Brothers)

PROCESSIONAL AND BRIDAL MUSIC

(played as the family, wedding party, and bride walk down the aisle)

1. "Bridal Chorus (Here Comes the Bride)" from *Lohengrin* (Wagner)
2. "Trumpet Voluntary in D (The Prince of Denmark's March)" (Clarke or Purcell)
3. "Canon in D" (Pachelbel)
4. "The Four Seasons" (Vivaldi)
5. "Water Music" (Handel)
6. "What a Wonderful World" (Louis Armstrong)
7. "Unforgettable" (Nat King Cole)
8. "I Can't Help Falling in Love" (Elvis Presley)
9. "When a Man Loves a Woman" (Percy Sledge)
10. "In My Life" (The Beatles)
11. "March" from *Lohengrin* (Wagner)

Sheet music, ca. 1900 **AUTHORS' COLLECTION**

INTERLUDE MUSIC

(played during the ceremony)

1. "Ave Maria" (Schubert)
2. "Amazing Grace" (traditional)
3. "La Traviata" (Verdi)
4. "Sheep May Safely Graze" (Bach)
5. "And I Love Her" (The Beatles)
6. First movement (allegro) of "Primavera" (Vivaldi)
7. "Love Me Tender" (Elvis Presley)
8. "Für Elise" (Beethoven)
9. "We've Only Just Begun" (The Carpenters)
10. "Have I Told You Lately" (Van Morrison)

RECESSIONAL MUSIC

(played as the new husband and wife walk up the aisle together)

1. "Wedding March" from *A Midsummer Night's Dream* (Mendelssohn)
2. "Ode to Joy" from the Ninth Symphony (Beethoven)
3. "Hallelujah Chorus" from *The Messiah* (Handel)
4. "Trumpet Tune" (Purcell)
5. "Magnificat in D" (Bach)
6. "The Long and Winding Road" (The Beatles)
7. "I Got You (I Feel Good)" (James Brown)
8. "How Sweet It Is" (James Taylor)

9. "Then He Kissed Me" (The Crystals)

10. "I Got You, Babe" (Sonny and Cher)

RECEPTION MUSIC

First-Dance Music
(first dance as husband and wife)

1. "Unforgettable" (Nat King Cole)

2. "Can't Help Falling in Love" (Elvis Presley)

3. "Can I Have This Dance?" (Ann Murray)

4. "The Way You Look Tonight" (Frank Sinatra)

5. "It Had to Be You" (Harry Connick Jr.)

6. "What a Wonderful World" (Louis Armstrong)

7. "Endless Love" (Diana Ross and Lionel Richie)

8. "I Cross My Heart" (George Strait)

9. "I Swear" (John M. Montgomery or All 4 One)

10. "A Whole New World" (Peabo Bryson and Regina Belle)

11. "As Time Goes By (A Kiss Is Just a Kiss)" (Tony Bennett)

12. "When You Say Nothing at All" (Allison Krauss)

13. "Faithfully" (Journey)

14. "No Ordinary Love" (Sade)

15. "Here and Now" (Luther Vandross)

16. "I Can Love You Like That" (John M. Montgomery)

17. "Power of Love" (Celine Dion)

18. "Tonight I Celebrate My Love" (Roberta Flack and Peabo Bryson)

19. "Everything I Do (I Do for You)" (Bryan Adams)

20. "When a Man Loves a Woman" (Percy Sledge or Michael Bolton)

21. "All My Life" (Linda Ronstadt and Aaron Neville)

22. "I'll Be There" (Mariah Carey)

23. "On Bended Knee" (Boyz II Men)

24. "At Last" (Etta James)

25. "Don't Know Much" (Linda Ronstadt and Aaron Neville)

26. "From This Moment On" (Shania Twain and Bryan White)

27. "Our Love Is Here to Stay" (Harry Connick Jr.)

28. "Unchained Melody" (The Righteous Brothers)

Father-Daughter Dance

1. "My Girl" (The Temptations)

2. "Thank Heaven for Little Girls" (Gigi)

3. "Just the Way You Are" (Billy Joel)

4. "Unforgettable" (Nat King Cole and Natalie Cole)

5. "The Wind Beneath My Wings" (Bette Midler)

6. "My Dad" (Paul Petersen)

7. "Hero" (Mariah Carey)

8. "Butterfly Kisses" (Bob Carlisle)

9. "Times of Your Life" (Paul Anka)

10. "A Song for My Daughter" (Steve Moser, Mikki Viereck, Ray Allaire)

11. "Can You Feel the Love Tonight" (Elton John)

Live or Memorex?

Choosing between a band and a DJ for a wedding reception was once a much more difficult decision than it is today, when DJs are seen as less a way of scrimping and more a way of providing guests with a greater range of entertainment.

Choose a DJ if . . .

You want a variety of music, especially if you want to throw in some ethnic or little-known family favorites. Hearing this music in its natural form, by original artists, is far different from hastily learned versions.

• You want continuous music. (Bands take breaks.)

• Space is at a premium. A five-piece band, including a drum kit, can take up valuable dance room. If the room is small to begin with, live music can overpower the event.

• You want flexibility. DJs can accommodate requests more easily than bands can.

• Money is an issue. A band can cost as much as $15,000 for a five-hour event; a good DJ can be had for $2,500.

Performance Fees for High-Profile Entertainers

There wasn't a dry eye in the house when Percy Sledge sang "When a Man Loves a Woman" at the wedding of rocker Steven Van Zandt to Maureen Santoro on New Year's Eve of 1982. The legendary Sledge has since retired, but if music soothes your soul and you have money to burn, here are the performance fees for 45 entertainers, all of whom have been known to play private parties. Note that these prices represent the artist fee only and do not include costs for all the ancillary expenses necessary to stage a performance (stage, sound, lights, stagehands, backline, artist catering, air, hotel and ground, etc.). Often these associated costs can run much higher than the artist fee.

1. Jennifer Holliday $12,500
2. Duke Ellington Orchestra $15,000
3. Ru Paul $15,000
4. Blood, Sweat and Tears $30,000
5. Peabo Bryson $30,000
6. Ladysmith Black Mambazo $30,000
7. Village People $35,000
8. Burt Bacharach $50,000
9. The O Jays $50,000
10. The Pointer Sisters $50,000
11. Max Weinberg 7 $50,000
12. Smash Mouth $65,000
13. Kellie Pickler $75,000–$100,000
14. Lucinda Williams $75,000–$100,000
15. Gypsy Kings $100,000
16. Allison Krauss and Union Station $100,000
17. Brian Setzer Orchestra $100,000
18. Yo Yo Ma $100,000
19. Aretha Franklin $125,000
20. Wynton Marsalis $125,000–$150,000
21. Tony Bennett $250,000
22. Mary J. Blige $250,000
23. Bob Dylan $250,000
24. Norah Jones $250,000
25. Pink $250,000
26. Kelly Clarkson $300,000
27. Alanis Morrisette $350,000
28. Usher $350,000
29. Alicia Keys $500,000
30. ZZ Top $500,000
31. Cher $1,000,000
32. Neil Diamond $1,000,000
33. The Eagles $1,000,000
34. Bette Midler $1,000,000
35. Billy Joel $1,000,000
36. Sting $1,000,000
37. Stevie Wonder $1,000,000
38. Elton John $1,500,000
39. Prince $1,500,000
40. Eric Clapton $3,000,000
41. Celine Dion $3,000,000
42. Madonna $3,000,000
43. Barbra Streisand $3,000,000
44. U2 $3,000,000
45. The Rolling Stones $3,000,000 +

12. "The Way You Look Tonight" (Frank Sinatra)
13. "Have I Told You Lately" (Rod Stewart)
14. "Because You Loved Me" (Celine Dion)
15. "My Heart Will Go On" (Celine Dion)
16. "Have I Told You Lately" (Van Morrison)
17. "What a Wonderful World" (Louis Armstrong)
18. "Through the Years" (Kenny Rogers)
19. "Daddy's Girl" (Peter Cetera)
20. "Sunrise, Sunset" (*Fiddler on the Roof*)
21. "Isn't She Lovely" (Stevie Wonder)
22. "Father's Eyes" (Amy Grant)
23. "In Your Eyes" (Peter Gabriel)

Mother-Son Dance

1. "Don't Know Much" (Linda Ronstadt and Aaron Neville)
2. "Butterfly Kisses" (Bob Carlisle)
3. "IOU" (Jimmy Dean)
4. "Moon Dance" (Van Morrison)
5. "Through the Years" (Kenny Rogers)
6. "Because You Loved Me" (Celine Dion)
7. "Just the Way You Are" (Billy Joel)
8. "Unforgettable" (Nat King Cole and Natalie Cole)
9. "What a Wonderful World" (Louis Armstrong)
10. "In This Life" (Bette Midler)
11. "You're the Inspiration" (Chicago)
12. "Hero" (Mariah Carey)

13. "Wind Beneath My Wings" (Bette Midler)

14. "Friends" (Elton John)

15. "Blessed" (Elton John)

16. "In Your Eyes" (Peter Gabriel)

17. "A Song for My Son" (Steve Moser, Mikki Viereck, Ray Allaire)

18. "Sunrise, Sunset" (*Fiddler on the Roof*)

19. "In My Life" (The Beatles)

20. "Ever I Saw Your Face" (Roberta Flack)

21. "I Wish You Love" (Natalie Cole)

22. "Stand by Me" (Ben E. King)

Bridal Party Dance Music
(the dance including the bride and groom, bridesmaids and groomsmen, and family members)

1. "That's What Friends Are For" (Dionne and Friends; Elton John; Gladys Knight; and Stevie Wonder)

2. "Can You Feel the Love Tonight" (Elton John)

3. "Friends in Low Places" (Garth Brooks)

4. "We Are Family" (Sister Sledge)

5. "Friends" (Elton John)

6. "Heroes and Friends" (Randy Travis)

7. "In Your Eyes" (Peter Gabriel)

8. "Celebration" (Kool and The Gang)

Cutting the Cake

1. "Cut the Cake" (Average White Band)

2. "How Sweet It Is" (James Taylor)

3. "Sugar, Sugar" (The Archies)

4. "I Wanna Grow Old with You" (Adam Sandler)

5. "Hit Me with Your Best Shot" (Pat Benatar)

6. "When I'm 64" (The Beatles)

7. "Recipe for Love" (Harry Connick Jr.)

8. "That's Amore" (Dean Martin)

9. "Happy Together" (The Turtles)

10. "Pour Some Sugar on Me" (Def Leppard)

11. "I Got You, Babe" (Sonny and Cher)

12. "Love and Marriage" (Frank Sinatra)

Garter and Bouquet Toss
(if you must)

1. "The Stripper" (David Rose)

2. "Legs" (ZZ Top)

3. "You Sexy Thing" (Hot Chocolate)

4. "Oh Yeah!" (Yello)

5. "Macho Man" (Village People)

6. "Theme" from *Mission Impossible* (Danny Elfman)

7. "Wild Thing" (The Troggs or Tone Loc)

8. "Let's Get It On" (Marvin Gaye)

9. "Bad Boys" (Inner Circle)

10. "Kiss" (Prince)

11. "Do Ya Think I'm Sexy" (Rod Stewart)

12. "Pretty Woman" (Roy Orbison)

13. "Hungry Eyes" (Eric Carmen)

14. "U Can't Touch This" (MC Hammer)

15. "Shameless" (Garth Brooks)

16. "Whipped Cream" (theme from *The Dating Game*) (Herb Alpert)

Last Dance

1. "Last Dance" (Donna Summer)

2. "New York, New York" (Frank Sinatra)

3. "Good Riddance (Time of Your Life)" (Green Day)

4. "From This Moment On" (Shania Twain and Bryan White)

5. "Save the Best for Last" (Vanessa Williams)

6. "Wonderful Tonight" (David Kersh)

7. "Could I Have This Dance" (Anne Murray)

8. "You're Still the One" (Shania Twain)

9. "Closing Time" (Semisonic)

10. "Unforgettable" (Nat King Cole and Natalie Cole)

11. "I've Had the Time of My Life" (Bill Medly and Jennifer Warnes)

12. "How Your Love Makes Me Feel" (Diamond Rio)

13. "Goodnight, Sweetheart" (David Kersh)

14. "The Party's Over" (Nat King Cole)

15. "Goodnight, Sweetheart" (Spaniels)

16. "What a Wonderful World" (Louis Armstrong)

17. "The Dance" (Garth Brooks)

18. "Truly, Madly, Deeply" (Savage Garden)

19. "Always and Forever" (Heatwave)

How to Choose a DJ

"They didn't play what I wanted."

"They played music that I specifically asked them not to play."

"The guy showed up with a home stereo system and some CDs."

"Mine never showed up!"

These are just a few of the common complaints people have had about wedding DJs. Now they know: not all DJs are created equal, just as no two bands are exactly alike. Being a great DJ isn't as easy as it looks. Neither is finding one. Your best bet is to go with someone who played at an event you enjoyed. Beyond that, get referrals from satisfied friends. When you do finally meet with your prospective DJs, keep these criteria in mind:

Professional DJs:

- Use professional equipment, not a home stereo
- Will meet with you and help you plan your reception
- Have many references available for you to talk to
- Do not subcontract out your event unless they tell you at the time of contract signing
- Are set up on time and ready by the time your first guest arrives
- Abide by your wishes and don't just play what they like
- Have liability insurance
- Do not drink alcoholic beverages on the job
- Do not try to be the life of the party (the bride and groom should never have to share the limelight)
- Do not invite potential clients to watch them perform at your event, since any DJ trying to sell his or her services to someone else cannot give your event 100 percent attention
- Use contracts, to protect both parties

7 Ways to Save Money on Entertainment

1. Keep it simple and go for a singular approach: hire just a keyboardist, a flutist, a harpist, or a blues or folk guitarist to handle all of the ceremony music.

2. DJs cost a lot less than bands and are more in fashion now than ever. They can play anything, thereby entertaining a range of guests, and are especially helpful in regard to ethnic music and customs.

3. Use less-experienced DJs who need the gig to build their careers.

4. For the ceremony, hire the church choir, or check with local music schools for string quartets.

5. For destination weddings, hire local performers.

6. Use canned music for the ceremony and dispense with live performers. Or use canned music for everything. In these technological times, there's liable to be a teenager on your guest list who can handle it all.

7. Limit the number of musicians and performers—hire a talented five-piece band instead of a seven-piece band.

Limo Basics

Don't even think of hiring a limousine for your wedding without getting referrals from friends. This is one area where extra care pays off, as the trade is filled with drivers who promise the world and show up with a lot less—if they show up at all. If personal recommendations are not possible, check with the Better Business Bureau before you book to make sure the company does not have outstanding complaints. Remember that, in a pinch, you can always call a cab. Some tips:

1. Make sure the driver knows the itinerary: who is being picked up, where they are located, and how they can be reached by cell phone. Guests should also have the contact information for the driver so they can report any problems.

2. Drive the limo route yourself before the wedding to determine how much time will really be needed. Do your dry run on the same day of the week and at the same time the wedding will take place.

3. Be sure your contract indicates exactly which car you are renting. It should also indicate a plan B in case the car becomes unavailable for an unavoidable reason.

4. Is the company properly insured?

13 Ways to Save Money on Transportation

1. Have out-of-town guests stay at the same hotel and negotiate a special price for the block of rooms you'll need.

2. Can the hotel arrange for shuttle service to the wedding site? Negotiate this as part of a package deal.

3. Shop around for limo services, as their prices vary widely.

4. Use minivans when possible to chauffeur large groups.

5. Instead of having expensive limos pick up wedding party members, consider a decorated "wedding bus."

6. Check with antique car societies in your area to find out if a vintage car can be rented. (Often the owner of the car will act as chauffeur.)

7. Hire limousines to bring the wedding party to the ceremony site, but arrange for cheaper transportation for the departure. Perhaps the groomsmen can lend rides.

8. White limos are more expensive than black limos. Town cars are cheapest of all.

9. If you want the limo bar to be stocked for guests, BYOB.

A Free Ride?

On April 10, 2006, bride-to-be Julie Henley, her bridegroom, and 16 members of the wedding party were rescued by and driven to the wedding in a Phoenix fire truck after the stretch Hummer they were riding in caught fire.

They arrived with the sirens and lights flashing. The wedding guests, who knew about the fire, were standing outside clapping and cheering.

10. Hire town cars instead of limousines for all but the immediate family.

11. Don't use the valet service; guests won't mind parking their own cars as long as there is ample space near the entrance to the venue.

12. If the wedding is near your home, honor tradition by having the wedding party walk to the ceremony. This is how it was done centuries ago. Your little parade will no doubt entertain onlookers. Don't forget to include a musician (anything from a guitar to a kazoo will do) in the entourage.

13. Funeral homes sometimes rent out their limos when they're not using them, and no, it's not bad luck—as long as you avoid the hearse.

It never fails: no matter how much money is spent on food, the bride and groom always leave the wedding hungry. Arrange to have a small meal waiting in the limo for them to share as they make their getaway.

On the Importance of Supplying the Chauffeur with Directions

In August 2005, eight wealthy and powerful guests flew into Atlantic City, New Jersey, to attend a wedding between two well-respected and well-connected members of a smuggling syndicate with whom they had all done business. But the limousines that met each guest at the city's airport took them to a different destination—straight to jail.

The "wedding" was in fact the climax of a sting operation. The happy couple whom the "guests" had known and trusted for so long were actually undercover FBI agents.

Chapter 4

Now and Forever

Here comes the bride—at last!

The months of planning and obsessing, the challenges of the color choices and logistics questions, and the biggest hurdle of them all—paying for it—have brought you here, to your wedding day. But questions remain: Where does everyone stand? What if something goes wrong? And most importantly, how do you relax and enjoy it all?

This chapter tells you how, offering scenarios for a variety of wedding processionals as well as a guide to who's who and what's what on the big day. If the in-laws have suddenly launched into an argument over the seating arrangement, if the flower girl has spilled soda on your wedding gown, if the thought of delivering a wedding toast makes you break out in hives, we've got you covered. And even if it all gets to be too much and you think you might faint at the altar, we've got a quick fix for that too.

Then, of course, there's the getaway—alone at last! But where to? The honeymoon capital of the world? There are three of them. A beach? There are literally thousands. We've covered the very best of these, but before you settle on one, you might want to consider our menu of more adventurous choices: the Grand Canals of Venice, a rain forest in China, a castle in Patagonia, or even a trans-Siberian train trek.

Even then, the wedding isn't officially over—there are thank-you cards to think about (we've included some creative ways to show your gratitude, not only to your guests but also to the community of which you are now a part), as well as the business and financial aspects of becoming a couple. Does a name change make sense? How are bank accounts best combined, and what sort of reception can newlyweds expect from the IRS?

Finally, there's the culmination of all the preparations and expense, the matrimonial prize toward which you have worked so hard. We've got some ideas on how to get you

"The Marriage," lithograph,
1846 LIBRARY OF CONGRESS

started, from tips on handling PNS (Post-Nuptial Syndrome) to putting the love that made you get married in the first place into every day of your life. Love, after all, is the most important tool you will need as you make the journey from Planet Wedding to Planet Married. May the stars in the solar system shine on you always.

Vintage postcard, ca. 1910 **AUTHORS' COLLECTION**

Religious Wedding Ceremonies

Most weddings throughout the world have their origins in one religion or another. But that doesn't make them the same or even similar, as even weddings of the same religion can vary within regions. Jewish weddings among Reform Jews are different from those of Conservative and Orthodox sects. Intermarriage and commerce have further blurred the lines between religions, and today a wedding ceremony can be officiated by more than one religious representative. Finally, ceremonies may vary among clergypeople, who may add their own unique imprints, and couples who choose to create "new traditions" are common today. Thus, the following should be viewed as basic configurations that can take a variety of forms.

The Protestant Wedding

The Protestant wedding provides what is probably the most common format for the majority of modern American weddings. Protestant elements have been used by almost every religion and culture, although sometimes with a different significance. Details such as the order of the processional, the manner in which rings are exchanged, and the prayers and vows spoken can change from one culture and preference to another, but the wedding service follows this basic order:

Musical prelude: Music is played and soloists perform as guests are seated by ushers.

Pre-processional: Ushers and groomsmen escort the members of the wedding party down the aisle. The parents of the bride and groom are seated. The person who will officiate over the ceremony enters. The groom and best man enter and take their positions at the altar.

Processional: Here comes the bride. The bridesmaids, followed by a maid or matron of honor, enter and approach the altar. A flower girl, tossing petals, and a ring-bearer make their way down the aisle. As the processional music begins, the guests rise as the bride is escorted down the aisle by her father, by both parents, or by whoever is "giving away the bride."

Giving away the bride: At the altar, a father may take the bride's right hand and place it in the hand of the officiant, who then passes it to the groom.

> "With this ring I thee wed, with my body I thee worship, and with my worldly goods I thee endow."
> — *The Book of Common Prayer*

Opening words: The officiant opens the ceremony with a prayer and invocation that welcomes the guests. A biblical theme usually suggests the importance of marriage.

Lighting of candles: Here or at another time in the ceremony, the bride and groom may carry a lit candle that is then used to light an unlit candle, signifying the union of the bride and groom in some cultures and honoring the departed in others.

> "...for fairer or fouler, for better or worse, for richer or poorer ..."
> — From an old Anglo-Saxon wedding vow

Exchange of vows: Vows are recited. In some cultures, the officiant reads vows and the bride and groom respond; in others, the bride and groom may make their promises to one another directly. Guests are asked whether anyone present objects to the union.

Exchange of rings: The bride and groom exchange rings, each placing a ring on the third finger of the other's left hand.

Marriage pronouncement: The officiant pronounces the couple man and wife. They kiss.

Blessing of the couple: A final prayer is read.

Recessional: Music is played as the wedding party and attendants move to the back of the room to form a receiving line, in which they greet each of their guests. As they leave the receiving line, guests congregate outside, where they throw rice, a symbol of fertility, at the newlyweds when they exit.

Reception: A grand banquet (held at another venue if the ceremony took place in a house of worship) featuring music and dancing follows. A first dance is reserved especially for the bride and groom. The bride then dances with her father as guests join in. The newlyweds feed one another pieces of wedding cake. The groom may remove a garter from the bride's leg and toss it into the crowd. The bride then throws her bouquet to the eligible women in attendance; she who catches it is believed to be the next to marry.

Getaway: Amid well-wishing and happy tears, the bride and groom leave for their honeymoon in a decorated car. Alone at last!

The Buddhist Wedding

Whereas in many religions, both Asian and Western, marriage is a sacrament and an essential aspect of religious duty, the Buddhist marriage is purely a secular affair. A Buddhist's decision to wed is not affected by or intertwined with a desire to continue the Buddhist faith. Marriage is considered a personal concern; there are no religious directions on whether or not one should marry or remain unwed. There is also no formal wedding service. This does not mean, however, that Buddhist weddings don't have a rich tradition. Buddhist communities have fashioned a variety of creative wedding ceremonies out of Asian and Buddhist rituals.

Pre-wedding rituals: Many Buddhist weddings are arranged. A wedding broker suggests a match and is normally responsible for the match between the bride and groom. The wedding broker visits families of the area, assessing their wealth, health, social status, and prospects. When visiting families, the broker can easily suggest a match and have the parents of the two families meet. After several more visits, including one with an astrologer, the couple to be wed meet and (hopefully) agree to the union. A dowry is negotiated, and an astrologer chooses a wedding date.

The wedding ceremony: The wedding day is begun at a local temple where the bride and groom separately ask for the blessings of Buddha. Both bride and groom are then dressed in outfits traditional to their region.

At the astrologically designated wedding time, the bride and groom are individually taken to the shrine room of their local temple or a hall hired for the occasion. Here the bride and groom see each other for the first time.

The ceremony begins as the entire assembly recites the Vandana, Tisarana, and Pancasila readings. Monks may be present. The couple then light the candles and incense sticks surrounding Buddha's image and offer him the flowers within the shrine. There is no assigned set of marriage vows, but the bride and groom do recite their expected undertakings using the *Sigilovdda Sutta* as a guide.

After the vows are spoken, the bride and groom can exchange rings. If monks are present, the marriage vows are both preceded and followed by their chanting.

After the wedding: Once officially married, the couple receives their guests at a festive reception.

The Jewish Wedding

Most Jewish wedding ceremonies are held under a chuppah, a kind of canopy, under an open sky to recall God's blessing to Abraham that his children would be "as the stars of Heaven" (Genesis 15:5). Although today most weddings are held indoors, the chuppah is still used, and the sentiment remains the same.

Pre-wedding fast: The bride and groom fast on the day of their wedding and say special prayers for the occasion. Some grooms place ashes on their forehead, a practice mentioned in the Talmud, to recall the destruction of the Holy Jewish Temple.

Signing of the ketubah: Just prior to the wedding ceremony, in a special area apart from the seated guests, the rabbi who will perform the ceremony reviews the *ketubah,* the written marriage contract. The groom accepts its terms, and it is signed by two

---

The Catholic Wedding

Many Catholic couples marry in April, as that is when Lent is over. According to a popular rhyme, "Marry in Lent, you'll live to repent."

The wedding takes place during a full Mass.

The priest blesses the Catholic couple's wedding rings.

The bride may place her flowers in front of the statue of the Virgin Mary.

The Catholic wedding party allows for many individuals to participate, as readers, altar boys, deacons, and ministers of the Eucharist.

A Jewish couple prepare to marry beneath a chuppah. COURTESY OF GARDENSTATEPHOTO.COM

Circling the groom: Before she takes her place at the groom's side, the bride circles him seven times. Some say this is a reference to Jeremiah 31:22, in which the prophet says that a woman encompasses and protects a man. Others claim it is done just as Joshua circled the wall of Jericho seven times, after which the walls of Jericho fell. It is said that once the bride has circled the groom, the walls between them will fall and their souls will be united.

Kiddushin: This is the first part of the Jewish marriage ceremony and includes the betrothal blessings said over wine and the giving of the ring. The groom places the ring on the bride's right forefinger, the right side symbolizing love. (She may move it to another finger after the ceremony.) Because this portion of the ceremony represents a special gift given by the groom to his bride, Jewish law does not provide for a double-ring ceremony. If the groom chooses to wear a ring, it may be presented at another time.

Reading of the ketubah: The rabbi reads the ketubah, then hands it to the groom, who presents it to his bride. At this point in the ceremony, the rabbi may make his comments.

Nesuin: The second part of the ceremony consists of a reading of the Seven Blessings from the Talmud by honored guests. Each passage celebrates the joy that is felt for the couple and the hopes of harmony and love for the future.

witnesses. It is said that from this moment the couple is actually married.

Bedekin: This custom dates back to the biblical story in which Jacob was deceived into marrying Leah, who was hidden behind a veil, instead of his chosen bride Rachel. To make sure he isn't repeating Jacob's mistake, the groom confronts the bride and then covers her face with her veil as a special blessing is read. The custom also refers to a story in the Torah of Rebecca seeing her husband Isaac for the first time and immediately covering herself with a veil in modesty.

Processional: There are no hard and fast rules about the order of the processional. Members of the wedding party stand beneath the chuppah, and once they are in place the groom enters, most typically escorted by his parents. Brides are not "given away" in Jewish weddings; instead, the bride is escorted to the chuppah by her parents, and this signifies her entrance into her husband's domain.

> "I'm going to marry a Jewish woman because I like the idea of getting up Sunday morning and going to the deli."
> — Michael J. Fox

Breaking the glass: After final comments are made, the ceremony ends with a ritual in which the groom shatters glass (usually a drinking glass and usually wrapped in cloth to prevent injury).

Recessional: As in other weddings, the bridal party proceeds to the back of the room to receive guests.

Yichud: Before the bride and groom are swept away in the frenzy of the celebration, they are escorted to a private room where they may share a small meal and their first precious moments as husband and wife in privacy.

Reception: Music, dancing, and a feast, complete with their own traditional rituals, follow.

Getaway: Mr. and Mrs. Newlywed are off on their honeymoon.

4 Possible Reasons for Breaking the Glass at a Jewish Wedding

This final act in the ceremony is usually accompanied by cheering and well-wishing all around. Its origin lies with an incident recorded in the Talmud in which Mar, the son of Ravina and Rav Ashi, deliberately smashed costly glass at their sons' weddings to put a stop to the raucous dancing and celebrating. As is typical of so many wedding traditions, there is much debate as to the significance of the rite. Here are four contenders.

1. The broken glass reminds Jews that even at joyous occasions, one must recall those individuals, Jew and non-Jew alike, who do not have the freedom to celebrate either religiously or publicly.

2. The glass represents the relationship of the couple. Just as glass cannot be unbroken, so too is the marriage between them binding.

3. It is a representation of the sexual consummation of the marriage by the breaking of the hymen.

4. It is an act of noisemaking designed to chase away demons that might attack the couple as they pass through that liminal period between unmarried and married status.

The Muslim Wedding

Islam recognizes marriage as an act of devotion to God and a solemn pact that must be respected by the couple throughout their lives. Muslim weddings attach great significance to customs. And as anyone who has had the good fortune of attending a Muslim wedding knows, festivity, traditional splendor, and lavish banquets make the occasion a great treat for the invitees.

Because Muslim weddings have perhaps more varied traditions than any other religion, owing to the widespread and largely decentralized nature of the Islamic faith itself, we have space to focus on just one culture. Here are the traditional Islamic wedding customs of India.

Mangni: Traditional Muslim wedding ceremonies begin with an exchange of rings well before the official wedding day in a ceremony called the Mangni. On this occasion, the bride's outfit is provided by the groom's family.

Mehendi ceremony: The mehendi (henna) ceremony is held at the home of the bride-to-be on the eve of the wedding ceremony or a few days before it. The female relatives of the girl anoint her with turmeric paste to bring out the glow in her complexion. A relative or a *mehendiwali* (henna artist) applies mehendi on the hands and feet of the bride-to-be.

The mehendiwali usually uses a mehendi cone to draw thin, artistic patterns on the hands and feet of the blushing bride-to-be. The mehendi is washed off after a few hours or kept on overnight. The event has a festive feel to it, with the women singing traditional songs. According to custom, the bride must not step out of the house until her marriage.

Sangeet: Besides the festivity and frolicking that mark the days leading up to the wedding, the families of the prospective bride and groom hold a special sangeet (singing) session. Friends and close family members are invited and traditional wedding songs are sung. Sometimes professional *dholwalis* (female musicians who play the traditional drum) are invited for a special touch. Both sides exchange gifts and sweets.

Welcoming the *baraat*: The groom (*baraat*) arrives at the wedding venue with his wedding procession (*baraati*). A band of musicians strike up some traditional notes to announce their arrival. The groom shares a drink of sherbet with the bride's brother. The bride's sisters play pranks and slap the guests playfully with batons made of flowers.

Nikaah **ceremony:** The nikaah or wedding ceremony can be conducted at the home of the bride or the groom, or at any other convenient venue. A *maulvi* (priest) conducts the ceremony in the presence of close family members and relatives. In orthodox Muslim communities, the men and women are seated separately. The *walis* (the fathers of the bride and groom) play an important role in the ceremony. As a father, each must ensure that the rights of his child are protected. The maulvi reads selected verses from the Koran, the holy book of the Muslims. The nikaah is complete after a proposal is made by the boy's family and the girl's family conveys its assent. The mutual consent of the couple is of great importance for the marriage to be legal.

On the day of the nikaah, the elder members of the families decide on the amount of *mehar,* a sum of money given by the groom's family to the bride.

Nikaahnama: The nikaahnama, signed by the groom, the bride, the walis, and the maulvi, is a document that spells out the marriage contract. It contains a set of terms and conditions that must be respected by both the parties. It also gives the bride the right to divorce her husband.

Blessing the groom: The groom receives blessings from the older women and offers them his *salaam* (a respectful salutation). The guests pray for the newlyweds.

Dinner, prayers, and *aarsi-mashaf:* Dinner is a lavish spread. Usually, the women and the men dine separately. After dinner, the newlyweds sit together for the first time. Their heads are covered by a *dupatta* (traditional scarf) while they read prayers under the direction of the maulvi. The Koran is placed between the couple, and they are allowed to see each other only through mirrors.

Rukshat: The bride's family bids the bride a tearful farewell before she departs for her husband's house. The bride's father gives her hand to her husband and tells him to protect and take good care of her.

Welcoming the bride: The groom's mother holds the Koran above the head of her new daughter-in-law as she enters her new home for the first time after the wedding.

Chauthi: On the fourth day after the wedding, the chauthi, the bride visits the home of her parents and is received with a joyous welcome.

Valimah: The valimah is the lavish reception that the groom's family hosts a few days after the nikaah. The reception is held in a club, on the grounds of a Muslim *gymkhana,* or in a banquet hall. It is a joyous occasion that brings together the two families, their relatives, and other well-wishers.

Henna designs on a Muslim bride **COURTESY OF GARDENSTATEPHOTO.COM**

Left to right: Indian Bride; A Hindu groom is escorted to his wedding; Sharing the blessings of a Hindu wedding ceremony **ALL COURTESY OF** GARDENSTATEPHOTO.COM

The Hindu Wedding

Grihistha Ashrama, one of the important stages of Hindu life, refers to the bringing together of two people in marriage to form a new household. Ceremonies differ so widely from region to region that it is impossible to make generalizations about their form. What they all have in common, however, is a series of the following rituals.

1. *Vara satkaarah:* This ceremony constitutes the welcome of the bridegroom and his relatives at the entrance of the wedding hall, where the priest chants a few sacred mantras and the bride's mother blesses the groom by applying *Tilak* made of vermilion and turmeric powder.

2. *Madhuparka:* During the welcoming of the groom at the altar, the bride offers him a mixture of yogurt and honey as a sign of purity. The bride then greets the groom by garlanding him, and the groom reciprocates.

3. *Kanya dan:* In this ceremony, the father of the bride gives away his daughter to the groom by pouring out a bit of sacred water.

4. *Vivah-homa:* This fire ceremony ensures that all auspicious undertakings of the marriage will start in an atmosphere of purity and spirituality.

5. *Pani-grahan:* The groom holds the right hand of the bride in his left hand. He recites some Vedic recitations praying for a long life.

6. *Pratigna-karan:* The bride and groom walk around the fire, with the bride leading, and make promises of loyalty, love, and fidelity to each other.

7. *Shila arohan:* The bride's mother helps the bride to symbolically step onto a stone to prepare her for a new life.

8. *Laja-homah:* The bride offers rice to the gods for their blessings.

9. *The mangala suthra dharana:* This marks the tying of the sacred thread, which is a mark of either Vishnu or Shiva, on the neck of the bride by the groom.

10. *Pradakshina:* The groom holds the hand of the bride and circles the nuptial fire seven times, thus completing the ceremony.

11. *Saptapadi:* The bride and groom are symbolically brought to-

gether through the marriage knot: the groom's scarf is tied to the bride's dress. Then they take seven steps, which represent nourishment, strength, prosperity, happiness, progeny, long life, and harmony.

12. *Abhishek:* This ceremony is done by sprinkling water as meditations are offered.

13. *Anna praashan:* The couple first offers food to the fire and then feed each other as a way of expressing mutual love and affection.

14. *Aashirvadah:* This ceremony marks the blessings received by the couple from the elders. All the people present in the ceremony express their happiness by showering flowers on the couple.

The Shinto Wedding

While most weddings in Japan are held in the Christian style, the traditional wedding of the Shinto religion is still practiced by some. This ceremony varied from family to family until 1900, when the wedding of Crown Prince Yoshihito and Princess Sado became something of a standard for the Shinto ceremony.

The ceremony takes place in a Shinto shrine or in a Shinto sanctuary constructed especially for this purpose. It is presided over by a priest and is attended only by family and close friends, including the *nakodo* (go-between) who may have participated in the mi-ai, a meeting between a possible bride and groom. If there was none, the bride and groom may select an elderly relative to stand in for ceremonial purposes only. The event is considered to be private, and the guests invited to the reception are asked to wait until the ceremony is over.

The Shinto wedding is accompanied by traditional music and attended by *miko* maidens who serve sake in red and white dresses.

Procession: The wedding party enters to traditional Japanese music. The bride and groom proceed to a small table at the front of the room near an altar. The members of the party take their places around the bride and groom.

Purification: All present stand for the first of the wedding rituals. The presiding priest offers a prayer and then presents a *harai-gushi,* a long stick with a great many white paper streamers attached to one end. He jerks the stick quickly to the left, then to the right, and back to the left again. The resulting whooshing sounds will purify the room and the wedding guests.

Prayer: The priest chants an invocation, addressing several deities and proclaiming the bride and groom united through the auspices of the nakoda; he prays for their happiness.

Sake ceremony: This special ritual, the Three-Times-Three Exchange of Nuptial Cups, creates bonds among members of the wedding party. While flute music is played in the background, three cups of sake are presented to the table at which the bride and groom are seated. First the groom and then the bride drink from one cup in a series of three sipping motions. The procedure is repeated with the second and third cups. The sake is then presented to the groom's parents, and next to the bride's parents. Finally, the two groups of relatives, along with the nakoda, drink together and proclaim their congratulations.

Wedding vows: This portion of the service is short and simple. The groom reads the vows from a text that is given to him. He expresses eternal trust and affection on behalf of himself and his bride.

Offerings: The groom's full name—and the bride's first name—are read aloud. Then the couple make an offering of *tamagushi,* a sacred evergreen branch, to Kami (the spirit that permeates the Shinto culture). Everyone in the room then bows twice, claps their hands twice, and bows again.

Ring exchange: A double-ring exchange follows, after which the priest makes his final invocation and announces the conclusion of the ceremony.

The Japanese Practice of Mi-Ai

The mi-ai interview is an ancient Japanese tradition in which a matchmaker brings together a prospective bride and groom for the possible purpose of a marriage. Although the meeting once presented a couple with a fait accompli, today it is practiced as more of a formality: once the mi-ai has ended, the future is left to the discretion of the couple.

Post-Wedding Traditions Around the World

When a post-wedding brunch just isn't enough:

An **Armenian** couple may break dishes, jars, or eggs before entering their new home to ward off evil spirits, or they may step over a flame to purify themselves.

When the **Austrian** bride leaves the church the day after the wedding, she is "captured" by friends who demand a ransom from the groom. The transaction is later settled at the local tavern.

In the **Czech Republic,** the bride is put up for sale in a mock auction held the day after the wedding. The groom must pay a steep price to "buy" back his bride. Some time soon after, the couple's friends sneak into their yard and plant a special tree from which they hang painted eggs and bright-colored ribbons. It is hoped that the bride will outlive the tree.

A bride in **Finland** is likely to use her wedding veil to make christening clothes for her children.

In the Burgundy region of **France,** guests practice a curious custom after the reception: they hoist a laurel tree over the roof of the groom's family home, pour wine over it, and dance around the chimney.

In **Germany,** as in many countries around the world and especially in Asia, it is respectful for the bride and groom to visit the graves of departed parents on the day after the wedding. (In Jewish practice, the bride does this before the ceremony.)

After a ceremony in **Greece,** a red flag is displayed outside the home of the groom. Before the bride can enter, she must throw a piece of iron onto the roof to symbolize the strength of her new home.

Haitian couples don't cut their wedding cake until after the party, when they can share it in the privacy of their own home.

A **Hindu** bride is kidnapped by her sisters after the wedding, and her husband has to buy her back with jewelry or some other acceptable offer.

After a wedding in **Holland,** some couples plant lily-of-the-valley in their garden so that they can renew their love for one another every year when the plant blooms. Others plant a pine tree to ensure fertility and good luck.

In **India,** when the newly married couple arrive home after the wedding, they play a game called *aeki-beki,* in which they must fish a ring out of a bowl of water tinted with milk and red ink. The first to find it four times will rule the roost. Once the fun is over, the Indian bride must start dressing like a married woman: in Punjab, she wears a nose ring and an ivory wrist cuff; in North India, she paints a red streak on her forehead; in the Kashmir region, a married woman identifies herself with tassels of silver thread worn from her ears; and a Bengali married woman sports conch-shell bracelets.

A newly married bride, entering her husband's family home for the first time, first has to knock down a container of uncooked rice and then enters putting forward her right foot first. This is to ensure that she brings good luck to the house.

Historically, at the end of the wedding day in **Italy,** a couple shattered a vase or glass into many pieces. The number of pieces represented the expected number of years they would be happily married to one another.

In **Jamaica,** guests who are not able to attend the wedding are sent slices of the wedding cake.

After the **Japanese** wedding, the common marriage system called *muko-iri* dictated that the bride went back to her own home, where the groom would visit her every night until she gave birth or the groom's family died, whichever came first. At that point, the groom would join the bride's family. In the thirteenth and fourteenth centuries, as Japan moved from the Age of Aristocracy to the Age of the Shoguns, muko-iri was replaced by *yome-iri,* in which the bride joined the groom's family.

Jewish couples enjoy a ritual known as "the week of *sheva brachas*" (the Week of Seven Blessings). The same seven blessings that were uttered during the wedding ceremony now kick off seven days of celebrations, each in the home of another family member or friend, with the purpose of entertaining the newly married couple and feeding them so that their first week of marriage is as carefree as it can be. Most Jewish couples delay their honeymoon for a week in order to enjoy this loving ritual.

In **Lithuania,** the married couple is likely to be awakened the morning after their wedding by revelers who will insist that the party continue at a wedding breakfast.

In **Morocco,** the bride must circle her new home (or, alternatively, its hearth) three times before she is officially the mistress of her house.

Although many traditional customs were destroyed when Communists came to rule Russia, some old rituals survived. When the new couple is welcomed into the groom's home, they are given a plate, which they must break with their feet. It is said that the first one to crack the plate will be boss. Festivities are taken seriously here: the bride and groom are treated like a king and queen at a celebration that can last for up to three days.

Brides in Siberia once came with an 18-month guarantee: the groom's parents had that length of time to return her to her family if they were not satisfied. The groom didn't even get a vote.

In South Africa, the bride's and groom's parents bring fire from their own hearths to light the fire of the new couple.

Friends of a married couple in Switzerland plant a young tree outside the door of their new home in the hopes that wood from it will be used to make the cradle for their first child.

Before guests leave a wedding in Thailand, they pour water over the hands of the bride and groom, who hold their palms together as if in prayer.

Why People Cry at Weddings

Dale V. Atkins, PhD, is a licensed psychologist with more than 25 years of experience as a relationship expert; she has also written several books, including *I'm Okay, You're My Parents: How to Overcome Guilt, Let Go of Anger, and Create a Relationship That Works* (2004). She frequently appears on NBC-TV's *Today* show and has a private practice in New York City. Dr. Atkins writes:

We can't all be allergic to the flowers! Maybe we're all basically sentimental at our core. Or perhaps it's hearing the first strings of Pachelbel's "Canon in D" that sends us rifling through our purses for a hankie. Then again, maybe we're all just suckers for the sheer beauty of the place—the sun shining through the stained glass and the aisle strewn with rose petals. We assume that people cry at weddings because they are just incredibly happy, overwhelmed with gratitude, and appreciate that they have come to this moment. But behind those tears, deep emotions may be at work.

1. For some of us, our tears well up because we are trying to reconcile our appreciation of the innocence of this new couple with the reality of what everyday life can do to their starry-eyed gaze. We tell ourselves, if we could only have some time to share our observations . . . our wisdom . . . we have so much more to teach them, to tell them, to guide them, to have them absorb before taking this step.

2. Similarly, we may cry for the loss of our own innocence, as we recall a time when we too made our way down the aisle with hopeful hearts and romantic dreams. We shed tears for what we have lost.

3. We may tear up because we are here, sitting across from our ex with his or her new love, and we are saddened that, for us, marriage was not all it was cracked up to be.

4. For some of us, our tears come because we are painfully aware of those people who are not with us, either because of death or other life circumstances, and we are sad to be experiencing this joyous day without them.

5. Some people may cry because they are faced with the reality that these young people have grown into adulthood, made their own choices, and no longer look to us—their parents, siblings, and friends—for constant guidance. Reluctantly we recognize that their first loyalties are now to each other and no longer to us.

6. Could it be that we just don't like our new in-law child or in-law family and we wonder how we are going to manage to live with these people as our relatives?

7. Brides and grooms cry at weddings too. Their lives are changing in every possible way, and as much as they want to be married, there can still be some doubt as to whether they've made the right choice. They may worry about losing their independence, their attraction, their feeling of love. Some couples cry because they are just plain scared in the face of overwhelming divorce statistics. Will Mr. Right remain interesting, fun, and sexy down the road? Will Mrs. (Always) Right stand up to the stress of married life?

Sometimes brides and grooms cry at their own weddings because they are overwhelmed with happiness at having found their true love, their life mate, the person they plan to live their life with, a thought that can truly bring tears to anyone's eyes.

13 Ways to Enjoy Every Minute of Your Wedding

If the flower truck breaks down, send someone out to the nearest supermarket or farmers' market for whatever they can find. If the photographer thought your wedding was next Saturday, raid the shelves at the pharmacy for disposable digital cameras. If the cake collapses, send someone out for a dozen sumptuous cakes—or about 300 doughnuts. The point is, there's a fix for everything, and after all the work you have put into your wedding, you deserve to enjoy the day. Here are some things you can do to make sure that every moment of your wedding becomes a treasured memory.

1. If a logistical problem arises, delegate it to someone else and put it out of your mind. Your concern would be reflected in the photographs, and there's probably nothing you can do that someone else can't handle just as well.

2. Say thank-you to all the important people before the party.

3. Spend a few minutes with each of your guests, especially those you don't see very often.

4. Take a bathroom break even if you don't need one. Spend a few quiet moments alone. Who is that beautiful bride in the mirror?

5. Eat something.

6. Dance a lot.

7. Dance with the little boys and the old men.

8. Dance with the women too.

9. Toast your guests.

10. Switch to comfortable shoes—or none at all—for the reception, even if it means soiling the hem of your gown.

11. Introduce people to one another. You may be planting the seed for another wedding!

12. Spend time with your new spouse, even if you have to sneak off somewhere to be alone for a short time. Can you believe it? You're married!

13. Pay attention to your in-laws and make sure they know that they are valued members of your new family.

20 Ways to Panic-Proof Your Wedding Day

Our thanks to USABride.com for these suggestions:

1. Tell everyone providing services exactly what your requirements are. Put everything in writing and make sure your wedding vendors sign the agreements.

2. Be sure to specify items you don't want as well (e.g., racy rap songs, too many posed photos, onion dip, whatever).

3. Two or three days before the wedding, call all your wedding vendors and verify your bookings. Have them read back to you the time, date, and location of the wedding as they have it noted, as well as the services or items they'll be providing. Make sure they know how to get to the site. It's a good idea to send a reminder letter as well. Bring contact information for each of your vendors to the wedding so that someone can make a phone call if one of them doesn't show up.

4. Avoid asking friends or family to provide food, flowers, or official photography. It will create an awkward situation if you're not pleased with the results. It's easier to expect perfection from someone being paid rather than a favorite uncle whose feelings may be hurt if you complain about anything. Nor will he have a spare camera to bring along if his camera breaks or an assistant to fill in if he catches the flu and can't make it, as would a pro.

5. Never let a guest serve as a bartender. He may pour too much liquor, which could quickly deplete a limited supply, run up the bill, or get guests too drunk. He might also get drunk, or leave the bar unattended to socialize.

6. Avoid heavy cake tops or too many tiers. These can make the cake unstable.

Day-Of Brownie Points for the Groom

Dancing with all her aunts, even the ones with no teeth: 10 points each

Dancing with the little girls: 2 points each

Remembering to thank all the parents during the speech: 6 points

Arranging to have flowers delivered to both mothers on the morning after the wedding: 20 points

Focusing on the bride, because this is all about her: priceless

7. Protect your wedding dress. Never iron it or attempt any kind of touchup. If it is badly wrinkled, contact the bridal shop for pressing. Do not eat, drink, or smoke after putting the gown on. Do not apply makeup, and keep away from pets. If you're traveling to the wedding in your gown, avoid exiting the car near dirt or bushes.

8. When you get your wedding dress, practice putting it on, walking, turning, and moving like you will during the ceremony. Get a feel for how the dress moves and how much extra time you'll need to handle the train.

9. Avoid having children under age three in the wedding party. If you do, let one of the attendants walk with the child, or pair the child with an older child.

10. Secure fake rings to the ring pillow so they won't fall off. Have the maid or matron of honor and the best man carry the real ones.

11. Make sure someone knows of any plans to use alternative entrances to the ceremony (side doors, back doors) so they won't be locked out.

12. Accompany the bridesmaids to their fittings to make sure the dresses are not altered to be too short, too loose, or too tight.

13. Advise out-of-town members of the wedding party to arrive early on the day before the wedding so they don't run the risk of missing or delaying the rehearsal.

14. Have attendants arrive early to get dressed at the wedding venue so there's no delay when the photographer arrives and no worry about making the wedding on time.

15. Have a spare tape recorder, batteries, and extra tape in case the one you're planning to use to record the vows acts up.

16. Get your marriage license in advance of the ceremony and have it with you on the wedding day. You'll need it to get married!

17. Have someone assigned to take care of the last-minute details and ensure the bridal party is dressed and ready to go. She can answer the phone, run errands, and make sure everyone has something to eat before the wedding.

18. Try not to stay up late the night before the wedding. Avoid drinking too much alcohol or caffeine.

19. If you are having a destination wedding, go to the location at least the night before. Rushing to the wedding site the day of the wedding only opens the door for tension and problems.

20. If something goes wrong, don't panic. You'll probably be the only one who notices that the ribbons in the bridesmaids' bouquets are the wrong color. Don't let little things ruin your day. Accept the idea that your wedding may not (and in fact probably will not) go as planned. Always hang on to your sense of humor!

9 Ways to Stay Relaxed During the Hours Before Your Wedding

Whether a couple has lived together many years or still live at home with their parents, all brides get some jitters just before the wedding. Here are some suggestions to make this time pass quickly and peacefully. It is a time to be selfish and not worry about anyone else.

You want to create a cocoon of warmth, love, and relaxation for yourself while knowing that your life is about to change. Here are some tips from Sandy Erzine.

1. If you can afford it, find a beautician who will do your hair and makeup and help get you dressed. (Basically all you have to do is show up and be pampered.)

2. Have a close friend, your mother, or a limo take you directly from the beauty shop or home to the wedding location.

3. If you are getting dressed at home, put some relaxing music on the stereo.

Take a bubble bath and leave yourself plenty of time to get dressed in a relaxed manner.

4. Make a list of everything you need ahead of time and tape it to the bathroom mirror. Then don't forget to look at it.

5. While you are getting ready, allow only people you are very comfortable with in your space. This is your day, and Aunt Doris can wait to pinch your cheeks until after the ceremony.

6. Forget about the wedding and reception for those few hours and pamper and focus on yourself.

7. If someone is making you tense, ask that person nicely to leave. You can be assertive without being aggressive.

8. If there are last-minute details, assign them to someone else. Everyone wants to help a bride.

9. Put a "Do Not Disturb" sign on the door.

Who's Who at the Wedding

The Maid of Honor

From the late Middle Ages on, marriages required two witnesses, including a close friend of the bride's who could vouch for the fact that she was marrying of her own volition. This was the first maid of honor, who accompanied the bride in the weeks before the wedding, helping her with all the preparations and acting as her confidante.

Today the maid of honor is still the bride's right-hand gal. She is the bride's sister, best friend, mother, or daughter. She acts as the bride's therapist both before and after the event, and she is trusted to make decisions on behalf of the families involved. A good maid of honor knows when to run with the ball and when to hang back. Choose her carefully and treat her with loving kindness—her duties are many! Here are 18 of them:

1. Advising the bride on wedding details—everything from the venue, seating arrangements, and color scheme to the music and favors—and accompanying the bride on shopping and browsing expeditions

2. Helping the bride choose invitations

3. Coordinating the bridesmaids, which involves everything from communicating with them about their dresses, the jewelry that has been chosen for them, and their responsibilities both before and at the wedding to making sure they all have their hair and makeup done on time and are all carrying the correct flowers

4. Shopping for a wedding gown with the bride

5. Hosting the bridal shower, with the help of the bridesmaids

6. Letting guests know where the couple is registered

7. Attending the rehearsal dinner

8. Acting as the bride's personal assistant on the day of the wedding, dispensing everything from therapy to tissues, as needed

9. Making sure that the bride's dress, train, and veil are perfectly arranged before the ceremony and being ready at the last minute with safety pins, hair clips, and whatever else might be needed

10. Arranging the bride's veil before the ceremony begins and holding her bouquet during the ceremony

11. Marching down the aisle, escorted by the best man

12. During the ceremony, holding the groom's ring until it is called for

13. Signing the marriage certificate as a witness

14. Participating in the receiving line if there is one and generally circulating to make sure all the guests are comfortable

15. Helping the bride adjust her train and prepare for the reception

16. Cohosting the wedding reception by greeting guests, helping vendors with questions and logistics, and generally handling all crisis management

17. Giving a toast during dinner

18. Helping to collect gifts and making sure they are safely stored

The Bridesmaids

The Greek woman who married as early as age 15 needed a flotilla of friends to protect her, not only from evil fortune but also from heckling strangers who might approach her as she traveled from her old home to the new one. Women who had had good fortune themselves were selected as her protectors and dressed in outfits similar to hers so as to confound the gods and anyone else who might want to single her out for mischief. In the weeks before the wedding, the bridesmaids followed the bride everywhere, assisting her with all aspects of wedding preparation.

It helps to appoint bridesmaids who get along with one another. Their tasks can be chores or fun, depending on how they view it. Here are their duties:

1. Helping the bride shop for her dress and the bridesmaids' dresses

2. Paying for their own attire

3. Assisting the maid of honor in all ways possible—for example, by offering advice, running errands, facilitating invitations, and communicating with vendors

4. Spreading the news as to where the couple is registered

5. Helping the maid of honor plan the shower or bachelorette party

6. Attending the rehearsal dinner

7. Marching down the aisle before the bride, escorted by the groomsmen

8. Participating in the reception line if there is one and generally acting as a hostess

9. Acting as a cohostess at the wedding, welcoming guests, facilitating conversation, and inviting shy guests to the dance floor

The Best Man

Even as Anglo-Saxon warriors on horseback swooped down to steal young girls for marriage, they were accompanied in this mischief by close friends who helped make sure the raid was a success. Today the duties of the groom's main attendant reflect a more civilized approach to marriage. The best man takes care of the following:

1. Organizing the bachelor party

2. Helping the groom choose his tuxedo as well as those for the groomsmen

3. Coordinating the groomsmen and ushers so they are prompt and properly dressed on the day of the wedding

4. Attending the rehearsal dinner and making the first toast

5. Assisting the groom on his wedding day by helping him dress and making sure that both the marriage license and the ring make it to the ceremony

6. Arranging and assisting with transportation for the departing couple

7. Keeping the bride's ring safe until it is time for it to be presented to either the groom or the ring-bearer

8. Standing next to the groom during the ceremony

9. Signing the marriage certificate as a witness

10. Participating in the receiving line if there is one

11. Making the first toast at the reception

12. Acting as a host at the reception, making sure all guests are comfortable

13. Helping to collect gift envelopes and keeping them safe

Groomsmen, aka Ushers

1. Help the best man plan the bachelor party

2. Rent their own attire, per the best man's instructions

3. Attend the rehearsal dinner

4. Escort guests to their seats before the ceremony

5. Act as hosts during the wedding, directing guests to rest rooms, answering vendors' questions, and running interference if problems arise

6. Escort bridesmaids down the aisle

7. Decorate the getaway car

The Flower Child

The first flower children were young boys and girls who actually scattered grains, not flowers, and they did so to ensure the bride's fertility. By medieval times, the job was given to a pair of girls, and flowers were mixed in with the grains. Usually age four to eight, the flower child today precedes the bride down the aisle, scattering flower petals from a basket. On the care and feeding of flower children:

1. The bride usually pays for the flower child's outfit, though this is not required.

2. Boys may act as flower children too, and there may be more than one. Or none at all.

3. Instead of scattering petals, these attendants can proceed down the aisle holding single flowers or bouquets, scattering birdseed, or blowing bubbles from tiny bottles.

4. Make sure the child knows what is expected of her and that she is comfortable with it all. Buy her a book on the subject, and make sure she attends the rehearsal dinner. If she is shy, perhaps this is not a job for her. Similarly, you take chances when you appoint a rambunctious, unpredictable youngster as a flower child—he may steal the show!

5. Seat the parents of the flower children on the aisle and near the altar so the child can see them; it will put her at ease.

6. Ask one bridesmaid to take charge of the flower children, seeing to it that they have the items they need for the ceremony, that they know what they are to do, and that they've visited the rest room just before the trip down the aisle.

The Ring-Bearer

Traditionally a boy age four to eight, the ring-bearer marches down the aisle holding a small pillow with the two wedding rings on top of it. As a safety measure, these rings are often inexpensive fakes; the real rings can be held until needed by the best man or maid of honor.

9 Ways to Settle an Argument

Wedding planning can bring out the worst in us all. BFFs can find themselves at odds, and old wounds can reopen under the pressure of wedding stress. Whether you're the bride, the groom, the maid of honor, or just an innocent bystander, here are some guidelines for getting the members of the wedding to behave.

1. Do a little homework before you attack the problem. Listen to both sides and find out if there's a history to the dispute. Is this a chronic quarrel between the parties or are nerves just getting in the way? Think about what you want to say before you speak.

2. Put pen to paper. Write down your solution and send it to both parties simultaneously so that you maintain an impartial position. Be fair to both sides.

3. Don't criticize or insult anyone.

4. Think about the big picture. Is there some way to make everyone happy by making a compromise?

5. Is there another family member who is in a better position to mediate the dispute? Perhaps a senior member can play the guilt card to get them in line.

6. Play the bride card. Ask them to put their dispute aside just for one day so that you can all enjoy your wedding.

7. Control your emotions. Losing it will only exacerbate the problem. Set an example for the warring parties by remaining calm and logical. Keep your solutions simple and practical.

8. Bring in the experts. Go online and find out how the etiquette experts view the dispute. Share your findings with both sides.

9. Rock, paper, scissors.

Standing on Ceremony: Who Sits Where?

According to EZWeddingPlanner.com:

• In a Christian wedding, the bride's family and friends are seated on the left side of the church facing the altar. The groom's family and friends sit on the right side of the church. If the church has two center aisles, the bride's side sits on both sides of the left aisle, the groom's on both sides of the right. The parents sit in the center section; the bride is on the left, and the groom is on the right.

• In a Jewish wedding, this is reversed and the bride's guests sit on the right (the side the bride stands on as she faces the rabbi). All parents remain standing under the chuppah (canopy) throughout the wedding ceremony. If parents are divorced, their new partners are seated in the second and third rows. At Orthodox Jewish ceremonies, where guests are divided by gender, women sit on the left and men on the right.

• The ushers generally ask the guests if they are a friend or relative of the bride or groom to determine the correct seating. If they are friends with both the bride and groom, they get the best available seats. The usher gives his right arm to the lady to escort her to her seat. If she has a male escort, he generally walks a few steps behind, although a couple can walk together if the usher simply says, "Please follow me."

• If one family has many more guests than the other, everyone may sit together without assigned sections. The usher may let guests know that both families are sitting together and then show them to the best available seats.

• When the bride's parents are divorced but not remarried, if they are congenial they might sit together in the left front row at a Christian wedding. Otherwise, the parent who raised the bride or groom (and guest or spouse) sits in the left front pew and the other parent (and guest or spouse) sits in the third row on the left side. This can also be an individual decision, depending on relationships and preferences. For the groom's parents, simply reverse the seating (using the right side).

• Parents of both sides sit in the first or second pew on their respective sides. (Often the first pew is left empty in case someone from the bridal party must sit down during the ceremony.) Grandparents sit in the next pew on the outside (next to the aisle). Siblings can also sit in the grandparents' pew. You can reserve additional pews for other honored guests.

The reserved pews can be marked with flowers, reserved signs, ribbons, etc., or the ushers can just seat the guests behind the reserved pews. You can send pew cards or "within the ribbons" cards to those guests you wish to honor with special seating.

• Guests who arrive after the bride's mother has been seated should not be seated by the ushers. This usually applies to guests who arrive later than ten minutes before the ceremony begins. They may simply slip into an empty pew behind the other seated guests. If the procession is already under way, late-arriving guests should remain in the rear of the church or synagogue until the wedding party reaches the altar, then seat themselves. It's helpful to have an usher at the back to help these late guests after the procession is complete.

A Guide to Table-Hopping

Promote exchanges by placing a seating chart at each table. On one side, it can list every guest, in alphabetical order, with the table number next to their name. On the other side, list each table and give the names of the people sitting there. This will allow people who haven't seen each other in a while to seek each other out, and it will help shy guests connect with their tablemates and others.

> "I can't believe it. You make someone a bridesmaid and they shit all over you."
> — Ginny Baker, Sixteen Candles

13 Seating Tips

1. Don't automatically assume that factions of family and friends are better off sitting together. Nor should your tables be limited to either the bride's or groom's relations. Mixing things up can make for lively table discussion and may lead to—who knows?—more weddings.

2. Seat people with others who are approximately the same age. No matter which side of the family they are from, teens, for instance, will appreciate the company of others of their ilk.

3. If guests are bringing babies and toddlers, seat them at the same table as their parents, who should be encouraged to watch them at all times.

4. Place people of similar interests and in like industries at the same table.

5. Separate divorced couples, unless they are friendly, at different tables, and position these tables on different sides of the room.

6. Seat the liveliest groups near the dance floor, where they can set a good example for everyone else.

7. Seat elderly people as far as possible from the speakers; inevitably they complain about the noise.

8. Try to keep your tables of similar sizes, but go ahead and be creative if it means that guests have a better shot at enjoying themselves. There's no law against a table of 8 next to a table of 14. You might have to mix table shapes in order to accomplish this (14 would be better seated at a long banquet table as opposed to a round one), but as long as you're not planning on any aerial shots of the room, it can work out fine.

9. If you're playing matchmaker by seating certain singles together, make sure that you or a bridesmaid takes the opportunity to introduce them formally.

10. If you're using place cards to assign specific seats (not recommended, except for the most formal affairs), alternate men and women. But don't be bothered if some guests choose to ignore your assignments.

11. Seat out-of-towners who look forward to seeing each other at the same table.

12. If rude people make special seating requests, do the polite thing and let them know you'll make every effort to accommodate them.

13. If you're completely unsure as to how certain pairs of guests might react to being seated at the same table, call and ask them before you finalize the seating plan.

17 Ways to Honor Special Guests

Whether they are a would-be bridesmaid for whom you just didn't have room, someone who has traveled a great distance, or a parent or mentor who deserves a special place in your heart, here are some ways to say thank-you.

For special guests who are attending the wedding:

1. Ask them to act as ushers who will escort guests to their seats before the wedding ceremony.

2. At a Jewish wedding, have four people hold up the chuppah and invite another to say the blessing over the challah.

3. Have them light a special candle at the ceremony (in honor of a departed loved one, for instance).

4. Ask them to give special readings during the ceremony.

5. If they have a special talent, ask them to perform at the reception.

6. Invite them to offer a special toast during the ceremony.

7. Ask them to sit at the head table, if there is one.

8. Invite their small children to participate in the ceremony as junior bridesmaids and groomsmen, who can precede their senior counterparts down the aisle. Don't worry if these little ones screw up—the laughter will dispel the generally nervous atmosphere.

9. Incorporate a lesson they have taught you or a favorite saying into your comments, either during the ceremony or after. Acknowledge the distance they have traveled or the contribution they have made to your life.

If your honorees are deceased or unable to attend:

1. Light a special candle during the ceremony or prior to the reception to honor their memory.

2. Read their favorite poem or include their favorite song in the festivities.

3. Serve their favorite food at dinner.

4. Wear an article of their clothing or jewelry.

5. Display a photo of them at the table where table cards will be placed or somewhere in the venue.

6. Include a short bio of the person in the wedding program.

7. Dance to their favorite song at the reception.

8. Tuck a photo of the person in the bridal bouquet.

Someone other than the bride should bring a file containing copies of all vendor contracts as well as contact information for all members of the wedding party.

14 Things to Put in the Courtesy Basket

Wedding venues charge as much as $150 for a basket that you can assemble far more cheaply with just one visit to the dollar store. Here are some suggestions for the contents of a ladies' room basket; use a smaller version for the men's room.

1. Hair spray
2. Combs
3. Some pairs of pantyhose
4. Lip gloss
5. Cold medication
6. Clear nail polish
7. Tissue packs
8. Aspirin
9. Breath mints
10. Scotch tape
11. Tampons and panty liners
12. Band-Aids
13. Foam shoe inserts
14. A pair of scissors

11 Guest Book Alternatives

There's a lot to be said for the traditional handsomely bound blank book that will preserve forever the thoughts of well-wishers. These days you'll find simple versions at discount stores as well as embossed leather bindings that hold delicate handmade papers—and which can set you back hundreds of dollars. Then there are some offbeat ways to get the job done:

1. Unfired pottery (dishes, mugs, vases, etc.) that are signed with special pens and then fired for preservation after the big day

2. Loose sheets of paper that can then be bound into your wedding album

3. Polaroid photos taken of each guest as they arrive, signed by each

4. A large sheet of wallpaper that will be incorporated into your furnishings

5. An enlargement of a photo of the bride and groom, with the image "ghosted" so that the signatures are legible

6. A picture frame and mat that will later be used for your wedding portrait

7. Squares of cloth that can be made into a quilt

8. A silver tray or box (to be signed with a jeweler's engraving tool)

9. Small pieces of paper that are incorporated into a wedding collage

10. A pair of his-and-hers T-shirts, for wearable art

11. A tablecloth

Internet sites such as photoworks.com allow guests to send in photos and messages that are bound into a book for the bride and groom.

9 Ways to Make Out-of-Towners Comfortable

You don't have to pay for your guests' travel and accommodations, but it is traditional for you to find and suggest appropriate hotels at reasonable rates and to try to obtain group rates on their behalf. Be sure to point these guests to your website, where you can post everything they need to know to feel comfortable in an unfamiliar city.

1. Have a gift basket waiting in their hotel rooms when they arrive. Include some fruit, a map of the city on which you have indicated the route from where they are to where the wedding is, and a schedule of local events.

2. Give them their party favors ahead of time—tickets to the theater or a regional event they might enjoy.

3. Let them know which of your other guests may be in the same hotel and suggest that they contact one another for rides to the wedding venue.

4. If they have children, arrange for a bridesmaid or trusted friend to act as a babysitter as needed.

5. Make sure they have information on local transportation and car rentals. Or better yet, can anyone in your wedding party act as a chauffeur?

6. Provide a directory of personal services available in the area—hair salons, manicurists, stores for last-minute shopping needs.

7. Invite them to the rehearsal dinner. Make every effort to introduce them to the members of your wedding party, especially those who might be able to help them with logistics.

8. If language problems exist, make sure they have access to someone in the family who will be able to translate.

9. At the wedding, in your comments, include your thanks to them for the great effort to which they have gone to be with you at your wedding.

Out, Out, Damn Spot!

Wedding Dress Stains

If you have time before the wedding (yet one more reason to shop early), put this in the hands of professionals. First consult the store where you purchased the dress; it may have a quick fix, or clever alterations may hide the damage entirely. If you're on your own, take the dress to a cleaners that specializes in wedding gowns. This solution is an expensive one, but it's by far the most reliable.

But if the accident happens at the wedding and you don't have weeks, let alone hours, to deal with the stain, you need to first assess the situation (is it that noticeable? have the important photos already been taken?) before you proceed. Emergency measures can make matters worse by spreading the stain; ask yourself if you really want to take the risk. Even if you do get the stain out, you're still liable to be sporting a giant wet spot for at least part of your wedding, although a hair dryer will speed up the process. (Just be careful to use the no-heat setting, as fabric can burn easily.) Know that many happily married women started out with wedding dress stains that no one noticed. They went on to live normal lives. Life goes on, and it would be the foolish bride indeed who allowed a spot to ruin her wedding day.

If you decide to tackle it, know that the sooner you treat a stain, the better chance you have of getting rid of it.

Red wine stain: Dab at—don't rub!—the stain with a clean cloth to soak up as much of it as you can, then pour club soda or water onto the cloth and continue dabbing. The stain should slowly fade. Cover any remains of the stain with talcum powder or chalk.

Oil stain: Sprinkle lots of talcum powder on the stain and leave it for about ten minutes. Then shake off the powder, which should have absorbed the oil if you acted quickly enough.

Ink stain: This is tricky, so you want to test it on an inside hem of the dress before you try it on the stain. Place a cloth under the stain and lightly spray the stain with hair spray. Wait for about five minutes, then dab the spot with a damp cloth.

Lipstick stain: Cover the stain with baking soda or talcum powder. You could try using a cleaning solvent, but this can discolor the fabric, and there's no way to tell how harsh chemicals and your dress will react. If you do use a solvent, test it on a hidden portion of the dress first.

Blood stain: If the blood is still wet, moisten a cotton swab with the saliva of the person whose blood it is and gently rub the area. If the stain is dry, moisten it with cold water applied to a washcloth. Hold the cloth down on the spot. If that doesn't work, you can apply hydrogen peroxide (there's one in most first-aid kits), diluting it one part peroxide to nine parts water, but know that you are taking the risk of bleaching the dress.

Fresh food stains: Those stain-remover pens work well on these, but test first.

Water-based stains (coffee, soda): Dab at the spot with a cold, damp (not saturated) washcloth.

31 Things to Put in the Bride's Wedding Day Emergency Basket

Any one of these items can save the day, and most can be purchased at dollar stores. Even if you never use any of them, you will sleep better for days before the wedding knowing that you're prepared for anything.

1. Aspirin
2. Baby powder
3. Band-Aids
4. Breath mints
5. Brush/comb
6. Cell phone
7. Chalk
8. Clear nail polish
9. Deodorant
10. Double-sided scotch tape
11. Emery board
12. Hair dryer
13. Hairpins
14. Hair spray
15. Iron
16. Krazy glue
17. Lint brush
18. Makeup kit for retouching
19. Masking tape
20. Moisturizer
21. Pantyhose/stockings (an extra pair!)
22. Perfume
23. Safety pins
24. Scissors
25. Sewing kit
26. Slippers
27. Static-cling spray
28. Talcum powder
29. Tampons
30. Tissues
31. Toothbrush/toothpaste

18 Jobs for Kids

The youngest members of the wedding party have more to do than simply strew flower petals and carry the ring. Here are a number of other chores for them. (When they're "off-duty," however, keep them occupied by supplying each one with an activity kit: a basket of games, markers, books, and treats.)

1. Serving as junior bridesmaids and ushers

2. Handing out programs

3. Holding the bride's bouquet during the ceremony

4. Carrying the bride's train as she walks down the aisle

5. Acting as a flower child

6. Being the ring-bearer

7. Passing out candles, rice, or birdseed

8. Reciting a poem at the ceremony

9. Reciting a special vow accepting their role in the new family, if this is the case

10. Lighting a special candle during the ceremony (with adult help if it's needed)

11. Distributing wedding favors

12. Distributing directions to the reception (if it's at a different location than the ceremony)

13. Turning pages for the organist or soloist

14. Encouraging guests to use their table cameras

15. Carrying a basket and collecting the disposable cameras toward the end of the reception

16. Acting as a "people pointer," directing the photographer/videographer toward special guests

17. Being a gopher

18. Helping distribute wedding cake

A young attendant at a Hindu wedding **COURTESY OF GARDENSTATEPHOTO.COM**

"A good idea is to put your wedding gown on early, so that the sweat stains can expand from your armpit areas and cover the entire gown, and thus be less noticeable." —DAVE BARRY

What to Include in the Wedding Program

Your wedding program can be an elaborate booklet that leaves the invitation in the dust, or it can be a photocopied sheet of plain paper. The important thing is that it functions as a program and not a fan. The more you tell your guests about what is going on, who the key players are, and why you've made certain choices, the more involved they will feel. If you're going for a soup-to-nuts approach, include all the items listed here. Or pick and choose what feels right. There are no hard and fast rules regarding wedding programs, despite what many stationers would have you believe. In fact, most guests enjoy the programs during the ceremony and then leave them behind. Consider this when you're up at 3:00 A.M. hot-gluing tiny flowers to the cover of each of your 250 programs.

1. The full names of the bride and groom, the wedding date, and the venue, city, and state where the wedding is taking place

2. The order of the service

3. The names of the people in the wedding party

4. Short bios of each participant

5. Mention of family members who are attending in spirit only

6. The name of the officiant

7. The names of the musicians, along with the titles of the music they will play

8. An explanation of special traditions that will be followed

9. The names of the people who will offer readings and the titles of the readings

10. Poems or biblical passages that have special meaning for the bride and groom

11. A thank-you note from the bride and groom to all guests

12. A list of all the guests, by table and by alphabetical order (including a note to the effect that the list does not include the inevitable last-minute changes)

13. An explanation of how you have chosen the wedding theme and the ways in which you have interpreted it throughout the wedding

14. The names of friends who might have helped prepare the program

Vintage postcard, ca. 1940 AUTHORS' COLLECTION

5 Reception Rituals

Certain moments at the wedding might be embarrassing for some and tear-jerking for others. None of these reception rituals are mandatory.

1. Announcing the entrance of the bride and groom once everyone is seated

Who does it: The bandleader or DJ
When it is done: After guests are seated at their tables
Why they do it: To announce the first appearance of the bride and groom as man and wife

2. The first dance

Who does it: The bride and groom, followed by:
• The bride and her father, the groom and his mother
• The bride and her new father-in-law, the groom with his new mother-in-law
• The bride and the best man, the groom and the maid of honor

When it is done: At the beginning of the reception—right after the bride and groom enter the reception hall, or after the opening toasts and/or prayers
Why they do it: Again, to present the bride and groom as they dance for the first time as man and wife, and to unite the families as others join in

3. The first toast

Who does it: The best man offers the first toast, the groom offers the next, the bride may follow with another one, and then it's every man for himself
When it is done: When everyone is seated, after the first course has been served or after everyone has had a chance to visit the buffet line
Why they do it: As a way for all guests to share in wishing the new couple a lifetime filled with joy and for the bride and groom to thank their guests for attending

4. The tossing of the bridal bouquet

Who does it: The bride throws the bouquet to a waiting group of single women
When it is done: Toward the end of the party, before the cake is cut
Why they do it: Whoever catches the bouquet is said to be the next

to marry. Historically, the bridal bouquet included herbs, many of which were considered lucky. The bride passed her bouquet on to a friend for good luck—and what could be better luck, it was believed, than to marry?

5. The tossing of the bride's garter

Who does it: The groom, who removes a garter from the bride's leg before tossing it to a crowd of single men
When it is done: Toward the end of the party, before the cake is cut
Why they do it: Whoever catches the garter is allowed to place the garter back on the bride's leg. Less generous grooms offer up a dance with the maid of honor instead. The practice harkens back to an old tradition of guests crowding into the bride and groom's bedchamber after the reception for further merriment. The women would line up and throw the groom's stockings backward over their heads, and the men would do the same with the bride's stockings. Whoever came closest to hitting the bride and groom would be the next to marry.

6 Reception Rituals That Are (Thankfully) Disappearing

At some point, a clever bride finally put her foot down once and for all, and that was the end of the chicken dance forever. Some other dated practices:

1. The receiving line. It was just too formal.

2. Garter toss. Too sexist.

3. Bouquet toss. Too pathetic.

4. Line dances. Too dumb.

5. Cake-in-the-face. Too gross.

6. Roast-toasts. Too rude.

How to Deliver a Toast

It's said that toasting goes back to a time when slipping poison into the glass of an enemy was considered business as usual. To the relief of guests everywhere, honorable hosts started pouring from a common pitcher and sipping the wine first—proving it was not poisoned—before offering a toast to the health and happiness of their guests.

Today's toasts are motivated by goodwill rather than fear. At weddings, it is customary for various members of the wedding party to offer their congratulations publicly. The creative toast-maker incorporates lines from appropriate poems, films, and books, or he or she can choose from the following popular choices, suggested by Rick Pieczonka of InstantWeddingToasts.com, in addition to the zillions more that can be found online.

1. Plan to speak from one to three minutes. Know that a toast is not a speech, and this is not the time to narrate the story of anything. A short toast delivered with sincerity will be remembered and appreciated.

2. When you get ready to deliver the toast, make an announcement to the guests, or have the emcee do it, then ask that all glasses be filled. Give the guests a few minutes to get settled.

3. Stand to give a toast (sit to receive one) and hold your glass with your right hand as you toast. Then lift your glass to your audience and take the first sip.

4. Humor works, but keep it G-rated. Using this opportunity to embarrass the bride or groom in any way is an exhibition of very bad taste.

5. Speak in your normal voice and avoid unnatural hand gestures or weird affectations. Wedding audiences want to hear what you have to say, not watch a drama unfold.

6. Practice your toast. Unless you are an accomplished public speaker, just "winging it" for the wedding toast is always a bad idea.

7. Look around the room at the audience and to the bride and groom as you toast. Eye contact is important for any public speaker.

8. Speak clearly and don't rush. Take your time and remember to breathe. If you speak too fast, no one will understand you.

9. And finally, finish your toast with a wish, a blessing, congratulations, or cheers.

8 Ways to Overcome Your Fear of Making a Speech

The fear of public speaking is second only to the fear of snakes and the fear of dying. That alone should help you relax: you have plenty of company and certainly are not the only one to experience dry mouth at the very thought of facing a large group of people. The reason for the fear is simple: no one wants to look foolish in public, and we imagine that our minds will go blank as soon as we begin to speak. Wedding speeches are no different, and even the most confident FOB has been known to sprout hives before it was his turn to address the guests. By the way, that idea about picturing everyone naked doesn't work; it's just distracting.

Here are some ways to get past the stuttering:

1. **Be prepared.** You should know what it is you want to say. That doesn't mean memorizing or reading from cards, but it does mean that you should have a brief outline in mind that will guide you through your speech. You can use cards if you have prepared a list of names of the people you want to thank and you're afraid you might omit someone without it.

2. **Practice.** Don't overdo it to the extent that it starts sounding meaningless, but do say your toast out loud in front of a mirror a few times before showtime. You can also try saying it into a tape recorder, to your roommate, or even to the dog.

3. **Relax before you begin.** When it's your turn to speak, take some deep breaths, thank the person who introduced you, and then count to ten. This will allow the audience to get settled and ready to hear you. It also is a way for you to gain control of everyone's attention.

Our favorite toast

The one uttered by Amy Tan at her wedding in 1974: "I am like a falling star who has finally found her place next to another in a lovely constellation, where we will sparkle in the heavens forever."

4. **Look at the audience.** Make eye contact with them. Remember that every single person is present because they want to celebrate this event. Don't be afraid to look them in the eye as you speak. Try to take in a range of people. If you're all nerves, it's okay to focus on one or two people who know exactly how you feel.

5. **Body language is important.** Don't over-animate, but move naturally and stand up straight. Use your hands as you would in normal conversation.

6. **Speak from the heart.** If you really mean everything you're saying, your sincerity will override any other problems you may be experiencing. Respond to the audience. If you've said something funny, give them a moment to laugh. Give both yourself and your audience a chance to reflect on your words.

7. **Use humor when you can.** Everyone enjoys a good laugh, and it will make you feel as though you are in control of the audience.

8. **Thankfully for shy speakers, a good speech is usually a short one.** Have a punch line at the end of your speech (perhaps something that ties in with your opening comment), give the audience a moment to react, and say thank-you as you exit the spotlight. Whew!

The 5 Biggest Toasting Mistakes to Avoid

1. Having one too many drinks to calm your nerves beforehand

2. Swearing and/or lying

3. Apologizing for being a bad speaker

4. Mentioning previous girlfriends, past marriages, or past relationships

5. Telling off-color stories about the bride or groom

So You Think You Can't Dance

You're at the reception. The music is pumping, and people are on the dance floor. You want to join the fun, but you're clueless. Not to worry: you can fake it. Here are some tips that will help you overcome your fears and make you look as though you actually know what you're doing.

1. You don't have to go it alone at first. Start by joining a line dance that has prescribed steps you can follow—these are usually pretty easy. The macarena, for example, is a cinch. Just do what everybody else is doing and don't worry if you mess up. You'll feel a lot more relaxed and comfortable on the dance floor afterward.

2. When you're ready to take the next step—dancing with a partner—approach the situation calmly and with confidence. Psych yourself up! Begin by dancing to a song that has a slow or medium-paced beat. Snapping your fingers, clapping your hands, swaying from side to side, or moving your feet from side to side are simple elements of dance that anyone can do. Don't try any fancy stuff, just follow your partner's moves.

3. Start out by nodding your head to the beat. Watch others dance and move your body along with the rhythm. This will help you establish the groove of the music. Let the beat be your guide. Feel the music.

4. Talking to your partner while you are dancing will distract her, and it's a good excuse to keep your moves to a minimum.

5. As you become more at ease, move your arms with your body, but be sure they are slightly bent and not rigid. Once you get in the groove, lift your arms up into a sort of boxing stance, with wrists crossed but not touching.

6. Move your shoulders up and down with the beat, but not at the same time—alternate your shoulder movements.

7. If you're feeling comfortable, add some attitude by shaking the junk in your trunk, but don't go overboard with fancy moves—stick to the basics. Remember that less is more. Don't wave your arms wildly, jump up and down, or scream and yell. This will attract more attention than you're probably ready for.

8. Steer your partner toward the middle of the dance floor. Your movements will be less visible to folks who are just looking on.

9. Try not to worry too much about how you look. Being self-conscious is really your greatest hurdle. Looking down at your feet will make you look more awkward than anything.

10. Whatever happens, keep a smile on your face and keep swaying to the music. You might actually enjoy it.

The 69 Rules of Wedding Crashing

1. The Rules of Wedding Crashing are sacred. Don't sully them by improvising.

2. Never leave a fellow crasher behind. Crashers take care of their own.

3. Never use your real name.

4. Never confess.

5. No one goes home alone.

6. Never let a girl get between you and a fellow crasher.

7. Do not sit in the corner and sulk. It draws attention in a negative way. Draw attention to yourself, but on your own terms.

8. Blend in by standing out.

9. Be the life of the party.

10. Sensitive is good.

11. Bridesmaids are desperate—console them.

12. You're a distant relative of a dead cousin.

13. Fight the urge to tell the truth.

14. Always have an up-to-date family tree.

15. Every female wedding guest deserves a sexy wedding night.

16. You love animals and children.

17. Toast in the native language of the bride or groom.

18. Always have an early "appointment" the next morning.

19. Definitely make sure she's 18.

20. If you get outed, leave calmly. Do not run.

21. Don't drink too much. A drunk crasher is a sloppy crasher.

22. Know the playbook so you can call an audible (a post-huddle football play that is changed orally after both teams have assumed their positions at the line of scrimmage).

23. If you call an audible, always make sure your fellow crashers know.

24. Never go back to your place.

25. Be gone by sunrise.

26. Your favorite movie is *The English Patient*.

27. Never hit on the bride! It's a one-way ticket to the pavement.

28. Dance with old folks and the kids. The girls will think you're "sweet."

29. Try not to break anything.

Always have an extra umbrella for Mr. Johnson.

30. At the service, sit in the fifth row. It's close enough to the wedding party to seem like you're an invited guest. Never sit in the back. The back row just smells like crashing.

31. Always remember your fake name.

32. You forgot your invitation in your rush to get to the church.

33. Make sure all the single women at the wedding know you're there because you've just suffered either a terrible breakup or the death of your fiancée.

34. Always work this into the conversation: "Yeah, I have tons of money. But how does one buy happiness?"

35. Get choked up during the service. The girls will think you're "sensitive." Bring artificial tears if necessary.

36. Always have an extra umbrella (condom) for Mr. Johnson.

37. Avoid virgins. They're too clingy.

38. If pressed, tell people you're related to Uncle John. Everyone has an Uncle John.

39. Don't fixate on one woman. Always have a backup.

40. When seeing a rival crasher, do not interact—merely acknowledge each other with a tug on the earlobe and gracefully move on.

41. The Ferrari's in the shop.

42. No chicken dancing. No exceptions.

43. No more than two weddings a weekend. More than that and your game gets sloppy.

44. Always save room for cake.

45. Dance with the bride's grandmother.

46. Research, research, research the wedding party. And when you are done researching, research some more.

47. Girls in hats tend to be proper and rarely give it up.

48. Keep interactions with the parents of the bride to a minimum.

49. Is the unmarried female rabbi fair game? Of course she is.

50. The tables farthest from the kitchen always get served first.

51. Bring a gift. If you get kicked out, demand to have it returned.

52. Don't let the ring-bearer bum your smokes. His parents may start to ask questions.

53. Stay clear of the wedding planner, who may recognize you from another wedding.

54. Don't use the "I have two months to live" bit. It's not cool or effective.

55. Wear nice shoes. They say a lot about the man.

56. Always choose large weddings. More choice. Easier to blend.

57. You're always from out of town.

58. Know something about the place you say you are from.

59. Of course you dream of having children one day.

60. Try not to show off on the dance floor.

61. Etiquette isn't old-fashioned. It's sexy.

62. The newspaper wedding announcements are your racing form. Choose carefully.

63. Be judicious with cologne. Citrus aromas are best.

64. Be well groomed and well mannered.

65. Never interrupt a fellow crasher.

66. Know when to abandon ship if it ain't floating.

67. Always carry an assortment of place cards to match any wedding design.

68. Make sure your magic trick and balloon animal skills are not rusty. If the kids love it, the girls will too.

69. Never, ever reveal your true identity.

The Blended Family Ceremony

Larry James is a minister, professional speaker, relationship coach, and author of *How to Really Love the One You're With*. To subscribe to his free monthly newsletter, visit CelebrateIntimateWeddings.com. We are grateful to him for these thoughtful ideas.

Most often we think of marriage as the joining of two people to be wife and husband. In reality, marriage is often much more than that. It is also the coming together and merging of family and friends. When the bride and/or groom have children, it is appropriate for the children to be included in the wedding ceremony. With children present, the wedding ceremony also becomes the proclamation of a new family or a "family wedding."

Generally speaking, children will accept a parent's remarriage more readily when they feel included in the wedding and are given a tangible symbol of being embraced by a new family; consider a piece of jewelry, such as a charm bracelet, that includes the names of all the new family members.

Blended families are often referred to as stepfamilies or co-families. The following ceremony can easily be incorporated into any wedding ceremony.

OFFICIANT REMARKS: It is the desire of _____ and _____ to extend their commitments to each other by making some promises to the children of this family. As you all join hands to form a new circle of love, we will seal this union with spoken promises like the rings this bride and groom have exchanged.

OFFICIANT TO THE BRIDE/GROOM: Do you, _____ and _____, promise to be faithful, loving, tender, and nurturing parents, always there for _____ (child/children's name), providing for not only their/her/his physical needs but their/her/his emotional needs as well, always a good listener, a loving counselor, and a friend?

BRIDE AND GROOM: We do.

OFFICIANT TO THE MOTHER/FATHER (SPEAKING TO THE CHILD/CHILDREN): (Repeat after me). _____, I want you to know that I love your mother/father very much. I will not and cannot replace a mother/father loved by you; however, I can promise you that I will love you and care for you as if you were my own. I promise to be a committed listener. I promise you my trust, to be fair, my support, what knowledge I can share, to be your friend, and to provide a shoulder to cry on. I promise to be available to you as I am to your mother/father.

BRIDE/GROOM TO THE CHILD/CHILDREN: _____, I give you this _____ [gift] as a sign of my loving promises made this day.

OFFICIANT TO THE CHILD/CHILDREN: Do you accept the promises made by _____?

CHILD/CHILDREN: I/We do.

OFFICIANT: May a kind God now bless you all as family and bless this marriage and this home, wherever you may be. And so it is.

The Unity Candle

Fire is one of the great forces of nature. It has been essential to human survival, and it has symbolized the heart of the home. Roman and Grecian girls alike were escorted to their futures by the same candlelight that still flickers at ceremonies today. The unity candle ceremony, nonsecular and practiced in a variety of forms, revives that historical tradition.

Cynics claim (and historians don't seem to disagree) that the unity candle ceremony is just another "tradition," like the double-ring ceremony and bridal registries, that was invented by the wedding industry to drum up business. It seems to have emerged during the 1960s in the United States and soon became trendy among Protestant couples. (The Catholic Church does not sanctify the unity candle ceremony.) But it wasn't until *General Hospital*'s Luke and Laura sealed their union over a glittering unity candle that the practice caught on like, well, wildfire. Today the lighting of a unity candle is considered a nondenominational ritual and is practiced by couples from many ethnicities and religions.

The ceremony itself symbolizes the joining of two families. Typically, after vows are read, the mothers of the bride and groom both light tapered candles; sometimes grandparents join in with candles of their own. Each set of parents passes their tapers on until they reach the bride and groom, who use it to light a pillar candle, thus creating one new family unit.

Appropriate candles can be found in any dollar store, or go online to check out personalized, decorated, and largely overpriced varieties. Today sand ceremonies have challenged the popularity of the unity candle. Time marches on.

Beyond the Unity Candle

Blake Kritzberg of Favorideas.com has some other ideas for unification ceremonies:

By now, surely everyone's familiar with the unity candle, but did you know there are other unification ceremonies to choose from when planning your wedding?

Although the unity candle seems to have been with us forever, in reality it's only about ten years old. During those years, more "two-become-one" motifs have arrived to round out the theme.

Unification ceremonies are not only a symbol of togetherness, they're also flexible elements of a wedding. These ceremonies can be "opened up" to include important family members, such as the bridal couple's parents. Children from previous marriages can play a part, as can the entire congregation in a smaller wedding. Candle and rose ceremonies are common choices for adapting in this way.

Unification ceremonies can also be "stacked." It's not unusual to find a wedding that includes a hand and water ceremony, for example, or a wine and rose ceremony. Some couples play music during these ceremonies and others don't.

The timing of unification ceremonies varies by wedding, but they most often take place directly before or after the exchange of vows. These ceremonies may be especially important in nonreligious weddings, which may end too quickly otherwise!

Let's look at some alternatives to the unity candle ceremony:

The Rose Ceremony: The rose ceremony is a flexible, informal ceremony especially suited to an interfaith or nonreligious wedding, not to mention a garden wedding! In the rose ceremony, the bride and groom exchange a single rose as their first married gift to each other. They are asked to recall this symbol of their love during the more trying seasons of marriage.

The Hand Ceremony: In the hand ceremony, the bride takes the groom's hands in hers, palms up. The officiant invites her to view his hands as a gift and says: "These are the hands that will work alongside yours as together you build your future, as together you laugh and cry, and together you share your innermost secrets and dreams." The groom then takes the bride's hands, palm side up. The officiant says, "These are the hands that will passionately love you and cherish you through the years, for a lifetime of happiness, as she promises her love and commitment to you all the days of her life."

The Knot Ceremony: In the knot ceremony, the mothers of the bridal couple are given a cord, which the officiant later asks them to give to the bridal couple. The couple ties a lover's knot, which they may save to look back on later.

The Sand, Water, and Wine Ceremonies: These are all mixing ceremonies suited to a Unitarian or interfaith wedding. The sand ceremony is said to arise from Apache customs and is popular in beach weddings. In each case, the bride and groom pour sand or liquid from two separate vials into one. In the wine ceremony, they drink the mixed wine. A nice touch is to have the bride pour white wine while the groom pours red. You can then serve rosé at the reception to remind everyone of the ceremony.

The Salt Covenant: The salt covenant is an ancient tradition, well described in the Bible and appearing regularly in Indian-national and Jewish weddings. Like the Jewish chuppah, the salt covenant (a mixing ceremony with ancient connotations of loyalty, protection, and hospitality) is beginning to show up in non-Jewish weddings as well.

The Foot-Washing Ceremony: The foot-washing ceremony (not to be confused with the Scottish bridal foot-washing ceremony, a raucous pre-wedding event) is a fascinating, solemn custom emphasizing the role of dual servitude in a marriage.

Tired of Tossing Rice?

Leaving your wedding in a shower of rice is the traditional grand exit. However, many brides are creating other options—something more dramatic, more romantic, or more environmentally friendly. Our thanks to Elizabeth Watts for these suggestions:

TOSS BIRDSEED

Pros: Organic and easy to clean up if the birds eat the free meal

Cons: Think how hard it will be to pick little grains out of your hair—not how you imagined spending your wedding night, huh?

TOSS COLORED CONFETTI OR PAPER STREAMERS

Pros: Pretty and relatively cheap

Cons: Rather wasteful (unless you recycle) and lots of sweeping up afterward

BLOW BUBBLES

Pros: Gives an effect of childlike innocence and fun; bottles decorated with your names and wedding date can double as favors; lots of fun for kids; environmentally safe

Cons: Can leave soap marks on delicate fabrics as bubbles land on people's clothing and burst

RELEASE BUTTERFLIES OR DOVES

Pros: Very dramatic

Cons: Live animals can be unpredictable; may not fly the way you want them to; "accidents" can happen

THROW ROSE PETALS

Pros: Can be super-romantic if you use petals from flowers your fiancé gave you during your courtship

Cons: May be expensive; may require pickup and sweeping later (but can there really be anything bad about roses?)

WAVE SPARKLERS

If you are going all out, this option is particularly effective for a late-summer evening. Light up the night with fireworks in the background and exit with a bang and a flash.

What to Expect at a Military Wedding

HudsonValleyWeddings.com, launched in 1996, is a complete resource for bridal couples in upstate New York, near West Point Military Academy. According to Judy Lewis, the site's founder, military weddings are a privilege of cadets and others in the armed forces. Here is what you can expect if you ever have the pleasure of attending a military wedding.

1. All weddings are formal, with military personnel in dress uniform and commanding officers seated according to rank.

2. Guests attending a military wedding are most likely to remember the "crossed sabers," also known as the "arch of sabers," or the "arch of steel."

3. Traditionally the bride and groom walk through the arch of swords. This passage is meant to ensure the couple's safe transition into their new life together. The arch of swords is formed by an honor guard. Should one of the honor guards also serve as a wedding attendant, he or she must be in full uniform. That includes wearing a sword or saber while in the wedding party.

4. The couple enters the arch, kiss, and then pass through. They then salute the honor guard, who then sheath their swords, or sabers, and return them to a carry position. Depending on church rules and the particular branch of service, the arch can be formed either outside or in the foyer of the chapel, synagogue, or church.

5. During Naval services, the head usher gives the command "Of-ficers, draw swords!" The bride and groom pass under the arch and pause for a moment. The head usher gives the command "Of-ficers, present arms." Swords are returned to the scabbard for all but about three or four inches of their length. The final inches of travel are completed in unison, the swords returning home with a single click.

6. When the arch of swords ceremony is held indoors, it occurs just as the couple rises after receiving the blessing. All members of the bridal party wait until the ushers' swords are returned to their scabbards before the recessional proceeds.

7. During Army or Air Force ceremonies, the arch of sabers is carried out differently. As the bride and groom rise from their kneeling position after the benediction, the senior saber-bearer gives the command "Center face." This command moves the saber-bearers into position facing each other. The next command is "Arch sabers." Each bearer raises his saber, rotating it in a clockwise direction so that the cutting edge will be on top, thus forming a true arch. Once the bride and groom have passed under the arch, the

command "Carry sabers" is issued, followed almost immediately by the "Rear face" command. The saber-bearers are now facing away from the altar and toward the front of the chapel. They re-form again with arched sabers on the steps to the chapel as the couple leaves the chapel.

8. Six or eight ushers or designated officers act as sword-bearers, but other officers can step in. Although the chaplain's office usually furnishes swords or sabers for the ceremony, it is customary, at West Point for instance, for the cadets to furnish their own attire.

9. It is traditional for the wedding cake to be cut with a saber or other type of military sword.

10. Then there is the gentle "swat to the backside" that the bride receives from the last swordsman. It's up to the groom to warn the bride of this impending love tap or suffer the consequences.

The 10 Essentials of a Wiccan Wedding

The Wiccan wedding, known as a handfasting (see page 59), is one Wiccan occasion when non-Wiccan friends and family members are most likely to be invited. We are grateful to Janus of Spawnfar.net for providing these details of this lovely ritual. Those details can vary tremendously, but all Wiccan ceremonies have these elements in common:

1. The ritual will likely be conducted by both a high priestess and a high priest, possibly assisted by four additional priests and priestesses for the four directions: east, west, north, and south.

2. All Wiccan rituals start with a "circle casting." Since Wiccans don't tend to have church buildings, they often worship outdoors. Circle casting is how they declare a place to be their church for the duration of the ritual. The circle may be cast with great ceremony and fanfare and waving of swords, or it may be done simply by gathering the participants in a ring where the ceremony is going to take place.

3. There will usually be some sort of invocation of the four elements, earth, air, fire, and water, in the four directions mentioned above. This may involve spoken invocations, or it may consist of holding up or carrying or placing physical objects that are symbols of the elements. The elements represent the Wiccan connection to the forces of nature and the variety and range of their experiences in the material world. Wiccans make heavy use of the symbolism of the four elements, which is meant to bring balance and harmony to the occasion.

4. There is also likely to be an invocation of the divine forces, in the form of the Goddess and the God, expressing the creative aspect of the divine. Just as Christians view the divine as a trinity of Father, Son, and Holy Spirit, so Wiccans view the divine as a duality of Goddess and God.

5. There may be a wine blessing, in which a chalice of wine or juice is blessed either by the high priestess and high priest or by the bride and groom. One of them will hold the chalice, while the other lowers a ceremonial knife into it. This symbolizes the creative union of opposites—female and male, Goddess and God, earth and heaven, life and death. After the wine has been blessed, it may be passed around the circle for all to partake. Although this is very similar to the Christian transubstantiation and communion rite, Wiccans won't be offended if a non-Wiccan takes some of the blessed wine. Don't be afraid to participate in the ceremony, although it is acceptable to decline.

6. It is possible that the bride and groom will enter the circle separately, and each may be challenged at its entrance with a dire-sounding "this is your last chance to back out" speech. The purpose is to impress upon the bride and groom that they are embarking upon a major life transition.

7. The bride and groom will probably exchange vows, which they may have written themselves.

8. During the handfasting, the bride's and groom's wrists are tied together to symbolize their union. Each participant in turn gets to tie a ribbon around their wrists and offer them a personal blessing.

9. The bride and groom will probably leave the circle by jumping over a broom that has been laid on the ground or is being held at ankle height at the edge of the circle. The custom symbolizes the crossing of the bride and groom into married life, and is said to contain a bit of fertility "magic" as well. Jumping the broom is also common at African-American weddings (see page 39).

10. Once the bride and groom have left the circle, the four elements are formally dismissed and the circle is opened, declaring that the ritual is officially at an end.

Double Bind

On September 10, 2005, Northside Tri-Ethnic Community Center in Fort Worth, Texas, played host to a double wedding as Leo Tate and his bride, Annie Lee, and James Nelson Jr. and Donna Mathis tied the knot. The couples had known each other for only a few days, and the wedding was planned in just two. But they shared a need to bring hope to their dismal surroundings as well as another important bond: they had all survived Hurricane Katrina. "We were thinking how we needed something to rejoice in, something to cry happy tears over," Mathis said. Local businesses provided all the fixings, including the bridal gowns, the bouquets, and the photography. Each couple did, however, have to scrape together the $41 needed for a marriage license in the state of Texas.

Double Weddings

We've heard of double weddings of sisters, sets of twins marrying sets of twins, and even a mother-daughter combo. Double weddings are special for the generosity they usually demonstrate; it takes a couple with kind hearts to share their wedding day—and the spotlight—with others. And it takes even more goodwill for everyone to agree on everything from the nature of the ceremony and a budget to the color of the programs. But it can be done! Double weddings are, of course, easier on guests, who are spared having to travel and dress for two weddings. Not to mention the unique photo opportunities. Here are some of the major issues you'll encounter.

Who goes first? Whether it's the listing on the invitation or the order of the ceremonial pronouncements, the older bride usually goes first, although she might want to relinquish the position for at least a few of the rituals.

How should invitations be configured? Consider going with an invitation that has three panels. The middle panel can list the location, date, and time, and the two side panels can be reserved for the individual couples. Or each couple can send out their own invitations on which they indicate that they are sharing their wedding day (and noting that invitees will not be expected to bring a gift for the other couple). If the couples do not include siblings, whoever is closest to the host of the wedding should be listed first.

Only in India

In 2008, billionaire industrialist Subrata Roy shelled out some $128 million for the double wedding of his two sons, Sushanto and Seemanto. Bollywood had to close down operation for a week, as most Indian film stars were guests at the weeklong extravaganza. Eleven thousand guests were flown to Lucknow, India, a lakeside setting where replicas of a castle, a fort, a Greek temple, and even the White House had been erected. The menu included fare from over 100 different cuisines, and the entertainment featured a 120-piece orchestra that had been flown in from England, four dance troupes, and a company of acrobats. There were tons—literally—of flowers.

Even the starving masses who lived in the dirt-poor surrounding province were included in the celebration. Meals were doled out to 140,000 locals, and 101 local girls were given $5,000 each (an unthinkable sum for people who regularly earn a dollar a day) toward their own marriages.

How should the wedding parties be dressed? The bridal parties of each bride do not have to wear the same thing; they merely have to complement each other. Choose different complementary colors or different shades of the same base color. Or agree on one color and use different styles for each bridal party.

> *In the Philippines, it's bad luck for siblings to marry within the same year.*

What about the processional? If the brides are sisters, their father can walk them down at the same time. The wedding parties can be interspersed, or there may be two separate processionals, with the older bride going first. It's helpful to include in the program descriptions of the relationships of the members of the bridal parties to the brides and grooms.

It's best if the brides choose two different maids of honor. In one wedding, however, that just wasn't possible, and so the maid of honor did the honors twice, separated by what the FOB called "halftime."

Most officiants allow couples to pronounce their vows in unison, but the ring exchanges must take place separately. If one couple is writing their own vows, it makes sense for both couples to do so, just to keep the ceremony as structured as possible. When the ceremony is completed, the officiant will say, "Now you may kiss the brides."

One cake or two? A creative pastry chef can create a shape that accommodates both couples, and they can cut the first piece at the same time. Or two different cakes can be used, preferably ones that complement each other at least in flavor (one chocolate, one vanilla).

12 Tips for Decorating the Getaway Car

Decorating the getaway car seems like a harmless and fun tradition, but it can be the cause of stress and unforeseen angst for the newlywed couple. Traffic violations, permanent car damage, fines, and even accidents could put a serious damper on the happiest of occasions. Here are some suggestions for decorating the car safely.

1. Speak with the couple beforehand. Be considerate of your friends' wishes. It's their day — don't do anything to spoil it.

2. Inquire about rentals. If the couple plans to leave in a rental car, check with the company about possible restrictions, like tying things to the bumper. You wouldn't want your newly married buddy to get slapped with a fine.

3. Don't damage the car's finish. Avoid using shaving or whipped cream on the body of the car— they eat away at paint and may leave a permanent message. Also avoid glue, cellophane tape, and electrical tape, since these can also damage the finish.

4. Invite others to help out. Kids will especially delight in this ritual.

5. Surprise the bridal couple with your thoughtfulness. Toss (not literally!) some drinks and snacks into the car. They'll probably be starving! If they have a driver, include some champagne as a special touch.

6. Keep attachments short. Make sure streamers don't get stuck in the wheels.

7. Be safe. Don't do anything that will obstruct the driver's view, cause the couple to get a ticket, or worse, cause an accident.

8. Get in the car after decorating. Check for visibility and falling debris.

9. Shop around. Complete car-decorating kits are the ultimate time-saver. Glass or window chalk is cheap and easy to clean. Vinyl window "clings" stick and peel off and come with pre-written wedding messages.

10. Tying cans to bumpers may be a tradition, but it's illegal in some areas. Check with the local police department.

11. Don't obscure the license plates.

12. If it's a rental, note the time it's due back. The happy couple shouldn't have to incur a late fee because extra time was needed to clean up.

Tipping Guidelines

Many of the vendor fees you agree to most probably include gratuities. Still, even though it is not required, it is customary to tip for services over and above what you have paid, especially if staff members have been exceptionally responsive to your needs. Thus, additional gratuities are not required, but they will be appreciated and expected by those who have worked hard on your behalf.

Remember to read your contracts carefully to see if tips have been included. If you have any questions, don't hesitate to ask the banquet manager about tipping policies. It's helpful to place tips in envelopes before the event, mark them clearly, and appoint someone (the best man, for instance) to distribute them. Here are some suggestions for appropriate tipping.

1. **Maitre d':** 15 to 20 percent of the catering bill

2. **Banquet manager or event planner:** 15 to 20 percent of the catering bill

3. **Food servers:** $20 each (given to the maitre d' for distribution to the staff)

4. **Bartenders:** 10 percent of the total liquor bill, distributed among the servers

5. **Coatroom attendant:** $1 per guest

6. **Limousine driver:** 15 percent

7. **Parking attendants:** $1 per car

8. **Ceremony musicians:** $50 to $75 each

9. **Reception musicians, DJs:** 15 percent of the entertainment charge

10. **Delivery truck drivers:** $5 to $10 each

11. **Decorating staff:** $50 each

12. **Officiant:** $100 if another fee has not been stated, given as a donation

Saying Thank-You

Your thanks will be the last memory people take away from the experience of your wedding. It will tell them how much you valued their participation and, ultimately, what kind of person you are. Your wedding was the result of hundreds of hours of teamwork. Now it's your turn to make your guests and helpers feel special.

• **Everyone gets a thank-you card,** even if you thanked them in person, even if they didn't send a gift ("We loved having you there"), and even if their gift was a charitable donation. People who hosted parties for you should receive cards as well.

• **Make sure you know who sent each gift** so you can send the right card to each recipient.

• **Send them promptly—no excuses!** By the time the wedding rolls around, you should already have sent thank-you cards for the gifts you received by mail. These should have been sent out within a week—no more than two—of receipt of the gift. After the wedding, you have a month to send thank-you cards for those gifts you received at the event or later. If you send them out late, apologize for being remiss.

• **The job of sending out thank-you cards belongs to both the bride and the groom.** Commit to writing a few each day after the wedding to make sure they go out promptly.

• **They have to be handwritten notes.** No preprinted cards, even if they are Hallmark's best, no e-mails, and no typewritten letters. They should be written on fine stationery. If you want your cards to match your invitations, order them when you place the initial stationery order. Couples often claim that the photo cards they ordered took months to arrive, thus the belated note. That's no excuse and only points to poor planning.

• **Start out by thanking the person for sharing your special day** with you ("Seeing your face there really made us feel special"), then thank him or her for the gift. Be specific. Refer to the gift and tell how it will be used ("The poodle-shaped vase will look great next to the fireplace," "Your generous gift will go toward the house we've been dreaming about"). If the person you're thanking provided extra help, mention it in the note: "How would we have put out that fire without you?"

• **Send out separate cards for shower gifts.**

How To Preserve Your Wedding Gown

Every bride should protect her investment by having her wedding gown professionally cleaned and stored. An expert dry cleaner or gown preservationist can make certain that your heirloom dress is protected from soil and age so that it looks as new in 20 years as it did the day you wore it.

It's all too common to find, years later, that your wedding gown wasn't properly cleaned. Spills are lethal to a dress. Body oils turn the fabric yellow. You may not even have seen them, but white wine and champagne stains can discolor fabric months after the spill.

Not every bride chooses to pack her wedding gown away in a box. It is perfectly acceptable to have your gown altered for use as a dress for special occasions. You should have your dress properly cleaned within one to six months after the wedding to preserve its beauty.

Here are more tips from USABride.com:

1. Find a dry cleaner who advertises as an expert cleaner of wedding gowns. Ask the cleaner if he or she uses different solvents on gowns than on regular clothing. Standard solvents are too harsh for wedding gowns. These gowns must be cleaned with the gentlest cleaners in an acid-free environment.

2. Ask to see the dress before it is packed. That way, you can see for yourself if all visible stains have been removed prior to storage.

3. Wedding gowns should be stuffed with clean, acid-free tissue placed between the folds of the dress and stuffed in the bodice to prevent permanent wrinkles and folds as well as help stabilize the environment of the box.

When Las Vegas photographer John Michael Cooper coined the phrase "Trash the Dress," he pioneered a new creative and artistic trend in the world of wedding photography. This nontraditional approach is intended not so much to destroy the bride's gown (although that's usually the result), but rather to create a memorable artistic moment.

His "Joan or Arc," seen here, is probably the most recognized of all of his post-wedding photographs. The image debuted at the Digital Wedding Forum Convention in Las Vegas in 2006. "Trash the Dress" photos have become popular with brides who want to add something a bit edgy to their wedding albums.

To see some more of John's inspired visual creations, visit Altf. com or his blog at Earth13.com.

COURTESY OF JOHN MICHAEL COOPER

6 Ways to Donate Your Wedding Gown

You can store your wedding gown in a closet for the rest of your life or you can make your day even more memorable by passing it on to someone in need. Whoever paid for the dress can take the tax deduction, and you'll be setting a great example for your bridesmaids (see page 319).

1. **Making Memories** sponsors Brides Against Breast Cancer. Proceeds from the sale of bridal gowns go toward bringing a bit of joy to the lives of breast cancer victims (visit MakingMemories.com).

2. **Africa Street Kids** sells wedding gowns and uses the proceeds to feed thousands of kids who live on the streets throughout Africa (visit DonateWeddingGowns.com).

3. **WedAlert.com** helps brides who cannot afford wedding gowns.

4. **I Do Foundation** donates 10 percent of the profits from gowns to the bride's charity of choice, and the rest funds the group's continued effort to encourage charitable giving at weddings (visit IDoFoundation.org).

5. **The Bridal Garden** in New York City offers wedding gowns at a fraction of their original price and donates the profits to shelters and day care centers that serve kids in need.

6. **Heavenly Angels in Need** will work with a seamstress to turn your dress into a burial gown for parents who have nothing in which to bury their babies (visit HeavenlyAngelsInNeed.com).

21 Uses for a Used Bridesmaid's Dress

1. Baby's coverlet
2. Bath scrub
3. Book cover
4. Chair cover
5. Curtains
6. Doll's clothing
7. Drawstring bags for shoes or gifts
8. Hair scrunchies
9. Halloween costume
10. Kite
11. Lampshade
12. Lining for a jewelry box
13. Napkins
14. Pillow shams
15. Ribbon for wrapping gifts
16. Ruffles to edge a tablecloth or towel
17. Seat cushion
18. Skirt for a vanity
19. Table runner
20. Tea or toaster cozy
21. Tent for a cat

We know that the earliest bridesmaids protected the bride by surrounding her before the wedding, keeping her hidden from the eyes of mischief-makers. Perhaps it was felt that frightening costumes would further help keep trouble at bay. Could this be the origin of the ugly bridesmaid's dress?

3 Charities That Seek Out Donations of Bridesmaids' Dresses

1. **The Cinderella Project** collects bridesmaids' dresses and tuxedos and distributes them among high school students in Los Angeles who cannot afford outfits for proms and graduations (visit CinderellaProject.net).

2. **The Glass Slipper Project** performs the same service for kids in Chicago (visit GlassSlipperProject.org).

3. **Fairy Godmothers** groups around the country collect wedding dresses and other formal attire for distribution to needy kids in various cities (visit FairyGodmotherInc.com).

6 Ways to Preserve Wedding Flowers

If you haven't tossed them, you can enjoy your wedding flowers for decades. However you choose to preserve them, make your decision right after the wedding, as preservation processes must begin within one to four days of the wedding for the best results.

Be sure to handle the flowers carefully; if possible, keep them in the refrigerator until you are ready to work with them. If professional methods seem pricey, consider having just a few representative buds preserved instead of a whole bouquet. You have a few options, although the DIY variety can be tricky. When flowers are professionally preserved, a bouquet is taken apart and then reassembled after the process is done. Do you really want to try this at home?

1. Have a bouquet professionally preserved by one of the many Internet companies that handle the delicate chemical process of placing the flowers in a special chamber and removing the moisture from them. This happens slowly; it can take a month or more. Expect to pay anywhere from $100 to $300 to have a bouquet freeze-dried. Once your flowers have been preserved, they are placed in the arrangement of your choice: under a glass bell jar or framed, with or without other wedding memorabilia.

2. You can imitate the above method by filling a box with dry river sand, placing the blossoms on the sand, and sifting more sand

over all the flowers until they are completely covered. Then cover the box and place it in a warm, dry place for about a week. It's a good idea to experiment with this method before you try it on your bridal flowers.

3. The simplest way to preserve flowers is by air-drying or hanging. You need only remove the leaves and hang the flowers upside down in a warm, dry, dark place. An attic or closet is perfect; avoid damp basements and porches. The flowers can be hung from a coat hanger, a clothesline, or a hook. The method takes about two weeks. Any blooms that become damaged in the process can be saved to make potpourri.

4. Silica gel, a granular substance available at garden centers, can also do the trick. Similar to the sand method, place the flowers in an airtight container, and just as in the sand method, cover them with the gel crystals for an extended period (depending on the variety of the flower). The method has pitfalls: the flowers sometimes reabsorb moisture once they are displayed, so it's best to keep them under glass.

5. You can also use silica gel to dry flowers in your microwave oven, though this method is tricky. Place the flowers in a microwave-safe container and cover them completely with silica gel. Use a toothpick to prod the gel granules around each flower petal. Then place the container in the microwave along with a cup of water for a short period. (Detailed "cooking" times for various flowers can be found on the Internet.) After cooking, allow the flowers to "rest." They can be removed once everything has cooled.

6. If you can't stand clutter, consider framing a beautiful photo of the bouquet instead of keeping the real thing around, or ask a talented friend to paint its portrait. The memory of your flowers, at least, will be preserved forever.

8 Ways to Protect Your Wedding Photos

When preserving or archiving your wedding photographs, be aware that they are fragile objects that can easily be damaged by improper storage, careless handling, or exposure to the environment.

1. Keep photographs in enclosures that protect them from light and dust and provide physical support, such as matting and framing, during display or use. Chemically stable plastic or paper enclosures, free of sulfur, acids, and peroxides, are recommended. Plastic sleeves should be constructed of uncoated polyester, polypropylene, or polyethylene.

2. Unbuffered or acid-free paper enclosures are preferred over the buffered variety. Alkaline buffering is added to archival storage papers to absorb acidity from the stored material or the environment surrounding it. However, some photographs may be altered by the buffering in alkaline papers, so unbuffered paper is recommended for most processes. Your archival album should be made with acid-free paper, acid-free prints, acid-free adhesive, and even acid-free photo corners. Acid-free materials will help preserve your photos for 75 to 100 years.

3. Storing photographs in albums serves the dual purpose of organizing groups of images while protecting them from physical and environmental damage. Preserve them intact when possible and store them in custom-fitted archival boxes. Magnetic or self-adhesive albums can be detrimental to photographs and should not be used.

4. Black-and-white prints last longer than color. The materials used in making color prints make them more susceptible to fading due to surrounding conditions such as temperature and moisture.

5. Most damage to photographs results from poor handling. A well-organized and properly housed collection promotes respect for the photographs and appropriate care in handling.

• View photographs in a clean, uncluttered area, and handle them with clean hands.

• Keep photographs covered when they are not being viewed.

• Do not use ink pens around photographic materials. Mark enclosures with pencil only. If it is necessary to mark a photograph, write lightly with a soft lead pencil on the back of the image.

6. Light damages photographs. You obviously have to expose photos to light to view them, but when you store them, place them in light-proof boxes. The pictures you hang on your walls should be thought of as disposable; don't hang the original if it is especially important to you—make a copy and hang that instead. Avoid placing any photos in direct sunlight.

7. Keep areas where photographs are handled or stored clean and pest-free. Paper fibers, albumen, and gelatin binders in photographic materials provide an attractive food source for rodents and insects. It is vital that your album be free of debris that might entice pests that can damage treasured photographs. Food and beverages should not be allowed while looking at photos. Accidental spills can damage most photographs.

8. Disaster preparedness begins by evaluating the storage location and the potential for damage in the event of a flood, fire, or other disaster. It is vital that you create a disaster preparedness plan that addresses the specific needs of the photo collection before a disaster occurs. The location and manner in which photographs are housed can be the first line of defense.

A History of the Honeymoon

We're grateful to Erica Tevis, proprietor of LittleThings WeddingFavors.com, for this slice of wedding history.

The post-wedding vacation that we have come to know as the honeymoon was not always such. Many sources say that the history lies somewhere in northern Europe, where for a month's time after the wedding, the newly married couple would drink a wine known as mead, which was made from fermented honey. This is where part of the term, "honey," comes from. A month's time during this period was also referred to as a moon; hence the term "honeymoon."

Honeymoons were first related to travel during the bride-by-capture era. Grooms would abduct their brides for a period of one month and take them into hiding. Friends and family assured their safe return. However, it was imperative that no one should find them during this period, although very often the family of the bride would go out looking for her to bring her home. It was the husband's hope that his bride would be pregnant before they located her.

It was not until the sixteenth century and later in the nineteenth-century Victorian era that the honeymoon became the romantic trip that it is known as today. During Victorian times, the bride and groom were kept separated during the engagement period, and the honeymoon was the first chance the couple had to go away together and get to know one another. Thus they began to take the form of romantic excursions.

During the latter part of the century, "bridal tours" were introduced, typically paid for by the groom's family. The couple would take a wedding trip that lasted anywhere from several weeks to several months. With the rise of industrialization, the middle class sought to emulate the upper-class bridal tours, and so they took small trips that lasted a few days after the wedding. Once automobiles, trains, and airplanes became commonplace, couples were able to increase the distance of the honeymoon trip and seek out exotic locations. Thus the modern-day honeymoon was born.

18 Great Honeymoon Tips

1. Your honeymoon is an important event, so talk to your travel agent and ask plenty of questions, the more specific the better. Ask questions about the hotel or resort, the room, your flight. Don't leave anything to chance.

2. If you can avoid it, don't book your flight for early the next morning after the wedding, particularly if you're planning an evening reception. Once you finally get to sleep, it may be hard to wake up at 5:00 A.M. for that early-morning flight, or worse, you may not even hear the alarm!

3. Splurge a little—it's your honeymoon! Do something special that you wouldn't normally do on a regular vacation. Spend a little extra for a room upgrade or the honeymoon suite. Plan a romantic dinner at a gourmet restaurant or go on a sunset cruise. Go on a few excursions or tours.

4. When packing for your honeymoon, think about packing some romantic items like candles, massage oil, and some new lingerie.

5. Give yourself plenty of time to pack, and make a list of all the items you'll need. Anything that you forget, such as suntan lotion, aspirin, or toothpaste, will always cost more to purchase at your destination.

6. The new security procedures at airports require you to show a current picture identification. It is important to purchase your airline tickets with your maiden name in order to match your photo ID, license, or passport.

7. If you are using disposable cameras at your wedding, buy a few extra and take them on your honeymoon! Disposable cameras are great when you don't want to risk losing or damaging your expensive digital camera.

8. When making reservations for your honeymoon, let your hotel, resort, or cruise line know that you are newlyweds. You're likely to receive lots of special treatment, like free champagne, breakfast in bed, a "goodie basket," or even the honeymoon suite!

9. Check your existing homeowner's insurance policy and credit cards to find out what sort of coverage you have. When you purchase your tickets, make sure they can be exchanged in case of an illness or other emergency. Be sure that your contract with any tour operative covers failure or default by the company.

10. Be sure to choose your honeymoon destination together, considering the preferences of both bride and groom. If each of you

makes a list of what you imagine would be the perfect honeymoon, you can then compare the lists. Visit HoneymoonersReviewGuide.com for a questionnaire that will guide you through the process.

11. Websites can sometimes be deceptive or lack information. Do your research and do it well. Don't let beautiful photographs lull you into a false sense of security. You definitely don't want to arrive at that "dream" location to find out that you can't swim there because the currents are too strong or the water is contaminated. Search for additional photos on the Internet. Find out if the resort features the "family vacation," kids and all. If so, it might not be the best place for a honeymoon. It's also a good idea to check customer reviews on the Internet—sites such as Travelpost.com will let you read what other guests have written about the resort you are interested in.

12. Why spend hours online searching for your perfect hotel when an agent can quickly narrow down the choices, steer you away from trouble, and handle all the ticketing all for free?

13. Passport dilemmas can be a pain. If you need a passport, apply for it well in advance. If you already have one, make sure it's current. Some countries require that your passport be valid for a certain period of time (as long as three months) once you've entered a foreign country, even if you are going home before the passport expires.

14. Find out if there are any necessary or recommended immunizations for your honeymoon destination. Check your own records to see if you need to update your immunizations. The Centers for Disease Control and Prevention is a great source of information regarding this (visit cdc.gov).

An advertisement from *Brides* magazine, 1940
AUTHORS' COLLECTION

15. Make sure you have enough time to pack so that you don't forget important items. Buying items at your destination will usually be more expensive and a waste of your precious honeymoon time. Start packing at least a week in advance and be sure that you are working with a thorough list.

16. Find out if the water is potable. Severe stomachaches or diarrhea could put a real damper on your honeymoon. Food and water can be contaminated with diseases such as cholera, typhoid, or hepatitis A. Let your doctor know where you are traveling and find out if there are any medications you should take along in the event of a problem.

17. Those stories you've heard about purse snatchers and pickpockets are true. Never keep anything in your wallet that you absolutely don't need. Before departing for your honeymoon, remove all unnecessary items from your wallet, especially those extra credit cards that you won't be using. Don't bring too many valuables with you. Leave your expensive diamond ring at home and sport a fake. When you go out at night, put your money and identification in a money belt or in your front pocket, protected by your hand. Open bags are easy targets. This is especially important in crowded areas. Don't be totally reliant on room safety. Put locks on bags while you're out of your room and use the safe.

18. No matter what happens, have a wonderful trip and enjoy your time together. Something is always bound to go wrong, but with a positive attitude and a little advance preparation, you can turn almost any situation around. And even if the honeymoon is a disaster, you have the rest of your lives to make up for it. Plus you'll have great stories to tell the grandchildren.

9 Ways to Save Money on a Honeymoon

7. Register at websites such as honeymoonwishes.com or honeyluna.com so that your guests can contribute to your honeymoon fund.

8. Set a budget for your honeymoon just like you've done for your wedding. Determine how much you want to spend on hotel, transportation (airfare, car, or taxi), meals, entertainment, and shopping. When you set a budget and put it in writing, the chances that you will stay within it and not overspend are much better.

9. If you are looking to save money on a vacation, in most cases an all-inclusive package will be the best value. It is one price that usually includes your airfare, hotel accommodations, food, drink (including alcoholic beverages), and some water sports (such as snorkeling and sailing).

1. Use a travel agent. Agents can send you to resorts that are tried and true and save you tons of time if you need to change your itinerary at any point. Tell them what you're looking for and be open to their suggestions.

2. If it's off-season, there's a reason. Check the local weather patterns carefully.

3. Rent a private home instead of staying at a hotel. You'll have to do your own cooking, but you'll have tons of privacy, and the price break could make even an exotic location affordable. (Plus, in many honeymoon destination spots locals can be hired to cook.)

4. When looking into travel packages, make sure you intend to use everything you're paying for—do you really want three meals a day and access to the golf course? Ask if gratuities are included; don't be trapped into double-tipping.

5. Make sure you're aware of all cancellation policies.

6. Don't book the honeymoon suite. The regular rooms at three- and four-star hotels can do nicely.

Above: Vintage postcard COPYRIGHT © 2008 BY JUPITER IMAGES CORP.

3 Ways to Get a Free Honeymoon

1. Complete a contest form at Win-Wedding.com and receive an automatic entry to win $50,000 for your dream wedding. The wedding will include the dress, the venue, the rings, and a honeymoon in the Bahamas, Hawaii, Mexico, or Las Vegas.

2. If you have your wedding at the Westin New York Times Square and spend more than $20,000, you'll get a free five-night stay at the Westin Rio Mar Beach and Golf Club in Puerto Rico (visit WestinNY.com or call 212-201-2700).

3. Wyndham Hotels and Resorts offer a free honeymoon if you book your wedding at one of their locations. The package includes a four- to seven-night stay at a participating Wyndham hotel or resort, $100 credit each day of your stay good toward any on-property food or beverage outlet, complimentary champagne upon arrival, and a honeymoon keepsake memento. Palm Springs, Orlando, the Virgin Islands, St. Thomas, the Bahamas, the Dominican Republic, Mexico, and St. Maarten are just some of their resort locations. Unfortunately, air-fare is not included in this "free" package (visit Wyndham.com).

7 Winners of Thrifty Car Rental's "Honeymoon Disasters Contest"

In July 1993, Thrifty Car Rental's senior manager of corporate communications, Chris Payne, and his wife Susan had the Jamaican honeymoon from hell. The succession of disastrous events they experienced inspired Thrifty's "Honeymoon Disaster Contest." Now Thrifty receives thousands of stories every year. To enter the contest, visit HoneymoonDisasters. com. You could win a second honeymoon!

Here are some of Thrifty's prize-winning stories:

1998

After a blissful first night in Niagara Falls, Lori and Ron Stagg of West Valley City, Utah, flipped their Subaru in a freak accident while road-tripping through the wilds of Canada. The wedding gifts left in the car-top carrier—including fine china—were smashed to bits. Covered in Day-Glo orange flavoring from the snacks they had been eating at the time of the accident, the Staggs were rescued and treated at a nearby hospital.

Barefoot, bandaged, and stranded, they boarded a cross-country bus bound for Chicago that turned into a "48-hour experiment in the amount of suffering a human being can endure," according to Lori. No air conditioning in the August heat and a broken toilet were just the beginning. Fellow passengers included a gospel singing group who spent the time preparing for their upcoming performance.

2000

What do you do when you are stuck on a boat in the middle of the Caribbean with passengers dropping like flies so fast that you begin to wonder if the Grim Reaper wasn't on the guest list?

Dylan and Amber Oles, of Rochester Hills, Michigan, had to do just that when the dream cruise they booked for their honeymoon played host to five onboard deaths in less than ten days. Things got so bad that even passengers and crew nicknamed the vessel "the Ship of Death."

The first sign of trouble was at the pier. The line for customs was as long as the eye could see, according to Amber, and it didn't appear to be moving.

"We were looking forward to having fun with other young couples or honeymooners," said Amber. "One look at the line, and we knew that wasn't going to happen. We were also on a ship in the middle of being remodeled, which meant the hot tub, gym, and other facilities were off limits."

Initially depressed by the situation, the pair decided to do what they could to enjoy their trip. Once they cleared customs and were on their way to dinner, a man collapsed and died in front of them. The ship was forced to turn around and drop off the body, making them late for their first port of call.

After two more ports and four more deaths, even the ship's comedians were cracking jokes about the growing body count. The highlight of the trip was the moment at which the ship's steward decided to ignore the "Do Not Disturb" sign plainly hanging on their doorknob and barge right in—at a very awkward moment.

2001

"Who's been sleeping in my bed? More importantly, who's been using my bath towels?"

That's the question Debbie and Steve Meyer of Sudbury, Massachusetts, asked themselves when they arrived at their honeymoon hideaway in Maui prior to the wedding. They discovered the place in shambles and the previous renters still in residence—and in no hurry to leave. After playing bellhops to the interlopers and helping them out with their bags, the Meyers discovered a paradise of unmade beds, grimy floors, greasy pans, and refrigerators filled with science experiments.

Things didn't get much better once the squatters cleared out. With the wedding only hours away, the couple decided to clean up and went in search of towels. Finding none, they called the owner, who returned with towels. Shaking and sniffing them, he finally declared, "I think this one's clean." That's when they left in search of more appealing accommodations.

Once they lucked into a nice, clean condo, the Meyers had only 20 minutes to shower and dress before meeting the minister. They greeted him with wet hair, and Debbie realized she had forgotten her shoes. After finding them, they returned to a locked church and were forced to have an impromptu outdoor wedding in a graveyard next to the church.

It wasn't until the next morning that the minister delivered the real kicker: due to a technicality, they weren't really married. Once the papers were signed (for real this time), they spent their first day as husband and wife on a secluded hike in the rain forest. While admiring the scenery along a steep path, they heard a scream and were enlisted by rescue personnel to find a person who had fallen from a rocky cliff.

Having had enough excitement for one day, the couple returned to the condo expecting to sip mai tais and instead found that the place was completely enclosed in a giant tent for insect fumigation.

2002

The earliest sign that Amy and Dave's honeymoon might not go as planned was when they landed at their "always sunny" Caribbean destination—and were greeted by buckets of rain.

Using trash bags for umbrellas, they arrived at the hotel only to find their honeymoon suite so cramped that there wasn't room for them and the luggage. So they paid an extra $60 for a larger room that held everything, "as long as you held your breath," according to Amy.

On their first evening out, they returned to the hotel after dinner and were mugged by two masked men who escaped with Amy's purse. Nearby, an apartment security guard watched the entire episode from behind a fence. Amy pleaded in Spanish for him to help but was told, "Inside the fence is my problem, and outside is yours."

Despite the never-ending rain, the couple decided to make the most of their time together by stargazing when the clouds parted briefly. They fell asleep in their lounge chairs by the pool until an amorous hotel employee awakened Amy by snuggling in beside her.

A few days later, and despite the incessant rain, Amy decided to go swimming, but she lost her footing on a rock and seriously bruised her foot. They rushed to the emergency room and found that the hospital was without electricity except for the emergency generator used only for essential functions. The doctor on duty ordered a muscle-relaxing shot for Amy. With no electricity and no light, Dave was asked to shine a flashlight on Amy's backside.

After copious amounts of paperwork, the couple returned to the hotel with Amy wanting nothing more than a shower. When she turned on the shower and nothing came out, she grudgingly settled for a cold sponge bath of water salvaged from the ice chest they had taken to the beach earlier that day.

2003

Katie and Ben Buchanan of Oregon should have seen it coming when Katie, a nurse, was feeling ill before the wedding and attributed it to wedding day jitters. The pair made it through the ceremony without incident, but that was where good fortune left them behind.

After spending most of the wedding night looking for their missing passports, they were finally able to get three hours of sleep at the hotel before their 5 A.M. departure to Mexico.

While waiting in line to check their baggage, Ben discovered that his wallet was missing. After dumping all the clothes out of their suitcases and scrambling all the way back to the hotel to look for it, he discovered the wallet wedged in a crevice of their car.

After one good evening at their hotel, Katie's illness worsened, but staying inside didn't seem to be a problem, since Hurricane Lane was now bearing down on them. Later that night the pain turned to lower-right quadrant pain—something she immediately recognized as an appendicitis attack.

After a local doctor concluded that surgery would be required, the couple made their way to his six-bed clinic. The doctor told Ben that the surgery would cost at least $10,000 and that he required some up-front cash before he could perform the operation. With the hurricane canceling all flights back to the United States and his new bride in excruciating pain, Ben emptied his wallet.

As Katie lay strapped to the narrow operating table, she panicked when the doctor began unwrapping the surgical instruments without any gloves on. Two hours later, Ben heard screaming coming from the operating room—Katie's anesthesia had worn off while the doctor was stitching her up.

After two days at the clinic, with Ben sleeping on a piece of foam on the floor, Katie had improved enough to leave—but not, the doctor insisted, before they paid the remaining $8,000. Ben didn't have the money; the doctor insisted that he come up with it within one day.

The next morning the couple met the doctor not knowing how they were going to come up with the $8,000. After Ben was threatened with jail, the doctor finally relented after Katie's mother promised to wire the money later in the day.

2004

Following a small reception in a mobile home, Cyndy and Roger Wilber of Ravena, New York, were escorted to a tent located behind the cabins of a church summer camp. The groom's dad had pitched the tent on a slope so that if it rained the water would run away from their possessions. Inside was a huge rock in the center of the floor, with cots set up on either side—not exactly what the newlyweds had in mind for sleeping arrangements. The couple wasted no time folding up the cots and squeezing together two sleeping bags on one side of the rock. Well-wishers from the wedding party had set up emergency flares around the tent so that "every shadow could be observed," according to the bride. "Bring on the show!" the onlookers catcalled. It was midnight before the flares finally burned out and the wedding party went home.

Then torrential rains paid a visit. To simplify things, the newlyweds brought the portable toilet inside. In the heat of passion, the toilet got knocked over, soiling their clothes, food, and sleeping bags. As it was still raining, the clever couple decided to harness the forces of nature and strung a rope between two trees to wash their clothes in the rain.

The next morning, Roger and Cyndy awakened to the sounds of children singing. As luck would have it, nobody had warned them that the church camp was still in session. Trapped by the singing von Trapp children, the Wilbers, wrapped only in blankets, were stuck in their tent until two o'clock in the afternoon.

As the porta-potty had contaminated their meager supplies, the couple were forced to eat berries and fish for blue gills using a safety pin suspended from nylon thread unraveled from one of the blankets.

2006

Honeymoons are supposed to be a time of romance and moonlit walks, but not for Jeff and Rhonda West of Bessemer City, North Carolina. Their honeymoon began with a torrential downpour. Headed for the hotel in Jeff's mint-condition 1968 Camaro RS, they lost a hubcap. After chasing it down, they resumed their journey, until they heard a very loud thud. Jeff, still dressed in his tuxedo, got out of the car to survey the blown-out back tire when the car, along with his new bride, started rolling down the hill; he had forgotten to put the car in park.

"I could hear my beautiful bride screaming at the top of her lungs," said Jeff. "'Help! Help!' Then I started chasing the car until it came to rest in a bunch of bushes. By now my wife is in tears, wondering what's going to happen next."

After changing the tire and double-checking the hubcap, the newlyweds were off again. But they still weren't home free.

"We finally get to our hotel, only to find out that it had caught on fire the day before and was completely shut down," said Jeff. "This almost pushed my new wife completely over the edge—sitting in a parking lot at three o'clock in the morning on our wedding night without a place to bed down for the night."

The couple started driving around searching for a room. They finally stopped at a small hotel outside the city limits and went into the office to inquire about a vacancy, at which point their car was stolen.

Honeymoon Weather Guide

When choosing a honeymoon destination, the most important factor of all will be the weather. Some couples even schedule their weddings around the weather of the location they've chosen. Here's a list that will help you choose. Note that weather conditions can always fluctuate, but the locations listed here for each month represent typical annual patterns. Still, it's always a good idea to purchase travelers' insurance in case weather conditions interfere with your plans and you have to reschedule or change locations.

WARM-WEATHER HONEYMOONS

Good weather can also mean crowds and peak-season pricing, so if you're looking for seclusion, shop carefully.

January
Australia
Caribbean and Florida Keys
Central America
Maldives
Mexico
New Zealand
North Africa
South America
Southeast Asia

February
Australia
Caribbean and Florida Keys
Central America
Maldives
Mexico
New Zealand
North Africa
South America
Southeast Asia

March
Australia
Caribbean and Florida Keys
Central America
French Polynesia
Maldives
Mexico
North Africa

South America
Southern United States

April
Australia
Caribbean and Florida Keys
Central America
French Polynesia
Maldives
Mauritius
Mexico
North Africa
South Africa
South America
United States

May
Canada
Caribbean and Florida Keys
Europe
Fiji
French Polynesia
Madagascar
Maldives
Mauritius
Mexico and Belize
Seychelles
South Africa
Thailand
United States

June
Bermuda
Canada
Europe
Fiji
French Polynesia
Madagascar
Maldives
Mauritius
Northern United States, including Alaska
Seychelles
South Africa
Thailand

July
Bermuda
Canada
Europe
Fiji
French Polynesia
Madagascar
Malaysia
Mauritius
Northern United States, including Alaska
Seychelles
South Africa
Thailand

August
Bermuda
Canada
Europe

Fiji
French Polynesia
Kenya
Madagascar
Malaysia
Mauritius
Northern United States, including Alaska
Seychelles
South Africa
Thailand

September
Australia
Bermuda
Canada
Europe
Fiji
French Polynesia
Madagascar
Malaysia
Mauritius
Seychelles
South Africa
Thailand
United States

October
Australia
Bermuda
Canada
Fiji
French Polynesia
Madagascar

Maldives
Mauritius
Mexico and Belize
North Africa
Seychelles
South Africa
Southeast Asia
Southern Europe
United States

November
Australia
French Polynesia
Mauritius
Mexico and Belize
New Zealand
North Africa
Seychelles
South Africa
Southeast Asia
Southern United States

December
Australia
Caribbean and Florida Keys
Central America
Mexico
New Zealand
North Africa
South America
Southeast Asia

COLD-WEATHER HONEYMOONS

Many locations from Colorado to the Swiss Alps make for great snow-packed honeymoon adventures. Check yearly averages of snow on the ground during your time of travel to be certain that the slopes are ready when you arrive. The following are favored cold-weather locations from November through April.

Asia
Iran
Japan
Kashmir
Kazakhstan
South Korea

Europe
Austria
France
Germany
Italy
Norway
Spain
Sweden
Switzerland

Canada
Alberta
British Columbia
Quebec

United States
California
Colorado
Idaho
Michigan
Montana
Oregon
Utah
Vermont
Wisconsin
Wyoming

The 10 Most Romantic Cities in the World

HoneymoonersReviewGuide.com, which provides a contemporary perspective on honeymoon and destination wedding planning, from the basics to a full-scale hotel search, has compiled this list of the most romantic places to say, "We did!"

1. Paris, France
2. Venice, Italy
3. San Francisco, California
4. Prague, Czech Republic
5. Rome, Italy
6. London, England
7. New York, New York

8. Vienna, Austria
9. Miami, Florida

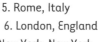

10. Sydney, Australia

3 Honeymoon Capitals of the World Right Here in the U.S.A.

When it comes to honeymoon destinations, you have a mind-numbing number of options. You can narrow the search by just deciding on "the honeymoon capital of the world"—but which one? Three famous destinations have claimed the title. For more suggestions, visit Every1Loves2Travel.com, where you'll find useful ideas from other travelers. We're grateful to Diana McCalley for this list.

1. **Niagara Falls** It may not be the tallest waterfall in the world, but it is certainly the most famous, located on the border between New York and Ontario. Niagara Falls is actually a collection of three waterfalls: Horseshoe Falls (called by some the Canadian Falls), the American Falls, and Bridal Veil Falls, with Horseshoe Falls considered the most spectacular of the three. Niagara Falls has hosted honeymooning couples Theodosia Burr, daughter of U.S. vice president Aaron Burr, who honeymooned with her new husband, Joseph Aliston, in 1802, and Jerome Bonaparte, brother of Napoleon, who honeymooned with his new wife, Elizabeth Patterson, in 1804.

2. **The Pocono Mountains** Each year over 200,000 honeymooning couples begin their married life in the Pocono Mountains of northeastern Pennsylvania, which boasts 2,400 square miles of wooded peaks and valleys with crystal clear lakes, rushing rivers, and some of the most spectacular waterfalls in the eastern United States. Think about it: what could be more romantic than this, the home of the heart-shaped waterbed?

3. **Gatlinburg, Tennessee** Located in the Bible Belt on the edge of the Great Smoky Mountains, Gatlinburg is something of an industry unto itself, hosting about 18,000 honeymoons a year. The breathtaking views and activities available (skiing, anyone?) are the main attraction, but that hasn't stopped the industrious folks in Gatlinburg from offering plenty of other amenities: Hillbilly Golf, the Cupid's Chapel of Love Hotel, and the Garters & Guns Old Tyme Saloon, all with a Christian flavor.

Round beds were all the rage among honeymooning couples in the 1950s.
AUTHORS' COLLECTION

10 Unusual Honeymoons

Cuddling in bed at home for a weekend can make for the most romantic honeymoon ever. But if you're looking for a once-in-a-lifetime trip to mark the start of married life, consider these choices.

1. **Alyeska Resort, Girdwood, Alaska (GuestServices@Alyeska Resort.com)** You're asleep in the Royal Suite, having spent the day dog sledding, rock-climbing, bear-watching, glacier-hiking, or cross-country skiing; relaxing in a spa; then dining in one of several restaurants (or did you call room service?). A staff member gently awakens you, per your request, so you can see the northern lights. Heavenly!

2. **Sheraton Sanya Resort, Sanya, China (Sheraton.com)** Gaze out over Yalong Bay in Sanya, China, from the private balcony of your honeymoon suite; indulge in a rain-forest shower; take a banana boat ride; spend the day at the luxurious spa; shake your newly relaxed booty at the Samba Night Club; or enjoy any of the hotel's numerous restaurants and bars. Within 100 miles of the hotel you can day-trip to the Luhuitou (Turn-Round Deer) Park, the intriguingly named End of the Earth, the Seven Fairy Hot Spring, Nanshan Temple, Wuzhi Mountain, Pacific Waterfall, and Jianfengling Tropical Rain Forest.

3. **Auberge du Soleil, Rutherford, California (aubergedusoleil .com)** View California's Napa Valley from a hot-air balloon; wave down to Auberge du Soleil on Rutherford Hill, where your private cottage amenities include a Jacuzzi, two fireplaces, and a two-person steam shower. Pamper yourself at the Spa du Soleil, admire the sculpture and photo galleries, then dine handsomely, as the Auberge du Soleil began its life as a restaurant. Napa is wine country, so make some time to visit a few of the 200 wineries in the area.

4. **Las Hayas Resort Hotel, Ushuaia, Argentina (lashayas@ overnet.com.ar)** Buenos Aires is nice, but hop a plane from there down to Islas Mavinas Airport in the southernmost city in the world, Ushuaia, in tax-free Tierra del Fuego, Patagonia. Book the presidential suite at the five-star Las Hayas, set in its own beech-forested park, your home base from which you'll explore a lighthouse and train (both at the "end of the world"), a famous jail (closed since 1947 but still a reminder of Ushuaia's longtime Spanish domination), and the Andes, glaciers, cliffs, lakes, and steppes. Hobnob with ostriches, albatrosses, doves, and penguins or snorkel, skin-dive, or sail in the Beagle Channel. Oh, and did we mention the dinosaur graveyards?

5. **Palazzo Sant'Angelo, Venice, Italy (palazzosantangelo@ sinahotels.it)** Still sleepy-eyed, gaze at the Grand Canal of Venice from the balcony of your suite at the four-star Palazzo Sant'Angelo. Once you can tear yourself away, spend some time in the marble bathroom: a hydro-massage awaits. The breakfast room overlooks the canal too, and the whole sparkling city, with about 150 other canals and 400 bridges, awaits you. Smooch in a *vaporetto* on the canal, drifting under the Rialto Bridge toward the palatial Ca' d'Oro (Golden House) and its art-laden Galleria Franchetti. Cross the Grand Canal in a *traghetto* and wander through the six Venetian neighborhoods. There are islands to explore, the Doge's Palace, and St. Mark's Basilica in St. Mark's Square. Lace-making and glass-blowing are two fine arts still practiced in this watery world.

6. **Pension Páv, Prague 1, Czech Republic (pension-pav@ prague.st)** Dying to visit Czechoslovakia? Too late! It no longer exists. But Prague still stands in all its golden glory on the Vitava (Muldau) River, serving as the capital of the Czech Republic, a relatively small nation that nonetheless boasts nearly 1,000 castles. Pension Páv is centrally located and charmingly decorated, and bustling Prague offers a plethora of dining experiences. You won't need a car because everything is easily reached on foot or by tram or subway, including huge Prague Castle, right in the heart of town, with its monasteries, cathedrals, churches, a convent, palaces, a toy museum, towers, and the Royal Garden. The Jewish Quarter (Franz Kafka's hometown) is just one of many historical neighborhoods.

7. **Trans-Siberia Railroad, Leningrad Station, Moscow, Russia** You'll be gently rocked to sleep in your first-class sleeper by the hypnotic rhythm of the Trans-Siberian Railroad, a whopping

6,152 miles in seven days from Moscow to Vladivostok. Watch the scenery speed by. Stop over in Omsk, or elsewhere along the way, just to soak up the local culture. (You'll need a Russian visa.)

8. **Chobe Chilwero Lodge, Chobe National Park, Kasane, Botswana (southernafrica@sanctuarylodges.com)** After a delightful swim and a spa treatment by the pool, sip fine wine on the private balcony of your luxuriously appointed cottage. Enjoy high tea on the shady lawn and gourmet meals in the lodge, where you can, but won't want to, check your e-mail. Take a sundowner cruise on the Chobe River at sunset. Be driven through the Chobe National Park and see lions, hippos, and the largest concentration of elephants in all of Africa. Day-trip to Victoria Falls. You won't run out of delights at Botswana's famous all-inclusive resort.

9. **Vatulele, Fiji (res@vatulele.com/info@vatulele.com)** Only 19 couples at once may be spoiled rotten by the staff of 110 at Vatulele, the award-winning, all-inclusive, Fijian private-island hideaway that eschews your shoes and declines your tips. You're not the only ones who'll want to book the Varle Vinge, the air-conditioned pink honeymoon bure (villa), with its plunge pool and private deck; you'd better reserve it about a year in advance. All the bures are beachfront yet have natural jungle settings. Both the diving and the dining are spectacular.

10. **Jolly Hotel Lotti, Paris, France (lotti.fr@jollyhotels.com)** Everything about the Jolly Hotel Lotti in Paris has a golden glow about it, from the lobby to the bar to the restaurant to your suite with its heated towel rack and Italian marble bath. You'll be seduced by the luxurious furnishings as well as the overall effect of sheer elegance right in the heart of Paris. You're a stone's throw from some of the best sights in the city, including l'Opera, the Musée d'Orsay, and the Champs-Élysées. The City of Lights awaits you.

How to Change Your Last Name

We have the Romans to thank for making name changes possible. Under Roman law—which, oddly enough, is still reflected in current U.S. law—people could change their names whenever they wanted, unless fraudulent purposes were intended. Unfortunately, the process is arduous and involves a great deal of paperwork and legwork. But if you follow the directions below, you should be able to get through it without too many hassles.

1. Make sure you've ordered and obtained multiple original copies of your marriage certificate. Your local Department of Motor Vehicles, for instance, may not accept a copy.

2. Go to the Social Security Administration website and download its change-of-name form, or call the SSA (800-772-1213) to obtain a hard copy. Once you've completed the form, you'll have to take it to your local Social Security office to obtain a new card.

3. When you get your new Social Security card, be sure to let your job know that you've changed your name so that all your financial information is corrected. Ask human resources to change your e-mail address and business cards.

4. The Department of Motor Vehicles is your next challenge. Call your local DMV and ask which documents will be needed to get a new driver's license. Some DMVs will let you use a copy of your marriage certificate. Play it safe! Bring an original with you.

5. Get a complete passport amendment/validation application at your nearest passport agency. When you file your application, you'll need to provide the agency with your current passport, a marriage certificate, and a check for administration fees.

6. Replace your checks, business cards, and credit cards as well as any other documents that contain your maiden name. There should not be a charge for any of these services.

7. Contact your local post office for a change-of-name-and-address form.

8. Send friends and family an announcement with your new name. If you're still in a buying mode, you can even order name-change cards designed specifically for this purpose.

Before you get married, make all your honeymoon reservations using your maiden name, since your name change won't appear on your current driver's license or passport.

The Pros and Cons of Changing Your Name — and 4 Alternatives

It has been estimated that about 70 percent of brides adopt their husband's last name after marriage. The decision is a highly personal one and there is no right or wrong choice.

Pros

1. It will make life easier for a family. Parents having two different last names can lead to confusion at school, for instance.

2. Most brides are more comfortable following tradition and therefore assume their husband's last name just as their mothers and grandmothers did before them.

3. Some women prefer their husband's last name to their own.

4. People often assume that a married woman has changed her name and call her by her husband's name anyway. Making the change keeps things simple.

Cons

1. Some women prefer the sound of their own last name to that of their husband's name.

2. Some women feel that once they've married they are still the same person and a name change would constitute a loss of identity.

3. Adopting her husband's name may go against a woman's politics. She may view taking the man's last name as a symbol of inequality. She might even ask her husband to change his name.

4. She may not wish to be perceived as more old-fashioned or traditional than she really is.

5. If a woman is the last of her family to carry her maiden name, she may not wish to abandon it.

6. A woman with a successful career may wish to remain identified by her own name. Reestablishing a reputation may be difficult with a different last name, especially if her diplomas and degrees were earned with her maiden name.

Alternatives

1. A husband and wife can hyphenate their last names. It's up to them to decide whose name should go first.

2. She can choose to keep her maiden name as a middle name.

3. If a bride is concerned about being the last in her family with her maiden name, she might consider adopting her husband's last name but using her original name as a first or middle name for a child. If her name, for instance, is Wendy Sarah Ashton and she has married Wayne Delroy Kutcher, she may wish to name her son Ashton Kutcher.

4. Although their numbers are few, some men will take their wife's maiden name if their wife is a well-known celebrity.

What She Said, What She Meant

The reluctant groom's cake topper COURTESY OF GARDENSTATEPHOTO.COM

You want . . .

We need . . .

It's your decision.

Do what you want.

We need to talk.

Sure . . . go ahead.

I'm not upset.

You're . . . so manly.

You are certainly attentive tonight.

I'm not emotional . . .
and I'm not overreacting.

Let's be romantic and turn off the lights.

This kitchen is so inconvenient;
I want new curtains and carpeting, and
furniture, and wallpaper . . .

I heard a noise.

Do you love me?

How much do you love me?

I'll be ready in a minute.

Is my butt fat?

You have to learn to communicate.

Was that the baby?

I'm not yelling.

All we are buying is a soap dish.

You want . . .

I want . . .

The correct decision should be obvious by now.

You'll pay for this later.

I need to complain.

I don't want you to.

Of course I'm upset, you moron!

You need a shave and you sweat a lot.

Is sex all you ever think about?

I'm on my period.

I have flabby thighs.

I want a new house.

I noticed you were almost asleep.

I'm going to ask for something expensive.

I did something today you're really not going to like.

Kick off your shoes and find a good game on TV.

Tell me I'm beautiful.

Just agree with me.

Why don't you get out of bed and walk him until he goes to sleep.

Yes, I am yelling because I think this is important.

It goes without saying that we're stopping at the cosmetics department, the shoe department, I need to look at a few new pocketbooks, and omigod there's a sale in lingerie, and wouldn't these pink sheets look great in the bedroom? and did you bring your checkbook?

12 Ways to Beat Post-Nuptial Syndrome (PNS)

The party's over, you've hung up your veil, and you find yourself pretty much broke. Experts estimate that one out of every ten newlywed couples suffers from post-nuptial depression.

But you don't have to fall victim to the malady. Feeling a bit depressed after your wedding day is normal. You've been running around busy for months, being the center of attention, getting lots of love from family and friends, having a great time at your reception, and relaxing during your honeymoon. All of a sudden it's over. Once-romantic weekends are now filled with chores and errands, and overnight, it seems, you have lost your youth.

It shouldn't last more than a few days or a couple of weeks (everybody is different), but if you are still feeling depressed after a month, you should consider professional help. In the meantime, these tips from Hugh Durkin of WeddingsIreland .com will help you over the rough patches:

1. **Don't let money be an issue.** Adjust to a budget while planning so you will not feel so suffocated by bills and debts.

2. **Share the chores.** Make lists of each of your responsibilities so you each know what is expected. Do some chores together.

3. **Plan nights out with friends** and other social events for after your wedding and honeymoon.

4. **Consider having your honeymoon a few weeks after the wedding day,** so the celebrations won't come and go all at the same time.

5. **Don't open all the presents in one go.**

6. **Keep yourself active:** go back to work and your normal activities.

7. **Engage in a new project together,** like learning a language, taking a course, or joining a fitness club.

8. **Pack away your gown** and put aside the wedding accoutrements. It's time for a new beginning.

9. **Make time for sex and romance.** Go on "dates," and indulge in all the activities you did when you were "young and in love."

10. **Keep the lines of communication open** and talk honestly about how you feel. Even if you're having second thoughts, talking them out will help.

11. **Be patient with yourself and your partner.** Treat one another with love and know that PNS comes with the territory and that it is not a reflection on how you feel about one another.

12. **Crash a wedding**—just to recapture "the moment" (see "The 69 Rules of Wedding Crashing," page 308).

Advice to Newlyweds from the IRS

It may not be high on the list of wedding planning activities, but there are a few simple steps you can take to help keep tax issues from interrupting newly wedded bliss, according to the Internal Revenue Service.

When the June wedding season is in full swing, the IRS advises the soon-to-be married and the just married to review their changing tax status. Choosing the right tax form and filing status can help save money and prevent problems like missing refunds.

One of the tax-related changes that newlyweds should think about now is notifying the IRS about changes of name and address. Later, as filing season approaches, they should consider itemizing their deductions, selecting the right tax return form to use, and choosing their filing status.

No one should delay the cake-cutting or honeymoon because of taxes. But here are some helpful hints for later:

1. **Use the correct name.** Taxpayers must provide correct names and identification numbers to claim personal exemptions or the Earned Income Tax Credit on their tax returns. A taxpayer who changes his or her last name upon marrying should let the Social Security Administration know and should update his or her Social Security card so the number matches the new name. Form SS-5, "Application for a Social Security Card," is available through the SSA website at www.ssa.gov or by calling toll-free 1-800-772-1213.

2. **Report your change of address.** If one or both spouses are changing their address, they should notify the IRS, as well as the U.S. Postal Service, to be sure they receive any tax refunds or IRS correspondence. It's a simple process. All they have to do is send in form 8822, "Change of Address Form," which is available by calling the IRS at 1-800-TAX-FORM (1-800-829-3676), at most local IRS offices or on the IRS website at www.irs.gov. They can also write to the IRS center where they filed their most recent return. They should include their full name, old and new addresses, Social Security numbers, and signatures. And they should remember to let their employers know about any changes to their name or address so they can receive their paychecks and W-2s.

3. **Get that refund check.** Each year thousands of tax refund checks are returned to the IRS as undeliverable, usually because the recipient has moved. Notifying both the post office and the IRS of an address change in a timely manner can help ensure the proper delivery of any refund checks. To check the status of a tax refund, use the "Where's My Refund" service on the IRS website or call the toll-free automated refund line at 1-800-829-4477. If a refund check was returned to the IRS as undeliverable, call the IRS toll-free customer service line at 1-800-829-1040 to arrange for reissuance of the check.

4. **Select the right form.** Choosing the right individual income tax form can help save money. Newly married taxpayers may find that they now have enough deductions to itemize on their tax returns.

Deductions for money paid for medical care, mortgage interest, contributions, casualty losses, and certain miscellaneous costs can reduce federal taxes. Form 1040, which is used to report all types of income, deductions, and credits, is the one to use if itemizing. Forms 1040EZ and 1040A do not allow such itemization.

Taxpayers who do not receive their preferred form in the tax package sent to them during filing season may obtain the form from the IRS website, at a local IRS office, or by calling the toll-free forms and publications line at 1-800-TAX-FORM (1-800-829-3676).

5. **Choose the best filing status.** A person's marital status on December 31 determines whether the person is considered married for that year. The tax law allows married couples to choose to file their federal income tax return either jointly or separately in any given year. Choosing the right filing status can help save money.

A joint return ("married filing jointly") allows spouses to combine their income and deduct combined deductions and expenses on a single tax return. Both spouses must sign the return, and both are held responsible for the contents. With separate returns ("married filing separately"), each spouse signs, files, and is responsible for his or her own tax return. Each is taxed on his or her own income and can take only his or her individual deductions and credits. If one spouse itemizes deductions, the other must also.

Figuring the tax both ways can determine which filing status will result in the lowest tax; usually it's filing jointly. More detailed information on filing status can be found in publication 501, "Exemptions, Standard Deduction, and Filing Information," on the IRS website.

Savings Advice for Newlyweds

Janet Bodnar is deputy editor of Kiplinger's *Personal Finance* magazine, for which she has written articles on a wide range of topics, including investing, money management, and the economy, and the author of *Money-Smart Women: Everything You Need to Know to Achieve a Lifetime of Financial Security.* This is her wise advice:

Eager to start your marriage off on the right financial foot? Start saving as soon as possible. Even small amounts of money will grow into big piles later. Retirement may sound like a long way off, but look at it this way: the longer you put off thinking about it, the longer you put off retirement itself. How to get started:

1. Rather than save a specific amount, I'd recommend that you each sign up for your employer's retirement plan, such as a 401(k) or 403(b). If your employer matches your contribution, aim to kick in at least enough to capture the match (say, 3 percent or 5 percent of your salary).

2. If your employer doesn't offer a match, each of you should open your own Roth Individual Retirement Account (IRA). It's easy to do. Just get in touch with an investment company and fill out some simple paperwork. In 2007 you could each contribute $4,000 to a Roth as long as your joint income was less than $156,000.

3. At your age, you should both invest nearly all of your retirement money in the stock market. (Another mistake newlyweds make is being too conservative.)

4. A great investment that is also simple is a so-called target-retirement fund. It's a mutual fund that puts your money in a variety of investments that are tied to your anticipated retirement date. The mix automatically changes over time, becoming more conservative as you get older.

5. Top-notch companies that offer target-retirement funds include T. Rowe Price, Vanguard, Fidelity, and American Century (for lots more on retirement planning, go to Kiplinger.com).

6. Husbands and wives should always contribute to and manage their own retirement accounts; don't depend on your spouse to do it for you. If you don't feel you can afford to put aside 5 percent of your salary or the full $4,000 each in an IRA, you can always start with less and boost your contribution as your income increases.

7. Have your employer or the mutual fund company automatically deduct money from each paycheck, and you'll never miss it.

74 Tips for a Happy Marriage

1. Talk a lot—about everything.
2. Make time for the things you did together before you got married.
3. Be patient.
4. Return the "something borrowed."
5. Don't put off the honeymoon.
6. Be yourself.
7. Choose your battles.
8. Take a course together.
9. Be honest about the past.
10. Make time for sex.
11. Try new things.
12. Work on the thank-you cards together.
13. Let your old friends know that your priorities have changed.
14. Treat your in-laws with respect.
15. Make plans.
16. Get counseling, even if you don't think you need it.
17. Admit when you're wrong.
18. Put the cap back on the toothpaste.
19. Ask questions.
20. Learn to cook new dishes that you both like.
21. Stick to your budget.
22. Hang out with old friends.
23. Fight fair.
24. Don't hog the closets.
25. Ask your honey to teach you to do something that he or she does well.
26. Avoid power struggles.
27. Don't get mad just because you have a right to.
28. Divide the chores.
29. Talk about how you want to raise the kids.
30. Compromise.
31. Decide together just how clean the place needs to be.
32. If you want one thing and she wants another, don't choose either. Pick something altogether different.
33. Let your parents know how happy you are.
34. Turn off the TV.
35. Accept criticism.
36. Keep your word.
37. Shower together.
38. Plan surprises.
39. Take nude photos of each other.
40. Don't hog the remote.
41. Memorize your wedding vows.
42. If your honey has to get up before you in the morning, get up at that time too.
43. No name-calling. Ever.
44. Don't go to sleep mad.
45. Tell her how nice she looks without makeup.
46. Once in a while, do his chores for him.
47. Don't sweat the small stuff.
48. Once in a while, insist on phone sex.
49. Use the fancy dishes just for the two of you.
50. Don't make threats.
51. Be forgiving.
52. Don't snoop. (Well, maybe just a little.)
53. Don't fight when you're really angry.
54. Eat together.
55. Pray together.
56. Don't cheat emotionally.
57. Read your sweetie's favorite book.
58. Don't interrupt.
59. Make new friends together.
60. Write down your in-laws' birthdays.
61. Apologize.
62. Laugh at yourself.
63. Laugh at yourselves.
64. Don't share intimate details about your marriage with anyone.
65. Be a friend.
66. Accept that there are many different ways to make a bed.
67. Don't live with your in-laws.
68. Sleep on the wet spot.
69. Don't listen to advice from people who (a) don't like your spouse, and (b) have never been married.
70. Kiss in public.
71. Don't ever argue in public.
72. Cook together.
73. Make a lunch date.
74. Remember your anniversary.

> "When I meet a man I ask myself, 'Is this the man I want my children to spend their weekends with?'"
> — Rita Rudner

The One Question That Will Ensure a Happy Marriage

It's going to be a roller coaster. Sometimes you'll be up and sometimes you'll be down. Remember that the ups and downs are all part of the same ride. There will be times, though, when you will find yourself completely perplexed as to what you were thinking when you said "I do." At these times, ask yourself this one question. It is a powerful question that will put everything in perspective, and if you're at all human, it will humble you. Answer the question honestly—your marriage could depend on it:

What's it like to be married to you?

Vintage postcard, 1907 COURTESY OF GARDENSTATEPHOTO.COM

Annulment Basics

Some marriages are made in heaven. Others never should have been made at all.

Like a divorce, an annulment is a court procedure that dissolves a marriage. But unlike a divorce, an annulment treats the marriage as though it never happened. For some people, divorce carries a stigma and they would rather pretend it never happened. Others prefer an annulment because it might make it easier to remarry later in a church that may not recognize divorce. Grounds for annulment vary slightly from state to state.

The following list describes grounds for civil annulments. Within the Roman Catholic Church, a couple may obtain a religious annulment after obtaining a civil divorce, so that one or both people may remarry within the church or anywhere else and have the second union recognized.

Most annulments take place after a marriage of a very short duration—a few weeks or months—so there are usually no assets or debts to divide, or children for whom custody, visitation, and child support are a concern. When a long-term marriage is annulled, however, most states have provisions for dividing property and debts, as well as determining custody, visitation, child support, and alimony. Children of an annulled marriage are not considered illegitimate. Generally, an annulment requires that at least one of the following reasons exists:

1. **Misrepresentation or fraud:** If a spouse lied about the capacity to have children, falsely stated that he or she had reached the age of consent, or failed to say that she was still married to someone else.

2. **Concealment:** If a spouse has concealed an addiction to alcohol or drugs, conviction of a felony, children from a prior relationship, a sexually transmitted disease, or impotency.

3. **Refusal or inability to consummate the marriage:** If a spouse has refused or is unable to have sexual intercourse with the other spouse.

4 **Misunderstanding:** If one spouse, for example, wanted children and the other did not and didn't let the other know.

Bibliography

Baldizzone, Tiziana, and Gianni Baldizzone. *Wedding Ceremonies: Ethnic Symbols, Costume, and Ritual.* Paris: Flammarion, 2001.

Cole, Harriette. *Jumping the Broom.* New York: Henry Holt and Co., 2003.

Coontz, Stephanie. *Marriage: A History.* New York: Viking, 2005.

Donovan, Mary. *The Thirteen Colonies Cookbook.* New York: Praeger, 1975.

Howard, Vicki. *Brides, Inc.* Philadelphia: University of Pennsylvania Press, 2006.

Ingram, Leah. *The Anxious Bride.* Franklin Lakes, NJ: Career Press, 2004.

Marg, Susan. *Las Vegas Weddings.* New York: HarperCollins, 2004.

Mead, Rebecca. *One Perfect Day.* New York: Penguin, 2007.

Melendez, Crystal, and Jason Melendez. *E-Plan Your Wedding.* San Jose, CA: Mediasoft Press, 2006.

Mellon, James. *Bullwhip Days: The Slaves Remember.* New York: Grove, 2002.

Mitchell, John. *What the Hell Is a Groom and What's He Supposed to Do?* Kansas City, MO: Andrews McMeel, 1999.

Monsarrat, Ann. *And the Bride Wore. . . .* New York: Dodd, Mead, 1974.

Mordechai, Carolyn. *Weddings: Dating and Love Customs of Cultures Worldwide.* Phoenix, AZ: Nittany, 1999.

Naylor, Sharon. *1,001 Ways to Save Money and Still Have a Dazzling Wedding.* New York: Contemporary Books, 2001.

Primerano, Lisa. *Off the Beaten Aisle.* New York: Citadel, 1998.

Roney, Carley. *The Knot Complete Guide to Weddings in the Real World.* San Francisco: Chronicle, 2004.

Safier, Rachel. *There Goes the Bride.* San Francisco: Jossey-Bass, 2003.

Scheu-Riesz, Helene. *Will You Marry Me?* New York: Simon & Schuster, 2008.

Spangenberg, Lisl M. *Timeless Traditions.* New York: Universe, 2002.

Stallings, Ariel Meadow. *Offbeat Bride.* Berkeley, CA: Seal Press, 2006.

Stewart, Arlene Hamilton. *A Bride's Book of Wedding Traditions.* New York: Morrow, 1995.

Waggoner, Susan. *I Do! I Do!* New York: Rizzoli, 2002.

Walker, Cindy. *101 Uses for a Bridesmaid Dress.* New York: Morrow, 1999.

Wallace, Carol McD. *All Dressed in White.* New York: Penguin, 2004.

Index

Page numbers in italics refer to text pictures.

Boleyn, Anne, 92
Bollywood wedding (2007), 99
Bonaparte, Jerome, 330
bouquet toss, 202, 279, 305
Bouvier, Jacqueline, 91, 109
    See also Kennedy, Jacqueline
Bow, Clara, 118
Bowditch, Eden Unger, 224
Bowles, Camilla Parker, 85, 107, 110, 117
Boyd, Patti, 111
Boyesen, Hjalmar Hjörth, 81, 132
Bracebridge Hall (Irving), 130
braiding of hair, 36
Brandy (singer/actress), 107
Bratman, Jordan, 107
Bratten, Millie Martini, 194
Brazil, 60
Brennan, James, 157
Brian Boru, High King, 179
Bridal Bargains (Fields), 232
"Bridal Chorus"/alternative lyrics, 133, *133*
bridal gown/attire
    ancient Rome, 5
    around the globe, 97–99, *97, 98, 99*
    color choices, 211–12, *213*
    donating, 318
    dressing the bride, *57, 57*
    fabrics, 212
    foundation garments, 251
    gown selection, 243–44, *243*
    hidden costs, 246
    history, 52–53, *53, 54,* 55–56, *246*
    knitting your own, 252–53, *253*
    miniature replicas of, 214
    most expensive, 127
    necklines, 246
    once-only dress, 55
    parachute wedding gown, *249*
    for pregnant brides, 194
    preserving, 317
    quality determination, 250, *250*
    record holders, 126, 127
    saving money on, 248–49, *248,* 256
    second weddings, 185
    shoes, 256
    silhouettes, 245
    skin tone and, 211, 244
    sleeves, 244

something old, new, borrowed, blue, 50
stain removal, 302
superstitions with, 52–53, 56, 213
Toilet Paper Wedding Dress Contest, *248*
train lengths, 126, 247, *247*
"Trash the Dress," *317*
when to buy, 243, 244
white variations, 211
bridal showers, 213, 214–15
bridal shows, 205
bridal trousseau history, 66
bride fattening custom, 36, 60, 64
bride price/wealth
    description, 4
    in different cultures, 4, 7, 14, 15, 18, 25, 30, 34, 37, 38
Brides magazine
    history, 10, 66, *66,* 148
    wedding industry and, 10, 148, *229, 323*
bridesmaids
    donating dresses, 319
    dresses, 253, 319, *319*
    dress uses, 318
    duties, 255, 296–97
    oldest bridesmaid, 127
    parties, 213
bride's pie, 76
bridezillas
    about/preventing syndrome, 198
    from film/books, 117
    television show on, 142
    test on, 199
    wedding industry and, 11, 146
Bridges of Madison County, The (Walker)/weddings, 169
British royal weddings overview, 82–85, *82, 83*
Brontë, Charlotte, 130
broom jumping ceremony, 38, 39, *39,* 165
Brosnan, Pierce, 179
Browning, Elizabeth Barrett, 84
Brown, Myra Gale, 89
Bruderman, Thomas, 106
Buchanan, Katie/Ben, 326–27
Buck, Pearl S., 130, 132
Buddhist traditions, 16, 17, 18, 166, 286
Budinger, Victoria May ("Miss Vicki")/daughter, 102

Bulgaria, 16
bundling, 61
Burr, Theodosia/Aaron, 330
Burton, Richard, 101, 107
Burton, Tim, 120
Bush, George W., 45
Buydens, Anne, 121

C

Cage, Nicolas, 101
Cajun traditions, 16–17
cakes
    around the world, 78, *78*
    examples, *78, 100, 144–45, 166, 170, 185, 216, 268, 269, 270*
    glossary, 268
    groom's cake, 77, *216,* 268
    history, 76–77
    largest cake, 126
    life-like cake, *268*
    most expensive cake, 270
    recipe (1747), 77
    saving money on, 269–70
    superstitions with, 76, 77
    "wacky cake," *170*
cake toppers, *167, 185, 206, 210, 334*
Cambodia, 17
canceling/postponing weddings, 195
Capshaw, Kate, 116
Carey, Mariah, 122
Casanova, 91
Cash, Johnny, 180
Cassidy, David, 120
castle weddings, 177–79, *178, 179*
Castro, Fidel, 19
Catherine of Braganza, 52
Catholic weddings, 286
Cavanaugh, John, 84
cave weddings, 168
celebrities
    big weddings/divorces, 122
    inviting to wedding, 242
    with most marriages, 123
    possible unions/names, 123
    prenuptial agreements, 115–16
    shortest marriages, 125
    wedding dates, 124–25
    See also specific celebrities

bride price/dowry, 4, 7
post-wedding traditions, 292
wedding customs, 22, 23, 24–25, 33, 290–91, 290
See also India
Hispanic traditions
wedding customs, 22, 23, 97–98, 166
See also specific countries
history of weddings/marriage
ancient Rome, 3, 5–6, 7
early Egypt, *2, 3*
incest and bloodlines, 3, 22, 29
individuality (1960s/1970s), 11
love and, 2, 6, 14
Middle Ages, 6
nineteenth century, 8–9
Paleolithic period, 2
today, 11
twentieth century, 9–11
Hitchcock, Alfred, 103
Hixson, Bill, 262
Holland, 24, 61–62, 79, 292
Holliday, Jennifer, 101
Holloway, Angela, 201
Holmes, Katie, 90, 107, 116
honeymoon capitals (U.S.), 330, *330*
honeymoons
free honeymoons, 324
history, 322
ideas for, 331–32
insurance and, 195, 229, 322, 328
movies on, 140–41, *140*
musical comedy ad, *327*
romantic cities, 329
saving money on, 324
Thrifty's "Honeymoon Disaster Contest" winners, 325–27
tips on, 322–23
vintage postcards, *284, 324*
weather guide, 328–29, *329*
Hopi customs, 30, 63
hot-air balloon weddings, 168, *168*
Hungary, 24
Hurley, Dorothea, 119
Hurricane Katrina, 313
Hurt, William, 115
"husband" slang words, 106

Ice Hotel, Quebec City, Canada, 169–70
Iceland, 74, 79
ice sculptures, *181*
Inca traditions, 29, 40
incest and bloodlines, 3, 22, 29
India
bride price/dowries, 4, 14
post-wedding traditions, 292
wedding/marriage customs, 24–25, 62, 65, 98, *98*, 166
See also Hindu traditions
Indonesia, 25
in-laws
books on, 224
tips on, 226
insurance for weddings, 229
Internet and weddings
Knot, The, 11, 190–91
mail-order brides, 42
parents marrying off daughters, 41
pregnant bride and, 194
websites summary, 190, 205
your website details, 190
invitations
to celebrities, 242
divorced parents and, 225
doing your own, 68, 241
eco-friendly ideas, 67, 202, 239
fonts, 240–41
history, 67–68
in-laws and, 226
printing advances and, 67, 68
printing techniques, 238
saving money on, 68, 239, 242
for second weddings, 185
selecting tips, 238
trends in, 239, *239*
Iran wedding customs, 79
Ireland
castle weddings, 177, *178*, 179
wedding customs, 25–26, 62, 78, 79, 98, 166
IRS/tax issues, 195, 231, 234, 336
Irving, Amy, 116
Irving, Washington, 130
Islamic marriages
bride price, 4

wedding customs, 25, 28–29, 35, 37, 65, 288–89, *289*
See also specific countries
Israel wedding party, *63*
Italy
marriage proverbs, 26
wedding customs, 26, 59, 79, 292

Jackson, Michael, 100, 180
Jamaica, 26, 292
James, Harry, 121
James, Larry, 309
Jane Eyre (Brontë), 130
Japan
engagement/pre-wedding traditions, 62
mi-ai interview, 291
post-wedding traditions, 292
Shinto wedding ceremony, 26–27, 291
wedding customs, 26–27, 58, 65, 78, 98, 166
Java, 25, *99*
Jawara, Sir Dawda, 104
Jaymes, Jessica, 106
Jeaffreson, John Cordy, 72
Jewish customs
breaking glass, 288
bride price, 14
engagement/pre-wedding traditions, 62, 63
Ethiopian Jews, 20
ketubah, *20*, 286–87
post-wedding traditions, 292
wedding traditions, 6, 58, 79, 167, 286–88, *287, 298*
Joel, Billy, 96
John, Sir Elton, 106, 110
Johnson, Lucy Baines, 102
Johnson, Lynda Bird, 108
Johnson, Lyndon Baines, 91, 102, 108, 109
Jolie, Angelina, 116, 119
Jordan almonds, 81
Jordan, Eric Benet, 116
Jordan, Michael, 119
Jovi, Jon Bon, 119, 121, 174
Juan Carlos, King of Spain, 104

Kalina, Princess of Bulgaria, 101
Kanawa, Kiri Te, 104

O'Neal, Shaquille, 96
Oneida Community group marriages, 40
Ono, Yoko, 110, 111
orange blossom legend, 71–72
Osbourne, Ozzy, 106
Otnes, Cele, 152
Outer Mongolia weddings, 170
outer space weddings, 170
Owens, Buck, 180
Owens, Mary, 92

P

Packham, Jenny, 113
Pagan, Angelo, 119
Paleolithic period, 2
palimony, 162
parachute wedding gown, *249*
Parker, Jeffrey W., 101
Parker, Tony, 107
parties, pre-wedding, 213
    See also specific parties
Parton, James, 8
Patterson, Elizabeth, 330
Payne, Chris/Susan, 325
Peabody, Sophia, 101
Perelman, Ronald, 116
Peru, 29
Pessagno, Rev. Jo Ann, 169
Peters, Jon, 120
Pettibone, Claire, 113
Pheifle, Allison, 170
Philip II, Prince of Spain, 101
Philippines
    engagement/pre-wedding traditions, 63
    mail-order brides, 29
    wedding customs, 29, 79, 166, 314
Philip, Prince (Duke of Edinburgh), 55, 83, *83*
Phillips, Mark, 84, 85
photography
    finding photographer, 271
    high-definition videography, 275
    history, 80, *80*
    preserving, 321, *321*
    record holder, 126–27
    saving money on, 273
    tips for looking good in, 274
    tips on, 187, 205, 271–72
    videographers, 274, 275

Pink Weddings, 176
Pitt, Brad, 107, 116, 122
"placage marriage," 1, 21–22
planning
    flowers/bouquets, 265–66
    multi-faith weddings, 210, *210*
    outdoor weddings, 164
    preserving sanity and, 186
    preventing disasters, 196–97, 294–95
    second weddings, 185
    settling arguments on, 298
    tips for grooms, 219
    your job and, 206, *206*
    See also Internet and weddings; *specific
        components*
Plastique, Renee, 224
Plato, 14
Plutarch, 49
Poland, 29, 31, 59, 64, 79
polyandry, 12, 22
polygamy, 1, 12–13, 18, 22, 30, 32, 37
polygyny, 12–13
Polynesian customs, 22, 32, 64, 65
postcards, vintage, *48, 86–87, 128, 192, 284,
    304, 324, 339*
Post, Emily, 68
Post-Nuptial Syndrome (PNS), 335
postponing/canceling wedding, 195
post-wedding traditions, 292–93
Powell, Cynthia, 111
pregnant bride, 194
Prelutsky, Burt, 101
premarital counseling, 201
*Prenuptial Agreements: How to Write a Fair and
    Lasting Contract* (book), 161
prenuptial agreements
    myths about, 161–62
    of rich/famous, 115–16
    for second weddings, 185
Presley, Elvis, 100, *100*, 120, 121
Presley family, 100
Presley, Lisa Marie, 100, 101
Princess Wedding Chapel, Las Vegas, Nevada,
    105
Prinze, Freddie, Jr., 101
Prolman, Gerald, 183
proposals
    about, 61

famous/historical proposals, 91–92
    in various languages, 90
Protestant wedding/reception, 285–86, 298, 310
Puck, Wolfgang, 122

Q

Qagyuhl wedding party, *31*
Quakers, 31, 64
Quant, Mary, 55
Queen Mother (Lady Elizabeth Bowes-Lyon), 83,
    85, 107
Quiche Maya people, *98*
quilts, 75

R

Rai, Aishwarya, 99
Rainier, Prince of Monaco, 96, 101, 102, 103,
    103
Rajasthani people, *98*
Ramsay, Sir Alexander, 178–79
Rase, Betty Jane, 121
Rashaayda people of Sudan, 38
Rathbone, Basil, 177
Reagan, Nancy, 104, 179
Reagan, Ronald, 174, 179
reception cards, 67
receptions
    ancient Egypt, 3
    cash bars, 236
    first dances, 305
    food around the world, 79
    largest banquet, 126
    Medieval wedding feast menu, 6
    Norse wedding feast, 81
    rituals, 305
    seating at, 225, 299
    serving styles, 237
    times for eating, 237
    tips on food/beverages, 236, 237
    wedding feast (1726), 80
Reed, Donna, 91
Register, Donnie, 223
rehearsal dinner, 213, 219
religion and weddings
    Bible verses, 208–9
    communism and, 35
    Middle Ages, 6
    multi-faith weddings, 210, *210*

About the Authors

SANDRA CHORON is a writer, editor, literary agent, book packager, and designer. She and her husband, **HARRY CHORON**, a graphic designer, are the authors of *Planet Cat*, *Planet Dog*, *College in a Can*, *The Book of Lists for Teens*, and *The All-New Book of Lists for Kids*, among other works.